MACROECONOMICS

5th Revised and Enlarged Edition

MACROECONOMICS

5th Revised and Enlarged Edition

K.R. GUPTA
R.K. MANDAL
AMITA GUPTA

Published by

ATLANTIC

PUBLISHERS & DISTRIBUTORS (P) LTD

B-2, Vishal Enclave, Opp. Rajouri Garden,
New Delhi-110027
Phones : +91-11-25413460, 25429987, 25466842

Sales Office
7/22, Ansari Road, Darya Ganj,
New Delhi-110002
Phones : +91-11-23273880, 23275880, 23280451
Fax : +91-11-23285873
web : www.atlanticbooks.com
e-mail : info@atlanticbooks.com

Branch Office
5, Nallathambi Street, Wallajah Road,
Chennai-600002
Phones : +91-44-64611085, 32413319
e-mail : chennai@atlanticbooks.com

Printed in India
at Nice Printing Press, Delhi

Preface

Macroeconomics is the study of the total economy – the national, regional or even the world economy. It is a fascinating subject that touches our daily lives. We are invariably interested in news about what is happening in the macroeconomy because changes in economic variables impinge upon our well-being. We follow news about unemployment and growth because our standard of living and ability to find jobs depend on these indicators. We also follow developments pertaining to interest rates and inflation because these variables determine our mortgage payments and the purchasing power (how much we can buy) of our income and savings, as well as the profitability of our investments.

The book has been out of print for the last two decades. In spite of great demand for the book I could not bring out the revised edition because of my preoccupation with other books. Now the fifth edition of the book has been thoroughly revised and considerably enlarged. It has a wide coverage and comprehensively deals with all the topics normally included in the subject, viz. National Income, Classical Theory of Employment, Determination of Income and Employment, Savings, Investment and Multiplier, Consumption Function, Marginal Efficiency of Capital, Rate of Interest, Saving-Investment Equality, Principle of Acceleration, Unemployment in an Undeveloped Economy, Secular Stagnation, Money and Prices, Inflation and Deflation, Credit Creation and Credit Control, Business Cycles, Economic Stabilization, Monetary Policy, Fiscal Policy, Fiscal Policy and Economic Development, Deficit Financing, Public Debt, Growth Models, etc.

The book would be found highly useful by undergraduate and postgraduate students of Economics.

K.R. Gupta

Contents

Micro and Macroeconomics

1

WHY STUDY MACROECONOMICS

As we have entered the new millennium, it has turned out that economic issues are gaining more and more importance everyday. The economic events have started affecting the everyday life of a common man. An office goer earns Rs. 12000 per month and after a month's hard work he finds out that his meagre income cannot satisfy even his basic needs as the prices of different goods and services are continuously rising. He wonders why the prices keep rising all the time while his own income does not rise at the same rate. An engineering student comes out of college, and hopes to get a handsome job with a fat paycheck. His efforts to find a job get frustrated because there is general unemployment in the country. He wonders why he cannot succeed in getting a job with his first class degree and good performances at the interviews?

Sometimes you experience that certain goods have disappeared from the market while certain other goods are available in large quantities. Have you not wondered why this is so? Have you noticed that different type of goods have shown more or less a permanent tendency to disappear from the market just few weeks before the Central Government presents its budget every year and have you not wondered why the Central Government has to keep on increasing the doses of taxation in every budget?

All these issues concern the basic functioning of the economy. By the word 'economy' we mean an organized system through which a society performs different types of economic activities, *i.e.*, produces different types of goods and services which it requires and distributes them among its members for consumption. In a way, economics is the study of how the economy works.

The economy is composed of individuals, households, and business firms. An individual is the smallest unit of economy. Many decisions he takes in his life, *e.g.*, what profession to enter? Where to work and where to live? etc. are largely governed by economic considerations. The next larger unit of economy is the household which is a group of individuals who fulfil their needs in unison. A common definition of household accepted in our country is that household basically constitutes of all those persons who are either related by blood or by bonds of marriage and share a common kitchen establishment. A household is basically a consumption unit. A firm, on the other hand, is also a household but it is basically a production unit. A firm is a collection of individuals, or of a group of individuals who produce some goods or service required by individuals or households for consumption. In other words, the firm is a productive household. The firm performs its economic functions, not as a social service but as a business proposition. It organizes production, hires workers, purchases raw materials and machinery, and thus produces as goods. The cost it has incurred on producing goods is known as cost of production. The firm sells its product at a price which is most often substantially, and sometime marginally higher than the cost of production. This surplus or difference between the selling price of a unit of product and its per unit cost of production is called profit which is firm's earning. In other words, this is the reward a firm gets of performing the socially useful function of organization of productive forces.

The next larger unit of the economy is the industry. An industry is a collection of several firms turning out identical or closely identical product. Thus, cotton textile industry refers to a number of firms, all of whom produce cotton textiles and cosmetics industry refers to a number of firms, all of whom produce different varieties of cosmetic products.

Closely linked to the concept of industry, is the concept of market. A market, in economics, does not mean a marketplace such as Connaught Place, or Sabzi Mandi, as is the usual connotation in everyday language. In economics, the term 'market', refers to an area over which the buyers and sellers of a particular commodity are spread and they determine the price of that commodity through mutual competition and bargain. The market for any good may be local, regional, national or international. Different types of fruits, vegetables, milk, curds etc. have only local markets in our country as they are perishable. But the same goods have a national market in the United States because they could be frozen, transported quickly and are sold in the completely airconditioned shops which are scattered throughout the continent. This reveals an interesting fact that extent of market could be changed by technological advance. Some goods which may be sold in one region but could not be sold in other regions have regional markets. The goods which are bought and sold within the national frontiers of a country have a national market. A good example of this would be the government securities issued by the Government of India which hold good only in India and in no other country. Then, there are goods like wheat, rice, gold, drugs, steel, aircrafts, guns, tanks, tractors, etc. which have international markets, because they can be bought and sold across the national frontiers.

A collection of several industries turning out products which may have some common characteristics is called a sector. The nomenclature of sector depends upon what purpose one has in mind. For example, all industries producing consumer goods may be called consumer goods sector. All industries producing for export may be called export sector. All firms engaged in export import business may be classified as foreign trade sector. There may be a number of sectors in an economy.

What we have been describing in preceding paragraphs is known in technical language as aggregation procedure. Industry is an aggregation of firms. Sector is an aggregation of industries and economy is an aggregation of sectors. The relationship between different levels of aggregation of economic unit is shown in Fig. 1.1. Fig. 1.1A depicts the production side of economy and Fig. 1.1B shows consumption side. The production side constitutes of firms, industries and sectors. A sector is a subset of economy. An industry is a subset of sectors and so on. Similarly, on the consumption side, household is a subset of economy and individual is a subset of household.

MACROECONOMICS AND MICROECONOMICS DISTINGUISHED

The terms microeconomics and macroeconomics were coined by Prof. Ragnar Frisch of Oslo University for the first time in 1933 and since then they gained popularity and were widely used by other economists. Now they have become an integral part of economic terminology.

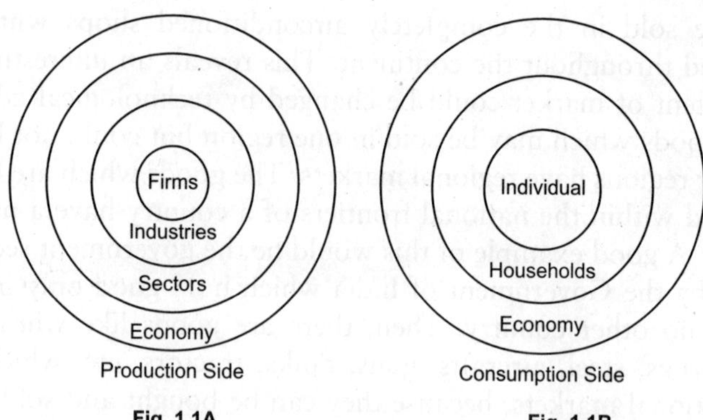

Fig. 1.1A **Fig. 1.1B**

The word 'micro' means a millionth part. Microeconomics means study of a small part or component of the whole economy. Microeconomics is the opposite of macroeconomics. It deals with the analysis of the constituent elements of an economy. It studies economic motives and behaviour of individual consumers and producers and the principles involved in organising and operating the individual firms and industries. It studies how an individual person, firm, or industry attains the equilibrium position. It may be the study of an individual consumer's behaviour or that of an individual firm or of a particular industry. In price analysis, for instance, under microeconomics, we study the price of a product or a factor of production and not the general price level. Similarly, in a demand analysis, we study demand of an individual person or that of an individual household, or that of a firm or industry and not the aggregate demand of the entire community. In income analysis, we study the income of an individual or household, or firm or industry and not the income of the whole country.

The microanalysis, while studying an individual element of the economy, assumes the prevalence of full employment in the economy as a whole. Given this assumption, an attempt is made to find out how a consumer or a producer attains equilibrium. As such it studies the division of total output among industries and firms and the allocation of resources among competing uses. It studies relative prices of different goods and services and the distribution of income. In other words, while studying the behaviour of a particular unit, it assumes the environmental data as given.

Macro and Microeconomics stand on two different branches of a same tree. Though there is a great deal of interdependence between them, they have many distinctions in their respective approaches.

The term microeconomics is derived from the Greek word, 'Mikros' meaning small and the term macroeconomics from the Greek word, 'Makros' meaning large. K.E. Boulding makes the distinction between them more clear and more specific when he says, "Microeconomics is the study of particular firms, particular households, individual prices, wages, incomes, individual industries, particular commodities" (K.E. Boulding, *A Reconstruction of Economics*, 1950, p. 3). "Macroeconomics deals not with individual quantities as such but with aggregates of these quantities; not with individual incomes but with the national income; not with individual prices but with the price level; not with the individual outputs but with the national output" (K.E. Boulding, *Economic Analysis*, p. 25).

Microeconomics should be carefully distinguished from macroeconomics. Microeconomics also does deal with some 'aggregates' but not of the type with which macroeconomics concerns. Microeconomics determines the product price, output and employment of an industry. Industry is also an aggregate of the various firms producing the same product. It also explains the determination of price of a product through the interaction of demand and supply of the market for that product. Market demand is the aggregate of individual demands of all consumers while the market supply is the aggregate of individual productions of all the firms producing the same product.

But the aggregates with which macroeconomics concerns are some what different from the aggregates with which microeconomics deals with. Macroeconomics deals with those aggregates which relate to the whole economy. It also discusses the sub-aggregates. But these sub-aggregates are not like the sub-aggregates with which microeconomics deals with. Examples of sub-aggregates with which macroeconomics concerns are the total production of consumer goods, total production of capital goods, etc.

Therefore, the subject matter of macroeconomics is to study aggregates or averages of the entire economy, such as national income, output and employment, total consumption, total savings and investment, aggregate demand and aggregate supply, etc. The macro-approach is essential, for what it is true of the parts may not be true of the whole. Prof. Ackley says, "Macroeconomics also uses aggregates smaller than for the whole economy but only in a context which makes them sub-divisions of an economy-wide total. Microeconomics also uses aggregates, but not in a context which relates them to an economy-wide total."

A separate and distinct microeconomic and macroeconomic analysis are essential to understand the true and actual function of the economic system of a country as a whole. None of these two approaches, *viz.* micro and macro economics, alone is adequate for the analysis of a economy. Thus, it is very much essential to integrate the two approaches to arrive at a correct solution for better understanding the economic problems.

IMPORTANCES AND USES OF MACROECONOMICS

There are several reasons for which we have to study macroeconomics separately. What are the main justifications in having it as a separate branch of modern economic theory? Is microeconomics not adequate in itself? To give answer to these questions we have to concern the following:

1. We cannot obtain the laws governing the macroeconomic variables such as total national product, total employment and total income, general price level, etc. by simple adding up, multiplying or averaging the results obtained from microeconomic variables. The macroeconomic aggregate is not merely a matter of addition or multiplication or averaging of microeconomic variables. Therefore, a separate macro-analysis is needed to study the behaviour of the economic system as a whole in respect of veriables of macroeconomic aggregates.
2. Macroeconomic analysis takes into account many relationships which are not applicable to individual parts at all. For instance, an individual may save more than that he invests or he may invest more than he saves, but for the economy as a whole it is one of the important principles of Keynesian Macroeconomics that actual savings are always equal to actual investment. Likewise, for an individual or a group of individuals, expenditure may be more or less than

his income but the national expenditure of the economy must be equal to the national income. In fact, the national expenditure and national income are two identical things.

3. The study of Macroeconomics becomes indispensable for the formulation and successful execution of government economic policies. Governments are concerned with the regulation of aggregates of the economic system such as the general price-level, the general level of production, the general volume of trade and so on. The Macroeconomics studies these statistics of the aggregative variables accurately and reliably to formulate the sound governmental policies.
4. The study of Macroeconomics is indispensable even for the purpose of building and developing Microeconomics. No Microeconomic law can be formulated without a prestudy of aggregates.
5. The popularity of Macroeconomics has greatly increased in recent years on account of the fact that it deals with most of the controversial and challenging issues of the day, such as, unemployment, deficit financing, inflation, taxation, planning and economic development. It is helpful in understanding the functioning of complicated economic system. It seeks to explain fluctuation in the level of national income, output, employment etc.

Although Macroeconomics gains a lot of popularity, yet it has some drawbacks which may not be avoidable. It may be discussed in several ways.

1. The aggregation may not influence all the sectors at a time in same direction. Some sections will be benefited and some sections affected adversely. For example, a general rise in prices for which some industries may be benefited more than other industries.
2. Sometimes the aggregative study gives us misleading conceptions. Suppose, the price of agricultural product falls by 50 per cent while that of industrial product rises by 50 per cent. These two types of price changes neutralize each other showing that the general price level remain same. One guided by macro analysis alone needs no new policy to help the agriculturist.

3. It takes into account an excessive generalization from individual experiences to the system as a whole. What is true of an individual component may not necessarily be true of the aggregate.
4. The attempt of aggregation of variables which are considered homogeneous in nature may not true in many causes. Sometimes, we may have to take into account aggregates which are rather heterogeneous in character.
5. The techniques of measurement of aggregates are very complicated. Many times it creates problem.

INTERDEPENDENCE BETWEEN MICRO AND MACRO ECONOMICS

Microeconomics and Macroeconomics are complementary to each other rather than being competitive. Actually Micro- and Macro-economics are so interdependent that one cannot approach without the other, again we cannot attain a complete understanding of the functioning of the economic system unless we integrate the two approaches in a judicious manner. Let us now examine this.

1. Macroeconomics depends on Microeconomics

The theories regarding the behaviour of some Macroeconomic aggregates are derived from the theories of individual behaviour, i.e. Theories of Microeconomics. The theory of relative prices of products and factors is essential in the explanation of the determination of general price level. Even Keynes used Microeconomic theory to explain the rise in price as a result of the increase in the money supply of the country. According to Keynes, as a result of the increase in money supply and consequently the aggregate demand, more output is produced, the cost of production rises. With the rise in the cost of production, the price rises. According to him, cost of production rises because of (1) the law of diminishing returns operates, and (2) wages and prices of raw materials may rise as the economy approaches full employment. Now, the influence of cost of production, diminishing returns, etc. to determine the general price level are the parts of Microeconomics. So, Microeconomic theory contributes to Macroeconomic theory in many times.

2. Microeconomics depends on Macroeconomics

The microeconomic topics: the determination of the rate of profit and the rate of interest depend greatly upon the Macroeconomic aggregates.

The magnitude of profits depends upon the level of aggregate demand, national income and the general price level which are the macroeconomic topics.

In the determination of rate of interest Keynes showed that the rate of interest is determined by the liquidity preference function and the stock (or supply) of money, both are macroeconomic topics. Again in the modern interest theory (i.e. intersection of IS-LM curves) along with liquidity preference and supply of money, the other two forces, saving and investment functions, which are macro terms, are used to explain the determination of interest. Thus, Microeconomics depends to some extend upon Macroeconomics.

Therefore, there is a good deal of interdependence between Micro and Macroeconomics. Microeconomics contributes to Macroeconomics and Macroeconomics, in its turn, contributes to Microeconomics. It is very essential to integrate the two approaches to get correct solution of our main economic problems.

THE NATURE OF MACROECONOMICS

The study of economy can be made at different levels of aggregation. For the sake of convenience, economic theory is classified into two separate branches—Microeconomics and Macroeconomics—Microeconomics is that branch of economic theory which analyses the economic phenomenon at small units of aggregation. It studies such issues as: How an individual spends his income? How should he allocate his scarce resources to satisfy his competing wants? How individual demand of a commodity be converted into market demand? How the price of a commodity is determined? Under what circumstance this price is stable? How firm decides what to produce, how much to produce and what technique of production to use? Is it better to have competition in one industry or monopoly or *vice versa*. All these questions have one common attribute—They are either concerned with the economic decisions of one single individual, or one single firm or one single market. Thus microeconomics is the study of either a single individual (such as theory of firm) or of a single market (such as perfect competition).

Macroeconomics, in contrast, is a study of aggregates of the entire economy, *e.g.*, national income, output, employment, total consumption, savings, investment, aggregate demand, supply, general price level etc.

Macro means big or large. Hence, in macroeconomics we study the economy as a whole. In this branch of economic enquiry, we deal with aggregate economic variables, such as national income, price level and employment level. It deals with questions such as: How the level of income is determined in an economy? Why does it fluctuate? Why the prices of all commodities rise at some time and fall at some other time? How the excess capacity develops? How the employment is determined and how can unemployment be reduced? In the analysis of all these issues, the basic unit of study is the economy itself. Hence, all this comes under the scope of macroeconomics.

Microeconomics is not necessarily restricted to individual units, say, a household or a firm. It also covers aggregates, *e.g.*, study of an industry which consists of several firms, consumer demand for cotton is an aggregate of the demands of several households. But the difference is that aggregates in microeconomics relate to only a part of the economy while the aggregates in macroeconomics cover the entire economy.

SOME MISCONCEPTIONS ABOUT MACROECONOMICS

The classification of economic theory into microeconomics and macroeconomics should not be taken as water-tight compartments. In many ways, they overlap each other. In fact, there cannot be any meaningful macroeconomics without micro-economics. It is just that group behaviour is not always the same as individual behaviour. Hence, with good reason, they should be kept separate for analytical purposes. It does not mean that group behaviour shall always be different from individual behaviour. In fact, many things which are said to be true about the individual behaviour may also hold good for the group behaviour. However, some economists like Gary Becker do think that this classification is unnecessary and there is no need for separate theories in order to deal with macro and microeconomic issues. Instead, both types of issues could very well be handled with what they call 'economic theory' encompassing both micro and macro theories. However, in this book we shall adhere to the distinction between micro and macroeconomic issues for several reasons: firstly, this is a book specifically, dealing with macroeconomic issues and we shall not have to say much about the microeconomic issues as such, except occasionally. Secondly, this is in line not only with age old tradition in economic analysis but also in conformity with the standard practice at the university departments where courses in micro and macroeconomics are offered separately.

It shall not be out of place to clear some of the misconceptions which people hold about the relative significance of micro and macroeconomics. It is not correct to say that macroeconomics is more useful, more relevant, and more realistic than microeconomics. Both of them are useful. Both of them are relevant and both of them may be equally realistic or unrealistic.

The truth of matter is that micro and macroeconomics are two different approaches to study the economic phenomenon. Sometimes, it is useful to adopt a micro approach to reach any meaningful conclusion. In treatment of some other problems the micro approach may not prove so useful and so productive. Consequently, a macro approach is required. It does not mean that one has become unimportant, irrelevant, or useless in comparison to the other: Both types of approaches are useful for the analysis of different type of issues.

METHODS OF MACROECONOMICS

The methods of analysis commonly used in economic analysis may be classified into three categories: (i) static method, (ii) comparative static method, and (iii) dynamic method.

The equilibrium in a model is defined as the balancing of some opposite forces involving some selected variables of the model, in such a manner that there is no inherent tendency in the system to change. The analysis of equilibrium in this sense is referred to as statics. Thus static analysis is characterized with the lack of change, *i.e.,* once the variables in the model assume a certain value, these values are adhered to until the position of equilibrium is reached. That is why static analysis is dubbed as analysis of how equilibrium is obtained. It does not concern itself with the questions such as: whether the equilibrium will be stable or unstable? What if there are changes in the parameters? Whether a new equilibrium will be established or not? How shall it compare with the original level of equilibrium etc. The static analysis is centered on a point of time. The moment equilibrium is achieved, its job is done. Probably, this was the consideration which led professor Hicks to remark: "......we call economic statics those parts of economic theory where we do not trouble about dating"[1] meaning thereby that time is not taken into account in static analysis.

Comparative statics is concerned with the comparison of two equilibrium positions. It addresses itself to the questions which have been raised above in pointing out the limitations of static analysis. In static method, certain initial values to parameters are assumed to be given, then the attainment of equilibrium is investigated. In comparative static analysis, it is assumed that initial equilibrium exists and there is a given change in the original parameters. Suppose that we can obtain a new equilibrium position with some values of parameters then it is the function of comparative statics to compare the new equilibrium position with the original equilibrium.

A dynamic analysis is one in which all variables of an economic model change with time in such a manner that their rate of change also becomes variable. The dynamic techniques of analysis are used in growth models. However, we shall remain concerned with statics and comparative statics only in the whole of this book.

Partial and General Equilibrium

Most of the economic activities do not depend only upon a single factor. They depend upon a number of factors. So in analysing a particular economic phenomenon, we may adopt any of the two different approaches available to us. One way is to consider all the possible relevant factors affecting the phenomenon. This is general equilibrium approach. The other way, sometimes more simple and straightforward way, is to consider a few selected factors which are considered to be crucial for the study of the problem. This is called partial equilibrium approach. Let us take the familiar example of a demand function for a commodity, *X*. Let

Q_x = Quantity demanded for *X*.

P_x = Price of the commodity *X*.

P_y = Price of the commodity *Y*.

---

1. J.R. Hicks, *Value and Capital* (1939), Oxford University Press, New York, p. 115.

$P_z \ldots P_n$ = Price of the commodity z and prices of all other commodities in the economy.

Y = Income.

T = Tastes, fashion etc.

Now the demand function of the commodity X can be written as:

$$Q_x = f(P_x, P_y, P_z, \ldots\ldots P_n, Y, T) \quad \ldots(1.1)$$

Eq (1.1) describes a demand function with a general equilibrium approach. It states that quantity demanded of goods X depends not only upon price of goods but also upon the prices of all other goods as well as upon income and tastes. The basic assumption in general equilibrium approach is that everything depends upon every thing. However, price of several goods may not affect the quantity demanded of goods X at all and it may be better to drop them from the model. Similarly, income, tastes, and other price may not change in course of time when we are studying the effect of a change in P_x upon Q_x. Therefore, equation (1.2) can be rewritten as:

$$Q_x = f(P_x, \overline{P}_y, \overline{P}_z, \ldots\ldots \overline{P}_n, \overline{Y}, \overline{T}) \quad \ldots(1.2)$$

where the bar on the variables $P_y \ldots T$ indicates that these variables remain constant. Therefore, Eq. (1.2) can be further rewritten as follows:

$$Q_x = f(P_x) \quad \ldots(1.3)$$

Equation (1.3) states that quantity demanded of goods x depends upon its price. Thus statement is valid only if we add another phrase 'other things remaining the same' implying that all other factors which may possibly influence the quantity demanded of goods x do not change in course of analysis. This is partial equilibrium approach which invokes assumption *'ceteris paribus'* which means nothing, but 'other things remaining the same'.

In course of study of macroeconomics we shall adopt a general equilibrium approach and employ the methods of static and comparative static analysis.

Aggregate Economic Variables

We have learnt above that macroeconomics is the study of aggregate economic activity. It studies the complete economy in its operation. How income is created? What governs investment and so on. Studying aggregate economic activity, macroeconomics deals with economic variables in their aggregate form. So let us explain what do we mean by aggregate economic variables. Here we are concerned with the variables such as income, consumption, investment, saving, employment, interest rate, etc.

In aggregate form these variables are related to the economy as a whole. By consumption expenditure we do not mean consumption expenditure of a single individual, or of a single family or household. It means the expenditure which the whole society incurs upon its consumption needs. Similarly, saving refers to total savings by the economy and investment is not amount invested by any single firm but is the total amount invested by all the firms. Price level refers to price of all goods and services. Of course, the economy is still divided into segments and sectors and some variables relate to the specific sectors. The basic function of macroeconomics is to study the interrelationships between different sectors and shed light on the working of the whole economy.

Macro-Dynamics and Macro-Statics

The traditional theory, when dealing with the economy as a whole, is concerned with certain aggregative relations which obtain in the stationary position without attempting to show how the economy reached there, temporally or spatially. This type of study is called 'macro-statics'. In contrast to this traditional theory of static equilibrium, Keynes considered his analysis 'dynamic', calling it "the theory of shifting equilibrium."[2] Keynes' theory is considered dynamic in the sense that it explains "a system in which changing views about the future are capable of influencing the present situation."[3] His emphasis on the role of 'expectations' lends some plausibility to his claim. Probably a more cogent interpretation of the 'dynamic' nature of Keynes' theory of shifting equilibrium is that he is thinking dynamically, because there can be no shift from one position of equilibrium to another without prior movement of variables through time. Keynes, however, made no formal attempt to trace the process of transition from one position of equilibrium to another. His method of comparing different equilibrium levels of

2. J.M. Keynes, *The General Theory of Employment, Interest and Money* (London, 1936), p. 293.

3. *Ibid.*

income corresponding to changes in the consumption and investment variables, that is, changes in the values of macro-variables, has been termed "comparative statics".

Macro-dynamics, in contrast, is concerned with discrete movements or rates of change of macro-variables. This method analyses the discrete or continuous changes in aggregates, the sequence of cause-and-effect events arising from some initial disturbance, and the time paths of macro-variables and aggregative relationships. Thus the macro-dynamic method enables one to see a 'progressive whole'. This technique has been developed by economists like D.H. Robertson, R. Frisch, M. Kalecki, J. Tinbergen, P.A. Samuelson, R.F. Harrod, J.R. Hicks etc. If Keynes' "comparative statistics" is concerned with the level of employment 'at any time' the macro-dynamics of those other economists is concerned with the fluctuations of employment "at instants of time". If the former is interested in the precise effects of change in some aggregate upon the stationary or equilibrium position of the economy as a whole, the latter may be said to describe the temporal process of deviations or disequilibria.

HISTORICAL DEVELOPMENT

Pre-classical Contribution: Even before Adam Smith, a group of economic thinkers known as 'Mercantilists" had been by and large concerned with the functioning of the whole economic system. They studied the cause and relation between a favourable balance of trade and national prosperity, between inflow of gold and the domestic rate of interest, between the rate of interest and the volume of investment and the level of employment. They were interested in practical policies aimed at promoting domestic prosperity and progress.

Classical Contribution: T.R. Malthus, better known for his *Essays on Population* (1798) than for his *Principles of Political Economy* (1820), was an important forerunner of macroeconomics. He ventured to put forward the view that aggregate demand could be inadequate in contrast to the then prevailing view of an automatic self-adjusting economy. He challenged Say's law on the reasoning that the parsimony which Adam Smith and others had sanctioned would, if pushed to excess, "destroy the motive to production" and lead to the 'stagnation of capital, and subsequent stagnation in the demand for labour'.

Karl Marx is probably the most important exception to the classical tradition roughly from Adam Smith to John Stuart Mill in more than one ways. He made the first attempt to deal with the problems of the whole economic system and to build a picture of economic life and relationships as a whole. Marx's aggregative analysis is considered predominantly 'organistic' in the sense that in is concerned with the organism of capitalism as a developing whole. In contrast, Keynes' analysis runs mainly in terms of 'mechanistic' equilibrium analysis since his method consists it investigating the equilibrium mechanism of capitalism in a historically given situation.

Neo-classicals: The neo-classical economists were concerned by and large with micro-analysis which culminated with Marshall. They took the economy as whole for granted and thus studied the determination of individual prices, outputs and employments, ignoring the general level of prices, output and employment.

Modern contribution: Though modern macroeconomic theory is associated with the name of Keynes, there are other writers also who before or along with Keynes contributed to macroeconomics, *e.g.* L. Walras, K. Wicksell, I. Fisher etc.

EQUILIBRIUM IN MACRO-ANALYSIS AND MICRO-ANALYSIS

Though the objectives are different, both the macroeconomics and microeconomics make use of the concepts of supply and demand and the equilibrium that may be established between the two. In micro-analysis, we study the market for a particular commodity. The buyers demand different quantities at different prices. Similarly, the sellers offer different quantities at different prices. The equilibrium is reached at the point where the demand and supply are equal and no one has the incentive to upset the position. If the price thus reached is so high that even the producers with the highest cost of production can earn abnormal profits, new firms will be attracted in the market which would result in an increase in supply. To induce the buyers to purchase the additional supplies, the price would have to be reduced. In this way the equilibrium would be attained by changes in price and in the quantities demanded and supplied.

In macro-analysis we study equilibrium between demand and supply for the economy as a whole. Supply consists of all types of goods and services available in the country while the demand is the aggregate of demands for all commodities. Since different commodities (*e.g.* cloth, shoes, wheat, cars) cannot be measured in terms of a single unit, in macroeconomics, the demand and supply are expressed in terms of money. The equilibrium will be reached where the aggregate demand is equal to aggregate supply. Inequality between aggregate demand and aggregate supply will cause changes in production and prices, and perhaps also in the volume of employment because less labour will be required if the level of production declines. It cannot be said with certainty, however, whether or not these changes will lead the economy towards an equilibrium position. Herein lies the difference between the single-commodity market and the economy as a whole.

This is because there are underlying relationships between demand and supply which can be ignored in micro-analysis but which are of vital importance when the economy as a whole is under study. In a single-commodity market, it is not unreasonable to assume that the buyers and sellers act independent of each other and the two sets of people influence each other's decisions only through the market itself. If the number of workers employed in a particular industry increases, it would be paying more wages and hence the recipients of wages would be in a position to spend more; but the effect of this on the product of the industry concerned may not be appreciable barring the exceptional cases when the industry employs an important portion of the community's workers or when the product of the industry is so important that the workers spend a considerable portion of their income on it. We can, therefore, safely ignore such behind-the-scenes 'feedback' of purchasing power from the supply side to the demand side. When, however, the supply of and demand for all the products are aggregated, the 'feedback' cannot be ignored; the buyers and sellers are more or less the same persons. The money obtained in exchange for goods and services on the supply side of the economy passes into the hands of spenders who appear on the demand side.

The aggregate demand and supply are thus linked through the intermediary of income. If the buyers, for instance, decide to spend less, the value of the commodities and hence the incomes of the suppliers of those commodities would decline which would cause a further decline in expenditure. Similarly, if the buyers decide to spend more, the value of the commodities and hence the incomes of the suppliers would rise which would lead to a further rise in expenditure. Thus while the market for a single commodity can be viewed to work in terms of the confrontation of the two forces of demand and supply, the functioning of the entire economy is to be conceived in terms of a triangular relationship—the three corners of the triangle being respectively aggregate supply, aggregate income and aggregate demand.

NEED FOR MACRO APPROACH

The need for a separate macro approach to the study of several economic problems arises from the fact that micro approach is not only inadequate but may lead to entirely misleading conclusions. In economics what is true of parts may not necessarily be true of the whole. The problem of aggregate is not simply a matter of adding or multiplying what happens in respect of the various individual parts of the whole. For example, in a period of recession, savings by an individual may increase his prosperity but savings by all the people would accentuate depression and bring misery for the country as a whole.

Wage cutting in a particular firm would increase employment in that firm but general wage cutting may fail to expand employment in the economy as a whole. An individual would become richer if he finds a few currency notes but the country as a whole cannot become richer by printing more notes. An individual depositor may withdraw his funds from the bank without doing any harm to it but if all the depositors act in the same manner simultaneously, the entire banking system would collapse.

Neither of the two approaches alone are adequate to analyse the multifarious problems facing an economy. To arrive at correct solutions, it is very necessary to integrate the two approaches. Even during the boom period, for instance, some industries may be dying because of a lack of effective demand for the products owing to number of reasons. Similarly, during a recession period, some industries may prosper fast. To apply solutions suggested by the micro-analysis to such industries would obviously be wrong. It would be equally wrong to apply solutions suggested by the micro-analysis of such industries to the economy as a whole. There are few macro problems which have no micro elements involved and there are hardly any micro problems without macro aspects. What is, therefore, required is a proper integration of the two approaches both in analysing economic problems and in prescribing policy measures for tackling them.

MEANINGFUL MACROECONOMICS

There arises the question whether a meaningful macroeconomics is possible.[4] It would be futile if confined solely to definitional relationships among macroeconomic variables. It must also study relationships among economic variables which express motivation and behaviour. Theories involving such relationships would obviously depend upon hypotheses concerning the behaviour of the individuals, families and firms which comprise the economy. The usefulness of macroeconomics would, therefore, depend on whether or not aggregative theories of behaviour are possible.

Experience tells us that individuals do react in certain generally common ways to changes in circumstances that confront them. With the increase in their incomes, other things remaining the same, for instance, most of the individuals will increase their expenditure. But the ratio of increase in expenditure to a certain increase in income would differ from person to person depending on a number of factors like total income, size of family, likely future needs for money, expected future income, thriftiness etc. It is not possible to have a theory which would accurately predict the behaviour of individuals to increase in their incomes. But while dealing with aggregates, the law of large numbers comes to our help. The law tells us that the vagaries of individual behaviour have a tendency to appear in a regular mass behaviour. While dealing with aggregates for the whole economy, we take advantage of greater regularity of mass than of individual behaviour.

The differences in individual behaviour may not, however, be of a random nature. There may be systematic and measureable differences of consumption behaviour as income changes between high and low income families, between rural and urban families, between wage-earning families and families living on profits etc. Even if each group of families reacted to changes in income in a regular and predictable manner, there may be no systematic and predictable response of aggregate consumer expenditure to a change

4. Gardner Ackley, *Macroeconomic Theory* (Tokyo, 1971), pp. 19-23.

in aggregate consumer income. If a given increase in aggregate income was received at one time primarily by one group and at another time mainly by another group, no reliable generalization would be possible in regard to the effect of a certain aggregate increase in income on aggregate increase in expenditure.

A regular aggregative relationship would exist only if the income distribution among groups with different responses remains unchanged or change in some systematic and regular way as the aggregate consumption-income relationship would be compound or product of two kinds of laws *viz.* (1) laws relating to consumer behaviour or several groups and (2) the laws relating to distribution of income. Fortunately, experience tells us that composition of several of our most important aggregates is fairly stable or systematic to allow meaningful aggregate theories and measurements.

Meaning is added to macroeconomics by another law, that is many variables that are important for explaining individual behaviour have a tendency to cancel out when we deal with aggregates. This is more true in the short run. Consumption behaviour of the individual family, for instance, depends, in addition to income, on many other things, *e.g.*, size of the family, age of the family head, age of its automobile and other durable goods, births, deaths, weddings, age-groups of children. While considering behaviour of aggregate families, many of these variables cancel out particularly in the short run. Birth and death rates of individual families, for instance, vary substantially but are fairly stable and predictable for the whole population. Similarly, the age structure of the total population changes very slowly.

The above discussion shows that macroeconomics is not meaningless. It can exist at least as a first approximation of reality because (1) it can depend upon certain macroeconomic truisms; (2) the composition of many aggregates is relatively stable, or varies systematically and regularly with changes in the magnitudes of the aggregates; and (3) many of the variables most significant in explaining individual economic behaviour cancel out, at least roughly when dealing with the entire economy.

IMPORTANCE

Macroeconomics is very essential for understanding the functioning of an economy and for proper formulation of economic policies. The causes of inflation, deflation, business fluctuations and underdevelopment, for instance, can be properly discovered only by techniques of macro-analysis and not by studying individual units. Similarly, the steps for remedying these maladies are based on macro-analysis.

LIMITATIONS

Macro-analysis cannot be very precise because of heterogeneous nature of different elements constituting an aggregate. For instance, 2 mangoes + 4 mangoes = 6 mangoes is a meaningful aggregate; but 2 mangoes + 4 books is a meaningless aggregate. The introduction of money as a common measuring rod has, however, added meaning to macro-analysis. The aggregate income, consumption, saving and investment are measured in terms of money and not in terms of heterogeneous goods and services. But the value of money itself continues changing which renders difficult comparisons of economic aggregates over time. But such limitations are more in the nature of practical difficulties in formulating meaningful aggregates rather than factors invalidating macroeconomic analysis.

STOCK AND FLOW VARIABLES

All the aggregate economic variables with whom we shall be dealing in this book may be classified into two kinds of variables: (i) stock variables; and (ii) flow variables. The distinction between these variables shall be basic to our understanding of functioning of aggregate economy.

Stock variables are those which are measured at a point of time. Flow variables are those which are measured in a period of time. A period is nothing but the difference between two points of time. Some examples may be helpful in making the distinction between these two concepts. The weight of a car is a stock as it is measured at a point of time but its speed (*e.g.* 80 km. per hour) is measured in a period of time. A student's weight on 1st January, 1983 was 65 kg. So the weight is a stock variable. Suppose that in preceding year he registered an increase of two kg. in his weight. This is a flow. Therefore, all changes in stock are flow as they have a time dimension.

Suppose that you keep Rs. 10,000 in a fixed deposit account in a bank. This is stock as its amounts shall be measured on a specific point of time. If you keep on receiving an annual interest payment the stock would remain the same even after several years. However, if you have instructed your bank to credit the interest payment in the same account, your stock of deposit will grow and change in deposit will be regarded as flow. Now, suppose that bank pays interest at the rate of 5% per year on its deposit, after one year you will earn Rs. 500 as interest payment. This is a flow as it is measured in a period of time, *i.e.*, one year. Since interest is a type of income, you can generalize that all types of incomes are flow variables. But the amount of capital for an economy has, at any given moment of time, is a stock.

CIRCULAR FLOW OF INCOME

We have seen above that income is flow variable. Now, let us see that how flow of income is generated in an economy. Let us assume that there is a simple economy composed of households and business firm. This is a two sector model of economy. It is assumed that there is no government which may impose taxes and incur expenditure. It is also assumed that there is no foreign trade sector, *i.e.*, nothing is imported from abroad and nothing is exported to foreign countries. A model of economy in which foreign trade sector is not taken into account is known as a model of closed economy.

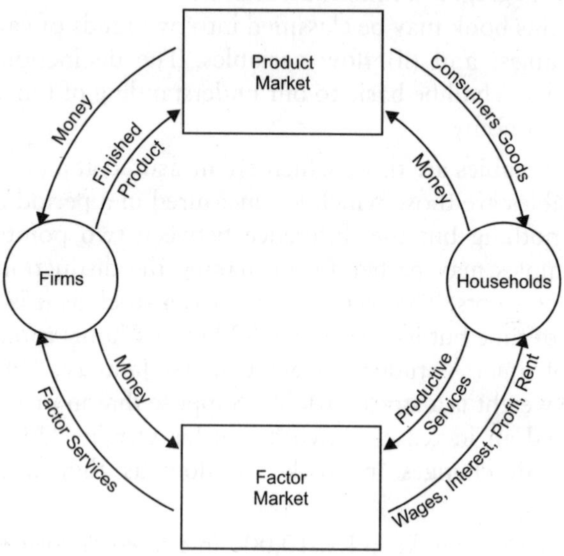

Fig. 1.2. Circular Flow of Income.

There will be two markets in our simple economy—Factor market and Product market. Factor market is one in which the productive services of factors of production are bought and sold. Households are also the owners of factor of production. They own labour power, capital stocks, buildings and lands and shares in the companies. They sell these services to firms who appear as buyers in the factor market. Thus money is transferred from firms to households. The firms get productive services of factors of production in return of their money. The money paid by firms to the households, for exchange of factor services becomes income for households. This income is in the form of wages, interest, rent, and profits.

The firms carry on the productive process with the help of factor services which they buy in the factor market. They produce various types of goods and services and sell in the product market. The households are the buyers of these products and they spend their income which they earned in the factors market to buy these goods and services in the product market. Thus money is transferred from households to the firms in the product market. The firms get their income in the product market from the households who obtain goods and services in exchange of their money. These flows have been depicted in Fig. 1.2 and direction of arrows show from whom to whom goods and income are flowing. Also notice that there is not one flow but there are two flows—one is the flow of goods and services and factor services. The other is the corresponding flow of income. The flow of goods and factor services is sometimes called the real flow and flow of income is called the money flow. The money flow is always in the opposite direction of real flow.

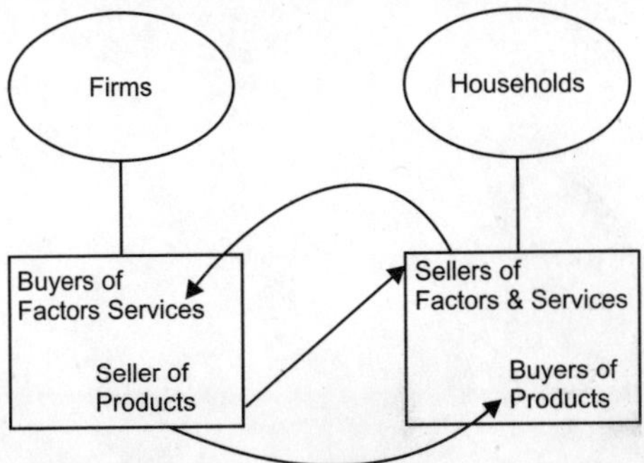

Fig. 1.3. Dual Role of Firms and Households.

It is also necessary to recognize the dual role of households and firms in order to understand the circular flow of income. These dual roles are explicitly shown in Fig. 1.3. The households are sellers of factors services and at the same time they are buyers of products. Similarly, firms are buyers of factor services and sellers of product. They switch over their respective roles in the factor market and product market. Thus, sellers in the product market become buyers in the factor market and *vice versa*.

The above model is the basic model of circular flow income. Macroeconomic theory is concerned with explaining this flow of income between firms and households. There is no doubt that this is a simple caricature of a complex reality. However, complications can be introduced as we start dropping the various assumptions made in the simple model one by one. As a first step, government and foreign trade sector may be incorporated. At a later stage various types of withdrawals from and injunctions into the circular flow may be introduced. However, this is a task which shall be taken up in later chapters of this book. Nevertheless, even the simple model is capable of showing the basic character of different types of flows in the economy.

National Income

2

The macroeconomics theory deals with broad national aggregates like national income, consumption, saving and investment. For a proper understanding of this theory, it is very necessary to be clear about the meaning of such terms. This is what we propose to do in this chapter.

MEASUREMENT OF AGGREGATE ECONOMIC ACTIVITY

It is by now clear that macroeconomics is the study of aggregate economic activity. Therefore, we need a measure by which we could determine the performance of aggregate economy. The total production of economy would be one such measure. But the problems of measurement and of aggregation are involved here.

An economy is an organization of the process of production and distribution where, in co-operation with others, people produce and acquire goods and services for the satisfaction of their wants. An economy is a collection of all the farms, factories, workshops, mines, roads, railways, banks, schools, cinema, houses and hospitals, etc. which provide the people with the goods which either they consume or use for further production or export to the foreign countries. Not only goods are produced, but services are also rendered by professional people, like doctors, teachers, lawyers, musicians, etc. These services are directly consumed by the members of the society. Each one of these individuals, who renders services, is an important production unit. Thus, the economy produces hundreds of thousands types of goods and services. These goods and services are measured in different types of units. Some goods like television sets, radios, fans etc. are measured in number. Foodgrains, rice, wheat etc. are measured in quintals. Cement and steel are measured in metric tons. Then economy produces different types of machinery which manufacture cloth, television sets, radio, steel, and tractors. How all these could be aggregated to arrive at a single measure of aggregate economic activity? An easy way out of this problem is to calculate the value of all goods and services (Value = price × quantity) and sum them over all goods and services produced in economy in a given period of time. The figure thus arrived at, is a measure of aggregate economic activity and is known as gross national product or GNP of which a more formal definition is given below:

GNP or gross national product is the value of all final goods and services produced by any economy during a given period of time, usually a year, and valued at current market prices.

We must keep the following facts in mind about GNP:

(1) GNP is the value of all final goods and services. A goods or service is considered final when it reaches the consumer who finally consumes it. For example, bread is a final good. The value of all bread shall be included in GNP. The baker uses flour, sugar, egg, and coal to make bread, but the values of these things are not included in the calculation of GNP. The reason is that the value of all these inputs is included in the price of bread. There are some goods which are final products of one industry but are used in production in some other industry as inputs. These goods are called intermediate goods. All intermediate goods are excluded from the accounting system of gross national product. It is necessary to do so to avoid double counting which shall greatly inflate our measure of aggregate economic activity and misrepresent the productive capacity of the economy. Consequently, to avoid double counting, intermediate products are neglected and only final products are counted. In the above example, flour, sugar, eggs and coal shall be included in GNP accounting only if they are bought by households for final consumption.

(2) We should note that GNP includes only such economic activities which are produced for market. In other words, only those goods and services which have a price tag on them are included in the calculation of GNP. Some economic activities may be performed outside the scope of market system, *e.g.*, a housewife prepares meals in her kitchen, an amateur gardener grows vegetables in his backyard, a test star cricketer participates in a friendly match in his home town, a film actor appears at a charity show in aid of a hospital etc. All these activities shall not be included in GNP. However, if the same activities were performed on a commercial basis, they would have been included in GNP. Now, we can state as

a rule that activities performed due to love, charity, entertainment and pleasure, patriotism etc. are not included in GNP but if the same activities were performed for a price, they would be included in GNP.

(3) It should also be clear that only legal economic activities are included in GNP. The illegal economic activities such as smuggled goods and services, the amount of goods stolen, the income obtained by theft, dacoity, cheating, etc. are not included in GNP.

We can establish an identity between gross national product (GNP) and gross national income (GNY) of an economy. GNP is the money measure of all the final goods and services produced during the year. Thus if $q_1, q_2, q_3;..., q_n$ are the qualities of all the final goods and services produced during the year and $p_1, p_2, p_3..., p_n$ are their per unit prices, then;

$$GNP = q_1 p_1 + q_2 p_2 + q_3 p_3 + ... + q_n p_n$$

Corresponding to every flow of goods, there is a flow of factor incomes. Production is a joint effort of factors like labour, land, capital and organisation which in turn for their contribution to production receive wages (*W*), rent (*R*), interest (*I*) and profits (*P*). The national income being a sum total of factor incomes can be expressed as,

$$GNY = W + R + I + P$$

Since both the production of final goods and the income of the factors arise out of the same production process, they are identically equal to each other. This can be proved by the following set of equations:

$$GNP = p_1 q_1 + p_2 q_2 + p_3 q_3 +... + p_n q_n \qquad ...(i)$$

$$GNY = W + R + I + P \qquad ... (ii)$$

In the equation (ii) *P* represents the profits of the entrepreneurs. The profits are a residue left over with the entrepreneurs after making payment to all the other factors *viz.* land, labour and capital from his total sale proceeds. Thus,

$$P = p_1 q_1 + p_2 q_2 + p_3 q_3 + ... + p_n q_n -(W+R+I) \qquad ... (iii)$$

by transposing the last point of the eq^n (iii) to the left hand side we get,

$$W+R+I+P = p_1 q_1 + p_2 q_2 + p_3 q_3 + ... + p_n q_n \qquad ... (iv)$$

Now the left hand side of the eq^n (iv) denotes national income while the right hand side is the gross national product. Thus

$GNY = GNP$

In other words, on the basis of the simplifying assumptions that we have made, the aggregate value of all the final goods and services produced in an economy during a given year is always equal to the aggregate of factor incomes generated during the year.

NNP AND NATIONAL INCOME

GNP can be produced by a combination of three factors of production—land, labour, and capital. Land is assumed to be fixed. Let us also assume that withdrawal from labour force (persons who retire every year) is exactly matched by new arrivals (persons who attain the working age and thus enter the job market). Thus, we are assuming that labour force is also constant. Thus GNP would depend mainly upon the capital stock. If the economy started with a given amount of capital stock in one year, in the next year GNP would decline. This will happen because capital stock will decline. There will be wear and tear of machinery in course of production. So the capital stock cannot remain constant. This is also called capital consumption meaning thereby that some amount of capital shall be consumed (lost) in the productive process. Unless some provision is made to replace this lost capital, the capital stock cannot remain intact at the initial level. Therefore, a special allowance is made to replace the capital and make up for the wear and tear of machinery. This is known as depreciation allowance or capital consumption allowance.

The Net National Product (NNP) is obtained from GNP after deducting the depreciation allowance:

$$NNP + D = GNP$$

or $$GNP - D = NNP \qquad ...(2.1)$$

where

NNP = Net National Product.

GNP = Gross National Product.

D = Depreciation or capital consumption allowance.

Closely related to the concept of *NNP* is the more popular concept of National Income which is the sum total of income of all individuals of the society. In fact, conceptually *NNP* and national income are the same thing.

DEFINITION OF NATIONAL INCOME

The national income has been defined by different persons in different ways. There is nothing absolutely right or wrong about any of these definitions. The most suitable definition of income would depend mainly on the purpose for which income estimate is required. Marshall defines national income as below:

> The labour and capital of a country, acting on its natural resources, produce annually a certain net aggregate of commodities, material and immaterial, including services of all kinds...and net income due on account of foreign investments must be added in. This is true net annual income or revenue of the country, or the national dividend.

Though this definition is theoretically sound, simple and comprehensive, it has serious practical limitations. It is not easy to make statistically correct estimates of the total production of goods and services particularly because of the difficulties of double counting and portion of the produce which is retained for personal consumption.

In the words of Prof. Pigou, "...the national dividend is that part of the objective income of the community including, of course, income derived from abroad, which can be measured in money.....". According to Prof. Pigou, only those goods and services are to be counted, avoiding double counting, of course, which are actually exchanged for money. Pigou's definition is practicable and convenient and avoids the difficulties of measuring national dividend inherent in Marshall's definition. But it has its own shortcomings.

NATIONAL INCOME AT FACTOR COST

The sum total of goods and services are produced by the cooperation of the factors of production and as such their money value is distributed among those factors of production. The national income can, therefore, also be conceived as the total incomes received by the factors of production for their contribution of land, labour, capital and entrepreneurship. Such receipts take the form of wages, rent, interest and profits.

The income of an individual may be defined as the amount of his earnings from the productive services currently rendered by him or by his property. National income is simply the sum of incomes of all individuals. It is a flow concept and relates to a definite period, normally a year.

Income defined as earnings should be distinguished from income receipts. The income earned during a certain period may not be received during the same period either because it is taxed away before receipts or is retained to be paid at a later date. Income received during a certain period may also exceed the income earned during that period either because delayed payment of past earnings exceeds current retentions or because of receipt of "transfer payment" which does not represent payment for productive services rendered in the present or past period, *e.g.*, relief payments which represent "government transfer payments", bad debts of consumers to business are a form of "business transfer payments", gifts in kind or money exchanged among individuals are a type of "interpersonal transfer payments".

Income should also be distinguished from simple asset transformation. The sale proceeds of a house, bonds, patent rights, for instance, are not income. Similarly, the amount received as a result of repayment of a debt is not income. All that has happened in such cases is the transformation of wealth from one form to another, that is, cash. In contrast, the current flow of services from the house, interest from the bond and royalties from the payment are income.

A special problem arises in case of capital gains resulting from sale of assets at prices higher than their purchase prices. This difference represents neither an asset transformation nor true income excepting in case of a person whose profession is buying and selling assets and who earns his livelihood by his ability to buy at prices lower than the sale prices. Normally capital gains, which are of the nature of a windfall and not earnings from current productive services, are not considered a part of income.

Theoretically, any costs which the individual incurs in earning his income should be deducted from his gross earnings. Examples of such costs are provided by the cost of tools which he must himself supply, union dues, travel to and back from the place of work, etc. In practice, however, most of these costs are not deducted because of the practical difficulties involved in clearly separating between expenses incurred in earning income and those for using or enjoying income. Part of the travel expenses, for instance, may be because the worker prefers to live at a distance from his place of work. In order to be able to work, a worker must have some clothing to wear, food to eat and shelter to live. To be efficient, he must have some entertainment and relaxation. If this argument is stretched further, we will reach the conclusion that a considerable portion of consumer expenditure is cost of earning income and should be deducted from the gross income. But the widely adopted convention is not to deduct such expenditure on the plea that the workers earn in order to consume and not consume in order to live. It would, however, be fair to deduct from gross income, at least, that expenditure which is obviously incurred for earning income, *e.g.*, cost of workers' tools.

In case of business enterprises, the expenses incurred in earning income are easily defined and are quite important and must be deducted from the gross income. Unlike most of consumer expenditures, most of business expenses are incurred for earning income. The usual practice, therefore, is to deduct business expenses in order to arrive at earnings of the business enterprise.

In short, national income is the sum of (1) wages, salaries, commissions, bonuses and other forms of employee earnings before deduction of taxes or social security contributions; (2) net income from rentals and royalties; (3) interest income; and (4) profits before deduction of taxes based on income.

The major significance of the concept of national income lies in revealing the distribution side of national economic activity or the manner in which the total product is allocated to the factors of production relatively to the productive services rendered. National income proper is considered to be the most satisfactory single measure of overall economic activity, not only because it has all the merits of net national product mentioned in the following pages but also because it shows how much total expenditure on consumer goods and capital goods (the latter being in excess of replacements) there must be in order to offset the total income of productive factors (total cost of production from the point of view of the producers).

PERSONAL INCOME

It is the total of incomes received by individuals from all sources. It consists of wages and salaries, interest, rent, dividends, incomes of self-employed people like farmers, doctors and shopkeepers, and receipts which are not payments for current productive services (*i.e.* government and business transfers). National income that is, total income earned and personal income, that is, total income received must be different because some income which is earned is not actually received (*e.g.* undistributed corporate profits, corporate income taxes, social security contributions) and conversely some income which is received is not currently earned (*e.g.* transfer payments). Thus,

Personal Income = National Income – Social Security Contributions – Corporate Income Taxes – Undistributed Corporate Profits + Transfer Payments.

The concept of personal income is helpful for the specific purpose of knowing the potential purchasing power of the household sector of the economy in a given period. Those inclined to regard consumer welfare both as a paramount economic end and as an essential means to national prosperity usually attach great importance to personal income data. But the concept of personal income fails to indicate what is actually available to the household sector for spending and saving purposes. This lacuna of the concept has necessitated another concept *viz.*, Disposable Income.

DISPOSABLE INCOME

A person does not have complete command over the personal income, as defined above, to spend, to save, to give away in any manner he chooses. He must pay taxes like income-tax, property tax etc. and other obligatory payments like national insurance contributions. The income which a person is free to dispose of in any manner he likes, therefore, is personal income minus taxes and other obligatory payments. This income is called disposable income. A person's freedom to dispose of even this income is limited by his contractual obligations, *e.g.*, life insurance policies, mortgages, instalment contracts.

The total of disposable income of all sectors must add up to the same total as the national income itself because the effect of the various taxes and transfer is merely one of redistribution. This process does not generate any new income. The only income available is that originally accruing to the owners of the factors of production.

The major usefulness of the concept of disposable income lies in the light it throws on the government's fiscal policy as an important factor affecting individual decisions to spend and to save.

REAL INCOME

The national income is expressed in terms of money but the purchasing power of money changes over time as a consequence of changes in the general level of prices. If the intention is to find out what the national income of any period is worth in terms of goods and services, then its 'normal' or 'money' value will have to be converted into its 'real' value by an adjustment or correction process known as 'deflating'. The money income can be deflated so as to obtain real income by the formula given below:

$$\text{Real income in terms of constant money} = \frac{\text{Nominal income in current money}}{\text{Price index for current period}}$$

GROSS NATIONAL PRODUCT (G.N.P.)

The gross national product is a basic social accounting measure of the total output or aggregate supply of goods and services. It is the total value of goods and services produced during a period, say, a year, at the market prices. Two things should be carefully noted in regard to G.N.P. In the first place, it is a monetary measure of the total goods and services produced during the period. There is no other way of adding up the heterogeneous types of goods and services. With a view to accurately measure the changes in physical output during different periods, the figures of gross national product are adjusted for price changes.

Secondly, in calculating gross national product, all goods and services produced during the period should be counted only once. Most of the goods pass through several processes of production before reaching the final market. Cotton, for instance, is spun into yarn which in turn is woven into cloth. Now while counting cloth in the G.N.P., we should be careful to avoid counting value of cotton which has gone into yarn and that of yarn which has gone into cloth. Similarly, if cloth is converted into ready-made garments and they are included in the G.N.P., we should avoid counting the value of cloth which has gone into the ready-made garments. Thus the G.N.P. includes the market value of only final goods and ignores transactions involving intermediate goods, because the value of final goods includes the value of intermediate goods which have gone into their production.

The gross national product at market prices may be obtained by adding up the following:

1. expenditure of private persons on consumption or what is called personal consumption expenditure;
2. expenditure of business enterprises on replacement, renewal and new investment or what is called gross domestic private investment;
3. expenditure of the government on the purchase of goods and services, *i.e.,* government purchase; and
4. expenditure of the rest of the world on the output of the national economy over and above what this economy spends on the output of the rest of the world, *i.e.,* export surplus or net foreign investment.

The definition of G.N.P. mentioned above assumes the existence of markets in which buyers are free to buy as much or as little as they desire, and in which the price is both a condition of supply and a reflection of the intensity of the buyer's desire for the commodity. But this is not true in case of some services, an important case being that of public services like education, external defence and the maintenance of internal law and order etc. Such services are normally provided without collecting a direct charge from the beneficiaries and cost of such services is met from the revenue of taxes, payment of which is compulsory, and whose amount in case of each citizen is not necessarily related to the value of the services rendered to him. It is not, therefore, possible to find out the market price of such services. As such their value can be measured only in terms of their cost. In the absence of evidence to the contrary, there is no alternative but to assume that the cost of provision of such services represents the value which the community attaches to these services.

A second case is that of owner-occupied houses, which obviously provide a service to the owner. Had the owners not owned those houses, they would have had to pay rent to others. Although no rent is paid in actual practice, the value of service can be assessed in money terms by assuming it to be equal to the rent paid by non-owning tenants who occupy houses of similar size and amenities.

Logically, a similar procedure should be followed for all durable goods which are used by their owners, *e.g.*, motor-cars, radios, television sets, etc. If a person hires a car on 'self-drive' terms, or rents a radio or a television set, the payment can be regarded as representing the value of the services rendered and counted as a part of the economy's production. The question arises why not count on a similar basis the imputed value of services yielded by cars and television sets used by their owners. This is, however, not done because of the obvious difficulties involved in calculating the imputed values.

A third case relates to the services rendered by housewives to their families. The housewives render valuable services by cooking, washing clothes, cleaning house, etc. Logically, these should be included in the aggregate output. Since the services of housewives are not sold in the free market for a wage, it is very difficult to impute proper money value to them. As such, the official statisticians normally do not take them into account.

There is further the difficulty of separating current from capital expenditure. The Department of Commerce of the United States arbitrarily defines as capital all expenditure on items that have a useful life of greater than one year. Before we can classify an expenditure as current or capital, we must know the life of the item for which the expenditure is being incurred. In case of many items, it is not possible to say with certainty as to whether or not their life will exceed one year till they are completely worn out. The Department of Commerce, for instance, excludes expenditure on repairs and maintenance from the definition of capital expenditure but some repairs may last for more than one year. In fact some of the Scandinavian countries use the concept of capital in a much broader sense than the United States. Maintenance of plant and machinery may considerably vary from period to period. There is a tendency to postpone repairs during periods of low profits and to catch up during periods of high profits when the firm can easily afford to spend on repairs and maintenance. The exclusion of maintenance and repairs from gross national product would underestimate true fluctuations in economic activity from prosperity to depression.

There also arises the problem of distinguishing between intermediate and final goods and services in regard to the services provided by the government. They may be considered as final products given to the economy or may partly represent intermediate products given to business firms. In both cases, since normally they are provided free of any charge, it is debatable as to whether or not they should be included at cost in the gross national product. Things like roads, conservation and information services provided by the government can be considered primarily as services consumed by producers in the process of their production. It could be argued that if business firms were required to directly pay for these services the market prices of the goods requiring such services would rise and as such these items should be included in gross national product at their cost. On the other hand, it could also be argued that business firms to pay for these services in the form of several taxes, or that the consumers would shift their choices to low-priced goods, if the cost of government services were included in the price of the goods and, therefore, the cost of government services should not be included. The normal practice, however, is to include in gross national product all government services valued at cost.

The G.N.P. concept has the merit that it reflects more accurately than any derived statistical concept, the actual conditions of production and employment during the period in question. In this concept the total production in the current period is not underestimated as would be in a derived figure excluding replacement investment nor is the total employment, considered as function of total production, understated, as it would be if the number of those employed in producing the new capital goods destined to replace the old depreciated one were to be excluded from the calculation. Another advantage of the G.N.P. concept is that it avoids many conceptual and statistical difficulties involved in estimating the value of capital consumed or depreciated as well as many arbitrary assumptions involved in reducing a product figure to an income figure. But the concept of G.N.P. has also its weaknesses. The most important weakness is that it obscures the current net gain in production over and above the capital consumed and replaced. To conclude, the concept of G.N.P. is particularly useful for the purpose of analysing national economic activity during a relatively short period, that is, for the type of analysis which proceeds by taking the physical stock of capital, technology and other fundamental conditions of supply as given.

'VALUE ADDED'

The Gross National Product can also be defined as the sum of 'values added' over a given period by the various branches of economic activity. This definition eliminates the problem of multiple counting. The increase in value which each sector imparts in the course of production to the materials which it uses as inputs is estimated. The sum of such increases in value for all sectors gives the value of Gross National Product. The economy is considered to be like a huge assembly line. At its starting point, agriculture and mining at home, and imports from abroad, provide primary materials. The primary products pass from one process to another until they emerge at the end in the final form of clothing, furniture, radios, machine tools and other durable instruments of production. Each process through which the materials pass adds to their value. The process need not necessarily be such as to change the form of the commodities. Transportation services, for instance, increase value of the commodities by carrying them from less to more convenient places without changing their form. Banks and other financial institutions, though not handling physical commodities, provide useful services which ease the process of production. Similar is the nature of services provided by the government and other public authorities. At each stage along the line, imports will be joining the stream of commodities emerging from anterior stages, and exports will be leaving the line instead of going on the next process.

The value added by a process to the commodities passing through it during a given period can be found by deducting the value of the inputs from the value of the products leaving the process. The sum of the values added by all the processes would give us the value of the gross national product.

The gross national product calculated by this method does not include the value of imports because the cost of imported materials is automatically deducted from the value of output of the industries using them. In computing value added, the value of stocks used in production is deducted from the value of products made from them; but the stocks accumulated during the period constitute a part of the current output which has not been sold by the end of the period.

To arrive at net national product, depreciation would have to be deducted from the sum of values added. In computing the value added, the value of the inputs of materials is deducted from the value of commodities at each stage of production. It is assumed that the materials are completely absorbed into the process to which they are submitted. But plant and machinery, which wears out partially and is not completely absorbed into the product, should also be treated as an input similar to the input of materials and accordingly deducted from the value of output.

The 'value added' method and the 'final products' method give the same results. While the former counts the flow of output past each process along the assembly line, the 'final products' method counts the quantity of commodities which are delivered at the end of the line during the given period, with appropriate adjustments for the goods still in transit at the beginning and the end of the period, and with a deduction to eliminate inputs of imported goods and services.

The 'value added' method is in accordance with the normal business accounting procedures because every firm must for its own purpose record the value of its output and value of materials used. The 'final products' method involves serious difficulties in that it requires a division of actual output into consumers' and producers' goods. Certain grades of coal, for instance, may be used by domestic consumers as well as the industry. It is difficult to say what part of coal output is to be classified as consumers' goods until it is actually in the possession of consumers. Motor-cars are mostly used by private consumers but a good number is also used for commercial purposes which would constitute producers' goods. Such examples can be easily multiplied. In fact, there are not many products whose entire output can confidently be put into one or the other of the two categories of goods. The only way to be sure whether or not a particular product is consumers' goods is to find out as to whether or not it is in fact bought by consumers. But this is a classification of expenditures rather than of products and since expenditures belong to a different side of the economy, they should not be included in an account which aims at estimating output.

In actual practice, however, it is very difficult to precisely estimate the depreciation during a particular period, say, a year. The depreciation during a year, for instance, can be calculated by dividing the value of equipment by the number of years of its life. But it is difficult to ascertain the life of equipment till it is finished. Further, if the price of the equipment rises over the year, there arises the problem as to whether it is the old or book value of the equipment or the current market price of that which is to be taken into account. Similarly, there arises a problem if the equipment becomes technically obsolete and has to be scrapped halfway through its previously expected life.

The major merit of the concept of Net National Product is that it clarifies the net increase in total production over and above current consumption and current replacement investment. Another merit lies in stressing the long-run significance of maintaining and improving the physical productivity of capital for economic growth. It is these merits which make the N.N.P. concept highly useful for the purposes of 'growth economics'.

RELATION BETWEEN N.N.P. AT MARKET PRICES AND NATIONAL INCOME FACTOR COST

The difference between national income at factor cost and net national product arises because indirect taxes and subsidies cause market prices of output to be different from the factor incomes resulting therefrom. For illustration, suppose that the actual cost of production of a table is Rs. 40 which is the payment made to different factors of production as wages, rents interests and profits. The government imposes a tax of Rs. 10 on the production of a table. The table would obviously be sold in the market for Rs. 50. Thus the market value of this output is Rs. 50 while the income payments received by the different factors of production amount to Rs. 40 only. Similarly, if the government gives a subsidy of Rs. 10 on the production of a table, the market value of the table would be Rs. 30 while the income receipt of different factors of production would be Rs. 40. It follows, therefore, that the national income at factor cost is equal to net national product minus indirect taxes plus subsidies.

Sometimes the government also renders productive services and earns profits. Since these profits do not go to the factors of production as incomes and are appropriated by the government treasury, they must also be deducted from the net national product in order to obtain national income at factor cost. Thus,

National Income at Factor Cost = { Net National Product at Market Prices – Indirect Taxes + Subsidies – Profit earned by Government.

NATIONAL EXPENDITURE

Gross National Expenditure is the sum of all 'final' expenditures during a certain period by the residents of the country. It consists of consumers' expenditure (C), public authorities' current expenditure on goods and services (G), gross capital formation at home (I) and the difference between exports (E) and imports (M). When these expenditures are shown at market prices, it is necessary to deduct indirect taxes minus subsidies.

National expenditure is not the sum of all expenditures made in the country during a given period. To count not only consumers' expenditure on bread but also manufacturers' expenditure on wheat, wheat flour, fuel etc. would involve the problem of multiple counting similar to that we eliminated in the calculation of Gross National Product. It is, therefore, necessary to exclude all purchases which are 'intermediate' in the sense that they are offset, within the same period, by the release of commodities bought, either in their original or after processing and absorption into other commodities. Thus only those transactions would be counted which relate to purchases of final goods and services which do not change hands again during the same period. Some final commodities will be completely used up in consumption or in public authorities' activities. Others may take the form of stocks of semi-finished goods or of durable plant and machinery which has been bought during the period but has not yet been absorbed into the commodities produced with its aid. Expenditure on new equipment and on increasing stocks is known as capital formation.

There arises a question as to whether 'stocks of materials' consist of goods held at the input end of each process, such as raw jute in case of jute mills, or also of stocks of finished products which the mills have not yet sold. Obviously, the purchases of 'input' materials must be counted but it is difficult to understand how the 'output' stocks can be counted since they have not been purchased by anybody and, therefore, no expenditure has been incurred. Nevertheless, the normal practice is to count them by assuming that the firms themselves have bought their stocks of finished commodities.

The second question relates to depreciation of old machinery and plant bought in the past years. To the extent the value of old equipment, is being embodied in current output, it would require to be replaced, and the amount spent on replacement can be thought of as 'intermediate' expenditure. But because of the usual difficulties involved in distinguishing the part of capital expenditure devoted to replacement and that devoted to expansion of productive capacity, business expenditure on new equipment is generally given "gross of depreciation" and the National Expenditure estimated on this basis is called Gross National Expenditure.

All expenditure on goods and services and capital formation by consumers as well as by public authorities does not constitute National Expenditure because it also includes payments for imported commodities. The National Expenditure generally includes only that part of expenditure which is spent on national products. At the same time, the National Expenditure includes expenditure by foreigners on the goods and services produced by the country concerned.

RELATIONSHIP BETWEEN INCOME AND EXPENDITURE

There exists a close relationship between income (Y) and expenditure (E). Income is the major source for incurring expenditure and expenditure necessarily generates income. But while expenditure necessarily generates income, all income need not necessarily be spent. The total money expenditure is not necessarily restricted to the income received in the preceding period. The aggregate expenditure may exceed aggregate income in the preceding period as a result of activisation of past hoardings or as a result of borrowing from the banks. Similarly, aggregate expenditure may be less than the aggregate income in the preceding period because a part of the income is hoarded of being spent. Thus the expenditure can be more or less than the income of the previous period.

RELATIONSHIP BETWEEN OUTPUT AND EMPLOYMENT

The flow of goods and services which constitute the national product can be increased either by employing larger quantities of labour and capital or using the existing resources in a more efficient way through improvements in the methods of production. Improved methods of production are partly the result of chance discoveries and partly of sustained operational research which is a very slow process and whose outcome cannot be guaranteed in advance. Even when improved methods have been devised, it takes time to implement these at the factory level. The changes in methods of production, therefore, cannot be much depended upon for increasing production in the short period. Over a short period, the techniques of production must be taken as more or less fixed and an increase in production can be obtained by increasing input of labour or capital equipment or both.

Though an individual firm can increase its capital equipment quickly, this is not possible for the economy as a whole. Before the economy as a whole can expand its capital equipment, the machines must be produced, buildings must be constructed to house them, sources of power must be installed, and provision for various ancillary services must be made, which requires time. Thus when a substantial increase (say 12 per cent) in production over a short period (say months) is under consideration, the total stock of capital equipment, like the techniques of production, must be taken more or less fixed.

Labour remains the only factor whose input can be increased rapidly. To attain a fast increase in production, more workers can be employed, or those already in employment can be asked to work longer hours or the two can be combined. Similarly, if output is to be decreased, some of the workers can be removed, or their hours of work can be reduced or both. Thus in the short period, during which techniques of production and the total stock of capital equipment are more or less fixed, changes in output are primarily attributed to the changes in the volume of labour employed.

An objection may, however, be raised that labour and capital are not being treated in the same manner. If the input of labour can be varied by the working of more or less man-hours, why can't the input of services of capital equipment be varied by use of more or less machine-hours? Fixed capital has been regarded as a stock of productive capacity. If labour is dealt with in the same manner, it would appear as a stock of 'labour power' rather than flow of services. Just as the country's total labour-power employed is measured by the number of man-hours worked, the stock of capital could be regarded as being used more or less intensively according to the number of machine-hours involved. Closing down the factory would be similar to the firing of a worker. According to this view, production will vary not only with the input of labour but with man-hours and machine hours taken together.

The above view is not entirely wrong but it does not invalidate our previous conclusion that, in the short period, the volume of output primarily depends on the input of labour. The capital equipment is owned by the enterprises and they have to bear its cost of maintenance whether or not it is put to use. In contrast, the labourers are not owned by them and they can hire as much labour as they desire within the limits of what is available. Neither the owners of capital equipment nor the owners of labour-power would like to allow their resources to remain unutilised. But since the control of production is in the hands of the owners of capital equipment they would make every effort to use their equipment as full as possible, even when they have decided to decrease production, by employing less labour and spreading it thinly over all the available equipment. In such a situation, output per worker may be fairly low because the volume of labour is too small to take the best advantage of the available equipment. If more man-hours are worked, output will increase in greater proportion because it will lead to a better utilisation of the equipment. If the input of labour is further increased so that the plant has to work above its capacity, the output would still increase but the increase will not be in proportion to the increase in man-hours. Finally, a stage would be reached at which further additions of labour would not lead to any increase in output at all. This sequence exemplifies the 'law of variable proportions', according to which successive additions of one factor of production to fixed quantities of other factors will lead to first increasing, then constant, then diminishing and finally zero marginal returns.

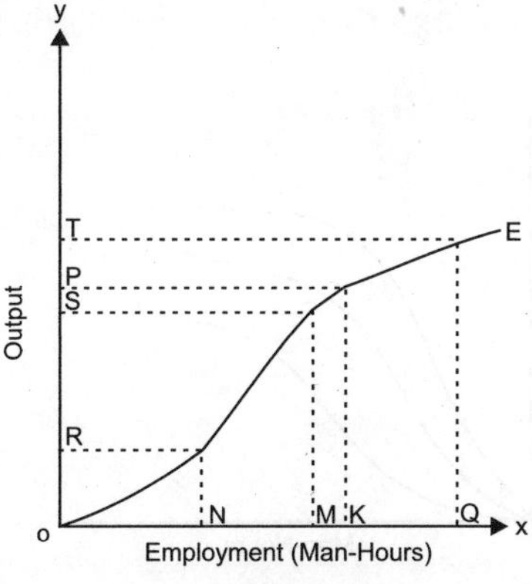

Fig. 2.1

In Fig. 2.1 the curve *OE* represents the relation between employment and output. At a low level of employment, say at *ON*, the output is small, that is, *OR*; at this level of employment, output per man-hour is *OR*/*ON*. As the volume of employment increases to *OM*, output rises to *OS*, and the proportionate increase in output is obviously greater than the proportionate increase in employment *i.e.* $\frac{RS}{OR} > \frac{NM}{ON}$. At this level of employment, output per man-hour is *OS*/*OM* and obviously exceeds *OR*/*ON*. If the employment further increases to *OQ*, the output rises to *OT*, and the proportionate increase in output is smaller than the proportionate increase in employment *i.e.* $\frac{ST}{OR} < \frac{MO}{OM}$. At this level of employment, output per man-hour has declined to $\frac{OT}{OQ}$ which is smaller than $\frac{OS}{OM}$. The flattening of the *OE* curve as it moves towards right indicates that input of additional man-hours will increase output by smaller and smaller amounts. Since the amount of capital equipment is fixed, only at one point the labour and capital will be in their most productive relationship, or in other words, only at one point the output per man-hour would be maximum; this point is represented at *K*. Where the volume of employment is less than *OK*, the number of man-hours is too small to make the best use of the available equipment; where more than *OK* man-hours are worked, the plant becomes inadequate to take the best advantage of the employed man-power.

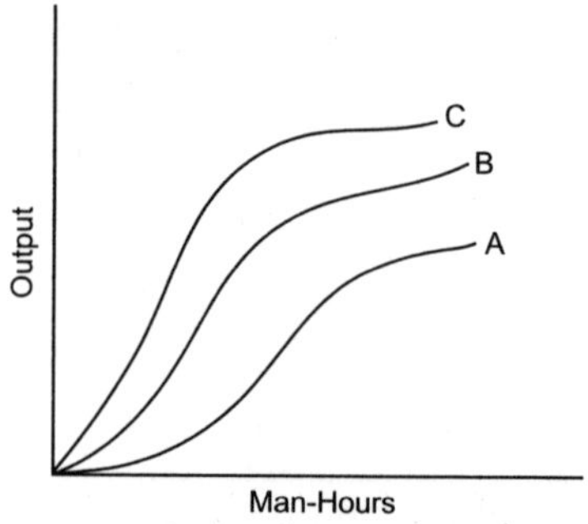

Fig. 2.2

If the time perspective were lengthened beyond the short period, it would be necessary to take into account the possible changes in the economy's stock of capital equipment and its techniques of production. This would give rise to a whole family of curves as shown in Fig. 2.2. Each curve shows the employment-output relationship for a given stock of capital equipment and given techniques of production. The larger the amount of capital equipment and the better the techniques of production, the higher would be the curve.

MEASUREMENT OF NATIONAL INCOME

The concept of national income, as seen above, has three interpretations. It represents a receipts total, it represents an expenditure total and it represents a total value of production. Thus three-fold interpretation arises; and if the goods and services bought are valued received equals the value paid, both of which equal the value of goods and services exchanged. Corresponding to this three-fold interpretation of income, there are three methods of measuring national income *viz.* (1) Product method, (2) Income method, and (3) Expenditure method.

PRODUCT METHOD

This method is also known as 'Inventory Method' or 'Commodity Service Method'. Under this method, the value of the gross product (sales + self-consumption + increase in stocks) of all the producers in an industry is summed up and from this total are deducted the purchases of these producers from other producers (*i.e.* value of intermediate products), and the depreciation of equipment involved in the process of production. This gives the net value contributed by these producers to the net value of aggregate national output. Such an estimate is made for each industry. The sum of all these estimates gives the net domestic product at factor cost classified by industrial origin. The addition of net income from abroad to this total gives net national product or national income at factor cost.

To measure national income by this method, we should consider the following points:

1. We include only final products in the estimation of national income. We exclude intermediate products. Otherwise, there will be double counting. On way to avoid this problem of double counting is the value added method. In

the value added method, we consider the value at each stage of production and add them up. This method will give us the value of the final products.

2. Inventories i.e., unsold stocks of goods are to be valued at the existing market price and included in the national income.
3. Services of owner-occupied houses are to be evaluated on the basis of imputed rents and these rents should be included in GNP.
4. The values of household services rendered by the members of the family is not included in the GNP. But the value of services rendered by paid workers in the household sector is to be included. Wages paid to such workers are taken as the value of such services.
5. Goods consumed by the producers themselves should be included in national income.
6. The values of the services of self-employed persons are to be included in GNP.
7. The cost of provision of public services, such as, defence, police, medical, education, etc. should be included in GNP.

In this way, in the product method, the problems of valuation of non-marketed goods are overcome. The money value of all final goods and services produced during the year are taken. By adding them, GNP of the country is obtained. We get NNP or national income by substracting depreciation of capital from GNP.

INCOME METHOD

Under this method, all incomes accruing to the various factors of production are added. This gives the national income classified by distributive shares as specified by the following equation:

$$Y = W + R + I + P \qquad \text{...(2.2)}$$

where

Y = National income.

W = Total wages before tax.

R = Total Rents.

I = Total Interest.

P = Total Profits.

Thus national income is the sum total of all wages, all rental payments, all interest payments and all profits in the economy during a year. The idea behind income received approach is that every earner in the society is the owner of at least one factor of production for which he receives payment—Wage is the reward for labour. Rent is the payment for the use of land. Interest is the payment for capital. Profits are the residual income for entrepreneurs. Thus, if we add the income payments of all the four kinds, we will arrive at an estimate of national income.

In modern times, profit accrues to business firms and companies. These firms retain a part of total profits which they may use for further investment in the next period. The other part of the profit is distributed among the shareholders and is known as distributed profits or dividends.

This is shown in the following equation

$$P = P_r + P_d \qquad ...(2.3)$$

where

P = Total Profits.

P_r = Retained Profits.

P_d = Distributed Profits or Dividends

Substituting equation (2.3) into equation (2.2)

We get

$$Y = W + R + I + P_R + P_d \qquad ...(2.4)$$

which shows that both retained profits and distributed profits are included in national income. However, we must note carefully, that national income is *not* the amount of income which is available to the individuals of a country for spending. The income which is available for spending is called disposable income and is defined below.

$$Y_d = Y - P_r - T_x + T_r \qquad ...(2.5)$$

where

Y_d = Disposable Income.

Y = National Income.

P_r = Retained Profits.

T_x = Taxes.

T_r = Transfer payments.

Disposable income as explained above is a measure of maximum purchasing power of household. This is the income which is available for spending. Since retained profits lie with the firms and are not distributed they are subtracted from national income. Next thing to be deducted is the tax paid to the government. Taxes which are paid to the government by the individuals and business firms constitute government income. They are included in national income as will be shown below but are excluded from disposable income. However, government pays some amount to individuals as old age pensions, scholarships, help to poors and unemployment compensations, etc. These types of payments are called transfer payments because they transfer income from government to the individuals. Since individuals are at liberty to spend this income also, transfer payments are also included in disposable income.

The composition of disposable income shall become clear if we substitute Eq. (2.4) into Eq. (2.5)

$$Y_d = W + R + I + P_d - T_x + T_r \qquad ...(2.6)$$

Equation (2.6) states that disposable income is the total of wages, rents, interest, dividends, and transfer payments minus total taxes.

There is another way to look at it. We can define net taxes imposed by the government as a difference between total tax revenue and transfer payment.

$$T = T_x + T_r \qquad ...(2.7)$$

where

T = Net taxes

T = Total tax revenue

T_r = Total transfer payment

New disposable income can be viewed as

$$Y_d = Y - P_r - T \qquad ...(2.8)$$

Eq. (2.8) states that disposable income is obtained after deducting retained profits and net taxes from the G.N.P.

Alternatively, the GNP can be viewed as

$$Y = Y_d + P_r + T \qquad ...(2.9)$$

which tells that GNP is the sum total of disposable income, retained profits and net taxes. From the point of view of use, the disposable income has only two possible uses. Either it may be spent on consumption or it may be saved. From a macro point of view, it is more likely that a part of disposable income will be spent upon consumption and other part of it will be saved. This can be shown as follows:

$$Y_d = C + S \qquad ...(2.10)$$

where

Y_d = disposable income.

C = Consumption expenditure.

S = Saving.

Substituting Eq. (2.10) into Eq. (2.9) the GNP can be seen as

$$Y = C + S + P_r + T \qquad ...(2.11)$$

where a part of GNP is shown as expenditure on the right hand side which takes us to expenditure approach for the estimation of national income.

EXPENDITURE METHOD

Under this method, we obtain 'gross national product at market prices' by adding up personal consumption expenditures, gross private domestic investment, net foreign investment and government purchases of goods and services.

The basic idea behind expenditure approach towards the estimation of national income is that total expenditure and total income would be the same for economy as a whole. Thus, an estimate of national expenditure would also be an estimate of national income. It may be possible for individuals to spend more than what they earn but it is not possible for the whole economy to do so. Imagine a simple economy with only two members—A.B. Suppose A and B earn one thousand rupees each and spend the whole of it without saving anything. Thus, national income as well as national expenditure of this simple economy would be the same Rs. 2000. However, if B spends Rs. 1500 and he borrows Rs. 500 from A then A's spending will be reduced by Rs. 500. Thus, A in the new situations, will spend Rs. 500 and B will spend Rs. 1500. Their total expenditure is still Rs. 2000 which is equal to their total income. Thus the national expenditure of any economy is by definition equal to its national income.

The society spends a major part of its income upon satisfying consumption needs such as food, clothing, shelters, entertainment etc. The expenditure on such items is called consumption expenditure and is a major component of national expenditure. The other most important component of national expenditure is investment expenditure. This is that part of expenditure which is incurred upon production, upon buying land, machinery, and raw materials, etc. So that production of goods and services as well as the production of more machinery etc. may be carried out. Here only net investment is counted because gross investment is component of GNP. Therefore, depreciation is not included in national income.

The total of consumption and investment expenditure by private individuals may be called private expenditure. But government also incurs some expenditure. First of all, this government has to buy different types of goods for its own consumption from the private economy, e.g., government buys paper for use in its offices, cloth to provide uniform to its soldiers and police, etc. It also buys services of individuals who could run the administration, etc. Sometime, the government undertakes production also and makes investment expenditure. Thus total government expenditure can be looked as:

$$G = G_c + G_i \qquad \text{...(2.12)}$$

where

G = Total government expenditure.

G_c = Government's consumption.

G_i = Government's investment.

Thus it is conceptually possible to distinguish between government's consumption and government's investment. However, to keep the analysis simple, we shall not make this distinction in this book and treat all government expenditure together.

A society not only produces goods and machines for its own use but also for sale to other countries. The amount of goods, services, and machines, which are sold to other countries by one country is called export. All exports transfer goods and services from producing country to the buying country and money income from buying country to producing country. Thus, exports raises a country's national income. However, the country may also have to buy goods, services, and machines etc. from other countries. Such purchases are called imports. Imports bring in goods and services in the buying country and transfer money income from buying country to the selling country. Thus net increase in income by exports can be known only if we subtract import from it. Suppose that we denote exports by the symbol *X*, and imports by the symbol *M*, then (*X*–*M*) would represent net imports. If exports are greater than imports, then net exports would be positive and it would raise income. However, if imports are greater than exports then net exports (*X*–*M*) would be negative and it would cause income to decline. Thus expenditure approach can be summarized in the following equation:

$$Y = C + I + G + X - M \qquad ...(2.13)$$

where

Y = national income = national expenditure.

C = Consumption expenditure.

I = Investment expenditure.

G = Government expenditure.

X = Earning from exports.

M = Expenditure on imports.

$X - M$ = Net exports.

In the theoretical model of macro-economic activities we shall make the following assumptions:

(1) Retained profits are zero. In other words, it shall be assumed that all profits are distributed in the form of dividend. This assumption is necessary to investigate the investment behaviour of the private firms.

(2) We also assume closed economy. This assumption does not mean that there is no foreign trade. There is foreign trade but we only assume that net exports ($X - M$) are zero, which means exports and imports all just equal to each other.

$$X = M \qquad ...(2.14)$$

Thus, in effect, we are assuming that foreign trade sector have no influence upon our economy. Thus, we abstract from the problems of balance of payment, exchange rate and money and other problems which are studied in international economics.

SOCIAL ACCOUNTING

Accounts maintained by private individuals are called "Private Accounting." Similarly, the accounts for the entire economy are known as "Social Accounting." Thus social accounting refers to that part of the descriptive economics which relates the production and distribution of national income. It is concerned with the statistical classification of the activities of human beings and human institutions in ways which help us to understand the operation of the economy as a whole. It helps us to understand how the entire economic system works and what are the relationships among the various sectors of the economy. Social accounts reflect changes in the health of the economy. They indicate fluctuations in economic activity and the performance of the economy. They help us in assessing the impact of government policy on various sectors. They also help us in knowing about the distribution of income among the various classes. Proper maintenance of detailed social or national accounts is very essential for having an idea of economic progress in different sectors and sub-sectors of an economy. Social accounts are helpful in comparing the prosperity, past and present, of nations, and of the various groups of persons and institutions comprising nations. In recent years they have been used for forecasting changes in the economic state of nations and in assessing the more probable economic consequences of government action.

Social or national accounts refer to a number of bodies of systematically arranged data, which have as their focus the economic activities taking place within a nation. The major five such bodies of data, treating different aspects of the nation's economic activity, are: (i) National Income and Product Accounts, (ii) Input-Output Tables, (iii) The Flow of Funds Statements, (iv) The Balance of Payments, (v) The National Balance Sheets.

(i) *National Income and Product Accounts*. In their simplest forms, national income accounts are no more than measurements of production, consumption and investment arranged in such a way as to emphasize the distinction between the decisions of people concerned with, the consumption of what has been produced. They are a statistical statement of national output or receipts, e.g. gross national product, net national product, personal income and disposable income. These accounts include consolidated business income and product account, personal income and expenditure account, rest of the world account, and gross savings and investment account.

(ii) *Input-Output Tables.* They are concerned with the current productive activity of the economy and focus attention on inter-industry relationships. They are also known as inter-industry analysis. It is a detailed and systematic analysis of the inter-relationship between an industry's or an economy's output of goods and services and the volume of goods and services required to attain a given volume of production. It shows the flow of goods and services represented by their money value during a given period (say a year) between different sectors (generally known as industry).

(iii) *Flow of Funds Statements.* They cover all money and credit transactions in the economy. They contain information on the creation of bank credit, the purchase of securities and other changes in the assets and liabilities of the different sectors of the economy, as well as on payments and receipts of income.

(iv) *Balance of Payments Tables.* They show foreign trade statistics by country of origin and destination of the commodity, as well as foreign financial transactions.

(v) *National Balance Sheet.* It shows the assets and liabilities of the different sectors of the economy. The assets included are both tangible and intangible. While the flow of funds statements deal with flows, the national balance sheet deals with stocks.

SECTORAL BREAKDOWN IN SOCIAL ACCOUNTING

National income estimates for social accounting can be presented in several ways. One of such ways is to divide the economy in four sectors, namely: (i) personal (household and institution) sector, (ii) business sector, (iii) government sector, and (iv) foreign (rest-of-the-world) sector. We have already seen that gross national product at market prices can be obtained by adding up the following: (i) expenditure of private persons on consumption or what is called personal consumption expenditure, (ii) expenditure of business enterprises on replacement, renewal and new investment or what is called gross domestic private investment, (iii) expenditure of government on purchase of goods and services, *i.e.*, government purchase, and (iv) expenditure of the rest of the world on the output of the national economy over and above what this economy spends on the output of the rest of the world, *i.e.*, export surplus or net foreign investment.

Personal Sector. This sector considers income and product originating not only in the households in the usual sense of the terms but also the income and product originating in non-profit institutions such as schools, colleges and hospitals, voluntary associations like temples, clubs and 'funds' like the Red Cross; trust funds benefiting consumers and private pension and welfare funds. When an institution—say a hospital—pays wages and buys supplies, these are considered as personal expenditure. The charges made by a private non-profit hospital and the donations received by it from private households to meet its deficits are considered as interpersonal transfers and, therefore, are not incorporated in the account. Gifts from business concerns will, however, be shown as business transfer payments. Similarly, the payments made by a private pension or welfare funds to its beneficiaries are treated as interpersonal transfers and not shown in the account. The payment made by an employer into the funds, however, is treated as personal income ("supplements to wages and salaries"). Similarly, the interest earned by the funds on its investments is treated as personal income. Table 2.1 shows the form of personal income and outlay account.

Table 2.1

Personal Income and Outlay Account

Personal consumption expenditures:	Wages, salaries, and Supplements from:
Purchases from business	business
Wages, salaries, and supplements	government
Purchases abroad	households
Interest paid	abroad
Personal taxes	less: employee and employer social insurance contributions.
Personal saving	Rental income of persons
	Proprietor's income:
	business and professional farm
	Dividends
	Personal interest income
	Government transfer payments
	Business transfer payments
Personal Outlay and Saving (total)	Personal Income (total)

In personal sector, there is no two-fold measurement in terms of both product and cost, as in case of business sector account shown below. This is because there is no transaction representing the sale of a product of a teacher employed by a private non-profit school or of a doctor employed by a charitable hospital and their product is measured by the wages received by them.

Business Sector. The business sector is defined to include in addition to corporate enterprise, all organisations producing goods and services sold at a price intended to cover at least the cost of production. The definition is broad enough to include government enterprises. It also includes unincorporated business enterprises like family businesses farm operators, independent professional practitioners, lessors of real property etc. Table 2.2 shows the income and product account for the business sector.

It is obvious from Table 2.2 that for business sector gross national product equals national income plus certain 'adjustment' and plus depreciation. Or net national product equals national income plus the adjustments.

Table 2.2
Business Income and Product Account

National income originating in business:	Consolidated net sales:
Compensation of employee	to persons
Wages and salaries	to government
Supplements*	to abroad
Net interest	to business on capital account
Net dividends	Increase in inventories
Corporate profits tax liability	
Proprietors' income	
Rental income of persons	
Adjustments to market price	
Indirect business tax liability**	
Business transfer payment***	
Current surplus of government enterprises	
Less: subsidies	
Net national product originating in business (sub-total)	
Depreciation	
Charges against business gross (Total)	Business gross product (Total)

* Supplements include employer's contribution to social insurance, employer's contributions to private pension and welfare funds, and miscellaneous kinds of "other labour income."

** All business taxes not based upon business profits. This includes, of course, all real estate taxes, even those paid by owner-occupants. All included are minor non-tax liabilities.

*** Includes bad debts inter-business bad debts out; this leaves net bad debts by persons to business, charitable contributions by business prizes, etc.

Government Sector. The national product and income originating in government sector can be presented by a simple statement of government receipts and expenditures which is shown in Table 2.3.

Table 2.3

Government Receipt and Expenditure Accounts

Purchases of goods and services:	Taxes:
from business	personal tax receipts
from abroad	corporate profits tax accruals
Transfer payments:	Contributions for social insurance:
to persons	
foreign	employer
Net interest paid	personal
Subsidies	
Less: current surplus of government enterprises	
Surplus or deficit (–) on income and product account	
Government outlays and surplus (total)	Government receipts (total)

The above is a consolidated statement, netting out all transactions among various levels of the government. Similarly, the social insurance funds are consolidated with other government accounts. The statement excludes all transactions in existing assets like government purchase or sale of land or buildings. The account also excludes government lending transactions as well as the current accounts of government enterprises. The purchases of capital goods by the government enterprises and the interest payments on any obligations of these enterprises are, however, included in the general government budget on the expenditure side. The current surplus of these enterprises forms a source of government revenues. It is, however, shown as a negative item on the expenditure side, instead.

Foreign Sector. Some of the income and product originating in a country say India accrues to foreigners who own the factors of production located in India. Similarly, some of the income originating abroad accrues to Indian residents who own the factors or production located in foreign countries. Income and product originating in the rest of the world sector is defined as the net foreign investment from the India side. Table 2.4 shows the foreign sector accounts.

Table 2.4

Rest-of-World Account

Net purchase of factor services (by rest-of world from India)	Net disinvestment (by rest of-world) in India
Wages and salaries	Transfer payments from Indian government
Interest	
Dividends	
Branch profits	
Net purchases from (Indian) business	
Net purchases from (Indian) government	
Net purchases from (Indian) households	
Net current payments to India (Total)	Sources of net current (Total)

Combining Sector Account. By combining the accounts in the four sectors, we can obtain the total national income. From business sector we have wages, salaries, and supplements; net interest; corporate profits, income of unincorporated enterprises, and rental income of persons. To this we add the wages, salaries, and supplements earned in government, and the same items earned in households, plus household interest payments. We further add net factor earnings from the rest-of-world sector.

Similarly, we can obtain the total national product by combining the sector national products. The gross national product tabulated by sector of origin is shown below:

1. Household output:
   (a) wages, salaries, and supplements
   (b) interest paid
2. Business output:
   (a) sales to consumers
   (b) sales to government
   (c) net sales abroad
   (d) sales to business on capital account
   (e) change in inventories
3. Government output:
   (a) wages, salaries and supplements
4. Rest-of-world output:
   (a) wages and salaries

(b) interest
(c) dividends
(d) branch profits

The above breakdown of national product is not, however, the one most useful for analytical purposes. We, therefore, generally rearrange these items into a tabulation of gross national product by type of expenditure, as is shown below:

I. Consumer expenditures
  A. on business products
  B. on household services
  C. on imports
II. Government expenditures
  A. purchases from business
  B. purchases from abroad
  C. wages, salaries and supplements
III. Gross private domestic investment
  A. sales to business on capital account
  B. change in inventories
IV. Net exports of goods and services

DIFFICULTIES IN THE MEASUREMENT OF NATIONAL INCOME

Measurement of national income involves certain conceptual and statistical difficulties. A few years ago, when the national income studies were not extensive, the difficulties were numerous. But in recent years some of the conceptual problems have been successfully solved. Simon Kuznets mentions the following theoretical or conceptual difficulties in the estimation of national income:

1. The definition of the term 'nation' as such in national income.
2. The method to be used in the measurement of national income.
3. The stage of economic activity at which national income should be measured.
4. The type of goods and services which the national income should include.

The first three of these difficulties have been resolved to a large extent. It is now generally agreed among economists that the concept 'nation' in national income measurement does not mean country as such and the national income is not restricted to income produced within the territorial boundaries of a country. The concept of national income cuts across political boundaries and includes, in addition to income produced within territorial boundaries of the country concerned, income earned by its nationals abroad by way of interest, banking, insurance, shipping charges etc. minus any such payments made to foreigners. This broad definition of the concept of 'nation' is now accepted by all economists.

The second problem relating to the choice between methods to be adopted for measuring national income has also been resolved. It is now generally believed that anyone or all of them should be used simultaneously depending upon the availability of relevant data.

In regard to the third problem, there exists common consensus that any stage of economic activity—production, consumption, or distribution—may be adopted depending upon the purpose of measurement of national income. If the purpose of measuring the national income is to assess the economic strength and potentiality of an economy, the production stage would be more suitable. If the objective is to assess the economic welfare of individuals as reflected by their incomes consumed, it would be better to adopt the consumption stage.

The problem which has not been successfully resolved is the fourth one which relates to the type of goods and services to be included in the national income. The problem particularly relates to the goods and services which are not exchanged against money, e.g. services rendered by housewives, owner-occupied houses. Since we have already discussed this problem in detail earlier, we will not dwell on it here any further.

The fifth difficulty relates to the problem of avoiding double or multiple counting in the calculation of national income. This problem has also been discussed above.

The sixth problem to the transfer payments, which is connected with the measurement of national income by income method. All transfer payments must be excluded from national income because they simply represent redistribution of income and not accrual of income as such. For instance, a person may earn an income of

Rs. 50,000 and out of it pay Rs. 10,000 as income-tax to the government. It would be double counting if we include in national income the individual's income of Rs. 50,000 and also government's income of Rs. 10,000. Thus all transfers of money between different persons, or groups of persons should be excluded from national income. This can best be done by taking into account only disposable incomes.

The seventh problem relates to the income generated by forcing firms. Is this income to be included in the national income of the country in which they are located or in that of the country which owns them? In this connection, the I.M.F.'s suggestion is that the income flowing from foreign firms should be ascribed to the country in which the production takes place but the profits earned by the foreign firms should be credited to their parent concerns.

The eighth problem relates to the value of services rendered by the government. This problem has also been discussed above.

DIFFICULTIES OF MEASUREMENT OF NATIONAL INCOME IN UNDERDEVELOPED COUNTRIES

The underdeveloped countries are characterised a marked degree of self-sufficiency in households. As such a considerable portion of their produce is consumed within the family and does not come to the market. This is particularly true of the small farmers who grow just enough for their family. A further portion of the produce is exchanged on barter basis without the introduction of money. It is very difficult to make a fairly reliable estimate of the value of the produce that is consumed within the family or exchanged on barter basis. This difficulty is particularly marked in the agricultural sector.

A large number of producers are illiterate and do not follow the practice of keeping regular accounts. The national income statistician, therefore, finds it difficult to get reliable information from them.

It is difficult to estimate national income by industrial origin because people lack specialisation of functions and occupational classification is not scientific. Many persons simultaneously engage in several economic activities. A farmer, for instance, may engage himself in some manufacturing business at home or take employment in a factory during the slack season in agriculture.

There is a general lack of statistical data which adds to the difficulties involved in estimating national income.

IMPORTANCE OF NATIONAL INCOME STATISTICS

National income statistics are a valuable instrument of economic analysis and a guide to economic policy. The emergence of planning and state intervention have further added to their value. A knowledge of national income trends is very essential for forming a realistic plan. National income statistics give us an idea about the structure of the economy. They throw light on the relative importance of various sectors in the economy. They help us in knowing about the distribution of incomes among the various classes. They indicate the manner in which national expenditure is divided between consumption expenditure and investment expenditure. This enables us to know whether or not reasonable provision is being made for depreciation to maintain the capital stock of a community. This also indicates the rate at which the economy would grow. The national income statistics help the government in knowing whether the economy or any of its sectors need any stimulus or regulation or control. They help in assessing the impact of government policy on various sectors. They help us in comparing the standard of living of people in different countries and at different times in the same country. They help in determining equitable contributions of different member countries towards the expenditure of international organisations like the United Nations International Monetary Fund and International Bank for Reconstruction and Development.

NATIONAL INCOME AS AN INDEX OF WELFARE: CONTROVERSIAL ISSUES

Generally, national income of a country is regarded as an index of welfare. According to Haberler, other things being equal, higher the level of national income, higher will be the level of welfare. But this idea has been now changed and put into question. That is why, national income is not a good measure of welfare for the following reasons:

1. GNP includes final output valued at market prices. But the services which are not valued at market prices, such as, service of a housewife, mother, sister, leisure etc. are not considered as part of rational income. But these affect welfare.

2. Distribution of wealth and income, stabilization of government, etc. are the factors which contribute to economic welfare. But these factors are not considered in national income. That is why, national income of a country is high, but her total welfare may less.
3. There are some social costs of industrialization, such as, air pollution, industrial disease, etc. These social costs reduce social welfare. Higher industrial output implies higher national income and higher welfare. At the same time, it implies more social cost and hence less welfare. Thus, more output does not necessarily imply more welfare.
4. If people have been forced to work against their will to increase national output, we cannot say that the welfare of the economy has increased with the increase in output.

For all these above reasons, GNP of an economy does not give a true welfare index. To make GNP a good welfare index Samuelson has suggested some modifications' in GNP measure. He has given a new concept called Net Economic Welfare (NEW) which takes into account all the major factors affecting welfare. For example, leisure should be counted as one which contributes to welfare and air-pollution as one which should be substracted from GNP to get the value of NEW.

In the measure of economic welfare, William Nordhaus and James Tobin have also evolved a new concept called Measure of Economic Welfare (MEW). It is similar to Semuelson's NEW. They have classified some items as regrettables and some items as intermediaries. Regrettables items are those items which have no direct utility but may be regrettably necessary and are counted as final products and included in GNP. These items should be excluded from the Measure of Economic Welfare (MEW). Intermediaries items are those items such as, defence, diplomacy, etc. which do not directly contribute to welfare.

If these modifications are made, national income may serve as an index of welfare.

Classical Theory of Employment

3

SAY'S LAW

The classical economists' belief in full employment as a normal condition of a free market economy is based on Say's Law of Markets. It was on the basis of this law that the classical economists thought that general over-production and hence general unemployment were impossible. The law (named after the French) economist, J.B. Say, (1767-1832) is very simple. It states "supply creates its own demand." In other words, every supply of output creates an equivalent demand for output so that there can never be a problem of general over-production. Thus the law denies the possibility of a deficiency of aggregate effective demand. It describes an important fact about the working of the free exchange economy that the main source of demand is the sum of incomes earned by various productive factors in the process of production itself. The employment of hitherto unutilised productive resources makes its own way because it simultaneously enlarges the market demand for goods by an amount equivalent to the income created and the value of output produced. Ricardo expressed Say's Law of Market as below:

> No man produces but with a view to consume or sell, and he never sells but with an intention to purchase some other commodity which may be useful to him, or which may contribute to future production. By producing them, he necessarily becomes either the consumer of his own goods, or the purchaser and consumer of the goods of some other person. . . . Productions are always bought by productions, or by services; money is only the medium by which the exchange is effected.[1]

1. *Principles of Political Economy* (Gonner ed.), pp. 273-75.

Say stated the law as below:

> . . . . a product is no sooner created than it, from that instant, affords a market for other products to the full extent of its own value. When the producer has put the finishing hand to his product, he is most anxious to sell it immediately lest its value should vanish in his hands. Nor is he less anxious to dispose of the money he may get for it; for the value of money is also perishable. But the only way of getting rid of money is in the purchase of some product or other. Thus the more circumstance of the creation of one product immediately opens a vent for other products.[2]

J.S. Mill states the law as below:

> What constitutes the means of payment for commodities is simply commodities. Each person's means of paying for the production of other people consist of those which he himself possesses. All sellers are inevitably and by the meaning of the word, buyers. Could we suddenly double the productive powers of the country, we should double the supply of commodities in every market; but we should, by the same stroke, double the purchasing power. Everybody would bring a double demand as well as supply; everybody would be able to buy twice as much, because every one would have twice as much to offer in exchange.[3]

As a corollary of the Say's law, it has been supposed that any individual act of abstaining from consumption necessarily leads to, and amounts to the same thing as, causing the labour and commodities thus released from supplying consumption to be invested in the production of capital wealth. In the words of Marshall:

> The whole of a man's income is expended in the purchase of services and of commodities. It is indeed commonly said that a man spends some portion of his income and saves another. But it is a familiar economic axiom that a man purchases labour and commodities with that portion of his

2. Jean, B. Say, *Treatise on Political Economy* (Princep edition), (Boston 1921).
3. J.S. Mill, *Principles of Political Economy*, Book III, Chap. XIV, p. 2.

> income which he saves just as much as he does with that he is said to spend. He is said to spend when he seeks to obtain present enjoyment from the services and commodities which he purchases. He is said to save when he causes the labour and the commodities which he purchases to be devoted to the production of wealth from which he expects to derive the means of enjoyment in the future.[4]

The doctrine is easily seen to be true in a barter economy, although its application was not supposed to be restricted to such an economy. What Say had in mind was that people work not for its own sake but only to obtain goods and services which yield satisfaction. The total production was limited by the fact that, at some point, or each individual, the satisfaction obtainable from a little leisure would outweigh the satisfaction obtainable from the consumption of goods and services which can be produced by foregoing that leisure, but such unemployment will be voluntary and not involuntary. If some productive resources are involuntarily unemployed, additional production will be undertaken which would yield an equivalent amount of income; whole of this additional income will be spent in the purchase of additional production. Say assumed that money is simply a medium of exchange and is never hoarded. As such the law framed in terms of barter economy would hold true in an economy using money. Money economy would behave in the same way as barter economy because rational individuals will not hold idle money. But in actual practice money is more than simply a medium of exchange. It is also a medium of store. Individuals as well as business firms have a tendency to hold cash for a number of purposes. If a part of the total supply of money is held as cash and not spent, the identity between buying and selling presumed in a barter economy will not hold true.

Say's law, of course, recognises the possibility that the individuals may not correctly direct their production in accordance with one another's wants. The person producing toys may produce more than people want to buy at the price which he assumed while deciding the number of toys to be produced. As a consequence, the toys would fetch in return quantities of other goods smaller than those he anticipated. This would lead him to produce some other

4. Alfred Marshall, *Pure Theory of Domestic Values*, p. 34.

goods which are in more demand or to have more leisure. But such maladjustments of relative outputs would be temporary and would be corrected soon by the operation of market forces.

ASSUMPTIONS OF SAY'S LAW

Say's law as described above is based on the following assumptions:

(i) There is no state intervention in economic activities because this obstructs the automatic and self-adjusting mechanism of the economy.

(ii) The size of the market is capable of expansion. It expands with the increase in the volume of products offered in exchange.

(iii) In an expanding economy new firms and workers make their way into the productive process not by supplanting others but by offering their products in exchange.

(iv) The free enterprise system based on price mechanism provides opportunities for the growing population and increase in capital.

(v) All savings are automatically invested and this equality between savings and investment is brought about by interest flexibility.

IMPLICATIONS OF SAY'S LAW

(i) Since there is automatic adjustment of every element with the working of the economy, there is no need for government intervention in the functioning of the economic system.

(ii) General over-production and general unemployment are not possible.

(iii) So long as there exist unemployed resources in the economy, it is profitable to employ them because they can pay their own way. In other words, when the unemployed resources are employed, they lead to more production which covers their own costs.

(iv) The mechanism of interest flexibility brings about an equality between savings and investment.

(v) The mechanism of wage-flexibility brings about full employment. Any unemployment would disappear if the workers are ready to accept a wage rate equal to their marginal productivity.

(vi) Money is no more than an instrument of overcoming the inconveniences of barter. It is simply a veil which conceals the fact what constitutes the means of payment for commodities is simply commodities.

CRITICISM OF SAY'S LAW

As the depression of 1929 deepened and years passed without signs of recovery, the validity of Say's law was called into question. The producers found it difficult to sell their entire output and there was a general glut in the economy. In 1936, Lord J.M. Keynes came forward with his *General Theory of Employment, Interest and Money* which rejected Say's Law on the ground that aggregate demand need not necessarily be equal to aggregate supply at full employment.

The incomes of the factors of production are necessarily equal to the value added in the productive process but this does not mean that the entire income will be automatically spent in goods and services created in a given time period. The recipients of the income spend a part of their incomes on consumer goods and save the other part. Unless the investors are willing to invest an amount equivalent to the amount of savings, the total effective demand which consists of demand for consumers' goods and producers' goods will not be sufficient to absorb the entire available supply of output. In such a situation, the producers will not be able to sell their entire output, their profits will fall and they will be compelled to reduce their production which will create unemployment. The savings and investment being done by different persons and for different motives, in the absence of any agency to ensure equality between intended savings and intended investment, a discrepancy between the two will not be an uncommon phenomenon. In contrast to the classical view that full employment equilibrium is the normal situation, Keynes, therefore, believed that in a free enterprise economy, there are more chances for the equilibrium to be established at less than full employment level. It may, however, be pointed out that rejection of Say's law by Keynes was not a new thing. It was rejected by Karl Marx much before Keynes.

SAY'S LAW AND CLASSICAL THEORY

The classical economists like David Recardo and Adam Smith believe that in a competitive capitalist economy there exists an automatic mechanism which brings about full employment of labour. This automatic mechanism is known as the 'invisible hand.' According to the classical theory, levels of income and employment are governed by fixed capital stock on the one hand and wage-goods fund on the other. The belief of classical theory regarding the existence of full employment in the economy is based on Say's Law propound by a French economist J.B. Say. According to Say's law, "Supply creates its own demand." This shows that every increase in production, will be sold in the market and hence there will be no problem of lack of demand.

In this way, classical economists rule out the possibility of overproduction. Say's Law states that over production automatically leads to a greater money income which creates the market for the greater flow of goods produced. In this way, deficiency in demand being no problem, the process of capital accumulation and expansion of productive capacity will continue till all people are employed. Thus, the income, which is not spent on consumer goods, is saved and will be invested in the production process. Therefore, investment equals savings. Thus, a given productive capacity continues to be fully utilized and no problem of deficiency of demand arises.

As per opinion of classical economists, there is always a tendency towards full-employment in a capitalist economy, if price mechanism is allowed to work freely without any interference by the government. Thus, the classical theory of employment is based upon two basic assumptions: (i) There is always enough expenditure or aggregate demand to purchase the total production at full-employment level of resources. (ii) Even when deficiency of aggregate expenditure or demand arises, the prices and wages would change in such a way that real production, employment and income will not decline. The classical economist thinks that there is no problem of deficiency of expenditure. Demand for goods was based upon Say's law.

Say's law says that every production of goods creates income equal to the value of goods produced and this income is spent on purchasing these goods. It can be said in other way that every production creates its own purchasing power, i.e., 'Supply creates its own demand.' Thus, the problem of over production does not arise. J.B. Say's argument is that when a new entrepreneur employs some factors of production and pay them their monetary rewards. The unemployed labourers when employed create their own demand. Thus, the new entrepreneur increases not only the supply of goods but also at the same time creates the demand for them. Production is the only source of demand. Dillard rightly writes that "'Say's Law of Markets' is the denial of the possibility of deficiency of aggregate demand. Therefore, employment of more resources will always be profitable and will take place to the point of full-employment, subject to the limitation that the contributors of the resources are willing to accept rewards not greater than their physical productivity justifies. There could be no general unemployment, according to this view, if workers will account what they are worth."*

WAGES AND EMPLOYMENT

The classical economists believed that there could be no involuntary unemployment in a labour market characterised by free and unhindered competition. In such a market, wage-rates would have a tendency to fall under the pressure of unemployment until all those who are willing to work can find employment. This follows from the definition of unemployment, for any man who is not in employment and who does not try to get work at a lower rate is no more considered to be unemployed than the man who refuses to work overtime or on Sundays. At the ruling wage, he prefers leisure to employment. He is idle but not involuntarily unemployed. If he really wanted employment, he would have offered himself at a lower wage which would have reduced the level of wages. Unemployment thus is incompatible with equilibrium. It can persist only if the State, or the trade unions, or some other institution prevents the unemployed from seeking employment at lower wages and thereby setting in motion the automatic mechanism which leads to equilibrium and full employment.

Prof. Pigou diagnosed the ills of depression mainly due to two causes *viz.*, (1) an improper allocation of people among jobs and (2) the prevalence of wage-rates above the level warranted by the general demand conditions. He, therefore, advocated a policy of wage cuts to cure unemployment. He held that given flexible wage-rates, the economic system has an automatic tendency towards full employment and the more rigid wages are, the larger would be the fluctuations in employment. He stated:

* D. Dillard, "Economics of J.M. Keynes."

> With perfectly free competition among work people and labour perfectly mobile, the nature of the relation (*i.e.*, between the real wage-rates for which people stipulate and the demand function for labour) will be very simple. There will always be at work a strong tendency for wage-rates to be so related to demand that everybody is employed. Hence in stable conditions everyone will actually be employed. The implication is that such unemployment as exists at any time is due wholly to the fact that changes in demand conditions are continually taking place and that frictional resistances prevent the appropriate wage adjustments from being made instantaneously.[5]

The process by which the reduction in wage-rates cures unemployment is described by the classical economists as below. In a free market economy, a reduction in wage-rates lowers the cost of production and hence prices which lead to an increase in sales. Increase in sales leads to increase in production which leads to an expansion of employment of the workers. Reduction in costs as a result of lower wages also increases profits of businessmen. Profits increase because it is assumed that the decline in wage-rates is larger than that in prices. The process of declining wages accompanied by rising profits and employment continues till equilibrium is reached at full employment. Thus the classical equilibrium is always at full employment equilibrium.

The main fallacy in the classical argument arises from the fact that the classical economists ignored the effect of a reduction in wages on the aggregate effective demand. They wrongly presumed that wage cuts leave the aggregate demand unaffected. They tried to extend to the whole economy the logic that was actually applicable to a single firm or industry. The classical theory is certainly true when applied to a single firm or industry. Take, for illustration, the case of a reduction in wage-rates in the watch industry alone. The reduction in wages will lower cost of production and hence prices in the watch industry. Decline in the prices of watches will lead to an increase in demand for them which will necessitate larger employment in the watch industry. No doubt, the reduction in the incomes of workers employed in the watch industry will decrease their demand

5. A.C. Pigou, *The Theory of Unemployment*, p. 252.

for all goods including watches, but the effect of this will be insignificant because they constitute a very small portion of the total buyers of watches.

In contrast, if the wage rates are reduced uniformly in all industries, the incomes of the buyers of watches as well as other goods will decline which would lead to a decline in the demand for all goods including watches. Thus the logic which is true in case of a single industry will not hold for the economy as a whole. While the reduction in wages in a single industry will not significantly reduce the demand for the product of that industry, the increased employment in that industry will also not significantly increase the aggregate employment in the economy as a whole. In fact, the increased employment in watch industry will be offset by small decreases in employment in all the industries whose products are bought by the workers employed in watch industry because reduction in their incomes as a result of wage cuts leads to a reduction in their demand for most of the goods they normally buy. Since one person's expenditure constitutes another person's income, the money incomes fall to the extent the general cut in wages reduces expenditure.

Decline in money wages may not necessarily result into a decline in real wages because the general fall in price resulting from a general reduction in wages may offset the decline in money wages and thus leave real wages unchanged. Keynes does assume that prices fall in proportion to the fall in wages. On this assumption, real wages will not decline and if real wages do not decline, profits cannot rise. If profits do not increase, there is no incentive for entrepreneurs to increase production. We again come to the same conclusion that the classical logic suffers from the drawback that it tries to extend to the whole economy what is true in case of only a single firm or industry.

Another version of the classical theory rests on the belief that the demand for labour is elastic. It is argued that a reduction in wage-rate per hour will increase the total earnings of workers because this will be more than offset by the increased volume of employment that results from it. The increased earnings would mean larger effective demand and hence greater volume of employment. Even if the profit per unit of output does not increase, total profits would increase as a result of greater output. This version of the classical theory also suffers from the same basic drawback as other versions. It assumes that supply creates its own demand for both consumption and investment output. We have already seen that Say's law is not valid and if that is so, wage-cut theory will not hold. No doubt, additional workers and others who share the newly created income will bring additional buying power in the market for consumption goods, it will not be adequate to absorb the entire output. A part of the additional income will naturally be saved and if this is not matched by additional investment, employment will not increase. But there is nothing automatic about increases in investment. This is the simple and basic point of Keynes' reaction to the classical theory of employment.

Keynes rejected the classical theory of employment more strongly on practical grounds. It is very difficult to implement a general cut in wage-rates because collective bargaining by labour unions, unemployment insurance minimum wage laws, etc., have come to stay. Keynes considered such a step immoral and anti-social.

According to Keynes, the volume of employment depends upon the volume of effective demand which in turn depends upon the propensity to consume and the relation between the marginal efficiency of capital and the rate of interest. A reduction in wage rates would, therefore, lead to an increase in employment only if it leads to an increase in the propensity to consume, or an increase in the marginal efficiency of capital, or a decline in the rate of interest. Let us briefly examine below the effect of a general reduction in wage-rates on these three independent variables.

Propensity to Consume: Consumption is the most important constituent of effective demand. Wage cuts lead to a transfer of income from wage-earners to rentiers, interest-recipients and enterpreneurs or, in other words, from the poorer classes towards the richer classes. Since the propensity to consume of the poorer classes is higher than that of the richer classes, the effect of wage cuts on consumption would be unfavourable. The decline in prices following wage cuts would, however, increase the purchasing power of people's fixed money wealth and thereby tend to increase their consumption.

Marginal Efficiency of Capital: The effect of wage cuts on the marginal efficiency of capital depends on what the entrepreneurs expect in regard to future wage-rates. If the reduction in wage-rates is once-for-all and is not expected to be followed by further wage cuts, the effect on the marginal efficiency of capital would he favourable. The entrepreneurs will be encouraged to make alterations and additions to plant and equipment and to build new plant when the wages are at the minimum. In case the entrepreneurs expect the reduction in wages to be followed by further wage cuts at a later date, the marginal efficiency of capital will be lowered because the entrepreneurs will have a tendency to postpone investment till the wages have fallen to still lower levels.

Once-for-all wage cuts are possible only in an authoritarian economy. Under a system of free labour and management, there is no way to ensure that a reduction in wages is not followed by further reductions in wages. Normally in such matters labour and management do not act as a whole and if labour is strongly organised, it would be almost impossible to effect reduction in wages. Generally, the weaker unions will be cut first and others will follow gradually. A gradually declining wage level will have adverse effects on the marginal efficiency of capital. A rigid wage policy will perhaps have more favourable effects on the marginal efficiency of capital than a policy of gradually declining wages.

Rate of Interest: A general reduction in wage-rates lowers the price level and thereby reduces the demand for money for transactions purpose. The total supply of money remaining unchanged, a decline in the demand for money for transactions purpose would release more money for inactive balances which would lead to decline in the rate of interest. Given the marginal efficiency of capital, a decline in the rate of interest will stimulate investment.

If money-wage reductions are expected to continue, people's liquidity-preference will probably increase, particularly to satisfy the speculative motive, that is, to hold money as a 'store of wealth' against the increasing uncertainty that deflation of wages generates. This may lead to two things. Firstly, the demand for consumer goods may be cut down in favour of the demand for money as a 'store of wealth', *i.e.*, to save and hold a larger portion of consumer income in the form of liquid assets. Secondly, the liquidity function may become so elastic with respect to interest that the monetary authority may not succeed in lowering the interest rate by varying the quantity of money. The first of these possible results obviously affects the consumption function whereas the second affects the investment function to the extent that investment decisions require a favourable 'monetary atmosphere.'

Open Economy: In an open economy, a change in the general wage rate and price level will affect the balance of trade. A cut in wage rates would lower the cost of production and hence prices. A decline in the price level would stimulate exports and discourage imports. A surplus in the balance of trade would be equivalent to an increase in real investment which would have multiplier effect on domestic real income and employment. This effect may be strengthened by a worsening of the terms of trade, which increases the employment necessary to obtain the equilibrium level of real income and real saving. These favourable effects may, however, be counteracted by similar wage adjustments or changes in exchange rates in other countries.

Public and Private Debt: Reduction in wage rates is also objectionable on the ground that the decline in the price level that follows it increases the real burden of private as well as public debt. Entrepreneurs find it difficult to meet their obligations and to pay the stipulated sums to the debenture holders. The real burden of the public debt is also increased which necessitates increased taxation.

Pigou Effect: Prof. Pigou contended that a decline in the price level raises the real value of the stock of liquid assets held by the people. As a result, the people would have a tendency to increase their consumption and to reduce savings because after the prices fall, a smaller amount of savings would be required to make purchases planned for the future. This means that so long as the market remains uncleared, wages and prices will fall, so that consumption will continue to increase until full employment is restored. This process has come to be known as "Pigou effect." But the modern economists have questioned the validity of the "Pigou effect" on a number of grounds. In the first place, a large number of persons do not possess money assets. Secondly, those who possess money assets want to possess still more. Thirdly, since the "Pigou effect" has only modest influence, considerable wage cuts would be required to affect employment appreciably, which would not be acceptable to trade unions. Fourthly, if the wages and prices are expected to decline further, expenditure may be postponed leading to an increase in unemployment. Fifthly, if the consumption changes only in response to changes in 'permanent' wealth and if the price level is expected to return to its previous level, the increase in wealth would be considered transitory and, therefore, the consumption may not increase. Sixthly, if there is a money illusion and people feel that a 'Rupee is a Rupee', consumption will not increase. Seventhly, with the decline in wages and prices, consumers' over-all asset position may be so impaired as to strengthen their desire to add more to their assets and less to their consumption, particularly if the real value of consumer durables and non-monetary assets is reduced much more than that of liquid assets is increased. Eighthly, although the value of liquid assets held by creditors increases with the decline in prices, there are also corresponding debtors, the real value of whose obligations increases. As such, the Pigou effect would fail to materialise at all if the "wealth effects" of price changes affect debtors and creditors symmetrically. It is, however, argued that the effects are not symmetrical because a large portion of the liquid assets held by the public is in the form of government obligations—the currency and governmental debt. Since government consumption is not supposed to be affected by a change in the real value of government obligations, there will be a net change in consumption resulting from a decline in the price level.

ASSUMPTIONS OF KEYNES

Keynes' money-wage theory is based on a number of assumptions, the important of which are[6]: (1) that labour is the only variable factor of production, (2) that pure competition exists throughout the economy or that the degree of monopoly is constant, (3) that "money illusion" affects the supply function for labour and (4) that "money illusion" does not occur in other supply and demand functions. It is necessary to remove these assumptions because they clash with other basic assumptions.

No Variable Factors Other than Labour: By assuming that labour is the only variable factor, Keynes rules out the possibility of substitution as a result of changes in money-wage rates. A reduction in wages, the prices of other variable factors remaining unchanged, would stimulate substitution of labour for other factors of production.

6. James Tobin, "Money-Wage Rates and Employment" in S.E. Harris (ed.) *The New Economics* (London, 1947), pp. 577-82.

Such a substitution would not only directly expand employment of labour but would also check or even reverse the transfer of income from labour to non-wage-earners and thereby raise the propensity to consume which would indirectly expand employment. In case the owners of other variable factors tried to avoid such substitution, they would reduce their prices in the same proportion as wage-rate and as a result their income would not increase at the cost of labour.

Pure Competition or Constant Degree of Monopoly: Keynes assumes that prices rise or fall in the same ratio as the changes in money-wage rates. This would be true only if there prevails pure competition or, under monopolistic conditions, if the degree of monopoly—the ratio of the difference between price and marginal cost to price—remains unchanged. Monopolistic conditions lead to price rigidity and stickiness. As such, a cut in money-wage rates will increase the degree of monopoly which would, other things remaining same, increase the relative share of national income going to non-wage-earners. Since the marginal propensity to consume of the wage-earners is usually higher than that of the non-wage-earners, such a redistribution of income reduces the real demand for goods and services, and thereby adversely affects the volume of output and employment.

Money Illusion in the Supply of Labour: Economic theory is usually based on the assumption that the people behave in a rational and consistent manner. A consumer, for instance, is not expected to change his pattern of expenditure if his income doubles and simultaneously the prices of all the goods he buys also double. Similarly, a business firm is not expected to change its output when the price of its product and the prices of all the factors which it employs change in the same ratio. The real wage being a ratio between the money-wage rate and the current price level of goods consumed by wage-earners, it would be expected that at a particular real wage the same amount of labour would be forthcoming irrespective of the level of money-wage-rate.

But because of a number of reasons, the "money illusion" does influence the labour supply function. In other words, the labour does attach importance to the money-wages rate, and more labour would be forthcoming at the same real wage, the higher is the money wage. Let us briefly state such reasons. In the first place, high money-wages-rates are a concrete and immediate accomplishment of the leadership of individual unions. The object of each individual union is to protect, and if possible to advance, their wages relative to other unions. The cost of living is a remote phenomenon over which a single bargaining unit has hardly any control. The unions have to bargain money wages for periods during which the cost of living may frequently change. Secondly, the wage-earners have obligations fixed in terms of money, *e.g.*, debts, taxes, contractual payments like insurance payments. A reduction in wages, even if accompanied by a proportionate decline in current prices, would increase the burden of such obligations. Thirdly, the labour may have inelastic price expectations. They may expect a certain 'normal' price level, or range of price levels, to prevail in the future irrespective of the current level of prices. With such price expectations, it is obviously in the interest of wage-earners to have, with the same current real income, the highest possible current money income. The higher are their money incomes, the larger would be their money saving and, therefore, their expected command over future goods. They will resist reductions in money wages even when prices are falling, not only because of their fear that wages will not rise again when prices rise but also because the expected price rise would reduce the real value of their current savings. Fourthly, the labour may be actually ignorant of the course of prices or naively deceived by the "money illusion." This argument might have some force in the past but in recent years the workers have become very much conscious of the cost of living and as such this argument does not carry much weight.

The "money illusion" may frequently affect not only labourers but also the suppliers of other factors of production. As such there can be price rigidities in all markets and consequently fluctuations in the use of all factors of production. In such an economy, the money-wage-rate is an independent determinant of the volume of employment.

The wage-earners may be affected by the 'money illusion' not only when they are selling their labour but also when they are acting as consumers. Not only wage-earners but all consumers may be influenced by the 'money illusion.' The Keynesian consumption function, which is crucial to the Keynesian solution to the money wage problem, however, is formulated in real terms. The real consumption expenditure is considered to be determined by real income. This is the significance of Keynes' use of wage-units. If 'money illusion' influences consumption and saving decisions, real consumption expenditure would depend on the level of money income as well as that of real income.

CONCLUSION

It is not easy to work out a clear-cut relationship between wage-cuts and employment. "Even Keynes found no simple answer. His analysis is pragmatic and leads to an agnostic position. In some circumstances, the effect will be favourable; in others not. All we can do is to apply our analysis to a variety of assumed conditions."[7] To cite from another book of Hansen, "there are few, if indeed any, economists now who will dogmatically assert either that wage cuts will surely increase employment or that such cuts cannot possibly have any favourable effect. There are too many unknowns that vary with special conditions and circumstances."[8] But there is certainly no simple rule as the classical economists envisage relating the level of employment to the money wage rates.

WAGE-BOOSTS

We have seen that a reduction in wages cannot cure unemployment. At the other extreme is what may be called the '"trade unionist argument" that the way out of depression is to raise money wages. It is held that an increase in wages will increase total effective demand and hence employment. This argument, however, has the same flaw as the one for reduction of wages. The rise in costs and prices that follows the rise in wages will offset the nominal increase in purchasing power. The increase will thus be only in nominal effective demand and not in real effective demand or, in other words, in employment.

As regards the indirect effects, rise in wages would redistribute income in favour of the wages-earners which would raise the propensity to consume. But it would have adverse effects on the marginal efficiency of capital and the rate of interest. An increase in wages at a time when the business is suffering losses from costs in excess of revenues would further impair the confidence of the

7. Alvin H. Hansen, *A Guide of Kenyes* (New York, 1953), p. 175.
8. ——, *Monetary Theory and Fiscal Policy* (New York, 1949), p. 128.

business community in the prospects for profitable operations. Higher prices resulting from higher wages would increase the demand for money for transaction purpose. Unless there is an expansion in the total quantity of money, it will decrease the quantity available as a store of value which will lead to a rise in the rate of interest. A rise in the rate of interest will discourage investment and thus adversely affect the total volume of employment.

FLEXIBLE WAGE POLICY VERSUS FLEXIBLE MONETARY POLICY

The process whereby wage cuts lead to a decline in interest rates is not different from that whereby the total quantity of money is increased in order to increase the amount of money available for inactive balances. Both do the same thing. In the words of Keynes himself, "We can......theoretically......produce precisely the same effects on the rate of interest by reducing wages, whilst leaving the quantity of money unchanged, that we can produce by increasing the quantity of money whilst leaving the level of wages unchanged."[9]

Though theoretically wage policy and monetary policy are very much the same, there is a world of difference between the two in actual practice. According to Keynes only "a foolish person......... would prefer a flexible wage policy to a flexible money policy; unless he can point to advantages from the former which are not obtainable from the latter."[10] There are important practical difficulties with the flexible wage policy which do not apply to flexible monetary policy. Important of such difficulties are mentioned below.

It is almost impossible to affect a general wage cut. This is possible only in a dictatorial society. In democratic countries, the wages are determined by the system of collective bargaining between individual labour unions and employers' unions which means that the wage reductions, if any, would be only piecemeal, that is, the workers with weak trade unions would be the first and the largest victims of cut in wages. In contrast, it is very easy for the government to increase the quantity of money to lower the rate of interest.

---

9. J.M. Keynes, *The General Theory of Employment, Interest and Money* (London, 1936), p. 266.
10. *Ibid.*, p. 268.

Even if labourers can be compelled to accept a general cut in wages, such a step would go against the democratic ideal of social justice. The non-wage-earners, particularly the rentiers receiving incomes from land rents, bonds and other forms of contractual securities would benefit at the cost of wage-earners. In contrast, an increase in the supply of money would cause a reduction in the real income of all sections by raising the prices of almost all goods.

Lower prices brought about by a general cut in wage-rate increases the burden of private as well as public debt. As against this, an increase in the supply of money reduces such burden. The existence of a large public or private debt is often an important objection to a policy of general reduction in wages and prices.

In an open economy, a general wage cut, though strengthens the balance of payments position, would deteriorate the terms of trade and thus lead to a reduction in the real income of the country.

A flexible wage policy would cause great instability of prices which would make business calculations difficult and thus be injurious to the smooth functioning of the economy. In contrast, the use of monetary policy for attaining the same purpose would create less instability and thereby promote proper functioning of the economy.

Keynes was of the opinion that a flexible monetary policy is an alternative to and on both economic and political grounds preferable to a flexible wage policy. According to him, under certain conditions money wage cuts might lead to a small increase in employment but anything that can be attained by reducing wages, as a matter of practical policy, can be attained better by monetary policy. In the words of Prof. Lerner, "To seek alleviation of depression by reducing money wages, rather than directly reducing the rate of interest or otherwise encouraging investment or consumption, is to abandon the high road for a devious, dark, difficult and unreliable path, for no better reason than that the dangers that await one at the common destination are more clearly seen when it is approached by the broad way."[11]

11. A.P. Lerner, "The General Theory (1)" in Seymour E. Harris (ed.), *The New Economics* (London, 1960), p. 132.

KEYNES' WAGE POLICY

Keynes was of the opinion that for a closed economy the best short run policy was to keep money wages as stable as possible. As seen above, besides the serious practical difficulties, steadily declining wages adversely affect the marginal efficiency of capital and thereby the volume of employment. Stable wages would remove this type of adverse effect on the volume of investment. In the long run, when productivity is likely to increase steadily, a choice can be made between stable wage-rates and gradually declining prices or stable prices and gradually rising money wages. Keynes preferred the latter alternative because it will (i) have favourable effects upon the expectations of the entrepreneurs and hence upon the inducement to invest, (ii) lighten the real burden of debt, (iii) provide greater psychological encouragement to the active working class than will the real wages in the form of stable money wages and falling prices, and (iv) facilitate the transfer of resources out of declining industries into growing industries by raising money wages in the latter without having to lower them in the former.

WAGE-PRICE POLICY DURING DEPRESSION

During the depression period, the decline in aggregate demand exhibits itself immediately in a decline in output and prices. The decline in prices is greater in highly competitive industries where commodities are bought and sold in organized markets. In contrast, in oligopolistic industries, where firms have some control over the prices they charge, prices, at first, decline slowly or not at all. The result is that the decline in economic activity normally leads to distortions in the price structure. The past depressions show that farm prices have declined more than industrial prices and the costs and prices in construction industry (and also in other capital-goods industries) have tended to be sticky and to remain high when the demand for building falls off. A more balanced fall in prices, and particularly lower prices for investment goods, would tend to moderate the severity of a depression. This indicates the scope for government intervention in the field of prices. The government should take steps to prevent a demoralising decline in prices in competitive industries (particularly agriculture) and force down costs and prices in monopolistic industries (particularly in construction and other investment goods industries).

FULL EMPLOYMENT AND INFLATION

The inflationary aspect of the wage-price problem raises two critical and related questions. Firstly, when aggregate demand rises, whether during the natural course of a business upswing or as a consequence of government measures, is the increase in spending likely to push up wages and prices? Secondly, is there danger, if full employment is continuously maintained, that the demand of strong labour unions and other organised groups will cause wages and prices to rise steadily, so that the objective of price stability becomes unattainable? Or to put in a more simple way, may not full employment and price stability be incompatible as objectives of policy?

A continuously maintained full employment is likely to lead to a steady rise in wages and prices. If the fear of unemployment disappears and the government undertakes to take measures to stimulate aggregate demand in case there appears any unemployment, the trade unions are likely to press steadily for higher wages. In case, as is very likely, the resulting wage increases are in excess of the normal improvements in productivity, labour costs will rise and businessmen will raise their prices. With the rise in the prices of industrial products the farm groups will demand government help in raising agricultural prices. And the general rise in prices will lead to a fresh round of rise in wage rates.

It is widely accepted that a continuously maintained full employment policy invariably leads to one of the two results. Either the goal of price stability must be abandoned or else full employment can be maintained without involving open inflation only if the government interferes with the traditional economic liberties by depriving labour of its right to bargain freely with employers, by imposing wage and price controls, and by direct control of consumer and business spending through rationing, allocations, and similar devices. On the other hand, some economists are more hopeful and believe that organized labour and other groups can be educated to keep their demands within limits so that full employment can be maintained without a steady rise in the price level. Some people, while accepting that a full employment policy leads to inflation in the absence of controls, prefer to restrict the power of labour and other groups if necessary to attain both price stability and full employment.

MOVEMENT OF REAL AND MONEY WAGES

The theory of the firm teaches us that a firm in a competitive industry will hire workers up to the point where the value of the marginal product (marginal product multiplied by the price of output) just equals the cost of the factor. Assuming that pure competition prevails, this profit maximization condition may be written as:

$$\omega = px_n$$

or

$$\omega/p = x_n$$

where ω stands for the money wage, p for the price level, ω/p for the real wage, and X_n for the marginal product of labour. The demand for labour may therefore be written as:

$$N_d = D\left[\frac{w}{p}\right]$$

which states that demand for labour is a function of the real wage. Since the law of diminishing returns suggests that the marginal product of labour declines as more workers are hired, increase in employment cannot be brought about without a decline in the real wage. Most of the economists, accepting the labour demand function as written above, assume that a decline in real wages is a natural consequence of emergence from depression. Noting that money wages rise with an increase in output, Keynes expressed the opinion that "the change in real wages associated with a change in money wages, so far from being usually in the same direction, is almost always in the opposite direction."[12] In other words, Keynes and most economists believed that, even though money wages rise during recovery, prices rise even faster so that real wages fall. The empirical, analysis, however, showed that the real wages actually rise with the increase in output and employment.[13] Apparently there is something wrong with the idea that the demand for labour is a decreasing function of the real wage.

---

12. J.M. Keynes, *The General Theory of Employment, Interest and Money* (London, 1936), p. 10.
13. L. Tarshis, "Changes in Real and Money Wages", *Economic Journal*, 1939, pp. 150-54.

In a later article[14] Keynes conceded that real wages seem to increase, though he refused to abandon the assumption of diminishing returns in the short run. He suggested instead that real wage increases would be consistent with employment increases if the assumptions of pure competition were abandoned. While under pure competition a producer would hire workers up to the point at which the wage rate is equal to the value of the marginal product (marginal product multiplied by price), under monopoly he would hire workers up to the point at which the wage rate equals the marginal revenue product (marginal product multiplied by marginal revenue). Since marginal revenue (*mr*) can be written as

$$mr = p\left[1 - \frac{1}{e}\right]$$

where p is the price of output and e is the price elasticity of demand, we may write

$$\omega = p\left[1 - \frac{1}{e}\right]X_n$$

or

$$\frac{\omega}{p} = \left[1 - \frac{1}{e}\right]X_n$$

as the condition for maximum profit. This means that we can write the demand for labour as

$$N_d = D\left[\frac{\omega}{p}, e\right]$$

Under these conditions output increases are compatible with real wage increases so long as demand elasticities increase with increases in aggregate demand. In fact, under imperfect competition, even if demand elasticities remain unchanged, increases in employment are not inconsistent with the increases in real wage rates.

It should be recognised that though a certain stock of capital goods exists, this does not, unless the stock of capital goods is indivisible, mean that whole of it will necessarily be employed in the

14. J.M. Keynes, "Relative Movement of Real Wages and Output", *Economic Journal*, 1939, pp. 34-51.

sense that it is utilised in the production process. A factory having 40 machines may, for instance, in times of slack demand use only 30 machines because substitution between labour and machines is not perfect. 'The firm may, therefore, use only 30 machines together with some labour even though labour costs are variable while the machine costs are fixed in the short run.'

If the period of slack demand persists, the idle equipment may gradually be reduced. But since this can normally take place only by a slow process of depreciation and obsolescence, the typical depression can be expected to be characterised by widespread excess capacity, which, if equipment is divisible and production function is characterised by ranges of zero returns, may for purposes of analysis be considered umemployed. From this it follows that output can be expanded by hiring more labour, by bringing additional existing machines into use or by both. This means that there is more than one attainable marginal productivity of labour schedule and that employment can be increased both by a shift in the schedule and by a movement along it. From this it follows that there may be many possible real wage rates that are compatible with labour market equilibrium.

Keynes ruled out, in the short run, the possibility of changes in organisation, equipment and techniques. In fact, changes in techniques go on year after year with sufficient speed and as such an expansion in output may be accompanied by constant real wages even if we assume rising cost curves. This is so because improvements in technology may counteract the increase in marginal cost arising from the shape of the cost functions.

Contrary to Keynes' view, it is now widely believed that the variable and marginal cost curves are substantially flat over wide ranges of output. If this is accepted, the process of increase in output and employment may not lead to a decline in real wage rates even if improvements in technology are ruled out in the short period. In case the possibilities of improvements in techniques are taken into consideration, there may even be an increase in real wages.

WAGE POLICY FOR FULL EMPLOYMENT

The full employment situation that would be reached through a simple application of functional finance would be one of low full employment. Whenever the number of unemployed falls below a fairly high figure, as already seen, the bargaining power of labour becomes strong which leads to a rise in wage rates and consequently to inflationary pressures even though there is no technical reason, in terms of real limitations on the mobility of labour, why unemployment should not be reduced to a much lower figure. Attainment of high full employment requires a wage policy which prevents inflationary wage increases.

Such a wage policy should be directed not at real wages but at money wages. Basically real wages are much more important than money wage rates but it is only the money wage rates that policy can directly affect. It is possible to raise (or to lower) a money wage rate and to know that it is in fact raised (or lowered). The same is not true of real wage. An attempt to change the real wage by changing the money wage may be defeated. If an increase in money wage rate leads to an equal increase in the prices of goods, and services bought by the workers, the real wage will not in fact have been raised at all. And this type of phenomena is not unlikely in actual practice. Raising money wage rates always increases costs which naturally leads to a rise in prices.

Secondly, the wage policy should be directed not at the general level of money wage rates but at specific wage rates in particular industries, trades and regions. This is because an over-all change in wages in general without any change in the relation of particular money wage rates to each other brings about a proportional change in prices, leaves the real wage rates unchanged, and has no effect on the volume of employment.

Though the wage policy should be directed at particular wage rates in particular labour markets, it must be such as results in desirable general effects on the general level of wages and on the general level of prices and incomes.

An important effect of a rise in the general level of money wages and the resultant rise in prices is the effect on the relationship between debtors and creditors because of the reduction in the real value of the debts. There is also a monetary effect. At a higher level of money wages, prices, and incomes, a larger volume of money is required to carry on with the same convenience as before, the same level of real economic activity, that is, in employing the same number of men and producing the same quantity of goods and services.

If the monetary authorities do not increase the stock of money, money will become tight. The tightness of money can lead to curtailment of investment and other economic activity which would result in unemployment and a reduction in real output and income. Many people would hold increase in money wage rate responsible for such unemployment. But other would put the blame for unemployment on the monetary authorities for their failure to increase the stock of money. It would, of course, be easier and more practicable to increase the supply of money than to lower all wages and prices. Increase in the supply of money would keep the wages and prices at a higher level without any real change in the production and consumption of goods and services or in the volume of employment in comparison with the situation before the money wages were raised.

The raising or lowering the general level of wages and prices can be very disturbing not only to the debtors and creditors but to those in charge of monetary policy and to investors and all who are concerned about what wages and prices are going to be in future. The wage policy, therefore, should be such as keeps the prices and the value of money stable.

It is not possible to have a wage policy which would stabilise both the general level of wages and the general level of prices. This is because productivity is continually increasing. Improvements in techniques of production resulting from a continuous process of inventions and scientific discoveries reduce the costs and prices of products in relation to the wage rate. If with the improvements in productivity, a choice is to be made between stable wages with declining prices and stable prices with rising wages, the latter course would be preferable. The latter course makes the financial management of the economy much easier and most probably the workers would like to see their increased real income over time taking the form of more money in their pay envelopes rather than the less tangible form of being able to buy more goods with the same amount of money.

The function of wages is to induce workers to work and to make them do the kind of work that is most effective in satisfying the needs of consumers—to make them produce the goods and services which the consumers prefer. Higher wages are the means of attracting workers where they are needed more. Similarly, lower wages are the means of persuading workers to leave places where they are needed less.

Higher wages have to be offered to induce workers to go where there is an increase in demand for their product or to go where they would otherwise not like to go because the conditions of work are not very congenial or the nature of work is not to their taste.

According to Lerner, wage policy can be based on indices of relative attractiveness.[15] An index of relative attractiveness of any occupation is provided by the ratio between the number of people who are qualified and ready to work in the occupation but have not been able to get a job there and the number of people actually employed in the occupation. For the economy as a whole the corresponding figure is an average that may be called the "national average index" of attractiveness of all occupations The wage policy consists of rules indicating that wages should in general rise at a rate equal to the rate of increase in productivity, that wages should rise faster where the index of relative attractiveness is sufficiently less than the national average, and that wages should be frozen where the index of relative attractiveness is sufficiently greater than the national average.

The increases in wages suggested above can be effected either frequently (say quarterly, half-yearly or yearly) or infrequently (say after every three years). The increases in wages would be small in the former case and large in the latter one. The method of adjustment to be followed would depend on what is more satisfactory to the workers and to the employers and could very well be one of the matters for collective bargaining. The more continuous adjustment would involve least dislocation and would mean more complete adjustment to the current conditions. It is also felt that the workers would prefer less frequent but more exciting increases in wages. There might be some advantage in annual adjustments which could be considered together with other issues in the course of the collective bargaining agreements.

15. Abba P. Lerner, *Economics of Employment* (New York, 1951).

Some people may consider wage policy to be unfair to labour in that it seeks to check the inflationary spiral of wages and prices by checking the increases in wages. They may raise the question as to why not to check inflation by checking price increases instead of checking increase in wages. It is better to stabilise wages than to stabilise prices for two reasons. In the first place, a policy of stabilising wages does not impair the effectiveness of price mechanism. The price level can also be stabilised without fixing individual prices if it is done by rationing spending in general or by limiting total spending in some other manner. But this brings us to the second reason for preferring stabilisation of wages. If we stabilise prices by limiting spending, we are in fact keeping prices from rising by keeping demand down to the level where the bargaining power of the workers is no longer excessive. We are then back at the low level of full employment with the reserve army of unemployed that we want to avoid. We can attain high full employment only by checking inflation through wages instead of through prices.

PRICE FLEXIBILITY AND FULL EMPLOYMENT

The phrase "price flexibility" can be interpreted in two different ways, *viz.* (1) structural price flexibility, and (2) cyclical price flexibility. Structural price flexibility means the long-term secular adjustment in the price structure. It is concerned not with the level of prices but with the interrelation of individual prices. Changes in technology and the methods of production, for instance, continually alter the relative unit costs of production of different commodities. Structural price flexibility means an adjustment of prices to change in relative unit costs resulting from unequal rates of technological progress in different industries or from shifts in the pattern of wants. A structurally flexible price system operates to direct the productive resources into channels which will yield the largest social product. In the absence of structural price flexibility, there would prevail an uneconomic allocation of resources and as a result it would not be possible to realise the full gains of economic progress.

Cyclical price flexibility refers to the sensitivity of prices to fluctuations of the business cycle. Commodities whose prices move swiftly in response to changes in the national income and whose amptitude of fluctuations is relatively large are said to be cycle-sensitive commodities in regard to price. Experience shows that raw materials, agricultural as well as industrial, are to a large extent cyclically price sensitive while finished manufactured products are, by and large, insensitive to cyclical changes in employment, output and income. In the case of farm products the sensitivity is limited to price responses, while in the case of certain industrial raw materials the sensitivity relates both to price and to fluctuations in output.

There exists more or less consensus of opinion in regard to the desirability of structural price flexibility. Absence of structural price flexibility would lead to an uneconomic utilization of resources. Further, any marked dearrangement in the structural adjustment of the prices of important commodities in relation to unit costs may have a disrupting effect upon consumption and investment expenditures, contributing to the initiation of a decline in industrial activity. Thus, at times, structural price adjustments may contribute to cyclical movements.

Price Flexibility and the Cycle: There, however, exists a sharp controversy in regard to cyclical price flexibility. It is held that unemployment is caused, or at least intensified, by the depression insensitivity of a large and important group of commodities. It is suggested that depression might, to a large extent, be prevented or mitigated by making all commodities as price sensitive as per most raw materials. The deflationary movements cannot be remedied by chasing administered prices and wage rates down the level of agricultural and other flexible prices. If in the industry as a whole, and particularly in the capital goods and durable consumers' goods industries, prices and wages were reduced drastically to an extent commensurate with decline in the prices of cyclically flexible commodities—agricultural and other raw materials—it is to be expected that, by and large, such price and wage declines would merely reduce the gross volume of monetary expenditures made in capital goods industries and durable consumers' goods area, without appreciably affecting the physical volume of output. Since these cost payments are also income receipts of individuals, incomes fall along with a decline in costs. Further, cyclical price flexibility all round under conditions prevailing at the end of a boom might accentuate the downswing. The expectation by business and consumers that prices will fall tends to generate a cumulative decline in expenditures and to intensify the downswing. There results not only inventory disinvestment, but also the curtailment of investment and durable consumers' expenditures in the expectation of further fall in the national income and in costs and prices. It was not altogether an accident that the most violent deflationary movement in the Great Depression came in 1931 in the midst of wholesale wage cuts. A high degree of wage stability during the business cycle, therefore, is considered to be preferable to a policy of wage adjustments.

The effect would, of course, be different if the income and effective demand could be maintained or expanded at the moment the costs are reduced. Combined with monetary and fiscal policies designed to maintain the total volume of consumption and investment opportunities, an orderly programme of cost-price readjustment does facilitate recovery.

Just as forced cyclical downward adjustments of administrative prices are to be avoided, so also an increase in administrative prices in the upswing is to be avoided. Such an increase similarly creates business expectations which tend to cause the accumulation of excessive inventories, leading to subsequent relapses.

It is sometimes asserted that chronic unemployment of resources must indicate that prices are too high in relation to the level of purchasing power and the situation can be rectified by progressive reduction of prices. This type of reasoning is meaningful only in case of monopoly prices and technological innovations reducing the unit cost of production. High monopoly prices have a tendency to reduce the volume of employment. They tend to reduce the real purchasing power of wage earners and to enhance profits. The increase in inequalities in the distribution of income tends to reduce consumption expenditure and to increase savings. As such, a reduction in monopoly prices will stimulate consumption and raise the level of employment.

Level of employment would also rise when consumer goods prices fall as a result of technological innovation which reduces the unit cost of production. The cost-reducing innovation induces new investment, and this results in an increase in employment while the new investment is made, and, subsequently, in a reduction in consumer goods prices after the new investment yields increased supply of goods.

In the absence of monopoly prices or of technological change, price reductions can be used as a means of increasing employment. If competitive prices are arbitrarily reduced, wage rates remaining unchanged, marginal firms will be driven out of business, and disinvestment will occur, causing a reduction in employment. It is not possible to solve this problem of unemployment by relying upon the potentially larger purchasing power which, it is assumed, will appear if prices are arbitrarily reduced below the point determined by competition.

Conclusion. While the price policy does play an important role, it does not constitute an adequate remedy for the business cycle and for chronic underutilisation of resources. Price policy must be integrated with monetary and fiscal policies. It is by and large upon these latter that reliance must be placed to prevent any large decline in business activity and in the national income. If this is done, cyclical price dispersion between cycle-sensitive commodities and cycle-insensitive commodities will be minimised to a large extent. From the long-run point of view, a reasonably full utilization of resources will facilitate the adaptation of individual prices to structural changes incident to the differential rates of technical progress in different industries.

Simple Determination of Income and Employment

4

Having explained the basic concepts and methodological issues, we are now equipped to proceed to the analysis of our main issue: What determines the level of income, employment and output in a closed economy? Many of these ideas and concepts were first presented by a British economist John Maynard Keynes in his famous book *General Theory of Employment, Interest and Money* (1936). Some of the ideas which Keynes originally presented have undergone significant changes and modification as a result of continuous research on macro economics. However, one must concede that there was not much systematic thinking on these topics before Keynes and his contribution to this branch of economic science was so fundamental that modern macro economics is also known as Keynesian Economics.

The basic idea of Keynesian economics is very simple. Marshall taught that equilibrium quantity of any good in the market depends upon demand price and supply price of any commodity. The demand schedule is a schedule of different quantities of a good which shall be bought at different prices. These prices are known as demand price. The demand price is the price at which the buyers demand a particular good. Such a demand schedule is shown as the curve DD in Fig. 4.1. The supply schedule is a schedule of different quantities of same good which shall be supplied at different prices. The supply price of a good is the price at which the suppliers supply the good. The equilibrium quantity and prices are determined at a point where demand price becomes equal to supply price, *i.e.*, quantity demanded of good is exactly equal to the quantity supplied. In Figure 4.1, this has been shown as $\overline{Q}$ and $\overline{P}$ where DD curve intersects SS curve. This diagram is also known as Marshallian cross. Keynes was a disciple of Marshall and he used basically the same idea to explain employment determination in the economy. Keynes argued that employment like all other goods also has demand price and a supply price.

Since, Keynes is concerned with the economy as a whole, and he wants to determine total employment in the economy, therefore, he speaks of aggregate demand price and aggregate supply price of employment.

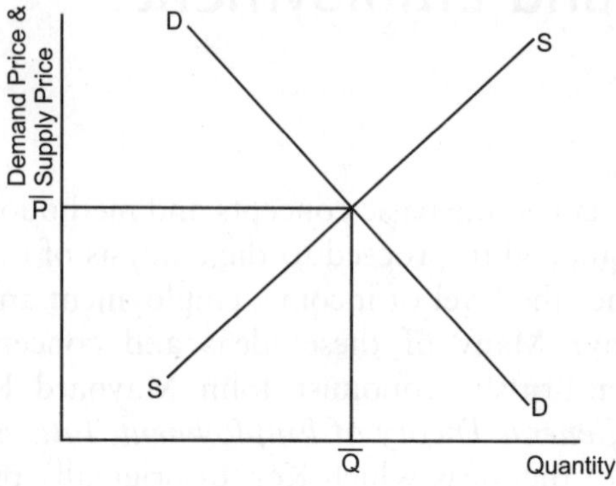

Fig. 4.1. Marshallian Cross showing price and output determination of good.

The aggregate demand schedule of the economy shows the amount of proceeds (income measured in Rupees) which all firms really expect to get if they can sell the output produced by different levels of employment. The aggregate supply schedule shows what all firms in any economy must expect to receive from the sale of output produced by the same number of men. The aggregate demand schedule and aggregate supply schedule are shown in Fig. 4.2. The Y-axis measures total receipts or income from the sale of output which is produced by a given level of employment. The X-axis measures the volume of employment. Each level of employment will have both, aggregate demand price and aggregate supply price. Aggregate demand price is a measure of revenue or (income) which all firms really expect to get. On the other hand, aggregate supply price is a measure of cost of employment in the economy (the proceed or receipts which all the firms must expect to spend in order to employ a certain number of people). Now let us consider point N_1. At this point of employment, aggregate demand price is greater than aggregate supply price. This means that employers (all firms) expect to get more than what they will spend to employ ON_1 people. In other words, the revenue obtained by ON_1 volume of employment exceeds the cost incurred upon it. Consequently, it is not only profitable to employ ON_1 volume of people, but also to expand it. Thus volume of employment will tend to move to the right hand side from ON_1. Now consider the point ON_2. At this point the aggregate supply price of employment is greater than its aggregate demand price which means that the cost of ON_2 amount of employment will be greater than the revenue or receipts which is expected to be obtained by the sale of output produced by this volume of employment. Consequently, it is not profitable for the firms to employ ON_2 people and employment will tend to move to the left hand side.

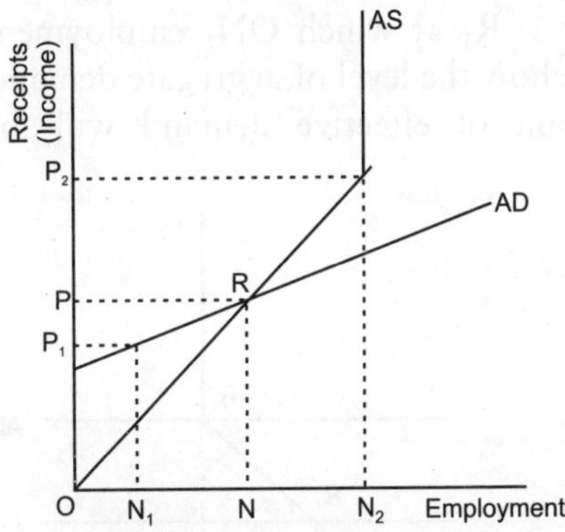

Fig. 4.2. Employment determination in the economy.

The equilibrium level of employment occurs where the aggregate demand curve intersects the aggregate supply curve, *i.e.*, aggregate demand price of employment is exactly equal to its aggregate supply price. In Fig. 4.2 this is shown at the point R where ON people are employed and they produce OP amount of income. At this point of employment there will be no tendency among the employers either to expand the employment or to curtail it, simply because, the income they expect to get from this level of employment will be exactly to the cost they will be incurring upon it. Consequently, there will be no tendency either to cut back the employment or to increase it.

THE PRINCIPLE OF EFFECTIVE DEMAND

Thus the essential idea of Keynesian Economics is that employment is determined at the point where aggregate demand is equal to aggregate supply. The point where aggregate demand is equal to the aggregate supply is called the point of effective demand

(This is also known as the break-even point). The principle of effective demand states that level of employment, given the aggregate supply, depends upon effective demand, which in turn depends upon aggregate demand. If effective demand is low, the level of employment will be low. If effective demand is higher, level of employment in the economy will be higher.

This is shown in Fig. 4.3 in which X-axis measures employment and Y-axis measures receipts or income. As is the aggregate supply schedule about which we have already learnt. If aggregate demand is AD_1, then point of intersection of aggregate demand and aggregate supply is R_1 at which ON_1 employment is determined. However, if somehow the level of aggregate demand could be raised to AD_2, the point of effective demand will move to R_2 and

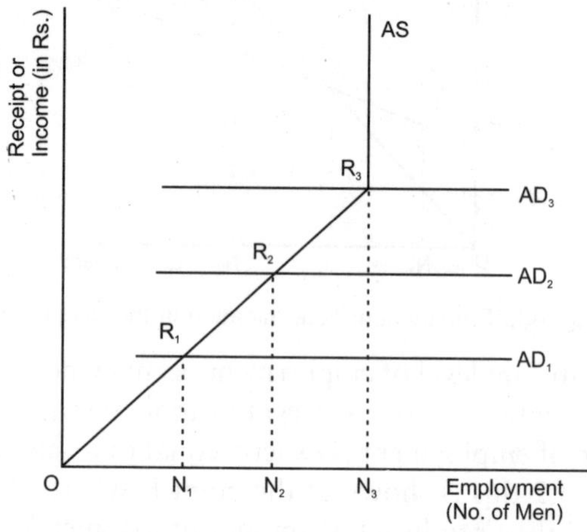

Fig. 4.3. Effective demand depends upon level of aggregate demand.

employment will rise to ON_2. Similarly, if aggregate demand rises to AD_3, effective demand is at R_3 and ON_3 employment will result. Note that employment cannot rise above ON_3 aggregate supply curve becomes horizontal to vertical axis (we will discover it later why this is so) and further increase in the aggregate demand will not result in any increase in employment. Thus when level of employment is reached to ON_3 we say that full employment has been achieved.

THE CONCEPT OF FULL EMPLOYMENT

Any economy cannot employ all the persons who are present. Generally speaking, children below a certain age (18 years in India) and old persons above a certain age (60 years in India) do not offer themselves for jobs. They are not included in the labour force. The persons coming in the age group 18-60 years are persons of working age. But all persons in this age group also do not constitute labour force. Some of them may be physically handicapped to do any kind of work. Some may be getting education and training. Some others may not be willing to work. Therefore, the persons who have ability (physical and mental) to work and are willing to do so, are included in the labour force. When all such persons who are willing to work find jobs, then it is said that full employment has been achieved. A more formal definition of full employment is that full employment exists when involuntary unemployment is zero. This raises the question: what is involuntary unemployment?

VOLUNTARY, INVOLUNTARY AND FRICTIONAL UNEMPLOYMENT

It is very natural to refer to unemployment while discussing the determination of employment, simply because the presence of one is the absence of the other. If employment is low, it means unemployment is high and if employment is high it means unemployment is low. Keynes has classified unemployment into following three categories:

1. Frictional unemployment.
2. Voluntary unemployment.
3. Involuntary unemployment.

Let us understand every one of these three types of unemployment.

1. Frictional Unemployment. Frictional unemployment is that type of unemployment which may come into existence because of less than perfect functioning of the economy. The people may be unemployed for short periods when they change over from one job to another. They may be unemployed because the flow of information about the job situation and about the conditions in the job market may not be very smooth. They may also become unemployed for sometime if firms switch over from one technology to the other technology. Unemployment may also result from the streamlining of organizational set up of firms etc. All these are illustrations of frictional unemployment.

2. Voluntary Unemployment. Keynes defines voluntary unemployment in the following words:

> "Voluntary unemployment (is) due to the refusal or inability of a unit of labour, as a result of legislation or social practices or of combination for collective bargaining or of slow response to change or of mere human obstinacy, to accept a reward corresponding to the value of the product attributable to its marginal productivity."[1]

Thus according to Keynes, voluntary unemployment is the result of a single individual's action who for one reason or the other refuses to accept the current market wage rate (which is in fact equal to the value of his own marginal product). Keynes outlines the following main reasons for voluntary unemployment:

(1) Legislation.

(2) Social customs.

(3) Labour unions.

(4) Slow response to change.

Because of any above reason the individual does not accept the job and prefers to remain unemployed. This type of unemployment is called voluntary unemployment.

3. Involuntary Unemployment. Involuntary unemployment has been defined by Keynes in the following manner:

> "Men are involuntarily unemployed if, in the event of a small rise in the price of wage-goods relatively to the money wage, both the aggregate supply of labour willing to work for the current money-wage and the aggregate demand for it at that wage would be greater than the existing volume of employment."[2]

Although the definition of involuntary unemployment given by Keynes appears to be cumbersome, the basic idea behind it is quite simple. Involuntary unemployment exists if people are willing to

---

1. John. Maynard Keynes: *General Theory of Employment, Interest and Money* (1936), Harbinger edition, p. 6.

2. Keynes, *op. cit.* p. 6.

work at the going market wage rate but there are no jobs for them. In this situation, people are unemployed because of scarcity of jobs. They are unwillingly unemployed. That is why it is called involuntary unemployment. In order to understand this concept clearly, let us go back to Fig. 4.3. Given the aggregate supply, ON_3 amount of labour is available for employment. Since the level of aggregate demand is AD_1 only ON_1 persons are employed and N_1 N_3 persons are involuntarily unemployed. If the level of aggregate demand rises to AD_2 employment rises to ON_2 and involuntary unemployment is reduced to N_2 N_3. Similarly when the level of aggregate demand rises to AD_3, all the available labour is employed, *i.e.*, full employment is achieved and involuntary unemployment is reduced to zero. Thus, following conclusions emerge out of the foregoing analysis:

1. In situations of full employment involuntary unemployment is zero.
2. Involuntary unemployment may be reduced or even eliminated by increasing the level of aggregate demand.

One must also mention that it is only involuntary unemployment which cannot exist with full employment. This is so because existence of full employment has been defined as absence of involuntary unemployment. Hence, their simultaneous occurrence would be contradiction in terms. However, frictional unemployment and voluntary unemployment may exist simultaneously with full employment. This implies that unemployment is not zero when economy achieves full employment. Some unemployment is tolerable even if the situation of full employment has been reached. How much is that 'some unemployment' which is consistent with full employment? Firstly, no magnitude of this type of unemployment may be given *a priori*. It is a question of empirical verification. For example, its has been estimated for the U.S.A. that magnitude of frictional and voluntary unemployment ranges between 4 per cent and 5 per cent per annum. Thus, if the American economy achieves 95 per cent to 96 per cent employment, it is regarded as full employment level. However, if the rate of unemployment reached to 10-12 per cent, the U.S. economy is taken as recessionary and involuntary unemployment is said to be present. Secondly, the magnitude of frictional and voluntary unemployment would differ from country to country and from time to time. This is so because the magnitudes of frictional and voluntary unemployment depend upon technological conditions, progress of science and technology and its application to productive processes, social customs and conditions, legislative framework etc. which differ from society to society.

UNDEREMPLOYMENT EQUILIBRIUM

Let us go back again to Fig. 4.3 which shows that involuntary employment may persist if the level of aggregate demand is low. The point R_3 at which there is no involuntary unemployment is known as full employment equilibrium. However, the economy is also in equilibrium at the points R_1 and R_2 simply because the aggregate demand and aggregate supply are equal at these points. Despite the fact that economy is in equilibrium this cannot be concealed that significant involuntary unemployment may be present in the economy. That is the reason that these equilibrium points are designated as underemployment equilibrium. In terms of Fig. 4.3, the points R_1 and R_2 show the situations of underemployment equilibrium.

Keynes was the first economist to show the possibility of underemployment equilibrium. The economists before Keynes, whom he calls classical economists used to believe that underemployment equilibrium is not possible. The classical economists were of the opinion that full employment shall always be maintained and involuntary unemployment cannot occur. This conclusion was based upon certain assumption about the labour market which shall be taken up later. At this moment, it is sufficient to know that classical economists assumed a vertical aggregate supply function which has been shown in Fig. 4.4(*b*). Employment as shown on the X-axis and Y-axis shows receipts or income. The point N_F shows full employment. Since the aggregate supply curve is vertical, therefore economy would always operate at the full employment level and the increases in the aggregate demand will not succeed in increasing the level of employment. In contrast to the classical aggregate supply function, Keynesian aggregate supply function has been depicted in Fig. 4.4(*a*). As you can see the aggregate supply function begins at the origin which means that employment can become zero in special circumstances. Thereafter, output or income rises with the increases in employment. As N_F full employment is reached and aggregate supply curve becomes vertical, which is similar to the classical aggregate supply function shown in Fig. 4.4(*b*).

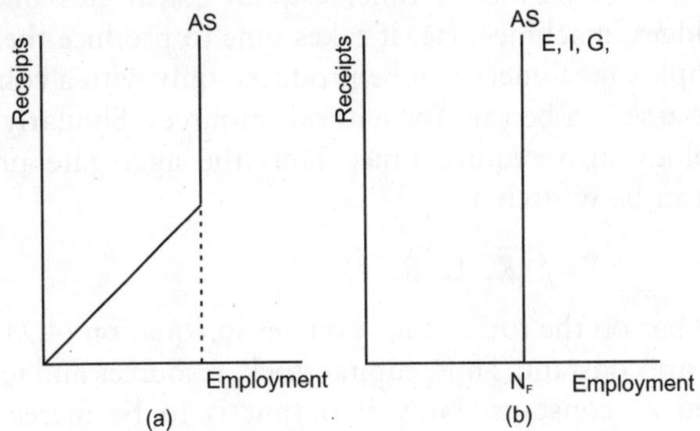

Fig. 4.4. Keynesian and classical aggregate Supply Functions.

WHY AGGREGATE SUPPLY IS NOT CONSIDERED?

We have seen that the level of employment depends on the aggregate demand and aggregate supply schedules. We have also shown that the level of aggregate demand shall determine the level of effective demand if the aggregate supply is given. Let us examine in this section how far the assumption of given aggregate supply is justified.

The aggregate supply function of an economy depends upon the physical conditions of production. It depends upon the amounts of capital stock, natural resources, technology, etc. It also depends upon the productivity of men, machines and natural resources. In other words, the aggregate supply depends upon aggregate production function of the economy which is given below:

$$Y = f(K, L, R, T) \quad ...(4.1)$$

where

Y = flow of output per period.

K = flow of machine services per period.

L = flow of labour services per period.

R = flow of services of natural resources.

T = Some appropriate index of technology.

If we want increases in output then we must increase either one or all or some of these variables. Now let us consider what variables we can increase in the short run (meaning thereby a short period of time such as a year). The capital stock cannot be increased within a reasonable short period of time. Capital constitutes of building, roads, bridges, machines, etc. It takes time to produce these things. Some complex machinery can be produced only with a considerable time lag. Same can be said for natural resources. Similarly, changes in technology also require time. Thus the aggregate production function can be written as

$$Y = f(\overline{K}, L, \overline{R}, \overline{T}) \qquad ...(4.2)$$

where the bar on the top of the variables in equation (4.2) indicates that these are constant. Thus, capital stock, resources and technology are treated as constant. Now if output is to be increased, only variable which we can raise in the short run is labour. Thus, the short run production function can be written as

$$Y = f(L) \qquad ...(4.3)$$

which means that income or output depends upon labour employed. By increasing the level of employment, the level of income and output can be raised. One may ask, "If capital and natural resources are constant, then how employment could be raised? After all labour works with the help of machine and materials?" This is a very legitimate question and this is also true that labour works with machines and materials. The clue to answer of this question lies in the fact that what do we mean by capital is constant. $\overline{K}$, $\overline{R}$, and $\overline{T}$ in equation (4.2) mean that their available supply is constant and cannot be increased. However, it does not say anything about how much of available supply is utilised. Whenever there is involuntary unemployment (remember that employment can be increased only in situations when involuntary unemployment is present) capital and other resources are also unemployed. The reason for this is that labour always works with some amount of machines and materials. Consequently, in the event of general unemployment of labour, the utilization of other resources is also at a very low level. This situation is known as excess capacity. When excess capacity is present, shortage (or scarcity) of capital is no problem. The total output can be increased only by increasing employment of labour because capital is already there working at less than its full capacity.

Thus, the essential thing about Keynesian economics is that it is essentially concerned with short run and its logical formulations and deductions are applicable only to the cases when excess capacity exists particularly in the machine building industries. In the presence of excess capacity, it is reasonable to assume that aggregate supply is given and aggregate demand shall determine the level of employment. Thus, in the following pages we shall evoke the assumption of given aggregate supply and concentrate our analysis on aggregate demands, its determinant and their role in the determination of income and employment in an economy.

COMPONENTS OF AGGREGATE DEMAND

In the last chapter, we have learnt that aggregate demand will determine the level of income and employment if aggregate supply is given. For reasons explained above we have also assumed the aggregate supply to be given. Now, let us proceed to find out the determinants of aggregate demand which in turn will determine the level of income and employment in the economy. To keep the analysis simple, let us make the following assumptions:

1. That there is no government. The government neither imposes a tax nor incurs any expenditure.
2. That there is no foreign trade sector in the economy.

With these two assumptions, aggregate demand can be decomposed into the following components:

1. *Consumption demand.* A part of income may be demanded by the individuals so that they could buy the goods and services they need. From expenditure point of view, this is called personal consumption expenditure. Thus, the expenditure on food, clothing, shelter, books, entertainment, transport, etc. constitutes consumption expenditure.
2. *Investment demand.* In order to produce the goods and services for consumption, one needs to make investment. One has to buy machines, raw materials, lands and buildings etc. so that the process of production may be carried out. This type of expenditure which helps production to rise is called investment expenditure.

Thus we have the following macro-economic equation:

$$Y = C + I \qquad ...(4.4)$$

where

Y = Income

C = Consumption Expenditure

I = Investment Expenditure.

The right hand side of equation (4.4) represents total expenditure and the left hand side represents income. On the one hand, this equation states that consumption demand and investment demand are the two components of aggregate demand and on the other hand, it tells that total expenditure (aggregate demand) and aggregate supply must be equal. Thus, equation (4.4) can be taken as an identity as well as an equilibrium condition.

CONSUMPTION FUNCTION

The idea behind the theory of consumption function is very simple. Have you ever thought upon what factor your consumption depends? For any student of economics, and for an intelligent layman as well, the answer would be obvious—income! So the theory of consumption function says only this: consumption is a function of income or in other words, consumption depends upon

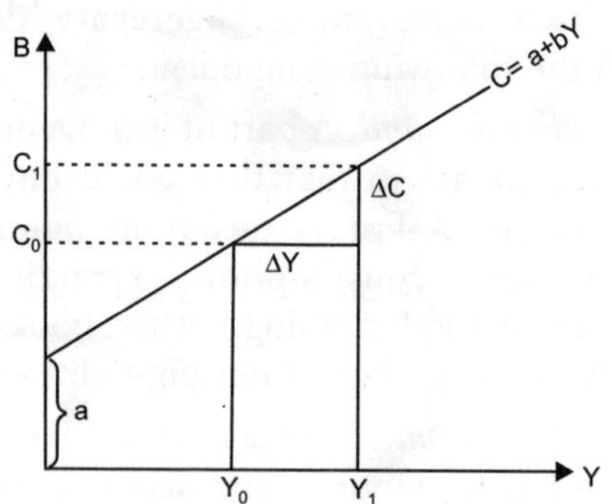

Fig. 4.5. A general linear consumption function.

income. Thus, consumption function specifies a certain relationship between two aggregate economic variables—Consumption and income. It states that consumption is an increasing function of income, *i.e.*, the consumption will tend to rise as income rises.

Figure 4.5 presents a consumption function which has the following form

$$C = a + bY \qquad ...(4.5)$$

In Figure 4.5 income is measured along the horizontal axis and consumption expenditure along the vertical axis. The consumption function described in equation (4.5) is called a linear consumption function because it is depicted in the form of a line. In Fig. 4.5, *a* is the intercept and *b* is the slope of line.

The data on the income and consumption expenditure of a hypothetical economy are presented in Table 4.1. In column (1) income is given and column (2) gives consumption expenditure. The ratio of consumption expenditure to income (*C/Y*) is given in column (3). This ratio is known as average propensity to consume. Not that average propensity to consume is declining as income rises. The reason for declining average propensity to consume (APC) is that consumption rises more slowly than income.

Table 4.1

Consumption Function of a Hypothetical Economy

Y	C	C/Y	ΔC	ΔY	ΔC/ΔY
(1)	(2)	(3)	(4)	(5)	(6)
100	125	1.25	—	—	—
200	200	1.00	75	100	0.75
300	275	0.90	75	100	0.75
400	350	0.87	75	100	0.75
500	425	0.85	75	100	0.75

MARGINAL PROPENSITY TO CONSUME

Marginal propensity to consume is the change in consumption from a given change in income. Let us go back to Table 4.1. Column (4) gives us the change in consumption (the symbol Δ is read as delta and is used to show change in variable. Thus, ΔC means change in consumption and ΔY means change in income). When income is 100 million consumption is 125 million when income rises to 200 million, consumption has also risen to 200 million. Thus the change in consumption is 75 million while the change in income is 100 million. Now, marginal propensity to consume (MPC) is defined as follows:

$$\text{MPC} = \frac{\text{Change in consumption}}{\text{Change income}}$$

$$\text{MPC} = \frac{\Delta C}{\Delta Y}$$

$$= \frac{75}{100} = 0.75$$

Notice that MPC remains constant when income rises.

The data of income and consumption which is presented in Table 4.1 has been plotted in Fig. 4.6 and the result is a consumption function of our hypothetical economy. Notice the marked similarity of Figures 4.5 and 4.6. The reason is obvious—both are linear consumption function. The consumption function depicted in Figure 4.2 has the following equation.

$$C = 50 + 0.75\,Y \quad \text{...(4.6)}$$

where 50 is intercept term and slope is 0.75. Also recall that MPC calculated in Table 4.1 was also 0.75. Thus, it is easy to see that MPC and slope the consumption function are the same. In other words, slope of consumption function represents MPC. In terms of Fig. 4.5, *b* is the slope as well as MPC. This can be shown as follows:

Let

Y_0 = Original level of income
Y_1 = New level of income
C_0 = Original level of consumption
C_1 = New level of consumption
ΔY = Change in income
ΔC = Change in consumption

But $$C_0 = a + bY_0 \quad \text{...(4.7)}$$

and $$C_1 = a + bY_1 \quad \text{...(4.8)}$$

Subtracting equation (4.5) from equation (4.6), we get

$$C_1 - C_0 = a + bY_1 - (a + bY_0)$$

$$C_1 - C_0 = a + bY_1 - a - bY_0$$

$$C_1 - C_0 = a + bY_1 - bY_0$$

$$C_1 - C_0 = b\,(Y_1 - Y_0) \quad \text{...(4.9)}$$

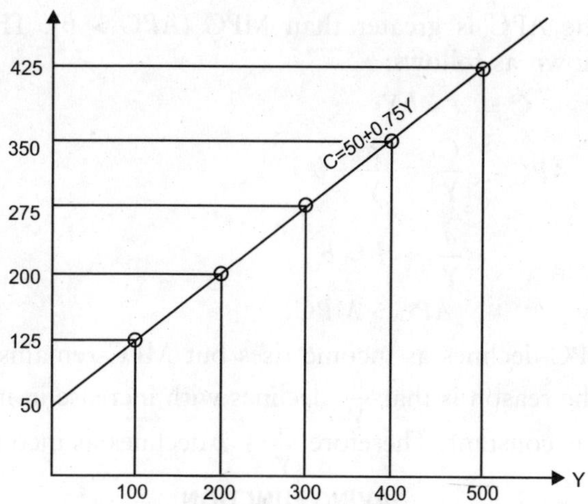

Fig. 4.6. Hypothetical consumption function.

Dividing equation (4.6) by $(Y_1 - Y_0)$, we get

$$\frac{C_1 - C_0}{Y_1 - Y_0} = \frac{b(Y_1 - Y_0)}{(Y_1 - Y_0)}$$

$$\frac{C_1 - C_0}{Y_1 - Y_0} = \frac{\Delta C}{\Delta Y} = b \qquad ...(4.10)$$

This b is marginal propensity to consume as well as slope.

Keynes propounded a psychological law of consumption which says that if there is a given increase in income then the resulting increase in consumption would be less than proportional than the original increase in income. The meaning of this 'law' is that MPC would be always greater than zero and its value would always be between the range zero and unity.

Now, the discussion about consumption can be summarized as follows:

(i) MPC is constant

(ii) MPC is greater than zero ($b > 0$)

(iii) The value of MPC is always between zero and unity ($0 < b < 1$).

(iv) The APC is greater than MPC ($APC > b$). This can be shown as follows:

$$C = a + bY$$

$$APC = \frac{C}{Y} = \frac{a}{Y} + b$$

$$\frac{a}{Y} + b > b$$

$$APC > MPC \quad ...(4.11)$$

(v) APC declines as income rises but MPC remains constant. The reason is that $\frac{a}{Y}$ declines with increase in income but b is constant. Therefore $\frac{a}{Y} + b$ declines as income rises.

SAVING FUNCTION

Whenever income accrues to a person, he may put it to any of the two uses. (*i*) A part of it, he may consume. This is consumption expenditure and we have studied above what governs it. A more thorough examination of determinants of consumption expenditure has been left for Chapter 7. (*ii*) The rest which he does not consume is saved. This is called saving. From this point of view income is to be either consumed or is to be saved. Thus, compared to equation (4.1) we have another macro-economic relationship.

$$Y = C + S \quad ...(4.12)$$

where

Y = Income

C = Consumption expenditure

S = Savings.

Since, we have defined saving as income not consumed, equation (3.9) can be modified as below:

$$S = Y - C \quad ...(4.13)$$

Equation (4.13) tells that saving is a residual. The income which is left after consumption is saving. Since consumption is a function of income, saving must also be a function of income.

$$S = F(Y) \quad ...(4.14)$$

The saving function can be obtained if we deduct consumption function from income.

$$S = Y - (a + bY)$$

$$S = -a + Y - bY \qquad \text{...(4.15)}$$

Taking Y common (4.12) can be written as:

$$S = -a + (1 - b)\ Y \qquad \text{...(4.16)}$$

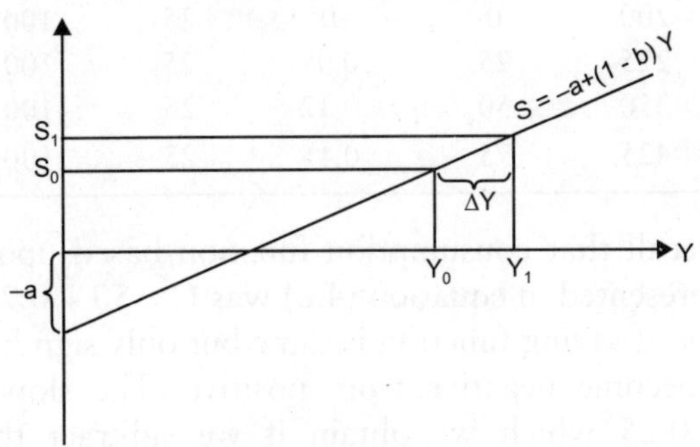

Fig. 4.7. A general linear saving function.

The saving function described in equation (4.16) has been drawn in Figure 4.8 in which income is measured on horizontal axis and saving has been measured on the vertical axis. This saving function has been derived from the consumption function described in Figure 4.5. Its intercept is $-a$ which is negative and its slope is $(1 - b)$. There two magnitudes really depend upon magnitudes of consumption function; a is numerically the same but its sign is different and $(1 - b)$ obviously depends upon b.

The income and consumption data presented in Table 4.1 can be used to generate the saving function. This has been done in Table 4.2. Columns (1) and (2) which provide data upon income and consumption are taken from Table 4.1. Column (3) gives the total savings of our hypothetical economy. Notice that saving is negative when income is too low. When income is 200 consumption and income become equal. This is zero saving point. Sometimes, it is referred as break-even point also. After this level of income, saving become positive and increase steadily with the increases in income. The saving function which is implicit in the Table 4.2 has been depicted in Figure 4.9. This saving function has the following line.

$$S = -50 + 0.25\ Y \qquad \text{...(4.17)}$$

Table 4.2

Saving Function of a Hypothetical Economy

Y	Y	$S = Y - C$	S/Y	ΔS	ΔY	$\Delta S/\Delta Y$
(1)	(2)	(3)	(4)	(5)	(6)	(7)
100	125	–25	–0.25	—	—	0
200	200	0	0	25	100	0.25
300	275	25	0.08	25	100	0.25
400	350	50	0.12	25	100	0.25
500	425	75	0.15	25	100	0.25

Let us recall that consumption function based upon the same data and represented in equation (4.6) was $C = 50 + 0.75\ Y$. Notice that intercept of saving function is same but only sign has changed, *i.e.*, it has become negative from positive. The slope of saving function is 0.25 which we obtain if we subtract the slope of consumption function (0.75) from unity.

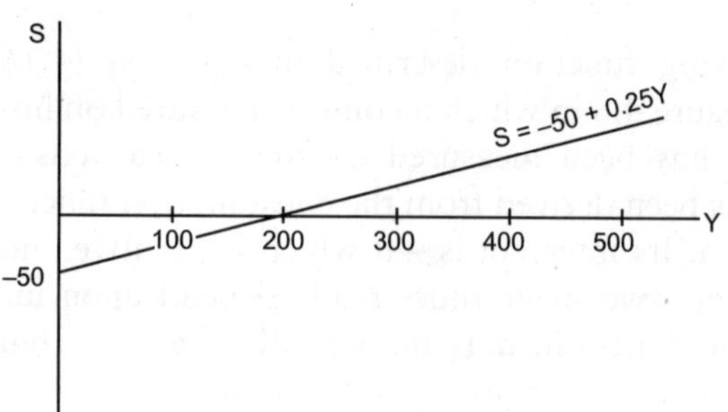

Fig. 4.8. Saving function of Hypothetical economy.

The concepts of average propensity to save (APS) and marginal propensity to save (MPS) are also similar to those of APC and MPC in case of consumption function.

$$\textit{Average propensity to save} = \frac{\textit{Saving}}{\textit{Income}}$$

$$\text{APS} = \frac{S}{Y} \qquad \text{...(4.18)}$$

In case of linear saving function APS is given by

$$S = -a + (1 - b)\ Y$$

$$\frac{S}{Y} = -\frac{a}{Y} + (1-b) \qquad ...(4.19)$$

Notice that average propensity to save tends to increase as income rises. This is so because the first term of the expression on right hand side in equation (4.19) tends to rise while $(1 - b)$ remains constant.

The marginal propensity to save, like marginal propensity to consume, is the change in saving due to a given change in income.

$$\textit{Marginal propensity to save} = \frac{\textit{change in saving}}{\textit{change in Income}}$$

$$MPS = \frac{\Delta S}{\Delta Y} \qquad ...(4.20)$$

In case of linear saving function MPS can be calculated as follows:

Let

Y_0 = Original level of income
Y_1 = New level of income
S_0 = Original level of saving
S_1 = New level of income
$Y_1 - Y_0 = \Delta Y$ = change in income
$S_1 - S_0 = \Delta S$ = change in saving

But

$$S_1 = -a + (1 - b)\ Y_1$$
$$S_0 = -a + (1 - b)\ Y_0$$

Therefore,

$$S_1 - S_0 = -a + (1 - b)\ Y_1 - [-a + (1 - b)\ Y_0]$$

or

$$S_1 - S_0 = -a + (1 - b)\ Y_1 - (1 - b)\ Y_0 + a$$
$$S_1 - S_0 = (1 - b)\ Y_1 - (1 - b)\ Y_0 \qquad ...(4.21)$$

which can be rewritten as

$$S_1 - S_0 = (1 - b)\ (Y_1 - Y_0) \qquad ...(4.22)$$

Dividing (4.22) on both sides by $Y_1 - Y_0$

We get

$$\frac{S_1 - S_0}{Y_1 - Y_0} \qquad \frac{(1-b)\,(Y_1 - Y_0)}{(Y_1 - Y_0)}$$

Thus,

$$\frac{S_1 - S_0}{Y_1 - Y_0} = \frac{\Delta S}{\Delta Y} = (1-b) \qquad \text{...(4.23)}$$

Thus, it is shown that $(1 - b)$ is the marginal propensity to save which is also the slope of linear saving function.

The discussion about the saving function can be summarized as follows:

(i) *MPS* is constant

(ii) *MPS* is greater than zero i.e., $(1 - b) > 0$

(iii) The value of MPS is always between zero and unity. i.e., $0 < (1 - b) < 1$

(iv) The MPS is greater than APS. This is easy to see. APS is $-\frac{a}{Y} + (1-b)$ while MPS is $(1 - b)$ obviously

$$(1-b) > -\left[\frac{a}{Y} + (1-b)\right]$$

(v) The APS declines as income rises but MPS remains constant.

RELATIONSHIP BETWEEN PROPENSITY TO CONSUME AND PROPENSITY TO SAVE

The propensity to save and propensity to consume are related with each other in a special way. It shall be useful to keep the following two theorems in mind.

(1) The sum of APC and APS is always unity.

This can be shown as follows:

We know that:

$$Y = C + S$$

Divide the both sides of above equation by Y

$$\left.\begin{aligned} \frac{Y}{Y} &= \frac{C}{Y} + \frac{S}{Y} \\ 1 &= \frac{C}{Y} + \frac{S}{Y} \end{aligned}\right\} \qquad \text{...(4.24)}$$

or $$APS + MPS = 1$$

(2) The sum of marginal propensity to consume and marginal propensity to save is also unity. This can be shown as follows. We know that

$$C + S = Y.$$

The same relation can be written for changes in consumption, savings, and income.

$$\Delta C + \Delta S = \Delta Y$$

Divide the above equation by ΔY on both sides, we get

$$\frac{\Delta C}{\Delta Y} + \frac{\Delta S}{\Delta Y} = \frac{\Delta Y}{\Delta Y}$$

$$\left.\begin{aligned} \frac{\Delta C}{\Delta Y} + \frac{\Delta S}{\Delta Y} &= 1 \\ MPC + MPS &= 1 \end{aligned}\right\} \qquad \text{...(4.25)}$$

DETERMINATION OF EQUILIBRIUM LEVEL OF INCOME

Now we have equipped ourselves to understand the process of income determination in a simple economy. The process of income determination is shown in Figure 4.9. In the construction of this diagram the thick break line is very fundamental. It is 45° line and its function is to divide the diagram into two equal parts. The advantage to this device is that we can turn the axes with the help of 45° line and the entries on horizontal axis can be read on the vertical axis. In Figure 4.9 income (aggregate supply) is measured On the horizontal axis and consumption and investment (components of aggregate demand) are measured on the vertical axis. Thus the 45° line has been labelled $Y = C + I$ because at all points along this line aggregate demand $(C + I)$ equals aggregate supply. That is the reason why some economists have dubbed it as a suppressed aggregate supply line.

The line C is a consumption function which was described in this chapter earlier. The C-Line intersects the 45° line at the point L. Before the point L, consumption exceeds income. Therefore, savings would be negative. This level of consumption cannot be sustained as consumption is more and income is less. Consequently income has to rise. At the point L consumption and income are equal. So this is

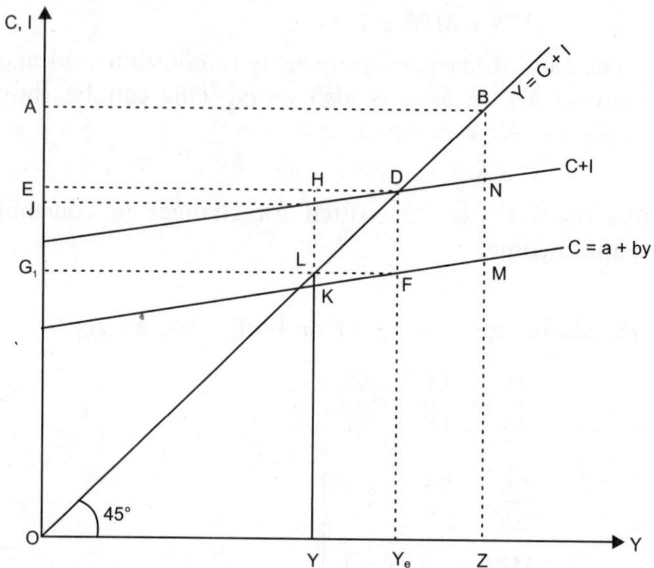

Fig. 4.9. Determination of Equilibrium level of income.

the break-even point. Beyond the point *L*, consumption is below income, therefore, positive savings must result.

The next line in the diagram is *C* + *I* line or the aggregate demand line. The vertical distance between the aggregate demand line and C-line is investment. Note that the amount of investment is the same at all levels of income. When the income is *OY*, *KY* is the consumption expenditure and *HK* is investment expenditure. When income is Y_e, consumption expenditure is $F\ Y_e$ and investment is *DF*. Similarly, when income is *OZ*, consumption is *MZ* and investment is *NM*. It can be seen through the diagram that amount of investment is the same, at all levels of income as *HK* = *DF* = *NM*. It would mean that amount of investment does not depend upon income. Such type of investment is said to be exogenous.

Note that aggregate demand line intersects 45° line at the point *D*. Before *D*, aggregate demand is more than aggregate supply. This situation prevails when the level of income is *OY*. This income level cannot be sustained and income would tend to rise. Suppose that income rises to *OZ*. At this level *MZ* is consumption expenditure and *NM* is the investment expenditure. The total amount of aggregate demand is *NZ* which falls short of aggregate supply which is BZ. At this level of income, excess capacity appears in the economy and the magnitude of excess capacity is BN. In fact, to sustain OZ amount of income, BM amount of investment must be made. But the actual amount of investment is only NM. Thus, income would tend to fall unless it reaches OY_e.

The only sustainable level of income is at the point D where $C+I$ line intersects 45° line. At this point aggregate demand and aggregate supply would be equal. Consequently, the equilibrium level of income is Y_e. The equilibrium level of consumption is FY_e and equilibrium level of investment is DF. This is equilibrium level because at this level of income there would be no inherent tendency for income either to rise or to fall.

A GRAPHICAL EXAMPLE

Let us apply the above theory to the case of our hypothetical economy for which the consumption function is $C = 50 + 0.75Y$. The process of income determination in a hypothetical economy has been shown in Figure 4.10. Income has been shown on the horizontal axis and consumption and investment expenditures have been shown on the vertical axis. The 45° line showing $Y = C + I$ has also been drawn. Then consumption function ($C = 50 + 0.75\ Y$) is plotted. It intersects the 45° line when the level of income is 200. At this level of income, consumption expenditure is also 200. Thus, before the income level of 200 is achieved C-line is above the 45° line and after that it is below the 45° line.

It is assumed that an autonomous investment of 50 takes place in our hypothetical economy irrespective of level of income. Thus, 50 is measured on the vertical axis on the top of the point when consumption function begins. From this Point, a line parallel to the C-line is drawn. This is the aggregate demand line of our hypothetical eeonomy. Since, $C+I$ line is parallel to C-line, the distance between two lines is the same at all points. This assumes that level of investment is 50 irrespective of level of income. The equilibrium level of income is determined where $C+I$ line intersects 45° line. If we draw a perpendicular from the point of intersection on the horizontal axis, it falls upon where the level of income is 400. Thus, equilibrium level of income is 400. The equilibrium level of income can also be found with the help of a little mathematics. We have the macro economic relations:

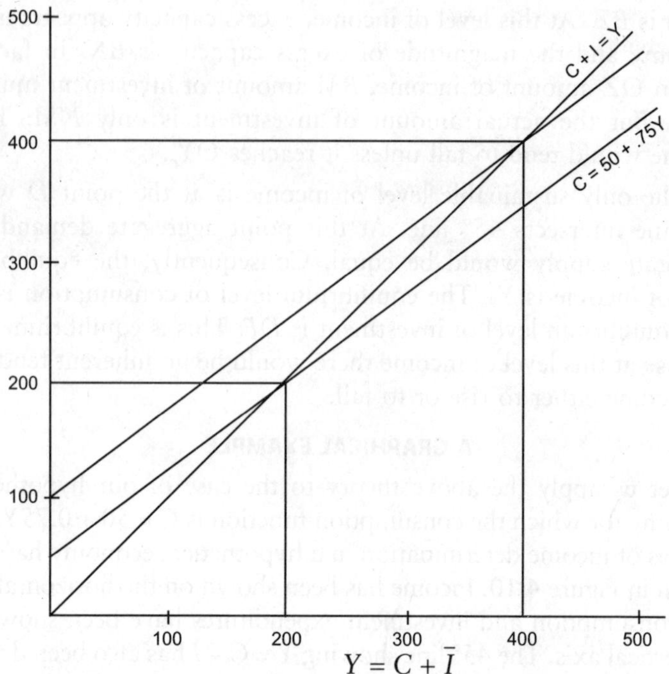

Fig. 4.10. Income determination in a Hypothetical Economy.

...(4.26)

and

$$C = a + bY \qquad ...(4.27)$$

Substituting the equation (4.27) into (4.26) we get

$$Y = a + bY + \bar{I} \qquad (4.28)$$

$\bar{I}$ in equation (4.28) indicates that investment is given exogenously. Collecting the terms which contain Y on the left hand side, (4.22) can be rewritten as

$$Y - bY = a + \bar{I}$$

$$Y(1 - b) = a + \bar{I}$$

$$Y = \frac{1}{1-b}\,(a + \bar{I}) \qquad ...(4.29)$$

Equation (4.29) gives the equilibrium level of income for a simple economy. If the amount of exogenous investment (I), and intercept and slope of the consumption function (a and b) are given, equilibrium level of income can be calculated.

In the example of our hypothetical economy the following values are given

$$a = 50$$
$$b = 0.75$$
$$I = 50$$

Thus equilibrium level of income would be

$$Y = \frac{1}{1-0.75}(50+50)$$
$$= \frac{1}{0.25}(100)$$
$$= 400$$

Note that equilibrium level of income obtained through this method is exactly the same as obtained through graphical method. The equilibrium level of consumption can be calculated easily by substituting the solution obtained in equation (4.26) into consumption function given in the equation (4.27).

$$C = a + b\left\{\frac{1}{1-b}(a+\bar{I})\right\} \qquad ...(4.30)$$

In case of our example

$$C = 50 + 0.75\ (400)$$
$$= 50 + 300.0$$
$$= 350.0$$

Thus equilibrium level of consumption obtained through this method is also the same as obtained through graphical method.

Saving, Investment and Multipliers

5

EQUALITY OF SAVING AND INVESTMENT

It has already been shown that equilibrium income is determined at the point where aggregate demand and aggregate supply are equal. However, the equilibrium condition can be stated in an another alternative way: Equilibrium level of income will be determined where saving and investment are equal. The equality of saving and investment can be easily seen. Saving depends on income, *i.e.*, Saving is a positive function of income. Income is, however, the aggregation of consumption and investment. That is the expenditure side of income determination is summarised in the equation

$$Y = C + I \qquad ...(5.1)$$

and income received approach is summarized in the following equation:

$$Y = C + S \qquad ...(5.2)$$

Since the left hand sides of equations (5.1) and (5.2) are equal the right hand side could also be equated.

Thus

$$C + S = C + I \qquad ...(5.3)$$

After eliminating C from the both side of equation (5.3), we get

$$S = I \qquad ...(5.4)$$

Equation (5.4) says that if income and expenditure in the economy have to be equal, saving and investment must also be equal.

The equality of saving and investment is an intricate and most puzzling aspect of income determination. Hence, one must be very careful in understanding this concept which occupies a fundamental position in the theory of income determination. Most of the time this confusion is the result of a failure of making a distinction between identity and equilibrium conditions. $Y = C + I$ and, $Y = C + S$, which have been written above as equations (5.1) and (5.2) are identities. An identity is a relation which is true by definition. Thus total expenditure is composed of consumption expenditure and investment expenditure. It is so, because it is defined that way. If the situation demanded, it could have been defined in any other way. Thus another identity would have been written. On the other hand an equilibrium condition states a relation, which is not true by definition but becomes true when certain conditions are fulfilled, *i.e.*, it becomes true when equilibrium is achieved.

The relationship described in equation (5.4) is an identity as well as an equilibrium condition. However, it does not play a significant role in income determination, as an identity but as an equilibrium condition. To understand the dual role of saving and investment, let us first understand the concepts of desired and realized magnitudes of savings and investment.

DESIRED AND REALIZED SAVING AND INVESTMENT

To begin with let us state that we must distinguish between four concepts: desired saving, desired investment, ritualized saving and realized investment. Thus both saving and investment have two set of magnitudes—desired and realized. Let us also state that desired is used here in the same meaning as expected or anticipated. Similarly, realized means actual. Some writers prefer to use the term ex-ante for desired and ex-post for realized or actual. Thus, we must always remember that

ex-ante = desired = expected = anticipated = intended and
ex-post = realized = actual

It may also be clear just by the choice and nature of words that desired magnitude of some variable points to the future and realized to the past. Thus, by realized saving, we mean the level or amount which was actually saved in a given period. Similarly, realized investment refers to the amount which was actually invested.

In an accounting sense, saving and investment are always equal. Income which is received but not consumed, is saved and invested. Thus, net investment and saving are equal to each other. This is an identity which refers only to realized saving and realized investment.

$$S^R = I^R \qquad ...(5.5)$$

However, the equality between the desired saving and desired investment is not so easily achieved.

$$S^d = I^d \qquad ...(5.6)$$

Equation (5.6) is an equilibrium condition. There is no reason why desired saving and desired investment would always be equal. On the other hand, it is more likely that there would be discrepancy between desired saving and desired investment. The desired level of saving is the amount which the individuals would like to save at any level of income. Similarly, desired level of investment is the amount which the investors would like to invest under some given condition. It is not difficult to see that the groups of savers (individuals who save) and investors (individuals and firms who invest) are not the same in a modern economy.

Saving is done mostly by the households depending upon their level of income. They do not know how much investors are planning to invest in the next periods. Similarly, investors are also not aware that what amount of saving would be forthcoming in the next period and be available for investment. They have to take their investment decisions about the next period right here and now. Hence the investment decisions are not dependent upon savings. Thus the discrepancy between desired saving and desired investment is in the logic of things. The equality between ex-ante saving and investment shall not come automatically. However, if the system works in a certain manner this equality may be achieved. That is why the equality of desired saving and desired investment is taken as an equilibrium condition as described in equation (5.6).

To understand its working, let us assume that net investment takes the form of changes in inventories. (Inventory means stock of goods for sale.) If desired saving is greater than desired investment then actual investment will be greater than desired investment. This is because desired savings will instantaneously be translated into actual saving. Since actual saving and actual investment are always equal, the actual investment will be greater than desired savings. Symbolically, this can be shown as follows:

$$S^d = I^d$$

$$S^a = S^d$$

$$S^a = I^a$$

$$I^a = I^d$$

$$I^a = I^d - I^a \qquad ...(5.7)$$

The difference between actual investment and desired investment is called unintended investment where:

I^u = unintended investment.

This is obvious from equation (5.7) that when actual investment becomes equal to desired investment, the unintended investment is zero. Similarly, when desired investment exceeds actual investment, then unintended investment is negative. Thus, in a situation where desired saving is greater than desired investment, the goods will not be sold and investors would like to cut down the production in order to meet this situation. Consequently, income would decline. Since saving is function of income, desired saving will also decline with the decline in income to the extent that desired saving and investment become equal and unintended investment becomes zero.

If the level of desired saving is less than desired investment, there would be a deficiency of inventories. It means that there is demand for more goods by the households and entrepreneurs are not keeping up the supply with the demand. This will encourage the entrepreneurs to increase the production which will raise the level of income. The desired saving will also rise with rising income to the extent that desired investment and desired saving become equal.

Thus the equilibrium condition of income determination can be stated either in terms of equality of aggregate demand and aggregate supply or equality of desired saving and investment.

AN ALTERNATIVE TREATMENT OF INCOME DETERMINATION

The process of equality between the desired saying and desired investment described above can also be used to illustrate income determination. In Figure 5.1 income has been measured along the horizontal axis. It is assumed, as before, that level of investment is given exogenously and is constant with the level of income. In terms of figure 5.1 OG amount is invested irrespective of level of income. Note that this is also the level of desired investment. Since it remains constant, it has been depicted in the figure as a line parallel to the horizontal axis. The saving function S is given by the line $S = -a + (I - b) Y$, where $-a$ is the intercept and $(I - b)$ is the slope of saving function. When income is Y_1, desired level of saving $AY_1 = OB$ is less than desired level of investment which is OG. Thus, unintended investment is negative. At this stage, inventories are deficient and there is unsatisfied demand. (In other words,

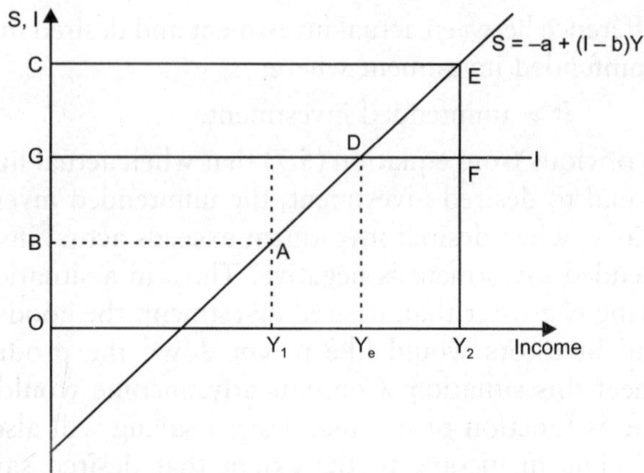

Fig. 5.1. Income determination by equality of saving and investment.

aggregate demand is more than aggregate supply). Consequently, production would expand and income would rise. Thus, we move along the horizontal axis from left to the right. With increases in income, saving also rises and we move along the saving function *S* from the point *D* and onwards. As we reach the income level OY_2, the desired level of saving is *OC* but desired level of investment is only *OG*. Now desired saving exceeds desired investment. Thus unintended investment takes place and its magnitude is equal to *EF* or *GC*. The inventories would be piled up. Consequently, entrepreneurs would begin reducing production. Thus OY_2 level of income cannot be sustained and income would start falling.

The equilibrium level of income would be determined at the point *D* where the income level is OY_e. At this level of income, desired saving is *OC* and desired investment is also *OC*. Both are equal. The amount of unintended investment is zero at this level of income. Consequently, there would be no tendency in the aggregate demand to change and thus equilibrium would be established.

The aggregate demand and aggregate supply approach and saving investment approach would give the same solution to equilibrium income determination.

This can be easily seen with the help of example of our hypothetical economy. This has been done in the Figure 5.2. The saving function of our hypothetical economy is $S = -50-0.25\ Y$ where –50 is the intercept and 0.25 is the slope. The level of investment is 50 which remains constant at all levels of income. At income levels less than 400 desired saving is less than desired investment as the saving line is below investment line. So income would tend to rise at income levels lower than 400. At income levels higher than 400 desired saying exceeds desired investment as saving line is above the investment line. Thus income would tend to decline for the reasons mentioned above. The equilibrium level of income is determined when income is 400. At this level of income, saving line intersects investment line. This is the equilibrium level of income because desired saving and desired investment become equal here.

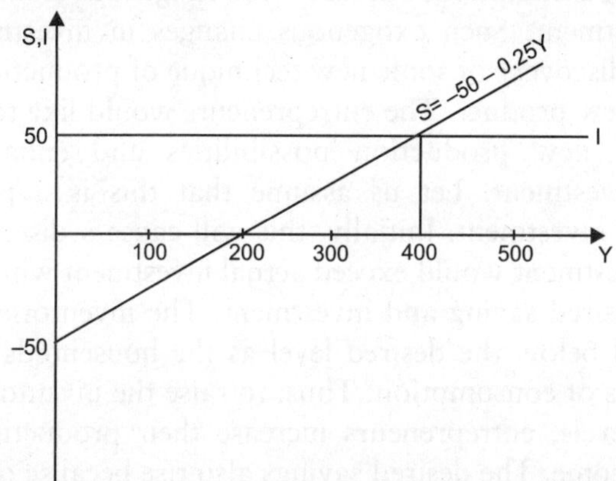

Fig. 5.2. Alternative approach to income determination in a hypothetical economy.

The same process of income determination is depicted in Table 5.1 when income is 100, saving is –25 and desired investment is 50. When income rises to 200, saving is zero and desired investment is 50. Since desired saving is much less the desired investment, unintended investment is negative.

Table 5.1

Saving Investment and Income determination in a Hypothetical Economy

Y	*S*	*I*	*Unintended Investments*
100	–25	50	–75
200	0	50	–50
300	25	50	–25
400	50	50	0
500	75	50	25

Aggregate demand is more than aggregate supply and income keeps on rising. If income rises to 500, saving rises to 75 but desired investment is 50 only. Hence the amount of unintended investment occurring at this level of income would be 25. There will be unsold stocks of goods. Consequently, equilibrium level of income would be determined at 400 where desired saving and desired investment both are 50 and unintended investment would be zero.

CHANGES IN INVESTMENT

It has been assumed so far that investment is exogenous. We still retain that assumption, but allow for exogenous changes in the level of investment. Such exogenous changes in investment may occur due to discovery of some new technique of production, a new market or a new product. The entrepreneurs would like to take the advantage of new production possibilities and enhance their exogenous investment. Let us assume that this is a permanent change in net investment. Initially, this will cause a disequilibrium as desired investment would exceed actual investment which in turn is equal to desired saving and investment. The inventories held by producers fall below the desired level as the households maintain their old levels of consumption. Thus, to raise the inventories up to the desired levels, entrepreneurs increase their production which increase in income. The desired savings also rise because of increase in income and once again equilibrium between desired saving and desired investment is achieved.

The changes in investment and its impact upon aggregate demand are shown in Figure 5.3. As before, income is shown on the horizontal axis and consumption and investment expenditure on the vertical axis. The *C*-line represents consumption function which has the break-even point at the point A where it intersects 45° line. The old aggregate demand line is shown by $C + I$ line which intersects 45° line at the point B. The original equilibrium level of income is determined at this point. The vertical distance between *C*-line and $C+I$ line shows the original level of investment.

Now, let us suppose that exogenous investment changes and there is an increase in investment. This is shown as the vertical distance between $C + I + \Delta I$ line and $C + I$ line where ΔI is the change in investment. The increased level of investment pushes the aggregate demand line upward (*i.e.* aggregate demand is increased).

The new aggregate demand line is depicted whereas $C + I + \Delta I$ line which intersects the 45° line at C. As it has been said before that 45° line represents a suppressed aggregate supply line, aggregate demand and aggregate supply are again equal at the point C and new equilibrium level of income Y_1 is determined at this point. The difference between Y_1 and Y_0 is ΔY, the increase in income as a result of change in investment, ΔI.

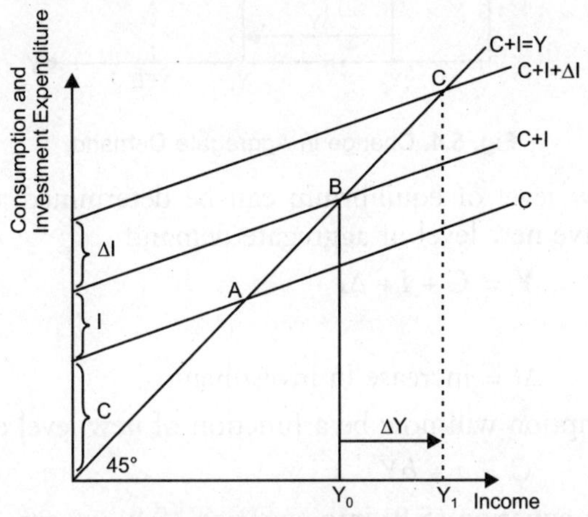

Fig. 5.3. The effect of a change in investment upon aggregate demand.

It should be kept in mind that increase in investment can cause income to rise only in case aggregate supply function is Keynesian. Only in this case, an underemployment equilibrium exists and idle resources are available. These idle resources are put to use with the new investment and more income is generated. This is illustrated in Figure 5.4 in which income is measured along the horizontal axis and price level is measured along the vertical axis. Aggregate supply function is represented by the curve AS. As full employment income Y is achieved aggregate supply curve becomes perfectly inelastic with respect to price level When aggregate demand is at the level AD_0, income is Y_0. When there is a given increase in exogenous investment the AD curve shifts to the right. New level of aggregate demand is AD_1 and new level of income is Y_1.

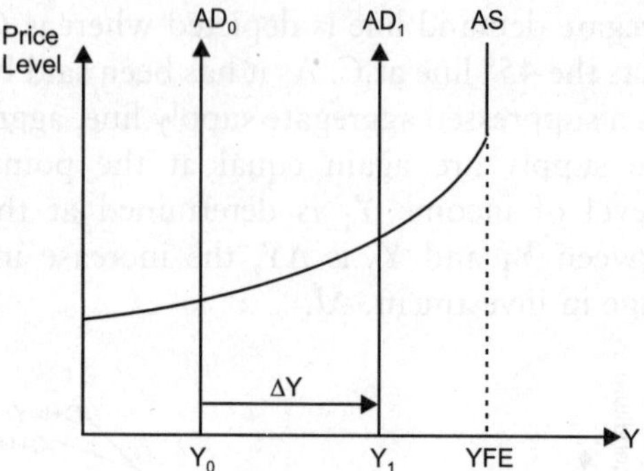

Fig. 5.4. Change in Aggregate Demand.

The new level of equilibrium can be determined algebraically also. We have new level of aggregate demand

$$Y_1 = C + I + \Delta I \qquad ...(5.8)$$

where

ΔI = increase in investment.

The consumption will now be a function of new level of income,

$$C = a + bY_1 \qquad ...(5.9)$$

Substituting equation (5.9) into equation (5.8) we get

$$Y_1 = a + bY_1 + I + \Delta I \qquad ...(5.10)$$

$$Y_1 - bY_1 = a + I + \Delta I$$

$$Y_1 - (I - b) = a + I + \Delta I$$

$$Y_1 = \frac{1}{1-b}(a + I + \Delta I) \qquad ...(5.11)$$

Y_1 is new equilibrium level of income. Let us recall that original level of equilibrium is

$$Y_0 = \frac{1}{1-b}(a + I) \qquad ...(5.12)$$

The change in income will be

$$Y_1 - Y_0 = \frac{1}{1-b}(a + I + \Delta I) - \frac{1}{1-b}(a + I)$$

$$\Delta Y = \frac{1}{1-b}(\Delta I) \qquad ...(5.13)$$

A NUMERICAL EXAMPLE

In case of our hypothetical economy, the consumption function was

$$C = 50 + 0.75\,Y$$

and the exogenous investment I was Rs. 50. Thus original level of income was calculated.

$$Y_0 = \frac{1}{1-b}(a+I)$$

$$Y_0 = \frac{1}{1-0.75}(50+50)$$

$$Y_0 = \frac{1}{0.25}(100)$$

$$Y_0 = \text{Rs. } 400$$

Let us now assume that investment rises by Rs. 25. Thus, new level of equilibrium income would be

$$Y_1 = \frac{1}{1-b}(a+I+\Delta I)$$

$$= \frac{1}{1-0.75}(50+50+25)$$

$$= \frac{1}{0.25}(125)$$

$$= 500.$$

Thus change in income is Rs. 100 when investment rises by Rs. 25.

INVESTMENT MULTIPLIER

The concept of multiplier occupies an important place in the modern theory of income and employment. The concept of multiplier was first developed by R.F. Kohn who discussed the concept of employment multiplier in his well-known article, "The Relation of Home Investment to Unemployment", published in *The Economic Journal* in June 1931. Keynes borrowed this concept from him and later refined it further.

The theory of multiplier tells us that if there is any given change in investment, then income caused by increased investment will be more than the original increase in investment. Multiplier is exactly that proportion by which income rises as a result of increase in investment. In the example given above investment has increased by Rs. 25. The previous level of income was Rs. 400 and the new level of income was Rs. 500. Thus income increased by Rs. 100. The increment in income is four times greater than original increase in investments. Thus one Rupee of additional investment leads to four rupees of additional income. It is not difficult to know that value of multiplier in this example is 4.

Symbolically, this idea can be represented in the following formula:

$$K = \frac{\Delta Y}{\Delta I} \qquad \text{...(5.14)}$$

where

ΔY = change in income.

ΔI = change in investment.

K = Multiplier.

Thus, multiplier is a ratio between change in income and in investment. It tells us if investment rises by a given amount, then how many times the income will rise. Equation (5.14) can be rearranged as

$$\Delta Y = K.\ \Delta I \qquad \text{...(5.15)}$$

which says that if investment rises by the amount ΔI, than change in income will be K times of ΔI.

DERIVATION OF MULTIPLIER

Equation below tells that change in income as a result of increase in investment will be

$$\Delta Y = \frac{1}{1-b}(\Delta I) \qquad (5.13)$$

Dividing both sides of equation (5.13) by ΔI we get

$$\frac{\Delta Y}{\Delta I} = \frac{1}{1-b}$$

or

$$K = \frac{1}{1-b} \qquad \text{...(5.16)}$$

where K = Multiplier

b = Marginal propensity to consume.

The above formula can also be derived in another way. We have by now familiar relationship

$$Y = C + I$$

Which says income is composed of consumption and investment expenditures. Same relationship must also held for changes in all the three variables. Thus,

$$\Delta Y = \Delta C + \Delta I \quad ...(5.17)$$

which says that change in income is composed of change in consumption expenditure and change in investment expenditure. Transporting, ΔC on the left hand side equation (5.17) can be written as:

$$\Delta I = \Delta Y - \Delta C \quad ...(5.18)$$

We know that multiplier is the ratio of change in income and change in investment. Thus,

$$K = \frac{\Delta Y}{\Delta I} \quad (5.14)$$

Substitute Equation (5.18) into equation (5.14) we get

$$K = \frac{\Delta Y}{\Delta Y - \Delta C} \quad ...(5.19)$$

Dividing each term on the right-hand side of equation (5.19) by ΔY, we get

$$K = \frac{\Delta Y/\Delta Y}{\Delta Y/\Delta Y - \Delta C/\Delta Y} \quad ...(5.19A)$$

$$K = \frac{1}{1 - \Delta C/\Delta Y} \quad ...(5.20)$$

or $$K = \frac{1}{1 - MPC} \quad ...(5.21)$$

Also, recall that

$$MPC + MPS = 1$$

and thus

$$MPS = 1 - MPC \qquad ...(5.22)$$

Substituting (5.22) into (5.21) we get

$$K = \frac{1}{MPS} \qquad ...(5.23)$$

The expressions for multiplier obtained in (5.16), (5.20), (5.21), (5.23) are all the same. All of them say that multiplier is the inverse of value of marginal propensity to save. Since saving is defined as a residual, the marginal propensity to save itself depends upon marginal propensity to consume. Thus, multiplier itself depends upon marginal propensity to consume.

DERIVATION OF MULTIPLIER: ALTERNATIVE TECHNIQUE

The multiplier can be derived in the following way.

For equilibrium level of income we can write

$$Y = C + I \qquad ...\text{ (i)}$$

Rewriting the equation (i) due to changes in the variables *i.e.*, changes in income followed by changes in investment, we can write

$$\Delta Y = \Delta C + \Delta I \qquad ...\text{ (ii)}$$

In simple Keynesian model of income determination, changes in consumption are function of changes in income considering change in investment as autonomous or independent.

Consumption function,

$$C = a + bY \qquad ...\text{ (iii)}$$

Where a is a constant term, b is marginal propensity to consume (MPC) assuming as constant. Hence, change in consumption is a function of change in income.

Therefore,

$$\Delta C = b\ \Delta Y \qquad ...\text{ (iv)}$$

Substituting (iv) into (ii), we get

$$\Delta Y = b\ \Delta Y + \Delta I$$

or $\quad \Delta Y\ (1-b) = \Delta I$

or $\quad \Delta Y = \dfrac{\Delta I}{(1-b)}$

or $$\frac{\Delta Y}{\Delta I} = \frac{1}{1-b}$$

or $$K = \frac{1}{1-b}$$

where $K = \frac{\Delta Y}{\Delta I}$ is the multiplier which is the ratio of change in income and change in investment.

or $$K = \frac{1}{1-b}$$

or $$K = \frac{1}{1-MPC} = \frac{1}{MPS}$$

Where $b = MPC$ and $MPC + MPS = 1$

This is the same formula of multiplier obtained above. We mention that the value of multiplier $\frac{\Delta Y}{\Delta Y}$ remains same as long as marginal propensity to consume remains the same.

VALUE OF MULTIPLIER

We can find out the value of multiplier if we know the value of either merginal propensity to consume (*MPC*) or marginal propensity to save (*MPS*).

If $MPC = \frac{1}{3}$, we can calculate the value of multiplier as shown below:

$$\text{Multiplier,} \quad K = \frac{1}{1-MPC} = \frac{1}{1-\frac{1}{3}} = \frac{1}{\frac{2}{3}}$$

$$= \frac{3}{2} = 1\frac{1}{2}$$

Or, if $MPS = \frac{3}{2}$, we can also find out the value of multiplier as under:

$$\text{Multiplier,} \quad K = \frac{1}{MPS} = \frac{1}{\frac{3}{2}} = \frac{2}{3}$$

The various values of multiplier corresponding to different values of *MPC* can be worked out as follows:

$MPC\ \left(\frac{\Delta C}{\Delta Y}\right)$	Multiplier (K)
0	1
$\frac{1}{3}$	$1\frac{1}{2}$
$\frac{1}{2}$	2
$\frac{3}{4}$	4
$\frac{4}{5}$	5
$\frac{9}{10}$	10
1	∞

EMPLOYMENT MULTIPLIER

The concept of employment multiplier was first put forward by Prof. Kahn in 1931 when he was discussing the favourable effects of public investment on aggregate employment. The employment multiplier is the ratio of increase in total employment (N) to the increase in primary employment (N_2) in the same way in which the income multiplier is the ratio of increase in income to the increase in primary investment. Thus the expression for the increase in employment, $\Delta N = K\Delta N_2$, is similar to the expression for increase in income, $\Delta Y = K\Delta I$. Prof. Kahn believed that an initial increase in employment leads to a very large increase in total employment. The discussions on public works recognize that besides the 'original' 'primary' employment in the public works, there will be 'secondary' employment resulting from public works. The 'secondary' employment is that which occurs in consumption goods industries as a result of the primary employment in investment goods industries. Suppose, for illustration, that 4 lakh people are employed for the construction of a canal. The newly employed people would demand more consumer goods which means greater demand for consumer goods industries. This will lead to additional employment in such industries. The additional workers employed in consumer goods industries would have additional income, part of which will again be spent on consumer goods; this would give a further fillip to secondary employment. Through the repetition of this process, the final total increase in employment would be much greater than the initial increase in employment which gives rise to the total increase in employment. If the magnitude of the multiplier is 4, an initial employment of 4 lakh workers will result in a total employment of 16 lakh workers.

Prof. Hansen believes that we do not do great violence to the fact if we take employment multiplier (*K'*) to be equal to investment multiplier (*K*), though we have no reason to presume them to be equal to each other. To simplify the analysis, we take them identical for practical purposes, particularly in the short period.

BACKWARD OPERATION OF MULTIPLIER

The process of income propagation through multiplier works not only in the forward direction but also in the backward direction depending upon the direction of the initial change in investment. Assuming the marginal propensity to consume equal to 3/4, a decline in investment by Rs. 100 for instance, will result in decline in national income by Rs. 400. The higher the MPC, the larger the value of the multiplier and hence the greater would be the cumulative decline in income. The same, as we have already seen, is true in case of a movement of income in the forward direction. Thus economies with a higher marginal propensity to consume would be subject to greater jerks and shocks as a result of changes in investment. The underdeveloped countries in which an overwhelming majority of people live from hand to mouth provide examples of such economies.

ASSUMPTIONS OF THE MULTIPLIER THEORY

The concept of multiplier is based on the following assumptions:

1. That the new, higher level of investment, is maintained long enough for the completion of the adjustment process;
2. that there is no induced investment (*i.e.*, the accelerator is inoperative);
3. that there is no change in the marginal propensity to consume during the adjustment process; and
4. that the output of consumer goods is responsive to effective demand for these.

Let us briefly discuss each of these assumptions one by one.

1. If the rate of investment suffers a decline before the completion of the adjustment process, income would experience a downturn before it could touch the equilibrium level corresponding to the rate of investment attained as a result of the stimulating increment of investment. Investment must, therefore, be maintained at the higher level long enough to attain the increment of income suggested by the multiplier.

2. The initial (autonomous) increment of investment and the resultant multiplication of income are very likely to have induced effects on investment owing to a number of reasons, important of which are mentioned below:

(i) Increase in demand for consumer goods would require an increase in output which would involve induced investment first in working capital and later in fixed capital. And according to the acceleration principle, discussed in a later chapter, such induced increase in investment would be more than proportionate to the increase in output which induced it.

(ii) The improved business outlook, and the prospect of a rise in the price of capital goods, may induce businessmen to carry out overdue replacement and renewal of plant. Further, businessmen may start enlarging their stock in anticipation of larger turnover and higher prices. Both these developments would increase the rate of investment.

(iii) If the initial autonomous investment takes the form of an accelerated programme of public investment, it may involve unbalanced budgets and a growing public debt. This might adversely affect confidence and thus discourage private investment.

(iv) The expansionary process generated by the initial autonomous investment may lead to a rise in the interest rates. If the banking system is unable to expand credit adequately, the increase in the transactions-demand for money resulting from a higher level of income may reduce the amount available for satisfying the liquidity demand for money and thus raise the rate of interest. A rise in the rate of interest would tend to discourage private investment.

The rate of interest, however, can also move in the reverse direction. If the expansionary process causes price rises which are expected to continue, the liquidity-demand for money might decrease leading to a decline in the interest rate. Similar would be the result if the banking section responds to expansion by new credit creation that more than offsets the increase in the transactions demand for money. The decline in the rate of interest might encourage private investment.

(v) The assumption of an absence of induced changes in investment is still more untenable in an open economy. In an open economy, part of the additional income may be spent on additional imports. If there is no induced increase in exports, the induced increase in imports will represent a corresponding decline in net foreign investment. The original increment of investment would be offset to the extent of this decline; in other words, the multipicand will be reduced by this amount. But it is very likely that there would be some induced increase in exports also. Decline in the net foreign investment of the country undertaking the initial increment of investment means an equivalent increase in the net foreign investment of other countries. This sets into operation the multiplier process into those countries. The resulting higher levels of economic activity and income in these countries are likely to increase their imports from the first country. The initial increment of investment in a given country is thus offset, in relation to the multiplier effect, only to the extent of the excess of induced increase of imports over the increase of exports. Thus when the original increment of investment induces changes in private domestic investment or net foreign investment, such changes must be taken into account in determining the total effect of the former on income.

3. The assumption of unchanged marginal propensity to consume may also not hold good in actual practice. Because of differences in the distribution of income, the marginal propensity to consume differs from person to person and from class to class. Thus the marginal propensity to consume of the community as a whole depends, *inter alia*, on the distribution of national income. It would,

therefore, remain unchanged only if the multiplication of income leaves unchanged the pattern of the income distribution. But thus is seldom true in actual practice, particularly when the changes in investment and income involved are large.

4. The multiplier is the ratio of increase in real income to the stimulating increase in the real investment. It can be greater than unity only if the increase in money investment associated with the increment of real investment stimulates, in response to the chain reaction of increased consumer spending thus generated, larger output of consumer goods. In case the output of consumer goods does not respond to increases in the effective demand for it, the multiplier effect will just be dissipated in inflationary price changes.

LEAKAGES

We have seen that whole of the newly created income is not spent and a part of it is saved. Income which is not spent for consumption is known as 'Leakage' in the cumulative income stream. The leakage limits the extent of the total increase in national income. If there were no leakage, that is, if the marginal propensity to consume were one, a small increase in investment would lead to full employment and inflation would start beyond that. But because of leakage, in actual practice, the successive increases in income resulting from a certain initial investment diminish at each stage and, therefore, the final total increase in income is a finite amount. The leakage can take several forms, important of which are stated below:

Debt Cancellation: A part of the income received by people may be used for paying off old debts to banks and individuals, who may, in turn, fail to spend. To this extent, the consumption is not stimulated and the value of the multiplier is correspondingly reduced.

Imports: If imports exceed exports, part of the Increased income resulting from increased investment will go abroad and would not, therefore, be available for expenditure within the country. This is particularly true in the short period. In the long period, increased income in foreign countries will increase their demand for exports of the importing country and will thus have favourable effects on the income of the latter country; this effect will, however, not materialise or materialise only partially if imports are restricted in the former countries.

Price Inflation*:* So long as there exist unemployed productive resources, an increase in investment has expansionary effects, but once the full employment or near full employment level is reached, increase in investment will go to rise in prices and to the cost of the factors of production because at this level factors of production become scarce and the consumer goods industries and investment goods industries outbid each other for obtaining the scarce resources. Thus a part of the increased income is dissipated in a rise in prices instead of expanding consumption, income and employment.

Hoarding*:* Hoarding and the tendency of the people to hold idle cash balances form another leakage. If the people have high liquidity preference and a tendency to hold cash balances, their expenditure on consumption would be less which would lower the magnitude of the multiplier.

Purchase of Stocks and Securities*:* A part of the newly created income may be used for buying old stocks and securities instead of being spent on increased consumption. Such financial investments diminish the magnitude of the multiplier because increased incomes instead of being spent on consumption, are spent on nominal (not real) investment.

Taxation: A part of increment in income received as a result of increase in investment is also used for payment of taxes. This part of income does not appear in the successive rounds of consumption expenditure in the multiplier process. This is an important leakage. But if the Government spends the money equal to the taxation, it would not have any adverse effect on the increase in income and investment and thus there would be no leakage in the multiplier process. It is not necessary that all the money raised through taxation is spent by the Government.

MULTIPLIER NOT NECESSARILY ASSOCIATED WITH INCREMENT OF INVESTMENT

Throughout the above analysis we have referred to 'investment' outlays the initiator of the process of income propagation. In fact, the initial outlay need not be on investment. The multiplier becomes operative whenever an outlay involves injection of purchasing power into the income stream from outside irrespective of the nature of the outlay, *i.e.*, irrespective of the fact whether such outlay is on public or private investment or on consumption. What is required is total expenditure in excess of the current flow of income irrespective of the nature of expenditure.

STATIC NATURE OF KEYNES' CONCEPT OF MULTIPLIER

Keynes' theory of investment multiplier has been criticised on the ground that is static in nature and has no connection with the dynamic process of income generation. It does not tell us what happens in between the initial increase in investment and the final increase in income. We do not know how and by what stages of time intervals the final increase in the total income is reached. Keynes' concept of multiplier shows the process of income expansion from one point of equilibrium to another and that too under static assumptions. No idea is given of the actual sequence of events and no time-lags are involved. The whole process of income propagation is automatic, unhampered by time or other factors. Post-Keynesians have pointed out that the value of the multiplier is affected by the fact that the particular doses of investment take time to exert their full influence in raising income. Because of the existence of time-lags, it takes longer time to reach the final position and the income rises at a rate slower than that at which it would have risen in the absence of time-lags. Keynes appears to have thought that the effect to such lags would be unimportant. He, however, was not unaware of the existence of time-lags. He, in fact, discusses, though briefly, three concepts of multiplier *viz.* (1) the logical theory of multiplier assuming no time-lags, (2) the period analysis concept of the multiplier based on the assumption of time-lags, and (3) 'comparative statics' timeless concept of multiplier in which the transition process or the path is skipped over completely.

DYNAMIC MULTIPLIER

If there is an economically significant time-lag between an initial investment expenditure and its reappearance as income, different equations expressing lagged consumption and investment must replace static equations so that the discrete steps involved in the multiplier process may be traced. We may build a simple dynamic system involving a consumption lag but no investment lag such as

$$C_t = a\,(Y_{t-1} - Y_0) + C_0 \qquad (5.24)$$

$$I_t = \bar{I} \tag{5.25}$$

$$Y_t = C_t + I_t \tag{5.26}$$

$$= a\,(Y_{t-1} - Y_0) + C_0 + I_t \tag{5.27}$$

where C_t stands for consumption at time t, a for the marginal propensity to consumer, Y_{t-1} for income in the previous period. Y_0 for income in the initial period, C_0 for consumption in the initial period, I_t for investment at time t, and I for constant autonomous investment.

The essential point to notice about the general multiplier equation (5.27) is that consumption is lagged, that is, it is dependent on the income of the preceding period over and above some arbitrary initial income.

Multiplier Sequence: Given the marginal propensity to consume and the investment multiplicand, national income will be found to grow exponentially although usually in dwindling series. The geometric progression of income involved can be shown in the following general system of equation:

$$Y_{(1)} = \Delta I$$

$$Y_{(2)} = \Delta\bar{I} + c\Delta\bar{I} = (1+c)\,\Delta\bar{I}$$

$$Y_{(3)} = \Delta\bar{I} + \Delta c\bar{I} + c^2\Delta\bar{I} = (1+c+c^2)\,\Delta\bar{I}$$

$$Y_{(n)} = \Delta\bar{I} + c\Delta\bar{I} + c^2\Delta\bar{I} + \ldots\ldots + c^{n-1}\Delta\bar{I}$$

$$= (1+c+c^2+\ldots\ldots+c^{n-1})\Delta I$$

Here $Y_{(1)}, Y_{(2)}$ and so forth are the national income of the first multiplier period, that of the second period etc. that is ${}^{n-1}Y = Y_{(t)}$ and t = 1, 2, r $\Delta\bar{I}$ is the investment multiplicand consider occurring once; c is the marginal propensity to consume governing the multiplier. The nth term of the above progression or the final sum of all the terms of the sequence will be found equal to the multiplier times the initial increment of autonomous investment:

$$Y(n) = \sum \frac{\infty 1 - c^{n-1}}{11 - c}\Delta\bar{I} = k\Delta\bar{I} = \Delta y$$

if $n = \infty$, as in the static multiplier theory.

Assuming $\bar{I} = 10$, $c = ½$ and $n = \infty$, the above system of equations can be made more explicit:

$$\gamma_{(1)} = \bar{I}\Delta = 10$$

$$\gamma_{(2)} = \bar{I}\Delta + \tfrac{1}{2}\,\Delta\bar{I} = 10 + (0.5)\,10 = 15$$

$$\gamma_{(3)} = \left[1 + \tfrac{1}{2} + \left(\tfrac{1}{2}\right)^2\right]\Delta\bar{I} = (1 + 0.5 + 0.25)10 = 17.5$$

$$\gamma_{(n)} = \left[1 + \tfrac{1}{2} + \left(\tfrac{1}{2}\right)^2 + \ldots\ldots\ldots\left(\tfrac{1}{2}\right)^{n-1}\right]\Delta\bar{I}$$

$$= (1+0.5+0.25\ldots\ldots\ldots)\ 10 = 20$$

$$= \frac{1}{1-c}\,\Delta\,\bar{I} = k\Delta\bar{I} = 2\times 10 = 20$$

The ultimate result in the *n*th period, that is, 20, is what we must expect since the marginal propensity to consume is assumed to be $\frac{1}{2}$ so as to give a multiplier coefficient of 2, given an additional autonomous investment of 10. Of greater analytical importance, though, is that the above sequence shows the cumulative increases of income above the base period, step by step, until a final total of 20 is reached.

Dynamic Process of Income Propagation: Let us now analyse the dynamic process of successive changes in income in terms of the Fig. 5.5.

We assume that consumption depends on the income of the preceding period, $C = C_t = a\,Y_{t-1}$ where a is the marginal propensity to consume and also that investment is a function of income and an

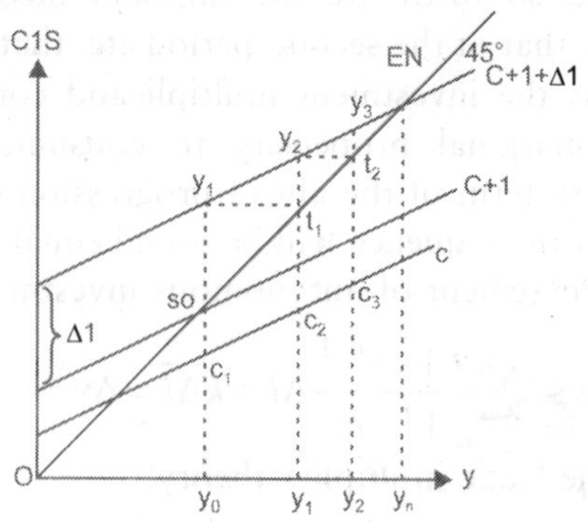

Fig. 5.5. Dynamic Multiplier

autonomous constant $I = I_t$. In diagram 5.5, consumption, investment, and savings are measured along the vertical axis and income is measured along the horizontal axis-all magnitudes being in real terms. The C curve relates consumption to the income of the preceding period had has a constant slope of 0.5. The original investment schedule is the vertical distance between the C curve and the $C + I$ curve, while the new investment schedule is that between the C curve and the $C + I + \Delta I$ curve, which gives a constant level of investment equal to ΔI. Savings out of previous income are measured by the vertical distance between the 45° line and the C curve. The system is initial settled at a equilibrium point E_0, where savings and investment are equal

$$(E_0C_1 = E_0C_1)$$

In period 0, before the change, consumption is C_1Y_0 and income OY_0 or E_0Y_0, thus leaving E_0C_1 both as saving and investment. Now investment increases by $\Delta\bar{I}$ from period 0 to period 1 and stays at this level. What is the effect of this? Consumption remains unchanged because consumers have not yet had an opportunity to adjust themselves to change. Similarly, intended savings remain unchanged. This means that investment exceeds intended savings by an amount equal to the increment of investment, or by y_1E_0. This excess of investment over intended savings for period 1 (equal to actual saving for period 0) account for the unexpected increment of income from period 0 to period 1.

In period 1 there is an equal horizontal change, Y_1t_1 $(=Y_0\ Y_1)$, for the vertical change of Y_1E_0. In other words, income increases over OY_0 by the amount of excess investment in period 1 after the injection of $\Delta\bar{I}$. The total income received in period 1 is therefore $OY_1(=OY_0 + Y_0Y_1)$. What would happen to saving investment relation in this period? Investment is again $I + \Delta\bar{I}$ or y_2c_2 and savings corresponding to previous income OY_0 are t_1c_2, thus making intended savings fall short of investment by Y_2t_1 $(=y_2c_2 - t_1c_2)$. This excess investment is what causes income to increase from period 1 to the next, that is, by Y_1Y_2 $(=y_2t_2 - y_2t_1)$.

Though consumption increases from C_1Y_0 to C_1Y_1 corresponding to the increased total income of OY_1, this extra consumption amounts to half of extra income Y_0Y_1. Similarly, savings increases by half of extra income Y_0Y_1. This explains why intended savings in period 1 fall short of investment. As such income expands by an amount equal to the above excess of investment over intended savings, or by y_2t_1, which amount is equal to the horizontal change of y_2t_2. It is thus that period 2 is ushered in and total income received is OY_2. But investment in this period still exceeds savings by y_3t_2 ($=y_3c_3 - t_2c_3$), since intended savings corresponding to previous income OY_1 amount to t_2c_3, which amount is y_3t_2 short of a total investment of y_3c_3 (constant $I + \Delta\bar{I}$). This excess of investment over intended savings in period 2 leads to an increase in income from period 2 to period 3.

The gap between intended savings and intended investment (the vertical distance between the $C + I + \Delta\bar{I}$ curve and the 45° line) becomes smaller and smaller, and the increment of income which it produces, until the gap is completely wiped out. The constant stream of new investment has developed its full effect, and aggregate income has reached the stationary higher level of Y_n in the nth period. The system has become stable at the new and higher equilibrium point E_n. Income has reached there via E_0, y_1, t_1, y_2, t_2, Y_3,......E_n. The multiplier has done its job, for it has caused income to expand to cause intended savings to expand up to the new level of investment, that is where $S_n = \bar{I}_n$. Thus in the *n*th period the savings gap (the vertical distance between the 45° vertical line and the *C* curve at Y_n) exactly equals the sum of old investment plus new investment (the vertical distance between the $C + I\,\Delta\bar{I}$ curve and the *C* curve at Y_n).

CRITICISM OF MULTIPLIER

Keynes' concept of multiplier has been severely criticised by many economists. In his famous article "Mr. Keynes' Theory of the Multiplier: A Methodological Criticism" published in 1936, Haberler criticised Keynes' concept of multiplier as being a mere tautology, *i.e.*, defining something as necessarily true and then proclaiming as a discovery the 'truth' of the relationship made inevitable by definition. Keynes defines multiplier (*K*) as below:

$$K \text{ (Multiplier)} = \frac{\Delta Y}{\Delta I}$$

We have already seen earlier that the above equation can also be written as:

$$K = \frac{1}{1 - MPC} \quad or \quad \frac{1}{MPS}$$

The above equation like other identity equations (*i.e.* $MV = PT$ or $I = S$) tells us nothing. It does not throw any light on the behaviour pattern of *MPC* over time or during transition from one equilibrium position to another. It is not subject to a verifiable behaviour pattern and as such is simply a tautology. If the concept of multiplier is to be used for estimating increase in national income during a specified period, it must be possible to advance reasonable hypothesis in regard to the behaviour of *MPC* or *MPS* over time; if this is not possible, the concept of multiplier will be of no use. Multiplier is a mere deduction as $K = \frac{1}{MPS}$ and *MPS* is not something independent which can be obtained independently of multiplier and then itself determining multiplier and through it determines income which would be created. In order to find out the value of the multiplier (*K*), we first find out how much income has been created and then divide it by investment. We have deducted that multiplier (*K*) is equal to $\frac{1}{MPS}$. We have found the magnitude of the marginal propensity to save and thus the size of the multiplier simply by finding what has actually happened and then using what has actually happened to predict what would happen. It is not surprising that in the investment (ΔI), times (X) the multiplier $\left(\frac{1}{1-MPS}\right)$ or $\left(\frac{\Delta Y}{\Delta I}\right)$ change should be equal to change in total income (ΔY). In other words, it does not make much to say that

$$\Delta I \times \frac{\Delta Y}{\Delta I} = \Delta Y$$

It is always true and there is no need to demonstrate it. If Keynes' concept of multiplier is to be freed from the criticism of being tautological, we must assume short-run normal behaviour pattern of MPC and MPS.

Prof. A.G. Hart considers the concept of multiplier a useless '*fifth wheel*'. The concept has also been criticised severely by Prof. Henry Hazlitt. He refers to it as "a strange concept about which some Keynesians make more fuss than about anything else in the Keynesian system." He dubs it as a 'myth' and asks "What reason is there to suppose that there is any such thing as the multiplier?" He points out that "there is never any precise, predeterminable or mechanical relationship between social income, consumption, investment and extend of employment." It is, therefore, just "a worthless toy", the type of thing made depressingly familiar by monetary cranks. Further the concept of multiplier rests on an assumption which is very unrealistic, namely, that there already exists unemployment in the economy. There is no reason why Keynes should assume that substantial unemployment is the "general situation" and "full employment" is only a "special situation." Another fallacy pointed out by Hazlitt in Keynes concept of multiplier is the assumption that the entire fraction of a community's income that is not consumed' is 'hoarded' and that no part of this 'unconsumed income is 'invested'. The "'propensity to consume" determines the multiplier only on the assumption that what is not spent on consumption is not spent on anything at all, or is hoarded, and not invested. But this is inconsistent with what Keynes had said earlier that savings and investment were not only equal but also identical; savings and investment can be equal only if what is not spent on consumption is invested. The acceptance of the concept of multiplier, however, gives rise to the problem of inequality between savings and investment.

To cite Prof. Hutt, "The practical harm brought by thinking along investment multiplier lines has been that it has caused investment (expenditure in the process of net accumulation) to be regarded as a causal factor and not, as it ought to be regarded, as the result of thrift which recovery normally includes." He further states, "But the intellectual harm has been indirectly even more serious. The conventional multiplier apparatus is rubbish. It should be expunged from the text books, its place being, taken by an exposition of the dynamic implications of the Say's Law."

In the words of Brooman, "Keynes' multiplier.....is a static concept. It gives little insight into the process by which the economy tries to achieve a new equilibrium. The process by which output adjusts itself to a new level of demand is assumed to take place instantaneously or at least so quickly that none of the parameters of the system has time to change—consumers' preferences remain unchanged, the distribution of income as before and so on. In real life, it is very unlikely that this would hold good."

Prof. Stigler considers multiplier to be "the fuzziest part of his (Keynes) theory." According to him, "The concept (of multiplier) often seems like nothing but a cheap jack way of getting some thing for nothing and appears to carry with it a spurious numerical accuracy."

Keynes' concept of multiplier concentrates exclusively on consumption. It would be more realistic to speak of "marginal propensity to spend" rather than "marginal propensity to consume" and then to consider the impact of an initial increase in investment not only on consumption but also on investment. Further, in a dynamic economy, the "marginal propensity to spend"—even if we use that term for the "marginal propensity to consume"—is not likely to remain constant. To cite Gordon, "Thus, it is not likely that in a dynamic world we shall be able to predict with much accuracy the multiplying effect over the cycle of a given increase in private investment or public spending."[1]

The Keynesian concept of multiplier assumes a linear relation between aggregate consumption and aggregate income. Lawrence Klein, however, points out that empirical studies regarding behaviour of aggregate consumption in relation to aggregate income show that the actual trends in spending have a much more complicated relationship which may be of a non-linear type. Further, consumption is not the function of only income and the marginal propensity to consume does not remain constant.

IMPORTANCE OF THE MULTIPLIER THEORY

The main justification for public investment or a programme of public works as an anti-depression measure lies in the multiplier theory. The multiplier being greater than unity, income increases by several times the increment of investment. In a deep depression when profitability might have sunk very low only public investment, being autonomous of the profit motive, might provide the key to a substantial and steady injection of new purchasing power for adequate multiplication of income.

Public investment can be directed more easily to those sectors of the economy where, the leakages from the income stream being small, the multiplier effect of the new injection of purchasing power on income and employment is the greatest. For example, if the new investment is directed to industries with a high ratio of wages to

1. R.A. Gordon, *Business Fluctuations*, pp. 118-19.

total cost, or to areas or sectors of the economy with the highest incidence of unemployment and only to a smaller extent to raise wages and prices, the stimulus to employment and income will be relatively large.

Owing to the multiplier effect, the cost of an employment motivated public works programme to the government, as distinguished from the community, may be very limited. For the increased expenditure of the government may be substantially compensated by larger revenue receipts that a higher level of income brings in and by the smaller needs of expenditure on the unemployed. As such the government may undertake investment considered not worthwhile by the private entrepreneur. The latter may, however, be provided with an equally strong incentive to undertake such investment if the government grants him a subsidy equal to the increase in revenue receipts, and the saving on `doles to the unemployed, that will result from it.

A knowledge of the concept of multiplier is very helpful in understanding the causes of the business cycle and also for its forecasting and control.

Government Expenditure, Taxation and Theory of Income Determination

6

GOVERNMENT AND SIMPLE INCOME DETERMINATION MODEL

In the previous chapters, we have presented a model of income determination which was based upon following assumptions:

1. There was no government expenditure and the government did not impose any taxes either.
2. There is no foreign trade in the economy.
3. All investment was assumed to be exogenously given.
4. The level of retained profit is zero.

Now, we relax our first assumption and incorporate the actions of the government into our analysis. All other assumptions are still retained. We may relax them one by one as we introduce new variables into our simple model of income determination. This method of analysis is known as the technique of successive approximation.

Currently, the government has become a force in the social and economic spheres to reckon with. There was a time, about two hundred years ago, when a limited role was assigned to the government. Under the influence of philosophies of individualism and liberalism, it was thought that the government which rules the least is the best. Translated in terms of economic principles, it was summed up in the philosophy of *laissez faire* which meant that the economy must be left alone. The government should not intervene in the economic system. It must confine its activities to have minimum or three activities *viz.*, administration, defence and judicial services. However, you must recognise that, under the modern conditions, government will have to intervene into economy to a large extent even if it confines itself to the provision of administration, defence and justices and restricts its role in other spheres and sectors, keeping in line with the liberal tradition. Let us take, for example, the case of defence which has been one of the most traditional though most important functions of the governments. In the modern times, a country requires not only a large military force but army, navy, and air force having a large number of guns, tanks, artillery, bombs, air crafts, bomber aeroplanes, war ships, anti aircraft guns, submarines, missiles, and rockets etc. To manufacture these, governments would require a large supply iron and steel, engineering goods, electric appliances, computors, and what not. This means that government will have to intervene in the economy in a big way in order to perform even its traditional functions.

In the modern times, the functions of the governments have been enlarged to a great extent. The government ensures that all essential goods of consumption must be available in the market at reasonable prices. To attain this objective sometimes, governments have to resort to price controls and undertake the direct distribution of goods. The governments spend huge sums of money on education, health care, and social welfare schemes. They have to run public administration and organise the judicial services in order to preserve law and order in the society. In the developed countries, the governments give unemployment bonus to unemployed. Thus, the range of governmental functions have been diversified. To fulfil these objective functions, governments sometime also undertake production of certain selected goods. For example, in our own country there is a sizable and significant public sector which produces not only utilities such as telephone, telegraph, postal services and transport but manufactures such basic goods as iron and steel and consumer goods such as bread and soft drinks. However, not all capitalist governments undertake the production of goods and services themselves. Mostly, they buy it from the private sector. The private sector produces goods and services and government sector generates demand for it. Therefore, the government expenditure should be taken as a component of aggregate demand of economy.

To meet its expenditure, the government imposes a number of taxes. A tax is nothing but a leakage from the circular flow of income. If the government would not have imposed the tax, the income would have remained available with the private individuals and the expenditure flow would have been strengthened. Hence a tax is a leakage from the flow in the same sense as saving is a leakage. But saving is invested and thus investment represents an injunction into the flow. Similarly, the revenue collected by the government through taxes is spent in the form of public expenditure and represents an injunction into the circular flow of income.

The modified system of income determination comprises of the following five equations:

$$Y = C + I + G \quad \text{...(6.1)}$$

$$C = a + bYd \quad \text{...(6.2)}$$

$$I = \bar{I} \quad \text{...(6.3)}$$

$$G = \overline{G} \quad \text{...(6.4)}$$

$$T = \overline{T} \quad \text{...(6.5)}$$

where

Y = Income

C = Consumption expenditure

G = Government expenditure

I = Investment expenditure

T = Total taxes

Yd = Disposable income.

The equation (6.1) is an identity which defines the components of aggregate demand. According to this equation there are three components of aggregate demands—consumption expenditure, investment expenditure, and government expenditure. The equation (6.2) describes a consumption function and states that consumption expenditure is a linear function of disposable income. The equations (6.3), (6.4) and (6.5) describe that investment expenditure, government expenditure and taxes are given exogeneously.

The above system of equation can be solved if we add another identity defining disposable income.

$$Yd = Y - T \quad \text{...(6.6)}$$

The equation (6.6) states that disposable income is that part of income which is left with the individuals after paying the taxes which are due to the government.

Substituting equation (6.3) and (6.4) into equation (6.1) we get:

$$Y = C + \bar{I} + \overline{G} \quad \text{...(6.7)}$$

Let us once again recall that a bar upon a variable means that related magnitude is given exogeneously. Substituting equation (6.2) into the equation (6.7) we get

$$Y = a + bYd + \bar{I} + \bar{G} \qquad (6.8)$$

Also substitute equation (6.6) into (6.8) and get

$$Y = a + b\,(Y - T) + \bar{I} + \bar{G} \qquad ...(6.9)$$

which can be simplified as

$$Y = a + bY - b\bar{T} + \bar{I} + \bar{G} \qquad ...(6.10)$$

collecting terms on the left hand side we can write

$$Y - Yb = a - b\bar{T} + \bar{I} + \bar{G} \qquad ...(6.11)$$

$$Y\,(1 - b) = a - b\bar{T} + \bar{I} + \bar{G} \qquad ...(6.12)$$

$$Y = \frac{1}{1-b}\left[a - b\bar{T} + \bar{I} + \bar{G}\right] \qquad ...(6.13)$$

The equation (6.13) gives the equilibrium level of income after incorporating government expenditure and taxes when both of these are given exogenously.

The level of government expenditure may not be constant over time. Like all other economic magnitudes, government expenditure is also subject to change. It may rise or fall. One may wonder what impact it will have upon aggregate economic activity. If the government expenditure rises then aggregate economic activity is likely to rise or fall or is not affected by at all? Since we have agreed to use income as a measure of aggregate economic activity, we shall investigate the impact of a change in the level of government expenditure upon the level of income of an economy.

Let us suppose that level of government expenditure rises. Since government expenditure is now taken as a component of aggregate demand, aggregate demand itself would rise as a result of an increase in government expenditure. Given aggregate supply, an increase in aggregate demand will cause income to rise. Thus the net result of an increase in government expenditure would be an increase in the level of income. However, the verbal argument shall not be able to show that how much increase in government expenditure will lead to how much increase in income. We can do so by resorting to the equation (6. 13). Let us assume that level of government expenditure rises from G to ΔG while all other magnitudes remain constant. Then, the equilibrium level of income would be

$$Y+\Delta Y = \frac{1}{1-b}(a - b\overline{T} + \overline{I} + \overline{G} + \Delta G) \qquad ...(6.14)$$

The equation (6.14) defines the new level of income. The resultant increase in income can be calculated if we substract the old level of income from new level of income. Thus by subtracting equation (6.13) from the equation (6.14) we get

$$Y+\Delta Y-Y=\frac{1}{1-b}(a - b\overline{T} + \overline{I} + \overline{G} + \Delta\overline{G}) - \frac{1}{1-b}(a - b\overline{T} + \overline{I} + \overline{G}) \qquad ...(6.15)$$

$$\Delta Y = \frac{1}{1-b}\Delta G \qquad ...(6.16)$$

The equation (6.16) states that if government expenditure rises by ΔG then income would increase $\frac{1}{1-b}$ times; where b is the marginal propensity to consume.

Dividing Equation (6.16) by ΔG on the both sides we get:

$$\frac{\Delta Y}{\Delta G} = \frac{1}{1-b} \qquad ...(6.17)$$

The relation described in the equation (6.17) is known as government expenditure multiplier. It is also the inverse of marginal propensity to save. We know that marginal propensity to save is always positive and less than unity ($0<b<1$) and so is marginal propensity to save ($0<1-b<1$). Therefore, the government expenditure multiplier shall never be zero unless marginal propensity to consume is unity. Since, marginal propensity to save cannot be one by definition, multiplier cannot be zero. Similarly, multiplier cannot be equal to unity because marginal propensity to save cannot be zero. Consequently, the value of government expenditure multiplier shall always be positive and greater than one.

You shall also notice that conceptually government expenditure multiplier described in equation (6.17) is the same as investment multiplier discussed earlier and obtained in equation (5.16). They differ only in explanation and interpretation, otherwise, both are identical.

A GRAPHIC EXAMPLE

The above analysis of impact of a change in the government expenditure can also be explained with the help of by now familiar Keynesian Cross diagram depicted in the Figure 6.1. The horizontal axis measures income and vertical axis measures consumption

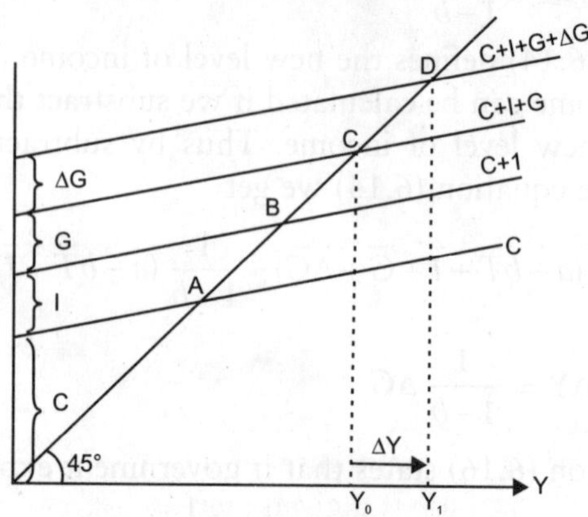

Fig. 6.1. The government expenditure multiplier.

expenditure, investment expenditure and government expenditure. *C*—line is the consumption function. The vertical distance from any point on this line to any point on the horizonal axis gives the amount of consumption expenditure at that level of income. The next line is *C+I* line which includes consumption and investment expenditure both. The vertical distance between *C*—line and *C+I* line gives the amount of investment. Since the amount of investment is constant (or invariant) with respect to income the *C+I* line has been drawn parallel to the *C*—line. This is so because all investment is assumed to be given exogenously at this point. The vertical distance between *C*—line and *C+I* line is the investment. The next line which is above *C+I* line is *C+I+G* line and includes consumption expenditures, investment expenditure and government expenditure. It is the original aggregate demand line. We already know that 45° line is nothing but an aggregate supply line. Equilibrium level of income is determined where aggregate demand and aggregate supply are equal. This is the point *C* in the Figure 6.1. We draw a perpendicular from the point *C* on the horizontal axis. This perpendicular cuts the horizontal axis at the point Y_0, hence OY_0

level of equilibrium income is achieved. Let us suppose now that government expenditure rises from G to ΔG. Consequently, aggregate demand rises and aggregate demand line is further pushed up from C+I+G line to C+I+4 ÷ ΔG line which shows the new level of aggregate demand. The vertical distance between lines C+I+G and C+I gives the amount of government expenditure. Similarly, the vertical distance between C+I+G+ΔG lines and C+I+G line gives the change in public expenditure. Both of these lines run parallel to each other because public expenditure is also given exogenously and does not depend upon the level of income. The new line C+I+G+ΔG cuts the 45° at the point D. This is the point where new level of aggregate demand and aggregate supply become equal. So new level of equilibrium income is determined at this point. If we drop a perpendicular from the point D upon the horizontal axis, it cuts it at the point Y_1 and OY_1 level of income is determined. The difference between OY_0 and OY_1 is ΔY. The ratio of ΔY and ΔG is the government expenditure multiplier which tells us how much the income would rise if there is a given increase in public expenditure.

LUMP SUM TAX MULTIPLIER

The above treatment of public expenditure is based upon the assumption that public expenditure is autonomous, *i.e.*, it does not depend upon the level of income. If the amount of tax is independent of level of income, it is called the lump sum tax. Its amount in money terms may be fixed. For example, the original level of tax was 10 crores rupees. It may be increased to 12 crores rupees. This is an increase in the lump sum tax. The lump sum tax multiplier helps us to find out the impact of a given change in the lump sum tax upon the level of income. It can be calculated as follows:

The original level of Equilibrium given by the equation (6.13) is

$$Y = \frac{1}{1-b}\left(a - b\overline{T} + \overline{I} + \overline{G}\right) \qquad ...(6.13)$$

Let us assume now that lump sum tax rises from T to ΔT. The change in income as a result of this change would be given by the following equation:

$$Y+\Delta Y = \frac{1}{1-b}\,[a - b(T+\Delta T) + \overline{I} + \overline{G}] \qquad ...(6.18)$$

which can be simplified as

$$Y+\Delta Y = \frac{1}{1-b}(a - bT - b\Delta T + \bar{I} + \bar{G}) \quad ...(6.19)$$

Subtracting (6.13) from (6.19), we get

$$Y+\Delta Y—Y = \frac{1}{1-b}\left[a - bT - b\Delta T + \bar{I} + \bar{G}\right] - \frac{1}{1-b}\left[a - bT + \bar{I} + \bar{G}\right] \quad ...(6.20)$$

$$\Delta Y = \frac{1}{1-b}[-b\Delta T]$$

or

$$\Delta Y = \frac{-b\Delta T}{1-b} \quad ...(6.21)$$

If we divide both sides of equation (6.21) by ΔT we get the lump sum-tax multiplier

$$\frac{\Delta Y}{\Delta T} = \frac{-b}{1-b} \quad ...(6.22)$$

Let us first note that sign of lump sum tax multiplier is negative which means that an increase in the amount of taxes would tend to reduce the income while an increase in public expenditure tends to raise income. The reason for this is that a tax, being a transfer of income from private individuals to the government lowers consumption. The reduction in consumption expenditure by a given amount of tax is M.P.C. × tax. For example, if M.P.C. is b and tax rises by the amount ΔT then reduction in consumption would be

$$\Delta C = -b\Delta T \quad ...(6.23)$$

Also notice that expression on the right hand side of equation (6.23) appears as the numerator of the lump sum tax multiplier given in equation (6.22). Another point which must be carefully noted is that absolute value of tax multiple is less than the government expenditure multiplier. Thus, an increase in government spending, matched by an equal increase in taxation, results in an over-all increase in aggregate demand.

BALANCED BUDGET MULTIPLIER

The government budget is balanced if the government expenditure is exactly equal to tax-revenue. A balanced budget is not neutral to increase in income. Instead, a balanced budget tends to increase the level of aggregate demand and thus increase income because the absolute value of government expenditure multiplier is more than the absolute value of tax multiplier. In other words, the expansionary effect of public expenditure is stronger than contractionary effect of taxes. Therefore, even if the amounts of public expenditure and tax are exactly equal, the net effect will be that of expansion. We can show it as follows:

Let us assume $\Delta G = \Delta T = \Delta E$

where E is the equal change in the government expenditure and taxes. Increase in aggregate demand caused by public expenditure will be

$$\Delta Y_G = \frac{\Delta E}{1-b} \quad ...(6.24)$$

where

ΔY_G = Increase in aggregate demand caused by government expenditure.

An equal increase in taxes will tend to lower aggregate demand. Making use of lump sum tax multiplier given in equation (6.23), the reduction in aggregate demand can be written as

$$\Delta Y_T = \frac{-b\Delta E}{1-b} \quad ...(6.25)$$

where Y_T = reduction in aggregate demand caused by equal taxes.

The over all change in aggregate demand caused by a balanced budget will be the algebraic sum of increases and decreases caused be public expenditure and taxes respectively. Hence, the net effect will be

$$\Delta Y = \Delta Y_G + \Delta Y_T = \frac{\Delta E}{1-b} - \frac{b\Delta E}{1-b} \quad ...(6.26)$$

or

$$= \frac{\Delta E - b\Delta E}{1-b}$$

or $$= \frac{\Delta E\ (1-b)}{1-b}$$

$$\Delta Y = \Delta E$$

or $$Y = E \qquad ...(6.27)$$

Dividing equation (6.27) by ΔE we get

$$\frac{\Delta Y}{\Delta E} = 1 \qquad (6.28)$$

which is balanced budget multiplier.

The balanced budget multiplier can be worked out in another way also.

The effect of public expenditure is

$$\Delta Y_G = \frac{\Delta G}{1-b} \qquad ...(6.29)$$

The effect of tax is

$$\Delta Y_T = \frac{-b\ \Delta T}{1-b} \qquad ...(6.30)$$

The net effect is given by

$$\Delta Y = \Delta Y_G + \Delta Y_T$$

or, $$\Delta Y = \frac{\Delta G}{1-b} - \frac{b\Delta T}{1-b} \qquad ...(6.31)$$

Since balanced budget implies $\Delta G = \Delta T$.

Substitute ΔG for ΔT and we get

$$\Delta Y = \frac{\Delta G}{1-b} - \frac{b\ \Delta G}{1-b} \qquad ...(6.32)$$

$$\Delta Y = \frac{\Delta G(1-b)}{1-b} \qquad ...(6.33)$$

$$\Delta Y = \Delta G \qquad ...(6.34)$$

Dividing equation (6.34) by ΔG we get

$$\frac{\Delta Y}{\Delta G} = \frac{\Delta G}{\Delta G} = 1 \qquad ...(6.35)$$

Equation (6.35) also describes the balanced budget multiplier which is the same as in equation (6.28). It is also interesting to note that the sum of public expenditure and tax multiplier is also unity.

$$\frac{1}{1-b} - \frac{b}{1-b} = 1 \qquad ...(6.36)$$

We have seen above that balanced budget multiplier is always equal to unity. On the one hand, it shows that balanced budget is not neutral to income. An equal increase in the level of taxes does not completely offsets the expansionary effects of public expenditure, though it is capable of retarding them to a great extent. Even then, balanced budget would be able to generate an increase in the aggregate demand equal to its own size. On the other hand, its significance lies in realizing the fact that in case of a balanced budget, most relevant variable to look at, is, its own size. It becomes important at what level the budget is balanced. Obviously, the effects of a budget balanced at Rs. 500 crores will be different from a budget which is balanced at Rs. 5,000 crores. The former will generate an income of Rs. 500 crores and the latter will generate an income of Rs. 5,000 crores. In the classical period, balanced budget was often favoured by economists on the ground that a balanced budget does not interfere with the functioning of private economy. The above analysis exposes that fallacy of classical economists and shows that it is not so.

TAX RATE MULTIPLIER

If you ponder a little, you shall discover that, in the ultimate analysis, all taxes are paid out of income. Hence, it is not reasonable to treat taxes as autonomous, or exogenously given. The tax revenue very much depends upon the level of income. If income is high, government will get more tax revenue. If income is low, the tax revenue would decline. If the taxes are made a function of income, the system of income determination could be written as follows:

$$Y = C+I+G \qquad ...(6.37)$$

$$C = a+bYd \qquad ...(6.38)$$

$$I = \overline{I} \qquad ...(6.39)$$

$$G = \overline{G} \qquad ...(6.40)$$

$$Yd = Y - T \qquad ...(6.41)$$

$$T = h + tY \qquad ...(6.42)$$

The equation (6.37) is an identity defining the various components of aggregate demand. Equation (6.38) shows that consumption expenditure is a linear function of disposable income. Investment and government expenditure are assumed to be exogenously given as shown in equations (6.39) and (6.40) respectively. An identity in equation (6.41) defines disposable income. You shall recall that equations (6.37) to (6.41) have appeared before also. The tax function is specified by equation (6.42). It is a behavioural equation because it shows the behaviour of a variable namely taxes.

The tax function specified in equation (6.42) is linear. Its intercept is *h* and its slope is *t*. The average rate of taxes can be calculated if we divide both sides of equation (6.42) by *Y*.

$$\frac{T}{Y} = \frac{h}{Y} + t \qquad ...(6.43)$$

The marginal tax rate can be calculated by differentiating *T* with respect to *Y*.

$$\frac{dT}{dY} = t \qquad ...(6.44)$$

The income-tax function can also be depicted in the form of a diagram as shown in the Fig. 6.2. Income is measured on the horizontal axis and taxes are measured on the vertical axis. The tax function is depicted in the form of a line *BT*. *OB* is the intercept of tax function while CY_1 is the amount of tax at the level of income OY_1. Hence the average rate of tax is CY_1/OY_1. When the level of income is OY_2, the amount of tax is DY_2, hence the average rate of

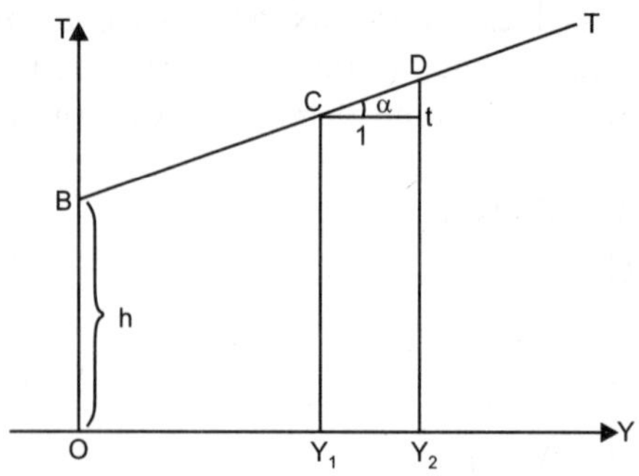

Fig. 6.2. Income-tax function.

tax is DY_2/OY_2. You shall notice the average rate of tax declines as income increases. This can be seen from equation (6.43) also and T/Y declines as income increases because h/Y declines with the increases in income. The slope of the line BT is

$$\frac{DE}{CE} = \frac{DE}{Y_1Y_2}$$

But $\quad DE = t$ and let $Y_1Y_2 = 1$

Therefore, $\quad \dfrac{DE}{CE} = \dfrac{DE}{Y_1Y_2} = \dfrac{t}{1} = t$

Thus the slope of the line BT is t which is also the marginal rate of tax. Total amount of tax can be changed either by changing the vertical intercept (h) or slope (t) or both.

Then equilibrium level of income in the presence of tax function can be calculated in the following manner.

Substituting equation (6.38) into equation (6.37) we get

$$Y = a + bYd + \overline{I} + \overline{G} \qquad ...(6.45)$$

Also substitute equation (6.41) into equation (6.45)

$$Y = a + b\,(Y - T) + \overline{I} + \overline{G} \qquad ...(6.46)$$

Also substitute equation (6.42) defining income tax function into above equation

$$Y = a + b\,[Y - (h + tY)] + \overline{I} + \overline{G} \qquad ...(6.47)$$

which can be simplified as,

$$Y = a + bY - bh - btY + \overline{I} + \overline{G} \qquad ...(6.48)$$

Collecting terms on the left hand side,

$$Y - bY + btY = a - bh + \overline{I} + \overline{G} \qquad ...(6.49)$$

or

$$Y - bY(1 - t) = a - bh + \overline{I} + \overline{G} \qquad ...(6.50)$$

or

$$Y\,[1 - b]\,(1 - t) = a - bh + \overline{I} + \overline{G} \qquad ...(6.51)$$

or

$$Y = \frac{1}{1 - b\,(1-t)}\left[a - bh + \bar{I} + \overline{G}\right] \qquad ...(6.52)$$

which is equilibrium level of income. Notice that $\frac{1}{1 - b\,(1-t)} < \frac{1}{1-b}$. Therefore, given the amounts of investment expenditure and public expenditure, more income will be generated if no tax is imposed, and if income tax is imposed, the amount of generated income will be comparatively low. This can be understood with the following example.

Let the behavioural equations be

$$C = 50 + 0.75Y$$
$$T = 15 + 0.20Y$$

and $\overline{G} = 50 \qquad \bar{I} = 50$

then

$$a = 50$$
$$b = 0.75$$
$$h = 15$$
$$t = 0.20$$

If stall income tax is imposed, equilibrium income is given by

$$Y = \frac{1}{1-b}(a + \bar{I} + \overline{G})$$

$$= \frac{1}{1-0.75}(50 + 50 + 50)$$

$$= \frac{1}{0.25}(150)$$

$$= 600$$

In case of income tax, equilibrium income is given by

$$Y = \frac{1}{(1-b)\,(1-t)}\left[a - bh + \bar{I} + \overline{G}\right]$$

$$Y = \frac{1}{(1-.75)\,(1-.2)}\left[50 - (.75)\,(15) + 50 + 50\right]$$

$$= \frac{1}{(.25)\,(.8)}\; 138.75$$

$$= 693.75$$

The tax rate multiplier can be computed from equation (6.52) which can also be written as

$$Y = [a - bh + \bar{I} + \bar{G}]\,[(1-b)(1-t)]^{-1} \qquad ...(6.53)$$

Differentiating the above equation with respect to t we get

$$\frac{dY}{dt} = -b\left[a - bh + \bar{I} + \bar{G}\right]\left[(1-b)\,(1-t)\right]^{-2} \qquad ...(6.54)$$

or

$$\frac{dY}{dt} = \frac{-b\left[a - bh + \bar{I} + \bar{G}\right]}{(1-b)\,(1-t)\,(1-b)\,(1-t)} \qquad ...(6.55)$$

which can be rewritten as

$$\frac{dY}{dt} = \frac{-bY}{(1-b)\,(1-t)} \qquad ...(6.56)$$

which is the tax rate multiplier. Note that tax rate multiplier has a negative sign suggesting that income will be lowered if the tax rate is increased, and t is a function of income.

BUILT-IN STABILISER

Tax rate multiplier is sometimes referred as built-in stabilizer simply because it is a function of income. Built-instability results because income would decline if there is a decline in investment. Since taxes are a function of income, they automatically fall with the decline in income. The fall in taxes increases the magnitude of disposable income. This sets in motion the operation of tax rate multiplier which operates in the opposite direction to investment multiplier. Thus, in a situation of contracting investment expenditure when income is declining, taxes fall. This expands disposable income and increases consumption expenditure and aggregate demand, which in its turn would raise income. Similarly, in a situation of expanding investment expenditure, when income is increasing, taxes increase. This contracts disposable income and cuts the consumption expenditure and aggregate demand, which in its turn would lower income. Thus, tax rate multiplier tends to stabilise the economy both in the situations of recession and inflation. That is why it is known as built-in stabiliser.

Thus, we can summarize the above discussions in the following propositions:

1. The change in government expenditure or the change in the amount of taxes affects aggregate demand.
2. The balanced budget is not neutral. It is likely to increase the level of aggregate demand and income.
3. The value of balanced budget multiplier is one.
4. A greater increase (or decrease) in Y can be achieved if ΔG is not matched by ΔT.
5. Taxes which are a function of income work as built-in stabiliser.

TRANSFER PAYMENT

Transfer payment is a special type of government expenditure. The government sometimes incurs certain expenditure which do not benefit the whole society (*e.g.* defence) nor do they are designed to provide some service (*e.g.* railways). Instead, they are designed to benefit some specific group of population. The examples of such expenditure may include unemployment bonus which benefits only those who are unemployed, old age pensions which are given only to those persons who have achieved a ripe old age and are not capable of earning their livelihood, educational scholarship given to meritorious poor students, and assistance towards health care etc. All these are welfare activities and the government carries them out because the society considers them to be good. Nevertheless, there are some important economic implications of such actions. Firstly, we must recognize that government is acting as a redistributive agent. These expenditures are incurred out of the tax revenue which the government collects from the private individuals. Thus, it is doing nothing more than this that it is collecting the money from some people and giving it to some other people. In other words, it is transferring the income from one segment of population to another segment. That is why it is called transfer payment. Secondly, we must see that transfer payments are mainly used for consumption purposes.

Incorporating the transfer payments following model of income determination could be worked out.

$$Y = C + I + G \qquad ...(6.57)$$

$$C = a + b\,(Y - T + R) \quad \text{...(6.58)}$$

$$I = \overline{I} \quad \text{...(6.59)}$$

$$G = \overline{G} \quad \text{...(6.60)}$$

$$T = \overline{T} \quad \text{...(6.61)}$$

$$R = \overline{R} \quad \text{...(6.62)}$$

In the above system of equations R is used to represent transfer payments. Equation (6.57) represents the components of aggregate demand. Equation (6.59) through equation (6.62) tell that investment, government expenditure, taxes, and transfer payments are assumed to be given exogenously. The consumption function described in equation (6.58) undergoes significant change in this model. Now, the disposable income does not constitute only of income minus taxes. The amount of transfer payment is added to it because this part of government expenditure is also available for consumption by private individual. Hence, it is very much component of disposable income and equation (6.58) takes account of this fact. Let us now solve this system of equation to determine the equilibrium level of income:

$\overline{R}$

Substituting equations (6.61) and (6.62) into (6.58) we get

$$C = a + b\,(Y - \overline{T} + \overline{R}) \quad \text{...(6.63)}$$

Also substitute equations (6.63), (6.59) and (6.60) into (6.57) to get

$$Y = a + b\,(Y - \overline{T} + \quad) + \overline{I} + \overline{G} \quad \text{...(6.64)}$$

and simplify

$$Y = a + bY - b\overline{T} + b\overline{R} + \overline{I} + \overline{G} \quad \text{...(6.65)}$$

Collecting terms we can write

$$Y - bY = a - b\overline{T} + b\overline{R} + \overline{I} + \overline{G} \quad \text{...(6.66)}$$

or

$$Y\,(1 - b) = a - b\overline{T} + b\overline{R} + \overline{I} + \overline{G} \quad \text{...(6.67)}$$

or

$$Y = \frac{1}{1-b}\left[a - b\overline{T} + b\overline{R} + \overline{I} + \overline{G}\right] \quad \text{...(6.68)}$$

which is the equilibrium level of income. Suppose that transfer payment R rises to ΔR while all other magnitudes remain the same. Then, the new level of income could be written as

$$Y + \Delta Y = \frac{1}{1-b}\left[a - b\overline{T} + b\overline{R} + b\Delta R + \overline{I} + \overline{G}\right] \quad ...(6.69)$$

Subtracting (6.68) from (6.69) we get

$$\Delta Y = \frac{1}{1-b}\, b\Delta R \quad ...(6.70)$$

Dividing both sides of equation (6.70) by ΔR, we get

$$\frac{\Delta Y}{\Delta R} = \frac{b}{1-b} \quad ...(6.71)$$

which is nothing but transfer payment multiplier. On comparing this multiplier with the government expenditure multiplier, you shall discover that transfer payment multiplier is smaller than government expenditure multiplier.

$$\frac{b}{1-b} < \frac{1}{1-b} \quad ...(6.72)$$

This can easily be seen by taking some numbers. Let $b = 0.75$ then

$$\frac{1}{1-b} = \frac{1}{1-0.75} = 4$$

But

$$\frac{b}{1-b} = \frac{0.75}{1-0.75} = 3$$

which shows that transfer payment multiplier is less than the government expenditure multiplier. Thus we can also say that ΔY due to government expenditure will be more than the ΔY due to an increase in transfer payment, provided that the absolute amount of government expenditure and transfer payment is the same.

$$\frac{\Delta G}{1-b} > \frac{b\Delta R}{1-b} \; \text{if } \Delta G = \Delta R \quad ...(6.73)$$

Now, let us suppose that transfer payment is financed by an increase of equal amount in tax. Then $\Delta T = \Delta R$. Notice that transfer payment multiplier and lump sum multiplier will operate in this case in opposite direction. The lump sum tax multiplier would tend to reduce income (hence, its sign will be negative) while the transfer payment multiplier will tend to raise the level of income. The net effect will be the algebraic sum of these two opposite magnitudes.

$$\Delta Y = \frac{-b\Delta T}{1-b} + \frac{b\Delta R}{1-b} \qquad \text{...(6.74)}$$

$$\begin{array}{l}\text{Total}\\ \text{change in}\\ Y\end{array} = \left\{\begin{array}{l}\text{Reduction in income}\\ \text{due to increase in}\\ \text{lump sum tax.}\end{array}\right\} + \left\{\begin{array}{l}\text{Increase in income due}\\ \text{to increase in transfer}\\ \text{payment.}\end{array}\right\}$$

Since the increase in transfer payment is exactly equal to increase in lump sum tax, put $\Delta R = \Delta T$ in the expression given in equation (6.74).

Thus we have

$$\Delta Y = \frac{-b\Delta T + b\Delta T}{1-b} \qquad \text{...(6.75)}$$

$$Y = \text{zero}$$

which means that, an equal increase in taxes and transfer payment will completely neutralize each other and there shall be no consequent increase in income. Let us note carefully that this result is based upon two crucial assumptions: (i) that tax involved is a lump sum tax, (ii) that marginal propensity to consume is constant and is same for all classes. If either of the two assumptions is relaxed, the above result shall no longer hold. It is usually found that poor people have a higher MPC and rich people have a lower MPC. If richer section of population is taxed, and poorer people are given transfer payment, it may have as expansionary effect upon income generation even though the absolute magnitudes of taxes and transfer payment may be exactly equal.

Consumption Function

7

PSYCHOLOGICAL LAW OF CONSUMPTION

Keynes' Psychological Law of Consumption is of basic importance in the analysis of income, output and employment. This law is a statement of common experience that with an increase in income, consumption also increases but not to the extent of the increase in income. Keynes states, "The psychology of the community is such that when aggregate real income is increased, aggregate consumption is increased, but not so much as income."[1] To cite Keynes again, "The fundamental psychological law, upon which we are entitled to depend with great confidence both *a priori* from our knowledge of human nature and from the detailed facts of experience, is that men are disposed, as a rule and on the average, to increase their consumption as their income increases, but not by as much the increase in their income."[2] This law is known as 'Propensity to Consume' or 'Consumption Function.'

This law consists of three related propositions. The first proposition is that when aggregate income increases, consumption expenditure also increases but by a somewhat smaller amount. This is because as a person's income increases, his more and more wants get satisfied and, therefore, lesser and lesser amounts are spent out of subsequent increases in income. The second proposition is that when income increases, extra income is divided in some proportion between spending and saving. This follows from the first proposition because what is not spent is saved. The third proposition is that with the increase in income, both spending and saving go up. It is very unlikely that an increase in income will lead either to less spending or less saving than before. It would seldom happen that a

1. J.M. Keynes, *The General Theory of Employment, Interest and Money*, (London, 1936), p. 27.
2. *Ibid.*, p. 96.

person decreases his consumption or his saving with an increase in his income. Normally, he would spend more and also save more than before.

Keynes' Psychological Law of Consumption is based on three assumptions: Firstly, it is assumed that habits of people regarding spending do not change or that the propensity to consume remains the same. Normally, the propensity to consume is more or less stable and does remain unchanged. This assumption implies that, only income changes whereas other variables like income distribution, price movements, growth of population etc. remain more or less unchanged. The second assumption is that the conditions remain normal, that is, there is no hyper-inflation or war or any other such abnormal condition. The third assumption is that of the existence of a capitalistic *laissez faire* economy. The law may not hold good in an economy where the state interferes with consumption or productive enterprise. The government, for instance, may not permit an increase in consumption with an increase in income. The above assumptions are more or less realistic in a short period and under normal conditions. Keynes' Psychological Law of Consumption is, therefore, a rough approximation to the actual macro behaviour of free consumers and it is true that normally consumption increases with an increase in income but to the extent of the increase in income.

IMPLICATIONS OF KEYNES' PSYCHOLOGICAL LAW

Most of the economists agree with Prof. Hansen's view that Keynes' most notable contribution was his consumption function. Keynes' formulation of the consumption function is considered to be an epoch-making contribution to the tools of economic analysis. This is obvious from the implications of Keynes' psychological law mentioned below.

Vital Importance of Investment: One of the most important implications of Keynes' psychological law of consumption is that it brings about the crucial importance of investment if we are to attain an increasing level of income and employment. The law tells us that with every increase in income, the gap between income and consumption widens; and if the increasing income is to be maintained, more and more investment must be forthcoming to fill up this widening gap; if adequate investment is not forthcoming, there would appear a shortage of effective demand and as a result the economy would slip down. Thus the law highlights the vital importance of investment.

General over-production: The law tells us that there can occur a general over-production and unemployment. Since the marginal propensity to consume is less than unity, with an increase in income, consumption would tend to lag behind income, which would result in over-production and unemployment.

Repudiation of Say's Law*:* With the help of his psychological law of consumption, Keynes repudiates Say's law of market which states that every supply creates its own demand. Since the marginal propensity to consume is less than unity, all that is produced (supplied) is not automatically spent (demanded). The supply fails to create its own demand and as such there results a glut of products in the market.

Need for Government Intervention: Since the entire income earned is not automatically spent, there is no automatic and self-adjusting mechanism to ensure maintenance of a circular flow of income and expenditure. The *laissez faire* policy will, therefore, fail to deliver the goods and the state will have to intervene actively to ensure that aggregate effective demand does not fall short of aggregate supply.

Over-saving Gap: Since the increase in consumption expenditure does not keep pace with the increase in income, there arises the danger of an over-saving gap. This danger is more for rich countries than for poor countries.

Decline in MEO*:* As a result of the propensity to consume remaining unchanged or failing to rise with an increase in income, the expected rate of profitability or the marginal efficiency of capital may tend to decline. Decline in the marginal efficiency of capital can be prevented only by increasing consumption with an increase in income because ultimately the decisions to undertake investment are guided by the volume of consumption.

Income propagation: Keynes' psychological law of consumption also explains the slow nature of income propagation. Since the marginal propensity to consume is less than unity, injection of increasing purchasing power into the income stream leads to smaller and smaller successive increments to income.

Underemployment Equilibrium: Equilibrium would be attained at full employment only if investment demand happens to be equal to the gap between aggregate income corresponding to full employment and aggregate consumption expenditure out of that income. But Keynes believed that the typical investment demand would not be adequate to fill the gap between the amount of income corresponding to full employment and the consumption demand out of that income, and, as such, the aggregate demand and supply schedules would interact at a point of less than full employment.

Secular Stagnation: With the increase in income, since consumption cannot be easily increased and investment demand becomes weaker and weaker, the economy may sooner or later reach a stage where it may not be able to provide outlets for its growing savings which is necessary for maintaining full employment. This stage is known as 'secular stagnation'. Such a situation could be avoided if the consumption function were not stable.

Turning Points of Trade Cycle: Keynes' psychological law of consumption is very helpful in explaining the turning points of the trade cycle. Before the publication of Keynes' General Theory there were several theories of trade cycle but none could offer a satisfactory explanation of turning points of the trade cycle. Keynes explained turning points of the trade cycle with the help of his stable consumption function. When the business cycle reaches the highest point of prosperity, income has increased, but marginal propensity of consume being less than unity, consumption does not increase correspondingly and the result is the downward start of the cycle. Similarly, when the business cycle reaches the lowest point, income has declined very low, but since people do not reduce their consumption to the full extent of decline in income, the upward phase of the cycle starts.

CONSUMPTION FUNCTION

The consumption function or the marginal propensity to consume is the relationship between income (Y) and consumption (C) and can be represented as $C = f(Y)$. At various level of income, there will be corresponding levels of consumption. A schedule of consumer expenditure at various levels of income is called the schedule of propensity to consume.

AVERAGE AND MARGINAL PROPENSITIES TO CONSUME

The relationship between income and consumption is measured by the average and the marginal propensities to consume. The average propensity to consume is a relationship between total consumption and total income in a given time period while the marginal propensity to consume is the incremental change in consumption as a result of a given increment in income. In other words, average propensity to consume is the rate of consumption to income while the marginal propensity to consume is the ratio of change in consumption to the change in income. Thus

$$APC = \frac{C}{Y}$$

$$MPC = \frac{\Delta C}{\Delta Y}$$ where ΔC is incremental change in consumption and ΔY is incremental change in income.

The normal relation between income and consumption is that when income rises, consumption also rises, but to an extent smaller than the rise in income. In other words, the ratio of an increase in consumption to an increase in income is always less than one. In technical terms, the marginal propensity to consume is less than unity.

The following table explains the relation between average propensity to consume (APC) and the marginal propensity to consume (MPC).

Income (Rs.)	Consumption (Rs.)	APC $(\frac{C}{Y})$	MPC $(\frac{\Delta C}{\Delta Y})$
1000	800	0.80	–
1100	870	0.79	0.7
1200	920	0.76	0.5
1300	950	0.73	0.3
1400	970	0.69	0.2

In Fig. 7.1, the function is represented by the curve *CC*. When the income is *OL*, the consumers desire to spend *ON*. If the income rises to *OM*, the expenditure increases to *OP*. The consumers would spend *OC* even when their income is zero. In other words, at zero income, instead of starving the people draw on past savings, sell property or borrow so as to buy consumer goods. The fact that CC is a straight line implies that as income rises, consumers' demand increases by an amount which always bears the same proportion to the increase in income, whatever the size of the increase and whatever the original level of income. In fact, the consumption function can take a number of shapes. Two more shapes are shown in Figs. 7.2 and 7.3. In Fig. 7.2, OC is a straight line starting from the origin, which implies that the consumers spend more with a rise in income but always spend the same proportion of income. The broken line marked Y=C indicates the position OC would take if the consumers spend whole of their income. The fact that OC slopes less steeply than the broken line means that the proportion of income consumed is always less than 100%. The curve $C_1C_2C_3$ in Fig. 7.3 shows a third shape of the consumption function. Even when the income is zero, the consumers incur a minimum expenditure of OC_1. This level of expenditure remains unchanged till the income does not rise above OY_1. At higher levels of income, consumption rises with a rise in income but by less than the increase in income. The diminishing slope of the curve between C_2 and C_3 shows that the proportion of income consumed falls progressively with a rise income. *APC* at any point on the income-consumption curve is the slope of the line drawn from the point to the origin. *MPC* at any point on the income consumption curve is represented by the slope of the tangent to the income-consumption curve at that point.

Figs. 7.1, 7.2 and 7.3 are based on the assumption that other things remain unchanged. If income is not the main determinant of

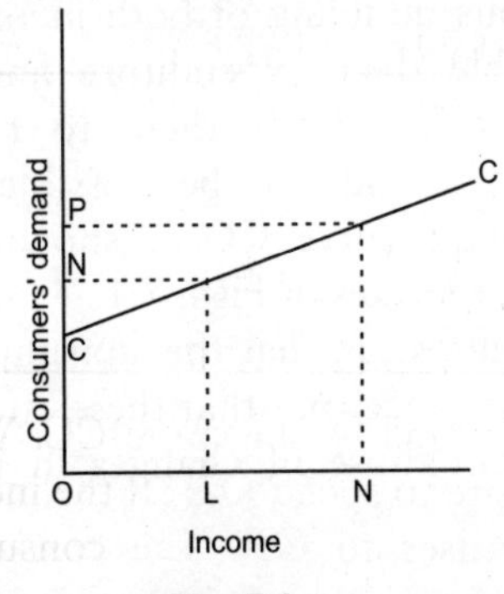

Fig. 7.1.

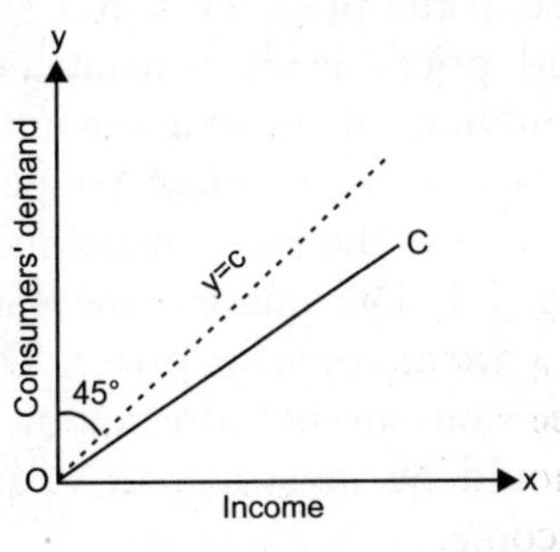

Fig. 7.2.

consumers' expenditure, its influence may be submerged under those of other stronger forces. If interest rates, for instance, are a much more powerful determinant of consumers expenditure than income, it would be necessary to show a separate consumption curve for each possible level of rate of interest. Instead of a single curve, like CC in Fig. 7.1, there would be a whole family of curves. In such a case the assumption of 'other things remain unchanged' would not be justified and as such the consumption function would not have much meaning; the direct relationship between interest rates and consumption would assume priority as an object of investment. The consumption function would be meaningful and useful only if it can be shown that income is, if not the sole determinant of consumers' demand, the most important of all the factors which influence it.

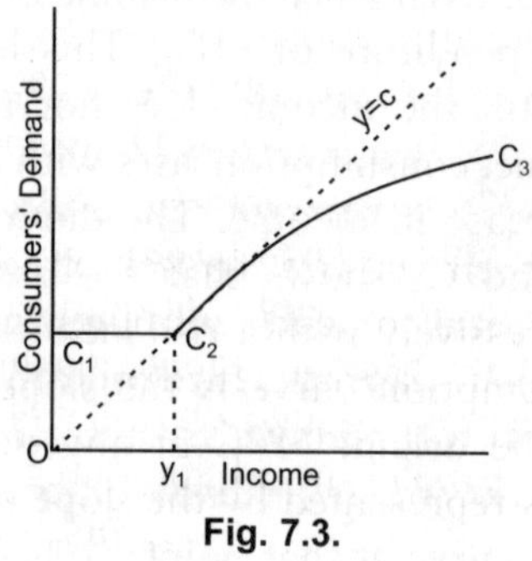

Fig. 7.3.

The relationship is normally expressed in terms of real income and real consumption. Consumers may respond differently to a rise in income, depending upon whether or not it is accompanied by a rise in the price level. If a simultaneous doubling of both incomes and prices leads consumers to double their expenditure and a doubling of income at unchanged prices leads them to raise expenditure by only 80 per cent, it would not be possible to represent the two situations by a single curve CC as shown in Fig. 7.1. The amounts measured along the axes of Figs. 7.1, 7.2 and 7.3 are at constant prices. This does not mean that the consumers' decisions are not affected by changes in prices but that these effects should be investigated separately from those of changes in real income.

Algebraically the consumption function can be written as:

$$C = C(Y_d)$$

where C stands for aggregate real consumption and Y_d for aggregate real disposable income. In case the consumption function is linear,

$$C = C_0 + aY_d$$

where b is the marginal propensity to consume and C_0 is the level of consumption at zero disposable income.

RELATIONSHIP BETWEEN *APC* AND *MPC*

Diagrammatic

With the increase in income, *APC* as well as *MPC* decline but the decline in *MPC* is more than that in *APC*. *MPC* is higher in poor countries than in rich countries. This is because in rich countries most of the essential wants of people have already been satisfied and, therefore, a major portion of the additional income is saved. In contrast, in poor countries people have many unsatisfied wants and as such a major portion of the additional income is spent for satisfying these wants. As pointed out by Prof. Hansen, sometimes *MPC* and *APC* in developed countries assume a constant ratio and become the cause of flattening of the consumption curve resulting in a shortage of effective demand and consequently leading to poverty amidst potential plenty.

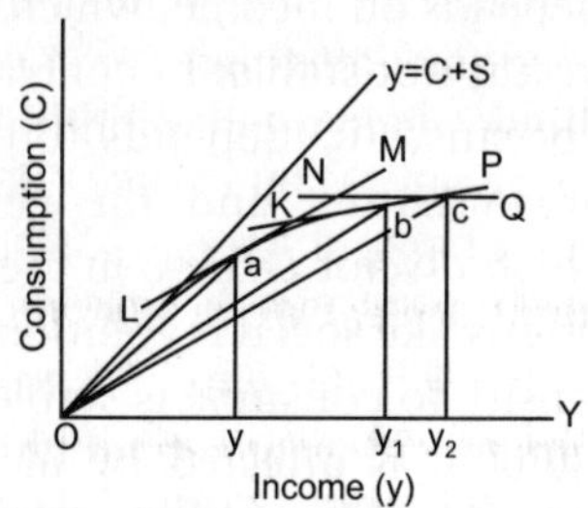

Fig. 7.4.

In the above figure, the curve *OQ* represents the consumption function. The *APC* at any point on this curve is shown by the slope of the straight line from this point to the origin. It would be seen that the slope of *Oa* is steeper than that of *Ob*, which means that the average propensity to consume is higher when income is *Oy* than when income is Oy_1. The *MPC* at any point on the curve *OQ* is shown by the slope of the tangent at that point on the curve. The slope of the tangent (or *MPC*) is greater when income is smaller (say *Oy*) than when it is larger (say Oy_2); in other words, *LM* is steeper than *KP*. It would also be seen from the diagram that when income increases from *Oy* to Oy_2, the decline in *MPC* (*i.e.* slope of *KP*) is greater than that in *APC* (*i.e.* slope of *OC*).

SAVING CURVE

Since income not consumed is income saved, the saving-income relation can be obtained from income-consumption relation. Savings at various levels of income can be obtained by subtraction consumption at those levels of income from the income. Since $MPC + MPS = 1$, $MPS = 1 - MPC$ or $1 - dc/dy$. Thus if we know the marginal propensity to consume, we can obtain the marginal propensity to save by subtracting the marginal propensity to consume from one.

FACTORS DETERMINING CONSUMPTION FUNCTION

A clear distinction must be made between two questions: (i) how much will be spent for consumption, given the propensity to consume? and (ii) how much will be spent for consumption out of a given income? In other words, distinction should be made between the amount of consumption and the propensity to consume, that is between an amount and a schedule. The amount of consumption is not stable because it depends on income, which is not stable because the inducement to invest is not stable. In contrast, the propensity to consume is stable because it depends on the psychological characteristics of human nature and the general structure and practices of society which do not change in the short period except under abnormal conditions like social revolution, war, hyperinflation etc. Though the propensity to consume is stable in the short period, it is not absolutely rigid. It is affected by factors like changes in government fiscal policy, significant changes in the rate of interest and capital values etc. Such factors are of two types, *viz.* (1) objective factors and (2) subjective factors. We first discuss objective factors.

Distribution of Income: This is an important factor determining the propensity to consume. Normally, the average and marginal propensities to consume of the poor people are higher than those of the rich. This is because the poor have a lot of unsatisfied wants and are likely to spend every additional unit of money that they obtain in satisfying those wants. In contrast, the rich have a high standard of living and relatively less urgent wants remain to be satisfied. Additional income in their case, therefore, is more likely to be saved than spent on consumption. Statistical studies show that a large portion of total saving is done by a relatively few high-income recipients and a small part of total saving is done by a large number of low-income recipients. Hence, the more equal the distribution of income, the higher will be the propensity to consume.

In a study of German time-series, Stachle[3] found that distribution of income was an important factor in determining aggregate consumption. The investigations using American "cross-section" data failed to find any significant relationship between income distribution and aggregate consumption.[4] These studies have led many economists to believe that policies aimed at reducing inequalities in the distribution of income will not be of significant help in raising the aggregate consumption.

Fiscal Policy: The fiscal policy of the government relating to taxation, expenditure and public debt appreciably affects the propensity to consume. A reduction in taxation will leave more post-tax incomes with people which would tend to increase their expenditure on consumption. In contrast, an increase in taxation will decrease consumption. A highly progressive tax system decreases inequalities in the distribution of income, which, as seen above, increases the propensity to consume.

Financial Policies of Corporations: If corporations and companies retain more reserves and distribute lesser profits in the form of dividends, the disposable incomes of the shareholders will be smaller. In contrast if more profits are distributed as dividends, more will be spent on consumption.

Changes in Expectations: If the consumers expect a shortage, or rise in price, of certain goods, they may rush to purchase such goods

---

3. H. Stachle, "Short Period Variations in the Distribution of Income", *Review of Economics Statistics,* 1937, pp. 133-43.
4. H. Lubell, "Effects of Income Redistribution on Consumers' Expenditure," *American Economic Review*, 1947, pp. 157-70 and Marschak, "Personal and Collective Budget Functions", *Review of Economics Statistics*, 1939, pp. 161-70.

far in excess of their current needs. This would raise the consumption function. Such a thing often happens during war time. On the other hand, if the people expect a plenty of a decline in prices, of certain durable goods, they would tend to postpone purchases of such goods, which would lower the consumption function.

The consumption of a person is also influenced by expectations as to what his income will be in the future. If he expects an increase in income in future, he will tend to consume more than if he expects it to continue at its present level. If he takes a really long view, he will look ahead to prospective income during the rest of his working life, and try to adjust his consumption so that it is smoothed out over his life-span in the most satisfactory way.

Windfall Gains or Losses: Sudden and unexpected gains and losses in income affect consumption function. It is believed that the beneficiaries of windfall gains increase in their consumption above the normal level. The boom conditions during the late twenties in the U.S. economy created huge windfall gains which are believed to have raised the consumption function.

Liquid Assets: Changes in liquid assets of people affect their consumption. With an increase in their liquid assets (*e.g.* cash-balances, shares, securities etc.), the people have a tendency to increase their consumption. Increased liquidity caused by the method of financing World War II had an appreciable stimulating effect on consumption during the years following the war.

It is easier for a person to dis-save if his wealth is in liquid form. Such a person is not protected from the temptation to spend beyond his income by the inconvenience and possible embarrassment or loss involved in first having to cash a non-liquid asset. This factor, however, is not likely to be very important for, at least, two reasons: Firstly, it applies only to potential dis-savers and not to those who could reduce their current saving without having to cash assets. Secondly, the 'consumers' whose portfolios may be shifted in a more liquid direction by the central bank open market operations include, by and large, trust funds, pension plans, insurance companies, endowed institutions, and a relatively small number of wealthy persons in whose case dis-saving temptation is not much relevant.

Rate of Interest: It is not possible to say with certainty as to which way a change in the rate of interest will affect the consumption function. One possibility is that a higher reward for saving (*i.e.* a rise in the rate of interest) may stimulate savings and thereby decrease consumption. But some persons save with the objective of providing a fixed income for themselves in old age or for their dependents. With a rise in the rate of interest, such people can get the desired income from a smaller amount of savings and may therefore have a tendency to correspondingly increase their consumption. For the rich people saving is almost automatic and a little higher rate of interest will be no attraction for the poor. The classical economists believed that the savings would vary directly with the rate of interest. Keynes, however, considered the effect of variations in the rate of interest on savings as highly complex and uncertain. In his view "the short period influence of the interest rate on individual spending out of a given income is secondary and relatively unimportant, except perhaps, where usually large changes are in question."[5] It is in the long period that considerable changes in the rate of interest influence social habits affecting consumption function. Changes in the rate of interest have more influence on the purchase of consumable durables which are purchased on instalment basis. A rise in the rate of interest makes instalment buying more expensive and thereby tends to discourage consumption. Thus whether or not a rise in the interest rates lowers consumption function will depend on the relative strength of the opposing forces.

Duesenberry Hypothesis: Prof. Duesenberry had made two important observations on the factors affecting consumption function which are called 'Duesenberry Hypothesis'.[6] In his view, consumption expenditure of an individual is determined not only by his current income but also by his standard of living in the past. If income falls, the expenditure on consumption also falls but not to the same extent because people find it difficult to adjust their expenditure to the changed income. Secondly, he has suggested that an individual's consumption depends not only on the absolute amount of his income but also in its size relative to the incomes of others. His reaction to a change in income will differ according to whether or not others' incomes have changed by a similar amount: if they have, his consumption will change in the same proportion as his income;

---

5. J.M. Keynes, *The General Theory of Employment, Interest and Money* (London, 1936), p. 94.
6. J.S. Duesenberry, *Income Saving and the Theory of Consumer Behaviour* (1949).

if they have not, his consumption will change in a smaller proportion. The consumption standards of low income groups are considerably influenced by the consumption standards of high income groups. The moment low income groups start using goods consumed by high income groups, the latter try to avoid consumption of such commodities and search for still better commodities. Such tendencies raise the consumption function.

Selling Effort: Those who advocate advertisement and other selling efforts as a means of increasing aggregate demand often overlook the fact that an increase in total consumer demand for one good or a class of goods may simply be at the cost of reduced demand for other goods. Nevertheless, given the level of income, an increase in selling effort may increase the total volume of consumer expenditure. But this factor has not been given much attention in the theory of aggregate demand because of three major reasons. In the first place, there is no independent measure of the volume of effective selling effort. Secondly, this volume probably does not fluctuate much in the short period. Thirdly, it has not been considered, at least, in the past, subject to social control.

Relative Prices: There is a tendency among economists to ignore the effect of changes in relative prices on the aggregate consumer demand in the belief that, like selling efforts, changes in relative prices increase demand for some products at the cost of that for other products. But, in fact, changes in relative prices can affect aggregate consumer demand. Much attention, however, has not been paid to this factor because there is no specific hypotheses as to whether this influence is important and in which direction it operates.

Volume of Wealth: The larger the wealth possessed by a person, the lower would be its marginal utility to him and as such the weaker would be the desire to add to future wealth by reducing current consumption.

Demographic Factors: Even at a given level of income, the consumption expenditure may differ widely from family to family. Such differences in consumption expenditure can partly be explained by "demographic factors" which include things like size of family, stage in the family 'life cycle', place of residence, occupation etc. Other things remaining unchanged, the large-size families would spend more than the short-sized families. Families with children college age would spend more than those with children of primary school age. Normally, the urban families have a tendency to spend more than the rural families. Farmers and small businessmen tend to spend less than the service people. Changes in demographic factors, however, occur over a long period and can, therefore, be ignored in the short-run analysis.

Terms of Consumer Credit: The terms of consumer credit exert an important influence on consumer purchases of durables and constitute possibly a strategic variable because of their susceptibility to social control, both through general monetary policy and through direct regulation. In recent years, there has been considerable increase in the volume of purchases of consumer durables financed by consumer credit and as such its cost and availability have assumed great importance.

It is generally recognised that the interest rate paid on instalment credit is not of so much importance as matters like the size of required down-payments, the length of the period over which the balance must be paid and the credit standards applied in judging request for credit expansion.

Permanent Income: A family's expenditure on consumption is determined not by its current income but by its permanent or normal income. Thus current changes in income do not affect consumption unless these changes also affect the household's belief as to what its normal income is likely to be. This approach provides an alternative explanation for the different behaviour of the long-run consumption functions. The apparent frequent shifting of the short-run consumption is to be explained largely by the fact the 'normal' income moves more slowly than current income and consumption is related mainly to the former. Over a long period, however, the trend in income, and consumption can be expected to rise more or less in proportion to such normal income.

Consumer Durables: The short-run instability of consumption expenditure in relation to income is considered to be concentrated in the area of consumer durables. The logic of the consumption function suggests that it is the current services rendered by durable goods which are desired in an amount related to current income. A small change in the desired level of current services of durable goods can lead to substantial changes in their rate of purchase. Large fluctuations in their purchases from year to year are quite consistent with only modest changes in the volume of current services rendered by consumers' stocks of durables because these stocks are the accumulation of a number of years' purchases. Thus factors affecting the timing of purchase of durable goods can significantly affect aggregate demand without involving any significant irregularity in the relationship between current consumption of the services of durable goods and income.

The purchases of durables are considerably influenced by the size of the existing stock of durable goods possessed by consumers and the age composition of this stock. The demand for durables, for instance, was very high in the post-war period because (i) during the war, consumer stocks of durables had either declined or had grown less in relation to consumer demand for their services on account of non-availability of durables and (ii) the stocks contained relatively old units. Similarly, in normal times if there are abnormally large sales of durables during a certain year, the sales may decline in the following years irrespective of the level of income or any other factor.

Though an important factor, the existing stock of durables is not the only factor influencing the volume of sales of durable goods. A recent study shows that the stock of automobiles on the road is an important variable for explaining new purchases of automobiles along with consumer incomes, relative prices of new and used cars and of cars relative to goods in general, and consumer credit terms.[7] Some other impair the significance of stocks by emphasizing style and performance changes, and consumers' comprehension and acceptance of them as important factors in the demand for durables. In other words, obsolescence can be as important as physical wearing out in creating a demand for new durable goods by people who already own them.[8]

Pigou Effect: Pigou effect says that the changes in the real value of liquid assets affect the consumption of the liquid asset holders. This is also known as 'Real value of money assets effect' or 'wealth

7. D.B. Suits, "The Demand for New Automobiles in the United States, 1929-1956", *Review of Economics Statistics* (August, 1958), pp. 273-80.
8. E. Mueller, "The Desire for Innovations in Household Goods" in L.H. Clark (ed.). *Consumer Behaviour, Research on Consumer Reaction* (Harper Bros., 1958).

effect'. A.C. Pigou proved first this effect in 1943. He showed that when money wages are cut, prices fall and then the value of money rises. As the value of money rises, the real value of assets increases. Such types of assets are stocks, shares, bank deposits, government securities, bonds, etc. whose values are fixed in monetary terms. The increase in the real value of these fixed assets will make the owners feel richer than before. As a result they will save less out of this present income and spend more on consumption. This will raise aggregate demand for output and thereby generate automatic full employment in the economy and the consumption function will shift upward. From the above discussion we observe that the Pigou effect is based on the following assumptions.

1. There is flexible wage.
2. There is flexible price.
3. There is constant stock of money.

The Pigou effect can be shown in figure 7.5.

In Figure 7.5(a), the economy is at y_1, level of income. As there is wage-price deflation. The consumption function shifts rightward from S_1 to S_2 and the level of income shifts from y_1 level to full employment level. Corresponding to y_1 and y_F in Figure 7.5(a) we get same y_1 and y_F in Figure 7.5(b). As explanation it is said that when the price falls from P_1 to P_2 with reduction in money wages, income increases from y_1 to the full employment level y_F and we get a downward sloping aggregate demand curve AD via consumption function.

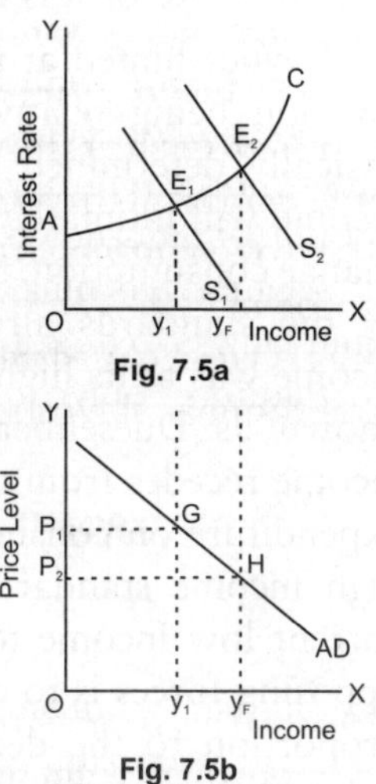

Fig. 7.5a

Fig. 7.5b

CYCLICAL AND SECULAR BEHAVIOUR OF CONSUMPTION FUNCTION

Keynes states that with an increase in income, the expenditure on consumption also increases but by less than the increase in income. Now the question arises: Does this relationship between income and consumption remain constant over time or is it subject to change? In other words, is there any difference between the cyclical and secular behaviour of the consumption function? In fact,

Keynes did not make a clear-cut distinction between the cyclical (or short-period) and secular (or long-period) consumption function. But whatever he said about the consumption function certainly throws some light on this distinction.

Historical experience shows that during the up-swing of business cycle, when income rises, the expenditure on consumption does not rise in the same proportion. Similarly, during the down-swing of business cycle, when income declines, the expenditure on consumption does not decline in the same proportion. Thus the cyclical increase and decrease in consumption is less than in proportion to the increase and decrease in income. In other words, there is a lagged adjustment between income and consumption. In the short period, consumption does not get enough time to adjust itself to changes in income. The result is a flat consumption function curve representing the normal behaviour pattern of consumption. In other words, the consumption function or the propensity to consume remains more or less constant over a short period of time.

Keynes hinted at two major explanations for the consumption function being relatively flat. In the first place, consumption is basically determined by primary needs and, while a rise in real income will ultimately induce increase in consumption, the urge to change consumption. Secondly, consumption is basically determined by the standards already attained in the recent past when the income was at its highest level. The second explanation is generally known as Duesenberry Hypothesis. To cite Prof. Hensen, "As income recedes from this level in the depression phase of the cycle, expenditure on consumption is subjected to two pulls—the former high income standard serves to hold consumption up, while the current low income tends to pull it down. The net effect of these opposing forces is to cause consumption outlays to fall less than in proportion to the decline in income. In the recovery, as current income rises the depressant force weakens and the pull of the formerly achieved standard becomes increasingly ascendant."[9]

While cyclically consumption rises and declines less than in proportion to the rise and decline in national income, over a long period consumption has risen more or less in proportion to a rise in national income To cite Hensen, "Even a little reflection on the

9. A.H. Hensen, *A Guide to Keynes* (New York, 1953), p. 81.

course of economic history is enough to disclose the unmistakable fact that consumption has risen, broadly conceived, more or less in proportion to the spectacular growth in productivity which the last 150 years have witnessed."[10] Bowley and Stamp have observed vast shifts in consumption standards over a long period more or less in proportion to the rise in income.

Some economists, among whom particular mention may be made of Arthur Smithies[11] and James Tobin,[12] hold the view that the basic relationship between income and consumption is non-proportional. They, therefore, believe that the basis of income along the average propensity to consume should decline with a rise in the level of income in the long run. The time-series data relating to consumption and income, however, does not corroborate their hypothesis. They reconcile their position by stating that while the basic income-consumption relationship is of a non-proportional type, still the long-run data exhibits relationship of a proportional type because the basic non-proportional consumption function has undergone upward shifts as a consequence of factors other than income influencing the level of consumption. Among such other factors mention may be made of the following: (i) with an increase in accumulated wealth of households, the utility of further accumulation of wealth has declined and as such the households have tended to spend a larger portion of their incomes leading to an upward shift in the aggregate consumption function; (ii) since the propensity to consume of the urban people is higher than that of the rural people, the movement of population from rural to urban areas has shifted the consumption function upwards; (iii) the age composition of population has so changed that the ratio of old-age people to the total population has tended to rise and as these people consume but do not earn, the ratio of aggregate consumption to total consumption has risen and given an upward shift to the consumption function; (iv) the introduction of new consumer goods considered as "essentials" by the typical household has also led to an upward shift in the consumption function.

10. *Ibid.*, p. 78.

11. Arthur Smithies, "Forecasting Postwar Demand", *Economica* (January 1956).

12. James Tobin, "Relative Income, Absolute Income, and Saving" in *Money Trade and Economic Growth* (Macmillan, 1951).

GENERAL THEORIES OF CONSUMER SPENDING BEHAVIOUR

There are three major general theories of consumer spending behaviour *viz.* (i) the absolute income hypothesis, (ii) the relative income hypothesis, and (iii) the permanent income hypothesis. The economists who have formulated these hypothesis have all started with a theory of individual consumer behaviour and then generalized to cover aggregate behaviour. In the testing of these theories cross-section data[13] provides empirical evidence on the way spending varies at different levels of family income in any one year, and time-series data provides empirical evidence on the way aggregate spending (or spending by all families taken together) varies as aggregate income (or income of all families taken together) changes from one year another of from one quarter to another.

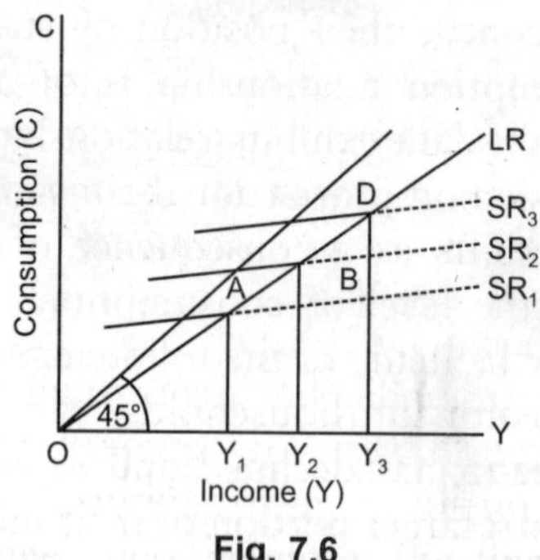

Fig. 7.6

The figure given above illustrates Duesenberry's relative income theory. Let us suppose that a recession takes place when the economy is at income Y_1' which we assume is the highest level of income yet attained by the economy when the income declines over the course of the recessions, the consumers as a group will try to mainain their consumption at the level which they enjoyed when income was at its peak. Consumers vigorously resist any reduction in their standard of living but ultimately find it necessary to reduce their expenditure gradually as their aggregate income declines. Thus consumption declines but not proportionally with the decline in income. The economy moves down the SR_1 curve and, as this

13. Cross-section data is that data which represents values of consumption and income for several different individuals or groups during a given year. Time-series data is that data which represents values of aggregate consumption and income over several different years.

happens, the *APC* rises and the *APS* declines. Thus shows that in an effort to maintain the previously attained higher standard of living, consumers would reduce their savings, more than proportionally and consumption less than proportionally when their income declines. When recovery replaces recession and the income level starts moving back towards its previous peak, consumption rises but less than proportionally with the rise in income. As such the *APC* declines and the *APS* rises. The movement of consumption upward along the SR_1 curve is just the opposite of the earlier movement downward along this curve. Just as consumers reduce saving more than proportionally to maintain the level of consumption on downswing, so they increase saving more than proportionally on the upswing in order to restore saving to its previous level.

The economic theorists have come up with several alternative explanations of consumption function. The major landmarks in the theory of consumption function are—Absolute Income Hypothesis (Keynes, 1936), Relative Income Hypothesis (Duesenberry, 1948). Permanent Income Hypothesis (Friedman, 1957), and Life Cycle Hypothesis (Modigliani & Brumberg, 1954 and Ando & Modigliani, 1963). In what follows, we shall present a brief summary of each theory.

Absolute Income Hypothesis

It is generally held that absolute income hypothesis (hereafter referred to as AIH) was formulated and put forth strongly by John Maynard Keynes in his General Theory. The AIH is composed of the following postulates:

1. Consumption is a stable function of income.
2. The marginal propensity to consume is less in the short run than in the long run.
3. In the long run, a smaller proportion of income will be consumed as income increases and hence marginal propensity to consume is less than average propensity to consume.
4. Changes in the stock of wealth of households will directly affect their level of consumption.[14]

---

14. F.R. Glahe, *Macro Economics—Theory and Policy,* Harcourt Brece Jovanovich, New York (1973), pp. 64-65.

We can do no better than to look to Keynes' General Theory to find the support for these postulates. The first statement is borne out by the following quote from Keynes:

> "The fundamental psychological law upon which we are entitled to depend with great confidence both *a priori* from our knowledge of human nature and from the detailed facts of experience, is that *men are deposed*, as a rule and on the average, to increase their consumption as their income increases, but not by as much as the increase in their income. That is to say if C_w is the amount of consumption and Y_w, is income (both measured in wage units) C_w has the same sign as Y_w, but is smaller in amount, *i.e.* $\frac{dC\omega}{dY\omega}$ is positive and less than unity."[15]

The above quotation from the general theory established that marginal propensity to consume is always positive and less than unity.... $\left(0 < \frac{dC}{dY} < 1\right)$. By corollary, same limits could be established for marginal propensity to save. $\left(0 < \frac{dS}{dY} < 1\right)$. Main contention of the AIH which can be supported by the statements in *The General Theory* is this: Absolute changes in income are responsible for changes in saving, though the changes in savings are not proportional to changes in income. Keynes wrote in the general theory:

> "......it is also obvious that a higher absolute level of income will tend, as a rule, to widen the gap between income and consumption... These reasons will lead, as a rule, to a greater proportion of income as real income increases. But whether or not a greater proportion is saved, we take it as a fundamental psychological rule of any modern community that, when its real income is increased, it will not increase its consumption by an equal absolute amount, so that a greater *absolute* amount must be saved,

15. J.M. Keynes, *The General Theory of Employment, Interest and Money* (1936) Harbinger edition, New York, p. 96.

unless a large and unusual change is occurring at the same time in other factors."[16]

Keynes was also prompt to recognise that a number of subjective factors were involved in the decision making process on savings. He listed eight different motives which lead individuals to save and refrain from spending the full amount of income.[17]

(i) *Motive of Precaution*: The individuals want to preserve a part of their current income to meet the unforeseen contingencies in the future.

(ii) *Motive of Foresight*: The individuals would like to provide for some anticipated needs which shall arise in future. These needs may be different from the present needs, or there may be no income when they arise. Hence, it is an act of foresight to save from the current income to satisfy these needs. The examples for such needs are family education, old age and maintenance of dependents etc.

(iii) *Motive of Calculation*: Individuals also like to save because they prefer larger consumption at a future date in comparison to a smaller consumption at present. Sometimes, individuals save to earn interest and keep their savings in the form of such commodities whose value is expected to appreciate, *e.g.*, gold, real estate etc.

(iv) *Motive of Improvement*: Individuals enjoy a rising standard of living. Hence they prefer to save and invest so that they could get larger incomes to improve their standard of living.

(v) *Motive of Independence*: Individuals would like to retain some portion of their income because the possession of money in this form accords a sense of independence and confers upon them powers to do things of which they may not have a clear idea at the time of saving the income.

(vi) *Motive of Enterprise*: Some individuals save so that they can speculate or carry out certain business projects.

(vii) *Motive of Pride*: Individuals have a natural desire to bequeath some assets for their descendants. Hence, they save and accumulate wealth to satisfy this motive.

(viii) *Motive of Avarice*: Some people save just because they are miser and have some natural inhibitions against spending.

---

16. J.M. Keynes, *Ibid*., p. 97.
17. J.M. Keynes, *Ibid*., pp. 107-108.

Keynes had also listed the comparable motives of consumption such as enjoyment, shortsightedness, generosity, Miscalculation and Extravagance. The economic research which followed the Keynesian revolution neglected these motives and was lacking in depth as far as the socio-psychological aspects of consumption and savings are concerned. Nevertheless, some of the motives indicated the direction which future research on the theory of consumption function might have taken. For example, the motives of improvement and significance of standard of living in saving behaviour becomes a cornerstone of the relative income hypothesis. The motives to bequeath a fortune to the descendants appears significantly in the life cycle formulations of saving behaviour. Keynes had also emphasized the importance of institutional and other social factors like education, population etc. as is evident in the following quotation from the general theory:

> "......the strength of all these motives will vary enormously according to the institutions and organization of the economic society which we presume, according to habits formed by race, education, convention, religion and current morals, according to present hopes and past experiences, according to the scale and technique of capital equipment, and according to the prevailing distribution of wealth and established standards of life."[18]

Keynes' theory as enunciated in the general theory and sketched above was not simplistic or one-sided. It emphasized the socio-cultural aspects as well as economic factors. Keynes' fundamental psychological law implied nothing more than that marginal propensity to consume was higher than the average propensity to consume. The early Keynesian writers ignored the qualifications Keynes had mentioned and adopted some simple version of the relationship between income and consumption. The simple 'Keynesian' formulation of consumption soon came into conflict with the observed facts. According to this version, the relationship between consumption and income (or between saving and income) is non-proportional and the relationship is postulated to be reversible in time. Though the earlier budget studies seem to confirm these conjectures, but the evidence from the time series data was found to

---

18. J.M. Keynes, *Ibid.*, p. 109.

be in conflict with the hypothesis. Firstly, if the relationship is claimed to be reversible then it must be possible to predict the future and past levels of consumption correctly. However, it was not possible to do so. The aggregate relation overestimates consumption if it is extrapolated back. Secondly, the empirical studies of saving done by Simon Kuznets and Goldsmith did not confirm the conjectures of hypothesis. Kuznets found that percentage of disposable income consumed had remained constant in the United States for a very long period (1867-1940) despite large growth in income. According to Kuznets estimates[19], the long run marginal propensity to consume ranged between 0.84 and 0.89 for different time periods between 1869-1940. The marginal propensity to consume in 1869-78 was 0.86, as well as for 1874-83. It was 0.85 for the year 1879-88 and declined a bit to 0.84 during 1889-98. For the period 1919-1928, he estimated the marginal propensity to consume to be 0.89. Raymond Goldsmith also calculated the long run marginal propensity to consume for the United States as 0.86 for the period 1897-1947 (excluding the such periods 1917-18 and 1942-45).[20] In this estimate Goldsmith used the consumption data which excluded the expenditure on consumer durables but included an estimate of the value of services rendered by the stock of durable goods.

The above findings have the following implications which are against the postulates of Absolute Income Hypothesis: (i) Intercept term does not exist in the saving function. (ii) The average propensity to consume and marginal propensity to consume do not decline with the increases in income as claimed by the *AIH*. Instead, they are constant. (iii) The marginal propensity to consume and average propensity to consume are equal to each other. The consumption function according to the *AIH* is

$$C = a + b\,Y \qquad ...(7.1)$$

where

C = Total consumption expenditure

19. Simon Kuznets, *Uses of National Income in Peace and War* (National Bureau of Economic Research), New York, 1942.

20. Raymond, W. Goldsmith, *A Study of Saving in the United States, Vol. III* (Princeton University Press) for the National Bureau of Economic Research: Princeton, N.J. 1956.

a = Intercept term

b = Marginal propensity to consume

Y = Real income.

Thus *APC* can be calculated as

$$\frac{C}{Y} = \frac{a}{Y} + b \qquad ...(7.2)$$

and *M.P.C.* can be calculated as

$$\frac{dC}{dY} = b. \qquad ...(7.3)$$

It is obvious to see that

$$APC > MPC$$

The consumption function implied by the empirical studies of Kuznets and Goldsmith is

$$C = b\,Y \qquad ...(7.4)$$

where $\dfrac{C}{Y} = b$

and $\dfrac{dC}{dY} = b$

or $\dfrac{C}{Y} = \dfrac{dC}{dY}$ or $APC = MPC$.

In other words, the consumption and income are proportional to each other and are not non-proportional as the AIH would have us believed. Moreover, the AIH also lacked the sound theoretical foundation. It did not investigate the relationship between consumption, saving, income and wealth. Once the role of saving in creating wealth was recognized, it would be imperative to include all these variables within a single theoretical model. In fact, all these variables interact with each other. Accumulated savings are nothing but additions to wealth which generate income, which in its own turn is used either for further consumption or to increase the level of savings, and so on. This phenomenon necessarily involves a temporal dimension which was not taken into account in the AIH formulation. Further theoretical breakthrough were required to do this.

On an empirical level, the researchers tried to resolve the conflicts between theoretical postulates and observed constancy of saving ratios and its proportionality with income by bringing in new explanatory variables into consumption function. Consumption of the previous year, possession of liquid assets by the households, interest rates, real assets, urbanization, population and its age composition were such variables which were used as independent variables in a regression of consumption upon income. Since most of these studies were empirical in nature, theoretical connections between these variables and saving behaviour were not very specific.

Relative Income Hypothesis

James Duesenberry's formulation of Relative Income Hypothesis (RIH) was one of the earliest attempts to resolve the differences between the predictions based upon the AIH and observed phenomena. Unlike the AIH, Duesenberry regards the consumption function as a reversible function. He begins with a critique of Keynesian consumption function which is based upon the assumptions (i) that every individual's consumption behaviour is independent of that of every other individual, and (ii) that consumption relations are reversible in time.[21] He builds his model around the following four assumptions:

(1) Physical needs and social culture require the consumption of certain goods.

(2) Each of the needs, whether physical or cultural, may be satisfied by a number of goods which are qualitatively different.

(3) Some of these goods are regarded superior and some as inferior.

(4) There is some scale of ranking of these goods which might be used for any specific purpose.[22]

Duesenberry argues that there is some basic drive to secure a higher standard of living in the western societies leading to higher consumption. "In a fundamental sense the basic source of the drive

21. *Ibid*., p. 1.

22. *Ibid*., p. 22.

toward higher consumption is to be found in the character of our culture."[23] He argues that introduction of new articles of consumption and the "demonstration effect" lead an individual to break his equilibrium and induce him to increase his expenditure on consumption. Duesenberry explains the demonstration effect in the following manner:

> ".........people believe that the consumption of high quality goods for any purpose is desirable and important. If they habitually use one set of goods, they can be made dissatisfied with them by a demonstration of the superiority of others. But more knowledge of the existence of superior goods is not a very effective habit breaker. Frequent contact with them may be. In this field it is not only true that "what you don't know won't hurt you" but that what you do know does hurt you."[24]

Through the operation of "demonstration effect" Duesenberry does away with the assumption of independent utilities which is implict in the AIH and introduce 'interdependence' in the utility function.[25] The utility function used by Duesenberry is

$$u_i = f_i\,(C_{i1}/R_1,\ C_{i2}/R_2,\ \ldots\ C_{in}/R_n,\ A_{i1}/R_1,\ \ldots A_{in}/R_n)$$

where u_i = utility function if ith individual.

C_{i1}..............C_{in} = Consumption of n goods by the individual i.

A_{i1}..............A_{in} = Values of n assets owned by the individual i.

$R_i = \Sigma a_{ij}\ C_j$ a weighted average of consumption expenditure of other individuals; a_{ij} is the weight applied to consumption of jth individual by ith individuals.

Using the above utility function Duesenberry formulated the RIH which has been summarized in the following propositions:

(1) "In periods of steadily rising income the aggregate saving ratio tends to be independent of income.

(2) The saving ratio will be affected by changes in interest rate, income expectations, the distribution of income, the rate of growth of income, and the ago distribution of population.

---

23. *Ibid.*, p. 26.
24. *Ibid.*, p. 27.
25. *Ibid.*, pp. 34-39.

(3) On balance, changes in these variables have not been sufficiently large to have had much effects on the saving ratio.

(4) Over the trade cycle the saving ratio is dependent on the ratio of current income to previous peak income."[26]

The aggregate saving function deduced by the RIH is

$$\frac{St}{Yt} = b\left(\frac{Yb}{Y_j}\right) + a \qquad ...(7.5)$$

where St = current saving, Y_t = current income. Y_j = previous peak income in case of time-series data. In case of cross-section data Y_j is income of other country or group.[27] A negative coefficient of b in the above equation would confirm the RIH. Thus, RIH was one of several attempts to reconcile the apparent inconsistencies of the AIH and to assert that consumers may not adjust their consumption (and hence savings) immediately and completely to the current level of income.

Duesenberry's RIH is criticised on the following issues.

1. The RIH assumes a proportional increase in consumption with increase in income.
2. This hypothesis assumes a direct relationship between consumption and income. But this may not happen every time.
3. This hypothesis assumes consumers' behaviour fully irreversible. But consumers' behaviour is slowly irreversible over time.
4. This hypothesis does not take into account other factors which influence consumers' expenditure such as asset holdings, urbanisation, age composition, the appearance of new consumer goods, etc.
5. The RIH assumes that consumers' preferences are interdependent and the consumer expenditure is related to his consumption pattern. But it is not always true.

---

26. *Ibid.*, p. 111.
27. D.B. Suits, "The Determinants of Consumer Expenditure: A Review of Present Knowledge", in D.B. Suits (ed.) *Impact of Monetary Policy*, Englewood Cliffs, N.J. Prentice Hall, p. 39.

The Permanent Income Hypothesis

Friedman's permanent income hypothesis (PIH) is considered somewhat like a breakthrough which has opened up new vistas of research on saving and consumption function.[28] The permanent income hypothesis (PIH) of Friedman is based on three fundamental tenets.

1. Friedman postulated that each household has some conception of his future expected income which is considered to be stable. This he calls permanent income. The actual income of the household (that is what is usually referred as income and termed by Friedman as measured income) may or may not coincide with the permanent income. The deviations between the measured income and permanent income are called the transitory income which may be either positive or negative. Thus we have the following identity:

$$Y_m = Y_p + Y_{tr} \qquad \text{...(7.6)}$$

which says that measured income is composed of permanent income and transitory income. The permanent income, according to Friedman, reflects "the effects of those factors that the unit regards as determining its capital value of wealth: the non-human wealth it owns, the personal attributes of earner in the unit such as their training, ability, personality, the attributes of the economic activity of the earners and so on. It is analogous to the "expected" value of a probability distribution.[29] Transitory component of income, on the other hand reflects the effects of 'chance' or 'accidental' factors which cause the measured income to rise or fall temporarily. For example, a person gets some extra income by winning a lottery ticket, or some windfall such as some unexpected rise in the prices of shares etc. The income earned through such windfall gains is purely temporary and the consumer recognises it to be such. So he will not base his consumption upon such transitory income as he would have to cut down his consumption as soon as the temporary effect disappears completely. Thus, it is more likely that consumer shall base his consumption (and therefore savings) upon what he regards his permanent income.

---

28. M. Friedman, *A Theory of Consumption Function* (1957), Indian Edition, Oxford & IBH Publishing House, New Delhi, 1970.

29. *Ibid*., p. 21.

Like income, measured consumption is also viewed as being composed of two elements—permanent consumption and transitory consumption:

$$C_m = C_p + C_{tr} \qquad ...(7.7)$$

Permanent income at a particular period is the product of two factors: w, the wealth of the consumer, which is estimated at discounted present value of a stream of future expected receipts and the rate, r at which these expected receipts are discounted.

Mathematically, $W = \sum_{t=1}^{n} \frac{y_t}{(1+r)^t}$

Therefore, where time, $t = 1, 2, ..., n$.

$$W = \frac{y_1}{1+r} + \frac{y_2}{(1+r)^2} + ... + \frac{y_{n-1}}{(1+r)^{n-1}} + \frac{y_n}{(1+r)^n}$$

For simple formulation,

Let $y_1 = y_2 = y_3 = ... = y_{n-1} = y_n = y$

$$\therefore W = \frac{y}{1+r} + \frac{y}{(1+r)^2} + ... + \frac{y}{(1+r)^{n-1}} + \frac{y}{(1+r)^n}$$

$$= \frac{y}{1+r}\left\{1 + \frac{1}{(1+r)} + \frac{1}{(1+r)^2} + ... + \frac{1}{(1+r)^{n-1}}\right\}$$

$$= \frac{y}{1+r}.1.\frac{1-\left(\frac{1}{1+r}\right)^n}{1-\frac{1}{1+r}}$$

$$\therefore n \to \infty$$

$$= \frac{y}{1+r}.\frac{1}{1-\frac{1}{1+r}}$$

$$\therefore \left(\frac{1}{1+r}\right)^n \to O \text{ as } r > 1$$

$$= \frac{y}{1+r}.\frac{(1+r)}{r}$$

$$\therefore W = \frac{y}{r}$$

Here y means permanent income.

Therefore, $y_p = rw$

2. Permanent consumption is a multiple, K of the permanent income. That is,

$$C_P = Ky_p \; [O < K \leq 1]$$

where K depends on i, w, u, i.e.,

$$K = f(i, w, u)$$

where, i = rate of interest, w= the ratio of human to non-human (physical) capital, and u = catch all variable. Hence, $C_p = Ky_p$ postulates a proportional relationship between permanent consumption and permanent income. The factor of proportionality is K.

3. Transitory income and permanent income, transitory consumption and permanent consumption, transitory consumption and transitory income are assumed to be uncorrelated.

That is $r(y_{tr}\ y_p) = r(C_{tr}\ C_P) = r(C_{tr}\ y_{tr}) = O$

where, r = coefficient of correlation.

As a result a consumer unit is assumed to be determined its standard of living on the basis of expected returns from its resources over its life time. This expected returns are assumed to be constant from time to time, though in actual practice, some fluctuation would result over time. Actual consumption and income deviate from the planned of permanent levels to the extent that transitory factors enter in.

From an empirical point of view this is a very difficult hypothesis to test but from the analytical point of view this is a very rich hypothesis. Under this hypothesis, the slope of the observed consumption function, $C = a + by$ can be shown to be equivalent to $b = K\ Py$ where Py is the ratio of variances of the permanent component of income (yp) to the total income (y), i.e.,

$$Py = \frac{\Sigma(y_p - \bar{y}_p)^2}{\Sigma(y - \bar{y})^2}$$

Since K is constant by assumption. This means that fluctuation in the slope of the measured income reflects the fluctuation in the permanent component of income.

The above version is regarded as a stricter version of PIH as it requires that marginal propensity to consume out of transitory income to be zero. However, several studies have reported positive but significantly different from zero marginal propensity to consume out of transitory income.[30] A rather mild version of PIH allows for marginal propensity to consume out of transitory income to be positive but it still requires that it must be less than the *MPC* out of permanent income.

The basic problem in the estimation of K is that being a 'theoretical construct' Y_p itself is unknown. In order to know K, it is imperative to estimate Y_P. For time-series data, permanent income can be viewed as a weighted average of present and past incomes. Friedman has given the following formula for estimation on permanent income.[31]

$$Y_p(T) = \beta \int_{-\infty}^{T} e^{(\beta-\alpha)(t-T)} \, Y(t)\, dt \qquad ...(7.15)$$

where β = coefficient of adjustment between measured income and permanent income.

α = Growth rate of income.

T = Present time period.

t = Index of time period.

$y(t)$ = Measured income at the time t.

---

30. J.G. Williamson, "Personal Savings in Developing Nations: An Inter-temporal cross-section from Asia." *Economic Record*, 44, (June 1968) pp. 198-210. Also see I. Friend and P. Taubman "The Aggregate Propensity to Save: Some Comparison and their Application to International Data" *Review of Economics and Statistics*, 48, (May 1948) pp. 113-123.
31. M. Friedman, *op. cit.*, p. 144.

The discrete analogue of the above formula is

$$Y_p(T) = \beta\left[Y_t + e^{(\beta-\alpha)}Y_{t-1} + e^{(\beta-\alpha)}Y_{t-2} + \ldots + e^{T(\beta-\alpha)}Y_{t-T}\right] \qquad \ldots(7.16)$$

The weights decline continuously. This means that higher weights are attached to present and more recent incomes and relatively lower weights are given to incomes of past periods.

The inverse of β is regarded as consumer's horizon, which is defined as the period required by the consumer to dichotomize the nature of abrupt and random changes. Friedman points out that the span of time which shall be relevant for calculation of permanent income depends upon the magnitude of β. If it is large, the discrepancy between measured income and expected income is removed at a rapid rate and the time span is shorter.[32] Conversely, a larger time span is required if β is small and thus rate of adjustment is low. For the United States, Friedman estimated the value of β to be 0.4 and the consumer horizon as 2½ years.[33] Williamson, in his study of saving function for a number of Asian countries also used a three year horizon.[34] Friend and Taubman also used three year horizon for pooled data from 22 developed and less developed countries.[35] The same practice was followed by Gupta in his study of per capita household saving in India.[36] Apparently it seems that these researchers have used a three year horizon simply because Friedman calculated the consumer horizon for close to three years in the United States. There is no reason why consumer horizon in developing countries which are so different not only in social and economic structures but also in behaviour pattern, has to be the same as in the advanced countries.

As pointed out earlier the forceful presentation of the PIH has been responsible for opening new vistas of research on consumption function. There has been a flood of research studies which have presented mixed types of evidences, sometimes supporting and

---

32. *Ibid.*, p. 144.
33. *Ibid.*, p. 147.
34. J.G. Williamson, *op. cit.*
35. I. Friend and P. Taubman, *op. cit.*
36. K.L. Gupta, "Personal Savings in Developing Nations: Further Evidence" *American Economic Review* 46, June 1970, pp. 243-49.

sometimes rejecting the PIH. The distribution of National Service Life Insurance in 1950 in the United States and restitution payment by Germany to Israel made it possible to test the PIH directly. On the basis of American data Bodkin argued that there is no significant difference between the marginal propensity to consume out of permanent income and marginal propensity to consume out of transitory income while he treated the payment of dividend as transitory income.[37] Thus Bodkin's finding did not provide any evidence in favour of the PIH. On the other hand, on the basis of Israeli experience, treating the restitute payment as transitory income, Kreinin presented evidence in support of the PIH.[38] Kreinin's results shows that there is a significant difference between the marginal propensities to consume out of permanent and transitory income, though the correlation between consumption and transitory income is not zero as claimed by the strict version of the hypothesis. Thus, it seems that strict version of the PIH postulating a zero marginal propensity to consume out of transitory income is not tenable. However, one could concede the PIH claim that marginal propensities to consume permanent and transitory income are significantly different from each other. Holbrook and Stafford have tried a general formulation of the PIH using three year panel data of a sample of United States families.[39] They distinguish five different types of income *viz.* husband's income, wife's income and other member's income, transfer income, mixed capital and labor income, and other income. They have concluded that marginal propensity to consume was significantly different in each case. Thus, the essence of PIH seems to be that (i) savings are proportional to income and (ii) propensities to consume for different types of income are different.

---

37. R.G. Bodkin, "Windfall Income and Consumption" *American Economic Review* 49, (September 1959), pp. 602-614.
38. M.E. Kreinin, "Windfall Income and Consumption" *American Economic Review* 51 (June, 1961) pp. 388-390.
39. R. Holbrook and F. Stafford. "The Propensity to Consume Separate Type of Income: A Generalized Permanent Income Hypothesis." *Econometrica* 39 (January, 1971), pp. 1-21.

Friedman's PIH has been criticised on following grounds.

1. PIH assumes that the coefficient of correlation between transitory component of consumption and transitory component of income is zero. This is not real. The natural behaviour of consumers is very much contrary. Suppose, a person who has gained a profit does not deposit the entire amount in the bank but spends a whole or part of it in his current consumption. Similary a person who has faced a loss does reduce or postpone his current consumption.

2. This hypothesis assumes that the APC of all families, whether they are rich or poor, is the same in the long run. But it is not practical. The consumption of the poor is higher relatively to their incomes while the saving of the rich is higher relatively to their incomes. Even consumption differs among the persons with same level of permanent income.

3. This hypothesis cannot make distinction between human and non-human wealth.

4. In this hypothesis, the concept of measured income creates confusion by bringing permanent and transitory components of income. Again, permanent and transitory components of consumption also create confusion.

The Life Cycle Hypothesis

The Life Cycle Hypothesis (LCH) is associated with the writings of Franco Modigliani, Richard Brumberg and Albert Ando.[40] The original formulation of LCH was in terms of cross-section analysis.[41] The LCH claims to maximize the utility function over life span subject to a wealth constraint. It has been assumed that individuals derive utility only from present and future consumption and from the assets which he wants to bequeath. It is noteworthy that

40. F. Modigliani & R. Brumberg, "Utility Analysis and the Consumption Function: An Interpretation of Cross-section Data" in K.K. Kurihara (ed.) *Post-Keynesian Economics*, London. (1955) Allen and Unwin, pp. 338-436. A. Ando and F. Modigliani "The Life Cycle Hypothesis of Savings : Aggregate Implications and Tests", *American Economic Review*, Vol. 53 (1963), pp. 54-82; E. Modigliani and A. Ando "Test of Life Cycle Hypothesis of Saving" *Bulletin of Oxford University Institute of Economics and Statistics*, Vol. 19 (May 1957), pp. 99-124.

41. See Modigliani & Brumberg, (1955) *op. cit.*

individual's utility function depends upon his own consumption. This utility function is maximized subject to the resources available to him. The resources of an individual are sum total of his current and discounted future earnings over his lifetime and his current net worth. Thus an individual's consumption is given as follows:

$$C_T = f\,(V_t,\ t,\ T)\ T = t,\ 1 + t,\ \ldots\ldots\ldots\ldots,\ L$$

$$V_t = \sum_{T=1}^{N} \frac{Yt}{(1+r)\ T+1-t} + a_t \qquad \ldots(7.17)$$

C_T = Consumption r = discount rate.

T = index of time. N = earning span.

t = Present age.

L = Life span.

Y = Income.

a_t = asset at time t.

Thus an individual's consumption is a function of his current income and future income (which in fact depends upon the rate of return on capital) with parameters depending upon age. The individual consumption function obtained above is then aggregated to get community's consumption function.

The LCH also implies that proportion of income saved is essentially independent of income. Thus proportionality hypothesis of the RIH and PIH is confirmed while AIH is rejected. Furthermore, LCH maintains that proportion of income saved would depend upon the age-composition of the saver and his earning span. Thus, it brings age composition and family size as determinant of saving behaviour. Yotopoulos and Nugent have very cogently summarized the LCH position on this issue:

> "The life cycle hypothesis is cast in terms of an individual household member, with each member's consumption flow equalized through life. Savings, however, are measured per family and saving ratios are expressed as a proportion of income. Family incomes are observed to follow roughly parabolic paths over the earning span, rising sharply to a peak in the 35-54 age range and declining thereafter. Family size is also correlated with household age, reaching a peak at ages 35-44 and declining thereafter as children

establish their own households. As a result of these two forces, income per household member reaches a low at ages 35-44 and rises thereafter. After considering the age-of-household correlates of income and family size, equalization of consumption per household member would predict that average savings as a proportion of family income are high in the age group 45-64 and low in the age group 25-44 and at retirement."[42]

There have not been several attempts to test the LCH for developing countries, with two notable exceptions. Landsberger applied the LCH type model to Isreal.[43] He estimated the linear consumption function which discriminates between different age-groups of head of households. He took family consumption, family current income, windfall income and the age of the head of family as key variables. Regression equations were estimated for four age groups and for two types of consumption (consumer durables and non-durables) for two time periods. Landsberger wanted to investigate whether marginal propensity to consume changes with age. His results indicated that marginal propensity to consume increased with age for five out of the eight pairs. These were the only pairs for which the estimated parameters were statistically significant.

Kelley and Williamson have made an attempt to test the applicability of LCH formulation to Indonesia. They had cross-section data of 490 families collected through a sample survey in Jogjakarta region in Indonesia. Kelley and Williamson regressed per capita household saving against per capita household income for five household age groups, using the following equation:

$$S_h/N = + b(Yd/N) \qquad ...(7.19)$$

where S_h = household saving. N = Family size

Y_d = disposable income.

42. P.A. Yotopoulos and J.B. Nugent, *Economics of Development: Empirical Investigations* (1976) Harper & Row, New York, pp. 177-178.

43. M. Landsberger "The Life Cycle Hypothesis: A Reinterpretation and Empirical Test", *American Economic Review* (March 1970), pp. 175-88.

Statistically significant results were obtained for all but the 40-49 age group; estimated values of *b* the youngest group (20-29) to 0.599 for the oldest group (60-69). For the rural households they estimated marginal propensity to save increased from 0.133 in the age group 20-29 to 0.75 in the age group 60-69. Thus LCH formulation was considered to be confirmed by the data.[44]

The life cycle hypothesis has been criticised on the following reasons.

1. The consumers, generally, do not always make plan for their expenditure on consumption over their life time. They stress more concentration on present consumption rather than on future consumption.

2. This hypothesis pre-supposes that consumption is directly related to the assets possessed by the individual. Consumption increases with the increase in asset holding and vice versa.

3. Consumption also depends upon individual's attitude towards life. Two persons having same income and assets may not consume same, i.e. one may consume more than the other.

44. A.C. Kelly and J.G. Williamson, "Household Saving Behaviour in the Developing Economics: The Indonesian Case," *Economic Development and Cultural Changes*, Vol. 16, No. 3 (April 1968), pp. 385-403.

Marginal Efficiency of Capital

8

ITS MEANING

The word 'efficiency' in the term "marginal efficiency of capital" represents the earning power, or rate of return over cost or profitability, of a capital asset. The marginal efficiency of a particular type of capital asset is the highest rate of return over cost expected from an additional, or marginal unit of that asset. The marginal efficiency of capital in general is the highest rate of return over cost expected from producing an additional, or marginal unit of the most profitable of all types of capital assets. Any available investment opportunity would be utilised so long as the expected rate of return over cost exceeds the rate of interest. Since the marginal efficiency of capital refers to the expected rate, rather than the current rate, of profit, it is liable to great fluctuations in the short run.

While deciding to make investment, the businessmen compare the expected rates of net return over the entire life of the capital asset with its supply price or the "replacement cost". If the former exceeds the latter the businessman will make investment, otherwise not. The prospective yield of a capital asset is what a businessman expects to obtain from selling the output resulting from that asset. These yields are in the form of a flow of money income over a period of time. If the total expected life of the new capital asset is divided into a series of periods, say years, the annual return may be referred to as a series of annuities represented by Q_1, Q_2, Q_3 where subscripts refer to the years of the respective annuities. If the values of Q's are estimated and if the cost of production of the asset which yields these returns is known, comparison of the expected returns with the cost gives the rate or ratio known as the marginal efficiency of capital. In other words, marginal efficiency of capital refers to the rate of discount at which the prospective yield of an asset is discounted so as to make it just equal to the supply price of the asset. Keynes[1] states, "More precisely, I define marginal efficiency of capital as being equal to the rate of discount which would make the present value of the series of annuities given by the return expected from the capital asset during its life just equal to its supply price." This definition can be expressed as below:

Supply price = Discounted Prospective Yields

$$C_R = \frac{Q_1}{1+r} + \frac{Q_2}{(1+r)^2} + \frac{Q_3}{(1+r)^3} + \ldots + \frac{Q_n}{(a+r)^n}$$

where C_R represents the supply price or replacement cost of the new capital asset; Q's indicate the prospective yields in the various years 1, 2, 3,...,*n*; and *r* stands for the rate of discount which will make the present value of the series of annual returns just equal to the supply price of the capital asset. Let us illustrate this with the help of a numerical example. Suppose the prospective annual yields from the use of the new capital asset having a life of only three years are as follows:

First year	Second year	Third year
Rs. 150	Rs. 100	Rs. 50

Further suppose the current supply price or the replacement cost of the capital asset is Rs. 264.30. Now, 8 per cent would be the unique rate of discount which will equate the sum of the discount values of the prospective annual yields to the current supply price of the capital asset because

$$\text{Rs. } 264.30 = \frac{\text{Rs. } 150}{1.08} + \frac{\text{Rs. } 100}{(1.08)^2} + \frac{\text{Rs. } 50}{(1.08)^3}$$

In actual practice, it is very difficult to correctly estimate the expected return from a capital asset over its life time. Not only that, it is difficult to precisely estimate even the life of the capital asset. At best we can perhaps do not better than just guess "An estimate of what an investment will earn in five, ten or twenty years hence is based largely on guess work, on animal spirits, on adapting estimates to the average estimate, which in turn, is based on

1. J.M. Keynes, *The General Theory of Employment, Interest and Money* (New York, 1936), p. 135.

uninformed guesses."[2] Further the values of the Q's are not necessarily equal in all years, as assumed in our algebraic formulation stated above, except in a static society. In a dynamic world it is only by the rates accident that may one of them would turn out to be identical with some other.

If 8 per cent is the highest rate of return expected on any newly produced capital asset, it is the marginal efficiency of a capital in general. Since the marginal efficiency of capital is expressed as a certain per cent per year, it can be directly compared with the rate of interest. In the above example, if the rate of interest on money is less than 8 per cent, it would be more profitable to construct the new capital asset in question than to lend money at interest or to buy an old capital asset of that type. People who can obtain money at less than 8 per cent would make a profit by borrowing and constructing such assets. The market value of an asset which promises to yield Rs. 150 at the end of one year, Rs. 100 at the end of second year and Rs. 50 at the end of third year would be greater than Rs. 264.30, if the rate of interest is less than 8 per cent. If the market rate of interest, for example, is 5 per cent, the capital asset in question will have a present value of

$$\frac{\text{Rs. } 150}{1.05} + \frac{\text{Rs. } 100}{(1.05)^2} + \frac{\text{Rs. } 500}{(1.05)^3} = 276.70$$

This is what Kenyes calls the demand price, in contrast with the supply price, of a capital asset. The demand price of any asset is defined as the sum of the expected future yields discounted at the current rate of interest. In contrast, the supply price is the sum of prospective yields discounted by the marginal efficiency of capital.

The greater would be the demand price, the lower the rate of interest at which it is discounted. The lower the rate of interest, therefore, the larger will be the number of capital assets for which the demand price will exceed the supply price and the higher will be the rate of investment in new capital assets.

The market value of a capital asset cannot, however, be determined from a knowledge of the marginal efficiency of capital.

---

2. Seymour E. Harris, "Ten Years After: What Remains of the *General Theory*" in Seymour E. Harris (Ed.), *The New Economics* (London, 1948), p. 50.

Nor can the rate of interest be deducted from the marginal efficiency of capital. Before the present market value of an asset can be worked out, the rate of interest must be determined independently from a knowledge of the quantity of money and the state of liquidity preference. The rate of interest as well as the marginal efficiency of capital must be known before the volume of investment can be determined. These two rates are determined independently of one another. The marginal efficiency of capital is determined by the supply price and the prospective yields of assets while the rate of interest depends upon the schedule of liquidity preference and the quantity of money in circulation. There is a sense, however, in which the marginal efficiency of capital adjusts to the rate of interest rather than the other way round. Changes in the quantum of investment directly affect the marginal efficiency of capital but not the rate of interest, and it is changes in the quantum of investment which bring the two rates to equality.

INVESTMENT DEMAND SCHEDULE

The different marginal efficiencies of capital at different levels of investment in a certain type of capital asset during a particular period can be represented in the form of a schedule. A curve representing such a schedule would take the shape of an ordinary demand curve slanting down towards right which indicates that as the investment in a certain type of capital asset during a particular period increases, its marginal efficiency decline. Keynes mentions two reasons for this:

> If there is an increased investment in any given type of capital during any period of time, the marginal efficiency of that type of capital will diminish as the investment in it is increased, partly because the prospective yield will fall as the supply of that type of capital is increased and partly because, as a rule, pressure on the facilities for producing that type of capital will cause its supply price to increase;....[3]

An aggregate of demand schedules for all different types of capital would give us a schedule relating the rate of aggregate investment to the corresponding marginal efficiency of capital in general which is also known as the investment demand schedule.

---

3. J.M. Keynes, *The General Theory of Employment, Interest and Money* (London, 1936), p. 136.

The position and shape of the investment demand schedule is of great importance in determining the volume of employment because it shows the extent to which the amount of investment will vary in response to changes in the rate of interest. The greater the elasticity of the schedule of the marginal efficiency of capital, the larger will be the increase in investment in response to a given decline in the rate of interest. Similarly, the smaller the elasticity of the marginal efficiency of capital, the smaller will be the increase in investment in response to a given decline in the rate of interest. The position and shape of the investment demand schedule depends upon many complex factors which are subject to different estimation by each entrepreneur and to frequent revision. It is, however, not impossible to draw an approximate schedule of the marginal efficiency for particular industries and for the economy as a whole at any given time. Experience shows that the schedule of the marginal efficiency of capital has a tendency to be less elastic rather than being more elastic. The variations in the rate of interest, therefore, do not much affect the flow of new investment. Much more important in this respect are the dynamic forces of growth and technological progress.

INVESTMENT

Marginal Efficiency of Capital and Rate of Interest

Income and employment in the Keynesian world are determined by mainly two factors: Consumption and Investment. By investment Keynes means new investment. When price of shares, capital, stocks, etc. are rising, original investment may show a higher monetary value—this should not be taken as additional investment. To the classical economist, investment is determined by two factors: marginal productivity of capital (MPC) and interest rate.

MPC is the actual marginal yield of investment. But Keynes is rightly of the view that the actual yield of investment takes place only when investment has been made and it has started yielding productivity. So MPC cannot determine factor of investment. The investment decision is based not on actual yield of investment but on the expected yield and the market rate of interest.

Keynes is right from the beginning of the view that expectation plays a major role in the case of investment decision. Based upon expectation, he modifies the classical conception that determines investment demand. In place of MPC, marginal efficiency of capital (MEC) is substituted. The MEC is the ratio of the expected yields or returns from an income-yielding capital asset to the supply price or replacement cost of this capital asset.

Keynes defines, "The MEC as being equal to that rate of discount which would make the present value of the series of annuities given by the returns expected from the capital asset during its life just equal to its supply price." Supply price may be determined by the following formula:

$$C_R = \frac{Q_1}{1+r} + \frac{Q_2}{(1+r)^2} + \frac{Q_3}{(1+r)^3} + \ldots + \frac{Q_n}{(1+r)^n}$$

Where Q_1, Q_2, Q_3, ..., Q_n are series of prospective or expected annual returns or prospective yields, C_R is supply price or replacement cost, i.e. C_R indicates the price which the seller of the machine wants to charge as price by selling the machine. r is the rate of discount which will equate the present value of the prospective annual returns to the cost of capital goods. In other words, r is the marginal efficiency of capital (Keynes) or the rate of returns over cost (Fisher).

Let us now introduce the concept of demand price of investment. Let v stands for the value of capital goods or demand price, i be the market rate of interest.

Then, $$V = \frac{Q_1}{1+i} + \frac{Q_2}{(1+i)^2} + \frac{Q_3}{(1+i)^3} + \ldots + \frac{Q_n}{(1+i)^n}$$

Keynes compares MEC, r with the market rate of interest, i to find out whether a particular investment is profitable or not.

In order to make investment profitable we have to get $V > C_R$ which shows $i < r$. On the other hand if $i > r$, $V < C_R$ making investment unprofitable. In other words, given the objective of profit maximisation, an investor will increase the amount of investment so long as MEC > the current rate of interest. So, equalibrium amount of investment will be determined at the point where the MEC equals the rate of interest ($r = i$) indicating the equality between the demand price and the supply price of capital ($C_R = V$). Therefore, as long as the MEC is greater than the rate of interest the investor will invest till the MEC and rate of interest get equalised. In order to understand the relationship between the MEC and the rate of interest, a table given below is discussed.

MEC (%)	Rate of Interest (%)	Effect on Investment
5	4	Favourable
4	4	Neutral
3	4	unfavourable

In the first case, MEC > rate of interest implies that the effect of investment is favourable and the investor will go for new investment. In the second case, MEC = rate of interest shows that the effect of investment would be neutral. In this case the investors will not go for new investment. In the third case, MEC < rate of interest depicts that the effect of investment is unfavourable and the investors would clearly suffer loss if they go for new investment.

According to Keynes, MEC and the amount of new investment are inversely related. There are two main reasons for such inverse relationship: (i) As the amount of new investment increases, the 'prospective yields' from this capital decrease. Because as the production increases with increased investment, the product prices may be decreased. (ii) As the input price increases due to increased demand for investment, the prospective yields from the capital asset decline. Besides these two factors, there is another important factor which makes inverse relationship between the MEC and investment. The MEC or the expected rate of yield is based on subjective calculation, but the rate of interest is the actual cost of borrowing fund. Hence, greater the amount of investment, the greater may be amount of loss if things do not happen in accordance with expectation. Therefore, the investor has to take risk for increasing investment. As investment increases, the risk would also increase. This increasing risk will make the MEC fall. The relationship between investment and rate of interest is shown in figure 8.1.

In this figure it is seen that when investment in capital asset is equal to OI_1, *MEC* is r_1. When the investment is increased to OI_2, *MEC* is r_2. Likewise, when investment rises to OI_3, *MEC* is r_3. That is, as investment increases, *MEC* decreases. Hence, inducement to invest depends upon the *MEC* and the rate of interest. Now what will be the equilibrium level of investment when the rate of interest and *MEC* curve are given. In this figure, both rate of interest and *MEC* are shown along the *Y-axis*.

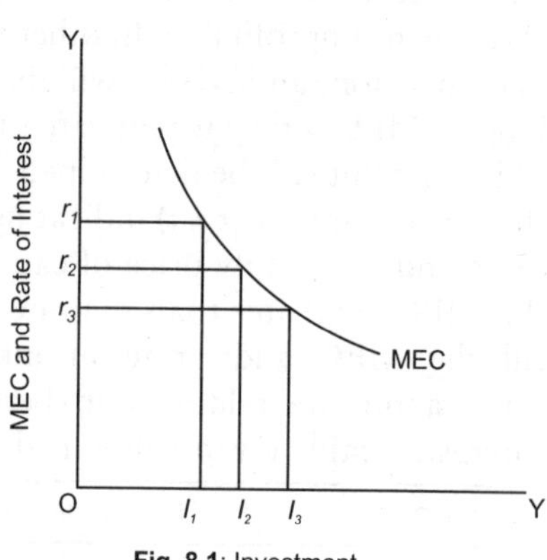

Fig. 8.1: Investment

The equilibrium level of investment will be established at the point where *MEC* equals to the current rate of interest. Thus, if the rate of interest is r_1, then I_1 investment will be undertaken. Hence, at OI_1 level of investment *MEC* is equal to the rate of interest. If the rate of interest falls to r_2, investment will rise to I_2 since at OI_2 level of investment the new rate of interest is equal to *MEC*. Thus, *MEC* curve shows the demand for investment at various rates of interest. Hence *MEC* curve represents the investment demand curve.

SHORT-RUN FACTORS AFFECTING MEC

The marginal efficiency of capital is influenced by a number of short-run as well as long-run factors. Among the former type of factors, the important are mentioned below:

1. Nature of Demand, Prices and Costs: A businessman's expectations about the rate of return from any given investment will decline if costs are expected to rise, or if prices and demand are likely to fall in the future. In contrast, MEC, will rise if the entrepreneurs expect a decline in costs, rise in prices, increase in demand or a combination of these.

2. Propensity to consume: Short-run upward shifts in the propensity to consume have favourable effects on the MEC because the demand for capital goods is, at least, partly derived from the demand for consumer goods.

3. Changes in Liquid Assets: An entrepreneur possessing a large volume of liquid assets and of different types is in a more favourable position to take advantage of any investment opportunity that comes his way. On the other hand, if his assets are not liquid, he will find it difficult to undertake new investment for exploiting such an opportunity.

4. Changes in Income: The marginal efficiency of capital is influenced by sudden changes in income caused by windfall profits or losses, tax concessions or levies. It will be affected favourably by a rise in income and unfavourably by a decline in income.

5. Current State of Expenditure: The business expectations are considerably influenced by the prevailing rate of return on investment. Entrepreneurs often invest on the assumption that the current state of affairs will continue indefinitely. It is not possible to base expectations and hence investment on the future course of events which are so uncertain. Current expectations thus have an important influence on investment.

6. Waves of Optimism and Pessimism: The marginal efficiency of capital is considerably influenced by the waves of optimism and pessimism. During periods of optimism, rates of return on future investment are unduly over-estimated while during periods of pessimism they are badly underestimated.

LONG-RUN INFLUENCES ON MEC

Following may be mentioned among the important factors which influence the marginal efficiency of capital in the long run.

1. Population: A high rate of population growth stimulates investments because the basic requirements of a growing population require larger investments in fields like public utility services, residential buildings and consumer goods industries particularly those producing necessaries of life.

2. Techniques of Production: Introduction of new techniques of production, particularly those of a capital-intensive nature and those which lower the cost of production, give rise to huge investments. Great technical progress in the manufacture of steel, cars, rubber, glass, textiles, electrical goods etc. has substantially expanded the market for these goods which has resulted in large amount of investment.

3. Supply of Capital Equipment: The effects of population growth, expansion of territories and markets and improvements in the techniques of production, depend upon the existing supply of capital equipment. To the extent the existing plant and machinery are adequate to meet the increased demand resulting from the above mentioned factors, the new or induced investment will not occur. In contrast, if there exists no unutilised capacity, such factors would lead to an increase in investment.

EXPECTATION AND MARGINAL EFFICIENCY OF CAPITAL

The marginal efficiency of capital, as we have seen, depends upon the supply price or costs and the prospective yield or return. The prospective yield is the most important factor responsible for the unstable nature of the marginal efficiency of capital. The expectations of prospective yield are based partly on the existing events which can be more or less ascertained and partly on future facts which cannot be anticipated with confidence. It is because of the uncertain events on which the prospective yields primarily depend that the marginal efficiency of capital is so unstable. The unstable economic behaviour under capitalism is mainly attributable to the unstable nature of prospective yields from capital assets. The investment decisions are governed by expected yields and not by actual yields.

A prospective yield is what an entrepreneur expects to obtain from selling the output of his capital assets. In regard to the yields of assets, there are two types of expectations *viz.* (1) short-term expectations and (2) long-term expectations. Short-term expectations relate to sales proceeds from the output of existing plant. In such expectations, the size of the plant is assumed to be fixed and only the output from it is variable. The long-term expectations, in contrast, relate to sales proceeds from variations in the size of the plant or from the installation of an entirely new plant. In the long-term expectations, the size of the plant as well as the amount of output from it are variable.

SHORT-TERM EXPECTATIONS

Short-term expectations are more stable than the long-term expectations because the realised results of the recent past are a relatively safe guide to what will happen in the near future. In contrast, the past experience cannot serve as a sufficiently reliable guide to what will happen in the distant future. In case of short-term expectations, there is a high degree of continuity because most of the conditions which affect current output remain more or less the same from day to day, from week to week, and from month to month. In the absence of definite evidence for expecting a change, the most recent events may be expected, to continue in the near future. Short-term expectations can be checked in the light of realised results. Since realised results are a fairly good guide to the near future, it is not very unsafe to substitute them for expectations pertaining to the near future. The short-term expectations are relatively stable and, therefore, are unable to explain fluctuations in investment.

LONG-TERM EXPECTATIONS

Long-term expectations regarding future yields, in contrast to short-term expectations, are highly unstable and, therefore, more important in explaining the fluctuations in aggregate investment and aggregate employment in the economic system. While it may be safe to assume that the economic activity next day or next week or next month will be more or less what it was during the previous day, or previous week, or previous month, experience warns us against assuming that the next three or four years will be like the past three or four years because the realised results of the past are not a reliable guide for the future.

There are, however, some factors affecting long-term considerations which do not depend upon uncertain things. Decisions to invest are partly based on facts regarding the existing stock of capital assets. The decision to build a new cotton textile mill, for instance, partly depends upon the existing total production capacity which is a fact and can be ascertained without much difficulty. Similarly, the power of the existing capacity to cope up with the existing demand at the prevailing prices are data of a more or less definite nature. But as we try to look into the distant future, the horizon becomes more clouded. The probable life and maintenance of the plant cannot be accurately predicted. Still less predictable are factors like possible changes in technology in the cotton textile industry which would govern the rate of obsolescence of the contemplated plant. There prevails uncertainty in regard to factors like level of effective demand twelve or fourteen years hence, the amount of new competition, the prices which would prevail from year to year, the possibility of war, the size of the export market, changes in tax burdens, conditions in the labour market, political climate in future years which will influence the extent of social control over industry etc. There is no probability calculus upon which to base scientific judgments in regard to such factors. The distant future can never be seen clearly. This is particularly so when entrepreneurial decisions are made by a large number of private entrepreneurs whose decisions are uncoordinated. The extremely uncertain conditions under which long-term expectations are formed result in great instability in the economic system. Long-terrn expectations are subject to sudden revisions. Periods of feverish investment activity tens to be followed by periods of extreme pessimism and depression in which investment in durable capital assets declines to very low levels. To quote Keynes:

> The outstanding fact is the extreme precariousness of the basis of knowledge on which our estimates of protective yield have to be made. Our knowledge of the factors which will govern the yield of an investment some years hence is

> usually very slight and often negligible. If we speak frankly, we have to admit that our basis of knowledge for estimating the yield ten years hence of railway, a copper mine, a textile factory, the goodwill of a patent medicine, an Atlantic liner, a building in the City of London amounts to little and sometimes to nothing or even five years hence. In fact, those who seriously attempt to make any such estimate are often so much in the minority that their behaviour does not govern the market.[4]

CRITICISM OF M.E.C.

Keynes' concept of marginal efficiency of capital has been severely criticised on a number of counts. Saulnier points out that marginal efficiency of capital cannot be used as an analytical tool without presupposing a whole structure of distribution theory which enables us to distinguish between and evaluate the contributions of different productive factors.[5] Keynes did not pay adequate attention to this conceptual difficulty. Further, Keynes assumes the existence of perfect competition in the market and does not consider the qualifications necessary for an imperfectly competitive market. Moreover, Keynes' analysis of investment function is related to the rate of interest and the marginal efficiency of capital because he assumed that wages are equal to the marginal productivity of labour. But if this assumption is dropped the wage rate becomes a more important element in the theory.

Keynes' concept refers to the marginal efficiency of capital as a whole. Saulnier believes, however, that the most illuminating data for economic analysis are those relating to the expected returns on capital investment in different sectors of the economy. This has special significance in a market characterised by imperfect competition.[6]

Saulnier further points out that the Keynesian analysis does not contain an adequate explanation regarding the determination of the shape of the aggregate investment demand schedule. It does not

4. J.M. Keynes, *The General Theory of Employment, Interest and Money* (London, 1936), pp. 149-50.
5. R.J. Saulnier, *Contemporary Monetary Theory* (New York, 1947), pp. 340-41.
6. *Ibid*., p. 341.

explain variations in the productivity of capital with consideration of certain problems involved therein, such as: how will the MEC change if all other factors, besides the quantity of capital, are held constant? How will the MEC vary if, along with the variation of the quantity of capital, the labour is increasing in quantity and improving in quality, if new and more productive natural resource are being opened up, and if improved techniques of production are being introduced? Further, the Keynesian analysis does not discuss the 'economies' or 'diseconomies' which are likely to influence the shape of the investment demand schedule.[7] Saulnier concludes that Keynes' analysis is not complete, nor it provides a satisfactory explanation of the factors which determine the productivity of capital.

Prof. Hazlitt points out that Keynes uses the term 'marginal efficiency of capital' in so many different senses that it is difficult, if not impossible, to keep track of them. He fails to stick to any fixed meaning of the term and plays fast and loose with it. The ambiguities and bad reasoning that Keynes fell into could have been avoided if he had dropped this term altogether and used instead anyone of half dozen different terms then in use. Among the terms then in use like the marginal productivity, yield or utility or efficiency of capital, Keynes uses the vaguest among them, that is, efficiency of capital.

Keynes fails to recognise that interest rate is no less influenced by expectations than the marginal efficiency of capital. In other words, Keynes includes the marginal efficiency of capital in the realm of dynamic economics and the rate of interest in the realm of static economics. There is no justification for this assumption, nor does it correspond to real economic facts. Acceptance of this assumption would imply that entrepreneurs are influenced by their expectations but the lenders are not influenced by those, for which there is no justification.

CONTROL OF FLUCTUATIONS IN INVESTMENT

The precarious nature of long-term expectations, as we have seen, leads to so great instability in the marginal efficiency of capital as cannot be counteracted by any practical change in the rate of interest. This leads to violent fluctuations in private investment. Keynes, therefore, felt that it would not be safe to leave entire investment in the hands of private entrepreneurs who are guided by

7. *Ibid.*, p. 342.

the marginal efficiency of capital or the expected rate of profit. The state, which is in a better position than private enterprise to calculate long-term needs in terms of general social advantage, should shoulder greater responsibility for directly organising investment. In other words, Keynes believed in the "socialisation" of investment to control fluctuations in the marginal efficiency of capital. Keynes, however, was never in favour of complete nationalisation of investment. What he advocated, in fact, was just supplementing private investment with public investment.

Rate of Interest

9

INTRODUCTION

Rate of interest is one of the important determinants of investment and hence of income, output and employment. It is one of the weapons in the hands of central banking authorities to fight problems of inflation, deflation and business fluctuations. It has also considerable influence on the rate of capital formation and hence on the rate of economic growth. A proper understanding of how the rate of interest is determined is, therefore, of vital importance.

THEORIES OF INTEREST

The important theories explaining the determination of the rate of interest are: (1) Classical or Real Theory, (2) Loanable Funds or Neo-classical Theory, and (3) Liquidity Preference or Keynesian Theory. All these theories attempt to explain the determination of the rate of interest through the equilibrium between the forces of demand and supply. In other words, in all these theories, rate of interest is the mechanism which brings about an equilibrium between demand and supply. The difference among these theories lies in the answer to the question: demand for what and supply of what? According to the Classical Theory, the rate of interest is determined by the demand for and supply of savings. Loanable Funds Theory states that the rate of interest is determined by the demand for and supply of loanable funds. In addition to current savings loanable funds also consist of dishoarding, bank credit and disinvestment. Keynesian Theory of Interest explains the determination of the rate of interest through the equilibrium between demand for money (*i.e.* liquidity preference) and the supply of money. Let us briefly examine these theories one by one.

CLASSICAL THEORY

The theory of rate of interest as propounded by classical economists like Ricardo, Marshall and Pigou is known as the classical theory of the rate of interest. Cassel, Walras, Carver, Taussig and Prof. Knight also subscribed to this theory. According to this theory, the rate of interest is determined by the demand for saving to invest in capital goods and the supply of savings under free and perfect competition.

The demand for savings arises from those who desire to invest, that is, to purchase or make new capital goods. Capital goods are demanded because they are helpful in the production of consumption goods or, in other words, because they have a revenue productivity like other factors. Since capital is scarce, it is subject to alternative uses and is first put to the most productive use. As the amount of capital increases, additional units of capital are put to less productive uses. In other words, as the amount of capital increases, its marginal productivity tends to decline. An individual producer will push his investment of capital up to the point where the marginal productivity of capital equals the prevailing rate of interest. Thus the producers would use more capital at lower rates of interest and less capital at higher rates of interest. The demand curve for capital, therefore, slopes down towards the right.

The supply of capital depends upon a number of psychological and institutional factors which are generally grouped under "will to save" and "power to save". Those who make savings available have to postpone consumption of a part of their income. In other words, saving involves an element of waiting. But people prefer present enjoyment of goods and services to future enjoyment of those. If people are to be persuaded to save money and lend it to entrepreneurs, therefore, they must be offered some interest as reward. In other words, to make people to overcome their time preference, inducement must be offered in the form of interest. The larger the savings people make, the larger the consumption they will have to postpone, the greater must be the rate of interest they will ask to make such a postponement worthwhile. Thus to induce people to save more, a higher rate of interest must be offered. A higher rate of interest will also have to be paid if savings are to come from those persons whose rates of time-preference are relatively more strongly weighed in favour of present satisfactions. The supply curve of capital will, therefore, slope upward to the right.

Senior stated the theory in terms of abstinence. Saving was an act of abstaining from consumption. Since to abstain was painful, it was essential to reward people for this act. The idea of abstinence was, however, widely criticised on the ground that it suggested positive discomfort while the rich people, who are the main source of capital, save without the least inconvenience. To avoid this criticism, Marshall and Cassel explained the theory in terms of waiting. Bohm Bawerk and Irving Fisher developed the premium theory of interest. According to them, because people prefer present goods to future goods, there is a premium on present goods.

The demand for capital is identical with the investment demand function while the supply of capital is identical with the saving supply function. Thus, in the classical theory, an investment function is a downward sloping function of the rate of interest, i.e., investment increases with fall in interest rate and a saving function which is an upward rising function of the rate of interest, i.e. saving increases with rise in the rate of interest. The rate of interest, at which saving and investment is equal, is called natural rate of interest or the real rate of interest or the equilibrium rate of interest. In the classical theory, we get a saving function,

$S + f(r)$, and $\frac{dS}{dr} > O$ and an investment function, $I=g(r)$ and $\frac{dI}{dr} < O$. The equilibrium condition requires, $S=I$. There are three unknowns (S, I and r) in these three equations. We can find out the values of these three unknowns solving these three equations. The classical theory of interest rate can be explained with the help of following diagram (Fig. 9.1). In this diagram, we plot saving and investment along the *X-axis* and the rate of interest along the *Y-axis*. The saving supply curve *SS* is a positively sloping, *i.e.* upward rising curve while the investment demand curve *II* is

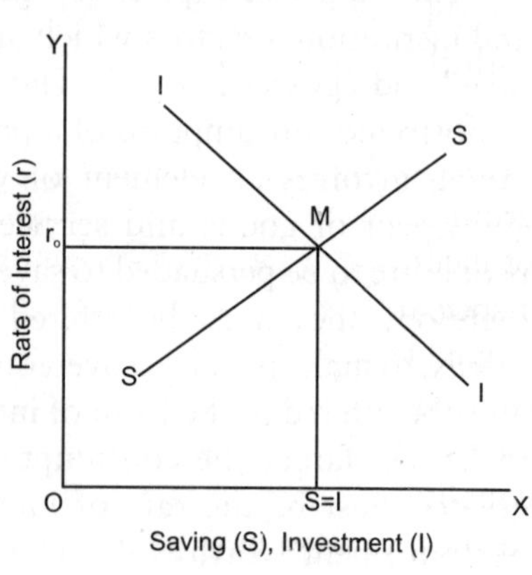

Fig. 9.1

negatively, *i.e.* downward sloping curve. They intersect at point *M* where the rate of interest is $O\ r_o$ and the saving supply equals to investment demand. $O\ r_o$ is the natural rate of interest or the equilibrium rate of interest, which will come to stay in the capital market. The market rate of interest is regarded as fluctuating around this long-run equilibrium rate of interest.

The classical theory of the rate of interest has three important features. First, it is a purely flow theory, because saving and investment variables which determine the rate of interest are the flow quantities as distinct from the stock quantities per period of time.

Secondly, both saving and investment are the real variables as distinct from the monetary variables. The rate of interest is a real phenomenon. It is not determined by the quantity of money in circulation. Money acts only as a mediating agent. Any change in the money supply in the economy is neutralised by equi-proportionate change in prices keeping the real quantity of money unchanged. Consequently, if the money supply changes, the rate of interest remains unaffected.

Thirdly, if the equilibrium between saving and investment is disturbed due to a shift in one of the functions, it is re-established through changes in the rate of interest without affecting any other variable. Hence, this theory is self-contained and is not connected with the monetary sector in the economy.

Criticism of Classical Theory of Interest Rate: The classical theory of interest was sharply criticised by Keynes on a number of grounds. In the first place, this theory neglects changes in the level of income and assumes it to be constant. Keynes calls this theory as a special theory of interest because it is based on the assumption of a fixed level of income corresponding to a fixed level of employment (full employment). By ignoring changes in the level of income, it views the rate of interest as the factor which brings about an equality between the demand for and supply of investible funds. Keynes, in contrast, asserts that the equality between savings and investment is brought about not by changes in the rate of interest but by changes in the level of income.

Secondly, the classical theory is indeterminate. According to this theory, the rate of interest is determined by the intersection of demand for and supply of capital schedules. But according to Keynes, saving schedule changes with a change in the level of income. As such, we cannot know the rate of interest unless we know the level of income and we cannot know the level of income until we know the rate of interest because the level of investment and hence that of income partly depends on the rate of interest.

Thirdly, the classical theory assumes full employment of all productive resources. According to Keynes, so long as there are unemployed productive resources in the economy, there is no need to reward people to abstain from consumption so as to release resources for employment for the production of capital goods. The obvious way would be to utilise idle resources rather than withdrawing already employed resources. The emergence of the rate of interest, therefore, has to be explained by something other than the theory of "waiting" or "abstinence" or "time-preference". According to Keynes, interest is a payment for the use of money and is determined by the demand for and supply of money.

Fourthly, the classical theory neglects the important role played by the quantity of money, created money and bank credit, in the determination of the rate of interest. Though less important in 18th and 19th centuries, the role of banking and created money in the determination of the rate of interest has assumed great importance in modern times. Money is no more neutral and does not act simply as a veil as assumed by the classicals. In Keynes' analysis, money plays an active role in influencing the rate of interest.

Fifthly, the classical theory assumes both investment and savings to be interest-elastic. Statistical investigations, however, show that both of them are not very responsive to changes in the rate of interest. In fact, the relation between the two, if any, is rather indirect and weak.

Sixthly, the classical theory, unlike moot partial analyses of the kind, does not even give the first approximation provided by a statement like "The price of shoes is determined by the supply and demand for shoes."[1] In the case of shoes, such a simplification from the Walrasian formulation of general equilibrium is permissible

1. Abba P. Lerner, "Interest Theory—Supply and Demand for Loans or Supply and Demand for Cash," in Seymour E. Harris (ed.), *The New Economics* (London, 1960), p. 656.

because an increase in the demand for shoes does not normally have a very important effect on the supply of shoes. In contrast, such a relative independence does not hold good in case of savings. When there is an increase in the demand for savings, say because businessmen want to borrow money in order to spend it, there is likely to result from this an increase in the supply of savings. The additional spending will lead to an increase in income, part of which will be saved and offered on the loan market. The part of these incomes that is not saved but spent will increase incomes still further and part of these further additions to income will be saved and offered on the loan market. Such induced increases in the supply of savings may partly or wholly offset the effects of the increase in the demand for savings. Similarly, if there is a decrease in the supply of saving because some lenders decide to spend their money instead of lending it, this would increase the amount of money in the hands of those from whom the purchases are made which may directly or indirectly increase the supply of savings; alternatively, the money spent by the erstwhile lenders may flow into the hands of erstwhile borrowers who will decrease their demand for loans.

Finally, the classical theory assumes that the demand for funds is for purposes of investment and would vary inversely with the rate of interest. Keynes, however, shows that this may not be true. The investors, for instance, would be prepared to borrow and invest more even at a higher rate of interest if the expected rate of profit is still higher. Similarly, the investors may not come forward to borrow even at very low rates of interest if the expected rates of profit are still lower.

NEO-CLASSICAL OR LOANABLE FUNDS THEORY

This theory was first formulated by the Swedish economist, K. Wicksell. Other Swedish economists who refined his ideas include G. Myrdal, Lindahl and B. Ohlin. In England, D.H. Robertson developed this theory. According to this theory, interest is the price paid for the use of loanable funds. It asserts that the rate of interest is determined by the demand for and supply of loanable funds. The supply of loanable funds comes from four basic sources namely savings, dishoarding, bank credit and investment.

Savings: Savings by individuals or households constitute the most important sources of loanable funds. The savings are visualised in two ways. Firstly, as *ex-ante* savings, that is, savings planned by individuals at the beginning of a period in the hope of expected incomes and anticipated expenditures on consumption. Secondly, in the Robertsonian sense, that is, the difference between the income of the preceding period and the consumption of the present period. In either case, the volume of savings varies at different rates of interest. At a given level of income, the larger would be the savings, the higher is the rate of interest and *vice versa*.

Like individuals and households, business concerns also do saving. A part of the profits of the business concerns is distributed as dividend. The remaining undistributed profits constitute business or corporate savings. Such savings partly depend upon the current rate of interest. A higher rate of interest would stimulate business savings as a substitute for borrowing from the loan market. But the business savings are often invested by the firms themselves and therefore, most of them do not constitute loanable funds.

Dishoarding: This is another source of loanable funds. People may dishoard money from their hoardings of previous periods and make it available as loanable funds. A higher rate of interest will stimulate people to dishoard money. At lower rates of interest people will have a tendency to hold on to money.

Banking Credit: Banks are a third source of loanable funds. By creating credit, banks advance loans to business concerns. The new money created by the banks adds to the supply of loanable funds. By contracting their credit; they can also reduce the supply of loanable funds. Normally, other things remaining the same, the banks will have a tendency to lend more money at higher rates of interest and *vice versa*.

Disinvestment: It takes place when due to structural changes or unsuccessful venture the existing stock of capital equipment is allowed to wear out without being replaced or when the inventories are permitted to deplete below the level of the previous period. When this happens, a part of the revenue from the sale of the products instead of going into capital replacement, flows into the market for loanable funds. A higher rate of interest encourages disinvestment. When the rate of interest is high, some of the capital equipment may not produce a marginal revenue product equal to this rate of interest. The firm may allow such capital equipment to run down and bring the depreciation funds into the market for loanable funds.

Demand far Loanable Funds: Loanable funds are demanded mainly for three purposes *viz.* (1) investment, (2) consumption, and (3) hoarding.

Investment: A major portion of the demand for loanable funds comes from business concerns which borrow funds for purchasing or making new capital goods or for building up inventories. The price of loanable funds needed for purchasing capital goods is obviously the rate of interest. It would be profitable for businessmen to demand loanable funds up to the point at which the expected net rate of return on capital goods equals the rate of interest. The business concerns will have a tendency to purchase larger amounts of capital goods at a lower rate of interest. The demand for loanable funds for investment purposes, therefore, is interest-elastic and slopes downwards to the right.

Consumption: The second major demand for loanable funds comes from people who want to borrow funds for consumption purposes. People demand loanable funds when they desire to spend more than their current incomes and cash resources. Normally, loans for consumption are demanded for buying durable goods like automobiles, radios, refrigerators etc. A lower rate of interest will stimulate demand for loanable funds for consumption purposes and *vice versa*.

Hoarding: The third demand for loanable funds comes from those who want to hold idle cash balances for satisfying their liquidity preference. At higher rate of interest, people will have a tendency to hold lesser amounts of cash balances because the loss involved in holding cash balances will be greater. Similarly, at lower rates of interest, people will hold more money because it will not involve much loss.

Equilibrium between Total Demand for and Supply of Loanable Funds: The rate of interest is determined by equilibrium between total demand for and total supply of loanable funds. In figure 9.1 the rate of interest is determined by the interaction of the demand for loanable funds curve *DL* and supply of loanable funds curve *SL*.

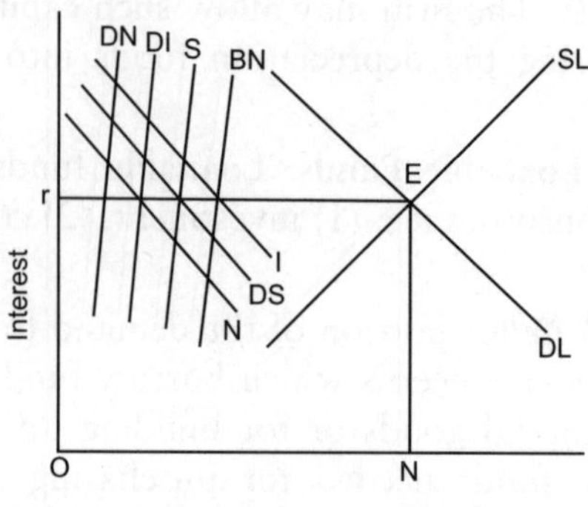

Fig. 9.1

The total supply curve of loanable funds *SL* is obtained by a lateral summation of the curves of saving (*S*), dishoarding (*DH*), bank money (*BM*) and disinvestment (*DI*). The aggregate loanable funds supply curve *SL* slopes upwards to the right showing a larger supply of the loanable funds at higher rates of interest. Similarly, the demand curve for loanable funds *DL* is obtained by a horizontal summation of the curves of investment (*I*), consumption (*DS*) and hoarding (*H*). The aggregate loanable fund demand curve *DL* slopes downwards to the right showing that the demand for loanable funds increases with a decline in the rate of interest.

DL and *SL* curves intersect at point *E* and thus determine the equilibrium rate of interest *Or*. At the equilibrium rate of interest *Or*, the supply of and demand for loanable funds are equal to *ON*. At any other interest rate either the demand for loanable funds will exceed the supply of loanable funds or the supply of loanable funds will exceed the demand for loanable funds and as a result the rate of interest will change until it reaches the level *Or* where the demand for and supply of loanable funds are equal.

It may be pointed out that at the equilibrium rate of interest where aggregate demand for and supply of loanable funds are equal, planned savings and investment may not be equal, as is evident from figure 9.1. In this figure, at the equilibrium rate of interest *Or*, the savings equal *rA* and investment equals *rB*. Investment *rB* is greater than savings *rA*. An excess of investment over saving will lead to an increase in income. The increase in income will shift saving curve *S* and the aggregate supply curve *SL* towards right. This shift in the savings curve *S* and loanable funds supply curve *SL* will lead to a change in the rate of interest. Thus the rate of interest as determined by the demand for and supply of loanable funds will not be a stable one if the savings and investment are not equal at that rate of interest and as such the interest rate will have a tendency to change. A stable equilibrium rate of interest will be attained only where the aggregate supply and demand curves of loanable funds determine the equilibrium rate of interest at which there also exists an equality between savings and investment.

We have explained above the various components of demand for and supply of loanable funds. It would be seen that saving (*S*) on supply side and dissaving (*DS*) on the demand side, dishoarding (*DH*) on supply side and hoarding (*H*) on the demand side and investment (*I*) on demand side and disinvestment (*DI*) on supply side are forces opposing each other. As these forces operate in the loanable funds market, it is their net effect which determines the market rate of interest. We can present the condition for an equilibrium rate of interest in a better and simplified manner if we use the concepts of net savings (*i.e.* savings minus dissavings), net hoarding (*i.e.* hoarding minus dishoarding) and net investment (*i.e.* investment minus disinvestment). This is shown below.

The equilibrium rate of interest is that at which the demand for loanable funds equals the supply of loanable funds. Writing the individual components on the demand and supply side in terms of symbols, the equilibrium rate of interest is determined when

$$S + DH + BM + DI = I + DS + H$$

In order to obtain net magnitudes we shift *DS* to the left side and *DH* and *DI* to the right side. The condition thus becomes

$$(S - DS) + BM = (I - DI) + (H - DH)$$

Or Net savings+Bank money = Net Investment + Net Hoarding.

Thus we find that the condition for equilibrium rate of interest is that the supply of net savings and bank money should be equal to the demand for net investment and net hoarding.

The classical theory did not take into consideration the importance of monetary factors like cash, credit, hoarding etc. It did not pay heed to the fact that the demand for money also arises from a desire to hoard. The non-classical theory, in contrast, considers monetary as well as non-monetary factors which have a bearing on the rate of interest.

Criticism of Loanable Funds Theory: Most of the criticisms made against the classical theory apply to loanable funds theory also. In fact, there is not such difference between the two theories. The major difference lies in the meaning of saving. In the classical theory, savings mean saving out of current income while in the loanable funds theory, savings refer to savings out of the income of the previous period. In the loanable funds theory, loanable funds consist of savings out of the income of the previous period plus borrowed bank deposits plus activated idle balances.

NATURAL AND MARKET RATE OF INTEREST

According to classical economists, natural rate of interest is that rate at which the demand for and supply of savings are in equilibrium. The market rate of interest will always correspond to this equilibrium rate of interest. The argument put forward in favour of the identity between the market and natural rates of interest is as follows: If the market rate of interest is higher than the natural or equilibrium rate of interest, supply of savings would exceed the demand of savings at that rate of interest. As a result of this, it would decline to the level of the natural rate of interest. Similarly, if at any time, the market rate of interest declines below the natural rate, the demand of savings would exceed the supply of savings, which would raise the market rate of interest to the level of the natural rate of interest.

Thus the classical theory did not conceive the possibility of the existence of a divergence between the market rate of interest and the natural rate of interest. This analysis was the direct outcome of a view which allowed money only a passive role. The classicists firmly believed that the introduction of money did not alter the real process of production and distribution. It simply increased the efficiency of a barter economy.

In the classical theory savings were the only source of the whole supply of loanable funds. The classicists failed to recognise the fact that created money, by increasing the supply of loanable funds, could independently affect real economic progress by lowering the rate of interest. Knut Wicksell (1851-1926) attacked the classical approach and recognised the positive role of credit or bank loans in influencing the market rate and making it different from the so-called natural rate of interest. In his book *Interest and Prices* published in 1889, Wicksell analysed the differences which could occur between the natural rate of interest and the market rate of interest.

While the classicists considered any divergence between the natural rate and the market rate of interest to be of a fortuitous nature, Wicksell argued that the divergence between the two was not of a fortuitous nature but owing to the intervention of the banks which by creating or destroying money cause the supply of loanable funds to deviate from the amount of real savings offered for investment in a barter economy. The creation of money by banks adds to the total supply of funds available for investors and as a result the market rate of interest is pushed below the natural rate of interest. In such a situation total investment will be in excess of total saving and the working of the famous Say's Law will be inhibited. Aggregate demand will exceed aggregate supply because a part of the aggregate demand which is financed by credit expansion has not made its own contribution to the supply of commodities: this will result in a rise in prices. Conversely, a restriction of credit by the banks will raise the market rate of interest above the natural rate of interest. Investment will fall short of the supply of saving. As a result, aggregate demand will fall short of aggregate supply and prices will decline.

LIQUIDITY PREFERENCE THEORY

Keynes put forward "Liquidity Preference Theory" of interest. According to this theory, the rate of interest is determined by the demand for and supply of money. Keynes' theory based on liquidity preference is known as *monetary* theory of interest as against the classical real theory of the rate of interest. Keynes' theory is called *monetary* theory because money plays an important role in it. Further, the rate of interest can be influenced or controlled by the central monetary authority through variations in the supply of money.

To Keynes, money is not only a medium of exchange but also a store of value. He laid more emphasis on the latter function of money. People desire to hold cash because it gives them a ready command over goods and services. People and business firms want to hold cash to meet day-to-day requirements, to provide against unforeseen contingencies and to earn from the future fluctuations of prices of bonds and securities. Thus those who have surplus money can either keep it in the form of ready cash or they may invest it in fixed income yielding assets like bonds and securities on which they earn a rate of interest, or they may purchase stocks on which they earn a rate of interest, dividend, or they may invest it in immovable property like houses on which they get rent. The desire to hold money as a store of wealth measures the extent of our distrust of our own calculation about the future. People do not want to hold all their wealth in interest-bearing assets because they are less liquid than cash and because their value is not fixed and varies from month to month, from week to week and from day to day. In view of this, it is rational to hoard money than to lend it. Interest is the reward which must be paid to overcome the liquidity.

The rate of interest depends on the strength of the liquidity preference in relation to the total quantity of money available to satisfy the desire for liquidity. The stronger the liquidity preference, the higher would be the rate of interest; and the greater the quantity of money, the lower would be the rate of interest. The rate of interest, like any other price, would be established at a level at which the demand for and supply of money are in equilibrium. An increase in the desire of the public to hold money may be met either by an increase in the price paid (rate of interest) or by an increase in the supply of money. Since the public cannot increase the supply of money, the direct result of an increase in its desire for money will not be to increase the quantity available but to increase the premium paid to those who give up their cash holdings. If the rate of interest did not rise with an increase in liquidity preference, the total quantity of money that public could desire to hold at the existing rate of interest would exceed the available supply. Similarly, if the rate of interest did not decline with a fall in liquidity preference, there would be surplus cash which no one would like to hold. In this manner, if the rate of interest tends to be too high or too low, an adjustment would take place equating the demand with the available supply. If the monetary authority agrees to expand the supply of money in proportion to the increase in liquidity preference, there would be no rise in the rate of interest.

LIQUIDITY PREFERENCE

According to Keynes, the demand for money or the desire to hold liquid cash arises out of three main motives *viz.* (1) the transanction motive, (2) the precautionary motive, and (3) the speculative motive. We discuss below these three motives in a little more details.

Transactions Motive: Money balances are held for the purpose of making transactions. Since the typical person is paid once a month or once a week and makes disbursements throughout the period, he must maintain some idle balance for transactions. A person who gets salary of y rupees at the beginning of the month makes consumption expenditures of c rupees at a uniform rate throughout the month will normally maintain a bank balance which averages one-half of his monthly expenditures *i.e.* $\frac{c}{2}$ rupees. If his income rises by Δy rupees, his consumption expenditure will rise by $b\Delta y$ rupees (assuming that his marginal propensity to consume is b) so that the average balance he must keep in his account will be $\frac{c+b\Delta y}{2}$. If the price level doubles, the amount he must maintain in his account will double. Thus the size of the cash balances depends upon the size of income, the frequency of income receipts and the frequency of income expenditure. If everybody received income in cash and simultaneously paid his expenses in cash, there would be no need to hold cash balances for transaction purposes. The greater is the length of interval between pay days, the larger will be the need for holding cash balances. Other things remaining the same, a person receiving monthly salary will require larger cash balances as compared with a person receiving daily wages.

It is quite possible that the transactions demand for money may depend not only on the level of income, frequency of income receipts and the frequency of income expenditure, but also, to some extent, on the rate of interest. Suppose that an individual plans to spend all his income at a uniform rate throughout the month. Of the y rupees which he receives at the beginning of the month, three-quarters will be idle for the first week (assuming that each month consists of four weeks); one-half of the balance will be idle for the first two weeks; and one-quarter will be idle for the first three weeks. He may, therefore, use these idle funds for purchasing an earning asset. At the beginning of the month he may use three-quarters of his income for purchasing bonds. At the end of the first week he requires some additional cash for transactions and therefore cashes in one-third of his bond holdings for expenditure during the second week. At the end of the second week he cashes in another one-third of his original bond purchases to spend during the third week; at the end of the third week he cashes in the remaining bonds. Instead of going into the bond market four times, he may go lesser times or more times. The more often he goes into the bond market, the less will be his average idle bank balance.

What governs the decision as to how many times to go into the market during the month? Since there is some cost of making each transaction, there is a definite disadvantage in going into the market which must be balanced against the desirability of holding earning assets as opposed to idle funds. Let us find out the optimum number of transactions. Let i be the rate of interest, n the number of transactions per income expenditure period, B the value of bond holdings, a the cost per transaction, c the transaction balance at the beginning of the month, and P the profit. Supposing that the cost of transactions depends only on the number of transactions and not on the size of the transactions, we have

$$C = na$$

At the beginning of the month, an individual will buy $\frac{(n-1)c}{n}$ bonds. Each $\frac{1}{n}$ days he sells $\frac{c}{n}$ bonds so that average bond holdings are

$$\overline{B} = \frac{(n-1)c}{2n}$$

Since the interest earnings on this average balance are $\frac{(n-1)ci}{2n}$, the total profit must be

$$P = \frac{(n-1)ci}{2n} - na$$

The optimum number of transactions is the value of n which makes P maximum. Accordingly,

$$\frac{dP}{dn} = \frac{2ci}{4n^2} - a = 0$$

So that

$$n = \sqrt{\frac{ci}{2a}}$$

Thus the optimum number of transactions depends on the rate of interest, the transactions cost, and the size of the beginning balance. It should be noted that when the rate of interest rises, the optimum number of transactions rises; this means that the transactions demand for money declines as the rate of interest rises.

Business firms, like individuals, also need to hold cash balances to bridge the gap between outlays for expenses and the receipt of cash from sales of finished products. As in the case of individuals, the longer is the interval, the larger will be the required size of balances. The business motive for holding cash will be stronger with an increase in the business activity. Payments from one entrepreneur to another will vary with the number of stages through which goods pass on their way to final completion, that is, the degree of integration in the economy as a whole. Other things remaining unchanged, an increase in integration will diminish the demand for money. Since factors like degree of business integration change slowly, fluctuations in the level of business activity are the only major factor responsible for changes in the demand for cash for transactions in the short run.

Precautionary Motive: Individuals, households and business firms normally have a tendency to hold more money than that required for transaction purposes. They hold more money because they want to take proper precautions against unforeseen future contingencies like sickness, unemployment, accidents; fire, old age etc. While going for shopping, an individual generally takes more money than just the amount he thinks will be needed for planned purposes. Plans may change, or opportunities may arise to make especially advantageous purchases if they are transacted on the spot without delay. The business firms require ready cash to meet contingent liabilities or to avail of unforeseen opportunities to make advantageous purchases. The amount of money held for precautionary motive varies widely with individuals and business firms according to their degree of financial conservatism, the nature of their enterprise, their access to the credit market, and the state of development of organized markets for conversion of earning assets like securities and stocks into cash. The demand for money for precautionary motive also depends upon income and the general level of business activity. Keynes takes the transactions and precautionary demand for money together because both are determined by the level of income.

Though the precautionary demand is probably quite closely related to the level of money income, as in the case of transaction demand, however, there may be some relation between the precautionary demand and the rate of interest. An increase in interest rates may make the purchase of earning assets so tempting that people may be willing to assume a slightly greater risk in the form of a lower precautionary balance in return for the added interest earnings.

Speculative Motive: The speculative motive relates to the desire to hold one's resources in liquid form with a view to take advantage of market movements. The object is to obtain profit from knowing better than the market what the future may bring forth. The speculative demand for money arises on account of the uncertainty regarding the future rate of interest. The individual investors are not sure of the terms and conditions on which the bonds owned by them can be converted into cash. If a particular individual, for instance, expects a decline in the prices of bonds, he would like to hold cash to take advantage of the situation when the prices actually decline. In this way, individuals safeguard themselves against possible losses. Similarly, if an individual expects a rise in the prices of bonds, he would buy bonds in anticipation of a rise in their prices. Thus the speculative motive for holding cash derives from a desire to keep one's resources in liquid form in readiness to take advantage of a turn in the market and to avoid a possible loss from holding securities in a falling market. This is known as the speculative demand for money. If there is no uncertainty about the future rate of interest, the rates at which debts of varying maturities can be converted into money at any future date would also be known with certainty. In such a situation, it would always be advantageous to own interest-bearing securities than possessing cash yielding no income and as such there would be no basis for liquidity preference for the speculative motive. This explains why the classical theory, resting upon static assumptions, attached no importance to the demand for money for speculative motive. It is here that Keynes' theory differs in a fundamental sense from the classical theory of interest. It is the speculative demand for money which introduces a dynamic clement in the analysis of the general price level and the volume of employment through a relationship between the current and prospective rates of interest and the profitability of investment. If the total quantity of money remains unchanged, speculative transactions affect output and employment by changing the rates of interest.

The size of the balances held for speculative motive varies inversely with the rate of interest. The speculative demand for money is less at a higher rate of interest and more at a lower rate of interest. What is the logic behind this proposition? When the rate of interest is low, security prices are high. As such, a large outlay would yield only a small amount of return. In such a situation, purchase of bonds is not very attractive. Further, if in the past the rate of interest was high but has since fallen to a lower level below which it is not expected to go, the balance of expectations will be in favour of a future rise in the rate. If the rate of interest rises, those holding bonds would suffer a loss. If the people expect that the rate of interest will rise, they would prefer liquidity, because this would enable them a better bargain at a later date.

The above argument has been criticised on the ground that it implies an all-or-none kind of behaviour. If the interest earnings of a bond exceed the expected capital loss, it will be profitable to invest all one's funds in bonds. In contrast, if the expected capital loss is in excess of the interest earnings, no bond will be held. As such the moment, the critical point is reached where the scales tip in favour of bonds, there would be expected a conversion of cash into bonds on a large scale. Keynes' explanation for the fact that this wholesale conversion does note take place was based on the assumption that different people have different expectations in regard to the future. This view, however, is open to the criticism that, if the low rate of interest persists long enough, it will begin to be considered as permanent so that expectations will converge, the fear of capital loss will vanish and the speculative demand for money will vanish.

If the above theory is open to criticism, is there anything to the idea that there is speculative demand for money which has an inverse relation with the rate of interest? Data for the United States economy certainly suggest that there is, for when short-term-paper rates are plotted against average idle deposits, a strong inverse relationship emerges.[2] Is there an alternative explanation? To state the argument of the economists who hold that there is, we must prepare the ground by abandoning the notion that there is only one kind of security, and recognise instead that there is in reality a wide range of securities varying in diverse ways in respect of extent of risk, rate of interest, and date of maturity. Since the investors are not likely to want to keep all their eggs in one basket, they will instead diversify their portfolios and hold some of several different kinds of assets.[3] The portfolios would also include some money which, although earns no interest, has the advantage of a high liquidity premium.

For the sake of simplification, suppose that there are only two kinds of bonds—long-term and short-term and assume that an individual's portfolio consists of some long-term bonds and some short-term bonds and some cash. If the rate of interest rises, the earnings which are lost by holding cash become greater. Some of the investor's risk aversion will be long-term bonds for short-term bonds and some short-term bonds for cash. If the interest rates decline, the income on long-term bonds no longer compensates for the risk, while the loss of interest on account of holding cash and short-term bonds becomes relatively smaller. As such, with the decline in interest rates investors will have a tendency to adjust their portfolios in the direction of increased liquidity.

The above form of liquidity preference argument is free from dependence on one-sided expectation of the future and difficult to justify assumption that expectations will not ultimately converge. It depends on the simple principle of not putting all one's eggs in one basket and thus appeals to the commonsense and every day experience.

---

2. J. Tobin, "Liquidity Preference and Monetary Policy", *Review of Economics and Statistics*, 1947, pp. 124-31.
3. J. Tobin, "Liquidity Preferernce as *Behavior towards Risk*", *Review of Economic Studies*, 1958, pp. 65-86.

If the total supply of money is represented by M, we may denote that part of M held for transactions and precautionary motives as M_1 and that part held for speculative motive as M_2 so that $M=M_1+M_2$. The demand for money for transactions and precautionary motives is virtually interest-inelastic except when the rate of interest is very high. Since the demand for money for these motives depends upon income, it may be expressed as $M_1 = f(Y)$ or $M_1 = L_1(Y)$. In contrast, the money held for speculative motive is very sensitive to changes in the rate of interest. It may, therefore, be expressed as $M_2 = f(r)$ or $M_2 = L_2, (r)$ where r stands for the rate of interest. The equation $M = M_1 + M_2$ may be written as $M = L_1(Y) + L_2(r)$. Thus we find that, given the supply of money (M), the rate of interest is determined by the liquidity preference ($M_1 + M_2$) and only that rate of interest will prevail in actual practice which brings about an equilibrium between the demand for liquidity and the supply of money. It may, however, be mentioned that though interest is related to the speculative motive only, the other two motives cannot be ignored because money held for one motive is a perfect substitute for money held under another motive.

In addition to the three motives mentioned by Keynes, the modern writers have mentioned three more motives which impel people to hold their assets in the form of money. They are: (i) deflationary motive, (ii) business-expansion motive and (iii) convenience motive. These three motives are briefly described below:

(i) *Deflationary Motive.* The deflationary motive for holding money appears when there is a general tendency towards a decline in prices. During periods of declining prices, both consumers and producers have a tendency to postpone their purchases expecting to buy cheaper at a later date. Thus, instead of buying goods, the people have a tendency to hold money. The deflationary motive for holding money is based on the speculative anticipation of people in regard to a decline in prices of goods and services. In a sense, this is also a speculative motive. But Keynes considers speculative motive for holding money in a narrower sense to mean speculation about future prices of only claims (bills, securities, bonds, shares etc.) while deflationary motive refers to speculation about future prices of goods and services.

(ii) *Business Expansion Motive*. The business-expansion motive for holding money refers to the tendency on the part of the business concerns to accumulate and hold money in order to finance their expansion plans. In recent years most of the companies have a tendency to depend on their own funds for expanding business in view of certain advantages involved in it. Similarly, the individuals have a tendency to accumulate and hold money to finance their purchases of expensive consumer durable goods like a refrigerator or television set. The business expansion motive is distinct from the transaction motive because the latter is used in narrower sense of current transactions.

(iii) *Convenience Motive*. The convenience motive refers to the fact that money is the most convenient way of keeping one's savings. If a person wants to keep his savings in the form of certain assets (like bonds, securities, furniture, house, precious metals), he has to undergo the inconvenience of going to the market, finding out the different goods available, searching the cheapest sources of supply of goods, making a choice between different assets available, and so forth and so on. The convenience motive for holding money is particularly important for people having small amounts of savings.

Since income (Y) partly depends on the rate of interest (r), changes either in r or M will affect the other indirectly. This relationship is important for monetary policy during periods of expanding output. If an increase in income or output is not accompanied by an increase in the total quantity of money (M), the increase in M_1 will take place by a transfer of funds from M_2. A decline in the amount of money available for speculative motive will push the rate of interest upwards which would have adverse effects on investment and hence on income. This rise in the rate of interest, which tends to inhibit expansion, can be offset by an increase in the total quantity of money (M) so that the increase in funds needed to meet the growing transactions demand will not be met at the expense of money needed to satisfy the speculative motive (M_2). Here the banking authority is required to act in such a way as will not permit a shortage of money to lead to a premature brake on expanding income and employment.

SUPPLY OF MONEY

Having analysed the demand for money, we now turn to the supply of money. The supply of money is different from the supply of a commodity. In case of a commodity, the supply is a *flow* over time. The commodity is being continuously produced. But in case of money, the supply is a *stock*. Money, unlike a commodity, is not being continuously produced and consumed. The supply of money, like the demand for money, is the supply of money to hold. Unless money is held by someone, it cannot exist. Thus the supply of money is the existing stock of money, all of which is held by someone or the other. An increase in the supply of money means not an increase in the sale of money by those who possess it, but an increase in the stock of money.

Unlike the demand for money, the supply of money is completely amenable to the state control because it is determined by the government and the central bank of the country. In his analysis of the rate of interest, Keynes assumes the quantity of money to be constant. In a short-period analysis, he considers this assumption to be quite reasonable.

The total supply of money consists of metallic coins, paper money and bank deposits. The first two constituents are completely under the control of the central bank which is generally a government-owned institution. In highly capitalist economies, bank deposits form the largest source of the total supply money. If money is defined as the perfectly liquid asset, the presumption would be against including saving and time deposits because the banks have a right to demand a certain number of days' notice for converting such deposits into legal money. Keynes, however, includes time deposits into money. Lending and borrowing activities of the banking system form the most important factor responsible for changes in the supply of money.

In diagram 9.2, *LP* is the curve of liquidity preference for speculative motive. Curve *LP* shows the demand for money for speculative motive. It slopes downward to the right showing that at higher rates of interest, the demand for speculative motive is less and conversely. *OM* is the initial quantity of money available for satisfying liquidity preference for speculative motive. *Or* is the equilibrium rate of interest because at this rate the amount of money demanded (*OM*) is equal to its supply (*OM*). Now let us

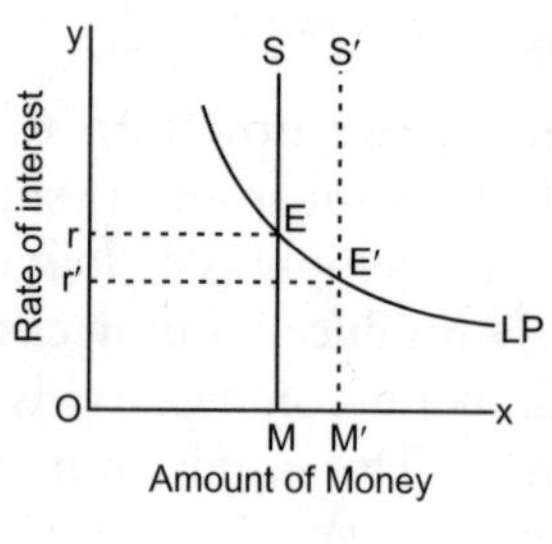

Fig. 9.2

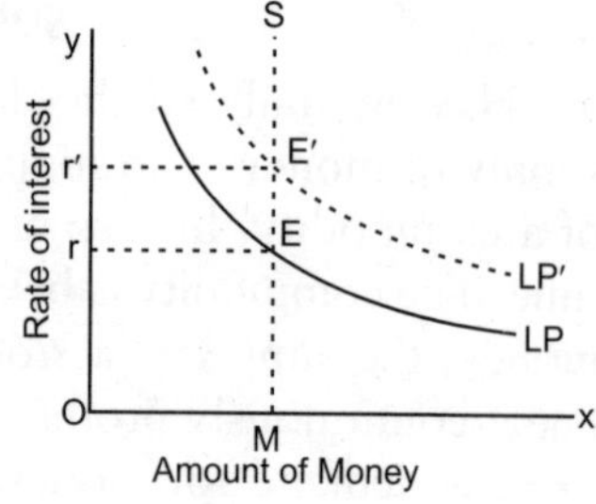

Fig. 9.3

suppose that the supply of money is increased from *OM* to *OM*' through open market operations. When the supply of money is increased to *OM*' the rate of interest would decline to *Or*' because the increased supply of money becomes equal to the speculative demand for money at *Or*' rate of interest. Similarly, if the supply of money is decreased, there would occur a rise in the rate of interest.

In Fig. 9.3, assuming that the supply of money remains unchanged, if the liquidity preference curve rises from *LP* to *LP*' the rate of interest would rise from *Or* to *Or*' because the increased speculative demand for money is equal to the supply of money at *Or*' rate of interest. Conversely, if the liquidity preference curve declines, there would occur a decline in the rate of interest.

IMPLICATIONS OF LIQUIDITY PREFERENCE THEORY

Interest Rate and Supply of Money: In the Keynesian analysis, the monetary authority is expected to stimulate employment by following a cheap money policy or, in other words, by lowering the rate of interest through an expansion in the supply of money. The logic behind easy monetary policy is that an expansion in the supply of money, other things remaining unchanged, will increase the money available for speculative motive (M_2) which would lead to a decline in the late of interest. A fall in the rate of interest stimulates investment which leads to a multiple increase in income and employment. With the increase in income, the amount of money required for transactions (M_1) increases so that the total increase in money (M) is divided in some way between M_1 and M_2. The effectiveness of money stimulation depends upon the extent of decline in the rate of interest in response to an increase in M_2 (*i.e.* upon the elasticity of L_2 function), responsiveness of investment to a decline in the rate of interest (*i.e.* the elasticity of the schedule of the marginal efficiency of capital), and the magnitude of increase in income resulting from a certain increase in investment (*i.e.* the size of the investment multiplier).

Such a policy of monetary management, however, has serious limitations. An increase in the quantity of money will not lower the rate of interest if the liquidity preference is increasing faster than the quantity of money. Similarly, a decline in the rate of interest will not expand investment and employment if the marginal efficiency of capital is declining faster than the rate of interest. Thus in a severe depression when the liquidity preference is high and the expectations of entrepreneurs for profitable investment are low, monetary policy may fail to lift the economy out of depression.

Long-term Vs. Short-term Rate of Interest*:* Although we speak of the rate of interest without mentioning the period of maturity of the debt, this does not mean that there is only one rate of interest prevailing in the market. We adopt this practice only for simplifying the analysis. In the real money market, there exists a complex of rates of interest differing among themselves depending upon debts of varying maturities. The rate of interest on daily loans will be different from the rates of interest on weekly, monthly or yearly loans. Similarly, debts of longer maturity like four, seven or twelve years, will bear different rates of interest. To overcome the difficulties involved in talking of a number of rates of interest, a distinction is made between the short-term rate of interest paid on bank loans and the long-term rate of interest paid on bonds and securities. Since the speculative demand for money over a short period changes very violently, the short-term rate of interest is subject to greater violations than the long-term rate of interest. The long-term rate of interest is comparatively stable because over a long period, expectations of a conflicting nature cancel themselves out leaving very little influence on the rate of interest.

It is much easier to lower the short-term than the long-term rate of interest. The major obstacle to a decline in interest rates is the expectation that they may rise later to such an extent as makes it worthwhile to hold cash in anticipation of buying on more favourable terms at a later date. If the banking authority launches a large-scale open-market policy to lower the interest rates, it is natural to assume that this policy would probably be pursued for some time. There would be hardly any reason to expect a rise in the rate of interest in the near future and, therefore, there would be little incentive to remain liquid with a view to buying later on more favourable terms. Further, commitments to debts on short-terms would not involve substantial losses even if expectations turn out to be wrong. The securities may be held for a short-time until maturity when they are redeemed at face value.

It is more difficult to lower the long-term rate of interest and it tends to become increasingly resistant to further reductions at every step on its downward path. At some level, say about 2 per cent, no further reductions may be possible. The loss from a rise in the interest rate from 2 to 3 per cent, for instance, is much greater than that from 4 to 5 per cent because the loss in capital value is greater and also because the interest income is less at the lower level.

The increasing risk of loss at lower rates of interest is reflected in the liquidity-preference schedule by a flattening out of the liquidity curve. The flattening of the curve indicates a growing elasticity of the liquidity-preference function which means a point will be reached below which it is very difficult to lower the rate of interest any further. Keynes suggested that at about 2 per cent, the liquidity curve may become horizontal, indicating perfect elasticity, and meaning that no further reduction in the rate of interest can be brought about through a mere expansion in the quantity of money. At this rate of interest, the demand for money is absolute in the sense that everyone prefers to hold money rather than long-term securities yielding a return of 2 per cent or less. A second reason for the liquidity preference curve becoming perfectly elastic at a certain minimum rate of interest is that this minimum rate of interest may not be adequate to compensate for the incidental out-lays and inconveniences involved in purchasing bonds. A third reason is that people may no longer expect any further fall in the interest rate and may expect it to rise in future. They, therefore, prefer to hold cash rather than bonds, securities and other earning assets yielding that minimum rate of interest or less than that. Thus, owing to the reasons mentioned above, the liquidity preference curve becomes perfectly elastic at a certain minimum rate of interest indicating that no further reduction in the interest rate can be attained merely by increasing the quantity of money.

Inverse Relationship between Rate of Interest and Bond Prices*:* There is a definite inverse relationship between interest rates and bond prices. In other words, when interest rates rise, bond prices fall, and when interest rates decline, bond prices rise. Changes in the prices of bonds in the organised securities markets reflect themselves in change in the liquidity preference of the people. A decline in liquidity preference is reflected in an increased desire on the part of people to buy bonds at current prices leading to a rise in the prices of bonds and a decline in the rate of interest. Similarly, an upward shift in the liquidity preference curve is reflected in an increased desire on the part of people to sell bonds in order to obtain more cash which leads to a decline in bond prices and a rise in the interest rate.

CRITICISM OF KEYNES' THEORY OF INTEREST

Keynes' theory of interest, like the classical theory, is indeterminate. The liquidity preference curve itself shifts up and down with changes in the level of income. The liquidity preference for transactions and precautionary motives cannot be known until we know the level of income. Thus we cannot know the liquidity preference curve and hence the rate of interest without knowing the level of income. The Keynesian theory tells us only the various schedules of liquidity preference at various levels of income and not what the rate of interest would be. To quote Hansen:

> In the Keynesian case the supply and demand for money schedule cannot give the income; in the classical case the demand and supply schedules for saving offer no solution until income is known. Precisely the same is true of loanable find theory. Keynes' criticism of the classical and loanable fund theories applies equally to his own theory.[4]

Prof. Hazlitt has pointed out that rate of interest is not purely a monetary phenomenon. Real forces like productivity of capital, thriftiness or time preference or savings also play an important role in the determination of rate of interest. While the classical economists were wrong in ignoring monetary factors, Keynes erred on the other side by ignoring real factors. In fact, as Wicksell has rightly pointed out, the theory of interest should take into consideration both money and real factors.

4. Alvin H. Hansen, *A Guide to Keynes* (New York, 1953), p. 141.

Keynes' theory of interest is self-contradictory. "For if a man is holding his funds in the form of time deposits or short-term treasury bills, he is being paid interest on them; therefore, he is getting interest and 'liquidity' too. What becomes, then, of Keynes' theory that interest is the reward for parting with liquidity."[5]

Keynes' theory goes contrary to the facts that it presumes to explain. If Keynes' theory were correct, the short-term interest rate would be the highest at the bottom of a depression when owing to declining prices, people's preference of liquidity is the strongest and lowest at the peak of the boom when due to all-round confidence the liquidity preference of the people is the weakest. But in actual practice, the interest rates are the lowest at the bottom of the depression and highest at the peak of the boom.

The rate of interest is not independent of the demand for investment funds as believed by Keynes. The amount of cash balances the businessmen will hold is considerably influenced by their demand for finance for investment purposes. The rate of interest, therefore, is not independent of the marginal efficiency of capital.

The distinction between liquidity and illiquidity is not so simple as assumed by Keynes. In fact, there are different degrees of liquidity and a complex system of rates of interest depending on the differences in the degree of liquidity. Keynes unnecessarily simplifies his theory by completely ignoring the time element and making distinction only between liquidity and illiquidity. In actual practice, we find that the rates of interest are different on daily, weekly, monthly, yearly and long-term loans.

Keynes' theory of liquidity preference is too narrow as an explanation of the rate of interest. In actual practice liquidity (or desire for money) arises on account of many factors and not only on account of motives mentioned by Keynes. It, for instance, also arises for investment. Further, the rate of interest influences and is in turn influenced by other important factors like the rate of saving, propensity to consume and the marginal efficiency of capital, which are neglected by the liquidity preference theory.

---

5. Henry Hazlitt, *The Failure of the "New Economics"* (New York, 1959), p. 193.

Keynes' ignores savings and explains interest as a reward for parting with liquidity. In actual practice, there can be no liquidity without saving. Prof. Jacob Viner pertinently remarks, "...without saving there can be no liquidity to surrender.... The rate of interest is the return for saving without liquidity."[6]

Prof. Patinkin points out that "Unfortunately, Keynes' analysis is repeatedly marred by a confusion.....between his basic proposition that the amount of money demanded is inversely dependent upon the rate of interest and the completely different proposition that the equilibrium rate of interest is inversely dependent upon the amount of money. His discussion of liquidity preference in the *General Theory* shifts uninhibitedly from one proposition to the other with never an indication that they are in any way not identical. More specifically, there is never a recognition that...the first of these propositions describes an individual-experiment and the second a market-experiment, and that the truth of the first need not imply the truth of the second."[7]

Prof. Patinkin further points that "Keynesian monetary theory never permits the speculative demand to absorb an increased supply of money except at a lower rate of interest. It never allows for the fact, provided the price level rises, such an absorption may take place even at an unchanged rate. Nor can this omission be explained as itself proving that the analysis of the *General Theory* proceeds on the assumption of absolute price rigidity. For there are passages in this work in which Keynes explicity assumes the wage or price level to rise, in which he explains how this rise affects the transactions and precautionary demands, and in which he overlooks the fact that it may also affect the speculative demand."[8]

Moreover, "Keynes should have taken account of the fact that shifts in liquidity preference can, in principle, also affect the demand for commodities...in such a case, the rate of interest need not be affected."[9]

---

6. Jacob Viner, *Quarterly Journal of Economics*, (1936-37), p. 157.
7. Don Patinkin, *Money, Interest and Prices* (Tokyo, 1966), p. 372.
8. *Ibid.*, pp. 373-74.
9. *Ibid.*, p. 375.

Despite all that has been said above the fact remains that Keynes' theory of interest is an improvement over the classical theory in that by introducing the dynamic concept of role of money namely 'as a link between the present and the future' and the consequent speculative demand for money, Keynes emphasizes how uncertainty and expectations exert an important influence on the levels of income and employment through the rate of interest.[10]

LIQUIDITY PREFERENCE *VS.* LOANABLE FUNDS

There has been an unnecessary controversy as to the choice between liquidity preference and loanable fund theories of the rate of interest. The advocates of the loanable funds theory claim that this theory is broader in scope and allows for more influences on the rate of interest than does the liquidity preference theory. An increase in consumption, for instance, decreases savings and thereby leads to a rise in the rate of interest. Similarly, a rise in the marginal efficiency of capital increases the demand for funds for investment and thereby leads to a rise in the rate of interest. The liquidity preference theory, in contrast, restricts the influences on the rate of interest to the demand for and supply of money for hoarding. The advocates of loanable funds theory admit that hoarding plays an important part in influencing the rate of interest but assert that this is not the only influence. On the supply side, while the liquidity preference theory is confined to the supply of money as determined by the monetary authority, the loanable funds theory includes not only bank money but also voluntary savings and dishoarded wealth. By linking the rate of interest with liquidity preference, quantity of credit, saving and investment, the loanable funds theory views the problem in a more practical way for it explains why market rate of interest is, and can be, different from the natural rate of interest.

The advocates of the liquidity preference, on the other hand, contend that this theory is an integral part of the analysis of the working of the economic system as a whole while the loanable funds theory is an exercise in partial equilibrium analysis and can hence be a square peg in a round whole in the general determinate system.

---

10. Kenneth K. Kurihara, *Introduction to Keynesian Dynamics* (London, 1956), p. 72.

The liquidity preference theory runs in terms of stocks, *i.e.*, supply of money in the short-run and demand for it in the short-run varying with the expectations of future interest rates while the loanable funds theory runs in terms of flows, *i.e.*, so much supply of loanable funds and so much demand for loanable funds per period of time. Many economists believe that the theory of the rate of interest should be in terms of stocks rather than flows.

> Scitovszky has pointed out that in ordinary supply and demand analysis, price is the allocating mechanism between two flows... But in the case in which stocks are significant and are dependent upon price, he claimed that the equation of supply-demand flows may not lead to the correct result.... It is certainly obvious that money and earning assets are commodities which possess very large stocks. We know that interest is earned on existing stocks of assets as well as on the current flows. Interest is not the allocating mechanism between the supply and demand for credit flows rather the allocating mechanism between the holding of stocks of earning and non-earning assets.[11]

The advocates of the liquidity preference theory contend that the rate of interest is a monetary phenomenon and has to be separated from the productivity of capital. In the words of Klein:

> In essence, the Keynesian contribution was to point out that people can make two distinct types of decisions. They may decide upon saving or consuming their incomes, and they may decide upon holding idle cash or non-liquid securities. Each decision requires an economic calculation. In the former case, individuals decide on the basis of their incomes how much they want to spend on consumption and at the same time how much they want to save. In the latter case, they may decide on the basis of alternative rates of return (*i.e.*, interest rates) whether they want to hoard their historically accumulated saving in the form of cash or securities. The distinction between these two sets of decisions clearly calls for a liquidity preference theory of interest.[12]

---

11. Lawrence R. Klein, *The Keynesian Revolution* (London, 1952), p. 123.
12. *Ibid.*

The liquidity preference theory not only brings forth the important role of money but integrates money into the theory of output and employment for the economy as a whole.

STOCKS AND FLOWS

Keynesian theory runs in terms of stocks, *i.e.*, the supply of money in the short-run and demand for it in the short-run varying with the expectations of future interest rates, while the classical and neo-classical theories run in terms of *flows*, *i.e.*, so much supply of savings or loanable funds and so much demand for savings or loanable funds per period of time. Many economists hold the view that the theory of interest should be in terms of stocks rather than flows T. de Scitovszky[13] points out that in ordinary supply-and-demand analysis, price is the allocating mechanism between two flows, and that this approach is appropriate when dealing with commodities for which there do not exist large stocks or for which the stocks are independent of the price. But in the case in which stocks are significant and are dependent upon price, he holds that the equation of supply-demand flows may not lead to the proper result. For illustration, suppose that current production and consumption flows for some good are in equilibrium at the current market price and that this price is also an equilibrium point for the supply and demand for stocks. If now the demand for the consumer goods changes, the establishment of a new price at which the two flows will be in equilibrium will be hindered by the adjustment of stocks to the new price. If the change in demand takes the form of a decline in consumer's desires for the good, price will tend to fall in order to bring the flow schedules into equilibrium. But then the holders of stocks may desire to increase their holdings at the lower price. Thus the stockholder behaviour may counteract the flow adjustment and can prevent it from taking place. If one or more of these interest rates on alternative assets rise, the demand for cash as a proportion of total assets declines, and *vice versa*.

A change in the interest rate of any money substitute affects not only the demand for money but also the demand for all other assets related to the money substitute. To put it in a general form, the demand for any asset, including money, is a function of not just one

---

13. T. de Scitovszky, "A Study of Interest and Capital" *Economica New Series*, Vol. VII, 1940, p. 293.

interest rate but of many interest rates. This means that a change in the supply of any asset, including money, will change not just one interest rate but many. Further, a change in the interest rate on any asset affects not only the demand for that asset but the demand for all related assets, of which money may be one. Thus the interest rate on any asset is determined not by the supply of that asset alone, but by the supplies of all related assets.

RECONCILIATION OF TWO THEORIES

The modern economists are of the view that the controversy in regard to the choice between the two theories is unnecessary and uncalled for. Economists like Hicks, Lerner and Fellner have made attempts to reconcile the two theories. They believe that the two theories are more or less similar and can be used to express the same thing. In the classical loanable funds theory, an excess of demand for loanable funds over their supply leads to a rise in the rate of interest. Similarly, in the liquidity preference theory an increase in investment leads to more use of cash for transaction purposes which, other things remaining unchanged, means less cash available for speculative purpose which results in the rise in the rate of interest. In the same way, an increase in consumption means more cash for transaction purposes which, other things remaining same, means less cash available for speculative purpose and hence a rise in the rate of interest. Thus the liquidity preference approach as well as the loanable funds approach lead to the same results. Prof. Hamberg remarks:

> In view of the interchangeability of the two approaches to the explanation of the interest, it is a matter of complete indifference and personal choice, which one of the two approaches is used. Because of the similarities too, it is probably best to say that Keynes did not forge nearly as a new theory of rate of interest as he and others at first thought. Rather, his great emphasis of the influence of hoarding on the rate of interest constituted an invaluable addition to the theory of interest as it had been developed by the loanable fund theorists who incorporated much of Keynes' ideas into their theory to make it more complete.[14]

---

14. D. Hamberg, *Business Cycles*, pp. 182-83.

In fact, both the theories considered individually are indeterminate. A determinate theory can, of course, be obtained by a synthesis of the two theories. In the words of Hansen, "The neo-classical (loanable fund) formulation and the Keynesian formulation, *taken together,*[15] do supply us with an adequate theory of the rate of interest."[16] Such a synthesis is given below:

The loanable funds formulation gives us a family of loanable fund schedules (or saving schedule in the Keynesian-Pigovian sense) at various levels of income. These together with the investment-demand schedule give us the Hicksian *IS* curve. In other words, the loanable funds formulation can tell us what the various levels of income will be (given the investment-demand schedule and a family of loanable fund schedules) at different rates of interest. But it does not tell us what the rate of interest will be. From the Keynesian formulation we get a family of liquidity preference schedules at various levels of income. These, together with the supply of money determined by the monetary authority, give us the Hicksian *L* curve (which Hansen prefers to call the *LM* curve). The *LM* curve tells us what the various rates of interest will be (given the quantity of money and the family of liquidity preference curves) at different levels of income. But the liquidity schedule alone cannot tell us what the rate of interest will be.

Derivation of *IS* curve is shown in figure 9.4(*a*). With the rise in income, the savings curve shifts to the right and the rate of interest which equalises savings and investment declines. In figure 9.4(*b*), income (Y) is measured along X-axis and the corresponding rates of interest determined by the equality of savings and investment are plotted. Thus when income is Y_2, the relevant saving curve is S_2Y_2 and the corresponding rate of interest equalising savings and investment is r_4. Similarly, for other levels of income, the *IS* curve slopes downward for with a rise in income, the rate of interest declines.

15. Italics in original.

16. Alvin H. Hansen, *A Guide to Keynes* (New York, 1953), p. 143.

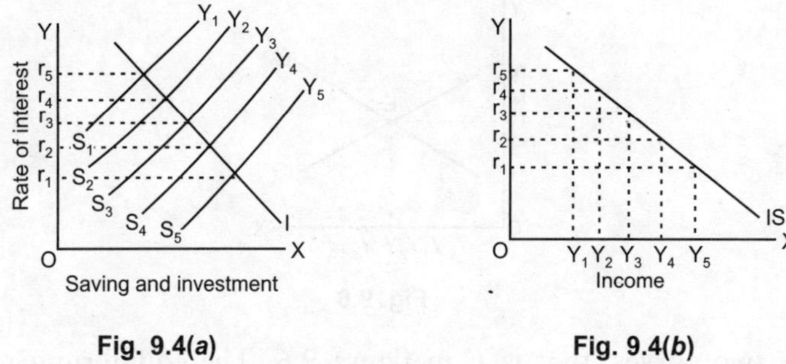

Fig. 9.4(*a*) Fig. 9.4(*b*)

From Keynesian theory we obtain a family of liquidity preference curves at various income levels. These, together with the supply of money fixed by the monetary authority, give us the Ricksian *LM* curve (Figure 9.5).

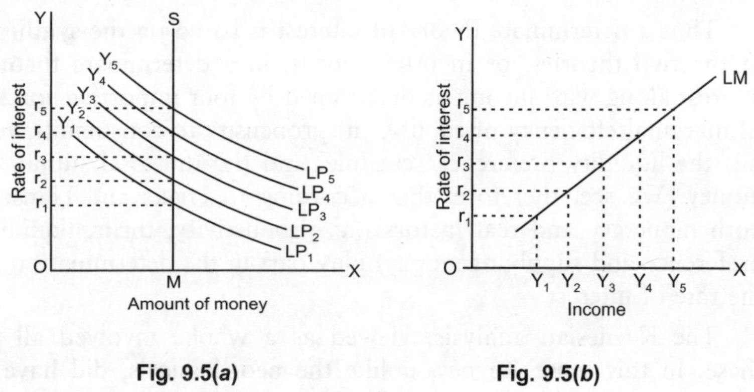

Fig. 9.5(*a*) Fig. 9.5(*b*)

The *LM* curve tells us what the various rates of interest will be (given the quantity of money and the family of liquidity preference curves) at different levels of income. In figure 9.5(*a*) we have derived the *LM* curve from a family of liquidity preference curves. With the increase in income, liquidity preference curve shifts upward and as such the rate of interest which equates supply of money with demand for money rises. In figure 9.5(*b*) we measure income on the *X*-axis and plot the income levels corresponding to the various interest rates given at those income levels by the quantity of demand for and supply of money in figure 9.5(*a*).

The *IS* and *LM* curves are schedules relating the two variables, (i) income, and (ii) rate of interest. Income and the rate of interest are therefore determined together at the point of intersection of

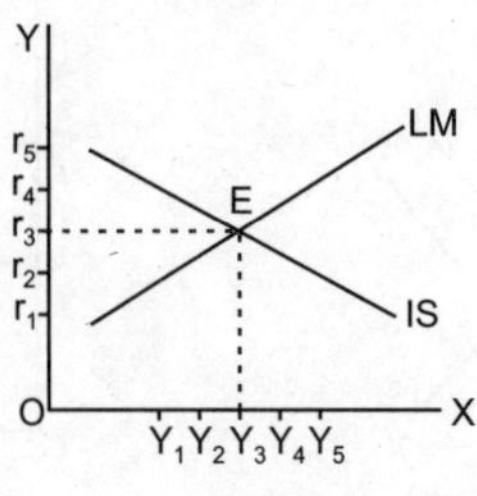

Fig. 9.6

these two curves, that is *E* in figure 9.6. The equilibrium rate of interest thus determined is Or_3 and the level of income, determined is OY_3. At this point, income and rate of interest are related to each other in a way that (i) investment and savings are in equilibrium and (ii) the demand for money is in equilibrium with the supply of money.

Thus a determinate theory of interest is based on the synthesis of the two theories, or in other words, in a determinate theory, interest along with income is determined by four important forces: (i) marginal efficiency of capital, (ii) propensity to consume (save), (iii) the liquidity preference schedule, and (iv) the total supply of money. We see, therefore, that according to Hicks and Hansen, both monetary and real factors (*i.e.* productivity, thrift, liquidity preference and supply of money) play part in the determination of the rate of interest.

The Keynesian analysis, viewed as a whole, involved all of these. In this sense Keynes, unlike the neo-classicals, did have a determinate theory of interest. But Keynes never combined all the elements together to form an integrated theory of interest. He failed to explicitly point out that liquidity preference combined with the quantity of money can give us only *LM* curve and not the rate of interest. It was Hicks who utilised the Keynesian tools and presented a complete picture combining productivity, thrift, liquidity preference and supply of money.

EVALUATION OF HICKS-HANSEN DETERMINATE THEORY

The Hicks-Hansen determinate theory of the rate of interest is a useful integration of the classical and Keynes' theories of interest. Further it has been used to explain several policy muddles which neither classical nor Keynesian theory could explain. Two important examples are cited below:

Firstly, it is observed that in underdeveloped countries the rate of interest is low in spite of the fact that the need and demand for capital are high. The classical theory can not explain this phenomenon. The liquidity preference of people in these countries is also high but the rate of interest is low. Thus the Keynesian analysis also fails to offer an explanation for the phenomenon. The Hicks-Hansen determinate theory tells us that the rate of interest and income are simultaneously determined. In underdeveloped countries, since the level of income determined by the real and monetary forces is low, the rate of interest which is simultaneously determined is also low.

Secondly, it has been observed in the present developed capitalist countries that during depression monetary policy alone fails to raise income while in a situation of near-full-employment it is successful in appreciably raising income and employment. This can be explained with the help of *IS-LM* diagram.

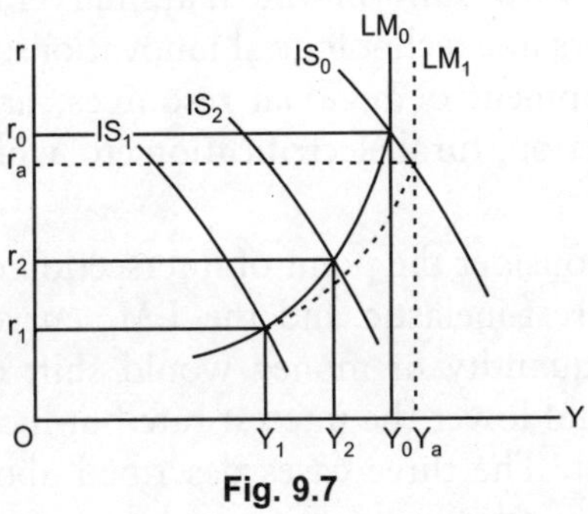

Fig. 9.7

In figure 9.7, the IS_0 curve which is relatively interest-elastic interesects LM_0 curve which is relatively interest-inelastic. At the point of intersection, the interest rate r_0 and income Y_0 are mutually determined.

Suppose that income at Y_0 is short of the full employment income. In order to increase income to full employment level, the monetary authority increases the supply of money so that LM_0 is shifted to LM_1. This leads to a decline in the interest rate to r_a and rise in income Y_a. This means boom conditions because Y_0 already represents a high level of employment (though not full employment). Thus it is obvious that if the *IS* curve is interest-elastic and the *LM* curve is interest-inelastic, an increase in the quantity of money will have an-expansionary effect and the monetary policy would succeed.

Now take the case of intersection of *IS* curve which is relatively interest-inelastic with LM_0 curve which is highly interest-elastic. In this case it is clear that income and employment cannot be raised by increasing the quantity of money, or in other words, monetary policy fails. In order to raise the level of income from Y_1 to Y_2 it is essential to shift the IS_1 curve to IS_2 and this would be possible only when the *MEC* schedule rises or when the consumption function is shifted upwards.

Under these circumstances the monetary policy fails and it is only the fiscal policy which can raise the *MEC* schedule and investment. This type of situation does arise in advanced countries which have large quantities of capital and hence a low marginal efficiency of capital and the low rate of interest under such conditions fails to induce new investment. The investment function I_1 being interest-inelastic, the *IS* curve would also have a tendency to be interest-inelastic. Investment outlets would, therefore, have to wait for an upward shift in the marginal efficiency of capital brought by factors like technological innovations, inventions of new products, development or regional resources, urban development, housing construction, rural electrification etc. which would shift IS_1 curve to IS_2.

Now let us consider the point of intersection of IS_2 curve which is relatively interest-inelastic and the LM_0 curve. In this case an increase in the quantity of money would shift the LM_0 curve to LM_1, which would lower the interest rate but increase income only to a small extent. The three cases described above represent near full-employment, underemployment and depression respectively.

But economists like Don Patinkin and Milton Friedman have criticised Hicks-Hansen formulation. They have pointed out that it is too simplified to be of any practical use. They hold the view that division of the economy into only two sectors—real and monetary—is an oversimplified presentation of the problem. They have suggested a general equilibrium analysis approach for determining the rate of interest and income. According to them, rate of interest is only one of prices which acts on and reacts to changes in the prices of all the commodities and services in the economy. In short, they prefer an integrated approach to the determination of not only income and rate of interest but of prices also.

REAL VERSUS MONETARY THEORIES OF INTEREST

The classical theories of interest concentrate on 'real forces' like productivity and thrift. The important role played by the monetary authorities in recent times and the existence of unemployment have considerably undermined the impact of real forces contemplated in these theories. As a result, the monetary theories of interest have assumed more importance. Today the popular theory of interest is either a liquidity preference theory, according to which the money rate of interest is determined by the demand for and supply of the stock of bonds, or a loanable funds theory, according to which the money rate of interest is determined by the demand for and supply of a flow of securities.

It is sometimes believed that there exists a conflict between the real and monetary theories of interest. According to real theories, interest is the yield of capital and a reward for foregoing present consumption. According to monetary theories, interest is the price of money and reward for parting with liquidity. Keynes himself believed that there exists a conflict between the real and monetary theories of interest when he remarked that interest is not a reward for waiting but a reward for not hoarding money.

In fact, the rate of interest is influenced by real as well as monetary forces. General equilibrium analysis shows that the rate of interest operates simultaneously, as D.H. Robertson has remarked, on "the threefold margin" of consumption decisions, investment decisions, and asset-portfolio decisions. In other words, interest simultaneously rewards waiting, reflects the pure yield of capital, and compensates for parting with liquidity. In actual practice, the rate of interest is influenced to some extent by all the elements expressed in the equation of Walras-Hicks general equilibrium. The loanable funds theory or the liquidity preference theory, therefore, represent only a form of partial equilibrium analysis of the determinants of the rate of interest. Determination of rate of interest can be properly viewed only by considering the rate of interest to be determined in a general equilibrium system.

PORTFOLIO BALANCE THEORY

This theory was developed independently but simultaneously by James Tobin, Gurley and Shaw, and others in the 1950s and early 1960s. The theory is a natural and logical extension of the theory of liquidity preference. Like the liquidity preference theory, the portfolio balance theory focusses attention on interest rates as being that which explains the demand for money and that which is directly and primarily affected by a change in the supply of money. But, unlike liquidity preference, portfolio balance theory does not assume that securities and other non-monetary assets are such perfect substitutes for each other that there is only one rate of interest. Instead it maintains that there are as many different interest rates as there are imperfect substitutes among earning assets. According to it relative interest rates on differentiated assets depend on the relative supplies of the assets.

Portfolio balance is basically a theory of asset choice. It is concerned with how individuals and the community allocate their holdings among alternative assets. It is a theory of the demand for assets, with the demand for each asset being measured as a proportion of total assets. To the extent money is an asset, portfolio balance is partly a theory of the demand for money.

The theory states that the demand for any asset, considered as a proportion of total assets, varies directly with its own interest rate and inversely with interest rates on substitute assets.[17] The demand for money varies directly with its own implicit rate of interest, and it varies inversely with interest rates on other assets.

NEGATIVE RATE OF INTEREST

The early theorists upheld the possibility of a negative rate of interest. Foxwell in a paper entitled '*Some Social Aspects of Banking*' read in 1886 before the Bankers' Institution imagined a situation in which the rate of interest may become negative. Irving Fisher, in his book '*The Theory of Interest*', argued in favour of the possibility of the rate of interest being zero or even negative. Marshall imagines a situation in which the rate of interest would be negative.[18]

> We can therefore imagine a state of things in which stored up wealth could be put to but little use in which many

---

17. Interest rates are here defined in a broad general sense to include rates of return, yields, and other percentage measures of benefits received. In this sense, all assets have interest rates.
18. Alfred Marshall, *Principles*, Reprint 8th Ed., pp. 192-93.

> persons wanted to make provision for their future while but few of those who wanted to borrow goods were able to offer good security for returning them or equivalent goods at a future date. In such a state of things the postponement of, and waiting for enjoyments would be an action that incurred a penalty rather than reaped a reward: by handing over his means to another to be taken care of a person could only expect to get a sure promise of something less and not of something more than that which he lent: the rate of interest would be negative.

Mill also conceived the possibility of an extremely low rate of interest owing to capital accumulation resulting from economic development.

In the real world, however, there is no possibility of the rate of interest becoming negative. So long as the demand for capital exceeds its supply, rate of the interest will always be positive. Some people hold the opinion that incomes in advanced countries are rising so fast that a stage may be reached when people's capacity to save increases so much that the supply of capital exceeds the demand for it. But in the real world, it is highly improbable that this stage will ever be reached. Actual experience shows that with the rise in income the demand for capital has not lagged behind its supply. The demand for capital has been rising quite fast as a result of factors like fast increase in population—at least in developing countries—increase in wants and change in tastes, innovations, development programmes of developing countries etc. On the supply side also, a positive rate of interest is necessary to induce people to forego their present consumption and save in order to provide funds to meet the demand for capital.

Keynes ruled out the possibility of reducing the rate of interest to zero even by a vast supply of money by the monetary authority. He held the view that there is a low positive rate of interest at which the liquidity preference curve becomes infinitely elastic, or in other words, becomes parallel to the horizontal axes. At a low positive rate of interest, there is what Keynes calls a 'liquidity trap'; or in other words, the demand of people for money is insatiable at this rate of interest. Even if the monetary authority goes on putting huge quantities of money in circulation, the rate of interest will not decline below a certain positive rate because at this rate people simply go on absorbing the additional money in their money balances. The monetary experience during the great depression corroborates the view held by Keynes.

Moreover, so long as capital remains productive, the rate of interest would remain positive and with economic progress the productivity of capital will increase rather than decrease. According to Prof. J.K. Metha the very phrase "negative rate of interest is an example of a curious contradiction in terms. Interest is the earning of capital. Capital, being a factor of production, is necessarily productive. Interest is, therefore, invariably positive."[19]

It may, however, be pointed out that although the money rate of interest cannot become zero or negative, the real rate of interest can and has in fact been negative during periods of rapidly rising prices. For illustration, if the money rate of interest is 4 per cent and the price level rises by 6 per cent, the real rate of interest will be—2.24 per cent.

CO-EXISTENCE OF INFLATION AND HIGH INTEREST RATES

Inflation is a situation characterised by an excessive quantity of money in circulation. A high rate of interest existing side by side with an excessive quantity of money in circulation appears to be a state of inconsistency. Apparently, this appears to contradict the law of supply which states that, other things remaining unchanged, an increase in the supply of a commodity leads to a decline in its price. In fact, inflation and high interest rates can exist side by side without involving any contradiction and this would be obvious if the assumption of "other things remaining unchanged" is removed.

The rate of interest is determined not only by the supply of money but by both the demand for and supply of money. If increase in the demand for money is greater than that in the supply of money, the rate of interest would rise in spite of an increase in the quantity of money in circulation. During inflation rising prices increase the marginal efficiency of capital and thus stimulate investment. Keeping in view rising profits, the entrepreneurs do not mind borrowing at higher rates of interest.

During inflationary periods, the demand for money for speculative motive also rises very fast. Rising prices eliminate the

---

19. J.K. Mehta, *Studies in Advanced Economic Theory*, p. 24.

risks of speculation and as such the entrepreneurs do not mind borrowing even at higher rates of interest to take advantage of the highly favourable conditions.

LOW INTEREST RATES IN UNDERDEVELOPED COUNTRIES

The underdeveloped countries are characterised by a shortage of capital. The existence of low interest rates in such countries appears to be quite paradoxical. The basic reason for low interest rates in underdeveloped countries is that, although the supply of capital is scarce, the demand for capital is not much. The shortage of demand for capital is explained by a low marginal efficiency of capital in these countries. The marginal efficiency of capital is low because of the small size of the market and lack of external economies like means of transportation and communication, power, supply of water, banking facilities, trained labour etc. Another reason for shortage of demand for capital is the availability of cheap labour in these countries. It is more profitable to make greater use of cheap labour than of scarce capital.

Saving-Investment Equality

10

INTRODUCTION

The equality between saving and investment has been a subject of great controversy in economic literature for quite a number of years. An analysis of the problem shows that the basic reason for the differences of opinion lies in the definitions adopted by different economists and not in any defects of logic. Those who quarrel with the definitions given by others do so mainly on the basis of the usefulness of the definitions put forth. We briefly discuss below the important definitions of saving and investment put forward by different economists.

(1) *Keynes in his General Theory of Employment, Interest and Money* defines *S* as the difference between income earned in a period and the consumption in the same period and *I* as the expenditure on investment in the same period (and therefore also the income earned in that period other than in the production of consumption goods). In this sense *S* is always equal to investment.

(2) Keynes in his *Treatise on Money* defines S_t as the difference between "normal" (instead of actual) income and consumption, and is as such less than the S of the *General Theory* by as much as "normal" income is less than actual income; I_t is defined just like *I* in the *General Theory*. $I_t - S_t$ (which is the same as $S - S_t$), therefore, represents the excess of actual over "normal" income—"abnormal profits."

(3) In Robertson's writings, S_r is defined as income earned yesterday (instead of today and therefore disposable today) minus today's consumption and is therefore less than *S* by as much as income earned yesterday is less than income earned today. I_r is defined in the same way as *I*. $I_r - Sr$ (which is the same as $S - S_r$), therefore, represents the excess of income earned today over income earned yesterday.

(4) The Swedish economists—Ohlin, Lundberg and particularly Myrdal-define S_e as *expected* or *ex-ante* saving and I_e as *expected* or *ex-ante* investment.

KEYNES IN GENERAL THEORY

Keynes, in the *General Theory* defines saving and investment in such a way that they are necessarily equal.

> Whilst, therefore, the amount of saving is an outcome of the collective behaviour of individual consumers and the amount of investment of the collective behaviour of individual entrepreneurs, these two amounts are necessarily equal, since each of them is equal to the value of current output, the current investment is equal to the value of that part of current output which is not consumed, and that saving is equal to the excess of income over consumption, ...the equality of saving and investment necessarily follows.[1]

To cite Keynes again, "...saving and investment have been so defined that they are necessarily equal in amount, being, for the community as a whole, merely different aspects of the same thing."

Keynes argues at times that saving and investment are not only always equal but "merely different aspects of the same thing." And yet he deplores saving while approving investment.

One of the drawbacks, though perhaps not a very important one, of adopting Keynes' concepts is that it means departing from the ordinary usage. "It is an uncommon use of terms to say that a newly employed workman who receives his wage at the beginning of the week, and spends it entirely in the course of the week, 'saves' the money in the meantime, and that as soon as he spends the money it is 'saved' by the next recipient...and so on."[2] Further, the Keynesian concepts do not distinguish between investment which is financed out of inflationary credit or dishoarding and that financed out of the current supply of voluntary savings. Beyond doubt, it makes a lot of difference whether investment is financed from one

---

1. J.M. Keynes, *The General Theory of Employment, Interest and Money* (London, 1936), p. 63.
2. Friedrich A. Lutz, "The outcome of the Saving-Investment Discussion", reprinted in The American Economic Association, *Readings in Business Cycle Theory* (London, 1950), p. 155.

source or the other; and the concepts which ignore this difference are not very useful. Moreover, Keynes' concepts are neither useful for the analysis of the cumulative process nor of any help in dealing with the problem of credit policy. The only advantage which these concepts appear to possess is that they avoid the necessity of defining the unit period which is the crucial problem in regard to other definitions.

KEYNES IN TREATISE

In the *Treatise*, Keynes had adopted a different definition of Y and, therefore, could maintain that S can be different from I. There all receipts do not form part of Y. Abnormal profits or losses are neither to be added to income nor are they to be subtracted from it. For this reason Keynes could state that when I rises, the only result is that total expenditure is more, so that profits (Q) rise. Since savings are coming out of normal income, the result is that $I > S$ by an amount equal to additional investment or profits Q. Similarly, if investment falls, abnormal losses take place and lead to a situation where $S > I$. Keynes was excluding occurrence of abnormal profits or losses from the income accounts to show the effect of changing investment on prices. His main purpose was to find out the way prices of consumption goods and capital goods get determined and fluctuate with changing investment leading to abnormal profits or losses.

The possibility of inequality of S and I in the *Treatise* was useful for Keynes because it could help in the explanation of fluctuations in prices. In his *General Theory*, on the other hand, the definitions adopted were of greater significance because there his purpose was not to discuss changes in prices but rather to eliminate them for finding out changes in real income and output.

ROBERTSON'S CONCEPTS

In Robertson's view, an equality between saving and investment can exist both at the top of the boom and at the bottom of the depression; and the same would be true of an equality between the money rate of interest and the natural rate if this is supposed to be identical with an equality between saving and investment.

Robertson's concepts can be used as instruments for analysing economic events over time, showing how the events of one period influence the events of the next. The relation between S and I at each moment tells us whether the system contains a tendency to an upswing or a downswing.

Since *S* and *I* may be equal in the depression, it is evident that their equality cannot provide a norm of monetary policy, at least not by itself. It can be used solely as an instrument of theoretical analysis, which is the only use to which Robertson himself puts it.

Dr. F.A. Lutz prefers the Robertsonian definitions to other definitions. He states, "In contradiction to Mr. Lerner's view, it is the contention of this article that the assumption of a time-lag between receipts and expenditure in Robertson's sense is closer to reality than the assumption of simultaneity between them and is necessary for the analysis of economic events over time."[3] To this Lerner replies that "Keynesian simultaneity between receipts and expenditure is implicit in the proposition that $I = S$ only in the sense that there is no interval between the moment *X* receives a payment from *Y* and the moment when *Y* makes this same payment to *X*. Hence the question of time-lag is not there. Robertson's time-lag is quite different which is the time elapsing between the moment that *X* receives his income from *Y* and the moment when he spends this income on consumer goods purchased from *Z*. Simultaneity between such receipt and expenditure is impossible. However this kind of simultaneity has nowhere been assumed by Keynes. Thus criticism based on this reasoning must be based on a confusion between the two meanings of a time-lag between receipts and expenditures."

Dr. Lutz prefers Robertsonian definitions also because they are dynamic and they permit to speak of gap between *S* and *I* which provide a guide for credit policy. Replying to this argument, Dr. Klein states, "Both claims are confused. Robertson's definitions are dynamic only in the most trivial sense. They define observed aggregates at different points of time, but they give no functional relation to economic behaviour so that one can solve for each variable in the system as a function of time alone. Robertson did not realise the existence of a consumption schedule, a saving schedule or an investment schedule. He has set up a few lagged definitions but has presented no truly dynamical relations."[4] Further Lutz's

---

3. F.A. Lutz, "The Outcome of Saving-Investment Decisions", *Quarterly Journal of Economics*, August, 1938.
4. Lawrence R. Klein, The Keynesian Revolution (London, 1952), pp. 116-17.

interpretation of Robertson's I and S consists of one or all the elements: (i) abnormal profits, (ii) excess of income earned today over income earned yesterday, (iii) unexpected income, and (iv) unexpected depletions. None of these can tell us ambiguously whether economic activity is going up or down and cannot provide us any guide for credit policy.

Another argument advanced by Lutz against the Keynesian concepts is, "They do not allow us to distinguish between investment which is financed out of inflationary credit or dishoarding from investment which is financed out of the current supply of voluntary savings...and a terminology that conceals this difference hardly seems commendable." To this argument, Prof. Lerner replies, "If this means that the use of the Keynesian terminology prevents us from discussing the effects of increases in the amount of money or of diminutions in liquidity preference or increases in the marginal efficiency schedule of investment it clearly is incorrect."[5]

The final argument put forward by Lutz in favour of Robertsonian approach is that it appears more impressive because it purports to provide an explanation of fluctuations both in income as well as in prices. Further, by varying the time interval between different "days" or by varying the lengths of the "days" for different sectors of the economy, it may be possible to weave out intricate patterns in which the fluctuations in income and prices occur in an economy. But in actual practice, the Robertsonian analysis, just like the Keynesian analysis, is not of much help. Robertsonian analysis does not tell us why I should exceed S or *vice versa*. It does not tell us what should cause such a change and in what direction this change should be expected to take place in the next period. If it is maintained that changes in I and S in the next period will depend upon prices and incomes respectively, we have to find out the causal relationships between income and consumption and prices and investment decisions. In other words, we have to study the causes which determine investment and consumption decisions and that is what Keynes does in his *General Theory* and Keynes certainly does it more systematically and more successfully.

---

5. A.P. Lerner, "Saving and Investment" in S.E. Harris (ed.), *The New Economics* (London, 1960).

Keynes' equality between *S* and *I* is not, therefore, meaningless. It has its own place and cannot be replaced by any substitute.

Prof. Lerner mentions the following reasons for criticism of equality between saving and investment by some writers.[6]

(i) They fail to recognise that all items involved are payments (or differences between payments) over a period of time and not amounts existing at some point of time. They represent flows which can be measured.

(ii) They fail to understand that while every person is free to save either more or less than he invests, all persons considered together are not free because the total investments are equal to total savings.

(iii) They fail to visualise expenditure as a flow with the flow of income during the same period.

(iv) They fail to recognise that the equation does not mention equilibrium.

(v) They fail to realise that the proposition (S = I) is only an analytical phenomenon and does not represent the working in the real world.

To cite Prof. Hansen, "Clearly it is not a question of one definition being wrong and another being right... The only question is their usefulness. In period analysis, Robertsonian definitions are useful and indeed necessary. In time-rates-of-change analysis, the Keynesian definitions are appropriate." Now all the countries use Keynesian definitions for calculating national income because in national income measurements all variables must apply to the same period.

EX-ANTE AND *EX-POST* CONCEPTS

Saving and investment are not always equal in the *ex-ante* sense of the terms. In a dynamic society where the savers and investors are different persons, and their decisions with regard to saving and investment are unco-ordinated, *ex-ante* (planned or desired) investments are not likely to be equal to *ex-ante* (planned or desired) savings. The two can be and often are unequal. Current investment can exceed the current saving. This is possible where the excess investment that cannot be financed out of current saving is

6. *Ibid*., p. 633.

financed through newly created money or through dishoarding, *i.e.*, by drawing upon past savings. Similarly, current saving will exceed current investment if people increase their hoardings. The system is out of equilibrium almost always in the sense that *ex-ante* investment is out of tune with *ex-ante* savings.

The equilibrium level of income is reached when both the savers and investors are in equilibrium. The savers would be in equilibrium only when they succeed in actually saving that amount which they intend to save. The investors would be in equilibrium when the actual investment equals the investment intended by them. The double condition of equilibrium would, therefore, be satisfied when

(i) Intended Saving = Actual Saving

(ii) Intended Investment = Actual Investment

Since saving is that part of the current product which is not consumed ($S = Y - C$) and investment is also equal to the part of current product not consumed ($I = Y - C$), it follows that the actual (ex-post) investment must be always equal to the actual (ex-post) saving. Thus by definition we nave:

Actual Saving = Actual Investment

It does not, however, follow from the above that *ex-ante* (intended) investment and *ex-ante* (intended) saving must also always be equal. In equilibrium, of course, where the intended saving equals the actual saving and the intended investment is equal to the actual investment, it follows from the identity of actual saving and actual investment that:

ex-ante (intended) saving = *ex-ante* (intended) investment.

The process through which the two *ex-ante* quantities are ultimately brought into equilibrium position from one of disequilibrium at the beginning of the period operates through multiplier repercussions on income variable. If *ex-ante* investment exceeds *ex-ante* saving, the level of income would rise, which in turn would increase the volume of savings and the two would become equal in the equilibrium. Similarly, if savings are in excess of investment, the level of income would decline, which in turn would decrease the volume of savings and the two would become equal in the equilibrium. This is illustrated by diagram 10.1.

SS represents the saving curve and *II* the investment curve. The two curves intersect each other at point *E* which gives the

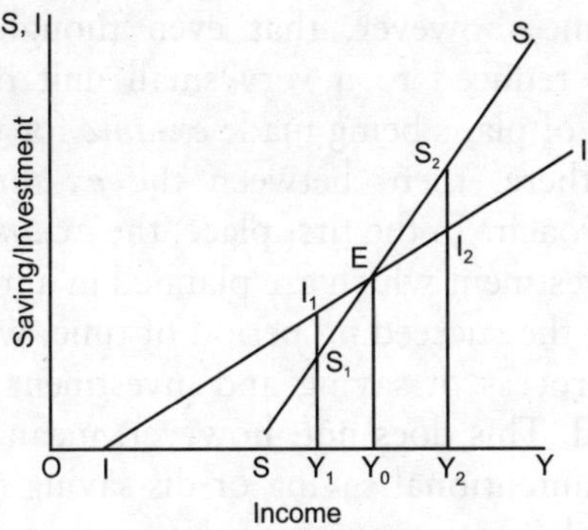

Fig. 10.1

equilibrium level of income or OY_0. At the OY_1 level of income Y_1I_1 is the *ex-ante* investment and Y_1S_1 is the *ex-ante* saving, which is less than *ex-ante* investment. Since *ex-ante* investment is greater than *ex-ante* saving, the level of income must rise and reach OY_0 where *ex-ante* saving becomes equal to *ex-ante* investment. When the income is OY_2, the *ex-ante* saving Y_2S_2 exceeds the *ex-ante* investment Y_2I_2. Since *ex-ante* savings are larger than *ex-ante* investment, the level of income must decline and reach OY_0 level, where the *ex-ante* savings become equal to *ex-ante* investment.

How useful are these *ex-ante* concepts of savings and investment as the analytical tools which Myrdal intends them to be? In Myrdal's treatment saving and investment are calculated *ex-ante* for a unit-period the length of which is arbitrarily chosen. It is, however, obvious that we are not free to choose the unit-period arbitrarily. If the intention is to talk about plans being fixed in advance for a certain period or time, the period must be so chosen that no changes in plans occur within it. This is the definition of the unit period which Ohlin and Lundberg adopt. But this is significant only when applied to an individual enterprise; there is no such period for all entrepreneurs in the aggregate. The length as well as the timing of their individual planning period vary, so that plans are stopping and starting at every moment. Any attempt, therefore, to analyse the *ex-ante* concepts leads logically to the identification of the period with an extremely short "finite but indivisible" unit of time. This appears virtually abandonment of the *ex-ante* concepts in favour of Robertson's approach.

Let us assume, however, that even though the period has ultimately to be reduced to a very small unit of time, it is still sensible to speak of plans being made *ex-ante* for this period. What differences are there, then, between the *ex-ante* approach and Robertson's approach? In the first place, the *ex-ante* concepts relate to saving and investment which are planned in a moment of time to be executed over the succeeding period of time, while Robertson is looking at the process of saving and investment as it takes place during the period. This does not, however, mean that Robertson's terms include unintentional saving or dis-saving (profits or losses) and unintentional investment or dis-investment (accumulation or depletion of stocks), which may be made during the period. Unintentional saving (or dis-saving) is not included because Robertson does not add profits (or substract losses) made during the period to the disposable income of that period but carries them forward to the disposable income of the next period. Unintentional investment (or dis-investment) is not included because he abstracts from stocks, on which this item depends. If he were to include stocks, he would have to specifically define his investment as intended investment carried out during the period, so as to arrive at consistent results.

Secondly, it appears as if the magnitude of S according to the *ex-ante* calculations might differ from the magnitude of S according to Robertson's calculation for the reason that the *ex-ante* saving is conceived of as being determined on the basis of the income that people expect to receive in the forthcoming period, while Robertson's saving is made out of the income actually received in the preceding period. But the difference is illusory. From Robertson's point of view, it does not matter whether the saving which people decide to do in the forthcoming period is determined by them as some portion of the income received in the last period or as some portion of the income which they hope to receive in the forthcoming period. Robertson is not concerned with the factors which influence people's decisions as to the amount of saving they want to do, but only with the actual carrying out of their plans; and these plans can only be executed out of the amount of income already received.

Thirdly, the *ex-ante* concepts refer explicitly to expectations while Robertson's concepts do not. The results of applying the concepts, however, are the same in both cases. If, for example, *ex-ante* investment is greater than *ex-ante* saving, we have an expansion in the period to which the *ex-ante* plans relate. According to Robertson's concepts also, an excess of I over S shows an expansion for this period.

HANSEN'S APPROACH

Hansen has made an attempt to resolve the saving-investment controversy. To cite him "One source of confusion arose from the failure of his (Keynes') critics to realise that while investment and saving are always *equal*, they are not always in *equilibrium*. All this could have been avoided had Keynes made it clear from the outset that the *equality* of saving and investment does not mean that they are necessarily in *equilibrium*. He was realistic enough to see this, as is revealed again and again in different sections of his book. But he never explicitly stated it, doubtless because the matter had not been clearly, thought through."[7] He continues, "If the economy is in a moving equilibrium, so that the variables are always in a normal (desired) functional relationship to each other, then indeed saving and investment will not only be *equal* but will also be in equilibrium. But if the process of change involves a lagged adjustment of certain-variables, this will not be the case. If, for example, there is an expenditure lag (*i.e.* if consumers adjust their expenditures slowly to changes in income), then, until the lag has worked itself out, *actual* consumption will not be equal to *desired* consumption (and actual saving will not be equal to *desired* saving). Similarly, if there is an output lag, producers being slow to adjust to increases (or decreases) in sales, then unintended disinvestment (or investment) in inventory stocks will occur. Thus actual investment will diverge from desired (intended) investment. Under either of these conditions (expenditure lag or production lag) saving and investment, though *equal*, will not be in equilibrium. There can obviously be no *equilibrium* condition until the lags have been worked through. In equilibrium conditions (lags having been overcome) saving and investment are both *equal* and in equilibrium, and this is true whether the system is in moving or in stable equilibrium. But if the system is not in equilibrium, saving and investment, while still *equal* will not be in *equilibrium*."[8]

7. A.H. Hansen, *A Guide to Keynes* (New York, 1953), p. 59.
8. *Ibid*., pp. 59-60.

KLEIN'S APPROACH

Dr. Klein states, "The entire confusion in connection with the saving-investment controversy can be traced to a failure to distinguish between *schedules* and *observables*."[9] According to him there exists a functional relationship between *S* and *Y* on the one hand, and between *I* and *Y* on the other hand. Thus *S* and *I* schedules represent various amounts of *S* and *I* respectively corresponding to the various levels of national income. If these schedules showing relationship between income, *S* and *I* (independent of each other) are smooth curves, there would exist a unique level of income at which *S* and *I* calculated from their respective schedules are equal. This is $S - I$ equality in the schedule sense. Observable $S(I)$ refers to that particular level of $S(I)$ calculated from the $S(I)$ schedule from a knowledge of the unique equilibrium value of national income which equates *S* and *I*. Observable values refers to a single point while schedules are series of points along curves. The observed levels of *S* and *I* are those two values on the schedules corresponding to the observed level of income; all other values of *S* and *I* along schedules are not observed.

When Keynes said that *S* is always equal to *I*, he was referring to the observable. But when he said, "when investment changes, income must necessarily change in just that degree which is necessary to make the change in saving equal the change in investment,"[10] he was referring to the process of adjustment which achieves an equilibrium. As observable over time *S* and *I* are always equal but there can be a divergency between them at a virtual or unobserved level of income.

HAWTREY'S CONCEPTS

According to Hawtrey, equilibrium exists if active *I* is equal to active *S*. If active *S* exceeds active *I*, the result will be passive investment owing to unintentional accumulation of stocks or, assuming: that there are no stocks, passive dis-saving due to losses. Similarly, if active *I* exceeds active *S*, there will result passive disinvestment owing to depletion of stocks or passive saving in the form of profits.

---

9. Lawrence R. Klein, *The Keynesian Revolution* (London, 1956), p. 11.
10. J.M. Keynes, *The General Theory of Employment, Interest and Money* (London, 1936), p. 18.

If a very long period is chosen, the passive savings which are made within the period can become active savings within the same period because those who possess passive savings may decide within this period whether to spend them or to save them "actively." The same is true of passive investment. If such a situation is to be avoided, there is no alternative but to take a very short period. In case a very short period is taken, we are back again at Robertson's concepts.

SAVING AND INVESTMENT EQUALITY (CLASSICAL POSITION)

Keynes was not the first person to visualise equality between saving and investment. Classical economists also talked of this equality. There are, however, important differences between Keynes and classicals. Firstly, according to classicals equality between saving and investment is brought about by the rate of interest. If savings exceed investment, the rate of interest declines. A decline in the rate of interest discourages savings and encourages investment and thus an equality is brought about between the two. Similarly, if investment exceeds savings, the rate of interest rises. A rise in the rate of interest stimulates savings and discourages investment and thus an equality is brought about between the two. In this way, changes in the rate of interest correct any disequilibrium that may arise between savings and investment. Secondly, the classicals believed that the equality between saving and investment is brought about at full employment level of income.

In contrast to the classical view, Keynes believed that the equality between saving and investment is brought about not by the rate of interest but by income. For instance, if investment exceeds savings, increased investment increases the aggregate income of the community to such a level that the increased saving out of increased income becomes equal to increased investment. Further, Keynes believes that saving and investment can be equal, in fact, normally are so, at less than full employment.

SAVING AND INVESTMENT (ACCOUNTING EQUALITY)

Accounting equality between saving and investment is also called logical identity. This is very similar to the identity between purchases and sales. Price is determined by demand and supply and at each price total amount sold is equal to total amount bought. This is so because every transaction has two aspects *viz.* buying and selling or income and expenditure. The identity between saving and investment holds true at all levels of income irrespective of the fact that saving and investment are done by different sets of people. Employment of labour at any time results in a certain amount of national output which, in turn, results in the creation of national income. This national output consists of (i) consumption goods and (ii) investment goods. In algebraic terms, $O = C + I$. Similarly, national income is divided between consumption expenditure and saving. In algebraic terms, $Y = C + S$. We know that by definition $O = Y$. From this it follows that $C + I = C + S$ or $I = S$. This equality between saving and investment can be expressed in another way also. Keynes defines savings as the difference between income and consumption *i.e.* $S = Y - C$. Further, investment is the difference between income and consumption, *i.e.*, $I = Y - C$. Since $Y - C$ is common in both the equations $S = I$.

What is the economic significance of the accounting equality between S and I ? The answer is that it shows the condition that must be satisfied in order to reach the equilibrium level of income, that is, a condition characterised by the equality of planned saving and investment. The accounting equality between S and I implies that unless the economy as a whole is willing and able to invest at the same rate at which the general public is disposed to save, producers will have to contract or expand output and employment in order to maximise their expectation of profit or to minimise their expectation of loss until the economy gains a position of equilibrium. Further the accounting equality has the richer implication that the determinants of consumer and entrepreneurial behaviour must be investigated if the economy as a whole is temporarily in dislocation.

SAVING AND INVESTMENT (FUNCTIONAL EQUALITY)

The accounting equality between saving and investment is not of much use for analytical purposes. It throws no light on the casual factors that go to determine savings, investment, consumption and income. It also does not show the mechanism by which an equality is brought about. Accounting equality shows simply the statistical result of the behaviour of the national income or economic system during a given period. Functional equality, in contrast, shows the actual behaviour and the process of adjustment of saving and investment in the economy as a whole. In other words, it puts life into dead statistics.

Though savings and investment in the statistical sense are identically equal at all times and at any level of income, saving and investment in the schedule sense are equal only in equilibrium, or in other words, at the equilibrium level of income. In order to facilitate exposition we may compare the equilibrium of savings and investment with that of supply and demand. Just as there can be inequality between supply and demand except in equilibrium, so can there be inequality between saving and investment except in equilibrium. Just as supply and demand are brought into equilibrium by the equilibrating mechanism of price, so are saving and investment in the schedule sense equilibrated by the income mechanism. Supply and demand are equal only at the equilibrium price, that is, the price at which the quantity demanded is precisely the same as the quantity offered. If the demand exceeds supply, the price would rise to the equilibrium level and if the supply exceeds demand, the price would decline to the equilibrium level. The supply and demand would remain unequal until and unless they reach the equilibrium price.

Let us construct a dynamical model for the equilibrium of savings and investment. The three variables involved in this model are independent variable Y and dependent variables S and I. The rate of change of income is functionally related to savings and investment in such a manner that income must rise when investment exceeds savings and decline when savings exceed investment. Savings and investment are equal only at the equilibrium level of income, that is, an income, which is neither rising nor declining. Thus the equality between saving and investment is brought about through changes in the level of income.

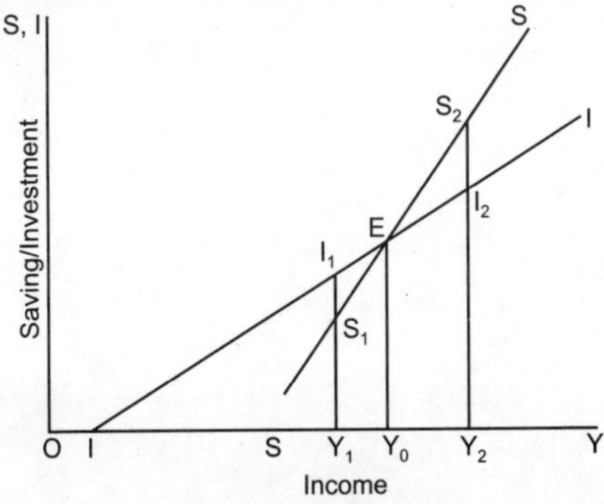

Fig. 10.2.

The diagram given above illustrates the equilibrium process of savings-investment adjustment. Both the saving and investment are along the vertical axis and income is measured along the horizontal axis. The savings function, *S*, intersects the investment function, *I*, from below, indicating that stable equilibrium is under study. The situation would be one of unstable equilibrium if the *I* curve intersects the *S* curve from below because in that case income would move away from the equilibrium level. If we start from income Y_2, investment is greater than savings by I_2S_2. This excess of investment over savings would cause the level of income to rise till it reaches the equilibrium level of income, at which savings and investment are equal. In contrast, if we start from an income Y_1, savings exceed investment by I_1S_1, which would cause the income to decline till it reaches the equilibrium level.

Thus saving and investment in the schedule sense are brought into equality, over time, by the equilibrating mechanism of income. This way of looking at savings and investment is consistent with the common-sense view that, though decisions to save and decision to invest are made by different people and for different motives in the course of time these decisions get somehow reconciled through the "invisible hand" of *income*. This implies that income, while influencing savings and investment, may itself be influenced by them.

Principle of Acceleration

11

INTRODUCTION

The principle is known by several names like "acceleration principle", "principle of accelerated or magnified derived demand", "The Relation" etc. Though casually mentioned in the *General Theory*, the principle does not form an important part of the Keynes' analysis of income, output, employment and business fluctuations. The principle as stated by Aftalion, Carver, Bickerdike and others is much older than the concept of multiplier. It is, however, generally associated with the name of J.M. Clark because it is he who made the concept popular. Interest in this principle developed when it was found that this principle combined with the Keynesian consumption function can explain self-generating cyclical mechanism. The concept was refined and developed by a number of economists including Harrod, Samuelson, Hicks, Goodwin, Robertson, Haberler, Pigou, Ragnar Frisch, Fellner, Hansen, Kuznets, Hayek, Mathews, Klecki and Kaldor.

MEANING

While the multiplier shows the effect of investment on consumption (and hence on income), the accelerator shows the effect of a change in consumption on investment. An increase in demand for consumption goods will lead to an increase in demand for equipment required to produce these goods. Since the production of a given amount of final output normally requires an amount of capital several times larger than the output produced with it during any short period (say a year), an increase in demand for final goods will result in an additional demand for capital goods several times larger than the new final demand. The principle of acceleration thus states that an increase in demand for consumption goods results in several times larger increase in demand for capital goods. The accelerator measures the change in investment goods industries as a result of changes in consumption goods industries. When incomes are rising, investment rises even faster; when incomes cease rising and stabilize at some level, investment may drop off very sharply. The principle of acceleration is based on the theory that the demand for services of capital goods industries is derived from current consumption demand and states that a given increase in demand for consumption goods in the economy generally results in an accelerated or magnified demand for capital goods, the latter bringing a stimulus to the whole economy. The acceleration coefficient is the numerical value of the relation between an increase in income (ΔY) and the resulting increase in investment (ΔI) via increase in consumption (ΔC). If, for instance, an increase in consumption expenditure of Rs. 4 crores induces businessmen to increase their investment by Rs. 16 crores, the accelerator would be 16/4 = 4.

Retailers and wholesalers may increase their inventories if it is their custom to keep their inventories in a fixed proportion to the rate of sales. New orders will, in this case, increase by more than the increase in sales. A similar but often much stronger effect is to be expected when the increased demand relates to durable consumers' goods. Durable consumer goods are demanded because of the services they render. To enjoy the services of durable goods through their life-time, the durable goods have first to be produced. Thus the increased demand for services leads to an accelerated demand for the goods which render these services. While the increase in income may be just enough to pay for the services which are rendered monthly or to make small payments on the instalment plan, the demand cannot be satisfied unless the durable consumers' goods are produced as a whole. The increased demand for services of durable consumers' goods (like furniture, automobiles, radio sets, television sets, refrigerators, houses) leads to an accelerated demand for the durable consumer goods themselves. The larger the difference between the sale price of the service (*e.g.* monthly rent) and the total cost of the durable goods (*e.g.* house) or the larger the number of instalments, the greater would be the magnification of an original change in demand and the greater the opportunity for new investments.

Sometimes, production of increased consumer goods resulting from a rise in their demand may not lead to an increase in the capital equipment producing these goods. The existing equipment may wear out on account of constant use with the result that the increased demand for consumer goods cannot be met. This actually happened in India during the Second World War. In the absence of induced investment, the increased demand for consumer goods levelled off and as such the accelerator did not operate during all these years.

The factual basis of the acceleration principle is the knowledge that fluctuations in output and employment in investment goods industries are greater than in consumption goods industries. The more capitalised the methods of production are, the greater would be the value of the accelerator. The accelerator, however, cannot and does not claim to be able to explain all types of fluctuations. The prices of raw materials, for instance, fluctuate more violently than the prices of investment goods because the supply of raw materials, particularly agricultural commodities, is much more inelastic in response to the changes in demand than is the supply of manufactured goods.

Acceleration Principle simply says that the amount of investment expenditure in any period of time depends on the change in level of income in the period. If I_t is investment expenditure in period t, Y_t and Y_{t-1} are the income levels in period t and period t_{-1} respectively. The change in the level of income is $(Y_t - Y_{t-1})$. The acceleration principle says that:

$$I_t = \beta (Y_t - Y_{t-1}) \text{ where } O < \beta < 1$$

Assumptions

The assumptions on which the acceleration principle is based can be enumerated as follows:

1. The total capital stock of the economy is fully utilised.
2. The firms increase their capital stock to meet the increase in the demand for their products.
3. The capital-output ratio is fixed. The optimum stock of capital is some constant proportion of output.
4. There is no ceilling on investment and the supply of capital goods is perfectly elastic.
5. Capital goods are perfectly divisible.
6. Capital stock is optimally adjusted in each period.
7. The increase in the demand for output occurs autonomously and not with response to the increase in investment.

8. There are either fixed coefficients of production or variable coefficients of production, production is subject to constant returns to scale.
9. There is no change of input prices.

The amount of optimum capital stock depends on the amount of output produced. The optimum capital stock increases with the increase in output. If output increases more quickly, the greater will be the demand for additional capital stock. It means that additional capital stock depends on the additional output produced, *i.e.* ΔK is a function of ΔY. Here ΔK is investment, I. Hence, I is a function of ΔY. This relationship can be analysed with the help of the following diagram. Suppose, output, Y is a function of capital, K and labour, L.

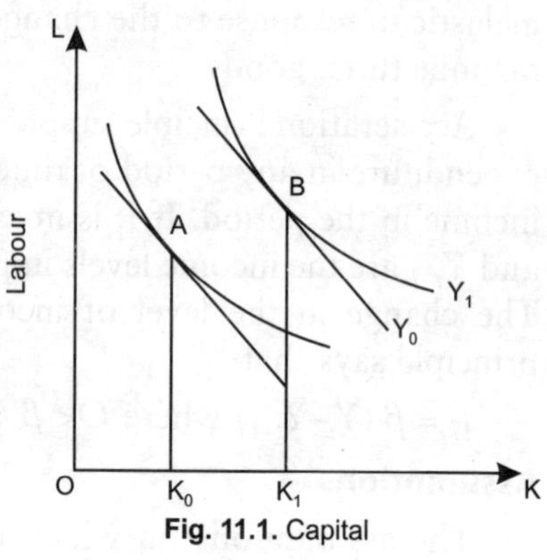

Fig. 11.1. Capital

In this Fig. 11.1, horizontal axis represents capital while vertical axis represents labour. Y_0 and Y_1 represent isoquant showing fixed level of output produced from different combinations capital and labour. We get optimum capital stock K_0 for output level Y_0 and optimum capital stock K_1 for output level Y_1. The optimum capital stock increases from K_0 to K_1 with the increase in output level from Y_0 to Y_1. That is, the change in the optimum capital stock depends on the change in the planned output level. This is the main reason behind the acceleration principle.

It makes again two further implicit assumptions. (1) It assumes that the firms are always in equilibrium in using of inputs having no excess capacity. If there is excess capacity, the level of output can be increased without increasing the stock of capital. (2) The supply of capital goods is infinitely elastic so that adjustment is possible without lags. If the supply of capital goods is not perfectly elastic and if the capital goods require sometime to be produced investment increases only after a time lag.

Generally, we assume a linear relationship between I_t and $(Y_t - Y_{t-1})$, i.e. $I_t = \beta(Y_t - Y_{t-1})$ where β is called accelerator or the acceleration coefficient and also represents optimum capital-output ratio. If there is a fixed proportionality between capital and output,

then $$\frac{K_t}{Y_t} = \beta \text{ or, } K_t = \beta Y_t$$

Similarly, $K_{t-1} = \beta Y_{t-1}$

$\therefore \quad K_t - K_{t-1} = \beta(Y_t - Y_{t-1})$

or, $\quad I_t = \beta(Y_t - Y_{t-1})$

where change in capital stock is called investment. If we assume that $K(t)$ and $Y(t)$ are continuous functions of time (t), then the acceleration principle can be written as:

$$\frac{dK(t)}{dt} = \beta.\frac{dY(t)}{dt}, \text{i.e. } I(t) = \beta.\frac{dY(t)}{dt}$$

In this form investment at time t is directly proportional to $\frac{dY(t)}{dt}$. So long as $\frac{dY(t)}{dt}$ is positive, $I(t)$ is also positive, when $\frac{dY(t)}{dt}$ is zero, $I(t)$ is also zero and $\frac{dY(t)}{dt}$ is negative, $I(t)$ is also negative. Therefore, $I(t)$ increases, decreases or remains constant depending on the value of $\frac{dY(t)}{dt}$. That is, $I(t)$ increases when $\frac{dY(t)}{dt}$ increases, $I(t)$ decreases when $\frac{dY(t)}{dt}$ decreases and $I(t)$ remains constant when $\frac{dY(t)}{dt}$ remains constant.

Hence, investment depends not on the absolute level of income but to the rate of change in the level of income. Thus, total output increases, but we cannot say that investment increases, investment may decrease, because investment is not related with total output but related with the rate of growth of output. In the following diagram (Fig. 11.2) we can explain the relationship between output and investment.

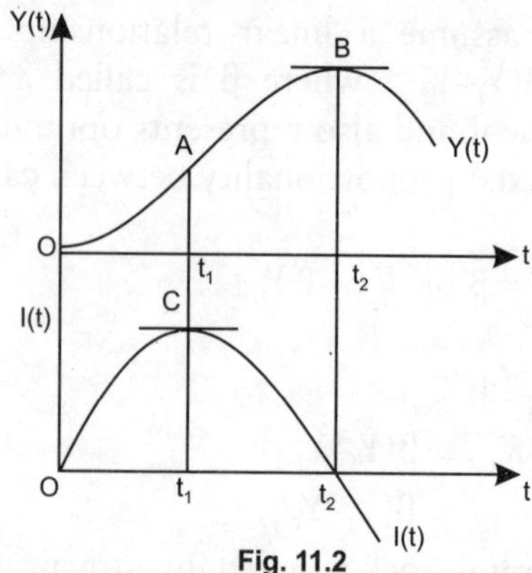

Fig. 11.2

In this Fig. 11.2, as t increases, the rate of growth of income first increases, reaches its maximum and then decreases. The curve $Y(t)$ is first convex from below and then concave. So long as $Y(t)$ is convex $\frac{dY(t)}{dt}$ is rising. At point of inflexion A, $\frac{dY(t)}{dt}$ is maximum, when $Y(t)$ is concave, $\frac{dY(t)}{dt}$ is decreasing. When $Y(t)$ is maximum at point B, $\frac{dY(t)}{dt} = O$ and $Y(t)$ is decreasing $\frac{dY(t)}{dt}$ is negative.

In the lower part of the diagram the $I(t)$ curve is derived from the $Y(t)$ curve from the upper part. How is it derived? It is shown below:

1. Up to point A in the upper part of the diagram, $\frac{dY(t)}{dt}$ is increasing and hence $I(t)$ is increasing up to point B in the lower part of the diagram both corresonding to the period t_1.
2. At the point of inflexion A corresponding to the period t_1, $\frac{dY(t)}{dt}$ is maximum and $I(t)$ is also maximum, at point C.
3. Between A and B on $Y(t)$ curve $\frac{dY(t)}{dt}$ is decreasing corresponding to the period between t_1 and t_2, hence $I(t)$ is also decreasing.

4. At point B on $Y(t)$ corresponding to the period t_2, $\frac{dY(t)}{dt}$ is zero and hence $I(t)$ is also zero.
5. Beyond B on $Y(t)$ corresponding to the period after t_2, $\frac{dY(t)}{dt}$ is negative and hence $I(t)$ is also negative.

Therefore, $I(t)$ depends not on $Y(t)$ but on $\frac{dY(t)}{dt}$. $I(t)$ increases when $\frac{dY(t)}{dt}$ increases. $I(t)$ is maximum when $\frac{dY(t)}{dt}$ is maximum. $I(t)$ decreases when $\frac{dY(t)}{dt}$ decreases. $I(t)$ is zero when $\frac{dY(t)}{dt}$ is zero. $I(t)$ is negative when $\frac{dY(t)}{dt}$ is negative.

MULTIPLIER AND ACCELERATOR DISTINGUISHED

The multiplier shows the effect of a change in investment on income and employment and the accelerator shows the effect of a change in consumption on investment. While the multiplier depends upon the propensity to consume, the accelerator depends upon the durability of the equipment. In other words, the former depends upon psychological factors while the latter is dependent upon psychological factors. In fact, accelerator is also psychological in its origin and content but becomes highly technical on operational plane.

CONCEPT OF INDUCED INVESTMENT

Traditionally, the accelerator refers to the investment induced by changes is consumption only; but it may also be viewed in terms of investment induced by changes in output as a whole which includes investment. Hicks, in fact, considers accelerator in the latter sense and rightly so. For the relation, he substitutes the investment co-efficient (v) defined as "the ratio of the induced investment to the changes in output which called it forth." The strength of the acceleration effect, if measured by the total amount of induced investment generated in a given period, would depend on the relevant change in output and the size of the investment co-efficient.

The above concept of 'induced' investment is based on the fundamental assumption that producers of capital goods as a whole adjust their investment programmes to the changing level of national income, considering the latter as the best single index of the profit outlook. The main justification for conceiving of 'induced' investment in terms of the *marginal propensity to invest* rather than in terms of the traditional *acceleration coefficient* lies in the fact that the former is a *behavioural* relation on a par with the marginal propensity to consume while the latter is a technological relation between the additional stock of capital equipment and the additional physical output. Thus the marginal propensity to invest can have as large or small values as business confidence, profit expectations and financial prudence are assumed to influence investment policies in given conditions of technology. When, however, a change in the stock of capital (positive net investment) must be considered as an explicit variable, as in a long-run growth analysis, then induced investment must be conceived in terms of acceleration coefficient or the capital-output ratio. A corollary justification for viewing 'induced' investment from the point of view of the marginal propensity to invest lies in the advantage it affords for analysing the behaviour of gross investment and hence of GNP, irrespective of whether the stock of capital and hence production capacity are thereby increased or decreased (which latter changes are the concern mainly of growth economics).

FORMS OF INDUCED INVESTMENT

The total induced investment consists of induced investment in fixed capital, in working capital and in inventories. Hicks defines working capital as "goods in process as well as such minimum stocks of materials and half-finished goods as are technically necessary in the production process." Inventories or what Hicks calls "liquid capital", is defined as "reserve stocks not technically necessary." Some minimum amount of liquid capital, consisting of reserve stocks of finished as well unfinished goods, would be necessary for conveniently carrying out production. Investment in the three forms, because of the differences in their nature, responds differently to changes in consumption or output. It is, therefore, necessary to study the response separately for the three forms.

INDUCED INVESTMENT IN FIXED CAPITAL

Strength of the Acceleration Effect: A change in output, by necessitating the adjustment of the capital stock to the new level of output induces investment in a given capital. The total amount of induced investment in a given period depends upon the relevant change (s) in output and the related Investment Coefficient (v). If it is assumed that the entire induced investment generated by a given change in output occurs in the period immediately following such change, induced investment in the nth period would be $v\ (Y_{n-1}-Y_{n-2})$ where Y_n is output in the nth period and v is the Investment Coefficient. If the induced investment effect of a given change in output extends over a number of periods, induced investment in the nth period would be

$$v_1(Y_{n-1}-Y_{n-2})+v_2(Y_{n-2}-Y_{n-3})+.....+v_p(Y_{n-p}-Y_{n-p-1})$$

where Y_n is output in the nth period, v_p is the induced investment which materializes p periods later as the result of a change in output of one unit in some particular period, and p is the number of periods following that in which the change in output occurs over which the induced investment effect of such change extends. On the same assumption the total induced investment generated by the change, in output in the nth period would be

$$(Y_n-Y_{n-1})\ (v_1+v_2+v_3+.....+v_n)$$

In this case the Investment Coefficient v would be the sum total of the partial coefficients v_1, v_2, v_3, ...v_p.

The larger the v, the greater (in absolute amount) is the total induced investment generated by a given change in output. In case of positive induced investment generated by an increase in output, the strength of v depends on (1) the degree of capital intensity of the production techniques employed, (2) the existence of unused plant capacity relevant to the given increment of output, (3) the scope for the utilisation of capital-saving inventions in effecting replacement and renewals of plant, (4) the nature of the expected increase in the demand for output, and (5) the proportion of increase in output foreseen and provided for in previous capital outlays. The higher the ratio of capital to output (*i.e.* the capital intensity of production techniques), the large would obviously be v. The existence of unused plant capacity in the lines in which the increase in demand for output occurs makes the required increase in output possible without addition to the stock of fixed capital. The existence of relevant idle capacity, therefore, lowers v. If the rate of capital-saving invention, and that of depreciation and obsolescence of plant, are high enough, it may be possible to replace the capital stock falling due for replacement and renewal by one with a higher ratio of output to capital at a rate that would enable the required increase in output to be achieved without net addition to the total capital stock. The larger the scope for the rise in this way of the ratio of output to capital, the lower will be v. Increase in the demand for output induces net addition to the capital stock only if it is expected to last. In case the increase in demand for output is not expected to continue, the producers would have a tendency to meet the increased demand by utilising the existing plant capacity more intensively, in fact even at a rate higher than the optimum rate of utilization. Lastly, to the extent the increase in demand has been foreseen and investment outlay undertaken in anticipation of it, it would not, when it occurs, induce further investment.

Time-shape of Induced Investment: Having discussed the factors on which depends the strength of the acceleration effect, now we turn to the shape of induced investment through time. Let us start from a stationary state characterised by constant output, zero net investment and gross investment equal to the constant rate of depreciation. Let us now assume that a once-for-all increase in output, expected to be permanent, takes place. The capital stock will need to be adjusted to the new level of output; increase in output would thus induce positive net investment. Assume that the additional capital goods can be produced within a single 'period'. During the first period gross investment would rise above its previous level by the value of the additional capital goods, and since depreciation, being based on the previously existing stock of capital, would remain unchanged, net investment would also be equal to the same amount. In the next period, when the additional capital stock has already been acquired, gross investment will decline to the level prevailing under the initial stationary equilibrium. But now there is the extra depreciation on the new capital stock. As such the net investment will become negative by this amount. When the new capital goods are due for replacement, and if they are replaced in a single period, gross investment will once again rise to the level of the period during which they were first created. But because of the extra depreciation of the now larger capital-stock, net investment in this period will be lower than in that period by the amount of this extra depreciation. In the next period, gross investment will revert to the initial level and net investment become negative and so on. The first phase of positive net investment induced by the increase in output is called the 'initial hump' and the subsequently altering phase of negative and positive net investment the 'tail' of the 'stream' of a new investment induced by such increase in output.

In case the capital goods comprising the additional investment, and their replacements, have different lives, there will be a 'stream' of net investment corresponding to each part of the investment. Since the flows and ebbs of each stream (*i.e.*, the alternating spans of positive and negative net investment) will occur at different times and be superimposed, fluctuations will be damped to the extent such ups and downs are mutually offset. Further damping will occur if actual life of each portion of equipment turns out to be different from its normal life. The more effective will be the damping, the longer is the period over which the initial investment spreads.

Now assume that the increase in output is not once-for-all but it is followed in latter periods by other increases in output, each inducing a fresh stream of net investment with the above time-shape. Since these streams begin at different periods of time, when added together, their flows and ebbs may mutually offset. A succession of increases in output may thus tend to damp fluctuations in net investment.

INDUCED INVESTMENT IN WORKING CAPITAL AND LIQUID CAPITAL

Let us assume a once-for-all increase in the demand for output at a time when both working capital and liquid capital are fully adjusted to a previously constant level of output. On the assumption of continuous production, requiring outputs at all stages of the production process, the rate of investment in working capital will rise from the beginning to the end of the production process. After that it will decrease sharply to zero because then total working capital would have been adjusted to the higher level of output. Investment in liquid capital will, however, respond differently to an increase in output. During the time taken by output to attain the higher level, increased demand will be met by drawing upon stocks. Thus the period of investment in working capital will be marked by disinvestment in liquid capital. The end of this period is characterised by the cessation both of investment in working capital and disinvestment in liquid capital so that taking the two together net investment falls to zero.

Unlike investment in fixed capital, there is no necessary asymmetry between rises and declines in output in their effects on investment in working and liquid capital. In the first phase following the decline in output, there is positive net investment in liquid capital and disinvestment in working capital. At the close of this period both positive investment in liquid capital and disinvestment in working capital ceases, leaving the total net investment zero.

Induced investment in fixed capital depends upon actual changes in output, for directly, in the Marshallian short period, business responds to changes in demand for output by varying the rate of utilisation of existing capacity. It is only the in-appropriateness of the existing stock of fixed capital for the new level of output that, in due course, causes this stock to be suitably adjusted. The induced investment in working and the liquid-capital occurs in response to changes in demand for output and precedes the actual change in output.

TOTAL INDUCED INVESTMENT

The above analysis shows that investment responds typically to increases in demand for output in three phases. During the first phase, there is positive investment in working capital and disinvestment in stocks, both falling to zero at its close. During the second phase, there is positive investment in stocks (necessary to rebuild them after the withdrawals in the first phase and to adjust them to the new higher level of output). During the third phase, extending to the distant future, there are oscillations in net investment or owing to altering periods of negative and positive net investment in fixed capital represented by the 'tail' of the induced stream of investment in fixed capital.

Similarly, the decline in demand proceeds in three phases: during the first phase there is disinvestment in working capital and positive investment in stocks, both falling to zero at its close; during the second phase there will be disinvestment both in fixed capital and stocks; during the third phase there would be oscillations in net investment represented by the 'tail' of the induced stream of disinvestment in fixed capital. Though total net disinvestment in the second phase is comparable, for an equal change in demand, to the total net investment in response to increase in demand, yet the existence of a ceiling to the possible rate of disinvestment may cause it to be spread over a longer period. Since the initial trough in the second phase of investment's reaction to decline in demand might be flatter than the corresponding initial hump produced by investment's response to an equal increase in demand, oscillations in net investment in the third phase would be damped, and hence less important in the first phase. Lastly, while the induced investment streams produced by successive rises in demand that supervene upon one another can be superimposed, such superimposition may not be possible when successive declines in demand supervene upon one another, for rate of disinvestment already may have touched its ceiling. The supervening declines in demand would not then intensify but prolong disinvestment.

Table 11.1

Working of Accelerator

(Figures in crores of Rupees)

Period	*Output of final goods*	*Capital goods required*	*New capital goods required*	*Replacement*	*Total new capital goods required*
1	2	3	4	5	6 = 4 + 5
1	1,000	500	0	50	50
2	1,200	600	100	50	150
3	1,300	650	50	60	110
4	1,300	650	0	65	65
5	1,200	600	—50	65	15
6	1,100	550	—50	60	10
7	1,000	500	—50	55	5
8	900	450	—50	50	0

Table 11.1 explains the working of the acceleration principle. Let us suppose that production of final goods worth Rs. 2 requires capital goods worth Re. 1; the life of the capital goods is 10 years and 10 per cent of them are accordingly replaced each year.

The first row in Table 11.1 shows the position in the first period. In the second period, output of final goods rises by Rs. 200 crores and the requirement of new capital goods by Rs. 100 crores (col. 4). The total amount of new capital goods required (col. 6) is Rs. 150 crores. Thus a 20 per cent increase (from Rs. 1,000 crores to Rs. 1,200 crores) in output results in a 200 per cent increase (from Rs. 50 crores to Rs. 150 crores) in capital goods. In the third period, the output of final goods rises, but only by Rs. 100 crores, over the preceding period. This requires an increase of Rs. 110 crores in the total new capital goods. In spite of an 8 per cent rise (from Rs. 1,200 crores to Rs. 1,300 crores) in output of final goods, there is a decline of 26.67 per cent (from Rs. 150 crores to Rs. 110 crores) in capital goods industry. This is so because the absolute increase of Rs. 200 crores in the output of final goods has not been maintained. In the fourth period, the output of final goods remains unchanged at Rs. 1,300 crores. No new capital goods are required except for replacement. Production in the capital goods industry drops by 40.09 per cent (from Rs. 110 crores to Rs. 65 crores). In the eighth period, the output of final goods declines by Rs. 100 crores and the capital goods industry collapses.

The above example leads to an important generalisation. When there is an absolute increase in the production of final goods, the rise in the capital goods industry is magnified. If the increase in the production goods is maintained, the capital goods industry will only manage to avoid a decline. As the increment in the final goods industry declines, the capital goods industry suffers an absolute decline and in greater proportion. Thus a depression can set in simply because consumption has stopped growing so rapidly. In other words, the depression can start even if the consumption has not dropped off absolutely but only levelled off at a high level. Any change in output of final goods causes a multiple change in the production of capital goods. This magnifying effect is the root cause of fluctuations in the capital goods industry. Thus the principle of acceleration provides a powerful explanation of the destabilising forces working in the economy during a trade cycle. This explanation teaches us a lesson that in order to keep the economy prosperous, mere standing still or running at a slow pace is not enough, we must run faster and faster to ward off the danger of a depression. "We have all heard of situations", says Samuelson, "where people have to keep running in order to standstill. In economic world, matters may be still worse: the system may have to keep running at an ever-faster pace in order to standstill."[1]

1. P.A. Samuelson, *Economics*, p. 191.

The strength of the accelerator primarily depends upon (i) the capital-output ratio or capital coefficient and (ii) the durability of the capital equipment. The higher the capital coefficient, the larger would be the increase in investment as a result of a given increase in consumption and conversely. Similarly, the greater the durability of the capital equipment, the larger would be the degree of magnification of the derived demand; when there are no durable means of production, there is no magnification at all.

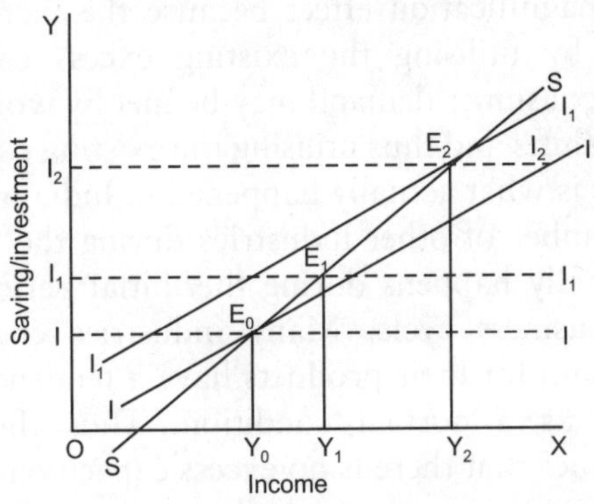

Fig. 11.3.

The figure given above illustrates the principle of acceleration. Since investment depends upon the level of national income, investment would be high when national income is high and investment would be low when national income is low. The investment schedule (*II*), therefore, is drawn in such a way that it is higher at a higher level of income. The investment may be negative at a very low level of income. If the investment schedule shifts upward from *II* to I_1I_1 because of an exogenous increase in investment, the multiplier effect would be greater than it would be if the investment were purely exogenous. If there were only exogenous investment (*i.e.* increase in income does not induce any investment) as shown by the dotted *II* which is parallel to the horizontal axis, the multiplier effect would have been only Y_0Y_1. But when there is induced investment as shown by rising *II*, super-multiplier effect or total multiplier-acceleration effect would be Y_1Y_2 which consists of Y_0Y_1 (multiplier effect) and Y_1Y_2 (acceleration effect). If there were no acceleration effect, Y_0Y_2 increase in income would have been obtained by I_1I_2 exogenous investment.

LIMITATIONS OF ACCELERATION PRINCIPLE

The operation of the acceleration principle is subject to the following qualifications, limitations or assumptions.

1. Non-existence of Excess Capacity in Consumer Goods Industries: The acceleration principle will not operate if there exists unutilised capacity in the consumer goods industries. When there is enough unutilised capacity in consumer goods industries, an increase in demand for consumer goods will not lead to any induced investment or magnification effect because the increased demand would be met by utilising the existing excess capacity. Many increases in the consumer demand may be met by working overtime or adding extra shifts and thus utilising the existing equipment more intensively. This is what actually happened in India in paper, sugar, textile and a number of other industries during the Second World War. This normally happens during the initial period of recovery phase of the business cycle. Many industries characterised by fluctuating demand for their products have a tendency to maintain excess capacity as a normal condition. Thus the working of accelerator assumes that there is no excess capacity and devices like double shift or overtime are not possible.

2. Excess Capacity in Investment Goods Industries: In the capital goods industries, on the other hand, it is assumed that there exists unutilised capacity. If there were no excess capacity in investment goods industries, an increase in the derived demand for equipment would not lead to an increase in the supply of equipment and thus the operation of the accelerator would be impaired. The working of the accelerator, therefore, is conditioned by the tough assumption that there exists excess capacity in the investment goods industry but no excess capacity in the consumer goods industry.

3. Fluidity: The operation of the accelerator assumes that the industry is in a fluid condition. It presumes that "....finished goods are turned out as fast as wanted and materials and means of production are instantly supplied as fast as the process of finishing requires them."[2]

---

2. J.M. Clark, "Business Acceleration and the Law of Demand: A Technical Factor in Economic Cycles" in The American Economic Association, *Readings in Business Cycle Theory* (London, 1950), p. 239.

4. Nature of Demand: The principle of acceleration will work only if the additional demand for consumer goods is of a lasting nature. If the entrepreneurs feel that the increase in demand is of a purely temporary character, they will not add to their capital equipment for meeting this demand. This also shows that the principle of acceleration is based not only on technological factor but also on profit expectation.

5. Constant Capital-Output Ratio: The principle assumes that there is a constant ratio between the output of consumer goods and the capital equipment required for their production, or in other words, that there is constant capital-output ratio. In the real world, this ratio is not constant. In addition to inventions and improvements in techniques of production which change the output per unit of capital equipment, the existing capital equipment may be used more or less intensively. Further, changes in the expectations of businessmen in regard to future trends in wages, interest, and demand, may lead to changes in the proportions in which the different factors are combined. The capital-output ratio thus varies in different phases of the business cycle.

6. Elastic Supply of Resources: The operation of the principle of acceleration is conditioned by the elastic supply of resources and the ability of the capital-equipment industry to expand its production. The capital-equipment industry would be able to expand its production in response to an increase in demand for its product only if adequate unemployed resources are available to it for employment. But once the full employment level is reached, it would not be possible to expand the production of capital equipment which would put a break to the working of the acceleration principle.

7. Elastic Supply of Credit: An elastic supply of money and credit facilitates the smooth working of the acceleration principle. Whenever there is induced investment, money and credit should be forthcoming in adequate quantities for investment in investment goods industries. A shortage of money and credit would raise the rate of interest and thereby the cost of investment financed by borrowed funds which would in turn inhibit investment. For the free and unhindered operation of accelerator, it is essential that sufficient funds are always available for investment purposes.

8. Inability of Investment Demand to Fall below the Value of Depreciation: Though accelerator works in the period of rising demand as well as in that of declining demand, its effect may be limited in the latter period. A decline in the demand for capital equipment (or disinvestment) is necessarily limited to replacement. An entrepreneur cannot reduce his demand for capital equipment below zero. The maximum that he can do in response to a decline in the demand for his product is to curtail replacement of his capital equipment and this cannot go below zero. Suppose the decline in demand for the finished product requires a 25 per cent reduction in the capital equipment but replacement demand in any year amounts to only 10 per cent of the capital equipment. In this case the accelerator cannot operate with full strength and its operation would be limited to a 10 per cent decline in capital equipment. The restraint on the free working of the accelerator in such a situation would be reflected in the generation of excess idle capacity.

9. Marginal Efficiency of Investment and the Rate of Interest: The acceleration principle does not take into account of the role of marginal efficiency of investment and the rate of interest in determining the level of investment.

10. Expectations: The role of expectations in investment decision is neglected in this theory. But investment is done on the basis of expectation. This vital part is omitted in this theory.

11. Divisibility of Capital: The vital leakage of this theory is that capital is completely divisible. But in reality, capital good is not perfectly divisible and many times it is indivisible.

MULTIPLIER-ACCELERATION INTERACTION

The multiplier and acceleration effects act and react on each other. Any change in investment has a multiple effect on national income which affects the level of consumption. Changes in the level of consumption, in turn, have magnified effects on investment. The change in investment again have multiple effect on national income and thereby on consumption and thus this chain of reactions goes on and on. Let us illustrate this chain of reactions with the help of a numerical example.

In Table 11.2 it is assumed that in each income period, there is an autonomous investment of Rs. 100, that the marginal propensity to consume is ½, and that the accelerator is 2.

Table 11.2

(Figure in Rupees)

Period	*Autonomous Investment*	*Increase in Consumption*	*Induced Investment*	*Total Increase in Income*
1	100	.00	.00	100.00
2	100	50.00	100.00	250.00
3	100	125.00	150.00	375.00
4	100	187.50	125.00	412.50
5	100	206.25	37.50	343.75
6	100	171.87	–68.76	203.11
7	100	101.55	–140.64	60.91
8	100	30.45	–142.20	–11.75
9	100	54.87	–72.64	21.60
10	100	10.80	33.34	144.14
11	100	72.07	122.46	294.53
12	100	147.26	150.38	397.64

Since there is a lag of one period, the rise in investment by Rs. 100 in the first period increases income in this period only by Rs. 100. In the second period, Rs. 100 income of the first period induces a rise of Rs. 50 in consumption because the marginal propensity to consume is assumed to be ½; this rise of Rs. 50 in consumption induces investment of Rs. 100 as the accelerator is assumed to be 2. Thus in this period the income rises by Rs. 100 + Rs. 50 + Rs. 100 or Rs. 250. In the third period this income of Rs. 250 induces a rise of Rs. 125 in consumption. Since this Rs. 125 constitutes a rise of Rs. 75 over the previous period, a new investment of Rs. 150 is induced. Thus in this period, the increase in income amounts to Rs. 375. In the same manner the increase in income is calculated for the succeeding periods.

Table 11.2 shows that the investments in income fluctuate widely. The increments in income rise up to the fourth period; thereafter they decline and become even negative in period 8. After the 8th period, they start rising again. Even the rates of changes are different in different periods. This explains the cyclical changes which take place in the economy as a result of the interaction of the multiplier and accelerator. It may be mentioned that different values of the marginal propensity to consume and of the accelerator would give rise to different cycles or patterns of series of increment in income shown in the last column of Table 11.2.

If both the marginal propensity to consume and the accelerator are very high, the process of expansion will go on to higher and higher levels until the ceiling of full employment is reached. At this level, the output will flatten out and induced investment will come to a stop. Besides this case, so long as the MPS is positive, the rise in income will be slowed down progressively as a continuously large part of the increase in income is saved. Ultimately there would occur a decline in induced investment. When this decline in induced investment exceeds the rise in consumption, a decline in income will start. Thus in spite of the acceleration effect, a positive marginal propensity to save will ultimately put a stop to the process of income propagation. Further, a continuous increase in investment tends to lower the MEC until further investment no longer remains profitable.

SAMUELSON MODEL

Prof. Samuelson shows that it is possible to have different types of business cycles or fluctuations from a continued injection of public investment by assuming different values of the marginal propensity to consume (α) and the acceleration coefficient (β).[3] The model sequence of national income for selected values of α and β are shown in Table 11.3.

Table 11.3

(unit: one dollar)

Period	$\alpha = .5$ $\beta = 0$	$\alpha = .5$ $\beta = 2$	$\alpha = .6$ $\beta = 2$	$\alpha = .8$ $\beta = 4$
1	1.00	1.00	1.00	1.00
2	1.50	2.50	2.80	5.00
3	1.75	3.75	4.84	17.80
4	1.875	4.125	6.352	56.20
5	1.9375	3.4375	6.6256	169.84
6	1.9688	2.0313	5.3037	500.52
7	1.9844	0.9141	2.5959	1,459.592
8	1.9922	–0.1172	–0.6918	4,227.704
9	1.9961	0.2148	–3.3603	12,241.1216

3. Paul A. Samuelson, "Interaction Between the Multiplier Analysis and Principle of Acceleration", *Review of Economic Statistics,* 1939, pp. 75-78.

1. $\alpha = 0.5$ and $\beta = 0$. This gives us purely multiplier effects with income approaching the peak. Here acceleration coefficient is zero.

2. $\alpha = 0.5$, $\beta = 1$. This gives us damped fluctuations, falling in value as they fluctuate about the multiplier level, gradually subsiding to that level. In this case, a constant continuing level of public expenditure will result in damped oscillatory movements of national income, gradually approaching the asymptote $\frac{1}{1-\alpha}$ times the constant level of public expenditure.

3. $\alpha = 0.5$, $\beta = 2$. This gives regular cycles about the multiplier level more or less unchanged values repeating themselves indefinitely.

4. $\alpha = 0$, $\beta = 2$. This gives us explosive cycles with variations about the multiplier level becoming larger and larger. In this case, a constant level of public expenditure will result in explosive ever-increasing oscillations, *i.e.*, the amplitude increases from cycle to cycle.

5. $\alpha = 0.8$, $\beta = 4$. This gives us an ever-increasing income gradually approaching a compound rate of growth. In this case, a constant level of public expenditure will result in an ever-increasing national income ("compound rate of interest growth") without oscillations.

Since even very simple models lead to entirely different results if we change our assumptions in regard to the coefficient of acclerator and the marginal propensity to consume, it is quite obvious that predictions as to the combined leverage effect of multiplier and acceleration principle in concrete circumstances is more or less impossible.

HICKSIAN MODEL

Relatively Static Case: Let us first examine the interaction of the multiplier and the accelerator in a stationary economy in which autonomous investment is nil. With a view to simplify the argument, we also assume:

(a) that disinvestment induced by a fall in output has the same time-shape as the investment induced by an equal rise in output;

(b) that the 'tail' of the stream of induced investment is of negligible importance so that only the initial hump or trough needs to be taken into account;

(c) that the initial hump or trough covers but one period, namely that immediately following the one in which the rise in output occurs; and

(d) that consumption is lagged one period behind income.

Now assume that the stationary equilibrium is disturbed in period 0 by, say, a once for all autonomous investment of amount A. In the next period autonomous investment again becomes zero. But, as shown below, owing to the interaction of the multiplier and the accelerator, the system may not return to stationary equilibrium.

Let Y_n be the excess of output in the nth period over the (stationary) equilibrium level of output (*i.e.* level of output in the period preceding the period 0 in which the disturbance occurs), s be the savings co-efficient or the marginal propensity to save, and v be the investment co-efficient. The consumption in the nth period will exceed its equilibrium level by $(1 - s)y_{n-1}$ and induced investment in this period will be $(y_{n-1} - y_{n-2})$. Since there is no autonomous investment, the excess of output in the nth period relatively to the equilibrium output, *i.e.*, y_n would be $(1 - s)y_{n-1} + v\,(y_{n-1} - y_{n-2})$.

$$y_n = (1 - s)y_{n-1} + v(y_{n-1} - y_{n-2})$$
$$= (1 - s + v)y_{n-1} - y_{n-2}).$$

As the autonomous investment takes place in period *0*, output is at its equilibrium level in period—1. In other words $y{-1} = 0$. In period *0* net investment is A against nil in the previous period while consumption remains the same. Output in period *0*, therefore, exceeds the equilibrium output by A. In other words $y_0 = A$. Given the values of s and v, by repeated application of the above formula, we can determine the excess of output in each successive period relatively to the equilibrium output.

Hicks identifies the following alternative ways, depending upon the value of v, in which output would react to the above disturbance.

(a) If the value of v is less than what Hicks calls the Lower Point, output may continue to increase for a few periods and then converge to the equilibrium level and stay there. The sequence is thus similar to the Kahn process (which, in fact, is the case where $v = 0$) except that there is the possibility of the initial rise.

(b) If v is above the Lower Point but below what Hicks calls the Middle Point, there is a larger initial rise than in the first case and damped oscillations (with decreasing amplitude) thereafter so that equilibrium is reached at the end.

(c) If v is above the Middle Point but below the Upper Point, the initial rise is not only larger than in the previous case but is also followed by fluctuations with increasing amplitude. Thus there will be an oscillation about the equilibrium position and no tendency to settle at it. All the while, as v increases, the initial swing is getting larger and larger.

(d) If v is above the Upper Point, the initial upward movement becomes so larger that it fail to turn round at all and the system moves relentlessly away from equilibrium.

The points which distinguish these four alternatives can be easily defined in terms of the value of s (the marginal propensity to save). Under the assumptions we have made, the middle point is to be always found where $v = 1$. The lower point is where $v = \left(1-\sqrt{s}\right)^2$ and upper point where $v = \left(1+\sqrt{s}\right)^2$.

The above conclusions remain essentially valid under assumptions which are less rigorous than those made in the simplified case above. This is so, for instance, when it is assumed that the initial hump of induced investment is spread out over a number of periods or is postponed to a period later than the one immediately following that which experiences the increase in output, or that consumption lags longer than one period, or that allowance is made for the 'tail'.[4] The interaction of multiplier and accelerator obviously holds the possibility of cyclical fluctuations. This possibility remains even under less rigorous assumptions though in this case the cycle would be less regular.

Interaction in a Dynamic Economy: Let us now turn to the interaction of the multiplier and the accelerator in a dynamic economy. With a view to simplify the argument we consider the simplest form of such an economy, namely, what Hicks calls the regularly progressive economy in which output increases at a constant geometrical rate so that in the nth period it is $(1 + g)$ of that in the $(n + 1)$th period where g is a positive constant. Assuming

4. J.R. Hicks, *A Contribution to the Theory of the Trade Cycle*, (London 1951), pp. 74-82.

a constant v and s, an essential condition of such an economy is that the rate of growth of autonomous investment must be the same as that of output so that the latter always bears a constant ratio to the former.[5] Hicks calls this ratio the super-multiplier.[6] Obviously in such an economy, given the level of autonomous investment at a given time and the constant rate of growth of such investment, the level of autonomous investment can be determined at different times. By applying the super-multiplier to the latter, the level of equilibrium output at different times can be obtained. In this way, we can determine the moving equilibrium path adjusted to the growth of autonomous investment along which output increases at a constant rate. The system can move along it if it is not disturbed. But if it is disturbed the results will be similar to those in the stationary case analysed above. This may be illustrated with reference to the elementary case mentioned above.

We have

Actual current output = current autonomous investment + current induced investment + current consumption.

Or $$Y_n = A_n + v(Y_{n-1} - Y_{n-2}) + (1-s)\, Y_{n-1}$$

If equilibrium output of the current period is E_n, we have

$$E_n = A_n + v(E_{n-1} - E_{n-2}) + (I-s)\, E_{n-1}$$

$$Y_n - E_n = v(Y_{n-1} - E_{n-1}) - v(Y_{n-2} - E_{n-2}) + (1-s)\,(Y_{n-1} - E_{n-1}).$$

Since $Y_n - E_n$ is the deviation from the equilibrium output in the period n, we may write it as in the stationary case as y_n. We then have

$$y_n = v(y_{n-1} - y_{n-2}) + (1-s)\, y_{n-1}$$
$$= (1-s+v)\, y_{n-1} - v y_{n-2}$$

This is the same relation as was obtained in case of a stationary economy. In other words, the deviation of the actual output from equilibrium output has precisely the same properties whether we have a stationary equilibrium or a regularly progressive economy. The results are, therefore, the same if the latter is disturbed, namely,

5. *Ibid.*, p. 59.
6. *Ibid.*, p. 62.

convergence to the equilibrium path if v is below the Lower Point, damped oscillations about the equilibrium path if v is between the Lower and the Middle Point, a regular cycle if v is at the Middle Point, explosive oscillations if v is between the Middle and the Higher Points, and relentless upwards divergence from equilibrium if v is higher than the Higher Point.

HICKS' 'REAL' THEORY OF TRADE CYCLE

We have seen above that if the investment coefficient (v) is at the Middle Point, any initial disturbance will generate regular fluctuations about the equilibrium path. But it would not be realistic to assume that v would always be at this point. Any realistic theory of trade cycle must show how cyclical fluctuations could arise and continue even when v had some other value.

Hicks believes that the cycle can be realistically explained only on the hypothesis of v being, as a rule, above its Middle Point.[7] This hypothesis does not appear to be inconsistent with the available statistical evidence.[8] There is, however, the consideration that on this hypothesis, a single disturbance should produce an explosive cycle. But throughout the 19th century, the trade cycle was not of this nature. The logical results of the hypothesis may, however, be made consistent with observed reality if there could be discovered some check which prevents the fluctuations from crossing certain limits. "The system", remarks. Hicks, "might then continue periodically breaking its head against these limits without running away altogether." Hicks believes that this hypothesis to a large extent corresponds to reality and, on its basis, proceeds to explain the cycle in outline.

Hicks' theory of trade cycle is based on the following assumptions:

(i) that v (the ratio of induced investment to changes in output which called it forth) lies above its middle point so that an upward displacement from the equilibrium path results either in explosive fluctuations about it or in relentless divergence from it;

7. *Ibid.*, p. 92.
8. *Ibid.*, pp. 92-94.

(ii) that the value of the multiplier (determined by the marginal propensity to consume) and the accelerator (which in Hicks' model is the ratio of induced investment to the increase in output or income) are constant and are such as to give a strong tendency to instability as a reaction to any disturbance so that any upward displacement from equilibrium will not be self-contracting (*i.e.* the equilibrium is not stable) but will cause continuing movement of the explosive variety away from equilibrium;

(iii) that there is a ceiling to the expansion of output in response to increase in effective demand on account of employable resources;

(iv) that the accelerator operates differently in response to decline in output because of the existence of a ceiling to the rate of disinvestment; and

(v) that (a) autonomous investment is increasing at a constant (geometrical) rate so that the system, if not disturbed from its equilibrium path, could remain in progressive equilibrium (with output increasing at the same constant percentage rate at which autonomous investment increases), and (b) that the rise in equilibrium output and in the output ceiling consequent on the steady increase in the rate of investment proceeds at the same rate as the latter.

The above assumptions are incorporated in figure 11.4.

Upswing and Boom: Suppose that an economy while proceeding along its equilibrium path experiences an upward displacement at P_0, say, owing to an abnormal burst of autonomous investment generated by an exceptional flow of new inventions. After the burst, autonomous investment returns to its old path. But on our "explosive" assumption of v being above its Middle Point, output will experience, perhaps after a lag, either explosive oscillations about, or relentless divergence from, the equilibrium path. It must, therefore, in due course touch the ceiling. The path P_0P_1 represents the particular upward movement which thus touches the ceiling. After output touches the ceiling at P_1, it can at best only creep along the ceiling. The phase in which output moves from the equilibrium path upward towards the ceiling may be termed the upswing, and that during which it creeps along the ceiling as the boom.

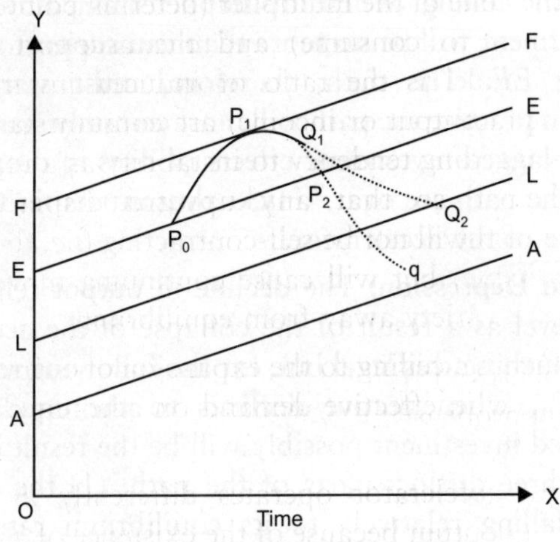

Fig. 11.4.

Downturn: The output can creep along the ceiling only for a limited period, ultimately it must start converging towards the equilibrium path. With the end of the assumed shortlived burst of autonomous investment, such investment would return to the normal level. This may be taken to happen at some point on the upper part of the path P_0P_1. After that the continued upward divergence of output from its equilibrium path would be entirely owing to investment induced by the previous rises in output above its equilibrium level. But once the path hits the ceiling and starts creeping along it, there is no further increase in the relative deviation from the equilibrium path. Now the induced investment which this rate of increase in output can induce can support a growth of output not along *FF* but *EE*. Output will, therefore, converge to *EE*. This conclusion remains valid even if induced investment is lagged, contrary to the assumption made above for more than one period. The effect of a longer lag is simply that induced investment remains larger than would support a growth of output no higher than along *EE* longer than previously so that the path may creep along the ceiling for a longer distance. Eventually, however, the time must come when even the longest lagged induced investment effect of rises in output during the P_0P_1 part of the path is over so that the current induced investment is entirely the result of changes in output represented by that part of the path where it creeps along the ceiling. When this happens, as pointed out above, induced investment will be no more than can support an increase in output along EE. The path, therefore, must start converging towards EE. In practice the path will most certainly start downwards before all the lagged investment effects of rises in output along the P_0P_1 part of the path are over.[9] Hicks thus attributes the downturn to the collapse of the accelerator.

Slump and Depression: The decline in output relatively to the equilibrium level as a result of the collapse of the accelerator will not stop on touching this level but, for the following reason, will go further. At P_2, when output declines to the equilibrium level, current induced investment possibly will be the result of changes in output over three distinct parts of the path: (1) the stretch when output was falling relatively to its equilibrium rate of growth, (2) the stretch where the path crept along the ceiling indicating a rate of growth of output equal to equilibrium rate of growth, and (3) the stretch when output was rising relatively to its equilibrium rate of growth. The induced investment generated by (2) might be sufficient to play its part in maintaining output at the equilibrium path, but that resulting from (1) would fall short of this requirement. This deficiency is not likely to be covered by investment in excess of this requirement coming from (1) because the stretch (1) being the farthest away from P_2, the relevant induced investment effect of rises in output during the period would be very much milder. The total current induced investment would, therefore, be insufficient to maintain output, when it reaches P_2, at the equilibrium path. There must be decline in output relatively to the equilibrium rate of growth.

In case the rate of growth is so large that output continues to increase in absolute terms even in spite of the above relative decline, the slump experienced by the system would be no more than slackening of the rate of progress. The system would then experience only mild 'cycles'. But such a high rate of growth is not realistic. The relative decline is thus most likely to involve absolute decline in output. Once that happens, on the "explosive" assumption made above, if the accelerator operated during the downswing in the same manner as during the upswing, the contraction could not end

9. *Ibid.*, p. 100.

(if at all) until output had fallen to a very low level. But the accelerator does not work in this manner. As stated earlier, there is a ceiling to the rate of disinvestment in fixed capital. Once the ceiling is reached, the rate of disinvestment becomes inelastic to further declines in output, *i.e.*, it becomes a constant. Total investment now being equal to autonomous investment minus a constant, disinvestment may properly be treated as but a downward adjustment in autonomous investment and represented by a downward shift of the *AA* line. We then have a situation in which *AA* line is somewhat depressed below its normal position while induced investment is zero. This gives a situation where the ordinary multiplier works free from the simultaneous operation of the accelerator. As such there will exist a moving equilibrium path corresponding to the adjusted *AA* line. In the above figure this is shown by *LL* which may be called the slump equilibrium line. Since the adjusted *AA* line lies below the original *AA* line, *LL* will lie below *EE*. The existence of the slump equilibrium line sets a floor to the slump.

From the point the negative rate of investment reaches the ceiling shown by Q_1, in figure 11.4, there must be a steady decline in output till it reaches the slump equilibrium line at P_2. The path Q_1Q_2 must lie above Q_1q (the path which would have been followed if the ceiling to the rate of disinvestment had not transformed the accelerator).

The above result would have to be slightly modified when we take into consideration also the induced disinvestment in working capital and stocks resulting from the fall in output. For the rate of such disinvestment has no technical ceiling. The accelerator continues working during the downswing to the extent of this part of capital stock. But when disinvestment in fixed capital has reached its ceiling, the investment coefficient relevant to further declines in output, being based only on additional disinvestment in working capital and stocks induced by such declines, will be rather small. And, as seen earlier, a small coefficient rules out the "explosive" possibility. Thus even when allowance is made for disinvestment in working capital and stocks, the path is likely to converge to the Slump Equilibrium.

After touching the Slump Equilibrium path, output starts creeping along it. Hicks calls this phase as "Depression." This phase is brought to a close by what Hicks calls "Recovery" which marks the movement of output upwards from *LL* to *EE*.

Upturn or Recovery: Recovery is inevitable provided autonomous investment maintains its upward trend (*i.e.* has the time-shape given by an upswing *AA* curve as in figure 11.4). For, given such a trend of autonomous investment, the *LL* line deduced from it would be up-sloping. As such when after reaching the *LL* line, output path starts creeping along this line the system experiences an absolute increase in output which must, after sometime, bring the old accelerator once again into operation. Once this happens, the equilibrium line is not *LL* but *EE*. The output must, therefore, after sometime, start rising to *EE*. This development marks the beginning of Recovery.

The exact point at which recovery begins is influenced by the speed of the slump and the slope of the Slump Equilibrium line. The speed of the slump is to a great extent influenced by consumption lags: the larger and longer the consumption lags, the slower will be the speed of the slump. The greater the speed of the slump, the larger will be the surplus capital stock (including both fixed capital and stocks) and Q_2 and, the longer will the system creep along the *LL* line before lack of replacement helps to work off the "surplus" capital stock. The slope of the *LL* line depends upon the slope of the *AA* line as the former line is deduced from the latter. The larger the slope of *LL*, the speedier will be the absolute increase in output as the system creeps along this line, and hence less will be the time required to absorb the "surplus" capital stock. Slower speed of the slump and larger slope of the *LL* line thus cut down the time required to work off and absolve the "surplus" capital stock adequately to make the accelerator strong enough to make the system start rising from *LL* to *EE*. In contrast, the higher the speed of the slump and smaller the slope of the *LL* line, the slower would be the adjustment and hence the longer the duration of the depression.

Thus Hicks attributes Recovery to the revival of the accelerator just as he attributed the downturn to the latter's collapse.

The Upswing Again: When the new upswing reaches the upper equilibrium *EE*, it cannot possibly stop there because output is necessarily expanding more rapidly than it would do along *EE*. The boom will therefore continue, apparently until it reaches the ceiling. Thereafter, the whole cycle goes on being repeated.

In the case of actual cycle, the downturn often occurs before the system touches the Full Employment ceiling. The downturn may thus be experienced again and again without the ceiling ever becoming operative. Hicks feels that it is possible to reconcile this observation with the "explosive" assumption that v is above its Middle Point. His reasoning is like this. If the investment coefficient were only slightly above its Middle Point, and if the initial displacement were small, there would be, to begin with, a series of small "free" cycles of increasing amplitude. The ceiling will be touched only when the amplitude has grown long enough. The above discussion of the course of the cycle started precisely at this point. Suppose on one of the earlier swings that are reversed before they touch the ceiling, the absolute decline in output during the downswing is large enough to transform the accelerator in the manner given above. The output would then fall to its slump equilibrium level and start creeping up along it. Recovery that begins, in due course, grows into boom, *i.e.*, the rise in output beginning as an upward movement from the slump equilibrium level (*LL*) will overshoot the equilibrium path (*EE*). The fact that the "free" cycle is explosive means that the divergence above *EE* would be longer than the distance between *EE* and the *LL* line. It may, however, be reversed before touching the ceiling if the latter is high enough. The transformation of the accelerator during the downswing once again brings the latter to an end when the slump equilibrium level is reached. Recovery once again starts at a point where the relative divergence from *EE* is the same as in the previous upswing; the relative divergence at the corresponding peak will, therefore, be exactly the same and so on. The cycle is thus kept going indefinitely even while v is above its Middle Point without ever touching the Full Employment ceiling.

A Snag in Hicks' Model: In actual practice, while recovery starts in a slow and imperceptible manner, the downturn involves a rapid decline in output. But Hicks' model suggests quite the reverse. If the accelerator operated identically during the upswing and the downswing, the process must take almost the same number of periods to drop from ceiling on to *EE* that it would take to rise from *LL* to *EE*. But as discussed above, during the downswing, there is transformation of the accelerator in a way that the decline in output proceeds at a rate slower than it would be if the accelerator were free from constraint as in the upswing. Actual experience thus is contrary to the conclusions that logically follow from Hicks' analysis. To resolve the conflict between the two, Hicks puts forward the view that though the downswing takes a larger number of periods yet the calendar time taken is shorter because of the shortening of the 'period' during this phase of cycle. Financial difficulties and the fear of heavy-losses compel businessmen to try to avoid surplus stocks. This necessitates reduction in output much below the level that would correspond to reduced demand. To affect this much decline in output in the near future requires a rapid decline in inputs. Thus there is rapid decline in the goods-in-process, which means a high rate of disinvestment in working capital. Since the 'period' measures the span of calendar time by the end of which, in case of increase in the demand for output, investment in working capital becomes large enough to offset the accumulation of stocks, or in case of decline in the demand for output, disinvestment in working capital becomes large enough to offset the accumulation of stocks, a higher rate of disinvestment in working capital during the recovery means that in the first case the length of the period in calendar time is shorter. Thus the downswing, even while taking a larger number of periods, takes less calendar time.

Thus Hicks provides a fairly satisfactory explanation of turning points as well as the periodicity of the cycle. As the system has a ceiling and a floor, changes in income and output oscillate between these two limits like the pendulum of the clock which moves between the two limits. At the lower turning point Hicks makes a significant contribution to the theory of trade cycle by showing how the existence of excess capacity in capital equipment tends to delay the upswing.

Hicks' theory also pinpoints the fact that in the absence of technological development and other powerful growth factors the economy will tend to languish in depression for long periods of time. There are two reasons for this. In the first place, without technological change, autonomous investment may not rise over time, and thus a positive change in output, required to set the accelerator in motion will not take place until equipment has worn out to the point where some replacement investment is necessary.

Secondly, if there is no technological change, the time at which this replacement is necessary will be deferred because no help is obtained from the obsolescence of existing equipment. The entire burden of setting the accelerator going is thus placed on the wearing out (or depreciation) of equipment. It is not surprising, therefore, that depressions are more severe and long-lasting during periods when long-run growth factors appear to be in abeyance.

Criticism of Hicks' Theory: The major weakness of Hicks' theory lies in treating the multiplier and accelerator as having fixed values (*i.e.* constant coefficients) during the different phases of the cycle. The constant multiplier is derived from the constant propensity to consume out of income. Recent studies, however, show that the marginal propensity to consume does not remain constant over different phases of the trade cycle, although permanent consumption is a stable function of permanent income. As Friedman has shown, there is no certain and predictable relation between the transitory income and consumption elements.

Similarly, the fixed value attached to the accelerator, a powerful tool in Hicks' apparatus, is not very appropriate. The relation between capital and output need not necessarily remain constant over time. There are large variations in this relation as between various sectors of the economy and these various sectors do not expand at a uniform rate. Further, the gestation periods for different types of capital goods differ. For example, while a plan to expand inventories might be completed soon, the construction of a steel plant takes a long time before it starts yielding production. While some upturns may be dominated by an initial expansion of durable goods industries, the dominant place might be occupied by agriculture or consumer goods industries in others. The expansion in output will invoke different investment responses and the assumed constant relation as employed by Hicks is subject to criticism.

Prof. Hutt remarks:

> I maintain that we cannot find in the relation between demand for goods of a lower order [consumption goods] and the demand for goods of a higher order [Investment goods] [and the supposed derivation of the latter from the former], an explanation of cyclical variation in the demand for growth. Nor can we find in those factors the source of

> great cyclical changes in entrepreneurial optimism affecting prospective yields, the rate of interest offered and the flow of savings. We can not even observe those factors to be influences which induce the cyclical withholding and release of capacity. In the study of all these issues, the relationship which the acceleration principle tries to express is wholly irrelevant.[10]

Another weakness of Hicks' theory is that the full employment ceiling as defined by him is independent of the path of output.[11] It depends rather on the population growth, technological progress etc., and is thus assumed to grow at the same rate as autonomous investment. But the full-employment level of output depends on the magnitude of the resources which are available to the economy. The capital stock is one such resource. This means that the ceiling is raised in any period during which the capital stock is increasing. Since the rate at which output increases determines the rate at which the capital stock changes, the ceiling level of output will vary depending upon the time path of output. It is not, therefore, possible to separate the long-run full-employment trend from what happens during a cycle.

A third important drawback of Hicks' theory is that in it autonomous investment plays a passive role. To cite Dernberg and Mcdougall[12]:

> It can, however, be argued that in a highly progressive capitalist economy the driving force may be the periodic disruptions introduced by technical progress. Indeed, there is reason to believe that the placing of primary emphasis on induced investment, while ignoring fluctuations in autonomous investment can be compared to the tail that wags the dog.

---

10. Hutt, *Keynesianism: Retrospect and Prospect*, p. 338.
11. Thomas F. Dernberg and Duncan M. Mcdougall, *Macro-Economics* (New York, 1960), p. 218.
12. *Ibid.*, p. 219.

Unemployment in an Underdeveloped Economy

12

INTRODUCTORY

Unemployment is a great economic waste. More serious are its moral consequences. The feeling of not being wanted by society demoralises a person. Unemployment breeds hatred, despair, fear and corruption. Full utilisation of the available manpower is very essential on economic and social grounds.

CONCEPT OF FULL EMPLOYMENT

What does the term full employment mean? The concept of full employment is a very ambiguous one. Different authors attach a different meaning to the concept. Literally speaking, full employment would prevail when every able bodied adult worked the numbers of hours considered normal for a fully employed person at the current return to labour. It is not, however, possible to attain this level of employment in private enterprise economies. In such economies quite a few have enough unearned incomes to be in a position to afford a life of well-paid idleness. Pigou, therefore, defined full employment as one when "everybody who at the ruling rate of wages wishes to be employed is in fact employed." But even Pigovian full employment appears to be unattainable because, at any given time, there is bound to be some seasonal and frictional unemployment. There will be a certain amount of irreducible unemployment as workers shift from one job to another and as plants are shut down for model changes, repairs and cleaning. The amount of unemployment necessary to reflect these adjustments within the economy may perhaps be set at one figure under certain circumstances and at another level in a different environment. Any attempt to give specific meaning to the concept of full employment must necessarily be an arbitrary one. For the sake of illustration, we may assume that an economy operating within a range of 3-5 per cent of its resources unemployed is operating within the full employment range. This would mean that with 95-97 per cent of its resources at work, an economy may be regarded as being at practical full employment. Whatever the exact figure may be, any economy which consistently moves at levels above this full employment range would bring upon itself the accompaniments of a condition of overfull employment, including rising price levels. The report of the delegation on economic depressions of the League of Nations suggested the concept that "in so far as possible, no man or woman able and willing to work should be unable to obtain employment for periods of time longer than is needed to transfer from one occupation to another or, when 'necessary, to acquire a new skill."[1] Keynes defines full employment as the absence of involuntary unemployment. He defines involuntary unemployment as a state in which "in the event of a small rise in the price of wage goods relatively to the money-wage, both the aggregate supply of labour willing to work for the current money wage and the aggregate demand for it at that wage would be greater than the existing volume of employment."[2] Thus full employment is reached when the real wage is equal to the marginal disutility of employment. No worker would offer himself for employment at a lower real wage. If a person does not work at this wage, it is evident that he is not interested in employment and therefore is voluntarily unemployed. Keynes considers both "frictional" and "voluntary" unemployment as consistent with his definition of full employment."[3] In fact, frictional unemployment, being involuntary (and not voluntary), cannot be consistent with full employment in Keynes' sense, *i.e.*, absence of involuntary unemployment. An alternative definition of full employment given by Keynes is "a situation in which aggregate employment is inelastic in response to an increase in the effective demand for its output."[4] The policy proposed by Keynes for achieving full employment is that of increasing effective demand to the appropriate level.

---

1. League of Nations, *Economic Stability in the Post-War World* (Geneva, 1945), p. 21.
2. J.M. Keynes, *The General Theory of Employment, Interest and Money* (London, 1957), p. 15.
3. *Ibid.*, pp. 15-16.
4. *Ibid.*, p. 26.

Beveridge's definition of full employment is broader than that of Keynes. According to him, full employment "means having always vacant jobs than unemployed men.... It means that the jobs are, at fair wages, of such a kind, and so located that the unemployed men can reasonably be expected to take them."[5] The policy proposed by Beveridge for achieving full employment consists not only of maintaining total outlay at an adequate level but also includes measures for securing controlled location of industry and organisational mobility of labour.[6] Measures for securing controlled location of industry and organising mobility of labour considerably decrease frictional unemployment. Frictional unemployment, therefore, is less consistent with the full employment concept of Beveridge than with that of Keynes. Mrs. Robinson goes still further and refuses to consider frictional unemployment as being consistent with full employment.

> It is commonly said that there is 'full' employment when the only unemployment which consists can be described as frictional. But it is impossible to give precision to the concept of specifically 'frictional' unemployment, because it is impossible to make a hard-and-fast distinction between unemployment which is due to frictions and unemployment which is due to a deficiency of effective demand.
>
> ...It seems preferable to say that full employment, in a precise sense, can never be attained so long as frictions exist, rather than to use 'full employment' in an imprecise sense in which it can be said to be attainable, such unemployment as remains being vaguely attributed to frictions.[7]

Lerner's definition of full employment is similar to that of Keynes. "Full employment is, therefore, that level of employment at which any further increase in spending would result in an inflationary

5. William H. Beveridge, *Full Employment in a Free Society* (London, 1945), p. 18.
6. *Ibid.*, p. 125.
7. Joan Robinson, *Essays in the Theory of Employment* (Oxford, 1953), pp. 41-42.

spiral of wages and prices."[8] He considers full employment to be consistent with frictional unemployment.

> The unemployment which results from a general insufficiency of jobs may be called 'deflationary unemployment' and the unemployment due to workers having the wrong skills or being located in the wrong places to get jobs is called 'frictional unemployment.' The frictional unemployment is the unemployment which exists when there is full employment.[9]

He maintains that the measures intended to reduce frictional unemployment do not contribute to full employment; these only raise the full employment level.

> All such improvements in the functioning of the economy in particular situations are ways not of moving towards full employment raising the full employment level itself.... It permits a greater level of employment to be attained before the inflationary point is reached. The full employment level comes to mean a greater level of actual employment. There is less residual frictional unemployment.[10]

The concepts of full employment mentioned above are not very relevant in the context of an underdeveloped economy. In an underdeveloped economy, a labourer employed in the physical sense may be unemployed in the economic sense, *i.e.*, his marginal productivity may be zero. This type of unemployment, often referred to as disguised unemployment, is particularly marked in the agricultural sector. The removal of a part of labour from the agricultural sector won't affect total production. Such unemployment cannot exist in a capitalistic economy because a capitalist won't employ an additional labourer if his productivity is zero or even positive but less that the prevailing wage rate. The problem in underdeveloped countries is not so much of increasing the quantity of employment as that of improving its quality (or productivity). In an underdeveloped economy, absence of lack of effective demand and frictions cannot mean a state of full employment in the

8. A.P. Lerner, *Economics of Employment* (New York), p. 24.
9. *Ibid.*, p. 18.
10. *Ibid.*, p. 25.

economic sense. Disguised unemployment is perfectly consistent with the concept of full employment of both Keynes and Beveridge. But this constitutes the main problem of unemployment in an underdeveloped economy. Full employment in the Keynesian sense—increase in effective demand leading to inflation—is reached at a very early stage because of lack of complementary factors. The main problem is not of reaching the full employment level but of raising the full employment level by increasing the amount of complementary resources. The emphasis in underdeveloped countries thus shifts from increasing effective demand to increasing complementary resources.

OVERFULL EMPLOYMENT

Full employment is reached at different times in different parts of the economy. During the early approaches to general full employment, only a few parts of the economy reach that level, with demand for their products in excess of their capacity. Firms in such industries find customers bidding for their products which are in short supply and as a result prices start rising. In a situation of rising prices, the management attempts to expand output by paying for overtime work; this increases the cost of production; the result is that the prices are pushed up by costs and pulled up by demand. Profits may rise for a while but excessive profits will lead to demands for higher wages. Thus, within this industry, the cost-price spiral starts gathering momentum.

The wage patterns established in the full employment industry and the prices charged for its products affect other industries also. A cumulative equilibrium spreads to more and more parts of the economy. Some firms may attempt to tackle their problems by undertaking the construction of new facilities. But this simply leads to diversion of resources into the construction industries from other parts of the economy; and these, in turn, find themselves in a situation of full employment. Ultimately, most of the economy enters the full employment situation and at this stage various rigidities become apparent.

When the full employment level is reached, all factors of production become short in supply. Faced with backing orders, the business firms will be reluctant to remove units of equipment for normal overhauling and maintenance, and tend to use such equipment on a round-the-clock basis. Overworking of equipment will lead to breakdowns in the production line which would tend to raise production costs and lower the general plant efficiency. Retired workers will be added to the labour force. There will follow a general decline in efficiency and a rise in cost structure.

Because of the excessive purchasing power which, by definition, is present in the economy at such times, consumers will not mind paying higher prices for goods in short supply. Being aware of this, the producers have a tendency not to resist the labour's demand for higher wages. They would prefer to grant an increase in wages rather than running the risk of a suspension of production. Promotion standards may be relaxed, piece-rate standards may be downgraded and other supervisory standards may be relaxed. Such measures would tend to raise costs and prices.

Over-full employment raises costs of production in other ways also. As materials become short in supply, the resulting scramble for goods leads to a great deal of crosshauling and of searching in distant supply markets, so that even when there is no increase in the price of materials, their costs to producers rise because of the increased costs of transportation involved in bringing them into the factory from distant sources. In view of the tight conditions, there is a tendency at all levels—producers, distributors, retailers, and even consumers—to build larger inventories of scarce goods. In this way, the pressure builds most heavily upon those sectors of the economy where these pressures are already great.

Ultimately, all these problems have a tendency to result in a disparity between the supply of money and that of goods. This imbalance leads to a rise in prices and profits which in turn push and pull wages and other costs to higher levels. There develops a general sellers' market not only for goods and services but also for factors of production. Such a situation leads to a wage-price spiral which results in a cumulative inflation. This is the danger inherent in any attempt to stabilise at too high a level of employment.

NATURE OF UNEMPLOYMENT

The nature of the unemployment problem in an underdeveloped country is widely different from that in a developed economy. In developed countries, unemployment is caused mostly by business cycles. Cyclical unemployment is not very important in an underdeveloped country. Recession affects mostly the money incomes and not the real output and incomes. Further the hardships caused by a decline in money incomes in underdeveloped countries are not very important because of an overwhelming degree of self-sufficiency. Producers retain most of their production for their own consumption and sell very little in the market. Similarly, they buy very little from the market. The most important factor responsible for the comparative stability of real income during the business cycle is the predominance of agriculture in these economies. Production in agriculture is comparatively stable not only in underdeveloped but also in developed countries. A major part of the total costs in agriculture consists of fixed costs and variable costs are small. Variable costs being small, prices during the recession, generally, do not fall below the marginal cost and consequently the restriction of production is unprofitable. Because of the competitive nature of agriculture, it is not possible to raise prices by restricting production. Further, in agriculture, the time lag between inputs and outputs is very long and, consequently, the limits within which production can profitably be restricted in the short period are comparatively narrower. On the contrary, there is some evidence to show that the supply curve in agriculture is backward sloping, *i.e.*, supply increases during the recession and falls during the boom. In developed countries, the number of wage earners is very high. Further wages are very inflexible because of contracts, social connections, legislation, trade union pressure etc. Business fluctuations, therefore, manifest themselves, mainly, in variations in employment and not in incomes. The incomes of those who are lucky enough to retain their employment remain almost unchanged. In underdeveloped countries, on the other hand, a predominant part of the population is self-employed. Business fluctuations in such economies, therefore, manifest themselves primarily in changes in money incomes and not in employment. Most of those who are employed on wages in factories, plantations and mines continue their contacts back in their villages and during a recession can go back to their homes and share agricultural employment along with their other family members. Cyclical unemployment, thus, is not very important in underdeveloped economies. Unemployment in underdeveloped countries is primarily of a secular nature and arises from inappropriate factor endowments, *i.e.*, excessive manpower in relation to capital and land. Inappropriate factor endowments won't be a cause of unemployment, if different factors of production were technically substitutable for each other. In actual practice, however, the possibilities for the substitution of different factors of production are considerably limited. Lack of flexibility in the co-efficients of production combined with abundance of labour relatively to other factors makes unemployment inevitable. The distinction between the nature of unemployment in advanced and underdeveloped countries has been well brought out by Majumdar:

> In contrast to the situation in advanced industrial countries visualised by Keynes, the problem in an underdeveloped country is one of underemployment rather than of unemployment; it is primarily agricultural rather than industrial; the phenomenon is chronic rather than cyclical; and moreover the incidence of unemployment spreads widely over the bulk of the population instead of being concentrated among a relatively limited number of workers.[11]

Unemployment in underdeveloped countries can be classified into four major categories *viz.* (1) cyclical unemployment, (2) disguised unemployment, (3) seasonal unemployment, and (4) technological unemployment.

CYCLICAL UNEMPLOYMENT

It takes place due to cyclical fluctuations in trade and industry. We have already seen above that this type of unemployment is not very important in underdeveloped countries.

DISGUISED UNEMPLOYMENT

Disguised unemployment exists primarily in two forms *viz.* (1) employment of people in less productive works than they are capable of or, in other words, an underutilisation of skills possessed by the people; (2) employment of people in a number larger than that required for doing the job. Mrs. Robinson uses the term 'disguised unemployment' to describe a situation in which the wage-workers take to less productive jobs because they lose their regular jobs owing to cyclical ebb in economic activity. The nature of the disguised unemployment, however, is very different in

---

11. N.A. Majumdar, "Some Aspects of Unemployment", *Indian Economic Journal* (July, 1957), p. 3.

underdeveloped countries. Firstly, if is chronic and not cyclical. Secondly, it relates more to self-employed workers than to wage-earners. Thirdly, it is caused by a shortage of complementary resources and not by a deficiency of effective demand. The experts of the Report on 'Measures for the Economic Development of Underdeveloped Countries' prefer to use the term underemployment to the term 'disguised unemployment':

> The use of the word 'unemployment' in this connection is, therefore, somewhat misleading, since it is more often confined to wage labourers whose status is recorded in unemployment statistics. We prefer to use, hereafter, the less precise but more familiar term 'underemployment'.[12]

Loss from disguised unemployment in developed countries arises primarily from an underutilisation of existing skill and de-skilling of labour during the period of unemployment. This kind of loss is not very important in underdeveloped countries. The main problem in these countries is not of preventing a waste and underutilisation of existing skills but of positive utilisation of underemployed manpower for the creation of skills and the formation of capital.

The fundamental reason for disguised unemployment in underdeveloped countries is that the capital and skill resources of these countries have not developed along with the growth of population. Population is increasing at a tremendous rate. Employment opportunities outside agriculture increase very slowly. The result is a growth in the number of people employed in agriculture. The additiorial labour force in agriculture adds little to the total output. Techniques, amount of capital and other complementary factors and the organisation remaining unchanged, a part of the working force can be removed without being followed by a decrease in total output. With minor changes in the organisation, techniques and the amount of capital, it is possible to remove a considerable portion of the working force without affecting production. Establishment of optimum sized holdings, for instance, will render surplus a considerable portion of the agricultural working force. The surplus manpower in agriculture is a great hindrance in increasing

12. United Nations, *Measures for the Economic Development of Underdeveloped Countries* (New York, 1951), p. 7.

productivity in agriculture. A part of the output which is consumed by the surplus mouths can be used for investment in agriculture for raising its productivity. Increase in number in agriculture increases the subdivision and fragmentation of land-holdings which is an important cause of low productivity in agriculture in underdeveloped countries. Mechanisation is not possible because it will render a large number of workers unemployed.

In underdeveloped countries, production is carried on, mainly, in family units. Almost all members of the family are associated in different capacities with the production processes. Consumption of different members of the family has very little relation to their contribution to the family product. If the productive unit is not sufficiently large to provide employment to all members of the family and cannot be expanded because of lack of land or capital, some members of the family may remain underemployed. These underemployed members continue being fed out of the family product without their underemployment being manifested to an outsider. Often, the underemployed workers themselves may not be conscious of their underemployment. Thus the under-development remains concealed or disguised, leaving its impact on the incomes. As the workers are not completely unemployed, they cannot be available for alternative employment at other places.

Disguised unemployment exists in underdeveloped countries not only in agriculture but also in other vocations, *e.g.* retail trading, personal services etc. In each locality, there is a large number of petty traders, each making a few sales. The number of shops in a locality can be reduced without causing any inconvenience to the buyers. The buyers may even gain if the retail margins are reduced with the increase in the amount of business conducted by each shop. Overcrowding of porters at railway stations, at bus stands, in markets and other places is a very common phenomenon. The same is true in case of several other casual jobs. Rich people keep an army of domestic servants just for prestige purposes. Reduction in the number of such workers won't affect national product.

Disguised unemployment though primarily existing among the self-employed workers is not absent in case of hired workers. Of course, it looks a little strange that an employer should employ labourers whose contribution to production is less than the wage paid to them.

> Social prestige requires people to have servants, and the grand seigneur may have to keep a whole army of retainers who are really little more than a burden upon his purse. This is found not only in domestic services, but in every sector of employment. Most businesses in underdeveloped countries employ a large number of 'messengers' whose contribution is almost negligible; you see them sitting outside office doors, or hanging around in the courtyard. And even in the severest slump the agricultural or commercial employer is expected to keep his labour force somehow or other—it would be immoral to turn them out, for how would they eat, in countries where the only form of employment assistance is the charity of relations.[13]

SOLUTION

Wherever there exists scope, more land should be brought under cultivation for affording employment to the additional workers. The best solution of the disguised unemployment in underdeveloped countries lies in rapid economic development which creates employment opportunities outside agriculture and thus makes possible a diversion of surplus labour from agriculture to other sectors. "The only remedy for this form of disguised unemployment is economic development, which constitutes the major economic problem of the world."[14]

SEASONAL UNEMPLOYMENT

Seasonal unemployment arises either from seasonal variations in demand or from those in production conditions. It is the later factor which causes the most serious problem. Seasonal unemployment is far more marked in agriculture than in any other sector of the economy. This is, to some extent, inevitable so long as the agricultural operations continue to depend on climatic conditions.

---

13. W. Arthur Lewis, "Economic Development with Unlimited Supplies of Labour" A.N. Agarwala and S.P. Singh (eds.), *The Economics of Underdevelopment* (Bombay, 1958), p. 403.
14. United Nations, *National and International Measures for Full Employment* (New York, 1949), p. 12.

The amount of work during sowing, transplanting and harvesting seasons is far larger than in other seasons. During busy seasons, the workers have much more than the normally required work; there, often, occurs even a scarcity of labour in some regions. But, owing to a number of reasons, the volume of seasonal unemployment is far larger in underdeveloped countries than in the developed ones. In underdeveloped countries, the agricultural operations are highly labour-intensive. The difference in the demand for labour between the busy and the slack seasons, therefore, is very large. In developed countries, on the other hand, the mechanisation of agriculture has considerably decreased the gap in the demand for labour between the busy and the slack seasons. In underdeveloped countries, the large demand for labour during the busy seasons gathers a large volume of labour around agricultural occupations. Because of a number of reasons, the labour force gathered during the busy seasons gets permanently attached to these occupations. In underdeveloped countries, occupation-structure is comparatively rigid. Because of certain economic and social factors, mobility of labour between different occupations is extremely low. There exists a bias for agricultural occupations. After elementary needs have been met, the marginal leisure preference of the agricultural labour becomes very high. In advanced countries, the difference in demand for labour during different seasons has been considerably reduced through intensive cultivation, double cropping, mixed farming and dovetailing of agriculture with other subsidiary occupations. Because of comparatively higher incomes, seasonally unemployed labour in developed countries can better afford leisure as a consumer good.

Seasonal unemployment exists, also, in the industrial sector. Employment in rice mills lasts for only a few weeks. Work in sugar mills lasts for four to six months. More important is the seasonal unemployment in cottage industries which either depend on seasonal supplies of perishable raw materials or cater to seasonal demand. Seasonal unemployment in industry, however, is not so important in underdeveloped countries because the total number of workers employed in industry is not large.

Seasonal unemployment results in an underutilisation not only of manpower but also of the available capital equipment. Underutilisation of the available capital presents a serious problem for an underdeveloped country marked by an extreme shortage of capital. The indigenous capital equipment used in underdeveloped countries is not very durable and, therefore, the rate of depreciation merely because of the passage of time is very high. Capital in the form of cattle not only depreciates with the passage of time but also requires a considerable amount of positive expenditure for maintaining it. Cattle have got to be fed and looked after even during the slack season.

Seasonal unemployment is another form of the underemployment in underdeveloped countries. While disguised unemployment is primarily confined to self-employed workers, seasonal unemployment concerns both the self-employed and the hired workers. Disguised unemployment is concealed whereas the seasonal unemployment is visible.

Remedies for Seasonal unemployment: The best remedy for seasonal unemployment lies in making the agriculture a full-time job. Measures should be taken to extend the period of employment in agriculture itself. Lengthening of employment period, however, should not be for its own sake but for increasing production. Lengthening of employment period for its own sake will deprive the people of leisure (which is an important consumer goods without providing them any compensation in the form of additional goods. The employment period in agriculture can be fruitfully extended through intensive cultivation, double cropping. mixed farming, dry farming etc. This, of course, requires large investments, for providing the cultivators with several facilities *viz.* irrigation, fertilisers, modern equipment, technical know-how etc.

A second remedy lies in reducing the demand for labour in busy seasons by mechanising the agriculture. This remedy will be useful only if employment opportunities can be created outside agriculture for absorbing the labour rendered surplus by the mechanisation of agriculture. Creation of employment opportunities outside agriculture requires stupendous amounts of investment which can be made only over a very long period of time.

Thirdly, to the extent the busy seasons occur at different times in different regions, the volume of seasonal unemployment can be decreased by facilitating inter-regional mobility of labour. If, however, labour is to work at different places during different seasons, it will give rise to several social and economic problems. There will be the problem of providing the labour with housing at different places. Food arrangements will have to be made for the migratory labour. If the labourers take their families with them from place to place, labour movements will involve considerable costs. If they do not keep their families with them, the family life will be disturbed.

Fourthly, the seasonal unemployment in agriculture should be dovetailed with the seasonal employment in the industrial sector. Seasonal unemployment in cane-growing, for instance, can be dovetailed with work in sugar factories. Sugar factories, however, can employ only a small portion of the cane-growing labour. A far larger amount of labour can be employed if the cultivators themselves produce sugar in small home units. Seasonal unemployment in tea-growing has been successfully dovetailed into tea-manufacturing. This has been possible because tea-growing and tea-manufacturing is done not only by the same firms but also by the same work-units. Seasonal unemployment in cotton-growing can be eliminated by combing cotton-growing with spinning and weaving. Cottage industries, particularly, those using primarily agricultural raw materials, have, often, been suggested as the best measure for providing employment to the seasonally unemployed labour in agriculture.

Encouragement of cottage industries, however, raises a number of difficult problems *viz.* provision of finance, raw materials and technical know-how, protection from competition from the mill sector, marketing products etc. It will result into an underutilisation of capital resources. Capital equipment of cottage industries will remain idle during the agricultural season and agricultural equipment will remain idle when the equipment of cottage industries is being used. A country highly deficient in capital cannot afford such a waste of its capital resources. A stupendous amount of investment will be required for providing the agriculturists even with the simplest form of equipment for cottage industries. An equivalent amount of investment in mill sector may contribute much more to the national income. The ultimate interest lies not in mere full employment of labour but in the total production that can be had with the available productive resources. The efficiency of persons who work as cultivators during certain seasons and as artisans in other seasons is likely to be lower than that of the full time cultivators and full-time artisans. Agriculture-cum-handicraft system will forego the benefits which arise from specialisation. For a fuller utilisation of limited capital resources and for reaping the benefits of specialisation, it is better to have full time cultivation and full time artisans. Extending employment period in agriculture, on the other hand, has the advantage that it not only avoids duplication of equipment but also uses the existing agricultural equipment more fully. In case cottage industries are to be developed for affording employment to the seasonally unemployed labour it will be better to develop such cottage industries as can be run either with the existing agricultural equipment (*e.g.*, dairy farming) or as require mostly manpower and little capital equipment (*e.g.*, basket making, soap making).

Fifthly, as far as possible, the government should concentrate its public works during the agricultural slack season.

Sixthly, seasonal unemployment in cottage industries producing non-perishable goods can be remedied to some extent if certain arrangements are made for the provision of finance to the artisans. If finance is available for purchasing raw materials, the artisans can produce during the slack season for building stocks.

TECHNOLOGICAL UNEMPLOYMENT

Technological unemployment arises from developments in technology. Other things remaining the same, the unemployment caused by changes in technology will be permanent if the new technology requires a smaller number of workers. Unemployment will be transitional if the new technology requires the same number of workers; in this case the problem will be only that of adapting to the new techniques. The workers experienced in old techniques may have to remain unemployed or seek employment in unskilled jobs till they learn the new techniques. Technological unemployment will be considerable if the changes in technology are very rapid and the difference between the old and the new technology is considerably large.

Normally, the technological unemployment is not a serious problem in developed countries because the change in technology in these countries is very slow and regular, the workers can adapt to the new techniques without much difficulty and distress. In underdeveloped countries, in contrast, the primitive technology has got to be replaced by an altogether new technology, existing in advanced countries. The difference between the old and new technology is so large that the knowledge of the old technology becomes almost useless. Further the new technology requires a number of workers far smaller than that required by the old technology. For these reasons, unless new employment opportunities are created for absorbing the unemployed workers, the technological employment is likely to be a serious problem in underdeveloped countries. Artisans employed in handicrafts in underdeveloped countries are the worst victims of technological unemployment caused by the introduction of the modern mill sector. Handicrafts unable to face competition from domestic and foreign modern mills are decaying fast. Technological unemployment may be caused not only by changes in the techniques of production but also by those in the techniques of organisation. In underdeveloped countries, the organisation of production is very defective. In some industries, it is possible to obtain the same output with the same amount of equipment, the same technique of production and a smaller amount of labour if the production is organised and managed more efficiently. Application of modern methods of management and organization will render a considerable amount of labour unemployed. The amount of technological unemployment depends upon the rate at which the concerned underdeveloped country wants to modernise its methods of production.

Changes in technology not only cause unemployment among workers but also render old capital equipment useless. Mechanisation of agriculture, for instance, renders useless the indigenous equipment and cattle.

Advances in technology increase the productivity of labour, capital and land. Increases in productivity increase the investible resources. Increase in investment increases the volume of employment. Thus advances in technology which initially cause unemployment would ultimately increase the volume and productivity of employment. This conclusion, of course, is based on the assumption that the increased productivity is utilised, if not fully, at least partially, for investment. If whole of the increased productivity is used for raising the consumption standards, the ultimate increase in the volume of employment through increased investment may fail to materialise. Advances in technology may also fail to increase the volume of employment if the increased productivity is utilised for increasing leisure instead of increasing total production. Somewhat different situation will arise if the leisure is involuntary in the form of forced unemployment. In underdeveloped countries, the possibilities of involuntary leisure through forced unemployment are much larger than those of voluntary leisure. In case the leisure is involuntary, the profits of the entrepreneurs are likely to rise because the same amount of output will be produced with a smaller amount of labour. Profits may rise further if the wages are flexible and with the decrease in demand for labour, wage rates are lowered. Changes in the distribution of income in favour of profits and against wages, howsoever justifiable on economic grounds, cannot be approved on political and social grounds.

Remedies for Technological Unemployment: The best remedy for technological unemployment lies in the creation of new employment opportunities through the rapid development of the country. "Rapid economic development is paradoxically the greatest cause of and the greatest cure for technological unemployment."[15]

Secondly, underdeveloped countries should be a little cautious in employing the techniques which have been developed in advanced countries keeping in view, primarily, their own needs. The need in advanced countries is to economise labour and to find out outlets for savings. The techniques which require more capital and less labour, therefore, best suit such countries. The needs of underdeveloped countries are quite the reverse. These countries possess vast amounts of unemployed labour and are very short of capital. The techniques best suited to these countries, therefore, are those which employ more labour and less capital. But the problem is from where to obtain such techniques. Development of new techniques is a very long-term process. The modern techniques in advanced countries have been developed over centuries. Development of new techniques suited to the needs of underdeveloped countries requires huge investments and talents of a very high calibre. It is doubtful if the underdeveloped countries can afford to spend so much on research for developing new techniques. Still more difficult is the problem of finding talented persons for carrying on such research programmes.

---

15. United Nations, *Measures for the Economic Development of Underdeveloped Countries* (New York, 1951), p. 27.

Frictional Unemployment

Frictional unemployment prevails in the economy among the workers who have voluntarily quit their previous jobs and are searching for new better jobs. They are said to be between jobs. The persons who have lost jobs and are in search of jobs are also included under frictional unemployment. Frictional unemployment occurs due to lack of market information about the availability of employment opportunities and lack of perfect mobility on the part of workers, shortages of materials, breakdown of machinery, etc. The distinguishing feature of frictionally unemployed persons is that the number of job vacancies equal to them is available in the economy. The workers remain unemployed for a short period of time before they are able to get new jobs. It takes some time required for job seekers to get information about the availability of jobs. When the problems of frictionally unemployed persons are solved, *i.e.* they are absorbed in new jobs, again the new frictionally unemployed persons come into the market. Thus, there is always some frictional unemployment existing in the economy.

Remedies too Frictional Unemployment

The problem of frictional unemployment will be solved by the availability of employment opportunities and perfect mobility of the workers. Overall market information about the employment opportunities should be available.

CONCLUSION

The only satisfactory solution of unemployment in underdeveloped countries lies in creating additional employment opportunities through rapid overall economic development. "It will be seen that we are led by the analysis both of technological unemployment and of underemployment to the same point, namely, that new employment must be created rapidly. This is the task of economic development."[16]

---

16. *Ibid.*, p. 9.

Secular Stagnation

13

INTRODUCTION

The theory of secular stagnation is also known as 'economic maturity', 'growing underemployment', and 'secular underemployment equilibrium'. Almost all economists have recognised that unregulated and uncontrolled capitalistic system cannot lead to endless growth. The classical school believes that ultimately every economy would reach a stationary state in which growth will cease. Marx and Schumpeter predict an ultimate downfall of the capitalistic system. Harrod-Domar model shows that as the economy grows, it becomes more and more difficult to maintain full employment. Hansen believes that in mature economies, in the absence of state intervention, at the full employment level, net savings have a tendency to exceed net investment which would result into chronic underemployment equilibrium or secular stagnation. Stable growth can be maintained in mature economies only if the state continuously pursues appropriate monetary and fiscal policies. Let us examine the secular stagnation thesis in a little more detail.

STATEMENT OF THE DOCTRINE

There is no better short statement of the stagnation thesis than that given by Keynes himself. "The richer the community, the wider will tend to be the gap between its actual and its potential production, and, therefore, the more obvious and outrageous the defects of the economic system. Not only is the marginal propensity to consume weaker in a wealthy community but, owing to its accumulation of capital being already larger, the opportunities for further investment are less attractive." When there had been no occurrence of secular stagnation in the past, say in the 19th century, the question may be raised as to why it should occur in future? To this Keynes replied:

> During the 19th century, the growth of population and of inventions, the opening up of new land, the state of confidence and the frequency of war over the average (say) each decade, seem to have been sufficient, taken in conjunction with the propensity to consume, to establish a schedule of the marginal efficiency of capital which allowed a reasonable satisfactory average level of employment to be compatible with a rate of interest high enough to be psychologically acceptable to wealth owners... Today and presumably for the future the schedule of the marginal efficiency of capital is for a variety of reasons, much lower than it was in the 19th century.[1]

In a mature economy, there is a log-run tendency towards a contraction in economic activity. Depressions are more intense and prolonged than booms. The essence of secular stagnation is "sick recoveries which die in their infancy and depressions which feed on themselves and leave a hard and seemingly immovable core of unemployment."[2]

Secular stagnation is not inconsistent with a rising trend of actual per capita income, and even with a rising trend of actual gross investment. It refers simply to a growing gap between the trend of full employment income (without inflation) and trend of actual income or between potential employment and actual employment. Secular stagnation may refer to a growing economy in which the rate of growth, though positive, is declining. It may refer to an economy in which actual employment is increasing if at the same time the gap between the attainable and actual employment is also increasing. Thus secular stagnation is compatible with a decline in per capita income, constant per capita income, or slowing down of the increase in per capita income. Secular stagnation originates from savings exceeding investment at the full employment level. The gap between savings and investment may be ascribed either to excessive savings (deficient consumption) or to deficient investment or to both. For explaining the tendency towards secular stagnation

1. J.M. Keynes, *The General Theory of Employment, Interest and Money* (London, 1936), pp. 307-08.
2. A.H. Hansen, *Fiscal Policy and Business Cycles* (New York, 1941), p. 353.

in mature economies, we have to analyse the causes responsible for excessive savings and insufficient investment opportunities. Let us first examine the factors which cause excessive savings.

FACTORS WHICH TEND TO WIDEN SAVINGS LEAKAGE

The aggregate private net savings consist of (i) undistributed corporate profits and (ii) personal savings. The secular tendency in advanced private enterprise countries has been to increase the size, measured in absolute amount and perhaps also as a percentage of the national income at full employment, of both these components. Let us first examine the secular tendency in respect of corporate undistributed profits.

The statistical evidence in advance countries shows that the ratio, at full employment, of corporate undistributed profits to national income has risen over the secular long-term. This together with the rise in national income has meant a large increase, even when allowance is made for the rise in the price level, in the absolute amount of corporate undistributed profits.

The rising secular tendency in the ratio of corporate undistributed profits to national income, at full employment, appears mainly on account of two factors. The first is the rise in the ratio of corporate profits before tax to national income, presumably because of growing predominance of corporate enterprise and within it owing to imperfectly competitive market structures resulting in ever larger excess profits. The second is the rise in the ratio of corporate undistributed profits to total corporate profits after tax, presumably owing to the ambition of those who control corporations to expand their respective business and of share-holders to receive a large portion of their profits preferably in the form of tax-free bonus shares issued through capitalization of reserves rather than in the form of taxable dividends. The rise in the ratio of corporate tax liability to corporate profits before tax, of course, has been a factor working in the opposite direction. But this has not completely offset the favourable effect of the first two factors on corporate undistributed profits and, therefore, the net result has been rise in the ratio of such profits to national income. As such the absolute size of the leakage represented by corporate net saving has increased at a rate higher than that of the increase in national income.

To turn to the second component, the ratio of personal saving to national income depends upon (i) the ratio of disposable personal income to national income and (ii) the ratio of personal saving to disposable personal income (*i.e.* the average propensity to save). The higher are these two factors at a given level of employment, the higher is the ratio of personal saving to national income.

The secular tendency in regard to the ratio of disposable personal income to national income is, undoubtedly, towards a decline. This is primarily because of two factors. Firstly, there has occurred a great increase in taxation, corporate and personal, because of the vast increase in government spending necessitated by the higher cost of defence and social services expected of a modern welfare state. No doubt, there are also factors operating in the opposite direction, *e.g.*, larger increase in government transfer payments relatively to private (personal and corporate) contributions for social insurance, and the vast increase in the net interest paid by government owing to the phenomenal increase in the size of the public debt. But the factors working on the side of a decline in the ratio of disposable personal income to total national income have been more powerful than operating on the side of a rise in it.

As regards the ratio of personal savings to disposal personal income, at full employment, economic development of present-day advanced private-enterprise countries has been characterised by the working of conflicting tendencies, some in favour of and others against the rise in the propensity to save. We examine below important of such tendencies.

Private enterprise countries, by definition, are characterised by private ownership of means of production. This implies unearned incomes. The amount of a person's unearned income depends, other things remaining unchanged, upon the amount of income- yielding assets owned by him. This provides a powerful incentive for saving with a view to accumulate income-yielding assets. As such the increase in per capita real income, by enhancing the earner's capacity to save, has been an important factor tending towards a higher propensity to save. But there have also been factors tending to promote consumption, *e.g.*, increasing urbanization of the population, progress of advertising, greater educational opportunities, progressive taxation, wider and fuller social security, better provision of social amenities, the rise in the habitual standards of living as a result of the increase in per capita income, and the fact that "the capitalists, thanks to their greater wealth and more important social position, have become more aristocratic and are obliged to display their wealth somewhat more lavishly than was necessary for the 'middle class of the nineteenth century."[3] But the factors unfavourable to personal saving (or favourable to personal consumption) have not completely offset the favourable effect on saving of the secular increase in per capita income.

The propensity to save also depends upon the extent of inequalities in the distribution of disposable personal income. The greater the inequalities, the higher would be the propensity to save. Though conceptual and statistical difficulties in the measurement of the degree of inequality of income-distribution bar a precise identification of the secular tendency in this regard, a few general conclusions can safely be stated. Large, and probably increasing, inequalities in the distribution of personal income before tax appear to be inherent in the private-enterprise system. The inequalities in the distribution of income arise firstly, because different workers earn different amounts depending upon the quality and quantity of work performed by each and secondly, because the ownership of income-yielding assets is very unequally distributed. The vast inequalities in the distribution of personal income before tax found in advanced private-enterprise countries are by and large on account of the second factor. And the inequality in the ownership of income-yielding assets has a tendency to widen with the process of economic growth. The groups getting larger incomes on account of ownership or control of income-yielding assets normally have a tendency to save a higher proportion of their income. The absolute amount saved by them per capita is, therefore, much larger than by the non-owning groups with smaller incomes. As such, at each round, the former tend to be richer.

The government transfer payments, which mainly go to the low-income classes, are one of the factors tending to reduce inequalities in the distribution of personal incomes. The amount of such payments has substantially increased in recent years as a result of wider coverage and higher rates of actual security benefits. But

---

3. Paul M. Sweezy, *The Theory of Capitalist Development,* 1946, p. 230.

the equilibrium effect of this development is narrowly restricted by the fact that, at full employment, government transfer payments are likely to exceed private contributions for social insurance only by a moderate amount and that such contributions are likely to impinge, directly or indirectly, on the relatively small incomes so that the net transfer of income from the rich to the poor is rather limited.

The tendency towards higher rate of tax on corporate profits and towards diversion of larger proportion of corporate net profits to reserves, through its adverse effect on dividend payments which mainly go to the relatively rich, is unfavourable to personal saving not only because it depresses the ratio of personal income to national income but also because it reduces the inequalities in personal incomes. The corporate taxation cannot be used as an instrument of reducing private saving beyond certain limits because of the resistance of the powerful owning classes to excessive corporate taxes, the difficulties involved in checking legal and illegal evasion, and the fears of adverse effects on investment. The higher rate of corporate saving, while undoubtedly unfavourable to personal saving, is worse than self-defeating from the point of view of the matter under study because it, in fact, means a rise in the rate of total private saving including both corporate and personal saving.

The above discussion shows that high, and probably growing, inequalities in the distribution of personal income before tax with favourable effects on personal saving appear to be inherent in the private-enterprise economies.

Another factor which has led to the oversaving is the growth of joint stock and corporate form of business organisations. Corporate savings are becoming more and more important. These savings consist of depreciation reserves for replacement and are reflected in the amount of undistributed profits of corporations. They may, in fact, be much more than those required for financing replacement of capital equipment and new capital formation. The growth of life insurance and other institutions has also given a fillip to saving and thereby enchanced the chances of secular stagnation.

Insecurity is still another factor influencing the will to save. It strengthens the precautionary motive to saving. In this regard, modern private-enterprise economies have exhibited conflicting tendencies.

Such economies appear to be more unstable now than in the nineteenth century. This factor tends to work in favour of promoting savings. But expansion of the system of social security has offset this factor to some extent because the social provision against the contingencies and the exigencies of life weakens the precautionary motive to saving.

The net result of the conflicting tendencies mentioned above seems to be a secular rise in the average propensity to save at full employment. The advanced private enterprise economies are, therefore, faced with an ever more serious problem of how to offset the widening saving leakage. The failure to do that means less than full employment.

FACTORS THAT WEAKEN INVESTMENT OFFSETS

A high and rising absolute rate of private net saving at full employment is not, however, by itself a sufficient condition of inadequate demand. There would be no shortage of demand if the investment increased correspondingly to the increase in savings at the full employment level. But in the present day mature private-enterprise economies, there are several factors that tend to weaken the propensity to invest with the result that investment falls short of savings at the full employment level. We briefly discuss below importance of such factors.

Large Accumulation of Capital: The mature private-enterprise countries have accumulated huge amounts of capital. The larger the existing volume of capital, the lower would be the prospective rate of return on new investment and hence the weaker the incentives for investment.

Decline in the Rate of Population Growth: In the twentieth century, in most of the mature economies, population growth has considerably slowed down; in some countries the rate of population growth is near zero. In the nineteenth century, population grew at a tremendous rate. Growing population stimulates investment in two ways. Firstly, it requires goods and services which give rise to huge amounts of investment. It expands the demand for housing and public utilities like waterworks, sewerage disposal, gas works. electric works, transportation and communications etc. Provision of housing and public utilities involves enormous amounts of investment. Secondly, growing population facilitates investment by increasing the supply of labour. In the absence of a growing population, increase in the demand for labour caused by an increase in investment would raise wage rates. Rise in wage rates would lower profits and thereby discourage investment. Even if technical progress throws up new capital-intensive techniques at the required rate, investment may still be retarded by another factor. If capital used per worker (*i.e.* capital-labour ratio) increases, the ultimate decline in the rate of profit can be prevented only by a rise in the ratio of profits to wages. But a rising profits-wages ratio tends to depress the propensity to consume at full employment.

Development of New Territories: What is true of population growth holds also for the discovery and development of new territories and new resources. Development of new territories requires enormous investment in highways, railroads, means of communication etc. Further a huge amount of investment is required for providing the communities which settle in the new territories with goods, services, housing and public utilities. Expansion of territory furthers the growth of population which in turn stimulates investment. The era of territorial expansion has, now, come to an end. This has resulted into a decline in investment opportunities.

Disappearance of Pre-capitalist Sector: Historically, the adoption of capital-intensive techniques in advanced private-enterprise countries has been associated with capitalist enterprise (one where production is carried on private account with hired as against self-employed workers). In the early stages of capitalist development, the labour supply for the capitalist sector came from the decline of the pre-capitalist sector releasing men, women, and children for employment in the capitalist sector. This facilitated investment in the capitalist sector in the same manner as the increase in the available labour force through natural increase in population. But in advanced countries the scope for such increase in labour supply available to the capitalist sector appears to have more or less exhausted with the virtual disappearance of the pre-capitalist sector.

Relatively Weaker Stimulus of Technological Progress: Technological progress in the form of invention of new products, machines and processes promotes investment by creating new outlets for it. The strength of the stimulus provided by the discovery of new products depends upon the degree of their novelty, the capital intensity or the production process involved, the time dimension (fruition-period) of the investment promoted, and the intrinsic importance of the wants served. Similarly, the investment-generating potential of new machines and processes depends upon their novelty, their capital-intensity, and the intrinsic importance of the wants served. Technological progress provided a powerful stimulus to investment from the second half of the 18th century to about the end of the first quarter of the 20th century. Inventions in the fields of manufacture, transport and mining created products and processes which were very different from the then known products and processes. In the early part of this period, there was the change from handicrafts to 'roundabout' capitalistic methods of production; in the latter part there appeared large, altogether new, electrical, chemical and automotive industries. The novelty of the new products and processes meant that these could not be introduced simply by minor changes in the existing techniques. The new industries, being highly capital-intensive, led to large investments. As a result of the factors mentioned above, the propensity to invest was strong enough relatively to the then rate of saving corresponding to full employment level.

The things, in contrast, are very different today. Some of the important changes bearing on the inducement to investment are briefly stated below:

(i) Highly efficient methods of satisfying man's basic wants—food, clothing, footwear, means of transportation and communication, facilities for recreation or cultural pursuits—have been discovered and adequately employed in advanced countries. The future technological progress, therefore, is likely to relate to intrinsically less important wants or simply to improvements in the existing capitalistic methods of satisfying basic wants. As such, leaving aside the possibilities of 'technological progress' in the field of war, new wants and processes are not likely to stimulate investment as strongly as they did in the nineteenth century.

(ii) While a century back private enterprise economies were by and large competitive, in present days there is growing predominance of imperfectly competitive market structures. The growing monopolization of such economies has had in some ways favourable and in others adverse effects on new investment outlets. The vast resources at the disposal of giant monopolistic and oligopolistic enterprise, for instance, make it possible for them to spend lavishly on research projects which stimulates technological progress and hence new investment. Monopoly profits are an important source of finance for the employment of new techniques of production whereas the competitive enterprises having smaller profits might lack funds for this purpose, particularly where large initial investments are required and the fruition period is rather long. It is possible that a monopolistic producer may adopt 'risky' innovations of product or "technique more readily than a competitive producer. Innovations will presumably be made by a producer because these are likely to increase profits by increased demand or reduced cost. The larger the profits from a successful innovation and the longer the period for which the producer can enjoy these, the stronger is the incentive to introduce innovations. Under competition, while unsuccessful innovation is as damaging, successful innovation, because of early imitation or entry by others, does not add to profits by as much for as long as under monopoly which precludes entry and competition.

On the other hand, the growing predominance of monopoly and oligopoly has had adverse effect on investment in several ways. Under such market structures, output is not extended to the level where price equals the marginal cost. Output will thus fall short of what it would be if the monopolised or oligopolised industry were to act like a purely competitive industry. Restriction of output in the monopolised and oligopolised sector decreases the scope for investment in those sectors. It follows that the flow of investment into the monopolised and oligopolised fields stop even when average return on capital is higher than the normal return obtainable in the competitive sectors; to be more concrete, it stops when the marginal return on capital, as distinguished from the average return, falls short of the rate of profit that can be earned in competitive fields. After that the monopolists and oligopolists invest even their own savings in other fields and seek to monopolise and oligopolise them. Thus the tentacles of monopoly and oligopoly spread ever wider, and the restrictive effect on new investment outlets is correspondingly strengthened. Monopolies also delay the introduction of technological innovations because the monopolist while deciding whether or not to adopt them, must take account of the consequential obsolescence of existing capital. Under competitive conditions, the gain from an innovation accrued to the innovator while the loss (as a result of obsolescence of capital) was shared by his competitors. To be more concrete, given the cost-reducing opportunity, the monopolist will make the innovation only when, output being given for future periods, the average total cost of production with the new technique is less than the average variable cost with the existing plant. Under competitive conditions in contrast, though established sellers will act in the same way, new entrants will tend to introduce new techniques as soon as the average total cost with them is less than the expected market price. Thus under monopolistic and oligopolistic conditions introduction of innovations tends to be delayed. In other words, the technological progress tends to be financed from depreciation accruals instead of from net saving. Taking into account the favourable as well as the unfavourable factors, the conclusion appears to be that the impact of growing predominance of imperfectly competitive market structure would be unfavourable to the inducement to invest.

(iii) In recent periods, the bias of technological innovations appears to be markedly towards capital-saving. The latest development (*e.g.* air conditioning and television) illustrates the trend towards more complex goods requiring less capital outlay. To cite Samuelson[4]:

> Thus the invention of airliner may make possible the development of Siberia without billions and billions of dollars of investment in public roads and rail-roads...Atomic energy may minimise the need in many parts of the world for costly hydro-electric reclamation projects...Science gives and takes as far as investment is concerned, and Hansen thinks these may continue to be—what he believes to have been true of the 1930s—a preponderance of capital-saving invention.

Since monopolies and oligopolies produce on a relatively large scale, they have a tendency to make greater use of complex, specialised and indivisible equipment to economise capital outlay per unit of capacity or output. Further development of safeguards against breakdowns and excess wear and tear has considerably

4. P.A. Samuelson, *Economics,* p. 404.

reduced the replacement demand incident to rapid depreciation. Still further, equipment has often been installed which increased productivity by merely speeding up the operation of the existing equipment. All such capital-saving innovations have inhibited the growth of investment-demand.

(iv) Financial prudence is now a commonly accepted tenet of corporate management. In pursuance of this, it is customary for corporate managements to amortize assets at higher than the actual rate of their depreciation. As such the depreciation provision contains an element of net saving. To the extent net investment is financed from such concealed net saving fewer net investment opportunities remain available to offset the statistically accepted private net saving.

Relatively Weaker Stimulus of Expanding Exports: Expanding exports stimulate investment in the export industries. But the net addition of exports to the aggregate opportunities for domestic investment open to the system depends upon the character of imports obtained in exchange. If the latter consists of commodities which the country must in any case import, (because either it simply cannot produce them or it is not worthwhile for it to produce them because the position of comparative costs is such) expanding exports create new investment opportunities for domestic investment without being off-set by the disappearance of potential investment opportunities in other sectors of the economy. For example, during the period from the Indian Mutiny (1857) to the First World War the expansion of British exports of textiles and other manufactured products to India stimulated investment in the export industries concerned, but the expanding imports of food-grains, raw cotton, raw jute, oil seeds, hides and skins, tea, spices, manganese ore, mica etc. obtained in return from India, did not diminish any investment opportunities in Britain. The stimulating effect of expanding exports on capitalist development is reinforced if the resultant expansion in imports causes a decline of the non-capitalist sectors, so that the capitalist sector is enabled to tap both the labour-power and the demands currently in the non-capitalist sector; it is further reinforced if expanding exports also involve a growing exports surplus. In contrast, if the imports consist of commodities which discourage the growth of industries that could in course of time be expected to become as efficient as the present export industries, the additional investment opportunities provided in the export industries are largely offset by the suppression of potential investment opportunities in other fields. Thus the stimulus to capitalist development from expanding exports is the strongest when they increase at a fast pace and are accompanied by a growing export surplus, and when the resultant expansion of imports not only does not impair potential investment opportunities but also brings about a rapid decline in the pre-capitalist sector. In all these respects, conditions are not so favourable as they were a century ago. Then there was a great scope for the expansion of foreign trade of the few capitalist countries within the pattern-structure most conducive to the development of their respective capitalist sectors *viz.*, export of manufactured products in exchange for food, raw materials and very simple manufactures. At that time vast territories were available for 'colonization', which term signifies reduction of a country into a buyer of manufactured goods and a supplier of primary products. Further, there were in these areas till that time large possibilities of the colonial type of development, *i.e.*, development which, being confined to agriculture, mining, transport and communications and public utilities increased their importance as sources of supply of primary products and markets for manufactured products. Export of capital to these areas for this type of development stimulated the exports of the advanced capitalist countries not only at the time when such exports occurred but also in subsequent years because the increase in exports of primary products from the relatively backward countries increased their capacity to absorb larger imports of manufactured products. The stimulus to capitalistic development in advanced countries provided by expanding exports from them is now very much weaker than it was a century back owing to the fact that, relatively to their aggregate output, the scope for expanding exports within the appropriate pattern structure of foreign trade (*i.e.* exchange of manufactured for primary products) is much smaller because of a number of reasons. In the first place, the relatively backward territories of the world have greatly shrunk in size. Secondly, some development has taken place even in the backward countries. Thirdly, the possibilities of development with the colonial-feudal framework have been largely exhausted; in fact, many of these countries, owing to expanding population and relatively stagnant primary production, have actually become importers of food and agricultural raw materials. Finally, the most important capitalist country of today (*i.e.* the United States) is a very large producer and also exporter of primary products. Moreover, the stimulus to private investment in the advanced countries has greatly weakened because it is no longer possible for these countries to raise capital exports to backward countries to the level at which they will stimulate a volume of exports from the former sufficient to absorb a significant production of their output.

Lesser Scope for Foreign Investment: Net private saving corresponding to full employment may also be offset by positive net investment abroad. In the pre-World War I period, capital exports provided a significant outlet for net private saving in those private-enterprise countries in which the volume of such saving had begun to press against investment opportunities available at home. From 1874 to 1914, for instance, the foreign long-term investments of the United Kingdom, France and Germany increased from $ 6,000 million to $33,000 million.[5] But because of the present international political climate and other factors,[6] there is hardly any hope for the revival of capital movements from advanced to the under-developed countries on the required scale.

Decline in population growth, virtual disappearance of territorial expansion, monopolistic competition, capital-saving innovations etc. have considerably decreased investment opportunities and thereby lowered the marginal efficiency of capital. Full employment can be maintained only if the rate of interest declines corresponding to the decline in the marginal efficiency of capital. While the marginal efficiency of capital can fall to zero or go even below that, the rate of interest cannot fall below a minimum level because the demand for liquidity becomes infinitely elastic at very low rates of interest and because of institutional borrowing costs. Thus, in mature economies there exists a deflationary gap at the full employment level of national income. The result is that national income would fall below the full employment level until the reduced savings are equalised to the investment opportunities forthcoming

5. United Nations, *International Capital Movements during the Inter-War Period,* 1949, pp. 1-2.
6. See K.R. Gupta, *Economics of Development* (Delhi, 1967), pp. 215-22.

at this low level of national income. This is the problem of chronic under-employment.

The figure given below illustrates the secular stagnation thesis. If the full employment is to be maintained, the investment opportunities must be adequate to absorb all the real savings which take place at that level of income—say at OY_0; otherwise there would occur a decline in national income. As the economy becomes more fully developed and investment opportunities decline, the propensity to invest will decline as shown by $C + I'$ curve which gives us a new level of income at OY_1. Income has declined from

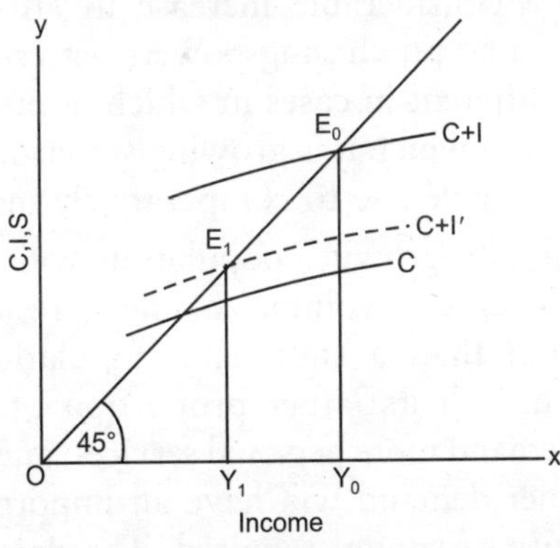

Fig. 13.1

OY_0 to OY_1 so that savings would not be larger than those for which the investment opportunities are available. This decline in income from OY_0 to OY_1 causes considerable unemployment and the economy continues in secular under-employment equilibrium for an indefinite period. Thus, we find that in order to maintain full employment, either the investment must be maintained at a level high enough to offset the volume of full-employment savings or savings must decline so as to raise the level of consumption high enough to reduce savings to be offset by investment. Otherwise, the economy will remain in a state of secular under-employment or secular stagnation.

AN APPRAISAL

The doctrine of secular stagnation has been sharply criticized by a number of economists. George Terbough, in a strong counter-attack, labels those who accept the doctrine as 'stagnationists' and 'professional pessimists'. Let us examine the important grounds on which the doctrine of secular stagnation has been criticised.

Some economists have challenged the relation between the rate of population growth and the rate of investment. Purchasing power remaining constant, mere increase in population won't expand market. "An increase in the number of paupers does not broaden the market."[7] Conversely, the decline in the rate of population growth may be accompanied by an increase in the per capita spending and thus may not lead to a decline in total expenditure. Purchasing power remaining constant, an increase in population may not lead to a considerable increase in effective demand in general. With the same purchasing power, pattern of expenditure, of course, will be different in cases in which population is growing rapidly and in those in which it is growing slowly and the pattern in the former cases will give rise to comparatively more investment.

> Thus a rapidly growing population will demand a much larger per capita volume of new residential building construction than a stationary population. A stationary population with its larger proportion of old people may perhaps demand more personal services; and the composition of consumer demand will have an important influence on the quantity of capital required. The demand for housing calls for large capital outlays, while the demand for personal services can be met without making large investment expenditures. It is therefore not unlikely that shift from a rapidly growing population to a stationary or declining one may so alter the composition of the final flow of consumption goods that the ratio of capital to output as a whole will tend to decline.[8]

Further, population growth may lead to an increase in aggregate income and even to an increase in per capita income if the population is below the optimum level. If population is small in relation to other productive factors, mere increase in population

7. Kalecki, *Theory of Economic Dynamics* (New York, 1954), p. 161.
8. Alvin H. Hansen, "Progress and Declining Population", *The American Economic Review* (March, 1939), p. 7.

would be accompanied by an increase in income and spending. The tendency for a growing population giving rise to increased expenditure will be stronger where increase in population is accompanied by an increase in income.

The optimist economists believe that there will always be spontaneous changes in the tastes of consumers and in the techniques of production which would create ample investment opportunities for absorbing current savings. Terborgh questions the vital importance of a 'few great innovations' as compared with 'many small ones'.

> There is no real evidence that one 'great new industry' is more dynamic in its impact on capital formation than ten small new industries. The important thing is the total flow of technological development, not its degree of concentration. Given an abundance of rising industries like aviation, mechanical refrigeration, air conditioning, radio, television, rayon, plastics, quick freezing, prefabricated housing, light metals, powered metals, high octave gasoline, gas turbines, jet propulsion, spun glass, cotton pickers, combined harvestors, electronics—to name only a few at random—the total volume of direct and induced investment can be tremendous... There is...no evidence of an increasing proportion of capital saving innovations.[9]

No doubt spontaneous changes in the pattern of consumer wants and techniques of production give rise to considerable investment but it is very doubtful if they alone would provide the required investment outlets.

Stagnationists believe that the propensity to consume is more or less stable. This has a considerable element of truth in the short run. But evidence shows that the consumption has a tendency to rise in the long run. In the long run, country's conception of a minimum standard of living has a tendency to shift upward. Things which were comforts and luxuries are now considered indispensable necessities. But the secular rise in the consumption function is not likely to be so rapid as to close or considerably reduce the gap between saving and investment at the full employment level.

---

9. George Terborgh, *The Bogey of Economic Maturity*, pp. 89-96.

We have examined above the important arguments of the proponents and opponents of the secular stagnation thesis. As the doctrine refers to a very remote future, it is very difficult to say anything definite about the possibility of the advent of a state of secular stagnation. Further the doctrine refers to a system of free enterprise which does not exist in any part of the world. Now, in almost all countries—whether capitalist or socialist—state plays an important role in economic affairs and tries to maintain full employment by all means at its disposal. Advent of socialist ideology pleading a more equalitarian distribution of wealth will considerably raise the consumption function and thus decrease the volume of savings and consequently the possibility of secular stagnation.

Prof. Martin Bronfenbrenner in a recent article has challenged the very concept of secular stagnation and asserts that it is the danger of secular inflation rather than secular stagnation that threatens the Western capitalist countries in the years to come. He states:[10]

> We look on secular inflation, not as strictly inevitable but as likely to dominate economic life in capitalist countries for the next few years... The world of secular stagnation is the world of sound finance and of the gold standard. It is not currently in existence. It passed into coma in 1933, when Roosevelt and Hitler came to power, and died completely on the several battle fronts of World War II. Its importance today may be largely academic... The world of secular inflation, however, is the pressure economy of the present, including the political necessity of maintaining high employment at whatever cost.

It is very difficult to say as to whether or not the predictions of secular stagnationists and secular inflationists are true and real. It would take a long time to test these theses against observations, To cite Koivisto, "The future contains too many imponderables. The subject remains a great guessing game...No one can say for sure. This is not a matter of economic analysis, but a prediction of

10. M. Bronfenbrenner, "Some Neglected Implications of Secular Inflation" in K.K. Kurihara (ed.) *Post-Keynesian Economics* (London, 1955), pp. 36 and 37.

exogenous factors. And the further into the future that we try to predict such matters, the more answers depend on our own particular crystal balls. Such forecasts accordingly must be taken with a large grain of salt, but it is nevertheless interesting to speculate about them."[11] To cite Prof. Samuelson, "Economic analysis must be prepared to understand the policies called for by stagnation; it must be no less prepared to meet the opposite situation of long range inflationary condition."[12]

MEASURES TO COUNTERACT SECULAR STAGNATION

We have seen above that in the absence of positive measures of public policy, present day advanced private enterprise economies may experience a shortage of demand. Such a tendency can be corrected in two possible ways, *viz.* (i) by reducing private net 'functional' saving corresponding to full employment, and (ii) by strengthening the offsets to private net saving, *i.e.*, by promoting private domestic investment, by inducing larger net foreign investment, and by creating or enlarging the budget deficit.

MEASURES TO DISCOURAGE PRIVATE SAVINGS

Private net savings consist of (i) corporate undistributed profit, and (ii) personal saving. To reduce private net savings corresponding to full employment, both of these components should be reduced. The important measures which can be used to reduce corporate undistributed profits are as follows: (1) The excess profits produced by monopolistic sale of commodities and monoposonistic purchase of factors should be reduced to the minimum by discouraging such combinations as aim at limiting competition and by forcing others, through fiscal and other measures, not to exploit their monopoly or monoposony power to maximise excess profits. (2) The corporate profits should be made to bear the highest practicable rate of tax. (3) The permissible provision for depreciation may be limited by law to the actual rate of depreciation and obsolescence so that depreciation provision contains no element of net saving. (4) Undistributed corporate profits may be taxed at a rate higher than that applicable to corporate profits distributed in the form of

11. Koivisto, *Principles and Problems of Modern Economics*, pp. 405 and 410.
12. P.A. Samuelson, *Economics,* p. 407.

dividends. But all these methods have their limitations. The fact that technological progress, by generally increasing the optimum size or the firm relatively to the size of the market, has a tendency to make monoploy and oligopoly natural, limits the scope for public policy to discourage monopolistic combinations. Monopoly on the sale side normally involves monoposony on the side of purchase of factors, both of which tend to generate excess profits. Further the administrative and political difficulties involved quite narrowly limit the extent to which public policy can prevent the full use of monopoly and monoposony power to obtain maximum excess profits. Moreover, besides the political difficulties involved, the fact that the tax on corporate profits, by reducing the net return on capital, discourages investment limits the extent to which it can be raised without adversely affecting investment. The adverse effect of a high rate of taxation on profits can, however, be lessened by levying the tax in the modified form suggested by Kalecki. Normally, the tax is levied on profits net of depreciation. Kalecki has suggested that tax should be levied on profits gross of depreciation, but all investment in fixed capital, whether for replacement or expansion, should be deducted from this taxable amount. The advantage of this form of the tax is that the rate of profit expected on new investment remains the same as it would be in the absence of the tax. Suppose tax is levied at the rate of 25 per cent and the entrepreneur expects a 20 per cent profit on investment. On an investment of Rs. 1000 he expects to make a profit of Rs. 200. The tax would reduce the expectation to Rs. 150. But the cost of an investment of Rs. 1000 would be only Rs. 750 because if this amount were not invested, he would have to pay Rs. 250 as tax and would be left with only Rs. 750. A return of Rs. 150 on an investment of Rs. 750 gives the same rate of 20 per cent. Thus the rate of profit expected on new investment remains the same as it would be if there were no tax on profits. Kalecki's suggestion, however, is not without its shortcomings. If the rate of tax is not much higher than that under the conventional system, the exemption of all reinvested gross profits, under Kalecki's scheme, would increase inequalities in the distribution of income which would in the long run aggravate the problem of shortage of demand. Kalecki's scheme would mean heavier taxation of the relatively less well-off companies which do not have much to plough back because of comparatively lower profits. The role which taxation of profits in either form can play in reducing private saving is limited. A high profits tax is likely to encourage socially wasteful expenditure at the expense of the tax. Huge amounts may, for instance, be spent on tax experts and lawyers with a view to find loopholes in the tax laws, and also on excessive advertisement, high pressure salesmanship and various 'prestige' items. Lastly, corporate saving may be discouraged through statutory limitation of the permissible provision for depreciation to the actual rate of depreciation and obsolescence, and through taxing undistributed corporate profits at a rate higher than that applicable to distributed corporate profits. Because of their extraordinary nature these measures do not appear to be very practicable.

Let us now return to the possible measures which can be taken to discourage the other component of private saving, *i.e.*, personal saving. Since such savings are made mostly by the rich people, one method of discouraging saving would be to encourage conspicuous consumption on the part of the rich. But in a society where material welfare, social esteem and political power are associated with ownership of wealth, the extent to which conspicuous consumption by the rich can be stimulated is strictly limited. Further increase in aggregate demand brought about in this manner may conflict with the pattern of demand required by the considerations of maximum social welfare. The better way, therefore, would be redistributive taxation, which, its incidence being mostly on the richer sections, heavily impinges on savings. Heavy taxes may be levied on the wealth, income and consumption and proceeds used to reduce taxes which impinge on lower incomes so as to raise the disposable incomes of the poor classes by conferring on them extensive social security benefits, to provide public sector goods and services of mass consumption at subsidised prices or to raise wages. The redistributive taxation, however, cannot be carried beyond certain limits because of legal and illegal tax evasion, resistance from the richer classes, discouragement to investment etc.

Social Security: A well-designed system of social security consisting of unemployment compensation, old age pensions, health insurance etc. can be an important method of raising consumption. Such a system would check the decline in consumption expenditure during depression when there is a decline in the incomes of the workers because additional purchasing power would be generated by unemployment allowances and doles etc. A well-managed system of social security would reduce the need for saving even during normal times by freeing the workers from the fear of insecurity.

Easy Credit Facilities*:* A large part of the durable consumer goods like radio sets, television sets, automobiles, refrigerators etc. are sold on credit basis and the demand for such goods is one of the most unstable constituents to effective demand. Easy credit facilities for instalment buying stimulate consumption of such goods.

Urbanisation*:* Studies in family budgets show that the people living in cities have a higher propensity to consume than the people living in rural areas. Process of urbanisation would, therefore, raise consumption function. Urbanisation can be promoted by measures like mechanisation of agriculture, crop rotation, slum clearance, low cost housing, setting up of industrial estates etc.

Advertisement and Salesmanship: A right type of advertisement, publicity and salesmanship go a long way in raising consumption by bringing to the notice of consumers many new products which would not be known to them otherwise.

MEASURES TO PROMOTE PRIVATE DOMESTIC INVESTMENT

The limitations of the various possible measures to reduce private net saving corresponding to the full employment level necessitate an examination of the measures which can be taken to strengthen the various offsets to such saving. We, therefore, briefly, examine below the measures which can be taken to promote private investment.

Cheaper and Easier Credit*:* Given the marginal efficiency of capital, investment can be promoted by making credit available cheaply and easily. Credit can be made cheaper and more easily available by the banking system, particularly by the central bank, following an expansionist monetary policy by the government itself, granting loans to private firms and individuals for replacement, renovation and expansion, or guaranteeing such loans to them by private agencies and by the government promoting, through low-interest loans, subsidies and other special facilities, the creation and expansion of such credit institutions as supply investment loans to small producers who generally lack approach to commercial banks. There are, however, limits to which cheaper and easier credit can stimulate investment. An important reason for this is that it is much more difficult, and takes longer time, to lower the long-term rate of interest, which is more relevant to investment in fixed capital. If the long-term rate of interest sags slowly, it may, in fact discourage investment in fixed capital and if it declines quickly, it may lead to rapid rise in capital values with huge windfall gains to the propertied classes, which does not appear to be very desirable. The League of Nations Delegation on Economic Depression remarked in their Report[13]:

> The experience of the Great Depression has made economists sceptical concerning the possibility of arresting a contraction and inducing an expansion by means of easy money and credit policies, although they still admit that an expansion can always be halted and turned into a depression, if credit is sufficiently restricted and interest rates raised. The role assigned to credit policy is thus rather that of a brake than of an accelerator.

Reduction or Adjustment of Taxes: A commonly suggested method is reduction in business profits tax. A high rate of tax checks enterprise by reducing expected profits. Further, since the payment made as interest on debentures is not subject to business profits tax, there is an inducement to financing by debentures rather than by equity. The resultant increase in the interest liability, which constitutes a fixed charge on the gross profits, makes the return on equity capital disproportionately low when business is depressed. This adversely affects the inducement to invest during bad times. A reduction in the rate of tax, therefore, is expected to encourage private enterprise both by improving profit expectations and by inducing a capital structure that does not accentuate instability. This method, however, is not without its shortcomings. A lower rate of profit tax may lead to large additions to reserves which would offset to that extent the inducement to invest. Further, under full employment this will lead to a transfer of income from the lower to the higher income classes, that is, in the wrong direction.[14] Lastly, this step would be self-defeating if it necessitated increases in

---

13. *Economic Stability in the Post-War World*, 1945, pp. 153-54.
14. The Oxford University Institute of Statistics, *The Economics of Full Employment* (Oxford, 1944), p. 48.

such other taxes as would lower the propensity to consume by more than the increase in the propensity to invest.

Business profits tax discourages enterprise in another way also. It makes the state, as businessmen would remark, share profits but not losses. The discouragement to risk-bearing would, therefore, be less if for purposes of computing the tax liability the deduction of losses from business profits were permitted not only for the year in which they occur but over a period of several years. This device has the shortcoming that it involves wasteful accounting and increases the opportunities for improper manipulation.

The creation of new industries and the introduction of new processes may be encouraged by permitting liberal depreciation allowances and full allowance for obsolescence. Sometimes, new enterprises are completely exempted from taxes for a certain initial period. Another device that may be adopted is the reduction of duties on imported machinery and raw materials.

Subsidies: The government may stimulate investment by subsidising the capital cost or the production cost. Government subsidies are a common method of promoting residential construction, particularly low-cost housing. In the case of industrial enterprises, the usual method is to subsidize production cost. But the League of Nations Delegation on Economic Depression was of the opinion that the exemption of earnings from taxation was a better way of stimulating industrial investment than the grant of subsidies. The former device is conducive to efficient management because to avail of the concession that the exemption provides, the enterprise must earn some profits.

Reduction in the Prices of Capital Goods: Other things being equal, a reduction in the prices of capital goods would raise the marginal efficiency of capital and thereby promote investment. During the recession period there is often considerable scope for reduction in the prices of capital goods. Prices of capital goods are often subject to monopolistic control which tends to keep them stable in the face of fluctuations in demand. As such, during the recession period, the prices of capital goods may be out of tune with the general price level. If the monopolists controlling the supply of capital goods can be compelled to lower their prices, it may provide considerable stimulation to investment activity. In addition to direct control of prices, another way of bringing about a decline in the price of capital goods would be to permit a free import of these and to reduce tariffs on their import.

Promotion of Scientific and Industrial Research: Technological progress in the form of discovery of new products and processes creates investment outlets. Promotion of scientific and industrial research would, therefore, stimulate investment. This can be done by government itself maintaining research institutions and by subsidising private research either by making direct grants for the purpose or by exempting from taxation that part of the profits which is spent on research.

Public Investment: Private investment may also be stimulated by public investment of suitable types. A well planned programme of public investment encourages private investment in a number of ways. To the extent such investment is deficit financed, supply of money, other things remaining unchanged, lowers the rate of interest which had favourable effects on the inducement to invest. Private investment would also be stimulated if the public investment is in social and economic overheads required by the private entrepreneurs. Public investment in power, for instance, may stimulate private investment in industries which springs up to take advantage of the availability of cheap power.

Government Guarantee of Adequate Demand: If the government can convince business of its intention and ability to attain and maintain adequate demand any recession would be considered to be a temporary phase. Investment activity will pick up in anticipation of better times ahead and would thus help to bring them nearer. To the extent the government can create favourable expectations regarding business prospects, its task of promoting private investment becomes easier.

Price Policy: Instability of prices is one of the important causes of instability of private investment. A certain measure of stability in prices would, therefore, promote private investment. To attain this end, it has been suggested that the government should follow a price-sport policy. Such a policy implies purchases and sales of commodities by the government with a view to maintain the prices at a certain specified level When there is excessive production and consequently prices decline, the government enters the market for bulk purchases and thus checks the decline in prices. During periods of short production when prices start rising, the government unloads the stocks built in the earlier periods and thus checks the rise in prices. In this way, the government stabilises the prices, which tends to promote private investment.

LIMITATIONS OF PRIVATE INVESTMENT

Private investment as a means of stimulating demand, however, has its limitations. The investment would ultimately lead to an increase in the production of consumption goods and services. It is, of course, possible that for some time the investment may not of accompanied by an increase in the production of consumption goods and services. This would be the case when growing production capacity resulting from investment is utilised not for increasing the supply of consumption goods but for the multiplication of productive capital at an ever faster rate. This may be a desirable and practicable policy for an underdeveloped or a war-devastated country or a country preparing for the war. But such a policy will not be practicable for a normal, peacetime and advanced private enterprise economy. In such an economy, sooner or later, consumption demand must expand in proportion to the expansion in production capacity. The rate of investment cannot be stabilised at a level that would expand production capacity at a rate higher than the rate of increase of consumption demand. In such a case there will be growing excess capacity which, by depressing the marginal efficiency of capital, will ultimately inhibit investment.

It is sometimes suggested that capital deepening can provide a solution of the problem. It is maintained that a high rate of investment will create not excess capacity but higher labour-productivity. Capital deepening, however, has its limitations. In the first place, the major stimulus to capital deepening is provided by technological progress. The former, therefore, cannot proceed at a rate faster than the latter. Secondly, if a rise in the current standards of living is accorded a higher place in the accepted scale of social priorities than an increase in labour productivity, the appropriate policy would be to step up current consumption rather than the pace of capital deepening. Thirdly, capital deepening does not solve but merely postpones the problem of lack of effective demand. A rising rate of capital deepening means an ever faster increase in labour productivity. This will obviously result in the full employment production capacity, and hence the need for consumption demand, in future being higher than would be the case if it were possible to devote a larger proportion of current production capacity to the satisfaction of consumption demand and a smaller proportion to its own multiplication. The problem of lack of effective demand, therefore, recurs in the future in a greater magnitude. The conclusion is that if the rate of investment is insufficient to ensure adequate demand, the solution lies in stepping up consumption rather than investment.

We may also briefly indicate other limitations of the policy. Firstly, in case the government measures do not create new investment opportunities but result merely in an earlier utilization of the existing opportunities, the present relief would be obtained at the cost of making the problem of deficient demand more acute in the future. Secondly, the policies aimed at improving investors' profits expectations might accentuate inequalities in the distribution of income. Such a tendency would not only go against an important objective of social policy, but also, by reducing the community's propensity to consume, would make it difficult to continuously ensure adequate demand.

Money and Prices

14

SIGNIFICANCE OF MONEY

Many economists, particularly those belonging to the so-called classical school whose main interest lied in the 'long-run' economics, did not attach much importance to the independent influence of money. For them money was simply a device. They believed that money did not affect the working of the economy. In their view in a money economy the total amount of employment, the volume of production, the types and proportions of the various goods and services produced and consumed, the exchange values of the various goods and services in the market, and the distribution of real wealth and income among the members of the community are normally the same as they would be in a highly developed and efficient barter economy, if such an economy could be devised. To cite J.S. Mill[1]:

> It must be evident, however, that the mere introduction of particular mode of exchanging things for one another by first exchanging a thing for money, and then exchanging the money for some thing else, makes no difference in the essential character of transactions.
>
> There cannot, in short, be intrinsically a more insignificant thing, in the economy of society, than money; except in the character of a contrivance of sparing time and labour. It is a machine for doing quickly and commodiously, what would be done, though less quickly and commodiously, without it; and like many other types of machinery, it only exerts a distinct and independent influence of its own when it gets out of order.
>
> The introduction of money does not interfere with the operation of any of the laws of value laid down in the preceding chapters. The reasons which make the temporary

1. J.S. Mill, *Principles of Political Economy*, pp. 332-33.

> or market value of things depend on the demand and supply, and their average and permanent values upon their cost of production, are as applicable to a money system as to a system of barter. Things which by barter would exchange for one another, will, if sold for money, sell for an equal amount of it, and so will exchange for one another still, through the process of exchanging them will consist of two operations instead of only one. The relations of commodities to one another remain unaltered by money: the only new relation introduced is their relation to money itself; how much or how little money they will exchange for; in other words how the Exchange Value of money itself is determined.

If money always performed its functions perfectly, the position assumed by classical economists would not be wrong. Unfortunately, however, no monetary system as yet evolved has functioned perfectly or even approached perfection. Each has exhibited a tendency to 'get out of order' and to exert 'a distinct and independent influence of its own'. The classical economists, of course, recognised this fact; but they believed that monetary disorders were infrequent enough to be ignored without invalidating an analysis couched in terms of barter, particularly since this analysis was concerned with long-run, rather than short-run phenomena. Modern monetary experts, in contrast, believe that money is almost always 'out of order'—though in different ways and to varying degrees—and this significantly affects the aggregate volume of employment and production, the relative amounts and exchange values of individual commodities produced and sold, and the distribution of real wealth and income among the members of the community. These effects are particularly important in the short-run and are capable of appreciably altering the long-run behaviour of the economy since long run is, after all, made up of a series of short runs, each of which is affected by monetary developments.

The disorderly working of money is closely bound up with fluctuations in its value. In case money is to satisfactorily serve as a unit of measuring the values of economic goods and as a standard of deferred payments, it must itself have a constant, or nearly constant, value. To quote Barbara Wootton[2]:

> One has only to imagine what would happen to business calculations and plans if the number of ounces in a pound, or inches in a foot, were variable, and then to remember that, whereas these measures enter only into contracts concerning goods sold by weight or length, the monetary unit enters to get an idea of the extent of the damage to economic efficiency for which a monetary system that is unreliable, or imperfectly understood, may be responsible.

But experience shows that money has never remained even approximately constant.

Keynes took a strong exception to the veil attitude of classical and rejected it as erroneous. He formulated a monetary theory which provided a full explanation of income or employment rather than a monetary explanation of production. To Keynes money is not merely a veil but something more vital, more crucial and more significant, the use of which as a medium of exchange, as a measure of value, as a standard of deferred payment and more particularly as "a link between the present and the future", has the capacity of influencing the magnitude and trend of economic activity. To Keynes, the monetary sector is an integral part of the general economic system. It is because of this reason that Keynes considers his 'General Theory' as 'theory of monetary economy' or as a monetary theory of production wherein the rate of interest, which is determined and influenced by the demand for and supply of money plays an important role. According to Keynes, money affects the rate of interest and through it investment and hence the general level of economic activity, output and employment. Dillard remarks "In Keynes' early years throughout money had significance in relation to price levels, but in the mature years monetary theory became the theory of output and employment as a whole."[3]

EFFECT OF CHANGES IN THE VALUE OF MONEY ON THE VOLUME OF EMPLOYMENT AND PRODUCTION

In a capitalistic society, the decisions in regard to the volume of production to be undertaken are made by entrepreneurs, whose

2. Barbara Wootton, *Plan or No Plan* (London, 1934), p. 142.
3. Dudley Dillard, "The Theory of a Monetary Economy" in Kenneth K. Kurihara (ed.), *Post-Keynesian Economics* (London, 1950), p. 30.

objective is to maximise their profits. More production is undertaken when profit prospects are bright and less when they are bleak. Changes in the value of money affect the prospects and thereby the volume of business activity by affecting the relationship between entrepreneurs' cost and selling prices. It is commonly observed that enterepreneurs' costs—which consist largely of wages and salaries, interest, rent, taxes, and allowances for depreciation and obsolescence—move more slowly than selling prices during both the upswing and the downswing. In a period of rising prices, therefore, costs lag behind selling prices; the consequent swelling of profits leads to an expansion in the volume of production and employment. The reverse happens in a period of declining prices.

MONEY AND PRICES

One of the basic problems is to find out the factors which determine the value of money or to explain cause of changes in the purchasing power of money. The views of the classical economists about changes in the general level of prices are found in what is known as the 'Quantity Theory of Money'. Hicks is of the view that Keynes' ideas about changes in the general level of prices are nothing but 'Quantity Theory much glorified'. In view of the above, it would be useful if we examine the quantity theory of money before we study Keynes' views on money and prices.

QUANTITY THEORY OF MONEY-TRANSACTIONS APPROACH

This theory is generally associated with the name of American economist, Prof. Irving Fisher, though its origin can be traced back to Devan Zatti, an Italian writer of the 16th century, Bodin, Cantillon and Hume, who gave vigorous formulations of the idea embodied in the theory. According to the Quantity Theory of Money, the value of money depends on its quantity in circulation, or in other words, the price level is a function of the quantity of money. Basically, the theory states that, other things remaining unchanged, changes in the general price level are to be explained with reference to changes in the quantity of money in circulation so that an increase in the quantity of money leads to an increase in the price level while a contraction in the quantity of money leads to a decline in the general price level. In its extreme form, the theory states that, other things remaining unchanged, the changes in the general price level are directly proportional to changes in the supply of money. In the words of Mill, "The value of money, other things being the same, varies inversely as its quantity; every increase of quantity lowers the value and every diminution raising it in a ratio exactly equivalent."[4] To cite Prof. Taussig, "Double the quantity of money and other things being equal, prices will be twice as high as before; and the value of money as one-half. Halve the quantity of money, and, other things being equal, prices will be one-half of what they were before; and the value of money double."[5]

Fisher formulated the Quantity Theory of Money in his book *Purchasing Power of Money* (1911). In his words, "The quantity theory asserts that (provided the velocity of circulation and the volume of trade are unchanged) if we increase the number of dollars whether by renaming coins or by increasing coinage, prices will be increased in the same proportion."[6] The credit of Fisher lies in presenting the theory in an algebraic equation called the 'equation of exchange' and clearly elucidating the assumptions underlying the theory. He puts it as:

$$MV = PT \qquad \text{... 14.1}$$

i.e. Supply of Money = Demand for money

or
$$P = \frac{MV}{T} \qquad \text{... 14.2}$$

where M stands for the quantity of money in circulation including both coins and bank notes but excluding bank reserves and the money held by the Treasury; V represents the velocity of circulation and is obtained by dividing the aggregate volume of money payments in a given period by the units of money in circulation; it shows the average number of times a unit of money changes hands; P refers to the general price level; T stands for the total volume of transactions for which money payments are made; it includes goods, services and securities and is equivalent to the physical volume of trade.

4. J.S. Mill, *Principles of Political Economy,* Vol. II, p. 15.
5. F.W. Taussig, *Principles of Economics,* Vol. I, p. 250.
6. Irving Fisher, *The Purchasing Power of Money,* p. 31.

The product of M and V (MV) gives us the aggregate effective supply of money during a given period. The product of P and T (PT) gives us the demand for money. The supply of money must, at any time, be equal to the demand for money. In other words, MV must be equal to PT. This equation broadly indicates that the total transactions effected during a given period of time multiplied by the price = total amount of money multiplied by its velocity.

The above equation was severely criticised by some of the monetary experts for ignoring credit money and its velocity, both of which were important in a modern economy. Fisher, therefore, extended his original equation of exchange to include bank deposits (M') and its velocity (V'). The revised equation was:

$$PT = MV + M'V' \qquad \text{... 14.3}$$

or

$$P = \frac{MV + M'V'}{T} \qquad \text{... 14.4}$$

VELOCITY OF CIRCULATION OF MONEY

The velocity of circulation of money (V) is equal to the total money value of all transactions divided by total quantity of money (PT/M). In other words, it is the money value of transactions per unit of money per period of time. It obviously expresses the velocity of circulation of per unit of money and not the velocity of circulation of money in general. For monetary units circulate at different average velocities according to the source of income and the purpose of expenditure. Further, the velocity of circulation of different kinds of money is different. For different kinds of money are not equally suitable to different types of transactions. The velocity of circulation of money is, therefore, in fact, an average of widely divergent velocities of different kinds of money supply. This average of averages is not free from statistical errors which may result from the difficulty of separating the deposits for the purpose of inclusion in the total quantity of deposit money. Besides this, there is the problem of defining the quantity of money.

The velocity of circulation of money is influenced by the liquidity preference of the people. The larger the volume of cash balances held for transactions motive, precautionary motive, and speculative motive, the smaller would be the rapidity of transactions and hence the smaller the velocity of circulation of money.

Conversely, the smaller the volume of cash balances held, the greater will be the rapidity of transactions and hence the larger the velocity of transactions and hence the larger the velocity of circulation of money. In other words, the velocity of circulation of money is considerably influenced by the volume of cash balances held. The amount of cash balances held depends on the organisation of the money market and the methods of income payment. The velocity of circulation of money will be greater if the wages are paid daily or weekly as against fortnightly or monthly because the time-lag between receipts and disbursements will be smaller in the former case. An improvement in the organisation of money market would increase the velocity of circulation of money by facilitating lending, borrowing and spending. The growth and composition of population, technological changes, monetary policy, fiscal policy, stock market policy, etc. affect the velocity of circulation of money by influencing the volume consumption, savings and investment. Short-run changes in velocity depends mostly on the state of business and expectations in regard to prices, interest and income. An increase in business activity will call the idle money back to activity and thus lead to a rise in the velocity of circulation of money. A rise in prices will make the money move faster in anticipation of further changes in prices. During the period of hyper-inflation, the velocity of circulation rises to an extremely high level. The rate of spending increases at a very fast rate owing to the fear among people that the value of money is declining with an increasing rapidity. Conversely during depression people spend less expecting a further decline in prices and incomes.

The velocity of circulation of money is low in economically backward countries or those countries where the credit and financial system has not fully developed. In recent decades, the velocity of circulation of money has shown a rising trend because of increase in number of financial institutions and their diversification.

ASSUMPTIONS OF THEORY

Before making a critical examination of the theory, it is very essential to understand the assumptions on which it is based. These are expressed by the phrase, "other things being equal" which relates to volume of trade, velocity of circulation of money, credit money etc.

(1) The theory assumes that V is constant and is not affected by the changes in the quantity of money (M) or the price level (P). The quantity theorists ignored the velocity of money because they were concerned with what Keynes calls transactions and precautionary motives for holding money. So long as we hold money for these purposes, the amount of money held may remain stable but as soon as we introduce the speculative motive for holding money, we cannot ignore the possibility of a change in the velocity of money.

(2) The theory assumes that the volume of goods and services (T) remains constant. It depends on natural resources, climatic conditions, techniques of production, productivity of labour, transportation etc. All these factors, it is assumed, have nothing to do with the changes in the quantity of money T, therefore remains constant. The assumption that total volume of goods and services (T) remains constant is based on an other assumption that there exists full employment; it implies that there are no unemployed productive resources which can be used to increase production of goods and services to be exchanged for money.

(3) The quantity theorists assume that price is a passive factor. Price is affected by other factors in the equation but does not affect or cause changes in those factors. The relation between P and other factors in the equation is one-sided in as much as P is determined by other elements in the equation but it does not determine them.

(4) Prof. Fisher considers a long period of time and assumes V and T to be constant over such a period. In the short period there can be changes in other variables like T or V. But when this short period or the period of transition is over, other variables will become constant so that a change in M or V is followed by a proportionate change in P.

CRITICISM

The quantity theory of money has been severely criticised by the modern economists on a number of counts, important of which are briefly stated below:

(1) The equation $MV = PT$ is an accounting identity or a simple truism. Everything is defined in terms of everything else so that the two sides of the equation must be equal. In other words, the two sides of the equation represent the two sides of transactions that take place in the economy. This equation shows that total quantity

of money given in exchange for goods and services (MV) = the money value of goods and services given in exchange for money (PT). In other words, the total money expenditure of buyers = the total amount of receipt of sellers. Thus the equation does not tell us anything new about money and prices; it only shows in a simple manner what is evidently true. As such, the theory has hardly any analytical or practical value.

(2) The assumption of *ceteris paribus* (other things remaining unchanged) is unrealistic and in the actual world 'other things' (*viz.* V, V', T and relation between M and M') rarely remain unchanged. They undergo changes not only in the long period but also in a comparatively short period. Regular changes are taking place in the size of population, volume of business transacted per velocity of circulation, policy in regard to ratio between cash and credit etc.

(3) The theory assumes that the volume of transactions and the velocity of circulation of money are independent of the variations in the general price level and the quantity of money. But in reality this is not so. It is quite possible that a change in the quantity of money (M) may cause a change in its velocity (V) and thus more than a proportionate change may be effective in the price level (P). There have been cases in the monetary history where increase in V and not in M has been the cause of increase in P. The immediate cause of hyper-inflation in the 1920s in Germany was not so much the increase in M but the increase in V, every body spending the fast depreciating Mark as quickly as possible. Similarly, a change in M may cause a change in T and a change in P may lead to a change in M. Again M may increase without any rise in P on account of the fact that T may have changed. The prosperity of 1920s in the United States shows that a rise in T can lead to increase in M without causing an increase in P. Further an increase in M may raise P, increase profits and thereby stimulate production beyond profitable limits and thus again depress P. Thus all the variables are mutually interdependent and it is difficult to know what affects what and what is the result of what. The quantity theory ignores this mutual interdependence and reaches the conclusion that M is the cause and P is the effect.

(4) The quantity theory is heterogenous in character. Some of the variables in the Equation of Exchange are non-comparables. M, for instance, refers to a point of time while V relates to a period of

time; it is not correct to multiply two different things. *P* includes all sorts of prices, wholesale as well as retail, wages and profits. Some prices move fast while others are rigid. It is difficult to say whether *P* represents highly fluctuating wholesale prices or rigid retail prices. Similarly, *T* includes goods as well as services. Thus the quantity theory of money consists of mutually inconsistent elements.

(5) Theory is static in nature. It may apply to a community which is living under static conditions. But we are living in a highly dynamic world. To cite Keynes, "The real task of such a theory is to treat the problem dynamically, analysing the different elements involved in such a manner as to exhibit the casual process by which the price level is determined and the method of transition from one position of equilibrium to another."[7]

(6) The theory does not explain the causal relationship between *P* and *M*. It does explain why the price level is what it is at any particular time but fails to explain the causes which bring about changes in the price level. In other words, it provides no tools for correct analysis of the hidden forces which produce variations in the value of money. The theory tries to establish an unrealistic direct causal relationship between *M* and *P* without realising the importance of other monetary factors and relative prices.

(7) Though the theory may be taken as a satisfactory explanation of the long-term trends of prices, it falls to explain the causes of the trade cycle. No doubt, the shortage of *M* and *M'* has brought a boom to a sudden end but sometimes it collapses without a shortage of money and credit. Further, the theory is not adequate to explain reversal of downswing at the bottom of slump. The theory appears to suggest that in order to raise prices during depression, the quantity of money in circulation should be increased. This suggestion was tested in the United States during the Great Depression, when the Federal Reserve System, with a view to arrest the downward movement of prices, carried on the process of expansion of money supply to fantastic extremes but without any substantial effect on the price level.

(8) The theory overemphasizes the role of the quantity of money in determining the price level Keynes points out that the change in economic activity or the price level is caused not by a change in the

---

7. J.M. Keynes, *A Treatise on Money* (1930), Vol. I, p. 133.

quantity of money alone but by other fundamental factors like income, expenditure, saving and investment.

(9) The theory ignores not only certain monetary factors but also non-monetary factors (*e.g.* diversification of industry, differentiation in human want, transport facilities, importation of money, use of book credit etc.) which have a significant effect on the price level. Irving Fisher himself elaborated these non-monetary factors; he observed that "transport facilities, diversification of industry and differentiation of human wants would lead to an increase in the volume of trade and thereby to a decline in the price level. Improvident habits, rapid transportation and the use of book credit would increase the velocity of circulation and thereby lead to a rise in prices. This shows that the exponent of the quantity theory was not ignorant of the limitations of the theory.

(10) The theory would hold good only if an increase in M leads to a corresponding increase in spending; in other words, the theory would be valid only if no part of the additional money created is kept in idle hoards. Obviously, there is no direct link between supply of money and spending.

(11) The theory assumes the existence of full employment which is not true in actual practice. The theory can be valid only if the increase in spending resulting from increase in supply of money faces a completely inelastic supply of output which would be true only under conditions of full employment. Beyond full employment an increase in M will increase P. But when there are unemployed resources, the supply curve of output would be elastic and as such the increase in M may lead to any increase in real income and output instead of that in P.

(12) According to Fisher T represents total transactions in the equation of exchange or the volume of trade. T simply represents commodity transactions but, as pointed out by Keynes, a large number of transactions which take place with the help of money are commercial, industrial and financial in nature. Commodity transactions form only a small percentage of them. The equation, therefore, measures only cash transactions and not the purchasing power of money.

(13) The theory may be useful to explain the long-term phenomenon but is not of much help in studying short-term

phenomenon. To cite Crowther, "the most we can say for the quantity theory is that the quantity in existence seems to be the dominant influence on the price level on the average of long period. But in the short period...it may or may not control the movements of prices. And whether it does or does not depends on whether changes in the quantity of money are offset by changes in velocity of its circulation."[8] Fisher, of course, recognises this. His reply is that variations in *V* and *T* do take place in the short or transitional period but over the long period, as the economy attains equilibrium, they become constant. But, as Keynes has pointed out, in the long-run we may all be dead. In this continuously changing world of ours, there is hardly anything like the long-run equilibrium. Long-run equilibrium is like to-morrow which never comes. The usefulness of a theory which ignores short-term fluctuations can well be imagined.

(14) *T* denotes the volume of transactions covering both final and intermediate transactions. *V* represents velocity of money, including all forms of transactions made by producers or consumers. *T* and *V*, therefore, do not help much in explaining the level of national income, which measures aggregate expenditure on final products only. Transactions equation neither indicates the national income nor measures the purchasing power of money in the proper sense.

(15) The equation of exchange can not express the changes in the structure of relative prices caused by monetary factors.

(16) Fisher ignores that rate of interest as a link between *M* and *P*.

(17) The theory explains how the changes in prices take place, but cannot explain why do these changes occur. In the words of Crowther, "It cannot even explain why it is that a creation of money will sometimes take and start off a rise in prices, while at another an equal creation may have no effect at all."[9]

(18) Some writers, including Alfred Marshall (*Money, Credit and Commerce*), have objected even to the concept of velocity of

---

8. Crowther, *An Outline of Money* (1942), p. 128.
9. *Ibid.*, p. 123.

circulation of money. It is said that during the period of falling prices, the rapidity of circulation of money is low; and during the period of rising prices, it is said to have increased or to be high. But the theory does not explain the causes that govern the velocity of circulation.

(19) Edwin Cannan has stressed the fact that unlike most commodities money is not governed by the strict laws of demand and supply. He is of the opinion that the demand for currency is furnished "not by the number and amount of transactions, but by the ability and willingness of persons to hold currency, in the same way as we think of the demand for houses as coming not from the persons who buy and resell or lease and sub-lease houses, but from the persons who occupy houses."[10]

In spite of the above criticisms, the theory contains, at least, some element of truth. A number of instances can be cited from economic history to prove its validity. Hyper-inflation in Germany (1923) and of China (1947-48) was to a great extent on account of excessive issue of currency. Discovery of gold mines in Australia and California towards the middle of the 19th century led to a rise in prices in the gold using countries and the prices declined after a decade with the reduction in world output of gold. The rapid rise in prices in India in recent years is associated with a substantial increase in the supply of money.

Covering the period 1879-1908, E.W. Kemmerer (*Money and Credit Instruments in their relation to General Prices*) tried to prove the validity of the theory, comparing the wholesale and retail price indices with the circulation of notes during the period 1914 to 1920. Gustav Cassel also attempted to prove with the help of statistical data that the changes in money supply and price level were proportional. Analysing all the relevant facts, he reached the conclusion that there was a "clear indication of general agreement between the rise in prices and the increase in circulation which is particularly striking since the agreement is, particularly speaking, absolute for the final quarter of 1920."[11] Cassel's statement simply shows that the prices increase with an increase in money supply and *vic versa*. It does not establish the fact that price variations are in

10. Edwin Cannan, *Money*, p. 72.

11. G. Cassel, *Money and Foreign Exchange After 1914*, pp. 58-59.

direct proportion to the variations in the quantity of money. This statement thus is different from the assertion of the theory.

QUANTITY THEORY OF MONEY (CASH BALANCE APPROACH)

Generally associated with the names of Cambridge economists like Alfred Marshall, Pigou, Robertson and Keynes, the cash balance approach found favour with the earlier economists like Adam Smith, William Petty, John Locke, Richard Cantillon etc. This approach depends upon the demand for and supply of money as obtaining at a particular moment instead of obtaining in a particular period of time. While the earlier economists laid emphasis on the supply side of money, the formulators of cash balance approach emphasized the demand side of money. According to this approach the value of money depends upon the demand for money; but the demand for money arises not on account of transactions but on account of its being a store of value. Money has two characteristics—flatness and roundness—money sitting and money on wings—to serve as a store of value and as a medium of exchange. The real demand for money comes from those who want to hold it on account of various motives and not from those who simply want to exchange it for goods and services just as the real demand for houses comes from those who want to live in them and not from those who simply want to construct and sell them. The essence of the cash balance approach has been clearly stated by Marshall as follows:

> In every state of society there is some fraction of their income which people find it worthwhile to keep in the form of currency; It may be a fifth or a tenth or a twentieth. A large command of resources in the form of currency renders their business easy, smooth and puts them at an advantage in bargaining; but on the other hand, it locks up in a barren form resources that might yield an income or gratification if invested...Every man finds the appropriate after balancing one against another; the advantages of a further ready command and the disadvantages of putting more of his resources into a form in which they yield him no income or other benefit...let us suppose that the inhabitants of a country...find it just worthwhile to keep by them on the average, ready purchasing power to the extent of a tenth part of their property; then the aggregate value of

the currency will tend to be equal to the sum of these amounts.[12]

Let us now examine two equations of cash balance approach, one put forward by Alfred Marshall and the other formulated by A.C. Pigou. Marshall's equation is:

$$M = KY \qquad \text{... 14.5}$$

where M represents the quantity of money, K stands for that portion of income which people want to hold in the form of money, and Y is the money income. K, in other words, is the reciprocal of velocity. If PO (price level times output) is substituted for Y,

$$M = KPO \qquad \text{... 14.6}$$

or

$$P = \frac{M}{KO} \qquad \text{... 14.7}$$

Criticising this equation, one of the monetary theorists has observed, "It does not follow from the mere fact that $V = I/K$ as an arithmetic identity, that therefore the Marshallian analysis is in fact the same thing as the Hume-Fisher analysis. To assert this is to miss entirely the significance of the K in the Marshallian equation."[13]

CAMBRIDGE EQUATION

The Cambridge Equation formulated by A.C. Pigou is:

$$P = \frac{KR}{M} \qquad \text{... 14.8}$$

where P represents the value of money, K stands for the proportion of total real income to be maintained in cash, R represents total real income, and M is the total quantity of money or the total number of units of money. But all people do not hold cash strictly in the form of legal tender money. Some of them hold part of it in the form of bank deposits. Keeping this in view the equation was enlarged as follows:

$$P = \frac{KR}{M}[C - h(1 - C)] \text{ or } M = \frac{KR}{P}[C - h(1 - C)] \qquad \text{... 14.9}$$

---

12. Alfred Marshall, *Money, Credit and Commerce* (London, 1929), pp. 1 and 3.

13. A.H. Hansen, *Monetary Theory and Fiscal Policy* (New York, 1949), pp. 49-50.

where C represents the proportion of cash people hold in the form of legal tender money, and h stands for the proportion of legal tender money which is kept in the form of bank deposits.

Prof. D.H. Robertson's equation is slightly different from that of Prof. Pigou. Robertson's equation is:

$$M = PKT \text{ or } P = \frac{M}{KT} \qquad \text{... 14.10}$$

where P stands for the price level, T represents the total amount of goods and services (like R of Pigou), K represents the fraction of T for which people wish to keep cash. Robertson's equation is considered better than that of Pigou because it is more comparable with that of Fisher. It is considered best of all the Cambridge equations because it is the simplest one.

COMPARISON OF TRANSACTIONS AND CASH BALANCES APPROACHES

The difference between the Fisherine equation and Cambridge equations is not as fundamental as is generally supposed. A closer examination of the two equations will show that they are more or less similar as both of them show that the price level depends upon the quantity of money. Further the two can be easily compared.

$$\text{P} = M\frac{V}{T} \text{ (Fisher) or } P = M\frac{1}{kR} \text{ (Pigou)} \qquad \text{... 14.11}$$

(We have converted Pigou's P, the value of money, into the price level p so that $P = 1/p$)

The two equations show that V and k tend to be the opposite of each other. The higher the fraction of the real income that people hold in money, the lower will be the velocity of money and *vice versa*. I and k are reciprocals (*i.e.* $V = 1/k$ or $k = 1/V$). It means that when people want to hold more (higher the k), the velocity of circulation of money will be less (lower the V). As such, if we want to enquire into the causes of the fluctuations in the velocity of money we should turn to causes which determine changes in the factor k. In fact, the two versions can be reconciled by substituting $1/V$ for k and $1/k$ for V in the two equations.

But there are also some notable differences between the two equations. In the first place, the two approaches give different interpretations to the demand for money. The cash balance approach emphasized what Robertson calls "money sitting" while the transactions approach stresses what Robertson calls "money on wings." Secondly, Fisherine approach emphasizes the velocity of money while Pigovian approach stresses idle balances kept as a part of the national income. Thirdly, while transactions approach looks upon money as a flow, the cash balance looks upon money as a stock. Fourthly, Fisher's equation is concerned with the amount of money required by the community during a period of time to finance its transactions while the Cambridge equation focusses attention on the amount of cash balances held by the individuals at any given time with a view to finance their future transactions. In other words, while the former refers to a period of time; the latter refers to a point of time. Fifthly, while Fisherine equation takes transaction velocity of circulation (*i.e.* number of times a unit of money circulates for performing all the transactions taking place in the economy in a year), the Cambridge equation takes income velocity of circulation (*i.e.* number of times a unit of money circulates for buying the final national product). Sixthly, T in Fisherine equation is the sum total of all transactions while R in the Cambridge equation is only the final product which comes to the market. Seventhly, P in the Fisherine equation is the average of the price level of each good and service at each stage of production and includes the average price level of all transactions while R in the Cambridge equation is the price level of only the goods finally brought to the market. Eighthly, the variables M, V, P, and T in the transactions equation are independent variables. In the cash balance equation variables P, K and T may not change at the same time and in the same direction. The change in one may offset the change in the other. Ninthly, the cash balance equation explains the value of money in terms of demand for and supply of money. In the case of transactions equation the value of money is artificially divorced from the general theory of value. Distinguishing between Marshallian version of the cash balance equation and Fisherine equation, Prof. Hansen remarks[14]:

14. A.H. Hansen, *Monetary Theory and Fiscal Policy* (New York, 1949), pp. 49-50.

> The Marshallian version of the quantity theory—$M = KY$—represents fundamentally new approach to the problem of money and prices: It is not true, as is often alleged, that the cash balance equation is merely the quantity theory in new algebraic dress...To assert this is to miss entirely the significance of the K in the Marshallian equation...The difference can be stated as follows: in the terms of the Marshallian approach, sudden and rapid shifts in the desire of the public to hold money may profoundly affect prices even though the monetary authority successfully maintains a high stability in the money supply. The desire of the public to hold cash balances—'liquidity preference'—enters as a powerful factor. Drastic and sudden shifts in the desire to hold money, reflected in a change in K, may produce large and quickly moving changes in the level of income and prices. Shifts in public psychology, in expectations, must be taken account of no less than changes in money supply. In the Marshallian analysis a shift in K may start an upward or downward movement. It is K, and not M, that holds the stage.

SUPERIORITY OF CASH BALANCES APPROACH

The cash balances approach is superior to Fisherine approach on a number of counts, important of which are briefly stated below:

(1) The cash balances approach lays stress on the subjective valuations and human motives which are the basis of all economic activities in sharp contrast to the highly mechanical nature of the concept of velocity of circulation of money in the transaction approach.

(2) The cash balances approach brings to light a new element, that is, the level of income and changes therein. Instead of being concerned with the total transactions, it is concerned with the level of income, which in turn, determines the level of economic development, employment and price level. In fact, the problem of price level cannot be studied in isolation of changes in income and output. Further what matters is not the velocity of money but velocity of circulation of money on account of changes in income and output.

(3) The cash balance approach emphasized the demand for money to hold whereas the Fisherine equation lays stress on the supply of money. In fact, the Cambridge equation was put forward to validate the classical quantity theory of money according to which the supply of money is the sole determinant of the price level.

(4) The cash balance approach links itself with the general theory of value since it explains the value of money in terms of the demand for the supply of money. The equation $P = kR/M$ is more useful than the equation $P = MV/T$ to explain the value of money for it is easier to know how large cash balances a community holds than to know how much it spends on various types of transactions.

(5) Cash balances approach brings out the importance of k. An analysis of the factors responsible for fluctuations in K offered scope for the study of many important problems like uncertainty, expectations, rate of interest etc., which were not considered in the transactions approach.

Speaking of the superiority of cash balances approach, Prof. Robertson remarks[15]:

> Broadly speaking, the sitting money exercise is the more useful for enabling us to understand the underlying psychological forces determining the value of money; while the money on the wing exercise is the more useful for equipping us to watch with understanding the actual process by which in real life prices of goods and services change for reminding us that the quantity of money and the quantity of goods do not affect the price level by some kind of occult planetary influence, but by modifying the capacity or willingness of human beings to buy or refrain from buying, to sell or refrain from selling. But in any case we have not reached the end of our task.

Comparing his equation with that of Fisher, Pigou remarks:

> Mine is not, of course, any 'truer' than its rival They are both equally true. The claim that I make on behalf of mine is merely that it is a somewhat more effective engine of analysis. It focusses attention on the proportion of their resources that people choose to keep in the form of titles of

15. D.H. Robertson, *Money* (1932), p. 39.

legal tender instead of focussing it on 'velocity of circulation'. This fact gives it, as I think, a real advantage, because it brings us at once into relation with volition—an ultimate cause of demand—instead of with something that seems at first sight accidental and arbitrary.

CRITICISM OF CASH BALANCES APPROACH

Despite the superiority of cash balances approach over transactions approach, it suffers from several shortcomings, important of which are briefly stated below:

(1) The introduction of the factor *R* which represents the current income of community suggested that a change in its quantity is one of those important factors which directly influence the demand for cash reserves. According to Keynes, it is fundamentally true in case of income deposits but its importance is considerably reduced when the total deposits are taken into consideration. "Indeed the chief inconvenience of the Cambridge Quantity Equation really lies in its applying to the total deposits considerations which are primarily relevant only to the income deposits, and in its tackling the problem as though the same sort of considerations which govern the income deposits also govern the total deposits."[16]

(2) According to Keynes, the prominence given to *K* (the proportion of bank deposits to the community's income) is misleading, when it is extended beyond the income deposits. The stress which this approach lays on the point that the mount of real balances held is determined by the comparative advantages of holding resources in cash, and in alternative forms, so that a change in *k* will be attributable to a change in these comparative advantages, is useful and instructive. But resources "in this connection ought not to be interpreted by Pigou, as being identical with current income."[17]

(3) Pigou measures the quantity of Real Balance in terms of wheat and is not able to solve the question of the measurement of price level. According to Keynes, "The object of any quantity equation is to discover, not the price of wheat, but in some sense or other, the purchasing power of money. But his equation either

16. J.M. Keynes, *A Treatise on Money*, Vol. I (1930), p. 232.
17. *Ibid.*

makes no contribution to this or does so by employing that relative prices are unchangeable", which is not proved by that facts.[18]

(4) The equation does not throw light on the disturbances which occur owing to a change in the proportion in which deposits are held for different purposes (savings, business, and income). In addition, "It is intractable for the task of analysing disturbances to the price level due to disparities between the rates of saving and investment."[19]

(5) The Cambridge approach ignored the speculative demand for money which turned out to be the most important motive for holding money. Ignoring the speculative demand for money meant that the linkage between the theories of the rate of interest and the level of income through the demand for money was not completed.

(6) Though the equation brought into the picture the level of income, it ignored other elements like productivity, thrift, liquidity preference, all of which are essential in a comprehensive theory of value of money.

(7) The Cambridge approach like the transactions approach assumes k and T as given and thus becomes subject to criticisms which were levied against transactions approach.

(8) The cash balances approach does not furnish an adequate monetary theory which could be used to explain and analyse the dynamic behaviour of prices in the economy, for it does not tell us by how much shall price and output change as a result of a given change in money supply in the short period.

(9) The approach fails to assign an explicit role to the rate of interest which leads to the impression that changes in the supply of money are directly related to the price level. A realistic theory of prices, however, cannot afford to ignore the important role which rate of interest plays.

(10) The theory assumes that the elasticity of demand for money is unity. The demand for money is said to be of unit elasticity when the change in price and the resultant change in the quantity of money are neutralised so that the total amount of money spent on goods remains unchanged. Modern writers do not agree with this

---

18. *Ibid.*, pp. 232-33.
19. *Ibid.*, p. 233.

view and feel that the volume of goods and services which money buys will change with the variations in the supply of money. As such the elasticity of demand for money cannot be unity excepting in a stationary state.

KEYNES' EQUATION—REAL BALANCE APPROACH

In the beginning, Lord J.M. Keynes also belonged to the Cambridge school. He, of course, was not satisfied with the equation known as the Real Balance Quantity Equation. According to him, a holder of money requires a quantity of real balances which is in appropriate relationship with the quantity of real transactions upon which those balances are spent. He measured real balances by consumption units and came to the conclusion that if this appropriate relationship remained unchanged, the amount of cash balances which he required would be equal to the amount of real balances as determined by the above relationship "multiplied by the price level corresponding to the prices applicable to the various real transactions against which the cash balances are held."[20]

$$n = p(K + rK') \qquad \text{... 14.12}$$

where n stands for the total quantity of cash, r for the proportion of banks' cash reserves to their deposits, p for the price level of consumptions units, K for the amount of real balances held in cash (or the number of consumption units which the people require in cash) and K' for real balances (number of consumption units) held in bank deposits. The proportion between K and K' depends upon the banking arrangements of the public while their absolute value would depend upon the habits of the people. The value of r would be a matter of reserve practices followed by the banking system. So long as these values remain unaltered, a direct nexus between the quantity of cash (n) and the price level (r) remains an established fact.

CRITICISM

This equation also suffers from a number of shortcomings. In fact, Keynes himself was not ignorant of these which he pointed out later in his *Treatise on Money*. In first place, the equation is faulty because p measures only the price level of consumption units

20. J.M. Keynes, *A Tract on Monetary Reform,* Chapter III, Section I.

implying thereby that money is held only to secure consumption goods. This implication is, however, incorrect since money is kept for a "vast multiplicity of business and personal purposes."[21]

The second defect of the equation, to use Keynes' own words, "lay in the suggestion that the possible causes of a variation of *K'* were limited to those which can be properly described as a change of habit on the part of the public. This use of language was not formally incorrect, but it is misleading in so far as it is intended to include, for example, a change in the proportions of the total deposits represented by Savings-deposits, Business-deposits and Income-deposits respectively, due to a change in the bank rate or in the business situation as a whole. In short, I was applying to the cash-deposits as a whole, conceptions which were only appropriate to the income deposits."[22]

Thirdly, the proportional relationship between *n* and *p* expressed in the equation does not exist, at any rate, in the short period, when *K*, *K'* and *r* all might and do change as a result of the change in ***n***. Recognising that change in *n* will affect *K*, *K'* and *r*, Keynes himself admits that in the short period there is no proportionate relationship between the quantity of money (*n*) and prices (*p*); though in the long run he feels that this relationship between *n* and *p* does hold. When a person's money income increases as a result of an increase in the quantity of money, the amount of bank deposits that he would keep for a vast multiplicity of business and personal purposes would also increase. Corresponding to increased bank deposits the reserves which the banks would keep in cash would also increase. This means that an increase in the volume of money would lead to an increase in, *K*, *K'* and *r*. As sum, there is no justification in holding a proportional relationship between the quantity of money (*n*) and price (*p*). Corresponding to an increase in the quantity of money (*n*), the level of prices (*p*) may increase (and even if it increases the increase may be more than, less than, or equal to the increase in the quantity of money), decrease or remain constant depending upon the behaviour of *K*, *K'* and *r* in the process of changes in the quantity of money.

21. J.M. Keynes, *A Treatise on Money,* Vol. I, p. 222.

22. *Ibid*., pp. 223-24.

KEYNES' FUNDAMENTAL EQUATIONS

With a view to treat the problem of the value of money more dynamically, Keynes made an attempt in the light of his. Saving-Investment Theory (in his *Treatise on Money*) to effect an improvement over his Real Balances Equation. Linking the rate of interest and the stock of cash to the determination of the price levels, he tried to show how the price levels are disturbed by a disequilibrium between savings and investment. There are two fundamental equations; one deals with the forces governing the price level of the output as a whole.

The first fundamental equation is

$$P = \frac{E}{O} + \frac{I' - S}{R} \qquad \text{... 14.13}$$

where p stands for the price level of consumption goods, E for the total earning of the community during a given period, O for the total number of units produced in the same period, I' for the cost of production of new investment goods, S for the amount of total savings of the community in the same period and R for the number of consumption units produced (or the volume of liquid consumption goods).

The second fundamental equation may be explained as follows:

From the point of view of the society as a whole total sum spent in buying goods and services = Total income of society

$$\pi O = Y \qquad \text{... 14.14}$$

where π = price level

O = output, and

Y = income

then $$\pi = \frac{Y}{O} \qquad \text{... 14.15}$$

the total income of society may be taken as consisting of two parts namely: (1) sums received by factors of production including normal profits of entrepreneurs, and (2) windfall profits, that is, extra profits arising out of appreciation in value of capital assets.

$$Y = E + Q \qquad \text{... 14.16}$$

where E = income of factors and

Q = windfall profits due to appreciation in value of capital assets.

Capital assets appreciate in value when demand for investment is in excess of supply of new investment. In any economy, supply of new investments is limited by its current savings. The savings go towards building up of new capital. As such, if the demand for new investment increases, while supply of new investments remains unchanged, the value of capital assets is bound to rise. Thus the owners of capital assets get a windfall profit. Keynes treats windfall profits as the excess of investment over saving. Thus

$$Q = I - S \qquad \text{... 14.17}$$

where I = investment

S = saving

Hence the Fundamental Equation may be written as:

$$\pi = \frac{Y}{O} = \frac{E+Q}{O} + \frac{I-S}{O} \qquad \text{... 14.18}$$

The equation, like the equation $MV = PT$, is a truism. It does not explain anything about fundamental economic behaviour. For income (Y) has only been conveniently broken up into parts: income paid out (E) and windfall profits (Q). Keynes, however, has attached certain hypothesis to some of the variables in order to study the process of price movement. In the equation $MV = PT$, any movement in M may be counteracted by the corresponding changes in V and/or T. The classical economists avoid this problem by assuming V and T as constant. Keynes also implicitly assumes that in the short-run output (O) is given. He further assumes that the ratio E/Q (*i.e.* rate of earnings of the factors of production per product) is stable. The windfall profits (Q) vary in accordance with the variation in the market and natural rate of interest. Natural rate of interest is the expected profit on new capital investments. Market rate of interest, in contrast, is the rate charged on borrowed money. If the expected rate of profit on new capital investments exceeds the rate at which money can be borrowed from banks and elsewhere, the people would tend to borrow more and invest the same in purchase of capital assets. This will result in an increase in the demand for capital assets which would lead to an appreciation in their value and hence windfall profits. If the natural rate is in excess of the market rate of interest, Q would be greater than zero; it would be equal to zero when the two rates are equal and less than zero when the market rate is higher than the natural rate of interest. From these hypotheses it may be concluded that the price level fluctuates around a rather stable equilibrium value, E/Q, in response to the fluctuations of the market rate of interest around the natural rate and induces fluctuations in the profit variable, Q. By definition Q is $(I - S)$. The mechanism of price fluctuation can thus be expressed in terms of the relative behaviour of savings (S) and investment (I).

Keynes' fundamental equations show that there is a unique functional relationship between the quantity of money and the price level of consumption goods (P) and the price level of output as a whole (π) in ideal conditions of equilibrium. To cite Keynes' own words: "This means indeed, that in equilibrium, *i.e.,* when the factors of production are fully employed, when the public is neither bullish nor bearish of securities and is maintaining in the forms of savings and deposits neither more nor less than 'Normal' proportion of its total wealth, and when the volume of savings is equal both to the cost (I') and to the value (I) of new investment goods there is a unique relationship between the quantity of money and price levels of consumption goods and output as a whole, of such a character that if the quantity of money were double the price level would be double also."[23]

The fundamental equations are useful tools which Keynes employs to explain the phases of the business cycle. They key force in the whole Keynesian analysis reflected in fundamental equations is the relationship between savings and investment. Though savings and investment as Keynes asserts, are not identical process, since the savings in a way facilitate investment, it is necessary to maintain equilibrium such that $\frac{I'-S}{R}$ and $\frac{I-S}{O}$ must be zero, for if S exceeds I of I' then prices decline, losses will ensure and output will be curtailed and *vice versa*.

23. J.M. Keynes, *A Treatise on Money*, Vol. I, pp. 146-47.

CRITICISM OF KEYNES' FUNDAMENTAL EQUATIONS

(1) Keynes' fundamental equations very much resemble the old quantity theory equation. As already mentioned, Keynes himself wrote that under ideal conditions of equilibrium the relationship between the quantity of money and the price level is such that a doubling of the quantity of money would lead to a doubling of the price level. He admitted that the fundamental equations were not intrinsically superior to other identities connected with monetary factors. He recognised that these elements could not be easily determined statistically.

(2) The conditions of equilibrium between I, I' and S envisaged by Keynes in his fundamental equations refer to the ideal state of reflation, *i.e.*, to a situation in which resources in the economy are fully employed. Thus according to Keynesian approach reflected in the fundamental equations, to establish reflationary stability in the economy, it is enough to bring the three variables—I, I' and S—into equilibrium. But this type of reasoning is in conflict with the later Keynesian approach (formulated in his General Theory) where he shows that these variables are in a state of equilibrium even when the economy is suffering from a depression.

(3) According to the fundamental equations, the rate of interest plays a dominant role in determining the volume of business activity and the level of prices. Expansion and contraction of business depends upon it because when saving exceed investment, the prices fall resulting in a decline in profits and production and *vice versa*. To control the ups and downs in business activity, Keynes suggested the manipulation of rate of interest by the central monetary authority. But this is in sharp conflict with the theory formulated in his *General Theory* according to which the volume of business activity depends not so much upon the manipulation of the rate of interest as on the changes in the marginal efficiency of capital.

(4) The fundamental equations do not mention all the factors which influence the price level. To arrive at a complete analysis, we have to look beyond these equations. In fact, they do not provide a satisfactory explanation.

(5) The fundamental equations hold true only under static conditions. This criticism becomes particularly sharp for Keynes claimed his equations to be dynamic. In the actual world production extends over a period of time and the earnings of a given period are

related not to the cost of producing goods purchased for consumption in the same period but to the cost of purchasing goods which would be purchased for consumption at some further date.

(6) The fundamental equations are based upon the unrealistic assumption of given or fixed output. This assumption would hold only under conditions of full employment. Thus the fundamental equations do not offer any scope for analysing changes in the level of output and employment as a result of changes in the supply of money. In this connection, Keynes himself wrote in his *General Theory* that his "so-called 'fundamental equations' were an instantaneous picture taken on the assumption of a given output. They attempted to show how, assuming the given output, forces could develop which involved a profit disequilibrium, and thus required a change in the level of output. But the dynamic development as distinct from the instantaneous picture, was left incomplete and extremely confused."[24]

(7) The definitions of income, profits and losses, as given by Keynes, give rise to absurdities. It is assumed, for instance, that the businessmen save the deficit which occurs as a result of earnings falling short of expectations. In reality, they do not receive it. Similarly, as suggested by the fundamental equations, the difference between the savings and investment can never be taken as the cause of profit or loss.

(8) In Keynes' equation $O = R + C$ where O stands for total output consisting of consumption goods (R) and investment goods (C). The units of quantities of both goods have been chosen "in such a way that a unit of each has the same cost of production at the base date."[25] But as Hansen points out, it is not necessary that cost of production of one unit of R (consumption goods) and C (investment goods) may be the same every year. Their cost of production is likely to differ on account of differences in technical and other progress recorded in the production of R and C. The same amount of money will not necessarily produce the same amount of consumption goods (R) and investment goods (C) every year. The

24. J.M. Keynes, *The General Theory of Employment, Interest and Money* (London, 1936), p. VII.
25. J.M. Keynes, *A Treatise on Money,* Vol. I, pp. 146-47.

fundamental equations are correct in the base year, but they may not necessarily hold true in other years. In other words, the fundamental equations apply to a static economy in which there is not technical progress but they do not hold in a dynamic economy where progress is the rule rather than an exception.

(9) The magnitudes of R, E and S refer to a stipulated period of time which helps us in determining the price level at any given moment. But this is simply a mechanical approach which can not govern the motives of human behaviour. The rumours of war, for instance, may upset the price level in the morning.

In spite of the shortcomings pointed out above, the fundamental equations are of special interest in as much as they represented a transition from the monetary theory of quantity equations to the modem theory of income, output and employment. The fundamental equations summarised the factors determining the price levels of consumption goods and output as a whole. With their help Keynes was able to distinguish between the normal profits and the "windfall profits" of the entrepreneurs.

INCOME THEORY

Modern monetary experts have discarded the old notion of the quantity of money as a causative factor in the state of business and a determinant of the value of money. In their opinion, Income Theory (also known as Income-Expenditure approach or Saving-Investment approach) is the best which provides a direct relationship between changes in the price level and the diverse phases of economic activity, namely, money income, expenditure on consumption goods, expenditure on investment goods, hoarding and dishoarding, creation and destruction of money, output, profit expectations etc. According to this approach price level or value of money is more a matter of total income rather than of the quantity of money.

Though the Income Theory is generally associated with the name of J.M. Keynes, in fact, it has a long history. Thomas Tooke in 1844 in his book *An Enquiry into the Currency Principles* stressed the fact that income rather than the quantity of money determined price levels. He stated the twelfth proposition in this book as follows: "That the prices of commodities do not depend upon the quantity of money...but on the contrary the amount of circulating medium is a consequence of prices."[26] The famous thirteenth proposition reads thus: "That it is the quantity of money, constituting the revenues of the different orders of State, under the head of rents, profits, salaries and wages, destined for current expenditure, that alone forms the limiting principle of the aggregate of money prices, the only price that can properly come under the designation of general prices. As the cost of production is the limiting principle of supply, so the aggregate of money incomes devoted to expenditure for consumption is the determining and limiting principle of demand."[27] In Tooke's proposition we have the most clear statement of the early exposition of the income theory of prices. The famous Swedish economist Knut Wicksell, considered to be an important member of the neo-classical school of economists along with Alfred Marshall, found Tooke's analysis of income, aggregate demand, and prices highly suggestive and made it the starting point for his theory of money and prices. Stating the income theory of prices he observed[28]:

> A general rise in prices is therefore only conceivable on the supposition that the general demand has for some reason become, or is expected to become, greater than the supply...Any theory of money worthy of the name must be able to show how and why the monetary or pecuniary demand for goods exceeds or falls short of the supply of goods in given conditions.

Wicksell stressed that to explain how the quantity of money affects "the general price level, it should be explained how the quantity of money makes its influence felt on the determination either of supply or demand for individual goods and services in the economy. It is this spirit of his approach, which seeks to remove the classical dichotomy by integrating the monetary and expenditure sectors, that entitles Wicksell to be called an important forerunner of the modern income approach.

---

26. Thomas Tooke, *An Enquiry into the Currency Principles*, pp. 123-124.
27. *Ibid*., p. 124.
28. Knut Wicksell, *Lectures on Political Economy*, Vol. II, *'Money'*, pp. 159-60.

In 1925, Aftalion effectively stated the income theory of money and prices and also elaborated it for the first time in the form of an equation $R = PQ$ where R stands for the money income, P for the price level and Q for the total production. Aftalion demonstrated the superiority of the income theory over quantity theory which, instead of viewing the problem in a mechanical manner as the old quantity theory did, studies the problem in a manner which explains why buyers and sellers act as they do. The income theory substitutes an explanation in terms of men for the one in terms of things on which the quantity theory is based. The theory takes into account individuals' incomes and the psychological effect of variations in income on demand imputable to human desires, aspirations and wants and that economic laws can best be explained in terms of human behaviour.

But neither Tooke, nor Aftalion made any systematic analysis of the determination of income. The task of formulating a systematic theory which explained the determinants of income, and not merely a theory of oscillations as Wicksell and Aftalion had done, was left for Keynes who successfully completed it in his *General Theory* published in 1936. He presented a systematic study of the components of income and put the equation as $Y = C + I$ or $Y = C + S$ and $E = C + I$, where Y represents income, C consumption, I investment, S saving and E expenditure. Everyone of us receives his or her income from one or more persons, for whom that income is an item of expenditure. Thus the only source of income is somebody else's expenditure and every expenditure creates somebody else's income. What is, therefore, needed for stability is the maintenance of the circular flow of money in the economic system. Money income refers to the sum of total payments made to the factors of production in the form of rents, wages, interests, profits etc. Money expenditure consists of expenditures on consumption goods (C) and on capital goods (I) (*i.e.* $Y = C + I$). In other words, all the incomes of the community can be divided into the same two categories according as they are derived from the production of consumption goods (C) and from the production of capital goods (I) (*i.e.* $Y = C + I$). Thus the income theorists proceed on the basis that all money expenditure on final consumption goods and finally purchased capital goods equals the sum of money incomes received in that period (*i.e.* $E = Y$). In other words, income received by all the factors of production in the economy is equal to the exchange value fetched by the goods and services produced by the community.

The Income Theory determines the value of money with the help of the identity between total money income and total money expenditure on consumption goods and capital goods. The flow of money income has generated a flow of real income (goods and services) and the value of money, therefore, depends upon the relative strength of the flow of money income and the flow of real income (goods and services). We can also say that the general price level depends on the rate of remuneration of the factors of production (net national income) which enter into marginal cost in relation to the scale of output. The flow of money income depends on the quantity of money and its income velocity[29] and the flow of real income (goods and services) depends upon a number of factors like techniques, productivity, resources, stage of economic development etc. The gist of the Income Theory of money can be stated thus: the higher the flow of money incomes generated by greater income velocity of money, and given the flow of real income (goods and services), the higher will be the price level and lower will be the value of money. But to the extent the flow of money income has been able to generate additional flows of real income (goods and services), price level as determined at the final end of purchase and sale will be lowered.

So far we have seen that it is the flow of income in relation to the flow of goods and services which determines the price level and not the changes in the quantity of money as such. Now we shall see as to why the income of the community varies up and down much more violently than the community's technical ability to produce

---

29. The income velocity of money must be distinguished from the circulation velocity of money. The latter refers to the number of times a unit of money on the average changes hands in a given period of time. But this changing of hands may not be creating an equivalent money income. Money income will be created only as and when the expenditure is received by final factors of production in the form of rent, wages, interests and profits. The income velocity of money is the average number of times a unit of money turns up in the form of somebody's income. It can be found out by dividing the total money income earned by all the economic units of a country a period of time by average quantity of money supplied.

goods and services (real income) so that income is sometimes more than enough and often insufficient to buy the goods and services which the community can produce; in the former case, prices will rise and the value of money will decline and in the latter case, prices will decine and the value of money will rise. The search for the cause of these fluctuations lies in the gigantic circular flow of income—each expenditure creating some income, which is again spent and creates another income and so forth right round in circle. So long as this circular flow of income is duly maintained, that is total expenditure (E) generates total income (Y), $E = C + I$, $Y = C + S$ $\therefore S = I$, or in other words so long as fundamental condition $S = I$ is fulfilled, there will be no fluctuations in income, output, employment and prices. It is this fundamental condition which according to Keynes is not fulfilled. For no doubt all expenditures automatically generate income but all income is not automatically spent.

Money expenditure in the market on the new goods and services produced may be more than or less than the money income given in their production. In other words, money expenditure is not limited to the income received because of hoarding, dishoarding, creation and destruction of credit money. The act of saving creates a gap in the flow of money payments which can be avoided only if money equal to the amount withdrawn is put back in the income-expenditure stream by an equivalent amount of investment. In Keynes' opinion relation between S and I which determines, Y, determines price level and it is their relationship which by causing fluctuations in income causes fluctuations in prices. If investment (I) exceeds savings (S) as a consequence of dishoarding or credit creation, both income and expenditure will rise, raising at the same time the level of employment and price and *vice versa*. The process is like this: when businessmen decide to make more capital goods, they begin to employ unemployed factors. The money incomes of these newly employed people will increase. So long as the unemployed resources are drawn into production, the volume of output will increase at the same time and prices may not rise. But normally some rise in prices will take place because it may not be easy to expand the production of all types of goods simultaneously. Once the full employment level is reached, any subsequent increase in investment will lead to a rise in prices. The reverse will happen if investment declines—unemployment will increase, money income will decline, expenditure on consumption goods will decline and prices fall.

Similarly, if savings exceed investment (on account of hoarding or destruction of credit), both income and expenditure will decline, lowering at the same time the level of employment and prices and *vice versa*. The process is like this: when a community decides to save a larger portion of their money income than before, their expenditure on consumption goods declines leading to a decline in the incomes of sellers of goods and services and thereby to a decline in the prices of goods and services. The reverse will happen if the savings decline, employment will increase, money incomes will rise, expenditure on consumption goods will increase and prices rise.

Prices are, therefore, governed by saving and investment during a given period. But the former is usually a suitable factor and remains more or less unchanged, depending as it does on the habits of the people. The most important factor determining the price level, therefore, is the volume of investment. It affects prices through its influence on employment and money incomes. Thus it is evident that the general price level is determined by total income and total economic activity than the quantity of money.

COMPARISON OF SAVING-INVESTMENT THEORY AND QUANTITY THEORY

The quantity theory of money is too mechanical. It cannot provide adequate explanation of a number of things about the behaviour of money. At the bottom of depression there is no shortage of money or goods; in spite of this, recovery starts. The quantity theory cannot provide explanation for this type of phenomenon. Again it cannot explain why a shortage of money can always nearly bring a boom to a halt. The saving-investment theory, in contrast, can explain the cyclical rise and decline in prices. If investment is in excess of saving, prices rise. Rise in prices and increase in investment proceed in a cumulative way sustained by increase in bank credit. When credit is restricted, the expectation of profit declines and as a result investment tends to fall short of saving. When saving exceeds investment, income tends to decline and as a consequence prices tend to deflate. Investment is undertaken in expectation of profit. When prices tend to fall, investment does not remain attractive even if money can be borrowed at a low rate of interest. The process of recovery begins as the businessmen shake off their indifferences to expectation of profit.

The velocity of circulation of money is not clearly explained in the quantity theory of money. The quantity theory states that the velocity of circulation depends on the proportion of the resources that the people desire to keep in the form of money. It is not understandable why once this proportion starts rising, it continues rising. Conversely, when it starts falling, it continues falling. But the quantity theory does not explain why these movements should ever start. The saving-investment approach however provides an explanation. When saving exceeds investment, the community as a whole is increasing the proportion of its income that it desires to keep in the form of money. This causes a decline in the velocity of circulation. Similarly, when investment exceeds saving, the velocity of circulation increases. In the words of Crowther, "This explains the puzzling phenomenon that when money is created at the bottom of a depression, it sometimes has no effect on the volume of investment so that in the terminology of the quantity theory, V goes down as rapidly as M goes up, leaving MV unchanged. When investment exceeds saving the contrary influences come into play."[30]

The saving-investment theory explains the step-by-step processes that influence the price level. The quantity theory holds that the quantity of money has a direct effect on the price level. It does not explain the casual relationship between different variables. In fact, there is a close relationship between the volume of money, the proportion of resources that the people desire to hold in cash and the rate of interest obtainable on near money stocks. If there is a change in the quantity of money, the proportion of resources desired to be held in cash remaining unchanged, there would occur a change in the rate of interest and hence that in the volume of investment. The equilibrium between saving and investment will accordingly be disturbed. There would occur a change in the level of activity and hence in that of prices. A similar chain of reactions can be brought about by a change in the proportion of resources which the people want to hold in the form of money, without any change in the quantity of money.

30. Crowther, *An Outline of Money* (1942), p. 158.

KEYNES' THEORY OF MONEY AND PRICES

The entire classical analysis suffered from a dichotomy relating to (i) the theory of relative prices and (ii) the theory of price level. According to the classical analysis, the relative prices were determined by the relative forces of demand and supply, while the absolute price level was considered to be determined by the quantity of money and its velocity of circulation. In contrast, Keynes' theory of prices is of a more general nature and his major contribution lies in integrating the theory of money with the general theory of value and output. He accepts the traditional conclusion that the increase in the quantity of money will be associated with a rise in the level of prices but differ fundamentally from the traditional analysis of the causal process by which changes in the quantity of money react upon the level of prices. As is clear from the earlier chapters, the initial impact of an increase in the quantity of money is to lower the rate of interest by increasing the amount of money available for satisfying the liquidity preference for the speculative motive. A lowering of the rate of interest tends to increase effective demand for investment which in turns is associated with rising income, employment and output. With the rise in income, output and employment, the prices may start rising even before the point of full employment is reached for four reasons. In the first place, since productive resources are not homogenous, an increase in output will generally involve diminishing returns and increasing supply prices even though the unit costs of all factors remain unchanged. Secondly, wage rates are very likely to increase with the increase in output. Thirdly, the prices of other factors entering into marginal costs will also rise in varying proportions. Finally, prices will also rise before full employment is reached because the short-period supply schedules in different markets will show varying degrees of elasticity with the result that supply in some markets will become completely inelastic while others are still quite elastic. With the increase in output, the emphasis is at first almost exclusively on increase in employment but shifting more and more to prices as the point of full employment is reached. Once the full employment is reached, further increases in effective demand become truly inflationary in the sense that they spend themselves entirely in rising prices.

The above link between money and the level of prices clearly shows that there is no direct and proportional relationship between the quantity of money on the one hand and price on the other as asserted by the traditional quantity theory of money. The relationship on the other hand is indirect and remote because a whole complex relationship is set in motion through chances in the rate of interest. But whether or not a change in the rate of interest will lead to a corresponding change in the investment demand and through it in the levels of employment, income and output and through these in the cost of production and prices will depend also upon the condition of two other main determinants of income *viz.* (i) the marginal efficiency of capital and (ii) the propensity to consume. For instance, if the marginal efficiency of capital for certain reasons suffers a decline, the decline in the rate of money may not lead to an increase in the volume of investment, output and employment etc. and as such the prices may not rise in spite of an increase in the quantity of money. In the same way, if the propensity to consume declines because of certain reasons, increase in the quantity of money may not be associated with increase in prices. Thus the relationship between the quantity of money and the level of prices is a complex one, established through a long chain of causation.

SUPERIORITY OF KEYNES' ANALYSIS OF MONEY AND PRICES

(1) The great merit of Keynes' theory of prices is that it integrates the monetary theory with the theory of value. The theory of value tells us that the price, which is value expressed in terms of money, is governed by the conditions of demand and supply. In connection with supply and demand, the most important concepts are marginal cost and marginal revenue (which determine the extent to which output will be carried since their equality designates the point of maximum profit) and the elasticity (which determine the relative changes in output which correspond to relative changes in price of the commodity in question). When Keynes comes to the theory of prices in general (price level), he still stresses cost of production, elasticity of supply, demand and other concepts which are important in the theory of value or individual price. Keynes shows that prices rise because of the rise in costs of production and the latter rise on account of inelasticity of short period supply of output and employment.

(2) The Keynesian theory integrates not only the theory of value and the theory of money but also the theory of output with the theory of money. In fact, it is through the theory of output that value theory and monetary theory are brought into juxtaposition with each other. Changes in the quantity of money can lead to changes in the level of output. With the variations in the level of output, costs change which in turn affect values (prices). Since the theory of money is part and parcel of the theory of interest and interest is intimately related to expectations concerning the future, it follows that discussions of the effects of changing expectations about the future must be stated in monetary terms. The emphasis shifts to money as a store of value as a link between the present and the future. This emphasis is lacking in the traditional presentations of the general economic theory of value and output and monetary theory and is responsible to a large extent for the lack of integration of monetary theory with the general economic theory in classical economics.

(3) The traditional quantity theory like all classical doctrines is based on the assumption of full employment. Under this assumption, increase in the quantity of money cannot bring about any increase in output and employment. Since by assumption changes in output are ruled out, the concepts of marginal cost and marginal revenue, elasticity of demand and supply etc. which figure so prominently in the theory of value or individual prices are not at all needed in the traditional theory of price levels. As such there is no occasion to integrate the theory of money with the theory of value. Since money cannot affect employment, it can influence only prices. This leads to the conclusion that all increases in the quantity of money tend to be inflationary, a conclusion quite valid under the assumption that resources are fully employed but having hardly any sense when this assumption is dropped. The extremely important relations between changes in the quantity of money and changes in employment are ignored. In contrast, for Keynes, full employment is an exception and less than full employment is the rule.

(4) The Keynesian theory enables us to look at inflation in its right perspective because it enables us to distinguish between an inflationary and a non-inflationary expansion of supply of money. It guides us when to dread inflation and when not. It tells us that there is no danger of inflation when monetary expansion takes place

in the context of unemployment, but once the level of full employment is reached, the danger of inflation becomes real. According to classicists every increase in the supply of money leads to inflation but to Keynes only that expansion in the supply of money leads to inflation which goes beyond the level of full employment.[31]

(5) A great merit of Keynesian theory lies in removing the old notion that prices are directly determined by the quantity of money. Keynes brings forth the true and causal process which exists between the quantity of money and prices. The relationship that exists is indirect, uncertain, complex and is brought through changes in the rate of interest.

(6) It differentiates between the determination of general price level and individual prices. Individual prices of various goods are determined by demand and supply with reference to the nature of competition and the type of market while a large number of considerations enter the determination of the general price level.

CRITICISM OF KEYNES' THEORY OF MONEY AND PRICES

Keynes' theory is too general and, therefore, it is difficult to study the actual price changes with the help of this theory. The market conditions of distribution of particular goods vary so widely, the technical conditions of production of various goods are so different, and variations in the conditions of demand affect various commodities so differently that the propositions stated in terms of total demand, total output, general technical conditions etc. are no more than the very first steps to a theory of prices.

Corporate policy and the economic policy of the government in regard to particular commodities introduce some amount of rigidities in prices. Any theory of money and prices, therefore, should adequately take into consideration the differences in price behaviour in the different parts of the price system. Keynes' theory does not take adequate account of special character of price behaviour of different parts of the price system.

Keynes holds that the level of output can be changed by changing the quantity of money through the change in the rate of interest. But this is conditioned by a long line of reasoning. The level

31. J.M. Keynes, *The General Theory of Employment, Interest and Money* (New York, 1936), p. 296.

of output can be changed by changing the quantity of money stock, and the rate of interest by changing the supply of money, if other conditions of costs and revenues operate appropriately.

THE REFORMULATED QUANTITY THEORY OF MONEY

By introducing an adequate number of qualifications, it is possible to formulate a simplified version of what may be called the reformed quantity theory of money. If there is perfectly elastic supply of productive factors when there is unemployment and perfectly inelastic supply when there is full employment, and if the increase in effective demand is proportional to the increase in quantity of money, the reformed quantity theory which takes into account the condition of unemployment as well as the special case of full employment may be stated thus, "so long as there is unemployment, employment will change in the same proportion as the quantity of money; and when there is full employment, prices will change in the same proportion as the quantity of money."[32]

This reformed theory of money, though not faultless, is more near reality and a better guide to practical policies than the old quantity theory. While the old quantity theory looked at every increase in the quantity of money as necessarily inflationary, the reformed theory tells us that so long as there exist unemployed resources, any increase in the quantity of money will not react upon prices but only upon unemployment. Thus it brings out the desirability of deficit financing by creating more money to fight deflation. It also sounds a note of warning that once the level of full employment is reached, inflation becomes an accomplished fact with every subsequent increases in the supply of money. Thus reformed quantity theory of money relieves us of the fear of inflation when the economy is suffering from unemployment and also warns us to be on the guard against inflation once the unemployment has been eliminated and the economy enters a state of full employment.

The proposition that "so long as there is unemployment, employment will change in the same proportion as the quantity of money; and when there is full employment, prices will change in the same proportion as the quantity of money" is, however, a mere approximation to the truth. It is a generalised statement subject to

32. *Ibid.*

so many qualifications that there is reasonable doubt as to its usefulness as a leading proposition of monetary theory. In fact, the prices may and do rise long before the level of full employment is reached, particularly in the latter stages of expansion. There are not mere chance increases arising from fortuitous circumstances. The increases in prices that occur as output expands are more or less inevitably associated with expanding output and can be explained in terms of well established principles of economic analysis. According to Keynes, the most important reasons for increases in costs and prices as employment expands are: (i) the enhanced bargaining power of the workers as unemployment declines resulting in increased wage rates without being followed by a corresponding increase in their productivity; (ii) the operation of the law of diminishing returns in the short period; (iii) the existence of bottlenecks in production on account of inelastic supply of certain resources; and (iv) non-homogeneity of resources.

CLASSICAL DICHOTOMY

The classical economists had a separate theory of *relative prices* and a separate theory of *absolute price level*. In their theory of relative prices, money was no more than an accounting media. Money was simply an accounting unit. Money was counted as one of the commodities whose determination of price was to be considered; then the value of money was assumed to be unity by definition and the prices of all other commodities were expressed in terms of money. The value of money in terms of money was always constant though the value of other goods in terms of money would not be so. The whole process of pricing was divided into two sectors. The relative prices of goods were expressed in terms of money but had no relation to the absolute price level. All prices could be changed by any proportion and the relative prices would remain unchanged. The second aspect of the process, *i.e.,* the absolute level of prices, was quite distinct from the one mentioned above. Here the relative prices were kept unchanged and study was made of the changes in the general price level.

This simplified approach had its sway. But soon the defects in this approach were realised and attempts were made to integrate the two sectors of analysis which appeared to be complementary rather than substitutes. It was obvious that an integrated view of the situation required synthesis of the existing monetary and real price theories. In the classical analysis, real price (though expressed in terms of money) were considered to depend upon the real demand and supply forces in the economy. These demand and supply forces were dependent not upon the expected changes in prices of the goods concerned. Price changes were neutral in creating any further waves of demand or supply. The function of all price changes was just to clear the markets. The level of demand and supply was determined by other forces like fashion, tastes, the supply of labour and capital, technological developments etc. It is curious to know how the classical economists ignored the effects of price changes on the future demand and supply. They completely ignored the price expectations. The growth theory, which is based upon the rates of changes of production factors and their utilization, cannot be complete without bringing in the role of expectations. In a dynamic economy no long-term investment can take place unless the expectations are brought in. The rate of interest bears a direct relation with the future prices of securities and other financial aspects. Even the classical economists admit that there can be no profits in a static society. From this, it is obvious that the two sides of the picture cannot be left unrelated and an effort must be made to integrate the real side with the monetary side so as to obtain a complete theory of price determination.

The need for the integration of real and monetary theory becomes obvious if we consider the sectoral behaviour of the economy. When we talk of relative prices or of the general price level, it does not mean that all goods in the economy must behave with an equal force. Whenever there are changes, they are of different degrees in different sectors. In fact, the concept of general price level does not have much meaning. What is required is the explanation of the sectoral price levels and the interaction between them. The reactions of every sector will be subject to a variety of forces including both real and monetary forces. It would be wrong to concentrate on only one type of forces and to ignore the other type of forces in explaining the prices.

PATINKIN ON MONEY AND PRICES

Don Patinkin's monumentally scholarly work[33] appeared in 1956. It, *inter alia*, demonstrates the rigid conditions necessary for

33. Don Patinkin, *Money, Interest and Prices,* 2nd Edition (New York, 1965).

strict proportionality rule of the quantity theory while at the same time launching a severe attack on the Cambridge analysis. Patinkin's main point of contention is that the advocates of the cash balance approach have failed to understand the true nature of the quantity theory. Their failure is obvious from the dichotomy which they maintain between the goods market and the money market. An increase in the stock of money is assumed to lead to an increase in the absolute price level but to have no real influence upon the market for commodities. One purpose of Patinkin's analysis is to show that only by exerting an influence upon the market for commodities, through the real balance affect, can the strict quantity theory be maintained.

Part of Patinkin's attack revolves round the nature of demand curve for money. According to Patinkin, the Cambridge school assumes the demand curve for money to be a rectangular hyperbola with constant unit elasticity of demand for money. In fact, such a demand curve is implicit in the argument that a doubling of the money stock would lead to a doubling of the price level. Patinkin uses the "real balance effect" to show that the demand curve for money can not be of the shape of a rectangular hyperbola (*i.e.* the elasticity of demand for money cannot be assumed to be unity except in a stationary state), and further such a demand curve would contradict the strict quantity theory assertion which the Cambridge quantity theorists are trying to formulate. Patinkin's main point is that the cash balance approach ignores the real balance effect and assumes the absence of money illusion under the assumption of 'homogeneity postulate'[34] and as such fails to bring about a correct relation between the theory of money and the theory of value. The homogeneity postulate implies that the demand functions in the real sectors are assumed to be insensitive to the changes in the absolute level of money prices (*i.e.*, with changes in the quantity of money there will be equi-proportional changes in all money prices), which shows the absence of money illusion and the real balance effect. This, however, holds true only in a pure barter economy, where there are no money holdings and as such the

34. It shows a relationship in which a *Proportionate change* in all of the variables (the prices) has no effect on the dependent variables (quantities supplied and demanded).

concept of absolute price level has no meaning. But the money economy cannot be without money illusion.

Patinkin first criticises the so-called classical dichotomy of money and then rehabilitates it through a different route. In classical dichotomy *relative prices* are determined by real demands (tastes) and real supplies (production conditions), and the *absolute price level* depends on the quantity of money in relation to the demand for money. There is a real theory of relative prices and a monetary theory of the absolute level of prices. The problem before Patinkin is how to reconcile these two theories and once this has been done, the second problem is whether the reconciliation permits one to arrive at the classical proposition that an increase in the quantity of money leads to an increase in all prices in the same proportion so that relative prices are not influenced by the quantity of money. This particular property is technically called *neutrality* of money. If money is neutral, an increase in the quantity of money will simply raise the level of money prices without changing relative prices and rate of interest (which is a particular relative price). Patinkin thinks that the two theories can be reconciled and the classical theory rehabilitated by making the demand and supply functions depend on real cash balances as well as on relative prices.

Thus the solution which Patinkin offers for the problem is to introduce the stock of real balances held by individuals as an influence on their demand for goods. The real balance effect is an important element of the mechanism which works to produce equilibrium in the money market. Suppose, for instance, that, owing to certain reasons, prices decline below their equilibrium level; this would increase the real wealth of the cash-holders, which would lead them to spend more money; this would push prices back towards equilibrium. Similarly, if the price level rises owing to certain reasons, it will reduce people's real balances and thus lead them to rebuild their balances by spending less, which would push prices back down. Thus the introduction of the real balance effect eliminates the classical dichotomy but nevertheless retains the classical proposition that the real equilibrium of the system will not be affected by the amount of money and all that will be affected will be the level of prices.

We give below the essence of Patinkin's theory in his own words, "Once the real and monetary data of an economy with outside money are specified, the equilibrium values of relative prices, the rate of interest, and the absolute price level are simultaneously determined by all the markets of the economy. It is generally impossible to isolate a subset of markets which can determine the equilibrium values of a sub-set of prices. In the true spirit of general-equilibrium economics, 'everything depends on everything else'...it is fatal to succumb to the temptation to say that relative prices are determined in the commodity markets and absolute prices in the money market. This does not mean that value theory cannot be distinguished from monetary theory. Obviously, there is a distinction; but it is based on a dichotomization of effects not on a dichotomization of *markets*. More specifically, both monetary theory and value theory consider *all* markets of the economy simultaneously. But, in each of these markets, value theory analyses individual-experiments which measure the substitution effect and that part of the wealth effect which does not stem from changes in real balances; and monetary theory, individual experiments which measure the real balance effect.

Correspondingly, value theory analyses market-experiments which do not (significantly) affect the absolute price-level and hence do not generate real-balance effects; and monetary theory, market-experiments which do not (significantly) affect relative prices and hence do not generate substitution and non-monetary wealth effects. Thus shifts in tastes, changes in technology, and the like are in the domain of value theory. Changes in the quantity of money and...shifts in liquidity preference are in the domain of monetary theory.

If we now examine this classificatory scheme, we will discover the grain of truth in the intuitive feeling that in some sense value theory is connected with the determination of relative prices and monetary theory with the determination of absolute prices. In particular, assume that by a *tatonnement* involving all prices and all markets the equilibrium values of money prices have been reached. We can now make use of this information to take a step backwards and approach the equilibrium position once again but this time by a restricted *tatonnement*. For example, holding the absolute price level constant at its already determined *equilibrium* value, we can arbitrarily shift relative prices from theirs, and then study the nature of the dynamic forces that—working simultaneously in *all* markets—

return the economy to its original equilibrium position. By the very definition of this procedure, such a return can be accomplished without any change in the absolute price level. Hence the restricted *tatonnement* by which equilibrium relative prices are thus redetermined need involve only these prices, need accordingly generate only substitution and non-monetary wealth effects, and can therefore be studied entirely within the confines of value theory.

Similarly, we can define a restricted *tatonnement* which—starting from a knowledge of the *equilibrium* values of relative prices and interest—works simultaneously through *all* the markets of the economy to redetermine the equilibrium value of the absolute price level. Such a *tatonnement* can clearly succeed without requiring any changes in relative prices and interest; that is, it need generate only real-balance effects. Hence, it can be studied entirely within the confines of monetary theory.

This decomposition of the overall *tatonnment* into two components is a convenient expository device.... It can be used safely provided we are clear in our own minds that it separates out effects and not markets. In particular, we must guard against the apparent tendency to slip over from this valid device into the invalid proposition of the false dichotomy that, starting with an absolute price level held constant at an *arbitary* level, a *tatonnement* on relative prices in the *commodity markets alone* can determine these prices; that, holding these relative prices constant at the values so determined, a *tatonnement* on the absolute price level in the *money market alone* can then determine this level; and that the absolute price level so determined, together with the relative prices determined by the first *tatonnement* in the commodity markets, must *necessarily* preserve the first equilibrium initially achieved in these markets. Clearly, this last statement will generally *not* be true unless the excess-demand equations of the commodity markets are actually independent of the absolute price level.

This is the crucial point. The dynamic groping of the absolute price level towards its equilibrium value will—through the real-balance effect—react back on the commodity markets and hence on relative prices. And it is precisely the constant failure to find this point explicitly recognised—and, indeed, the constant sensation of being just on the verge of having it explicitly contradicted—that is the basis of our original contention that the roots of the invalid dichotomy are to be found in the neo-classical analysis of Walras, Fisher, Pigou, and Cassel.[35]

Critical Evaluation

Patinkin model may be considered an elegant refinement of the traditional quantity theory and its value lies in precisely laying down the necessary conditions for the strict proportionality of the quantity theory to hold and in making detailed analysis of the mechanism by which change in the money stock takes effect—the real balance effect. The integration of product and money markets through the real balance effect represents a significant advance over the earlier treatments.

But Patinkin's analysis is incomplete and fails to provide a full long-run equilibrium. This was pointed out by Archibald and Lipsey[36] and conceded by Patinkin in the second edition of his book. They show that Patinkin's analysis of the real balance effect is inadequate to the extent he restricts his analysis to the impact effect of a change in a price and does not work the analysis through to the long-period equilibrium. The equilibrium obtained is only a short-term equilibrium because further changes will be induced for income recipients in future time periods. Further, if the analysis is extended to an infinite number of periods, general long-term equilibrium is found to be perfectly consistent with a unitary elastic demand curve for money—the real balance effect disappears. This raises again the complicated question of whether the quantity theory is a theory of short-run or long-run equilibria or indeed whether it should be considered a theory of equilibria at all.

Though Patinkin, for the first time, makes the nature of the wealth effect explicit, he does not analyse the manner in which the increase in monetary wealth comes about. A doubling of money balances is just assumed and the analysis entirely concentrates on the resultant effects. The failure to explain the manner in which the increase in monetary wealth is attained is a serious defect of the traditional statement. Obviously, if all money balances double

35. Don Patinkin, *Money, Interest and Prices* (New York, 1965), pp. 181-83.

36. G.C. Archibald and R.G. Lipsey, "Monetary and Value Theory", *Review of Economic Studies* (October, 1958).

overnight an immediate wealth effect is implied for all money holders throughout the economy. There is nothing to be surprised if the monetary expenditures increase as a result. But in reality monetary changes do not take place like this.

Traditionally, an increase in the monetary variable is not accompanied by an increase in net worth but instead by the exchange of one asset for another, *e.g.,* by the public's sale of government securities on the open market. In this case, there is no 'wealth' effect. The same is the case if the initial increase in the money stock is increased by the existence of fractional reserve banking system. Any resultant increase in bank deposits will be matched by an equal increase in liabilities. It may, therefore, be argued that there is no reason to assume that an increase in the money stock will exert any impact at all upon the economy unless it does so through the induced change in interest rates necessary to effect the increase. This is exactly the Keynesian position which leads to the conclusion that the net impact may be limited, particularly if the investment demands are interest inelastic, or at least unpredictable. Hence the rationale for the rejection of quantity theory by Keynes. In contrast, the revised version of the quantity theory maintains that an increase in the money stock will lead to fairly predictable increases in demands for commodities even in the absence of any change in net worth and acting independently of any interest-rate effect. This is the crux of the present dispute between the revised doctrine of the quantity theory and the Keynesian scepticism.

FRIEDMAN'S VERSION OF QUANTITY THEORY

The quantity theory has been revived mainly because of the work done by Milton Friedman and a group of adherents generally known as the 'Chicago School'. In 1956, there appeared a book entitled *Studies in the Quantity Theory of Money* edited by Friedman which signalled the re-emergence of the quantity theory. The modern quantity theory, as restated by Friedman, is a theory of the demand for money, not of output, money income, or prices; and that money is an asset or capital good, so that the demand for it is a problem in capital theory. In formulating the demand for money as a form of capital, however, Friedman differs from the Keynesian theorists in starting from the fundamentals of capital theory. He starts with the broad concept of wealth as comprising all sources of income, including human beings, and relates the demand for money to total wealth and the expected future streams of money income obtainable by holding wealth in alternative forms. Then, by a series of mathematical simplifications, approximations of non-observable variables (of which the most important is the representation of the influence of human wealth by the ratio of non-human to human wealth), simplifying economic assumptions, and rearrangements of variables, he arrives at a demand function for money which depends on the price level, bond and equity yields, the rate of change of the price level, income, the ratio of non-human to human wealth, and a taste variable; finally he makes neat use of the homogeneity assumption to show that the demand for real balances depends only on real variables and that it can be reformulated as a velocity function depending on the same variables.

Friedman maintains that money is only one of the five broad ways of holding wealth *viz.* (i) money, (ii) bonds, (iii) equities, (iv) physical goods, and (v) human wealth. Each of these has distinctive characteristics and each offers some return in money or kind. The ultimate wealth-owning unit is considered as dividing his wealth among them so as to maximise 'utility' subject to whatever restrictions affect the possibility of converting one form of wealth into another. This implies that he will seek an apportionment of his wealth such that the rate at which he can substitute one form of wealth for another is equal to the rate at which he is just willing to do so.

From the broadest and most general point of view, total wealth includes all sources of 'income' or consumable services. From this point of view, the rate of interest expresses the relation between the stock which is wealth and the flow which is income, so that if Y be the total flow of income, and r the interest rate, total wealth is $W = Y/r$.

Money may yield a return in the form of money, *e.g.*, interest on demand deposits. But it will simplify matters and involve no essential loss of generality if we assume that money yields its return solely in kind in the usual form of convenience, security etc. The quantum of this return in "real" terms per nominal unit of money clearly depends upon the volume of goods that unit corresponds to, or on the general price level, which may be designated as P. If the general price level falls, money appreciates and represents a capital gain in real terms which must be added to the nominal yield. Similarly, in case of a rise in the general price level, which is likely to be more common, the real capital loss has to be deducted from the nominal yield.

Bonds represent those assets which yield a perpetual income stream of constant nominal amount. The return to the holder of the bond can be of two forms: (i) the annual sum he receives—the "coupon" and (ii) any change in the price of the bond over time—a return which can be positive as well as negative. If the rate of interest on bonds is r_b, the nominal rate of return can be approximated by $r_b - (1/r_b)\ dr_b/dt$ where $(1/r_b)\ dr_b/dt$ measures the rate of capital appreciation owing to changes in the rate of interest; here *t* stands for time. This sum, together with *P* already introduced, defines the real return from holding of wealth in the form of bonds.

Equities represent assets which yield a perpetual income stream of constant 'real' amount. The nominal return to the holder of the equity can take three forms: (i) the constant nominal amount he would receive per year in the absence of any change in the price level (*P*), (ii) the increments or decrement to this nominal amount to adjust for changes in *P*, and (iii) any change in the nominal price of the equity over time, which may be caused by changes either in interest rates or in price levels. The nominal rate of return can be approximated by $r_e + 1/p\ (dp/dt)—1/r_e\ (dr_e/dt)$. This sum, together with *P* already introduced, defines the real return from holding of wealth in the form of equities.

Physical goods held by ultimate wealth-owning units are similar to equities except that the annual stream they yield is in kind rather than in money. In terms of nominal units, this return, like that from equities, depends on the behaviour of prices. In addition, like equities, physical goods must be considered as yielding a nominal return in the form of appreciation or depreciation in money value. If we suppose the price level *P*, introduced earlier, to apply equally to the value of these physical goods, then the nominal rate of return on physical goods is $1/p\ (dp/dt)$. Together with *P*, it defines the real return from holding wealth in the form of physical goods.

Human wealth is the discounted value of the expected stream of earned income. Since there is only a limited market in human capital, it is not easy to define in market prices the terms of substitution of human capital for other forms of capital. Nevertheless, some substitution is possible, *e.g.*, people can sell assets in order to pay for training which will increase their future earnings. The shifts between human capital and other forms take place mainly through direct investment and disinvestment in the human agent. In regard to this form of capital, therefore, the restriction or obstacles affecting the alternative composition of wealth available to the individual cannot be expressed in terms of market prices or rates of return. At any point of time there is some division between human and non-human wealth in his portfolio of assets; he may be able to change this over time, but it may be treated as given at a point in time. Let w be the ratio of non-human to human wealth or, equivalently, of income from non-human wealth to income from human wealth, which means that it bears a close relation to what is usually defined as the ratio of wealth to income. This is, then, the variable which should be taken into account so far as human wealth is concerned.

Y/r is the total wealth since Y represents the total return on all forms of wealth including money and physical capital goods owned and held directly by the ultimate wealth-owners. Some imputed income from the stock of money and directly owned physical capital goods is included in Y, where r is the rate of interest which applies to all types of assets. In the subsequent equation for the demand for money this has been dropped as an explicit variable on the assumption that its infleunce is taken care of by the inclusion of r_b and r_e in the equation.

We can say simply where

M = total demand for money

P = general price level

r_b = market bond interest rate

r_e = market interest rate on equities

$\frac{1}{P}\frac{dp}{dt}$ = size of nominal return from physical goods

w = ratio of non-human wealth to human wealth or ratio of income from non-human wealth to income from human wealth

$\frac{Y}{r}$ = total wealth

u = utility variable affecting the tastes and preferences of the ultimate wealth-owning units.

The tastes and preferences of wealth-owning units for the service streams arising from different forms of wealth must in general simply be taken for granted as determining the form of the demand function. In order to give the theory empirical content, it will generally have to be assumed that tastes are constant over considerable stretches of space and time. Explicit provision can, however, be made for some changes in tastes to the extent such changes are related to objective circumstances. For instance, it appears quite reasonable that, other things being equal, individuals want to hold a larger fraction of their wealth in the form of money when they are moving around geographically or are subject to unusual uncertainty than otherwise. Let u stand for any such variables which can be expected to affect tastes and preferences.

By combining the factors mentioned above, we can obtain the following demand function for money:

$$M = \int \left(P, r_b - \frac{1}{r_b}\frac{dr_b}{dt}, r_e + \frac{1}{p}\frac{dP}{dt} - \frac{1}{r_e}\frac{dr_e}{dt}, \frac{1}{p}\frac{dP}{dt}, w, \frac{Y}{r}, u\right) \quad \text{...14.19}$$

Friedman assumes r_b and r_e to be stable over time and states that the rate of change of prices is required separately. He replaces the variables representing the nominal return on bonds and equities $(r_b - \frac{1}{r_b}\frac{dr_b}{dt})$ and $(r_e + \frac{1}{P}\frac{dP}{dt} - \frac{1}{r_e}\frac{dr_e}{dt})$ in equation 14.19 by simply r_b and r_e. Hence the demand function for money (14.19) can be written simply as

$$M = \int \left(P, r_b, r_e, \frac{1}{p}\frac{dP}{dt}, w, Y, u\right) \quad \text{.. 14.20}$$

Friedman opines that if the unit in which prices and money income are expressed is changed, the amount of money demanded should change proportionately. The equation 14.20 pertaining to the demand function for money must be regarded as homogenous of degree one in prices (P) and the money value of wealth (Y) so that

$$\lambda M = \int \left(\lambda P, r_b, r_e, \frac{1}{p}\frac{dP}{dt}, w, \lambda Y, u\right) \quad \text{...14.21}$$

Putting $\lambda = \frac{1}{P}$ equation (14.21) can be written as

$$\frac{M}{P} = \int (r_b, r_e, \frac{1}{p}\frac{dP}{dt}, w, \frac{Y}{P}, u) \qquad ...14.22$$

This equation (14.22) expresses the demand for real balances as a function of 'real' variables independent of the nominal monetary values.

Putting $\lambda = \frac{1}{Y}$, equation (14.21) can be written as

$$\frac{M}{Y} = \int (\frac{P}{Y}, r_b, r_e, \frac{1}{p}\frac{dP}{dt}, w, u) \qquad ...14.23$$

$$\text{Or, } M = \int (\frac{P}{Y}, r_b, r_e, \frac{1}{p}\frac{dP}{dt}, w, u)Y \qquad ...14.24$$

According to Freedman, the most important factors influencing the demand for money are the rates of return on money and other assets, both real and financial, the level of permanent income, and the ratio of non-human to total wealth. Thus, for instance, an increase in the expectation of inflation would normally result in a decline in the demand for money holdings, that is, a rise in velocity. Far from velocity being constant, as was tacitly implied in many of the more naive versions of the traditional approach, it will respond to significant changes in the above variables in a predictable and rational manner. But—and this appears to be the essence of the modern approach—the above variables are generally subject to only slow change over time while the supply of money may undergo sudden changes. If this is so, and velocity is subject only to gradual change over time, while the stock of money may rise and fall rapidly, the obvious implication is that the demand for money is independent of its supply. The independence of supply and demand, *i.e.*, between the money stock and its velocity, is an important tenet of the revised theory.

If the demand for money does not show great variation in relation to the supply, which may experience considerable and rapid fluctuation, then changes in the value of money—which like anything else are to be explained in terms of supply and demand—are almost always supply determined. To cite Friedman, "It is clear from this discussion that changes in prices and nominal income can be produced either by changes in real balances that people wish to hold or by changes in the nominal balances available for them to hold. Indeed, it is a tautology, summarized in the famous quantity equation ...The quantity theory is not, however, this tautology. It is, rather, the empirical generalization that changes in desired real balances (in the demand) tend to proceed slowly and gradually or to be the result of events set in train by prior changes in supply, whereas, in contrast, substantial changes in the supply of nominal balances can and frequently do occur independently of any changes in demand. The conclusion is that substantial changes in prices or nominal income are almost invariably the result of changes in the nominal supply of money."[37]

Of basic importance to the modern quantity theory is the belief that the demand for money is normally insensitive to changes in the interest rate. If the demand for money were substantially interest-elastic, it would mean that any change in the money stock could be absorbed by a comparatively small change in the interest rates inducing people to extend their demand for money to match the supply. In such a case, a change in the money stock would not matter much; the impact upon commodity markets would be minimised and the additional supply of money would simply be held at the lower interest rate implying a significant decline in the average velocity of money. In contrast, if the demand for money were substantially interest-inelastic, additional supply of money would not be simply held at a lower interest rate and result in direct spending on goods and services, influencing the level of money incomes in the economy. The contention of interest-rate insensitivity implies that the transactions motive dominates the asset motive in the total demand for money. Nevertheless, it is because money is considered as an asset, able to serve as a temporary abode of purchasing power, that the relationship between changes in the monetary variable and increased expenditures is more indirect and more complex than the traditional theory had assumed. And it is precisely because the relationship is considered to be so complex and involve longer time periods of adjustment, that current advocacy of the importance of money does not necessarily imply that the monetary policy is a viable countercyclical device.

---

37. Milton Friedman, "Money : Quantity Theory" in *The International Encyclopaedia of the Social Sciences,* Vol. 10, 1968, p. 434.

Friedman's application to monetary theory of the basic principle of capital theory—that income is the yield on capital, and capital the present value of income—is perhaps the most important development in monetary theory since Keynes' *General Theory*. Its theoretical significance lies in the conceptual integration of wealth and income as influences on behaviour. Keynes ignored almost completely the influence of wealth, which was legitimate in short-period analysis. While subsequent writers in the Keynesian tradition have reintroduced wealth they have generally followed the Cambridge practice of restricting wealth to non-human property, a practice which encourages uncritical treatment of wealth and income as entirely independent influences on behaviour. The result has been that much of the monetary literature contains formulations of the demand for money relating it to income, wealth, and the rate of interest, variables which are in fact interdependent and the use of which in this way involves inelegant redundancy and promotes errors in both theoretical reasoning and empirical applications.

The most important implication of Friedman's analysis, however, relates not to the formulation of monetary theory but to the nature of the concept of 'income' relevant to monetary analysis, which, as stated above, should correspond to the notion of expected yield on wealth rather than the conventions of national income accounting.

LIQUIDITY APPROACH

This approach has become popular as a result of the publication of the Radcliffe Committee's Report on the Monetary System in Great Britain in 1959 and the views expressed by some economists like R.L. Sayers of England, Schmolders of Germany, and J.G. Gurley and E.S. Shaw of the United States. According to this approach, under modern conditions, causal relations between money and the volume of business activity or the general price level cannot be explained either by the quantity theory or by the so-called income theory. Its interest in the supply of money is owing to its significance in the whole liquidity picture. The ease with which money can be raised depends, on the one hand, on the composition of spender's assets and his borrowing power and, on the other hand, on the methods, moods and resources of financial institutions. Liquidity depends not only on the quantity of liquid assets available but also on the borrowing power, profit expectations, hopes and moods of the general public. Spending decisions are influenced by the entire structure of liquidity. It is, therefore, held that the theory of money and prices would be complete and realistic only if it incorporates not only the demand for cash or bank money but also the entire structure of liquid assets which, in some way or the other, serve as a substitute for money to satisfy the liquidity desire of the public.

Now it is widely recognised that there exists a close substitutability between money and a wide range of financial assets and as such the *quantity of money* gets a subordinate place and the *liquidity of the economy* comes to the forefront of the analysis. In a narrow sense, money may be defined as means of payments including currency and demand deposits. Then, obviously, all other liquid assets should be classified as "near-money" or "quasi-money." Near-money may be arbitrarily defined as claims other than demand deposits against financial institutions and central government. So defined, near-money would include time-deposits, different money market instruments like bills of exchange, treasury bills, gilt-edged securities, cash surrender values of life insurance policies, repurchaseable shares in savings and loan associations, travellers' cheques, saving bonds, deposits of building societies, deposits of savings and other banks, postal saving deposits, savings in 'units' of unit trusts, shares of investment trusts and all credit instruments of the financial sector of the economy. Such near-money assets are considered to be liquid because their prices are relatively stable and they can be easily converted into money as and when desired. The criterion for determining the liquidity of assets is the speed at which they can be converted into means of payment in relation to full value.

Source of Liquidity: The major source of liquid assets is the debt creating activities of the various financial institutions in the economy. Banks create first grade liquid assets like notes, coins, demand deposits etc. as well as second grade liquid assets like saving and time deposits. A considerable amount of liquidity is created outside the banking sector like treasury bills issued by the state treasury. In addition, there are non-bank financial intermediaries like insurance companies, building societies, saving banks, hire-purchase companies, land mortage banks, which provide liquid assets in exchange for short-term and long-term claims on the private and public sectors of the economy. The financial intermediaries enhance the liquidity of the financial sector of the economy and thus raise the velocity of spending money and hence the general business activity.

Radcliffe-Sayers Thesis: The essence of the thesis is that the supply of money, which the central bank can influence directly, is not the main plank of monetary action. The spending decisions of the public depend not only on the supply of money but also on the various alternatives of raising funds either by selling an asset or by borrowing. To cite Radcliffe Committee, "Decisions to spend on goods and services—the decisions that determine the level of total demand—are influenced by the liquidity of the spenders... The spending is not limited by the amount of money in existence, but it is related to the amount of money people think they can get hold of whether by disposal of capital assets or by borrowing."[38] In other words, the spending decisions are influenced not only by the supply of money but the 'general liquidity' of the entire economy.

The Radcliffe Model emphasises the likelihood of shifts in the liquidity function instead of its interest elasticity. The demand for liquidity is not treated as identical with the demand for money. The ready availability of interest-yielding substitutes broadens the demand for liquidity. Near-money substitutes like treasury bills, time deposits and loan shares are almost as liquid as cash and at the same time yield an interest return. The growth of highly competitive and liquid money markets, and the growth of non-bank financial intermediaries makes available a large quantity of earning assets. They have substantially increased the velocity of money. To the extent such money substitutes are available, an increase in income or the expectation of a rise in the interest rate may not lead to an increase in the demand for cash for the transaction and speculative motives.

The basic point stressed by the Radcliffe Model is that the *causal relations* existing between money and the general price level cannot be entirely explained either by the quantity theory of money or by the so-called income theory of money. The most important link between the general business activity (price level) and monetary conditions is provided neither by income nor by the *quantity of money* but by the general liquidity. In order to be successful, the monetary policy should, therefore, seek to control and influence not only the "supply of money" but the general state of liquidity of the

38. *The Radcliffe Committee Report,* paras 389-90.

entire economy. The Radcliffe-Sayers thesis suggests two alternatives *viz.* (i) imposition of 'liquidity controls' over a wide range of financial institutions and (ii) attainment of a control through the 'liquidity effect' of changes in the rate of interest. The first alternative, however, is difficult to administer because most of the financial intermediaries except commercial banks are normally outside the control of the central bank and even if an attempt is made to bring them within the scope of its regulation, new financial institutions are very likely to come up and there would be no end to this process. But the second alternative is also ruled out because it may cause serious disruptions in the financial sector. The Radcliffe-Sayers thesis, therefore, treats monetary policy as subordinate to fiscal policy in normal times and recommends its use only in inflationary situations.

Gurley-Shaw Thesis: These two authors stress the fact that in a growing economy, along with the process of economic growth in real terms, there is a proliferation of financial institutions and this makes a difference to monetary analysis. According to them what is significant is not the quantity of money but the entire *financial structure* of the economy, which makes the velocity function both complex and unstable. In order to be more effective, the monetary policy should control not only the quantity of money but also the activities of the non-bank financial intermediaries. The Gurley-Shaw thesis rejected the conventional division between commercial banks as creators of loanable funds and the financial intermediaries as brokers of loanable funds. They stressed the fact that all types of financial institutions can create loanable funds. In contrast to the Radciffe-Sayers thesis which gives monetary policy only a subordinate place, the Gurley-Shaw thesis recommends that the regulatory powers of the monetary authority should be broadened so as to cover also the activities of non-bank financial institutions.

Inflation and Deflation

15

DEFINITION OF INFLATION

Different economists have defined the term 'inflation' in different ways. According to Chamber's Twentieth Century dictionary inflation means a "disproportionate and as relatively sharp and sudden increase in the quantity of money or credit or both, relative to goods available for purchase. Inflation always produces a rise in the price levels." Crowther defines inflation as "a state in which the value of money is falling, *i.e.*, prices are rising."[1] According to Kemmerer, "inflation is a state in which the value of money is falling, *i.e.*, prices are rising."[2] In Pigou's opinion inflation takes place "when money income is expanding relatively to the output of work done by the productive agents for which it is the payment."[3] At another place Pigou says that "inflation exists when money income is expanding more than in proportion to income earning activity."[4] R.G. Hawtrey associates inflation with "the issue of too much currency"[5] and T.E. Gregory calls it a state of "abnormal increase in the quantity of purchasing power."[6] Coulborn says, it is a phenomenon where, "too much money chases too few goods."

All these definitions show that the basic phenomenon is that of quantity of money in circulation exceeding the total amount of goods and services which leads to an extraordinary increase in prices. Inflation is a situation in which the general level of prices keeps on rising primarily due to stimulus that is continuously being

---

1. G. Crowther, *An Outline of Money* (1958 ed.), p. 197.
2. E.W. Kemmerer, *ABC of Inflation*, p. 6.
3. A.C. Pigou, *Veil of Money*, p. 34.
4. A.C. Pigou, "Types of Inflation", *Economic Journal*, December 1941, p. 439.
5. R.G. Hawtrey, *Currency and Credit* (1928).
6. T.E. Gregory, "Inflation", *Encyclopaedia Britannica*.

administered by the ever-rising demand in the face of inadequate physical supplies. Thus inflation refers to a persistent rise in the general level of prices over a certain period owing to the continuous growth of demand very much in excess of the supply of goods and services.

No doubt a rise in prices is an important characteristic of inflation, every rise in prices may not be inflationary. A rise in prices resulting from a rise in production costs, for instance, can not be regarded as inflation. Further, as some writers have pointed out, inflation may exist without a rise in prices. When costs are falling but prices are kept stable (as in United States during 1924-29), or when the decline in prices is less than that in costs, the country may develop all symptoms of inflation. Such a phenomenon is described by Keynes as "profit inflation" to distinguish it from "commodity inflation" (meaning a rise in prices). In a state of repressed inflation prices are prevented from rising by an efficient system of controls and rationing. The inflationary pressure is held strictly under control and hidden from public view but the pressure is still there, dormant, but ready to manifest itself in the form of high prices the moment controls are relaxed or removed. Nevertheless, a rise in the general price level is a common characteristic of inflation and any definition of the term inflation must explain this phenomenon.

On this basis, inflation can be defined in two ways. Earlier writers based their definition on the well known Quantity Theory of Money and explained inflationary trends in prices in terms of an increase in the supply of money. Irving Fisher is of the view that the prices are affected much more by the supply of money than by the supply of goods. After an examination of the price trends in Europe and the United States in the nineteenth and the earlier part of the twentieth century, he concludes that "price level almost invariably shifts with monetary factors—gold, silver, paper, credit—and very little with commodity factors. The latter control only the deviations of individual prices from average price movement. In a word, supply and demand dictate each individual price level itself."[7]

But this definition, according to which expansion of money is the cause and rise in prices the effect is open to question. It is commonly known that during the inflation of early 1920s in

7. Irving Fisher, Inflation, 1933, p. 45.

Germany, prices, far from being pushed up by the volume of money, actually constituted the active factor drawing out into circulation an ever increasing volume of money. The prices were increasing at such a fast rate that the rate of expansion of money supply could not keep pace with the demand for it. As such the relationship between the money supply and prices was reversed. The writers at that time did not hold increase in money supply to be responsible for inflation. On the contrary, they emphasized the relative deficiency in the supply of money and attributed the rise in prices to the unfavourable balance of payments position of Germany and the consequent depreciation of Mark in terms of foreign currencies. Thus this definition of inflation is not very appropriate in a situation of hyper-inflation. This led Paul Einzig to distinguish between money inflation and price inflation, the first relates to that stage as it were, in which over-expansion of money beyond normal requirement for it pushes up prices; the second relates to the next stage in which prices get out of control and rise so rapidly that money supply lags behind. Paul Einzig defines inflation "as a state of disequilibrium in which an expansion of purchasing power tends to cause, or is the effect of, an increase of the price level."[8] This definition of inflation covers not only the familiar phenomenon of too much money chasing too few goods but also the other and the more vicious aspect of the problem of a wage, cost of production and price spiral in which each becomes at the same time the cause and effect.

A definition which attempts to explain inflation in terms of a relationship between money supply and price is at best a statement of one aspect of the problem. While mentioning the factors which help in an inflationary price movement, it does not explain the root cause of the trouble. A proper definition of inflation should indicate not only the factors responsible for an exceptional rise in the price level but also show how these factors work themselves out and produce an inflationary situation. In other words, it should cover not only the static but also the dynamic aspect of the problem.

This definition has another drawback. During the depression period if the government undertakes monetary and fiscal measures which lead to an expansion of money supply and a recovery in the

8. Paul Einzig, *Inflation,* 1952, p. 22.

price level, it would obviously be wrong to call such a situation as an inflationary one.

The second approach to the problem of inflation has been put forward by economists like Wicksell, Bent Hansen and J.M. Keynes. According to this approach, "general price level is determined by the total demand for and total supply of the group of goods concerned, the prices of which determine the general price level."[9] And the inflation is defined as that situation in which the total demand for goods, indicated by the volume of money offered, is in excess of the supply of goods at prevailing prices. Excess of demand over supply is a common factor to both repressed and open inflation. In the former case, it is concealed by devices like controls and rationing while in the latter it appears naked in the form of excessive money prices.

It can easily be seen that there is not much difference in the basic premises of the two approaches mentioned above in so far as excess demand, which forms the cornerstone of the analysis of the latter approach, can become effective only by means of increased money supply. The basic difference between the two approaches is that while the earlier quantity theory approach explains the position as it is, it fails to point out the origin of the trouble; the latter supply and demand approach not only indicates the source of the problem but also helps in visualizing the means by which the causal factors work themselves out in an-inflationary process.

Keynes makes a distinction between semi-inflation and full or true inflation. According to him, an expansion of the supply of money in circulation before the state of full employment is reached will exhaust itself partly in increasing employment and partly in increasing prices through an increase in production costs. He calls it the state of semi-inflation. Theoretically speaking, so long as full employment is not reached, any increase in the quantity of money should wholly exhaust itself in raising the level of employment and output and not in price level. Because of the existence of various frictions and bottlenecks in the economic system, however, a part of the increased supply of money exhausts itself in raising prices while the remaining part finds its way into productive channels raising the volume of employment and production in the country. It is only

9. Bent Hansen, *A Study in the Theory of Inflation*, 1951, p. 2.

after full employment is reached through a series of inflationary waves occasioned by an increase in the quantity of money that there is established a direct nexus between the increments in the quantity of money and the price level such that an increase in the quantity of money causes a direct and proportionate increase in the price levels. It is here that the true or full inflation comes into operation. Before the full employment is reached prices rise on account of rising costs associated with higher wages and diminishing returns as the scale of output increases in the short period.

CHARACTERISTICS OF INFLATION

In spite of the differences of opinion among economists in regard to the meaning of the term inflation, there is substantial consensus of opinion regarding the characteristics exhibited by the economic system as symptomatic of an inflationary situation. In the first place, inflation is popularly associated with a rise in prices. This is based on observation of facts and is by and large correct. Barring recovery of prices from the depression as a result of monetary and fiscal measures adopted by the government, it would be agreed that an excessive rise in prices has generally been the hallmark of inflation.

The second important characteristic of inflation is an excessive supply of money. In times of war or other national emergency when the tax resources of the state are not sufficient to meet the needs for funds, governments resort to banks which make advances on the basis of government bonds and securities. This results in an expansion in the volume of paper currency as well as of bank credit in the country.

An inflationary spiral once in operation has strong tendencies to feed upon itself. Since the prices are generally expected to rise, the incentive to save is diminished and the incentive to spend is increased. Consumers have a tendency to postpone savings and to buy goods which they do not require in the immediate period. During periods of rising prices money increasingly becomes a less desirable mode of holding assets. When the value of money is declining, people have a tendency to economise on their cash balances by increasing their spending. This leads to a spending spree and hence an increase in the velocity of money which reinforces increase in the supply of money and thereby further raises prices.

Businessmen likewise have a tendency to anticipate their growth requirements. Thus spending is increased on both accounts. But since the economy is already operating at more or less full capacity, further increases in spending result not in increased production but in rising prices, wages and costs. Rising prices and costs increase the demand for bank credit. More bank credit means more money to spend. Thus the vicious circle once started continues, ever after.

TYPES OF INFLATION

Inflation is of different types. These different types may be looked at by dividing them into different categories on different considerations. In the first place, we may distinguish between different types of inflation on the basis of degree or speed with which the prices rise. Secondly, the distinction may be based on the processes through which inflation is induced. Thirdly, different types of inflation may be distinguished on the basis of time. Fourthly, inflation may be either sporadic or comprehensive. Fifthly, inflation may be open or suppressed. On the basis of rapidity with which prices increase, inflation may be divided into four types: (1) creeping inflation, (2) walking inflation, (3) running inflation, and (4) jumping or galloping or hyper-inflation. The speed at which prices rise is significant from the point of view of the dangerous effects on the economy. Creeping inflation is the most mild form of inflation and some economists do not consider it to be dangerous for the economy. In fact, some economists consider it to be an important instrument of economic development. It is argued that it keeps the national economy free from the cankering effects of stagnation. Creeping inflation in which prices rise imperceptibly over a long period has been attracting a good deal of attention in Germany and the United States since 1956.

There is another school of thought which considers creeping inflation to be dangerous for the economy. According to this school, inflation is like conception which when once takes place goes on increasing till the baby is delivered. In course of time, the baby ceases to creep. It learns to walk, run and finally gallop. It should, therefore, be nipped in the bud.

In case of walking inflation, the rise in prices becomes more marked as compared with the situation obtaining under creeping inflation; in fact, it is danger signal of the occurrence of running and jumping inflation under which the rise in prices takes place by fits and starts. In hyper or galloping inflation prices rise every moment and there is no limit of the height to which the prices might rise. The post-war inflation in Germany and Austria, when the quantity of money increased many hundred quintillion times over the pre-war quantity and the prices increased many trillions over the pre-war prices, is a classic example of the runaway or hyper-inflation.

Hyper-inflation is an indication of the highest degree of abnormality in the monetary system of a country. After the First World War (1914-18), prices in Germany rose at one time by one milion times the pre-war level.[10] Under the condition of such an inflation all assets having a fixed income lose there real value. The best examples of such assets and incomes are provided by salaries, savings, mortgages, insurance policies, bonds etc. Hyper-inflation ruined millions of German families; it more or less wiped out the German middle class. Hyper-inflation was also experiened in Hungary, Poland, Greece, Austria, Russia etc. The question may be raised as to why the government issued such a large quantity of currency that led to hyper-inflation. The answer is that the large issue of currency served as a major source of funds for government expenditure. Statistical data has revealed beyond any doubt that in the final stage of hyper-inflation (1923) the half-yearly index of output in Germany declined by one-third in less than 6 months.[11]

On the basis of different processes through which it is induced, inflation is of three types:

(i) Deficit-induced inflation, which is caused by the adoption of deficit financing or by government spending in excess of its revenue receipts.

(ii) Wage-induced inflation, which result from an increase in money wages.

(iii) Profit-induced inflation, which occurs on account of an increase in the profits of the manufacturers.

Coming to the third category, we may have war-time inflation which emerges from the exigencies of war during the war period

10. Crowther, *An Outline of Money,* p. 108.

11. Philip Cagan, *Studies in the Quantity Theory of Money* (ed. Friedman), p. 53.

and the post-war inflation which exists in immediate post-war period and more often is the legacy of war. The hyper-inflation of Germany during the 'twenties' provides the classical example of war and post-war inflation. There is also peace time inflation which refers to the rise in prices during periods of peace resulting from increased government oulays.

Inflation is comprehensive or economy-wide when the price of every commodity rises throughout the economy. Sporadic inflation is of ephemeral and sectional nature. It occurs when a group of prices rises as a result of sporadic increases in individual prices owing to abnormal shortage of specific goods. The condition of sporadic inflation does not mean more market shortages of goods caused by distortions of price structure such as might take place when the prices of raw materials or wages increase but the prices of finished products are not adjusted in upward direction. It results in situations where supply is restricted by physical conditions and can not be expanded quickly. The shortages of current production are further accentuated by the backlog of deferred demand. Under such conditions, a rise in prices does not help in restoring supply in a high level of demand. A typical case of sporadic inflation would be an increase in prices of food products as a result of crop failure or a rise in the prices of manufactured goods resulting from the formation of a successful monopoly which aims at the curtailment of output, or rise in the prices of those goods whose production has been interrupted and capacity curtailed by war.

Inflation may be open or suppressed. It is open when prices rise without any interruption. The hyper-inflation during the 'twenties' in Germany, Austria, Russia, etc. and in China in the 'forties' provides an example of such an inflation. Suppressed inflation, in contrast, refers to conditions in which as a result of adoption of certain policies (*e.g.*, price control and rationing) by the government, prices are prevented from rising. When price control and rationing or other physical controls are removed, suppressed inflation bursts into an open inflation with vengeance. War-time controls are an example of suppressed inflation developed into an open inflation. The word suppression here means: (i) the postponement of the present demand to some future date; and (ii) the diversion of demand from one kind of goods to another—from those goods which are subject to price-control and rationing to those whose prices are uncontrolled and which are not rationed.

Suppressed inflation suffers from a number of evils. It gives rise to administrative problems. It leads to a hierarchy of price controllers and rationing officers whose duty is to administer rationing and controls. Efficient administration of rationing and controls requires that the administrative machinery should be competent, experienced and honest. War-time experience of actual working of controls and rationing even in advanced countries, however, shows that the administrative machinery is inefficient and easily corruptible. Under such conditions, there grows the most unpleasant phenomenon of black market through which the rationed and price-controlled goods are sold. The administrative machinery being a party to the activities of black-marketers, there soon develops hidden price inflation which is worse than open inflation. To cite Halm, "Excess purchasing power then causes a violent price inflation in the black markets, while the legal markets are drained of merchandise. Once the population finds that it cannot even buy its modest rations, black-market operations become the preoccupation of everybody. Where one such black-market transaction earns more money than a week's or a month's hard work, productivity will decline enormously."[12] Black-market demoralises national character.

Apart from all this, suppressed inflation causes uneconomic diversion of productive resources from essential-goods industries whose prices are statutorily fixed to those industries which produce relatively less essential goods but whose prices, being not subject to price control, are free to rise. Thus the scarce resources of the community have a tendency to move from more productive fields to less productive but monetarily more profitable channels. Such a deviation from the optimum utilisation of resources is very harmful for the community.

Sometimes, economists talk of the demand-pull, demand-shift and cost-push inflation.

DEMAND-PULL INFLATION

It emerges when the aggregate demand exceeds the level of full employment output. Consumers and investors seek to buy more

---

12. G.N. Halm, *Economics of Money and Banking,* p. 417.

than the total amount of output that can be produced. This type of inflation is also known as excess demand inflation. Excess demand may arise either in the public or private sector. The demand-pull inflation may be caused by an increase in the quantity of money. All increase in the quantity of money would lower the rate of interest which would stimulate investment. This will also lead to an increase in consumption expenditure through the multiplier. The demand-pull inflation can also occur without an increase in money supply. This would occur when aggregate demand increases either because of a rise in the marginal efficiency of capital or a rise in the propensity to consume.

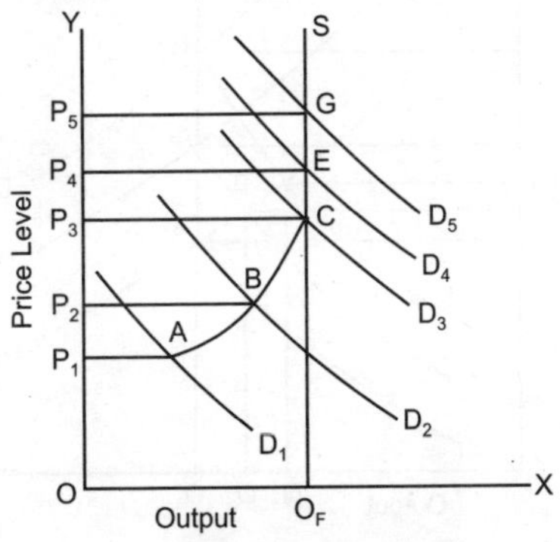

Fig. 15.1.

The figure given above illustrates the demand-pull inflation. In this diagram *D* curves show aggregate demand function and *S* curve shows the given supply function. As *D* curve rises higher and higher from D_1 to D_5, the price level rises higher and higher from P_1 to P_5. When the aggregate demand function rises from D_1 up to D_3, there takes place an increase both in the price level and the aggregate output because the full-employment level is not yet reached. This is known as bottleneck inflation. Full employment is reached at point *C* and, therefore, beyond *C* or above D_3, rise takes place only in the price level. This is known as true inflation.

COST-PUSH INFLATION

For a long time before the fifties, inflation theory ran mainly in terms of the generalised excess demand, explained either by quantity theory or Keynesian theory. During the fifties there occurred a revival of supply, or cost, theories of inflation. The general notion that price inflation can arise on the supply, or cost, side is not new. To cite M. Bronfenbrenner and F.D. Holzman, "Cost inflation has been the layman's instinctive explanation of general price increases since the dawn of the monetary system. We know of no inflationary movement that has not been blamed by some people on "profiteers", "speculators", hoarders", or workers and peasants 'living beyond their station.'"[13]

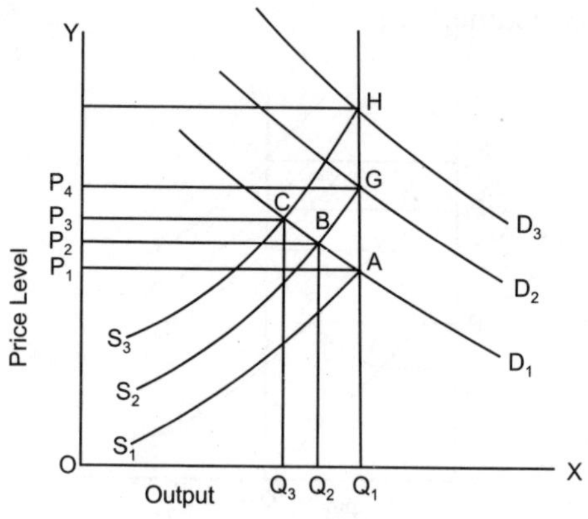

Fig. 15.2.

The figure given above illustrates the cost-push inflation. The full employment output equilibrium is determined at the point where the demand curve D_1 and the supply curve S_1 intersect each other. This is point *A* at which output is OQ_1 and price is OP_1. When the aggregate supply function shifts to S_2, output declines to OQ_2 and the price level rises to OP_2. Similarly, when the supply function further rises to S_3, output declines to OQ_3 and price level rises to OP_3. The process will continue for still further upward shifts in the supply function.

There are two main causes of inflationary shifts in the aggregate supply function, *viz.* (i) higher money wages secured by labour unions and (ii) higher prices secured by business firms in monopolistic or oligopolistic industries. The inflation caused by the first factor is

13. M. Bronfenbrenner and F.D. Holzman, "Survey of Inflation Theory", *American Economic Review* (September, 1963), p. 613.

known as *wage-push inflation* while that caused by the second factor is known as *profit-push inflation.*

Wage-push inflation: If the increase in wage-rate is faster than the increase in productivity, there will occur an upward shift in the aggregate supply function. One cause of a rise in wage rates is an excess demand for labour. Once the economy has reached full employment, any increase in the level of money income will reflect only in a rise in prices and no rise in output. Higher prices mean greater profits, and greater profits induce employers to expand output. For this purpose they seek more labour which is not available. Competition among employers leads to a rise in the wage rate. Thus there occurs a rise in wage rates without any rise in the productivity of labour. But it may be pointed out that this rise in the labour cost per unit of output is not the *cause* of the rise in the price level but the result. Wage rates rose because of an excessive demand for labour; this would have happened whether labour was organised or not.

The concept of wage-push inflation is restricted to increases in labour costs which are the *cause* and not the *result* of higher prices. Wage-push inflation is the result of "spontaneous" or "autonomous" upward shifts in the supply function as against those which are "induced" by excess demand for labour. Induced shifts may occur with or without the existence of strong labour unions but spontaneous shifts assume strong labour unions which are able to push up wage rates in the absence of any excess demand for labour. Wage-push inflation cannot occur in an economy in which wage-rates are determined by purely competitive market forces. In such an economy wage rates rise or fall only in response to variations in the demand for and supply of labour, which in turn depend on variations in aggregate demand for final output.

Profit-push Inflation*:* This is another form of supply inflation. Just as labour unions may exercise their market power by forcing wage increases, so oligopolists and monopolists may, in order to increase their profits, raise prices more than needed to offset any increase in costs. Again just as labour unions are a prerequisite to a generalised wage-push inflation, so the existence of imperfectly competitive markets in the sale of goods and services is a prerequisite to profit-push inflation. Where prices are determined by the competition among buyers and sellers, as is the case with agricultural commodities and raw material, the seller cannot influence the price significantly. But many goods are not sold through such markets and the sellers of these goods "administer" prices. In an economy where so-called administered prices abound, there is at least the possibility that these prices may be administered upward faster than costs in an effort to increase profits.

The cost-push hypothesis, however, rarely considers autonomous attempts to increase profits as an important inflationary element. In the first place, since profits are generally a small fraction of the total price, an increase in profits would not have much impact on prices. Secondly, monopolists and oligopolists generally hesitate to raise prices in the absence of obvious demand-pull elements. Finally, the motivation for a profit push is weak since, at least in corporations, those who make the decision to raise prices are not the direct beneficiaries of increase in price. The cost-push is, therefore, generally conceived as being synonymous with wage-push.

DEMAND-SHIFT INFLATION

A rise in the price level may occur without an increase in aggregate demand if the structure of demand changes so rapidly that the resources cannot be shifted equally fast. The year 1946 provides a typical example of demand-shift inflation in the United States. With the close of the War, there developed a simultaneous reduction in government expenditure and an increase in private consumption and private investment. Further, during the year, real net national product declined below the 1945 level, although money national product continued to rise. Thus, while the real output declined, the price level rose up. In this way, it is possible for changes in the structure of demand to affect the general price level even though there is no increase in aggregate demand. The basic idea behind demand shift inflation is that a shift in demand would raise wages and prices in fields in which demand has increased. But since wages and prices are inflexible in the downward direction, the rising wages and prices in some sectors are not matched by corresponding reductions in wages and prices in the sectors in which demand has declined. As such the general level of prices rises in spite of the fact that no increase in the over-all aggregate demand has taken place.

DEMAND-PULL VERSUS COST-PUSH INFLATION

According to some economists inflation is neither demand-pull alone nor cost-push alone and, in actual practice, it possesses elements of both. They point out that there cannot be such a thing as cost-push inflation because, without an increase in the purchasing power and demand, cost increases would lead to unemployment and depression and not to inflation. Similarly, there are assumptions for which it would be appropriate to say that demand-pull cannot cause inflation unless it is produced by cost-push. In other words, it is contended that there are conditions under which 'effective demand' is not effective and would not pull up prices unless cost-push produces inflation. But this position ignores an important distinction, namely, whether the cost-push is 'equilibrating' in the sense that it 'absorbs' a previously excess demand or whether it is 'disequilibrating' in the sense that it creates an excess supply (of labour and productive capacity) which would have to be prevented or removed by an increase in effective demand. To cite Prof. Harry G. Johnson, "The issue of cost-push versus demand-pull was...a spurious one...Neither cost-push nor demand-pull inflation models can generate a sustained inflation unless it is assumed either that the demand for money can be compressed indefinitely without adverse effects on demand and employment, which runs contrary to the theory and fact of monetary behaviour, or that the monetary authority permissively provides the additional money required to circulate the national income at ever-increasing prices, in which case the behaviour of the monetary authority becomes the crucial factor in inflation (and, in addition, the question arises for the cost-push theory as to what determines the pace of inflation). The two theories are therefore not independent and self-contained theories of inflation, but rather theories concerning the mechanism of inflation in a monetary environment that permits it."[14] Further, in actual practice, it is very difficult to devise a test capable of determining whether a particular inflation is of the demand-pull or cost-push variety.

No doubt the distinction between demand-pull and cost-push inflation is not very scientific, it cannot be denied that it does help in

14. Harry G. Johnson, *Essays in Monetary Economics* (London, 1967) p. 128.

separating two forces which might be in simultaneous and interdependent operation in any actual inflation. The distinction is also important for its policy implications. To cite Harry G. Johnson, "The importance of the debate stems largely from the difference between the recommendations for anti-inflationary policy to which the two views of the cause of inflation lead, the demand-pull explanation leading to the recommendation of monetary restraint and fiscal orthodoxy and the cost-push explanation leading to the rejection of macroeconomic measures of this sort in favour of policies directed at the processes of price formation and wage determination."[15]

INFLATIONARY GAP

Inflationary gap was defined by the Chancellor of the Exchequer in England in his budget speech of April, 1941 as "the amount of the government's expenditure against which there is no corresponding release of real resources of manpower or material by some other member of the community." As such it indicates an excess of total demand for goods over their total supply measured at constant prices. The concept of inflationary gap may be viewed in relationship to full employment level of real income and defined as the excess of the amount of aggregate spending over the amount of aggregate output at full employment level at the existing prices. Prof. Kurihara defines the inflationary gap as "an excess of anticipated expenditure over available output at base prices." According to Klein, this gap "is the difference between what the population will try to consume out of income (which is determined by the interaction of consumption function and the level of the government expenditure) and the amount available for consumption at pre-inflation prices."

Even if it is assumed that there exist some unemployed resources which can be commissioned to raise the level of income above the present level, an excess of demand over supply will lead to a rise in prices because production cannot be increased instantaneously. It takes time to build new factories and to commission new plants. Increased raw materials have to be obtained

15. *Ibid.*, p. 127.

by increasing agricultural and mineral production. Workers have to be trained in new skills. All this requires time. Thus even when production can be increased, such an increase would take place with a time-lag. As such when expenditure increases, prices would rise and inflationary gap would exist till the supply of goods is expanded.

To illustrate how the inflationary gap arises and how it is measured, we may consider the example of a war economy which is more or less a full-employment economy. The aggregate real national income would be equal to the sum of government and private expenditures incurred on investment and consumption. Let us suppose this amounts to Rs. 1200 crores in money terms calculated at the existing price level. Now if, out of this total output, the government takes away output worth Rs. 300 crores for war purposes, output only worth Rs. 900 crores would be available for civilian consumption. This output worth Rs. 900 crores constitutes the supply side. Let us suppose that the money income paid to the community during the same period is Rs. 1200 crores, out of which the government takes away Rs. 100 crores in the form of taxes. This leaves a disposable income of Rs. 1100 crores with the community. Obviously, the community would not spend the entire disposable money income on the purchase of goods and save a part of it. If people are in the habit of saving 10 per cent of their disposable income, the money income that would actually be spent on goods would amount to Rs. 990 crores (*e.g.* Rs. 1100 crores—Rs. 110 crores saved). As such, the inflationary gap at the current level of prices would be Rs. 90 crores, *i.e.*, Rs. 990 crores—Rs. 900 crores. Thus when disposable income of Rs. 990 crores chases goods available for civilian consumption worth Rs. 900 crores, there arises an inflationary gap to the tune of Rs. 90 crores. The process may be summarised as below:

Demand Side		*Supply side*	
	Rs. Crores		Rs. Crores
Money income paid to community	1200	Gross national product (GNP) at existing price (or at pre-inflation prices)	1200
Taxes	100		
Total disposable income	1100	War expenditure, *i.e.*, value of GNP appropriated for war purposes	300
Savings by community at the rate of 10 per cent	110		
Net disposable income (which represents total amount of anticipated expenditure)	990	Value available for civilian consumption at pre-inflation prices	900

A similar inflationary gap can arise during a period of development planning. The amount of money expenditure (and as such money income) may be high because of expenditure on development projects but there may not be a corresponding increase in the production of consumption goods because of the time-lag between the investment on development projects and the flow of goods from them. Thus, the basic fact is that so long as the amount of disposable income in the community and the amount of goods available are equal, price level could remain stable; but if the former exceeds the latter, an inflationary gap would appear. If, in contrast, the amount of goods is in excess of the disposable money incomes, a deflationary gap would appear.

Figure 15.3 illustrates the concept of inflationary gap.

In figure 15.3 total anticipated expenditure is measured along the vertical axis while the real income (gross national product) is measured along the horizontal axis. *C* represents consumption expenditure, *I* private investment expenditure and *G* government expenditure, so that the total expenditure of the economy is shown by the $C + I + G$ function. The 45° line *OE* is the equilibrium line showing that the economy is in equilibrium when the supply of goods and services (as reflected in real income) equals the demand for them (as reflected in the total spending function). The $C + I + G$ curve intersects the curve *OE* (equilibrium line) at point E_f which gives the equilibrium income Y_f, which may be assumed as the full

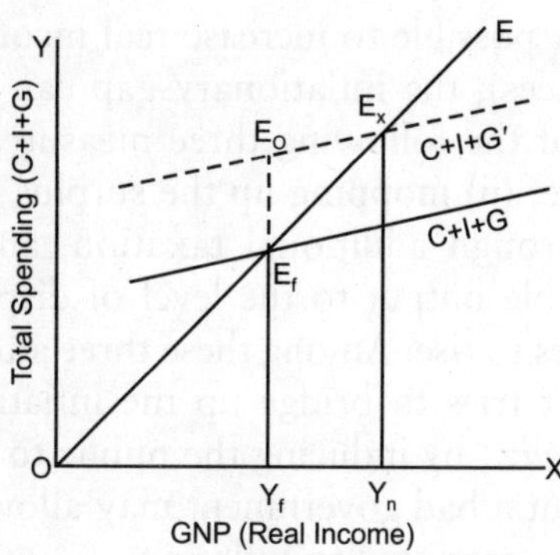

Fig. 15.3

employment income at current prices. At this point the aggregate monetary demand reflected by the $C + I + G$ function amounts to E_fY_f which is equal to the total amount of goods available, that is, OY_f. As such, there is no excess demand and no question of inflationary gap.

Now, suppose, for some reasons, the government expenditure increases by E_fE_o which gives the economy new function $C + I + G'$. Since Y_f is the real income at full employment level, it does not increase with the increase in government expenditure by E_fE_o. Thus E_fE_o represents an excess of monetary demand over the available quantity of goods (OY_f). In this case E_fE_o is the extent of inflationary gap which forces up prices. Thus inflationary gap occurs when, with the economy at full employment, the money income rises faster than the output of goods and services. When the expenditures are rising faster than the output of goods and services, prices will necessarily rise to equate expenditures with the money value of output at a higher price level. The inflationary gap is, therefore, defined as the amount by which full employment exceeds the value of current output at existing prices. This implies that if the prices are to be prevented from rising, the output of goods must increase by an amount which would be sufficient to absorb the excess demand generated by an increased expenditure. In the above diagram, the prices can be prevented from rising only if the real income is increased from Y_f to Y_x.

In case it is not possible to increase real income (or the volume of goods and services), the inflationary gap can be bridged up by any one or more of the following three measures: (i) inducing the public to save more, (ii) mopping up the surplus purchasing power with the public through additional taxation, and (iii) raising the value of the available output to the level of disposable income by permitting the prices to rise. Among these three alternative measures, a good government tries to bridge up the inflationary gap by the first two measures *viz.*, by inducing the public to save more and by increasing taxes. But a bad government may allow the prices to rise and thus expose the economy to inflation.

Significance of Inflationary Gap: The concept of inflationary gap is a highly useful analytical device because it indicates the direction and extent to which the various anti-inflationary measures should be carried out by the monetary and fiscal authorities. To cite Kurihara, "Analysis of the inflationary gap in terms of such aggregates as national income, investment outlays, and consumption expenditures clearly reveals what determines public policy with respect to taxes, public expenditures, savings campaigns, credit control, wage adjustments—in-short, all the conceivable anti-inflation measures affecting the propensities to consume, to save, and to invest, which together determine the general price level. It is by influencing those propensities, directly or indirectly, that the monetary-fiscal authorities hope to wipe out the inflationary gap and therefore prevent further price increases."[16]

UNEMPLOYMENT-INFLATION DILEMMA (PHILLIPS CURVE)

With remarkable prescience, both Keynes and Mrs. Robinson foresaw in the pre-war period the dilemma which most of the western countries face today; the possibility of attaining simultaneously, and without price or wage controls, the twin goals of full employment and price stability. The experience of many countries with strong producer pressure groups shows that as unemployment is reduced below a certain critical level, prices begin to rise, and that, when prices are stable, unemployment is above the level that is considered "socially tolerable" by countries committed in principle to a full employment goal.

16. Kenneth K. Kurihara, *Monetary Theory and Public Policy* (London, 1956), p. 45.

Thus we can not have price stability and full employment at one and the same time. If we want stable prices, we have to forgo a high level of employment. And if we want a high level of employment, we have to sacrifice stable prices. Thus we have to trade between unemployment and inflation.

A.W. Phillips has made an empirical study of the relationship between unemployment and the rate of change of money wage rates, which is known as "the Phillips Curve." The objective of his study is to investigate whether statistical evidence supports the hypothesis that the rate of change of money wage rates in the United Kingdom can be explained by the level of unemployment and the rate of change of unemployment and if so to form some

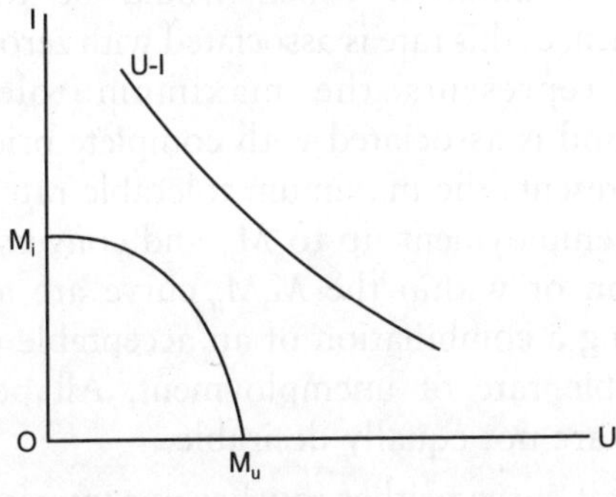

Fig. 15.4

quantitative estimate of the relation between unemployment and the rate of change of money wage rates. The empirical study appears in general to support the hypothesis that the rate of change of money wage rates can be explained by the *level* of unemployment and the *rate of change* of unemployment. The relation between unemployment and the rate of change of wage rates is likely to be curvilinear and not linear. Phillips has used this curve to determine that for the United Kingdom, a rate of 5½ per cent unemployment is needed if wages are to be held steady, and a rate of 2½ per cent unemployment is needed if prices are to be held steady; this means that wages would rise by the same percentage as the increase in productivity, which is estimated to be 2 per cent per annum. Samuelson and Solow have estimated a similar curve for the United States and have found a more pessimistic figure of 5½ per cent unemployment necessary for price stability, assuming that productivity increases at 2½ per cent per annum.[17]

In Fig. 15.4, the curve *U-I* represents the Phillips relationship. The curve can be derived from an economy's data for a period of years by plotting for each year the percentage money wage increase (vertical axis) against the percentage labour force that is unemployed (horizontal axis). The curve M_i—M_u represents the acceptable *trade off* between inflation and unemployment. This curve is concave indicating that as unemployment reaches low levels, more inflation is acceptable only if a relatively large decrease in unemployment can be traded for it and as the rate of inflation reaches low levels higher unemployment is acceptable only if increasingly large cuts in the rate of inflation can be traded for it. M_i is assumed to be the maximum rate of inflation which would be tolerated by the authorities concerned; this rate is associated with zero unemployment. Similarly, M_u represents the maximum tolerable rate of unemployment and is associated with complete price stability. The curve M_iM_u represents the maximum tolerable rate of inflation for every rate of unemployment up to M_u and conversely. All the *U-I* points located on or within the M_iM_u curve are acceptable, each point representing a combination of an acceptable rate of inflation and an acceptable rate of unemployment. All points inside the curve, however, are not equally desirable.

If the *U-I* limit curve neither touches nor intersects M_iM_u curve, the goals of full employment and price stability would be in effective conflict. A tolerable rate of unemployment would have to be paid for by an unacceptable rate of inflation and conversely. In contrast, if the macro boundary intersects the M_iM_u curve, an acceptable rate of unemployment can be combined with an acceptable rate of inflation. Although a trade off must still be made between a lower rate of inflation and a lower rate of unemployment, there is no effective conflict in the sense that one of the choices in the trade off must be unacceptable. Actual experience in most of the Western countries shows that high employment and price stability are in effective conflict.

17. Samuelson and Solow, "Analytical Aspects of Anti-Inflation Policy", *American Economic Review,* May, 1960, pp. 177-94.

Critical Evaluation: The Phillips curve has not been accepted by all economists and the empirical evidence is still a matter of great controversy. Many economists do not approve of an explanation of inflation which does not pay adequate consideration to the monetary conditions. Even if Phillips relation does exist, it does not necessarily imply that it will usefully lend itself to macroeconomic decision-making. They feel that changes in prices are at least as important as unemployment in determining changes in the wage rate. This is ignored in the Phillips Curve. The 'money illusion' among workers as suggested by Keynes is largely absent in today's bargaining because wage-earners would make every effort to retain their share of national income, if this has been eroded by rising prices. To cite Harry G. Johnson, "...there are some serious doubts about the applicability of the Phillips curve to the formulation of economic policy. On the one hand, the curve represents only a statistical description of the mechanics of adjustment in the labour market, resting on a simple model of economic dynamics with little general and well-tested monetary and value theory behind it. On the other hand, it describes the behaviour of the labour market in a combination of periods of economic fluctuation and varying rate of inflation, conditions which presumably influenced the behaviour of the labour market itself, so that it may reasonably be doubted whether the curve would continue to hold its shape if an attempt were made by economic policy to pin the economy down to a point on it."[18]

Friedman holds the view that a function relating the volume of employment to the rate of change in money prices is fallacious because it implies a relationship between real and nominal magnitudes.[19] Since the former is determined by real forces in the economy, and only temporarily influenced by the monetary variable, while the latter is determined entirely by monetary forces, it is obvious that there is no reason to assume any relationship between the two.

It has been pointed out that the degree of non-linearity between changes in the wage rate and unemployment is an empirical

18. Harry G. Johnson, *Essays in Monetary Economics* (London, 1967), pp. 132-33.

19. Milton Friedman, "The Role of Monetary Policy", *American Economic Review* (March, 1969).

question which needs further examination. Profits have often been suggested as another important determinant of the change in wage rates. This point needs serious consideration.

Phillips Curve and Control of Inflation: If we succeed in achieving full employment, we must find some way other than the use of monetary and fiscal policy to prevent the inflation which Phillips Curve suggests may well result. One of the ways is to link increases in wages to increases in productivity of the workers. Other measures include various forms of anti-union legislation, which at the extreme would abolish collective bargaining or prohibit industry-wide bargaining. Although all such measures have implications which go far beyond their possible anti-inflationary applicability, it may be emphasized that some such measures would be absolutely necessary if we want to attain full employment and rapid economic growth and at the same time avoid inflation.

CAUSES OF INFLATION

As seen above, basically speaking, the inflationary pressures arise when money income and corresponding expenditure or demand increase without being accompanied by a corresponding increase in the supply of goods and services. In other words, inflation results from factors which give rise to 'excess demand'. Broadly speaking, excess demand may be caused by two sets of factors *viz.* (i) those which shift the demand upwards and (ii) those which shift the supply downwards. These two sets of factors are briefly described below.

FACTORS CAUSING AN UPWARD SHIFT IN DEMAND

Deficit Financing: In recent years, there has been a tendency. Particularly in developing countries, to heavily resort to deficit financing to obtain funds for executing development plans. Deficit financing increases money in the hands of people and thereby increases demand for goods and services.

Increase in the Velocity of Money: This factor is particularly important during boom periods. The velocity of circulation of money increases on account of an increase in the marginal efficiency of capital or reduction in liquidity preference, or an increase in the propensity to consume.

Credit Expansion: The credit structure of a country is determined by the policy of the government as well as that of the commercial banks. The central bank of the country can cause an expansion of credit by lowering the bank rate or by purchasing government securities. Similarly, the commercial banks can expand credit by lowering their cash reserves; but they can do so only when there is demand for loans from borrowers. It may be pointed out that once the credit expands, as a result of either the policy of the government or the initiative of the commercial banks, it continues for a sufficiently long period of time.

Rapidly Increasing Public Expenditure: In recent years public expenditure has been growing fast, particularly because of increasing defence expenditure and expanding role of the state in economic activities; this considerably increases the demand for goods and services.

Expansion of Exports: An increase in exports would mean less available for domestic consumption. This would make the existing unchanged domestic demand excessive for the commodities whose exports increase and thus cause a rise in their prices.

Rapid Growth of Population: A rapidly growing population increases the demand for goods and services and thus pushes up their prices. To cite Prof. Coulborn, "If population increases rapidly, while the aggregate of money remains stable, the consequent rise in the velocity of circulation is likely to outweigh the countervailing decrease in the volume of money per head; further, a rapid increase of population may increase output less than proportionately—another factor tending to raise prices."[20]

War: This has been one of the most common causes of inflation. Financing of war leads to a considerable expansion in the supply of money. Further, it leads to a diversion of productive resources from the production of consumer goods to that of war materials and thus causes a shortage of consumer goods.

Trade Union Activities: The trade unions continuously agitate for higher wages, shorter hours of work, more holidays with pay and other amenities. In a democratic country, the government is often compelled to accept even unreasonably demands of the labourers. The increase in wages of labourers and other amenities

20. W.A.L. Coulborn, *A Discussion of Money*, p. 159.

provided to them beyond the increase in their productivity raises the cost of production and hence prices. Further, increase in wage increases purchasing power in the hands of labourers and reduction in working hours leads to a decline in the volume of production. This adds to the rise in prices.

Excise and Sales Taxes: Increased taxation is generally disinflationary because it mops up the purchasing power of the public. But if taxes are levied on the production and sale of goods which can be shifted to consumers, the prices of such goods will rise and add to inflationary pressures.

International Factors*:* Inflation in one country may be transmitted to other countries through trade. When prices are rising abroad, the importing country has to pay higher and higher prices for its imports. The rise in the prices of imported goods leads to a sympathetic rise in the prices of goods produced within the country.

Devaluation*:* Devaluation of the domestic currency increases the prices of imported goods. It stimulates foreign demand for export goods, which raises their prices. Rise in the prices of imported goods and exported goods causes a rise in the prices of non-treated goods also.

FACTORS CAUSING A DOWNWARD SHIFT IN SUPPLY

Natural Calamities: They can take a number of forms like floods, earthquakes, epidemics etc. They decrease production and thereby lead to a rise in prices.

Stage of Production: If the production has reached a stage where the law of diminishing returns begins to operate, the cost of production and hence the prices would start rising.

Hoarding: During periods of rising prices, dealers as well as consumers have a tendency to hoard commodities which aggravates shortages.

Shortage of Factors of Production: Non-availability of certain factors like capital equipment, land, skilled labour, raw materials etc., make it difficult to expand production in response to an increase in demand and thus leads to shortages.

INFLATION IN AN UNDERDEVELOPED ECONOMY

Basically speaking, inflation arises owing to a gap between effective demand and output. Inflation is normally considered to be a postfull-employment phenomenon because so long as unemployed resources exist, increase in effective demand is expected to lead to an increase in output and employment rather than to a rise in the prices. Theoretically, inflation starts only after the full-employment stage is reached. But in actual practice, prices may start rising much before the full-employment is reached because of lack of perfect elasticity of supply of goods and services and because of other factors which assist in raising the cost of production. Keynes mentions the following factors which cause an inflationary situation before full-employment is reached.[21]

(i) Effective demand will not change in exact proportion to the money supply.

(ii) Since the resources are not homogeneous and as such not perfectly substitutable, the law of diminishing returns starts operating as the employment of resources gradually increases.

(iii) Since various factors are not perfect substitutes for each other, some commodities will reach a condition of inelastic supply, while there are still unemployed resources available for the production of other are still unemployed resóurces available for the production of other commodities.

(iv) The wage-unit will tend to rise before the full employment has been reached.

(v) The remunerations of the factors entering into marginal cost will not all change in the same proportion.

Because of the bottlenecks mentioned above at various levels in the structure of the economy, an increase in the supply of money and hence in demand has a tendency to lead to a rise in the price level before the full-employment stage is reached. In addition to these general bottlenecks, an underdeveloped economy is characterised by various other forms of bottlenecks which cause a relative rigidity in the supply of goods and thus lead to a sharper rise in prices. Importance of these are briefly mentioned below:

21. J.M. Keynes, *The General Theory of Employment, Interest and Money* (London, 1936), p. 296.

(i) There exist several market imperfections which present an optimum allocation of resources and thereby extension of the actual production frontier to the maximum possible frontier. The important market imperfections include imperfect knowledge, imperfect mobility, specificity of factors and imperfect divisibility of factors.

(ii) In advanced countries the existence of unemployment leads to increased output as a result of increased demand. In underdeveloped countries what exists is not unemployment but disguised unemployment or underemployment which does not lead to increased production with an increase in effective demand. To the extent supply does not respond to an increase in effective demand caused by monetary expansion, the prices would tend to rise.

Apart from the bottlenecks mentioned above, there are other factors which cause inflationary pressures in underdeveloped countries. Because of lack of other sources of financing development plans, resort has to be made to deficit financing. High priorities given to the production of capital goods in development plans lead to a shortage of consumer goods. Thus while money incomes increase leading to a rise in demand, the consumer goods become inadequate, which results in a general rise in the price level.

INFLATION AND ECONOMIC DEVELOPMENT

There exists great controversy as to whether inflation promotes or retards economic development. Some economists, including Keynes, hold the opinion that inflation, in one form or the other, helps economic development. It is held that inflation helps mobilisation of resources by redistributing income and wealth away from wage-recipients towards the profit-recipients. Since the marginal propensity to save of the profit-earners is much higher than that of the wage-earners, transfer of income from the latter to the former class increases the volume of savings which can profitably be invested by the entrepreneurial class in productive channels, thereby raising the rate of economic development. Keynes favours mild inflation on the ground that slowly rising prices create an optimistic atmosphere resulting in high profit expectation which stimulates investment. Maurice Dobb remarks, "Inducements are necessary for large-scale movements of labour and for increased supplies of foodstuffs and raw materials to be made available by the village for the town."[22] Prof. Kaldor also remarks, "a slow and steady rate of inflation provides a most powerful aid to the attainment of a steady rate of economic progress."[23] Prof. Robertson also favours a mild inflation for economic growth. Such a policy is particularly important in underdeveloped economies where a great part of the labour force is self-employed and price incentives (through mild inflation) assume greater importance than wage incentives (at least in the initial stages of breakthrough). Professor Rostow believes that several 'take-off' processes have been assisted by inflation. Hamilton holds the view that inflation has been a powerful stimulant in a large number of historical instances and can perform a similar function in underdeveloped countries.

Many economists believe that a mild inflation is not necessarily an undesirable thing because the alternative to this would be unemployment and impaired economic growth. The argument is that since prices are flexible only in the upward direction in our present institutional set-up, resource allocation through the price system must operate through price increases in the sectors of the economy which are growing rather than through price decreases in the sectors which are stagnating. It is argued that since the monopoly power of unions and enterprises is such that price increases are inevitable, it is better for authorities not to adopt deflationary policies which might cause unemployment rather than a decline in the price level. Prof. Lewis believes that inflation for the purpose of creating useful capital is often ultimately self-terminating because sooner or later it would increase the supply of goods in the market.[24]

Some economists believe that inflation is a product of economic growth. Some inflation is considered to be unavoidable in the process of economic development. At least in the initial stages of development process, there is bound to be a time-lag between the increases in money incomes and the availability of consumption goods in the country and hence a rise in the price level. The

22. Maurice Dobb, *Some Aspects of Economic Development,* p. 48.
23. Nicholas Kaldor, "Economic Growth and Problem of Inflation", *Economica,* 1959.
24. W.A. Lewis, *The Theory of Economic Growth.*

inflationary pressures are considered to be almost certain if the planned investment exceeds the volume of real savings.

Another group of economists holds the view that inflation does not facilitate economic growth and, on the contrary, hinders the process of economic growth. Milton Friedman, for instance, completely disagrees with the policy of 'development through inflation'. He also holds the view that "inflation is not inevitable in the course of development."[25] He does not find much substance in the argument that inflation tends to stimulate development through its redistributive effects. No doubt, there were some circumstances in the past in which redistributive effects were favourable to development; but there is no guarantee that these favourable effects would operate in all cases.[26] The reason inflation had favourable effects in the past was that it was unexpected. The process of inflation was unanticipated because it was not planned by any body. Friedman believes that favourable effects cannot be obtained by a deliberate expansion in the supply of money without its degenerating into hyper-inflation. When the process of inflation is deliberate, many people would know about it and act in a way which prevents the occurrence of redistributive effects. Prof. Nurkse also observes that "the success of inflation as an instrument of capital formation depends largely on the degree of which rise in prices is unforeseen and unexpected. When a further rise in price is expected and seems certain, the velocity of circulation of money increases, saving gives place to dissaving and inflation loses its capital-forming power."[27] Further, inflation "invites development, if any, only through manipulation of markets rather than efficient production." This is obvious from the deterrent effects of inflation on productive enterprise, increasing cost of development, depreciating real value of cash holdings, accumulation of investment in real estates, decreasing investment in the export sector, speculation and hoarding resulting from rising prices.[28]

---

25. Milton Friedman, *Inflations—Causes and Consequences* (Bombay, 1963), p. 17.
26. *Ibid*., p. 13.
27. Ragnar Nurkse, *League of Nations: Course and Control of Inflation*, p. 13.
28. Indian Merchants' Chamber, *Inflation in a Developing Economy*, 1961, p. 82.

The decline in the real value of money resulting from inflation destroys the saving habits of the people and places a premium on improvidence and careless spending. Inflation may not only obstruct the process of capital formation but may drive the available capital out of the country. During inflationary periods business skill and efficiency tends to be used for speculative purposes rather than for productive purposes. Rising prices lead to a decline in the demand for export-goods resulting in unemployment in the export industries and balance of payments difficulties.[29]

EFFECTS OF INFLATION

Though inflation implies a general rise in the price level, this rise is not uniform throughout the economy. If the rate of increase in the prices of goods and services were uniform in all sectors of the economy, the relative position of the various earning groups would remain unchanged and as such the economic effects of inflation would be neutral. But in reality, during the inflationary process, the prices of different goods and services rise at different rates. This results in a change in the pattern of income distribution in the community which is the source of many evil effects normally attributed to inflation.

Inflation resulting from excess demand of the government in a state of national emergency, as during a war, amounts to a forced levy on the community and helps in the mobilisation of resources to meet the emergency by restricting civilian consumptions. From this special point of view, inflation is useful. In addition to this, it is claimed that inflation benefits two important classes of people in the community who form the backbone of the nation's economy *viz.* (i) farmers and (ii) entrepreneurs. It can easily be observed that both these classes of people gain from a rise in prices because they are primarily a debtor class. In an inflationary period, repayment of debt becomes easier because the real burden of debt falls with the rise in prices of goods and services. Farmers gain partly because the products which they sell are highly inflation-sensitive and partly because the costs which they incur in connection with their productive operations, such as interest charges, taxes, wages, etc. rise only to a small extent, at least in the early stages of inflation, in

29. Also see section on *Deficit Financing and Economic Development* in the Chapter on Deficit Financing.

comparison with the prices of the product which they offer for sale. Businessmen gain from a similar lagging of costs behind prices. They also gain from an appreciation in the value of their inventories. It is claimed that an increase in the profits of the entrepreneurial class stimulates capital formation, helps in the drawing up of idle resources for economic utilisation and in expanding production to the maximum capacity of the economy.

Though the advantages mentioned above have some validity in the short period, but it cannot be disputed that ultimately inflation has a harmful effects on the economy. The very forces which are helpful in stimulating capital formation start retarding investment after a stage is reached. A study[30] conducted by an economist of the International Monetary Fund points out that while no definite conclusions can be drawn, the evidence available broadly indicates that among the underdeveloped countries the rate of growth of the economy was higher when the rate of inflation was lower. In his study of the course of inflation in Europe in the nineteen twenties, professor Nurkse points out that the "success of inflation as an instrument of capital formation depends largely on the degree to which rise in prices is unforeseen and unexpected."[31] When a further rise in prices is expected and seems certain, velocity of circulation of money rises, saving gives place to dissaving and inflation loses its power of stimulating investment. Thereafter, there is cumulative process of inflation.

The declining value of the money and the failure of the wage level to adjust itself to the price level leaves the workers with a sense of frustration which impairs their incentives to work more with a view to earn more. Declining value of money also impairs the incentives to save and places a premium on improvidence and careless spending. Continued inflation or the knowledge that the government budgetary or monetary policy would maintain inflationary forces for long drives out capital from the country as happened in France and Germany at the close of the First World War. Thus, beyond a certain stage, inflation not only obstructs

---

30. U. Tun Wai, "The Relation between Inflation and Economic Development", *International Monetary Fund Staff Papers,* October, 1959, p. 302.

31. League of Nations, *Course and Control of Inflation,* 1947, p. 6.

domestic capital accumulation but also drives available capital out of the country. Nor is the attitude and behaviour of the entrepreneurial class in an inflationary period favourable to increased production. Cost accounting which is an important instrument of measuring efficiency, loses its meaning, when the value of money changes very frequently. There is a tendency to employ business skill and efficiency for speculative purposes rather than for productive purposes. The chances of earning wind-fall profits out of the rapidly rising prices of existing supplies encourage business community to indulge in hoarding and helps in the growth of black markets. When producers do not find much difficulty in transferring higher costs on to consumers, they have a tendency to be wasteful and lethargic. The transfer of income from the middle and lower income groups to higher income groups resulting from inflation leads to a decline in the aggregate consumption and thus generates instability.

During an inflationary period, the revenues of government fail to respond to the growing responsibilities of the state. The result is the starvation of developmental services like public works, education and public health, on which depends largely the growth and prosperity of the national economy.

Inflation affects different classes of society against the sound maxims of social justice. Comparing inflation to robbery, C.N. Vakil states, "Both deprive the victim of some possession with the difference that the robber is visible, inflation is invisible; the robber's victim may be one or a few at a time, the victims of inflation are the whole nation; the robber may be dragged to a court of law, inflation is legal."[32]

The people worst hit by inflation are those who are least able to protect themselves. Inflation causes hardships to all who live on fixed incomes, *e.g.*, pensioners, widows, teachers, civil servants, factory workers etc. Among the workers, the worst sufferers are those who are ill-organised. Long and sustained inflation corrupts the foundations of society. It erodes savings and undermines the provision for sickness, education and old age. It undermines the incentive for hard work and thrift. The investors in equities gain while those who invest in fixed interest yielding bonds are adversely affected. Since most of the middle class investors choose fixed

32. C.N. Vakil, *Financial Burden of War on India.*

interest bearing securities, insurance and saving accounts, inflation adversely affects the small investors. Angell describes the sufferings of the middle class during the post-war German inflation as follows: "The group which suffered most from the inflation, however, was the group which was also least able to defend itself; the middle classes among the town-dwellers... composed largely of people with small fixed incomes, such as salaried officials and clerks, recipients of pensions, and little investors living on interest and rent of whom the latter group were hit especially hard by the government control of city rentals—they were precisely the group most exposed to the evil consequences of currency depreciation, while they lacked both the knowledge and the opportunity to combat it."[33] Kemmerer makes similar observations about the impact of inflation on the middle class. "The middle class, however, which by hard work and thrift has built up a fund of savings to educate its children and to provide a livelihood for times of sickness and for old age, finds itself in a desperate situation in a time of serious inflation. The cost of living rises disproportionately to income; savings are wiped out; and hard work, independence, and thrift seem to be false gods. Under such conditions the middle class is all too often overwhelmed by a sense of futility and desperation."[34] Thus the people worst hit by inflation are those belonging to the middle class who form the backbone of modern democracy. The hyper-inflation in Germany, Austria, Poland and France after the First World War completely ruined the middle class.

Though businessman, debtors and producers gain from continuously rising prices, creditors are hit hard. The creditors are affected adversely because the purchasing power of the money which is returned to them is much lower than that of the money which they had lent.

Although slowly rising prices stimulate economic activity and increase the volume of employment, but if they start rising fast, they may lead to depression and cause widespread unemployment. To cite William McChesney Martin Jr., "If inflation is allowed to pursue its course it feeds upon itself in such a way that, when the

---

33. J.W. Angell, *The Recovery of Germany* (New Haven, 1929), p. 38.

34. Edwin Walter Kemmerer, *The ABC of Inflation,* p. 94.

inevitable correction finally comes, unemployment will be that much worse. It should not be difficult to see how inflation leads to unemployment. The danger becomes manifest when, as costs go up, it becomes increasingly hard to pass those costs along to the customer in the form of price increases, and it becomes increasingly easy to misjudge or miscalculate the market. Then for the first time volume dips, there is price-profit squeeze, and, at some point the profit-squeeze leads to a cutback in investment, income and production. The cutback in production leads to a cutback in employment."

Inflation makes business planning and long-term investment risky. It upsets calculations about depreciation costs and profits and thereby poses a threat to the solvency and sound growth of business. It deprives the economy of the benefits of a stable unit of account and store of value. It raises interest rates and creates a chaos in the money market. It causes a disequilibrium in the balance of payments.

Inflation lowers the moral standards of the people, particularly of business community and government officials. Black market, bribery and corruption become rampant. When people are robbed of their savings accumulated through hard work, they lose all confidence in the government. Andrew D. While depicts the impact of inflation on public morale at the time of fiat money inflation in France during the French Revolution as follows: "...with such masses of money and with such uncertainty as to its future value, the ordinary motives for saving and care are diminished, and a loose luxury spreads throughout the country. A still worse out-growth was the increase of speculation and gambling. In the leading French cities now arose a luxury and licence which was a greater evil than the plundering that ministered to it. In the country the gambling spirit spread more and more... Nor was this reckless and corrupt spirit confined to businessmen; it began to break out in official circles, and public men who a few years before, had been thought above all possibility of taint became luxurious, reckless, cynical and finally corrupt."[35]

A severe inflation not only disrupts the economy of the country but also sometimes leads to social and political upheavals. The

35. Andrew D. While, *Flat Money Inflation in France,* pp. 27-28.

hyper-inflation in Germany was one of the important factors which led to the fall of Dr. Cuno's liberal government and coming into power of Hitler. Constantino Bresciani Turroni beautifully describes the social and political consequences of inflation as follows: "The depreciation of the mark of 1914-23, which is the subject of this work, is one of the outstanding episodes in the history of the twentieth century. It was the most colossal thing of its kind in history; and next probably to the Great War itself, it must bear responsibility for many of the political and economic difficulties of our generation. It destroyed the wealth of the more solid elements in German society; and it left behind a moral and economic disequilibrium, apt breading ground for the disasters which have followed. Hitler is the foster-child of the inflation. The financial convulsions of the great depression were, in part at least, the product of the distortions of the system of international borrowing and lending to which its ravages had given rise. If we are to understand correctly the present position of Europe, we must not neglect the study of the great German inflation. If we are to plan for greater stability in the future, we must learn to avoid the mistakes from which it sprang."[36]

ANTI-INFLATIONARY MEASURES

The measures for controlling inflation can be divided into three broad categories: (i) monetary measures, (ii) fiscal measures, and (iii) direct controls and other measures. Since the first two categories of measures have been discussed in detail in chapters on Monetary Policy and Fiscal Policy, we shall make mention of these here very briefly.

Monetary Measures: The central bank of the country can curb inflation by restricting the supply of money and credit with the help of three important weapons available to it *viz.* (i) bank rate policy, (ii) open market operations and (iii) varying the reserve requirements of the member banks. Monetary measures, however, are not very effective in underdeveloped countries lacking a well-developed and integrated money market. In underdeveloped countries, selective credit control is preferable to the general credit control. Care should be taken that the credit control measures do not restrict the supply of credit for development projects.

---

36. Constantino Bresciani, *The Economics of Inflation*, p. 5.

Not to talk of underdeveloped countries, monetary policy has not been very effective in curbing inflation even in advanced countries. Prof. Hansen assigns monetary policy only a secondary role in controlling inflation. It cannot be the primary measure. No doubt, a sufficiently sharp reduction in the supply of money may quickly end an inflation. But stopping an inflationary development simply by reducing the quantity of money may involve dangerous consequences. To cite Hansen, "moderately used, monetary policy courts the failure of ineffectiveness; pushed to the needed fanatical extremes, it courts disaster."[37]

Fiscal Measures: The limitations of monetary measures make it important to make use of fiscal measures to curb inflation. Fiscal measures refer to taxation, government spending and public borrowing. Government should try to mop up through taxation as much purchasing power as possible without adverse effects on incentives to enterprise and invest. In underdeveloped countries, there exists considerable evasion of taxes. Measures should be taken to check this evasion.

Today the government accounts for a considerable portion of the total expenditure. It should cut down all its unnecessary and wasteful expenditure and try to work in the most economical manner.

Private savings have a strong disinflationary effect. The government should take measures to promote private savings. A strong savings drive reduces the spendable incomes of the people without involving harmful effects of the type associated with higher taxation. Further, public debt should be managed in such a manner that the supply of money in the country is controlled. The government should avoid paying back any of its past loans during inflationary periods so as to prevent an increase in the circulation of money.

Voluntary saving schemes may, however, be of limited success, particularly among poor classes who may not be able to avoid the temptation of spending their increased incomes on goods which they could not afford to buy for long. Keynes, therefore, suggested a programme of compulsory saving like "deferred pay" or "forced

37. A.H. Hansen, *Monetary Theory and Fiscal Policy* (New York, 1949), p. 163.

savings" to control inflation. "Deferred pay" implies that a part of the pay of the workers is credited to their savings account and would not be available for spending so long as the inflation lasts. Such compulsory saving schemes are expedient during war-time, or during post-war hyper-inflation, but are not practicable in peace time, particularly in democratic societies.

Direct Controls and Other Measures: Many countries have resorted to price control and rationing for checking a rise in prices, particularly, in case of essential commodities. Rationing and price control, however, have not been very effective in underdeveloped countries because of a lack of competent and honest machinery to administer these. These have often led to the disappearance of goods from the market, black marketing, bribery and corruption. Keynes objects to price control on the ground that it fails to bring about equilibrium between purchasing power and available output.[38] Further, it is also deterimental to the consumer's sovereignty, freedom and welfare. Prof. Kurihara observes that when administrative difficulties in enforcing price control and legal restrictions against black marketing are considered, price control becomes dim by the side of monetary-fiscal policy.[39] Keynes also objects to rationing because it "involves a great deal of waste, both of resources and of enjoyment."[40] Kurihara, however, suggests that "a sensible progress of rationing should aim at diverting consumption from particular articles whose supply is below normal rather than at controlling aggregate consumption."[41]

Measures should be taken to expand the production of necessary goods at the expense of luxury goods because a shortage of the former type of goods raises the prices much more rapidly than a shortage of the latter type of goods.

Control of wages has often been suggested to check a wage-price spiral. During galloping inflation it may be necessary to apply a wage-profit freeze. Control of wages and profits keeps down

38. J.M. Keynes, *How to Pay for the War*, p. 57.
39. Kenneth K. Kurihara, *Monetary Theory and Public Policy* (London, 1956), p. 100.
40. Keynes, *Op. cit.*, pp. 51-54.
41. Kurihara, *Op. cit.*, p. 101.

disposable income and, hence, the level of effective demand for goods and services.

Efforts should be made to obtain as much foreign capital as possible. Investment financed by foreign capital is less inflationary.

In some cases, relaxation of restrictions on imports may lighten inflationary pressures by increasing the supply of essential goods available in the country. Similar effects may be obtained by a curtailment of exports. But increase in imports and curtailment of exports are possible only if the country is having a very easy balance of payments position.

Every effort should be made to increase production. Preference should be given to investment in those projects which start yielding production earlier.

It is now widely believed that inflation can easily be controlled in the initial stages but when it goes beyond a certain stage, it assumes such dimensions that it becomes very difficult to control it. A hyper-inflation, for instance, can be removed only by replacing the old currency by a new currency.

Inflation is a hydra-headed monster and should be fought with many weapons. Dependence on a single measure may not help much in curbing inflation.

DEFINITION OF DEFLATION

Deflation is just the opposite of inflation. It is basically a phenomenon of declining prices. Deflation, according to Prof. Paul Einzig, "is a state of disequilibrium in which a contraction of purchasing power tends to cause, or is the effect of, a decline of the price level."[42] Thus, deflation is that state of declining prices when the output by productive agents is increasing relatively to money income. Deflation arises when the total expenditure of the community falls short of the value of the output at the existing prices. As such, the value of money goes up, and prices fall. But it may be emphasized that each and every decline in prices is not deflation. For instance, when the inflationary spiral is controlled by effective monetary and fiscal measures and, with the increased output and

42. Paul Einzig, *Inflation* (London, 1952), p. 22.

employment, prices start declining, this is not deflation. The process of reversing inflation without creating unemployment or reducing output is known as *disinflation* and not deflation. While deflation results from an insufficiency of effective demand and causes general depression leading to large-scale unemployment, disinflation aims at lowering costs and prices when they are abnormally high. The decline of abnormally high prices as a result of disinflation is desirable because with the decline in prices the level of production and employment does not decline. Deflation, in contrast, is bad for the community because it is a situation in which every decline in prices increases unemployment, reduces output and income of the community. Thus deflation is a situation when prices fall below full employment.

Reflation is defined by Prof. G.D.H. Cole as "inflation deliberately undertaken to relieve depression." It is a moderate degree of inflation which creeps in the economic system when efforts are made to lift it out of the depths of depression. Reflation is a function of full employment. Reflation is a function of full employment to the extent it is a special type of inflation which increases employment along with the rise in prices. Reflationary rise in prices is different from the inflationary rise in prices in that the former is *restorative* while the latter is *destructive*. To cite Prof. Brij Narain, "We might say, that it is reflation up to the point of optimum equilibrium, and *inflation* after that, and that if you go over to the optimum, you have got to have *disinflation* to get back there, and if you go beyond in a downward direction then it is

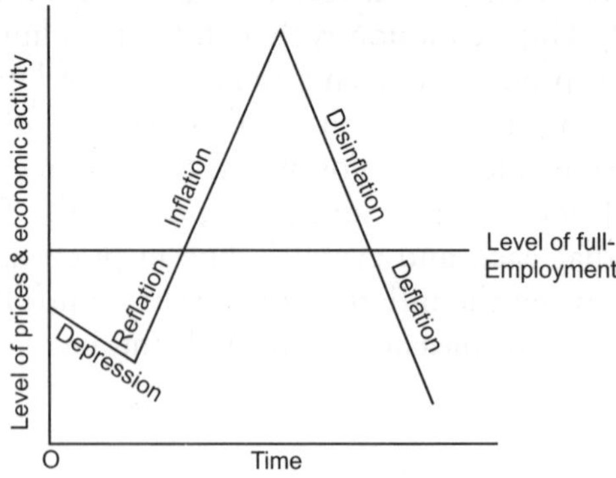

Fig. 15.5

deflation." Diagram 15.5 illustrates the terms reflation, inflation, disinflation and deflation.

EFFECTS OF DEFLATION

Deflation adversely affects the level of production, business activity and employment. During inflation when prices are falling rapidly and costs do not fall correspondingly, producers incur heavy losses and reduce employment and output. This results in a decline in aggregate income and hence in aggregate demand, which leads to a further decline in prices and this process goes on. There develops business pessimism which takes the economy towards depression. The consequences of depression are simply disastrous for the mankind. It not only leads to economic wastes through non-utilisation of productive resources and impairment of their efficiency but also to demoralisation. Unemployment corrupts the people who could otherwise have served the society as respectable working citizens. The unemployed persons become the worst enemies of society and are strong enough to corrode its basic foundations.

Deflation also affects the distribution of wealth and income. It favours consumers because with decline in prices they are able to buy a larger amount of goods and services with the same amount of money. It adversely affects the entrepreneurs and businessmen. While their gross earnings decline, the amount of payment which they have to make to labour and to government in the form of taxes remains unchanged. Some of the plants remain idle for months together because of lack of effective demand. Under these depressing conditions, financially weak business houses go bankrupt. During deflationary periods agriculturists lose because prices of agricultural goods decline much faster than those of manufactured goods. Deflation favours creditors at the cost of debtors because money can now purchase more than what it could when it was lent. It favours rentiers and investors in fixed interest bearing securities. In general, all flexible-income earners gain and all flexible-income earners lose during periods of deflation. During deflationary periods there is inducement for saving but because of the general decline in incomes the ability to save gets reduced. Deflation benefits the middle class at the cost of the richer classes. But its dampening effects on production are bad for the society because they reduce the level of output and employment.

CHOICE BETWEEN INFLATION AND DEFLATION

Both inflation as well deflation are social evils. Both indicate a state of economic disequilibrium. Both cause demoralisation in society. While inflation accentuates inequalities in the distribution of income and wealth by making the rich richer and the poor poorer, deflation hinders the creation of new wealth by causing unemployment and curtailment of production. Thus both inflation and deflation are bad and there is nothing to choose between them. We should try to achieve and maintain stability in the economic system and avoid both inflation and deflation. But if we have to make a choice between two evils, probably deflation is worse than inflation. To cite Keynes, "Inflation is unjust and deflation is inexpedient, of the two, perhaps deflation is the worse."[43] Of the two evils, Keynes preferred inflation to deflation. A mild inflation lubricates the wheels of industry and pushes up the total output but deflation leads to a decline in total output. Though inflation accentuates inequalities in the distribution of income and wealth, it does not reduce the total volume of real income as deflation does. Inflation may be unjust, yet it provides employment to all the factors of production in one way or the other. While under inflation, owing to rise in prices, people do not get enough, under deflation, owing to lack of income and purchasing power, many people do not get at all. It is not so difficult to control inflation as it is to control and check deflation. A mild inflation is generally preferred to a mild deflation because the losses to fixed income groups are generally less than the gains to the rest of the community. Even workers with relatively fixed wages are often better off because of improved employment opportunities and greater take-home pay; and a rise in interest rates on new securities may partly make up any losses to creditors. In deflation, on the other hand, the growing unemployment of labour and capital causes the total of the community's well-being to be less, so those few who gain receive much less benefit than those who lose. As a matter of fact in deep depression, almost everyone—including the creditor who is left with uncollectible debts—is likely to suffer."[44] Though Keynes preferred inflation to deflation, he never meant that inflation was good.

---

43. P.A. Samuelson, *Economics,* p. 302.

44. *Ibid.*

CONTROL OF DEFLATION

Deflation can be checked by raising the volume of effective demand which can be done by encouraging consumption and investment in the economy. Consumption might be stimulated by imposing progressive taxes on the rich and subsidising the poor. The measures to stimulate private investment include reduction in the rate of interest (or the adoption of cheap money policy), provision of tax relief, and of other facilities that might go a long way in improving the marginal efficiency of capital. To supplement private investment, the government may undertake public works programme. During deflationary periods, the government should undertake certain projects so as to provide jobs to the unemployed people. The public works programme should be so designed as does not replace private investment and rather stimulates private investment. For this, it is essential that the government should undertake only big projects (*e.g.* river valley schemes) which are beyond the capacity of private entrepreneurs or projects which are not profitable enough to attract private entrepreneurs. Further, effectiveness of public works policy considerably depends upon the manner in which such works are financed. Public works financed through taxation are less effective in counteracting deflation than those financed through public borrowing or through deficit financing.

Credit Creation and Credit Control

16

CREDIT CREATION

Bankers are not simply dealers in money; if they were so, they would have figured along with other financial institutions. They occupy a special position in the monetary system because of their power to create credit. To cite Sayers, "Banks are not merely purveyors of money, but also, in an important sense, manufacturers of money."

The credit creation is of multiple nature for the banking system, *i.e.*, taking the banking system as a whole a given increase in the cash-base causes increase in the total bank deposits by a certain multiple time. The power of an individual bank to create credit is very much limited. At best, it can create credit which is some fraction of the total original money deposit obtained by it. Its power to lend will be less than the amount of the original or primary deposits received by it from the public because it would have to keep a certain portion of such deposits as vault cash for performing its banking functions.

Process of Credit Creation*:* A bank's demand deposits are considered to be as good as money because every depositor can meet his obligations through cheques drawn on his deposit account. In a modern society, an over-whelming proportion of the total supply of money consists of banks' demand deposits.[1] Thus changes in the volume of bank deposits mean changes in the volume of money available to the community. In other words, creation of bank deposits means creation of money and destruction of bank deposits means destruction of money.

Bank deposits are created in two ways. A bank can create deposits passively against the cash or cheques it receives from its

---

1. In what follows, unless otherwise stated the term 'bank deposits' refers to 'demand deposits'.

customers. Such deposits are known as primary deposits. These have the true character of individual money reserves entrused to the banks to be drawn upon and replenished at the will of their owners. Primary deposits cause an increase in both the banks' assests as well as in their liabilities. In the creation of such deposits the banks play a passive role in determining the size of the deposits; the customers' decisions to deposit cash constitutes the real and active force in the creation of primary deposits. Creation of primary deposits, however, merely transforms the currency money into deposit money and leaves the stock of money available to the community unchanged.

The banks can create deposits actively by creating claims against themselves and in favour of borrowers or sellers of assets or securities acquired by the banks. Such actively created deposits are known as derivative deposits and arise from granting of loans or purchase of securities or assets by the bank. The size of derivative demand deposits is determined by the lending and investing activities of the banks to the extent the banks create such deposits in their books in favour of those to whom they grant loans or from whom they buy securities. When a bank grants a loan to a customer or purchases a security from a seller, normally it does not make payment in cash and opens a deposit account in the name of the customer or the seller for the amount of loan granted or the value of the security purchased; the customer or the seller is authorised to withdraw money from this account by issuing cheques as and when required. It is because of this custom that we have the banking maxim: "Every loan creates a deposit."

A derivative deposit, since it is actively created by the bank, increases the community's ownership of demand deposits without involving any decrease in people's holding of currency. Thus, it increases the total stock of money available to the community. The creation of derivative deposits is identical with what is commonly known as creation of credit by the commercial banks.

The banks generally create derivative deposits on the basis of the strength of primary deposits. Everyday, banks find that some primary deposits are received and some withdrawn. The banks require some cash to meet these withdrawals. But by experience they know that the total volume of cash required to meet these withdrawals is only a fraction of the total primary deposits because all depositors do not come forward at a time to withdraw all the money they have deposited. The banks, therefore, generally follow the practice of keeping cash reserves in what is known as "customary cash reserve ratio." The customary cash reserve ratio may be 10 to 20 per cent or so, depending on various factors. Cash reserves may be kept partly as till money (*i.e.* cash in hand) and partly as the banker's deposits with the central bank.

Now the party accounted with a derivative deposit by a bank will issue cheques out of this deposit to make payments arising out of business transactions; but the payees in these transactions may again deposit these cheques or cash with another bank. Now this other bank has primary deposit on the basis of which the excess over the minimum reserve may in turn create another derivative deposit. This may again go to some other bank as primary deposit and thus the process goes on until ultimately the total volume of credit or derivative deposits created by all banks are a multiple of the initial amount created by the initial bank.

Let us illustrate the process through which the commercial banking system creates a multiple expansion of credit by taking a hypothetical example. Suppose the customary cash reserve ratio observed by the commercial banks is 10 per cent. Now, a person deposits Rs. 10,000 in Bank *A*; the balance sheet of the Bank *A* will be as shown below:

Bank A

Liabilities		*Assets*		
Demand deposits		Cash reserves	...	Rs. 10,000
(Primary) ...	Rs. 10,000	Required reserves	...	Rs. 1,000
		Excess reserves	...	Rs. 9,000

since the reserve ratio is 10 per cent, the bank will keep Rs. 1,000 as cash reserve and creates derivative deposits to the tune of Rs. 9,000 which is the excess reserve. The balance sheet of the bank would then change to:

Bank A

Liabilities		*Assets*		
Demand deposits		Cash reserves	...	Rs. 10,000
(Primary) ...	Rs. 10,000			
Demand deposits				
(Derivative) ...	Rs. 9,000	Loans	...	Rs. 9,000

Now assume that the borrower Mr. *X* pays the cheque of Rs. 9,000 to Mr. *Y* who deposits it in his account in Bank *B*. Its balance sheet would be as shown below:

Bank B

Liabilities		*Assets*		
Demand deposits		Cash reserves	...	Rs. 9,000
(Primary)	.... Rs. 9,000	Required reserves	...	Rs. 900
		Excess reserves	...	Rs. 8,100

The above balance sheet shows that the Bank *B* has excess reserves to the extent of Rs. 8,100. on the basis of which it would create derivative deposits of Rs. 8,100. When Bank *B* expands its loans and deposits to the extent of its reserves, its balance sheet appears as shown below:

Bank B

Liabilities		*Assets*		
Demand deposits (Primary)	... Rs. 9,000	Cash reserves	...	Rs. 9,000
Demand deposits (Derivative)	... Rs. 8,100	Loans	...	Rs. 8,100

Now, assume that the borrower Mr. *Z* pays the amount of Rs. 8,100 to somebody who deposits it in his account in Bank C. Now the balance sheet of Bank C would be as shown below:

Bank C

Liabilities		*Assets*		
Demand deposits		Cash reserves	...	Rs. 8,100
(Primary)	... Rs. 8,100	Required reserves	...	Rs. 810
		Excess reserves	...	Rs. 7,290

The above balance sheet shows that the Bank C has excess reserves to the tune of Rs. 7,290 on the basis of which it can create derivative deposits of Rs. 7,290.

As the process described above continues, every time the liabilities with the banks go on increasing at a diminishing rate. This process will continue to work until all the original Rs. 9,000 excess reserves with the first bank have been distributed among the various banks and have become required reserves. As a result of the operation of this process, the sum total of all liabilities would be ten times the original amount of the primary deposit. The process is summarised below:

Multiple Expansion of Credit

(1)	(2)	(3)	(4)
Bank	*Liabilities (Primary Deposits)* Rs.	*Cash Reserve Requirements* Rs.	*Advances (Derivative Deposits)* Rs.
A	10,000	1,000	9,000
B	9,000	900	8,100
C	8,100	810	7,290
D	7,290	729	6,461
...	...	...	...
...	...	...	...
Total	100,000	10,000	90,000

Algebraically, column (2) = Rs. 10,000 + Rs. 10,000 $\left(\frac{9}{10}\right)$ + Rs. 10,000 $\left(\frac{9}{10}\right)^2$ + Rs. 10,000 $\left(\frac{9}{10}\right)^3$ +....+ Rs. 10,000 $\left(\frac{9}{10}\right)^n$. It is the sum of geometric progression $a + ar + ar^2 + ar^3 + ... + ar^n$, where $n = \infty$ (n tends to infinity) or $a\frac{1}{1-\gamma}$. In our example $\gamma = \frac{9}{10}$ or 90 per cent and a = 10,000. By substituting these values in the formula, we get:

$$\text{Rs. } 10{,}000\left(\frac{1}{1-\frac{9}{10}}\right) = \text{Rs. } 10{,}000 \times \frac{1}{\frac{1}{10}} = \text{Rs. } 10{,}000 \times 10$$

$$= \text{Rs. } 100{,}000$$

The above shows that the value of the deposit multiplier is inversely proportionate to the reserve requirements.

It may be pointed out that the process of deposit or credit expansion comes to an end when no bank has any excess reserves to lend after keeping aside the required reserve against deposits. In other words, the process of creating derivative deposits continues until the additional reserve is distributed among the various banks according to the reserve ratio and diffused.

It may also be pointed out that in this process of multiple expansion of deposits, three parties have been at work: (i) the public by keeping its money in the form of bank deposits; (ii) the banks by keeping only a fraction of their deposits in the form of cash; and

(iii) the borrowers (public or private) who enable the banks to find attractive earning assets to buy with their cash.

ALGEBRIAC TREATMENT FOR CREDIT CREATION

We can determine the amount of credit in two ways: (i) in case of no leakage of cash and (ii) in case of leakage of cash from the banking system.

(i) Case of no Leakage of Cash

Let us assume that initial increase in the cash reserves of the bank be Δa, the minimum legal cash reserves requirement ratio be r where $O<r<1$, an increase in the total deposits be ΔK. The whole process of the multiple credit creation by the banking system can be derived by means of the following equation.

$$\Delta K = \Delta a + (\Delta a - \Delta ar) + (\Delta a - \Delta ar^2) + (\Delta a - \Delta ar^3) + \ldots.+(\Delta a - \Delta ar^{n-1})$$

$$= \Delta a + (1-r)\Delta a + (1-r^2)\Delta a + (1-r^3)\Delta a + \ldots\ldots+(1-r^{n-1})\Delta a \quad \ldots 16.1$$

Here we have assumed that the expansion of credit continues for 'n' periods. The right hand side of the above equation (16.1) is in an geometric progression (G.P.) series. The summation of the above G.P. series is

$$\Delta K = \Delta a \left\{ \frac{1-(1-r)^n}{1-(1-r)} \right\}$$

Where $(1-r)$ is the common ratio and less than one.

As $n \to \infty$ implies $(1-r)^n \to O$

$$\therefore \quad \Delta K = \frac{\Delta a}{1-1+r} = \frac{\Delta a}{r} \quad \ldots 16.2$$

That is, expansion of credit by the bank in case of no leakage of cash

$$= \frac{\text{initial cash reserve}}{\text{minimum cash reserve ratio}}$$

Suppose a commercial bank has cash reserve of Rs. 1000. Minimum reserve ratio is fixed at 10%. At first the bank can lend out Rs. 900 to the borrowers after setting aside 10% as reserves. If there is no leakage of cash from the banking system, the bank can lend again rest Rs. 810 after setting aside 10% as reserves. This process of credit creation would be continuous which no bank in the banking system has cash reserves in excess of the minimum reserve ratio.

The maximum amount of credit will be

Rs. (1000 + 900 + 810 + 729 + ...)

$$= \text{Rs. } 1000 \frac{1-(\frac{9}{10})^n}{1-\frac{9}{10}} \text{ where } n \to \infty$$

= Rs. 1000×10= Rs. 10000

Therefore, the bank can expand credit of Rs. 10000 with initial cash reserve Rs. 1000 when the minimum cash reserve ratio is fixed at 10% with no leakage of cash from the bank.

(ii) Case of Leakage of Cash

Let us assume that

Δa = initial increase in the excess reserve;

ΔK = expansion of credit;

ΔN = part of ΔK which remains in the non-banking system;

ΔD = part of ΔK which is kept in the form of current amount with the commercial banks;

Δa_b = part of excess reserve which remains in banking system;

r = minimum reserve ratio ($O < r < 1$);

C = fraction of new credit which leakes out from the banking system in the form of cash.

We have the following relationship among the variables.

$$\Delta N = C\Delta K \quad ...16.3$$

$$\Delta K = \Delta N + \Delta D \quad ...16.4$$

$$\Delta a = \Delta a_b + \Delta N \quad ...16.5$$

$$\Delta a_b = r.\ \Delta D \quad ...16.6$$

From 16.6, we can write

$$r = \frac{\Delta a_b}{\Delta D} = \frac{\Delta a - \Delta N}{\Delta K - \Delta N} \text{ (From 16.4 and 16.5)}$$

$$\text{or, } r = \frac{\Delta a - C\Delta K}{\Delta K - C\Delta K} \text{ (From 16.3)}$$

or, $r(\Delta K - C\Delta K) = \Delta a - C\Delta K$

or, $r\Delta K - rC\Delta K = \Delta a - C\Delta K$

or, $r\Delta K - rC\Delta K + C\Delta K = \Delta a$

or, $\Delta K(r - rC + C) = \Delta a$

or, $\Delta K\{r + (1-r)C\} = \Delta a$

or, $$\Delta K = \frac{\Delta a}{r + (1-r)C} \qquad ...16.7$$

In this process of expansion of credit, there will be an outflow of cash and every bank should maintain a certain percentage of minimum reserve as deposits in order to meet unforseen circumstances, *i.e.* when outflow of cash will be larger than inflow. When cash reserves exceed the minimum reserves ratio, the bank can lend more even by reducing the rate of interest. When reserves fall short of the acceptable proportions, in this case the bank alters the rate of interest.

DESTRUCTION OF BANK CREDIT

Banks can destroy credit as easily as they create it. They can destroy credit by reducing their loans and investment. The extent of destruction depends upon the prevailing cash-reserve ratio. A reduction of cash below the reserves to support demand deposits results in a multiple contraction of bank credit throughout the banking system. The process of contraction of bank credit is the same as that of expansion, the only difference being that the process works in the reverse direction. It may be pointed out that sometimes the government intervenes directly with the creation and destruction of money by commercial banks. Under normal circumstances, the government need not do so, but under abnormal circumstances, to control inflationary and deflationary situations, the government may have to create or destroy money. It is in this sense that money is described as "a creature of the state." The government may interfere by creating or destroying the legal tender, resorting to printing press, monetary management through treasury, demonetization, etc. Out of the various instruments of creating or destroying money, the choice of any particular instrument depends on the nature of the situation, objectives of the monetary policy, monetary and banking conventions etc.

Limitations on Bank's Power of Credit Creation: The powers of the banking system to create credit are not unlimited and are circumscribed by certain well-defined limits. The important limitations on the powers of the banks to create credit are briefly described below:

Volume of Cash: The power of the banks to create credit is limited by the amount of cash which it can obtain from the public mainly through primary deposits. The larger the volume of the initial cash deposits with the banking system, the larger would be the excess funds and hence the capacity to create credit. To cite Crowther, "The banks' cash is the lever with which the whole gigantic system is manipulated." The volume of cash with the banks depends upon a number of factors like the total quantity of cash money in the country, the banking habits of the people, the rate of interest etc.

Cash Reserve Ratio: We have already seen that credit creation is the reciprocal of the cash reserve ratio. Thus, the higher the percentage of cash reserve ratio to be kept, the smaller will be the relative excess funds and smaller will be the volume of credit creation and *vice versa*. The cash reserve ratio depends on a number of factors like banking laws of the country, depositing and withdrawing habit of the people, the arrangement for accommodation among banks at the time of need, the nature of portfolios etc.

External Drain: An important factor limiting credit expansion is the "external drain." We have seen that commercial banks expand credit by creating demand deposits on the basis of 'excess reserves'. Then some borrowers from these banks are likely to withdraw a part of their deposits in currency. Every rupee that is withdrawn in cash from the banking system lowers the reserves of the banks and thereby restricts their capacity to expand deposits.

Willingness of the Customers to Borrow: The banks cannot create credit unless people are willing to borrow from them. The volume of credit, therefore, is limited by the willingness and needs of the borrowers. In other words, the banks' power to create credit depends upon the nature of business conditions and the state of the economy. For instance, credit creation will be large during prosperity (even if the rate of interest has a tendency to rise) and small during depression (even if the rate of interest has a tendency to decline). During prosperity, people approach banks for credit because of a general wave of optimism and banks are also willing to grant loans because of their faith in the ability of the borrowers to repay the loans. In contrast, during depression people do not approach banks for more credit because of a general wave of pessimism and banks' dwindling faith in their ability to pay. Because of this, the banker has been compared with a man who is prepared to lend his umbrella when the wheather is fine but refuses to do so just when it starts raining.

Supply of Collateral Security: The ability of the banks to lend depends upon the availability of good securities. Every loan made by a bank is secured by some valuable form of wealth, *e.g.*, bills, shares, stocks, etc. "Thus the bank does not create money out of thin air; it transmutes other forms of wealth into money."[2] When a bank creates credit, what it really does is to extend liquidity to holders of illiquid securities. The power of the bank to turn illiquid assets into money, therefore, depends on the volume of such assets or securities with the borrowers. If approved securities are not available, the banks cannot create credit without assuming great risks. To cite Sayers, "The banks put this newly created money into the hands, not of every body at once, but of those individuals who can offer to the bank the kind of asset which the bank thinks attractive."[3]

Banking Habits and Banking System: Growth of the banking system and banking habits among the people is an important factor determining the volume of credit. If people prefer to effect transactions with cash and not with cheques, multiple credit creation by the banks will not be possible. The banking habit among people becomes popular only if there is a developed banking system working on sound lines.

Behaviour of other Member Banks: An individual bank's power to create credit depends upon the policy followed by other member banks in regard to credit creation. No individual bank can prosper when the remaining banking community is in distress. This point is well brought out by Halm: "If an individual bank fails to keep up with the general rate of credit expansion, it will receive more cash

2. G. Crowther, *An Outline of Money* (London, 1958), p. 30.
3. R.S. Sayers, *Modern Banking* (Oxford, 1960), p. 17.

than it loses and it will, therefore, accumulate excess reserves which it will tend to loan out. If an individual bank expands loans or investments more rapidly than other banks, it will lose cash, may not be able to fulfil the reserve requirements and will tend to reduce its loans or investments."[4] Thus an individual bank can neither afford to go ahead nor lag behind the remaining community in regard to credit creation.

Monetary Policy of the Central Bank: The volume of credit creation also depends upon the policy of the central bank of a country. The central bank can regulate the volume of credit through a number of instruments like bank rate, open market operations, compulsory reserves, and margin requirements. In most of the countries, these days, the Central Bank plays an active role in regulating credit. The banking system functions under its direction and control.

CRITICISM OF THE THEORY OF CREDIT CREATION

Dr. Walter Leaf and Dr. Edwin Cannan have strongly objected to the above analysis of credit creation and have contended that banks do not create credit or money at all. They hold the view that it is wrong to say that the initiative in the creation of credit lies with the bank; on the contrary the initiative lies with the depositors whose money is lent by the bank. Banks cannot lend more than what people deposit with them. Walter Leaf, being a practical banker, contended that when a bank creates a deposit, the deposit amount is likely to be withdrawn sooner or later and as such it can lend more than what people have deposited with it. Thus, in real terms, a bank can not expand credits.

Dr. Cannan, in his book *An Economist's Protest*, compares the banking system with a cloak room. Suppose 100 members attend a night club regularly and bring one umbrella each which is deposited at the counter of the club. The counter attendant knows by experience that only 10 members demand umbrellas during an hour, and may rent out the other 90 umbrellas for the duration of the night and make some money. In such a case can it be said that the man at the counter has created 90 umbrellas ? Obviously, not. Similarly, a bank knowing that all depositors do not withdraw their

4. G.N. Halm, *Monetary Theory*, p. 43.

money at the same time, may lend a part of the deposits. But this does not mean that the bank has created credit. "The most abandoned cloak room attendant cannot lend out more umbrellas than have been entrusted to him, and the most reckless banker cannot lend out more money than he has of his own plus what he has of other peoples."[5] "Credit creation" thus is not a proper description of the method by which bank money comes into existence.

To the above objection, Crowther gives two answers, one theoretical and one practical. The theoretical answer is that the practical banker has not carried his analysis for enough. The argument may appear to be valid from the point of view of an individual banker but does not hold when we consider the banking system as a whole. When a bank creates credit, it may go to another bank, which enables it to start creating money further by making loans. In the process a part of the 'created' money would come back to the first bank, which would thus get some of its cash back. But if its original excess fund had come from somewhere outside the banking system it must be expanding the cash reserve of some bank, and until a multiple of new deposits has been created somewhere in the banking system, the cash reserve ratios of these banks on the average will be in excess of their usual figure. The swelling of deposits and the handling of cash back and forth must continue until the extra multiple amount has been 'created'.

On practical side, Crowther points out that the magnitude of bank deposists can be easily understood if we compare them with the quantity of money in circulation and the cash reserves of commercial banks. For example, in November, 1954, the total net deposits of commercial banks in Great Britain were £ 6,500 million. But the amount of money put into circulation was about £ 61,647.7 million, and the cash reserves of the banks were about £ 237 million. Thus, if the banks did not create credit, from where could the excess of £ 6,263 have come ? Obviously, therefore, the banks do create credit in a multiple ratio.

5. Edwin Cannan, *An Economist's Protest*, p. 250.

CREDIT CONTROL

NEED FOR CREDIT CONTROL

Credit plays an important role in a modern economy. The entire financial structure of a modern economy is founded upon the base of the credit system. It is the life-blood of modern business. Although credit is the concomitant of modern economic advancement, it is a delicate weapon the misuse of which can be simply disastrous. Credit, the source of many blessings in a modern economy, unless it is controlled, can also become a source of confusion and danger. In regard to the need for control of credit, De Cock writes, "For many years it has been almost universally accepted that the creation and distribution of credit, under the intricate economic organisation existing in most countries, should be subjected to some form of control. The main reason for this was that credit comes to play a predominant part in the settlement of monetary and business transactions of all kinds, and thus represent a powerful force for good or evil."[6]

METHODS OF CREDIT CONTROL

The major instruments of credit control at the disposal of the central bank can be classified into two categories: (i) quantitative or general and (ii) qualitative or selective. The quantitative or general instruments aim at influencing the total volume of credit in the banking system, without paying special regard to the use to which it is put. The selective or qualitative instruments of credit control, in contrast, aim at influencing the particular use to which credit is put and not the total volume of credit.

Following are the principal instruments of credit control:

1. Discount or Bank Rate.
2. Open Market Operations.
3. Minimum Legal Reserve Ratio.
4. Selective Credit Controls.

We briefly discuss below these various instruments of credit control one by one.

---

6. M.H. De Kock, *Central Banking* (London), p. 135.

BANK RATE POLICY

This instrument has arisen from the central bank's function as a lender of last resort. The bank rate is the rate at which the central bank in order to perform its function as a lender of last resort to commercial banks, discounts the first class or eligible securities. The discount rate policy seeks to influence both the cost and the availability of credit to member banks. The cost is determined by the discount rate charged and the availability depends mainly on the statutory requirements regarding the eligibility of bills for discounting and of advances, as also the maximum period for which the credit is available.

There is a direct and organic type of relationship between bank rate and other money-market interest rates, so that changes in the bank rate are followed by changes in the interest rates of commercial banks for loans and advances. This relationship arises from two conditions: (i) A traditional recognition of the leadership of the central bank by the commercial banks makes them follow the move taken by the central bank. (ii) The central bank, in discharge of its function as a lender of last resort, provides financial accommodation to commercial banks in times of credit stringencies and heavy seasonal strain. Therefore, when it changes the rate of interest it charges for advances, the commercial banks and other financial institutions have to make corresponding changes in their rate of interest.

When the central bank feels that the inflationary conditions in the economy should be curbed, it raises its bank rate which forces the commercial banks to raise their lending rates. This raises the cost of borrowing and thus discourages businessmen from borrowing from the banks either for holding inventories or for making fixed investment. Thus there occurs a contraction in business activity resulting in a decline in the demand for goods and hence in prices. If the inflationary rise in prices had led to an unfavourable balance of payments and loss of gold (under gold standard), this would also be reversed. Similarly, if the economy is suffering from deflation, the bank rate would be reduced and the effects would be quite the opposite of those described above.

Short-term *vs.* Long-term Interest Rates Controversy: Two different views have been expressed by Hawtrey and Keynes in regard to the operation of bank rate and its impact on investment and economic activity *via* changes in the interest rate. Hawtrey is of the view that investment and economic activity are mainly influenced by changes in the short-term rates of interest while Keynes holds the opinion that they are mainly influenced by changes in the long-term rates of interest.

According to Hawtrey movement in the short-term rates of interest, caused by a change in the bank rate, leads to changes in economic activities mainly through their influence on activities of dealers or stock-holders. When the short-term rate of interest rises in the money market as a result of the upward revision of the bank rates traders who generally keep stocks of goods with borrowed money tend to reduce their stocks with a rise in the cost of holding stocks. This leads to a reduction in their orders for goods from producers which compels the later to correspondingly reduce their production. The result is a decline in their investment activity and hence in the volume of employment. This results in a decline in income, consumption and demand in general and further reactions in investment and so on. Thus, by a series of actions and reactions, the economy enters a vicious circle of deflation. In contrast, if the bank rate is lowered, the reverse process takes place.

Hawtrey's view has been criticised on the ground that it attaches undue importance to traders holding stocks and to interest rate as the cost of holding such stocks while it is only one of the several components of the total costs.

Keynes, in contrast, holds the view that the bank rate affects economic activity through its influence on the long-term rates of interest. According to him, a change in the bank rate influences both short-term rates and the long-term rates of the money market because both are related in a security market. Variations in the long-term rates of interest affect the investment market. The volume of investment in fixed capital goods (like factories, machines etc.) depends upon the marginal efficiency of capital in relation to the long-term rate of interest. Marginal efficiency of capital remaining unchanged, the higher the long-term rate of interest, the less attractive becomes any form of new investment or the replacement of existing capital assets. The result is a decline in entrepreneurs' expenditure on the fixed capital goods. As such, the employment in capital goods industry declines and the total money income of the people in general declines. The decline in money income leads to a decline in consumption and in demand and in the general price level. As a result, production and employment in consumer goods industries also fall. Thus Keynes reaches the conclusion that a rise in the long-term rate of interest would lead to an all-round decline in prices and production and in the volume of employment and income. In contrast, if the long-term rates of interest decline, the reverse process would take place.

To conclude, it may be pointed out that the two explanations given above are not mutually exclusive so far as the effects of changes in bank rate on prices and production are concerned. A change in bank rate may cause a change in the holding of goods as well as in the volume of fixed capital goods because it affects both short-term rates and long- term rates of interest, and thus, influences the general economic activity. In short, a change in the bank rate affects the cost of borrowing and thereby influences the volume of credit. The changes in the volume of credit cause, in turn, changes in the various entities of economic activity *viz.* prices, production, employment and income.

Radcliffe Committee's View on the Working of Interest Rate: The Radcliffe Committee Report points out that variations in interest rates can have two types of effect *viz.* (i) the incentive effect and (ii) the general liquidity effect.

The incentive effect refers to changes in the rate of interest influencing the cost of holding stocks of goods whether commodities or capital goods like plant and machinery. When the rate of interest rises as a result of an upward revision of the bank rate, the cost of holding commodities increases and the profit margin declines; this induces merchants to get rid of some of their goods. Similarly, in regard to a project for capital goods, the promoter of the project hesitates to invest when the interest rates rise because the cost of money enters into his capital project over a period of time. He may reduce his project because the cost is rising above the level he can bear. This is the interest incentive effect. It makes the persons take into account the cost of money in holding goods. This is the position so far as the theory is concerned. In actual practice, however, the Radcliffe Committee observes that the cost of money is relatively so small in comparison with other costs of production, in relation to the element of risk in an undertaking, that a change in the cost of money within the margin in which the rate of interest and therefore the cost of borrowing varies, is not so big as to make merchants and investors change their plans. The Radcliffe Committee Report observes from evidence that the nationalised industries in the United Kingdom exhibit the same independence from variations in the interest rates. Their capital development has been decided often by the availability of material or labour, or by the administrative decision but not by the rate of interest. The Committee, however, does find some cases where the rise in interest rates has influenced the plans and projects and borrowings. But such cases were only marginal. In regard to the interest-incentive effect, therefore, the committee concludes that while the effects were real, they were not large or substantial.

The general liquidity effect, on the other hand, pertains not to the behaviour of borrowers but to that of lenders. It refers to the liquidity position of the near-money assets-holders owing to changes in the value of such financial assets as a consequence of variations in the rate of interest on the prices of such assets; there takes place a change in the behaviour of lenders which in turn influences the credit availability in the money market. With a rise in the interest rates, the lenders find that the value of their financial assets has declined and, therefore, they are less ready to realise it and lend more cash to the would-be borrowers. In contrast, if the interest rates decline and the value of their assets rises, the balance sheets appear more healthy and strong, and, therefore, the financial institutions start seeking opportunities for investment and contract lending activities. This is the general liquidity effect of variations in the interest rates.

The Radcliffe Committee observes that from the evidence it appears that the general liquidity effect has a little more weight perhaps than the interest-incentive effect. When considered together, the conclusion would be that while the pressure of interest rates, particularly if spread throughout the whole structure of interest rates (short-term to long-term), is real, is also graded, but not very substantial.

LIMITATIONS OF BANK RATE POLICY

The efficiency of bank rate in controlling credit depends on the *nature* of money market and the *degree of relationship* between bank rate and interest rates of commercial banks. In developed countries like England, the relationship is so close and intimate that any lead given by the central bank by changes in the bank rate is followed by corresponding changes in the money rates of commercial banks. In underdeveloped countries like India, however, there does not exit such a relationship between the bank rate and the interest rates of commercial banks. In such countries, the money market is not well organised and there prevails a wide range and multiplicity of money rates. This makes the bank rate policy ineffective.

The governments in underdeveloped countries frequently resort to deficit financing. This places large amounts of resources at the disposal of the banks which they can use for further credit creation undermining the effectiveness of bank rate.

The effectiveness of the bank rate policy also depends on the psychological reactions of the business community to a change in the bank rate. During a boom period, businessmen may be unduly optimistic and may be willing to borrow even at higher interest rates. Similarly, during depression they may be unduly pessimist and may not be willing to borrow even at lower interest rates. Thus, there is no direct relation between interest rate and investment as assumed under the theory of bank rate policy. No doubt, decisions of businessmen are influenced by interest rates but they are influenced more by business expectations.

If the gap between the interest rate and the discount rate is already sizeable, a small increase in the latter may not cause any readjustment of the former.

Greater rigidities like stability of prices, wages, interests etc. have come to stay in the economic structure of countries. This had reduced the effectiveness of bank rate as an instrument of credit control.

The canons of eligibility for rediscounting bills by the central bank presupposes, in the operation of bank rate policy, a well developed bill market, which does not exist in underdeveloped countries. This weakens the bank rate policy.

An increase in the bank rate increases the interest liabilities of the government. With the increase in bank rate, the rate of interest on public loans has also to be raised correspondingly. In underdeveloped countries, where the governments borrow on a large scale in order to finance the developed programmes, the bank rate policy becomes subservient to the fiscal policy.

While bank rate policy has not been successful in arresting deflationary trends, it has considerably helped in controlling inflation. After the Second World War, it has regained its importance as an instrument of credit control.

OPEN MARKET OPERATIONS

"Open market operations" is another traditional instrument of the central bank to control the volume of bank credit. Open market operations refer to buying and selling of eligible securities by the central bank in the money and capital markets. Transactions in the money market are restricted to those who deal in negotiable instruments falling due within a year. Those who participate in these transactions include the banks, business corporations, various public agencies, the central bank, and specialised financial intermediaries who deal both on their own account and on account of their clients. The instruments traded in this market are generally discountable at the central bank and as such are partial substitutes for high powered money. The transactions in the capital market are restricted to negotiable instruments falling due in a period of one year or more; in fact, some such instruments have no fixed maturity date, *e.g.,* fixed interest perpetuities and equities. The major participants in the capital market include banks, insurance companies, investment trusts, provident funds and specialised financial intermediaries who deal both on their own account as well as on account of their clients. The instruments traded in this market are not generally considered to be substitutes for high-powered money.

The theory of open market operations is quite simple. If the, central bank wants to reduce the volume of credit, it sells eligible securities in the market. Buyers of these securities—insurance companies, commercial banks or individuals—make payments to the central bank by drawing upon their cash deposits in the banks. Since the banks keep deposits with the central bank, payment by the former to the latter results in a decline in the volume of member banks' deposits held with the central bank. Decline in the cash reserves of banks compels them to reduce their loans and advances. In contrast, if the central bank wants to expand the volume of credit it buys approved securities from the market for which it makes the payment by issuing cheques drawn on itself to the individual and institutional sellers of securities. Those who receive the cheques deposit these in their accounts maintained with the commercial banks. This increases the cash reserves of the commercial bank which they can use for supporting additional loans. Thus bank credit is expanded.

LIMITATIONS OF OPEN MARKET OPERATIONS

The successful working of open market operations depends on certain conditions which may not all be present in a country at times. If the required conditions are not present, the operations may fail to attain their purpose. It is essential, for instance, that the central bank should have an adequate amount of the appropriate type of assets. This condition is by and large satisfied today because large amounts of government securities of varying maturities exist in all countries, and a large proportion of these are in the possession of central banks. What is probably more important for comprehensive open market operations is the existence of broad and active markets in short and long-term securities. This requirement is often not met, particularly in underdeveloped countries, where securities markets are limited to only a few types and central bank operations have only a limited scope. If broad and active markets do not exist, the central bank may be hampered by the loss it may incur owing to differences in its buying and selling prices of securities. Since the risk of loss is smaller in short-term securities, the open market operations are often restricted to dealings in short-term securities only.

Another requirement for effective open market operations is that the quantity of money in circulation and the cash reserves of the commercial banks are altered in accordance with the nature and extent of the central banks' open market operations. This requirement is not always met because one or more disturbing factors may be operating simultaneously. For instance, the effect of the purchase of securities by the central bank on the supply of bank cash may be offset partly or fully by the outflow of capital or unfavourable balance of payments or the withdrawal of notes by the public for hoarding purposes. Similarly, the sale of securities may be neutralised by an inflow of capital or dishoarding. Such disturbing factors can sometimes be offset by the central bank by carefully regulating the scale of its operations; but it is difficult to correctly judge the extent of all possible disturbing conditions and sometimes they may be beyond the control of the bank.

The third requirement for effective open market operations is that the commercial banks increase or decrease their loans and investment in accordance with the increase or decrease in their cash reserves, or in other words, that they maintain a rigid cash reserve ratio. This requirement is not always fulfilled. To cite De Kock, "there are many circumstances of a money, economic or political nature which may deter a commercial bank from employing increased cash reserves fully if at all or from contracting credit when its reserves are reduced." Further, in regard to the relation between an increase in cash reserves and the creation of credit, there are certain technical factors which must be taken into account by all banks. For example, unless the entire banking system adopts a policy of credit expansion, the expanding banks would tend to lose a part of their cash reserves to the non-expanding banks which might force them to contract again. In some countries (*e.g.* the United States), the commercial banks keep large amounts of excess reserves. Though the minimum cash ratio is fixed, any cash which the commercial banks come to acquire in excess of that is permitted to pile up without any change in bank deposits. This leaves a considerable range for commercial bank reserves to fall without affecting their deposits. Under such conditions open market operations can not be very effective.

The fourth requirement for effective open market operations is that the scope or demand for bank credit should increase or decrease in accordance with the increase or decrease in the credit base and the lowerwing or raising of money rates. In fact, the volume of credit does not depend only on commercial banks wanting to create more or less of it in accordance with changes in their cash reserves. The demand for credit is not the result of only interest rates. It also depends on the general economic and political conditions. During periods of economic or political uncertainty, businessmen have a tendency not to take risks even if cheap credit is available. Sometimes, the banks may not find an adequate number of creditworthy borrowers or borrowers who want credit for purposes acceptable to banks. Similarly, when money rates rise owing to a decrease in the cash reserves of banks, the demand for credit may continue to be high and there may be no shortage of projects that the banks are willing to finance. Business prospects may be quite bright to encourage investors and speculators to avail of large volumes of bank credit in spite of higher interest rates. Thus disturbing factors may be so strong as to considerably diminish the effectiveness of open market operations.

The fifth requirement for open market operations is that the velocity of circulation of bank deposits and legal tender money remains constant. This requirement, however, is not fulfilled in actual practice. Nor is the velocity of circulation of money and credit always directly controllable as it depends on human reactions and several such other factors. These factors frequently change and as such the velocity of money and bank deposits cannot remain constant. This requirement, however, is not fulfilled in actual practice. Nor is the velocity of circulation of money and credit always directly controllable as it depends on human reactions and several such other factors. These factors frequently change and as such the velocity of money and bank deposits cannot remain constant.

The sale of securities by the central bank may fail to reduce the quantity of money with the banks and the public so long as the possibility of rediscounting leaves the door open to replenish the reserves which are reduced by the open market (sales) operations. Similarly, the expansionist effect of open market (purchases) operations may be offset by the commercial banks by using their increasing primary indebtedness with the central bank.

The disturbing effect of open market operations on the security markets is another factor which should be taken in consideration, particularly in countries having underdeveloped banking systems. Large sales by the central bank lowers the prices of securities which adversely affects the assets of both the central bank and commercial banks, and upsets the government's borrowing programmes. In such a situation, the major job for the central bank is to stabilise the markets for various types of securities and, therefore, the scope for open market operations to control credit is limited.

In spite of the limitations mentioned above, open market operations are an important instrument of credit control, particularly in countries which have well developed and highly active money and capital markets. They constitute a more direct and effective way of controlling credit than bank rate policy. What is important is that the central bank should take quick action as and when required and avoid half-heartedness. To attain better results, the open market operations can be supplemented by other measures. If necessary, the monetary policy can be supported by the fiscal policy. It is, however, generally recognised that the limits within which and the circumstances under which credit can be effectively adjusted for specific purposes can not always be reduced to a rigid formula. This is a matter in which the central bank has to use its discretion, and in which it can profitably be guided by its past experience and current observations. Central banking in this sense is more an art than a science, and its effectiveness depends, more than anything else, on a careful and correct appreciation of the situation.

SUPERIORITY OF OPEN MARKET OPERATIONS

As an instrument of influencing supply of money, open market operations are superior to the bank rate because the initiative lies in the hands of the monetary authority in the case of the former while it rests with the commercial banks in the case of the latter. To cite Balm, "From the standpoint of their strategic value to the central bank, open market operations possess a degree of superiority over rediscount policy because of the fact that the initiative is in the hands of the monetary authority in the case of the former, whereas bank rate policy is passive in the sense that its effectiveness depends on the responses of commercial banks and their customers to changes in bank rates."[7] Thus, open market operations are superior to bank rate because they directly increase or decrease the money supply and show faster and more definite results than the variations in bank rate. Further, they are less harmful than the changes in bank rate to the extent they avoid the difficulties of international flows of capital which are caused by bank rate changes.

Some economists are, however, of the view that open market operations can hardly achieve anything. They can be successful only as a supplement to discount rate policy. Keynes, in contrast, held the view that open market operations undertaken extensively and skilfully can attain the objective without the help of a discount rate policy if they are supplemented by state organisation of investment or, failing this, by compensatory planning or public works. But the general view that prevails is that the open market operations must always be supplementary to the bank rate policy.

---

7. George N. Halm, *Monetary Theory* (Bombay, 1964), p. 59.

RELATION BETWEEN BANK RATE AND OPEN MARKET OPERATIONS

Bank rate policy and open market operations cannot be separated from each other. Each by itself may not be as effective as is desirable. For instance, an upward revision of the bank rate may not always lead to a contraction of credit. The commercial banks may be having surplus funds which they would go on lending at low rates even when the bank rate is raised. The bank rate may thus fail to attain the desired results. In such a situation it will be advisable for the central bank to sell some securities in the market and mop up the surplus funds of the banks. Once the surplus funds of the commercial banks are mopped up, they will be compelled to follow the lead given by central bank and reduce their loans. Similarly, the open market operations, if not backed by suitable changes in the bank rate, may not always be successful. Suppose that in order to control credit, the central bank sells securities, but has not raised its discount rate. Member banks may then replenish their reserves by rediscounting these securities with the central bank since the discount rate is low. Thus the policy of credit control will not be effective. But if the bank rate is also simultaneously raised, the member banks will find it unprofitable to rediscount securities. They would restrict their loans. Thus each of the two weapons may fail to attain the desired results unless it is backed by the other.

Open market operations are these days used to prepare the market for changes in the bank rate as well as to make the bank rate more effective. Before the bank rate is raised, securities are sold in the market to prepare the ground so that the market is compelled to follow the lead given by the central bank. Similarly, when the bank rate fails to have the desired effect, open market operations are used to make it effective. These days, it is being increasingly felt that it is not advisable to use bank rate policy for correcting a temporary maladjustment in the money market. The impact of changes in the bank rate is far reaching, and it should, therefore, be used to correct any permanent disequilibrium in the economic life of the country. Hence the open market operations are finding an increasing favour with the central banking authorities as an instrument of credit control.

CHANGING RESERVE REQUIREMENTS

The instrument arises from the idea that the central bank, in its capacity as a bankers' bank, must hold a part of the cash reserves of commercial banks. At present every commercial bank is required either by law or by custom to keep a certain percentage of its total deposit liabilities with the central bank in the form of minimum legal cash reserves, and the central bank is given statutory power to change these minimum reserves. The central bank can regulate the lending capacity of the member banks with the help of the instrument of minimum reserve requirements. Variations in the reserve requirements reduce or increase the liquidity and consequently the lending capacity of the banks. The ratio of reserves to be kept by the banks with the central bank is raised when a contraction in bank credit is desired and lowered when an expansion in bank credit is considered necessary.

The variable reserve ratio is a powerful instrument which influences the volume of excess reserves with the commercial banks as well as the credit creation multiplier of the banking system. Let us explain this point by taking a hypothetical example. Suppose the commercial banks have Rs. 10 crores of total reserve funds with the central bank and that the legal cash reserve ratio is 10 per cent of the total deposits. If with the existing deposits, the required reserves of the banks are Rs. 2 crores, the excess reserves of Rs. 8 crores will back a tenfold (the multiplier being 10 as the reserve ratio is 10 per cent) increase in deposits, *i.e.*, Rs. 80 crores of credit creation. Now if the reserve ratio is doubled, *i.e.*, it is raised to 20 per cent, the required cash reserves are Rs. 4 crores and the excess reserves would be Rs. 6 crores only. The excess reserves of Rs. 6 crores, the reserve requirements being 20 per cent, would obviously support only a five-fold (the multiplier now being 5) increase in bank deposits, *i.e.*, Rs. 30 crores of credit creation only. Thus, a rise in the reserve ratio would lead to a contraction in credit. Similarly, a lowering of the reserve ratio would lead to an expansion in credit.

The instrument of variable reserve requirements is more effective where open market operations have a limited scope either because the central bank does not possess enough suitable securities or because of the non-existence of broad and active markets in various types of securities. In such a situation, the traditional instruments of changing the cash reserves of banks cannot attain prompt results. Further, the surplus liquidity of banks is an obstacle to central bank's control of credit because the commercial banks can use excess reserves as shock absorbers to any changes resulting from central bank's open market operations. These excess reserves can be reduced by raising the minimum reserve requirements, and once this reduction has been attained, other methods can be more effective. This method, therefore, goes well with other instruments of credit control.

The method of varying reserve requirements is more direct and can attain more prompt results than open market operations. The cash reserves of the banks can be increased or reduced by just a stroke of the pen. A declaration by the central bank that the commercial banks must keep a larger percentage of their deposit liabilities as balances with the central bank than they have been keeping immediately reduces their lending capacity, compelling them to decrease their deposits. The commercial banks can replenish cash by selling some of their securities and this causes a reduction in their deposits. Further, the sale of securities lowers their prices and raises interest rates, which is quite consistent with the policy of the central bank. Similarly, an expansion of credit can be promptly achieved by decreasing the minimum cash reserves to be kept with the central bank.

LIMITATIONS OF VARIABLE RESERVE RATIOS

The method of variable reserve ratios has its limitations, some of which are described below:

When the banks are in possession of large excess reserves, the change in reserves caused by this method may not be very successful. Under these conditions when the reserve ratio is raised, the banks would satisfy the legal minimum reserves but their existing credit creation activities will not be reduced.

The banks do not determine their lending policy on the basis of only their cash reserves. They may determine their credit policy, for instance, on the basis of their foreign funds, or on the basis of the ratios of total advances to deposits. Under these conditions, changes in the reserve ratio may not be very effective.

The volume of credit depends not only on the supply of credit but also on the demand for it. A change in the credit-creating capacity of commercial banks may fail to achieve the desired objective if the demand does not change in the manner central bank wants it to change. During depression, for instance, a lowering of the reserve ratio may fail to bring about an expansion in credit.

Frequent changes in reserve requirements are very disturbing. This method can, therefore, be used only when a large change in credit is necessary on special occasions. It can not be used for frequent and small adjustments in current changes in money supply. It is a somewhat inflexible instrument. To cite De Kock, "While it is a very prompt and effective method of bringing about the desired changes in the available supply of bank cash, it has some technical and psychological limitations which prescribe that it should be used with moderation and discretion and only under obviously abnormal conditions."[8]

This device has been criticised for being discriminatory in nature. Since different banks have different amounts of excess reserves, any change in reserve requirements affects different banks differently. An increase in reserve requirements hits some banks harder than others. It is also discriminatory in the sense that its application is restricted only to commercial banks and non-banking financial intermediaries remain outside its purview. Changes in reserve requirements do not affect non-banking financial intermediaries like development banks, insurance companies, building societies etc. which compete with commercial banks in a way.

This method leads to an adverse psychological reaction. The changes in reserve requirements generate an element of uncertainty for commercial banks. Changes in it are unpredictable and sometimes shocking. Keynes, therefore, warned that the reserve requirements should be changed only in small degrees and after proper notice so that it does not cause a shock.

It is also criticised on the ground that it increases the cost of credit. Since the central bank does not pay any interest to the commercial banks on the fixed minimum deposits which they keep with it, they would be compelled to charge higher interest rates on their loans in order to cover the loss of interest on their deposits with the central bank. This criticism has some validity but maintenance of cash reserves is largely based on the grounds of safety and security and to create public confidence in banking; its use as an instrument of credit control emerges afterwards.

It has been pointed out that changes in reserve requirements are likely to cause a depressing effect on the security market. This is

---

8. M.H. De Kock, *Central Banking* (London), p. 251.

particularly likely when the banks are required to maintain a high cash reserve ratio because they may do that by selling their securities, which would depress the security market. To prevent a decline in security prices in such circumstances, it has been suggested that the central bank should simultaneously pursue an open market purchase policy.

In spite of the limitations mentioned above, the variable reserve ratio is a powerful and useful instrument of credit control. To cite Prof. Sayers, "It is a weapon which should always be placed in the hands of a central bank whose technique is circumscribed by the conditions hindering the effective utilisation of open market operations. Given such power, the central bank can perform useful functions that commercial banks cannot be expected to perform."[9]

SUPPLEMENTARY RESERVE REQUIREMENTS

In some countries, *e.g.*, Belgium, France, Sweden, Norway, the commercial banks are required by law to maintain a prescribed percentage of their deposit liabilities in government securities of specified types and maturities. In some cases, these supplementary reserve requirements can be imposed directly by the central bank, while in others this power is wielded by another body closely associated with the central bank. The objective of such requirements is to restrict the power of banks to convert these assets into cash in order to increase their capacity to expand credit to the private sector. It thus constitutes an important instrument of credit control.

Supplementary reserve requirements can serve as an important weapon for anti-inflationary policy. They reinforce the bank rate policy. But in some cases, their net effect has been to facilitate deficit financing by the government. When the law requires the banks to invest a part of their funds in government securities, it becomes easier for the government to resort to deficit spending. This method of finance, however, keeps public expenditure comparatively free of inflationary effects because to the extent the banks are required to finance government activity, they cannot create credit for the general business purposes. Thus this method can be a useful weapon for a disinflationary monetary policy when strong inflationary pressures have been generated by war, economic development, and other exceptional conditions.

---

9. R.S. Sayers, *Modern Banking* (Oxford, 1960), p. 261.

SELECTIVE CREDIT CONTROL

Selective credit controls are a comparatively recent development in monetary management by the central bank. They are sharply distinguishable from the general instruments of credit control in that they are directed towards particular *uses* of credit and not towards the total volume of credit. A general restriction of the volume of credit is sometimes unnecessary, or may be even harmful for the economy. But credit may be used in substantial volumes for activities which are not useful for the economy. The flow of credit into such activities must be restricted. Similarly, credit may have to be directed towards activities which are considered useful and desirable. For these purposes, central banks, in many countries, use a wide range of selective credit controls, either independently of, or sometimes in combination with, the general controls. These methods, which have a more direct influence on the credit situation, often show better results when they are applied at the appropriate time and in the appropriate manner. Experience shows that their effectiveness is substantially increased when they are used together with other more general methods.

OBJECTIVES OF SELECTIVE CREDIT CONTROL

The major objectives of selective credit control are mentioned below:

(i) To distinguish between essential and non-essential uses of bank credit and to discriminate against non-essential sectors of the economy in bank advances.

(ii) To influence only the sensitive spots of the economy without affecting the entire economy.

(iii) To discourage excessive consumer demand for certain goods resulting from instalment business. The regulation of consumer hire-purchases or instalment buying during inflationary periods constitutes a useful form of credit control.

(iv) To influence the balance of payments position of the country. In giving loans or in rediscounting bills of exchange, favour may be shown to export industries. In order to strengthen the balance of payment position by discouraging imports, the central bank may charge a higher rate of rediscount on import bills than on export bills.

(v) An important objective of selective credit control is to regulate all types of credit, commercial and financial, as against quantitative control which is limited to bank credit only.

TYPES OF SELECTIVE CONTROLS

A number of methods have been used for selective credit control. Some of these are of a dual nature, that is, they can be used both as general instruments and as selective ones. Moral suasion, direct action and publicity, for instance, can be used to control credit generally, but are more appropriately used for regulating its supply for particular purposes. Other methods, *e.g.*, control of instalment credit and of credit for stock market operations, are essentially selective in their effects. We briefly describe below important methods of credit control.

Moral Suasion and Publicity: In many countries, particularly in those having a small number of commercial banks, the central bank considerably relies on moral suasion to attain its objectives. Moral suasion implies persuasion and request made by the central bank to the commercial banks to cooperate with the general monetary policy of the former. The commercial banks are informed of what the central bank considers desirable banking policy at a particular time and are urged to take a particular line of action. Requests, warnings and threats, all may be used to make the banks fall in line with the central bank's policies. Pressure is exerted on individual banks not to lend in amounts and for purposes the central bank considers undesirable, and explanations are sometimes called for certain types of business the banks concerned have been doing. Often the commercial banks are persuaded or requested not to apply for further accommodation from her or not to finance speculative or non-essential activities. Moral suasion is purely informal and has, therefore, no legal force.

Moral suasion can work both as a general weapon and as a selective one. Directives can be given to the commercial banks regarding the general credit policy to be followed by them as well as regarding the supply of credit for particular purposes. They can be requested to limit lending during periods of undue expansion and increase it when contractionist tendencies appear. As an instrument of selective credit control, moral pressure can be exerted to restrict the supply of credit for speculative and non-essential purposes. Supplies of credit for stock market speculation, for instalment buying in respect of durable consumers' goods, and for transactions in real estate sometimes exceed limits considered desirable for the stability of the economy. In such a situation, the central bank can ask the commercial banks to reduce the supply of credit for these purposes.

Moral suasion can also be used for regulating the activities of institutions which normally do not borrow from the central bank, *e.g.*, investment houses, saving banks etc. Such institutions may follow its lead and agree to act on its suggestions about certain policies. This method has, therefore, a broader application than many other methods. But its real effectiveness is in respect of those institutions which borrow from it. The central bank's position as the ultimate source of credit gives importance to its directives. If certain institutions ignore its requests and warnings, it can always resort to direct action and make credit costly and difficult for them.

The central bank in modern times also exerts pressure on the banking system by giving publicity to what it considers to be undesirable in the credit system and what is the right and desirable policy. The central bank regularly publishes a statement of its assets and liabilities, money market and banking conditions and trends, reviews of credit and business conditions and so on. This provides guidelines to banks as to what they are expected to do and not to do. The announcement of a simple objective by the bank can help it to obtain the co-operation of the commercial banks.

Moral suasion can work successfully only in a well-knit money market, with large banking organisations of the branch banking type. When there exists a small number of very large banking concerns, the instructions of the central bank can be easily passed on to the smallest branches and the banks can take prompt action. This method does not work effectively in a banking system consisting of a large number of independent units.

Another weakness of moral suasion is that it is not a reversible weapon. Credit can be more easily contracted with its help than expanded. When credit is to be restricted, the advice of the central bank is readily accepted by the money market, but when it is to be liberalised, the banking system may find it difficult to accept the advice of the central bank. It is not difficult to restrict the supply of credit for unhealthy activities, but when it comes to expanding credit for activities considered desirable by the central bank, the commercial banks may find themselves almost helpless.

This method puts great responsibility on the central bank. The central bank has to decide when a bank is wrongly using its resources and should, therefore, be warned to change its lending policy. The central bank, in effect, assumes the responsibility of managing the affairs of the commercial banks. In some cases, the banks are not prepared to accept its advice as to how to run their business. In other cases, they have a tendency to become irresponsible and throw the blame of all wrong acts on the central bank.

A further weakness of this method is its discriminatory effect on different banking concerns. Some banks are more co-operative than others, and the central bank's directives have a tendency to drive business from the co-operative to the less co-operative banks. Some banks agree to go by the advice of the central bank and as a consequence lose some business. Others ignore central bank's advice and conduct their business as they consider it to be in their interest. Thus they gain business at the cost of those banks which accept the central bank's advice.

Direct Action: Direct action in more than one form has been used by the central bank either as an alternative to discount rate policy or open market operations or together with them. In a wider sense, direct action includes moral suasion also and many economists do not make a distinction between the two. But it would be desirable to make a clear distinction between the two. While moral suasion refers to the use by the central bank of only its moral influences and power of persuasion to regulate their activities, direct action involves taking coercive measures against the erring institutions. The measures may be only the issue of general directions to banks whose lending policy is not in accordance with the maintenance of sound credit conditions or whose borrowings from the central bank are considered to be excessive. The measures may, however, go beyond this, and the central bank may either completely refuse to rediscount for such institutions, or may charge varying penalty rates over and above the official discount rate. When bank credit is misused for speculation in securities, real estate, or commodities, the banks which are supplying excessive credit for such purposes are warned by the central bank, and if the banks concerned do not care for the warning, the central bank may refuse accommodation to them or charge penalty rates.

In centrally planned countries, the central bank is given direct control over the credit operations of the commercial banks. The credit institutions are required to follow the policy laid down by the central bank in making advances and investments. The amounts, the purposes for which loans are to be sanctioned and the interest rate to be charged, are all laid down by the central bank, which itself works under the direct control of the government. Such powers are granted to central banks in many countries during emergencies like war.

Direct action can be used as an effective method of credit control only in countries where the money market consists of the large institutions, each with many branches. Further the banks should also depend on the central institutions for the supply of funds. Rediscount ceilings and penalty rates on accommodation provided by the central bank are meaningful only when the commercial banks require these facilities.

This method involves many other difficulties. The central bank must possess vast information about the credit operations of the banks. It should be able to distinguish between reasonable and unreasonable operations. It should be able to know the use of credit by second, third and fourth parties. But all these conditions are not always present and as such the use of this weapon can lead to undesirable results. Excessive control has a tendency to kill the whole-hearted co-operation of banks. Great care and discretion on the part of the central bank are, therefore, essential when direct action is to be used.

Discussing the difficulties involved in the use of direct control for regulating credit De Kock remarks, "There are, however, several limitations to be reckoned with, namely, the difficulty for both central and commercial banks to make clear-cut distinctions between essential and non-essential industries, productive and unproductive activities, investment and speculation or between legitimate and excessive speculation or consumption; the further difficulty of controlling the ultimate use of credit by second, third or fourth parties, the dangers involved in the division of commercial banks for the soundness of the lending operations of the latter; and the possibility of forefeiting the whole-hearted and active co-operation of the commercial banks as a result of undue control and intervention."[10]

Rationing of Credit: It implies the power of a central bank to allow only a fixed amount of accommodation to member banks by means of rediscount facilities. When the supply of bank credit tends to exceed limits considered desirable by the central bank, and control through other instruments is not likely to be effective, this method can attain good results. Credit rationing may also be used when the total demand for rediscounting is in excess of the amount the central bank is ready to provide. In such a situation, the central bank's resources are distributed according to quotas fixed. In the U.S.S.R. credit rationing by the central bank has become an important factor in general economic policy. In fact, rationing of credit and capital is a logical concomitant of authoritarian planning.[11] It is used by the public authority to divert resources into the desired channels in furtherance of the objectives of planning.

Credit rationing may take two forms: (i) The central bank may fix a ceiling on the aggregate portfolios of commercial banks; loans and advances should not exceed the ceiling, called *variable portfolio ceiling*. (ii) The central bank may fix the minimum ratios which the capital of the commercial banks must bear to the total assets of specific catogeries thereof of the bank. The central bank can change such minimum ratios from time to time. This method is known as *variable capital assets ratio*. These two methods have both quantitative as well as qualitative effects.

Rationing of credit can be an effective method of control in countries where the money market consists of large institutions, each with many branches. Allocation of quotas can be effectively done when the resources of the central bank are to be divided among the few banks. Although his method can attain prompt results and is particularly useful when credit is used for the furtherance of a plan, it involves possibilities of serious inequalities and abuses. The requirements of the bank may not always be proportionate to the quota fixed by the central bank. Further, it involves a degree of regimentation of the banking system which is justified only in a completely planned economy or during periods of

10. M.H. De Kock, *op.cit.*, pp. 228-29.

11. *Ibid.*, p. 238

grave national emergency. In normal conditions, it may create heart-burning and resentment among banks. It is also inconsistent with the function of the central bank as the lender of the last resort.

Security Loan Regulation or Fixation of Margin Requirements. This is a typically American method, needed only in conditions prevailing in the United States. The method aims at regulating the volume of credit provided for purchasing and carrying securities. The Federal Revenue Board is empowered to prescribe rules and regulations for credit to be supplied for these purposes. Rules are laid down in regard to the margins for loans by brokers and bankers to customers. In order to regulate the volume of credit, the margin requirements can be changed from time to time. This method has been used in the United States for controlling the supply of credit for speculative dealings in the stock exchange. In underdeveloped countries, it has been used for regulating loans against certain goods, *e.g.*, grains, the hoarding of which was desired to be discouraged.

The term margin requirement refers to the proportion of the price of securities which banks and brokers are not permitted to lend. The maximum amount of loan which can be given against a security is only a part of the market price at the time the transaction takes place. The difference between the "loan value" and the market value is known as the margin. When the central bank is authorised to change margin requirements on security loans, it is able to control the supply of credit for speculation in the stock market. Stock market speculation has assumed high proportions in the United States; this method of selective control by the central bank has, therefore, become very necessary there.

This is a very effective selective device to regulate the supply of credit in speculative spheres without at the same time restricting the availability or cost of credit in other productive fields like industry, trade, agriculture etc. This method is also useful to check inflation in certain sensitive spots of the economy without affecting the other sectors.

Another distinct advantage of this method is that in practice it can be easily administered because the credit is well defined and enforceable on a number of banks and other dealers. This method will not, however, be effective if there exists scope for leakages of credit to finance security speculation through 'non-purpose' loans to speculators and to unregulated money lenders and several other ways.

Regulation of Consumer Credit: This is another important form of selective credit control which was originally used in the United States as a defence measure. The regulation of consumer credit consists in laying down rules in regard to payments and maximum maturities of instalment credit for the purchase of specified durable consumer goods. Thus this method of selective credit control used two devices, that is, (i) minimum down payments and (ii) maximum period of repayment. Both applied to consumer loans on listed articles. Raising the required down payment has the effect of reducing the demand for credit for this purpose as well as reducing the amount which could be legally supplied for it. Shortening the maximum period of repayment, with increased required instalment payments, has the effect of reducing the demand for such loans and thereby contracting consumer credit.

This is a useful supplementary tool for controlling inflation and maintaining economic stability. The need for this method is particularly strong when incomes are increasing and consumer goods are in short supply. The excessive demand has a tendency to cause inflationary rise in prices. The use of this instrument, in combination with other monetary and fiscal measures, helps in controlling inflationary situations. Similarly, contractionist tendencies can be checked by liberalising the terms of consumer credit. This method operates more directly than others in regulating movement of prices. In many countries, consumer instalment credit has grown so much that it substantially influences the economic activity in general. This method has special importance in such countries.

This method, however, does not have much significance in underdeveloped countries, where consumer credit through instalment payments and hire purchase is not very large. Further, the problems of administration, compliance, and enforcement represent a major task in this method, particularly during peace time when it is difficult to obtain public support for regulation.

LIMITATIONS OF SELECTIVE CREDIT CONTROL

Selective credit control is applicable mainly to commercial banks and thus to bank credit only. Non-banking financial institutions generally remain out of the purview of the central bank and, to that extent, the selective credit control may fail to attain the desired results. The success of selective credit control is also undermined by alternative sources of credit outside the organised money sector, *e.g.*, indigenous money-lenders, black market or unaccounted money with the people etc.

It is very difficult for banks to ensure that the loans given are not used for unintended purposes. The business concerns may use their own money for purposes for which the commercial banks are prohibited to lend and use bank loans to run their normal business for which the banks can provide finance.

Money is not only flat but also round, it has velocity. Thus, money given for a genuine purpose may be used for undesirable purposes in the second round.

Under the selective credit control, there are no restrictions on clean credit. The result is that measures like higher margin requirements can be adjusted by the borrowers through a clean loan. To cite Iengar, "the comparative lack of efficacy of the selective measures by themselves results in the difficulties of securing compliances by banks, when control is imposed after excessive lending has already taken place, or the difficulties of adopting the controls in advances to the future pattern of production, that is to say, of imparting the requisite flexibility in relation to changing credit demands in a system of control which is primarily regulated with reference to a base period or of curbing accumulation of inventories through alternative sources of finance, so long as the initiating cause of speculative wave *viz.*, scarcity of supplies in relation to demand, persists."[12]

12. H.V.R. Iengar, *Monetary Policy and Economic Growth* (Bombay, 1962).

Business Cycles

17

DEFINITION OF BUSINESS CYCLE

A business cycle refers to oscillations in aggregate economic activity, particularly in employment, output and income, prices, profits etc. It may, however, be pointed out that each and every oscillation in economic activity cannot be called a business cycle. Only those oscillations are called business cycle which occur periodically with a certain regularity. A business cycle has been defined differently by different economists. We state below some of the important definitions which throw light on the phenomenon of business cycles.

To cite Prof. Mitchell, "Business cycles are species of fluctuations in the economic activities of organised communities. The adjective 'business' restricts the concept to fluctuations in activities which are systematically conducted on commercial basis. The noun 'cycle' bars out fluctuations which do not occur with a measure of regularity." Thus, according to Prof. Mitchell, a business cycle (i) occurs only in organised communities which are money economies, (ii) refers to fluctuations in business conditions, and (iii) implies regular and periodical changes in economic activity. In the words of Keynes, "A trade cycle is composed of periods of good trade characterised by rising prices and low unemployment percentages altering with periods of bad trade characterised by falling prices and high unemployment percentages." R.A. Gordon defines business cycles more precisely as follows: "Business cycles consist of recurring alternation of expansion and contraction in aggregate economic activity, the alternating movements in each direction being self-reinforcing and pervading virtually all parts of the economy."

FEATURES OF A BUSINESS CYCLE

A business cycle has certain prominent features which clearly distinguish it from other types of fluctuations. Some of these features are briefly described below:

(i) A business cycle is synchronic. The entire business of a country or community is treated as an economic organism. Just as the entire body feels hurt when a limb is hurt, in the same manner when one part of economic or business organisation suffers depression or enjoys prosperity, the rest also experiences the same. Thus when one part of the economy suffers depression or enjoys prosperity, this is transmitted to other parts. Through the mechanism of international trade, booms and depressions in one country are transmitted to other countries and hence its effects are experienced throughout the world.

(ii) A business cycle is a wave-like movement. It is characterised by alternation of expansion (or prosperity) and contraction (or depression) in economic activity. A period of prosperity is followed by a period of depression and conversely.

(iii) Cyclical fluctuations are recurrent in nature. They have tendency to be repetitive. If prosperity is followed by depression, depression will again be followed by renewed prosperity. Thus, business cycles are rhythmic and have a recognised pattern.

(iv) The process of expansion and contraction is of a cumulative self-reinforcing nature. Each upswing or downswing of a cycle is self-reinforcing. It feeds on itself and creates further movement in the same direction. Once started, it persists in a given direction till forces accumulate to reverse the direction.

(v) The business cycle contains self-generating forces which have a tendency to terminate the phase of prosperity or of depression. In other words, there can not be an indefinite depression or an eternal boom period.

(vi) The peak and trough in the business cycle are not symmetrical. The movement from upward to downward is more sudden and violent than the change from downward to upward. The down-turn is sharp and steep. Speaking in statistical terms, the business cycle is relatively narrow at its peak and flatter at its trough.

(vii) Though business cycles are recurrent, they are not periodical. Some cycles are mild and others are severe. Some last for two, three or four years while others last for six or eight or even more years. In some cycles, the upswing is longer than the downswing; in others, the reverse may be the case.

Different cycles resemble each other but are not exactly similar. To cite Prof. A.C. Pigou, "A typical cycle constructed by making, as it were, a composite photograph of all the recorded cycles would not materially differ in form very widely from anyone of them. But this typical cycle is not an exact replica of any individual cycle. The rhythm is rough and imperfect. All the recorded cycles are members of the same family, but among them there are no twins."[1] In the words of Haberler, "Each cycle, each period of prosperity and depression, has its special features which are not present in any, or not in many, others. In a sense, each cycle is an historical individual; each is embedded in a social-economic structure of its own. Technological knowledge, methods of production, degree of capital-intensity, number, quality and age distribution of the population, habits and preferences of consumers, social institutions in the widest sense including the legal framework of society, practice in the matter of interventions of the state and other public bodies in the economic sphere, habits of payment, banking practices and so forth—all these factors change continuously and are not exactly the same in any two cases. It is therefore not at all surprising to find great dissimilarities between cycles in different countries and different periods."[2]

Prices and production generally rise or fall together. Agriculture is an exception, where during the downward phase of business cycle, when prices are declining the agriculturists may tend to produce more to offset the loss resulting from falling prices and thereby to maintain the same level of income.

Total output and employment fluctuate by a larger percentage in durable and capital goods industries than in non-durable and consumer goods industries.

Large changes in total output and employment and in the price level are generally accompanied by large changes in currency, credit and velocity of circulation of money in the same direction.

Prices of manufactures are comparatively rigid while prices of agricultural goods are generally flexible.

---

1. A.C. Pigou, *Industrial Fluctuations*, pp. 15-16.
2. G. Haberler, *Prosperity and Depression*, p. 275.

Profits fluctuate by a much larger percentage than other forms of income.

PHASES OF BUSINESS CYCLES

A business cycle is generally divided into four well-defined and inter-related recurring phases:

1. Prosperity (Boom) phase-expansion or the upswing.
2. Recession phase—the turn from prosperity to depression (or the upper turning point).
3. Depression phase—contraction or downswing.
4. Revival or recovery phase—the turn from depression to prosperity (or lower-turning point).

These four phases and shown in the diagram given below:

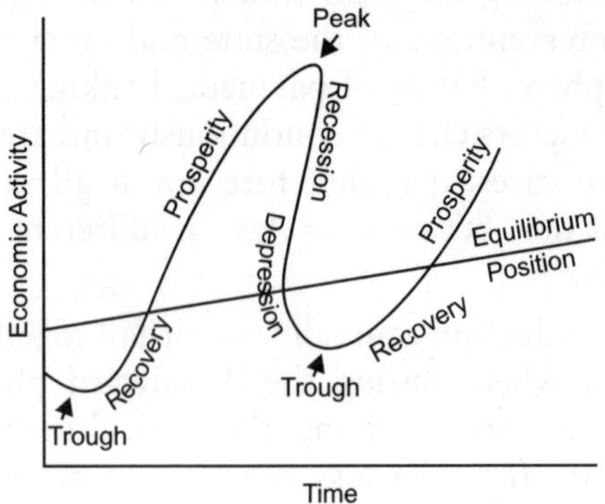

Fig. 17.1

We briefly describe these four phases below, one by one.

Prosperity: Prof. Haberler defines prosperity as "a state of affairs in which the real income consumed, real income produced, and level of employment are high or rising, and there are no idle resources or unemployed workers, or very few of either."[3] The important features of prosperity are: (i) a large volume of production and trade; (ii) a high level of employment and job opportunities enough to permit horizontal as well as vertical mobility; (iii) a rising price level; (iv) a rising structure of interest rates and bullish

3. *Ibid.*, p. 259.

tendency in stock exchanges; (v) a large expansion of credit and borrowing; (vi) a high level of real investment; (vii) a rise in wages and profits and hence a rise in community's income; (viii) overall business optimism; and (ix) operation of the economy at full capacity.

During the prosperity phase the dynamic forces operate in such a way that the expansion becomes cumulative. Rising prices lead to more profits which stimulates entrepreneurs to invest more. There prevails a wave of optimism. Business failures are very few. Inventories are usually large and heavy investment takes place in durable capital goods. New security issues are floated to finance new investment outlays. Every producer is engaged in expansion programme. Increasing rate of investment leads to increase in employment, income and output. Increase in incomes increases the volume of effective demand which further stimulates investment and increases employment. Thus, the expansionary phase is self-reinforcing and cumulative.

The prosperity phase comes to an end when the forces leading to expansion are progressively weakened. Bottlenecks begin to appear at the peak of the prosperity. As the tempo of investment activities countries to increase, a stage is reached when shortage of funds begins to be felt. This leads to a rise in bank's lending rates. Similarly, there appears a shortage of labour and other productive resources, leading to a rise in their prices. All these tendencies raise costs which affect both the consumers and the producers. In order to meet the rising costs, the producers raise prices of their products. Consumers start resisting higher prices which leads to a decline in sales and hence in revenues. The firms make efforts to liquidate their stocks. Though some firms may succeed in liquidating their stock at the same prices, all cannot liquidate their stocks at one and the same time without causing a crash in prices. When prices fall, firm after firm suffers losses. The wave of over-optimism gives place to the wave of over-pessimism. The producers start curtailing their production. Factors of production are thrown out of employment. Surplus funds accumulate with banks. Prices of raw materials fall. Retailers finding their sales declining cancel the orders which they had placed with the wholesalers who, in turn, cancel their orders placed with the manufacturers. Thus prosperity digs its own grave.

Recession: Where prosperity ends recession begins. Recession refers to a turning point rather than a phase. It is relatively for a shorter period of time. It marks the point at which the forces which account for contraction finally outweigh the forces of expansion. The entrepreneurs realise their mistakes and find that many of the ventures started in the rosy anticipations of prosperity are not profitable. This trend in thinking has cumulative effects. Over-optimism of prosperity gives place to over-pessimism characterised by a feeling of hesitation, doubt and fear. Investment is drastically reduced and the production in capital goods industries falls. The banking system and the people in general try to attain greater liquidity which leads to a contraction in credit. There is a general tendency to reduce the scale of operation which leads to an increase in unemployment and a decline in the level of income. Decline in incomes leads to a decrease in aggregate expenditure and hence in the level of effect demand, which, in turn, causes a decline in prices and profits. There is panic in the stock market and the equities continue to remain dull. To cite Prof. Lee, "A recession, once started tends to build upon itself much as forest fire, once under way, tends to create its own draft and given internal impetus to its destructive ability."[4]

Depression: The features of depression are just the reverse of prosperity. According to Professor Haberler, "Depression means a state of affairs in which real income consumed or volume of production per head and the rate of employment are falling or are subnormal in the sense that there are idle resources and unused capacity, especially unused labour."[5] There is a substantial decline in the production of goods and services and in the volume of employment. Though the decline is general throughout the entire economy, it is by no means uniform. Some fields like retail trade are little affected. Others like agriculture show irrational variations owing to weather and the relatively non-commercial nature of the occupation. Reduction is quite substantial in manufacture, mining, construction, and transport, particularly in the fields of capital goods, buildings, machinery and equipment.

In spite of a fall in the output of goods and services, the depression is characterised by a decline in the general price level. In

4. M.W. Lee, *Economic Fluctuations* (Homewood, 1955), p. 42.
5. Haberler, *op. cit.*, p. 259.

the earlier stages, the decline in the general price level may be caused by the liquidation of inventories accumulated during the expansion. As the depression proceeds, it is accompanied by a substantial reduction in the volume of money in actual use. The general decline in activity and the dark prospects of business result in a considerable decline in the volume of bank deposits. Loans are paid off, as far as possible. New loans do not take their place. Neither banks nor businessmen appear to be interested in continuing loans at the old scale. Throughout the economy there is a strong tendency to maintain positions of great liquidity and a strong disinclination to assume risks. The velocity of circulation of money declines. The prices of shares and securities decline substantially in the stock exchange.

The rate of decline in prices is not uniform. Some prices decline much faster than others. Prices of agricultural goods and raw materials fall more than those of manufactured goods. The terms of trade between manufacturers and agriculturists move in favour of the former but owing to low output and employment much of the advantage of the favourable terms of trade is denied to the manufacturing class. The decline is greater in whole-sale prices than in the retail prices. Some prices are held up by custom or by regulation. The unequal changes in the price level distort the price structure, change the distribution of income, which may prolong the depression.

Distortion takes place not only in the price structure but also in cost-price relations. Wages and salaries fall less than the price level. The decline in interest rates, rents, insurance and taxes is very slow. These distortions in cost-price relations transform profits into losses. This generated an atmosphere of pessimism which contributes to inactivity and stagnation.

Distribution of national dividend is also very much distorted. The reward of enterpreneurs—profits—which are the main force behind economic activity falls substantially or even becomes negative. The real wages of those who are able to retain their jobs are high in spite of a decline in money wages because of a greater fall in the prices of wage goods.

In a dynamic economy, depression cannot last for ever. In fact the very forces which caused depression are self-defeating. Since during depression the businessmen postpone replacement of their plant and machinery and consumers postpone the purchase of durable goods, the requirements for replacement and the purchase of durable goods gradually accumulate. This, after some time, causes a moderate increase in the purchases of durable goods by consumers and replacement of plant and machinery by the producers. This calls for increase in production, which in turn leads to increase in employment, income and aggregate effective demand. Banks become anxious to expand credit. Pessimism gives place to optimism and the economic activity gathers momentum. The stage of recovery sets in.

Recovery: Revival or recovery refers to the lower turning point at which the economy undergoes changes from depression to prosperity. During the recovery phase, things are not as bad as they have been during depression. Normally, the recovery begins with the revival of demand for capital goods. In order to meet this increased demand, the investment and employment increase in capital goods industry, which, in turn, leads to arise in incomes. The increase in incomes pushes up the level of effective demand, which, in turn, leads to rise in prices, profits, further investment, employment, and income. Thus, once the expansionary movement starts, the level of employment, output and income starts rising slowly and steadily.

During recovery, stock markets become more sensitive. Bullish tendency prevails in the stock exchange. A rise in the prices of stocks furthers expansion and strengthens revival. The expectations of the entrepreneurs improve and the business optimism grows, which stimulates investment. Bank loans and the demand for credit pick up. The expansionary effect of increasing bank credit is reinforced by the velocity of circulation of money which starts increasing as a consequence of increasing economic activity reflecting in increasing business transactions.

Process of recovery is cumulative. Increased business and factor incomes lead to increased expenditure resulting in further increase in incomes, which again leads to increased expenditure and so on. The wave of recovery once initiated soon begins to feed upon itself. When this happens, revival slowly merges with prosperity and the cycle repeats itself. When this happens, revival slowly merges with prosperity and the cycle repeats itself again.

The period of recovery may differ in strength and in length depending upon the differences in the nature and strength of the forces which initiate them. The forces may be varied in form. Recovery may be initiated, for instance, by innovations or by exploitation of new avenues of investment in new regions, new products and new methods, or by the mere need to replace capital which has depreciated during the inactive period of depression, or by additional expenditure undertaken by the government, etc.

BUSINESS CYCLE A RELIC OF PAST

Some people belive that business cycles are a thing of the past when there was complete *laissez faire*. The world has not experienced regular business cycles after the Second World War. Since the Second World War state intervention has increased in the economic sphere and attainment and maintenance of a high level of employment is considered to be an avowed objective of government in most capitalist countries. There is regulated or controlled capitalism. The government makes economic adjustments with the help of fiscal and monetary instruments. Since the Second World War, the contractions in economic activity have been rare and very mild; similarly, the speculative excesses of previous booms have not taken place. In view of all this, it may probably be thought that the standard business cycle is a relic of the past. In future, the capitalist economies may be free particularly of depression.

This pleasant suggestion, however, is not readily acceptable. No doubt, the governments in capitalist countries have considerably increased their capacity to control economic fluctuations by using anti-cyclical monetary and fiscal measures. If applied forcefully and at the proper time, these measures can prevent the occurrence of both rapid inflation and severe depression. But there is no guarantee that the things would always be managed well. And if the things are not managed properly, the possibility of too rapid expansion followed by a more a less severe depression can not be ruled out. According to A.F. Burns, "Men who wish to serve democracy faithfully must recognise that the roots of business cycles go deep in our economic organisation, that the ability of government to control depressions adequately is not yet assured, that our power of forecasting is limited and that true foresight requires policies for coping with numerous contingencies."[6] Prof. Moore observes that "the business cycle is not dead." The post-war experience with cyclical instability has been "sufficient to demonstrate that business cycle phenomena continue to exert a profound influence upon our economy."[7]

Depressions can be prevented only if a steady and satisfactory rate of economic growth is maintained. But what is a 'satisfactory' rate of growth is a matter of controversy. "It is clear that frequent or severe depressions make for an unsatisfactory rate of growth. Yet a very rapid rate of growth may create its own problems, among them an acceleration of inflationary tendencies and the development of economic maladjustments that will lead to a future depression."[8]

B. TRADE CYCLE THEORIES

The business cycle is a highly complex phenomenon and as such cannot be traced to any single cause. Generally, the business cycles are caused and conditioned by a large number of factors and circumstances. Different writers have given different explanations of trade cycles touching one or more aspects. Since the limited space does not permit discussion of all theories of trade cycles, we examine below only some of the important ones.

PSYCHOLOGICAL THEORY

The psychological theories of business cycle were developed by J.S. Mill, Beveridge, Marshall, Pigou, Lescure and even Keynes. These theories emphasize the role of psychological factors in the generation of business cycles. According to these theories, trade cycles are caused by the psychological behaviour of the entrepreneurs. Mill held the view that emotional factors are far more significant than economic factors in influencing business policy. According to Beveridge, the cyclical fluctuations originate out of the tendency of businessmen to react excessively to the changing conditions of the economy. It is this tendency of excessive reactions which gives rise to alternating periods of over- and under-production causing reversal changes in the economy. Writing in 1909, Lescure—a

6. A.F. Burns, *The Frontiers of Economic Knowledge*, p. 45.
7. G.H. Moore, "The 1957-58 Business Contraction: New Model or Old." *American Economic Review* (May, 1959), pp. 292-307.
8. R.A. Gordon, *Business Fluctuations* (New York, 1961), p. 8.

French economist—put forward the view that the actual cause of the origin of alternately recurring waves of over-production and under-production lies in the fluctuations in the profit expectations of the businessmen. His view is very similar to the view held by Keynes.

The chief architect of the psychological theory of trade cycle is Prof. Pigou, who makes the psychological factors exclusively originating force. According to Prof. Pigou, the sole cause of industrial fluctuations lies in the waves of over-optimism and over-pessimism which overtake the business community. The businessmen are guided by their impulse of optimism and pessimism and their decisions are accordingly affected. During periods of brisk trade and good business, entrepreneurs become over-optimistic and their confidence results into over-production. The confidence of one class of businessmen generates similar feelings among others because enthusiasm and despair are both catching. Both the optimism and despair tend to infect others. The entrepreneurs never bother to study the market conditions. Each one of them is extremely busy in introducing and improving his efficiency only in the expectation of higher profits. When demand and prices have continued for a while to rise, people get accustomed to expecting more and more confidently a further rise of equal or approximately equal extent, or in other words, they project current experience too confidently into the future. This leads to an excessive valuation of capital assets. To cite Keynes, "It is an essential characteristic of the boom that investments which will in fact yield, say 2% in conditions of full employment are made in the expectation of a yield of say 6%, and are valued accordingly."[9] The investments are carried beyond certain limits and it is difficult to find buyers for the products. The result is that the businessmen undergo losses. When they suffer losses, they at once grow pessimistic about the prospects of business and reduce their productive activities. The discovery of errors of optimism gives place to the opposite error of pessimism. To continue the above passage from Keynes, "When disillusion comes, this (optimistic) expectation is replaced by a contrary 'error of pessimism', with the result that investments which would in fact

9. J.M. Keynes, *The General Theory of Employment, Interest and Money* (London, 1936), p. 321.

yield 2% in conditions of full employment are expected to yield less than nothing ; and the resulting collapse of new investment then leads to a state of employment in which the investment, which would have yielded 2% in conditions of full employment, in fact yields less than nothing."[10] Professor Pigou says that "the extent of the revulsion towards pessimistic error, which follows when optimistic error is disclosed, depends, in part, upon, the magnitude of the preceding optimistic error...But it is also affected by what one may call the detonation which accompanies the discovery of a given amount of optimistic error. The detonation is greater or less according to the number and scale of the legal bankruptcies into which the detected error explodes."[11] In short, the theory holds that each phase of the cycle produces a state of psychology which sets into motion the forces that bring about a reversal of the train of responses, which in turn set the stage for another reversal, and so on.

CRITICISM

The theory contains much element of truth. Business conditions are closely influenced by business confidence. But business confidence itself is often the result rather than the cause of business conditions. In addition to business conditions, there are several exogenous factors which influence business community's psychology and the theory does not explain these. Monetary factors reflected in the changes in interest rate may also modify the business psychology.

The theory does not explain why a depression starts and recovery begins. It also does not explain why a boom starts and why confidence revives.

It fails to explain why optimism gives birth to pessimism and why pessimism gives rise to optimism. Thus it fails to explain the sequence of factors which cause alternate periods of prosperity and depression. The theory also does not explain the periodicity of trade cycle.

Schumpeter sharply criticises the theory and holds the view that much reliance cannot be put on it. "And since individual errors cannot convincingly be held to produce big disturbances, unless

---

10. *Ibid.*, p. 322.

11. A.C. Pigou, *Industrial Fluctuations* (London, 1929), p. 94.

they are overwhelmingly one way, we may put our trust in 'waves of optimism and pessimism', a version that was quite common and later on was to appeal to such authorities as Pigou and Harrod. There are many other variations of this theme none of which is entirely devoid of a modest element of truth and all of which are unequal to the burden put upon them."[12]

SAMUELSON'S THEORY OF TRADE CYCLE: MULTIPLIER-ACCELERATOR INTERACTION

According to recent thinking on trade cycle, the magnitude and direction of cyclical fluctuations in income and employment through time are determined by the interaction between the multiplier and the accelerator. The independent operation of the multiplier or the accelerator is not capable of causing cyclical fluctuation. This is the main proposition of Samuelson's theory, which has been taken into account by Hicks in his model of trade cycle. His theory is called Samuelson's Theory of Trade Cycle or Multiplier-Accelerator Interaction.

Prof. Samuelson has successfully demonstrated that when the acceleration principle is 'crossed' with dynamic multiplier process, the movement of income through time and its fluctuation may be shown realistically. The introduction of one period lag both in the accelerator and consumption will generate cyclical movement of income through time.

The acceleration principle states that new induced investment in a given time period depends upon the value of acceleration, say β with the increased in income in time period *t*, i.e.

$$I_t = \beta\,(y_t - y_{t-1})$$

Generally, we assume a linear relationship between I_t and $(Y_t - Y_{t-1})$ where β is called accelerator or the acceleration coefficient and also represents optimum capital-output ratio. If there is a fixed proportionality between capital and output,

then $$\frac{K_t}{Y_t} = \beta \text{ or, } K_t = \beta Y_t$$

Similarly, $$K_{t-1} = \beta Y_{t-1}$$

$$\therefore \quad K_t - K_{t-1} = \beta\,(Y_t - Y_{t-1})$$

12. J.A. Schumpeter, *History of Economic Analysis* (1954), pp. 1133-34.

or, $I_t = \beta (Y_t - Y_{t-1})$

where change in capital stock is called investment.

But the multiplier principle states that any given change in investment affects the income in the subsequent time periods. Furthermore each change in income and output during each one of these following periods will, through the acceleration principle, affects investment in the subsequent periods. Thus over time there will occur an endless series of changes in income and output, consumption and investment as a result of interaction between the multiplier and accelerator.

For the sake of simple demonstration we assume a closed economy, in which there is no government intervention and no output lag, that income at period t may be written as

$$y_t = C_t + I_t \quad \text{...17.1}$$

Let us assume one period lag between income and consumption, so the consumption function in period t may be written as

$$C_t = A + Cy_{t-1} \quad \text{...17.2}$$

where A is autonomous consumption, *i.e.* the level of consumption is independent of the level of income and C is marginal propensity to consume (*MPC*).

Now if we assume induced investment I_t depends on changes in consumption demand only, the acceleration principle may be written as

$$I_t = \beta (C_t - C_{t-1}) \quad \text{...17.3}$$

where β is the accelerator.

Now putting the value of C_t and C_{t-1} in equation (17.3), we get

$$I_t = \beta (A + Cy_{t-1} - A - Cy_{t-2}) \; [\because C_{t-1} = A + Cy_{t-2}]$$

$$= \beta (Cy_{t-1} - Cy_{t-2}) \quad \text{...17.4}$$

Putting the values of C_t and I_t from equations (17.2) and (17.4) respectively in equation (17.1), we get

$$y_t = A + Cy_{t-1} + \beta (Cy_{t-1} - Cy_{t-2})$$

$$= A + Cy_{t-1} + \beta \, Cy_{t-1} - \beta \, Cy_{t-2}$$

$$\therefore \quad y_t = C(1+\beta) \, y_{t-1} - \beta \, Cy_{t-2} + A \quad \text{...17.5}$$

This is the second order linear non-homogeneous difference euqation with constant coefficients. The solution of the above equation and their different values in different time periods indicate the growth and the fluctuations of income.

For the sake of simplicity, we are assuming stationary economy which means

$$y_t = y_{t-1} = y_{t-2} = y_E \qquad \text{...17.6}$$

The equilibrium income level of this model is associated with any given value of A, β and C. Putting the equation (17.6) in equation (17.5), we get

$$y_E = C(1+\beta)\, y_E - \beta\, Cy_E + A$$

$$= Cy_E + \beta\, Cy_E - \beta\, Cy_E + A$$

or, $$y_E = Cy_E + A$$

$$\therefore \quad y_E = \frac{A}{1-C}$$

This is the usual multiplier formulation in a modified form in which equilibrium income equal to autonomous consumption $(A) \times$ multiplier $\frac{1}{1-C}$. It is important note that the acceleration coefficient β is vanished from the expression of equilibrium income. The reason is simple that investment occurs only when income changes; equilibrium income means stable income, therefore, no role exists for the acceleration principle in equilibrium. Samuelson has depicted that changes income and fluctuation over time may follow one of the four alternative path depending on the different pairs of values of C (MPC) and accelerator β. Samuelson's famous diagram is shown in Fig. 17.2.

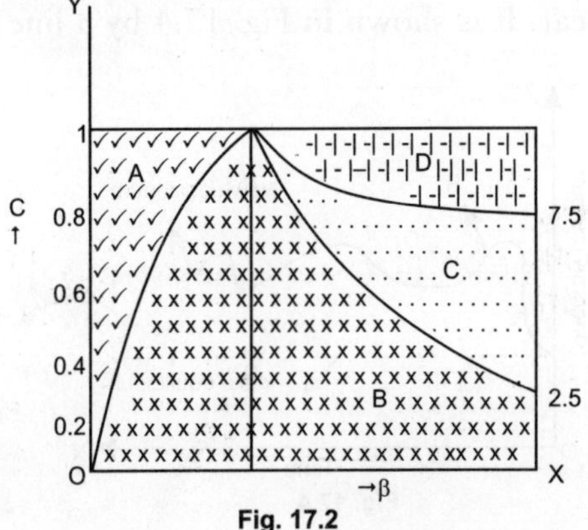

Fig. 17.2

In this Fig. 17.2, marginal propensity to consume (*C*) is measured along *Y*-axis and capital-output ratio, *i.e.* accelerator (β) along *X*-axis. Any point in the quadrant represents a pair of values of the two variables. By taking different combinations of the values of marginal propensity to consume (*C*) and capital-output ratio (β), Samuelson has shown different paths which the economy follows. The four paths of movements depends upon various combinations of the values of marginal propensity to consume (*C*) and capital-output (β).

When the combinations of the value of marginal propensity to consume (*C*) and capital-output ratio (β) lie within the region *A*, the initial equilibrium income moves upward or downward at a decreasing rate and finally reaches a new equilibrium approximated by a monotonic path as shown by a line *A* in Fig. 17.3.

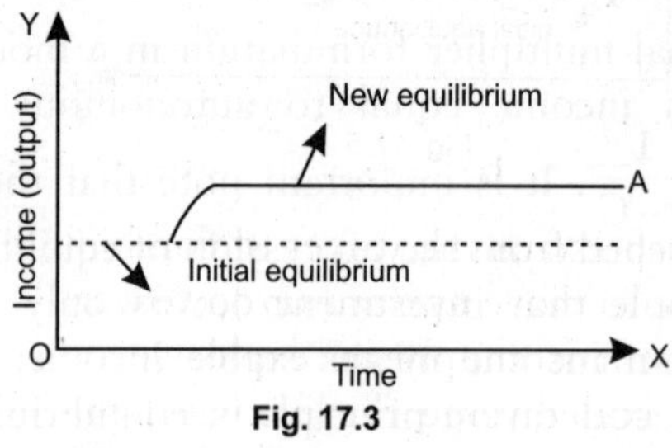

Fig. 17.3

If the values of C and β lie within the region *B*, the change in autonomous investment or autonomous consumption will generate fluctuations in income, the path to equilibrium follows the pattern of a series of damped cycles whose amplitudes go on declining until the cycles disappear. It is shown in Fig. 17.4 by a line *B*.

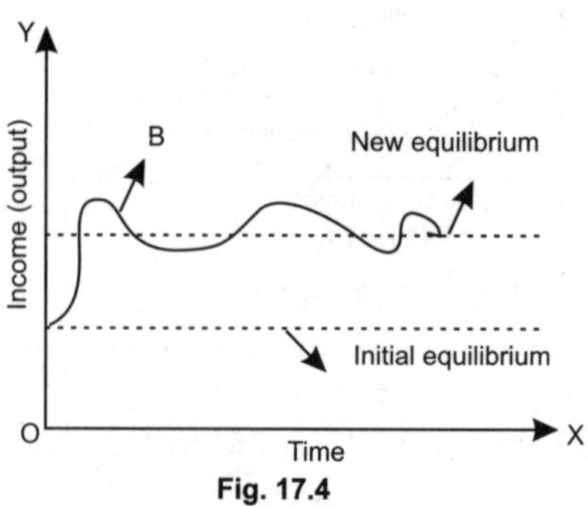

Fig. 17.4

In the region C, the values of combinations of C and β represent relatively higher than those of region B. This region determines such values of C and β which follow a cyclical path with cycles of progressively greater amplitudes. That is, the fluctuations of income with successively greater and greater amplitude. This situation tends to explode and diverges greatly from the equilibrium level. This situation is depicted in Fig. 17.5 by a line C.

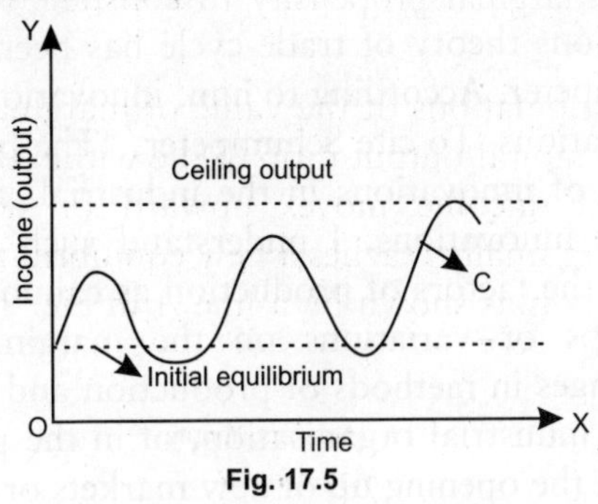

Fig. 17.5

The region D represents the values of combinations of C and β which cause income to move upward or downward at an increasing rate whose movement is simply an explosive one. This situation causes to explode and diverge the income from the equilibrium position by an increasing amount. It is shown in Fig. 17.6 by a line D.

Fig. 17.6

From the figures 17.2, 17.3 and 17.4 we see that region A and B are alike in nature, the level of income, after a disturbance caused by a change in the values of marginal propensity to consume (C) and capital-output ratio (β), come to stable equilibrium in the system. But the values of combinations of C and β falling in the region of C and D cause the level of income great instability with greater divergence from the equilibrium level of income and hence the system tends to explode.

Thus the model offers a simple and logical explanations to the theory of trade cycle. So the economists are greatly attracted to this model.

SCHUMPETER'S INNOVATIONS THEORY

The innovations theory of trade cycle has been formulated by Joseph A. Schumpeter. According to him, innovations are the cause of cyclical fluctuations. To cite Schumpeter, "The booms consist in the carrying out of innovations in the industrial, and commercial organisation. By innovations, I understand such changes of the combinations of the factors of production as cannot be effected by infinitesimal steps or variations on the margin. They consist primarily in changes in methods of production and transportation, or in changes in industrial organisation, of in the production of a new article, or in the opening up of new markets or of new sources of materials. The recurring periods or prosperity of the cyclical movements are the form progress takes in capitalistic society."[13] Schumepeterian innovations should not, however, be confused with inventions. Invention is the discovery of novelties. Innovation is simply the commercial application of new techniques of production, new materials and new methods of organisation and management. Thus the cornerstones of Schumpeter's trade cycle are (i) innovations and (ii) entrepreneurs who introduce innovations. The entrepreneurs have revolutionary attitudes and capacity to take new factor combinations, new methods or techniques, new products, new ideas, and thus they innovate business activity.

The cyclical upswing starts when the innovators begin investment in the commercial application of their ideas. This may start radually when a few leading entrepreneurs with drive make vestment. Once the initiative is taken by a few leaders, others follow in an increasing number and the path gets progressively smoothened for successors by an accumulation of experience and removal of obstacles. The innovating activity is helped by the banking system's readiness to give credit. The 'swarm-like'

13. J.A. Schumpeter, "The Explanation of the Business Cycle", *Economic*, (December, 1927), p. 295.

appearance of entrepreneurial activity raises the demand for productive resources. There being no unemployed resources before the development process starts, competition among entrepreneurs for the existing productive resources will raise their prices. Consequently, money incomes will rise and a positive rate of interest emerge. Detachment of a part of productive resources of the existing firms by new entrepreneurs will lead to a diminution of the output of consumption goods. Demand for consumer goods remaining the same their prices will rise leading to an increase in the revenue of the businessmen.

The innovational activity induces a second economic wave which is superimposed on the primary wave. Additional consumer spending encourages old firms to expand their production. Speculation develops as many people think that a rise in prices and income will continue indefinitely. New borrowing, then, finances not only entrepreneurs but also general expansion which is partly the result of speculative activity. Generally, in terms of quantity, the secondary wave is more important than the primary wave. The secondary wave covers a much wider surface and can be seen more easily. This is one reason why the element of innovation has been so much neglected in the traditional analysis of the business cycles. The primary process is free from cyclical clusters of errors, excess of optimism and pessimism but these have an important place in the secondary wave. This leads to many unproductive loans and over-indebtedness.

During the early stages of the upswing, the composition of total output shifts from consumer to producer goods. But as the new plants start functioning, new commodities flow into the market. Here starts a process of 'creative destruction'. The new commodities cannot be smoothly absorbed into the economic system. There appears a disequilibrium and the process of adjustment begins to take place.

The expansion, however, can not continue indefinitely. In addition to several accidents and incidents, there are two important tendencies inherent in the process of economic expansion which cause a decline in economic activity. Firstly, entrepreneurial activity characteristically starts off in a definite direction and does not distribute itself equally over the whole economy. There are limits to which a particular industry can advance without a corresponding development of other industries. Secondly, innovations disturb the existing equilibrium leading to a constant revision of the values of different elements in the system with a view to adapt to changing temporary situations. It becomes very difficult to estimate costs and receipts. Uncertainty increases the risk of failure of new enterprises. Before embarking on additional innovations, the entrepreneurs tend to wait until the equilibrium is established again. Thus innovational activity ceases not because no more innovations are available but because the economic climate is unfavourable to further innovations. Further, as the innovations start yielding fruit, entrepreneurs repay the loans to banks. Repayment of loans causes deflationary effects. Decline in innovational activity and the repayment of loans by entrepreneurs lower prices and money incomes and thereby intensify the adjustment process. All this, however, is not sufficient to cause a full-fledged depression. It causes only a painful readjustment process or recession and, before long, the economic environments, again, become favourable for further entrepreneurial activity.

It is the cessation of innovational activity on the secondary investment wave which precipitates a full-fledged depression. As seen earlier, a major portion of the investment in the secondary wave is of a speculative nature (*i.e.* investments are based on expected price rises) which would collapse at the slightest impairment of prices. Further, in the secondary wave of prosperity, there develop reckless, fraudulent or otherwise unsuccessful enterprises which cannot stand the test of the adjustment during the recession. Consequently, as soon as the prices begin to fall, a part of the debt structure crumbles. This would not necessarily lead to panic or crises. But when the prices begin to fall, there takes place a vicious spiral. Prices fall simply because they have fallen. Fall in prices enforces liquidation which in turn again leads to a further fall in prices. People begin to wonder as to how much there is to liquidate. They even go into hysterics about it. This pessimistic expectation may for a time acquire a causal role. Thus there occurs a vicious spiral of falling prices and contraction. Under the pressure of the breakdown of the secondary wave and of the bearish anticipation induced by it, the process out-runs and misses the neighbourhood of the equilibrium to which it was moving and the abnormal liquidation leads to the conditions of depression.

When the depression has run its course, the system tends to work its way towards a new neighbourhood of equilibrium. This new neighbourhood of equilibrium is not the same which would have been reached in the absence of abnormal liquidation. Firstly, abnormal liquidation destroys many things which could and would have survived without it and thus produces a pattern different from that which would have evolved under a normal process. Secondly, depression may take considerable period of time. During this period economic data changes and what would have been a neighbourhood of equilibrium when the depression started is no longer one when all is over. The process from depression to new neighbour of equilibrium is known as Recovery.

It can be shown that depressive process has a tendency to stop itself. As seen earlier, the spiral process occurs because of a number of unfavourable individual events like bankruptcies, breaks in individual markets, shutdowns etc. These induce similar events but each of them taken by itself loses momentum as its effects spread. Further, certain firms go bankrupt and close down creating possibilities for others to expand. Schumpeter calls it depression business. This spells not only actual and potential losses but also actual and potential gains. These tendencies lead to petering out of spiral.

Though it can be shown that a restrictive tendency will develop to contract the spiral, it cannot be proved that it will invariably succeed in breaking it. "....we must recognise the possibility of a system so conditioned and of a spiral so violent that tendency may fight a loosing battle at any given moment and that, theoretically, the system may never conquer the breathing space in which it would recover itself."[14] In such cases, help outside the economic system is necessary for bringing out recovery. Once the equilibrium is restored, the stage is set for a new wave of innovation and a repetition of a cycle.

CRITICISM

Schumpeter's theory of business cycles suffers from several drawbacks. In the first place, his theory is highly institutional. For its validity, it requires the existence of a typical institutional

14. Joseph A. Schumpter, *Business Cycles* (New York, 1939), p. 15.

framework of the society. Secondly, it overemphasizese the importance of innovations in generating business cycles. In fact, innovations are only one among the many factors causing business cycles. Thirdly, it overstresses the role of bank credit by maintaining that innovations are financed solely by means of bank credit. In fact, they may be financed out of voluntary savings. In short, Schumpeter's innovation theory fails to provide an adequate explanation of the phenomenon of business cycles.

UNDERCONSUMPTION (OR OVERSAVING) THEORY

This theory is the oldest explanation of the cyclical fluctuations. The crises which appeared in the nineteenth century were explained in terms of deficiency of effective demand resulting from the failure of consumption to keep pace with increasing production that was made possible by industrial revolution. Malthus had rejected the validity of Say's Law and Sismondi had found the cause of crises in the low consumption of the workmen which was owing to low wages. Thus the lack of adequate purchasing power with workers by causing accumulation of goods led to fall in prices with subsequent unemployment and, eventually a crisis. Sismondi's explanation was borrowed by Karl Marx to explain that crises were inevitable in a capitalistic system of society.

Though explanations of crises were given by Malthus, Sismondi, Lauderdale, Marx and other early writers, it was Hobson who made a sharp departure from the Say-Ricardo mill thesis which held that there could not occur general overproduction or general unemployment. In *The Physiology of Industry* which was published in 1819 and of which Hobson was co-author with A.F. Mummery, he severely criticised the orthodox theory which held that a general glut cannot take place. In the preface to the book the authors state that the purpose of this book was, "to show that...an undue amount of saving is possible (that it) impoverishes the community, throws labourers out of work, drives down wages, and spreads the gloom and frustrations through the commercial world which is known as Depression in Trade..."

In this latter work entitled *The Problem of the Unemployed* published in 1896, Hobson presents a complete explanation of the business cycle. Criticising the Say-Ricardo-Mill thesis, Hobson states that although "bad trade appears as a general lowness of prices and profits, but regarded as a disease of the industrial structure it takes the shape of a general slackness or under-use of the various factors of production."[15]

Hobson dubbs the view that overproduction in one sector reflects underproduction in the other sectors of the economy as unrealistic and an imagination of the minds of Ricardo and his followers. He points out that the problem is of explaining the existence of the simultaneous surplus (or deficiencies) in all sectors of the economy. He states, "All avenues of sound investment are already occupied. In trade after trade it has been made manifest that the capacity of production is far in advance of the current or expected demand at a profitable price."

Criticising Say's law of market—which holds that there can be no general overproduction because every supply creates its own demand—Hobson points that many individuals produce more than they require for their consumption. This leads them not to match their individual share of total demand for production with their individual share of total supply of production. In a money economy, it is possible for one to be a seller of goods without simultaneously and to an equal extent being a buyer of goods. The act of creating the supply (selling) gives the supplier the power to create demand (buying) but this does not necessarily mean that the owners of the power will use it in entirely by consuming as much of goods as they have produced. In other words, demand and need not necessarily be equal to supply and hence some saving can take place.

According to Hobson, the trade depression occurs due to 'over-saving'. The modern society is characterised by great inequalities of income and a large portion of the total wealth is owned by a small class. During the course of economic prosperity profiteers share larger part of increased income than the wage-earners. This increases inequalities. The large income recipients, however, consume only a portion of their income and save the rest. This savings in the economy increases. The wealthy businessmen continuously invest their savings in productive enterprises. The increase in investment leads to an increase in the total production capacity of the economy. This causes an increase in the volume of goods available for consumption for which the effective demand is inadequate at the prevailing prices. As a result, there appears a general glut of goods

15. J.A. Hobson, *The Problem of the Unemployed* (1896), p. 59.

in the market. These goods can be disposed of only at the reduced prices. A decline in the prices of goods results in a considerable decline in entrepreneurs' incomes and purchasing power. This further depresses the economy. Thus Hobson explains that business cycles are caused by the phenomenon of under consumption.

Though Hobson fails to put his theory on a high theoretical level and all his arguments are not convincing, yet his explanations go very near the recent rigorous analysis done by Evsey D. Domar, R. F. Harrod and other builders of growth models, who lay down the condition necessary for the equilibrium rate of growth. In fact, Domar praises Hobson for his keen observation of the problem and considers him superior to Keynes to the extent he clearly visualises that any increase in investment would increase the productive capacity of the society. While in Keynes' view it is enough for equilibrium if savings are invested, but according to Hobson, unless consumption continues to grow at a rate fast enough to absorb the additional productive capacity, the mere fact of savings being invested would not ensure full employment equilibrium. To cite Domar, "Even though both Keynes and Hobson were students of unemployment, they actually addressed themselves to two different problems. Keynes analysed that happens when savings (of the preceding period) arc not invested. The answer was unemployment, but the statement of the problem in this for.n might easily give the erroneous impression that if savings were invested, full employment would be assured. Hobson, on the other other hand, went a step further and stated the problem in this form: Suppose savings are invested, will the new plants be able to dispose of their products ? Such a statement of the problem was not all, as Keynes thought, a mistake. It was statement of a different, and possibly also a deeper, problem. Hobson was fully armed with the σ[16] effect of investment, and he saw that it could be answered only by growth. His weakness lay in a poor perception of the multiplier effect and his analysis lacked vigour in general. He gave a demonstration rather than a proof. But the problem to which he addressed himself is just as alive to today as it was fifty and twenty years ago."[17]

16. The Greek letter σ (sigma) indicates the increase in the productive capacity of the economy which results from each rupee invested. It is the ratio of output to capital.

17. E.D. Domar, *Essays in the Theory of Growth* (1957), p. 104.

CRITICISM

The theory explains only the upper turning-point from prosperity to depression. It does not say anything about recovery. Critics have further pointed out that the tendency to under-cunsumption or over-saving by itself can only explain the under-employment equilibrium and not the business cycles. Even as an explanation of depression, it is defective. There is no reason why the business class would continuously go on saving.

The theory assumes that the amount saved would automatically be invested. But this is not always true. In fact, savings would be invested only if there is a prospect of earning profits thereby.

According to the theory, depression appears because more consumers' goods have been produced than can be sold. We should expect, therefore, that the first sign of depression would be a decline in the prices of consumer goods. But empirical evidence shows that depression in its first phase is characterised by a decline in the prices of producer goods and prices of consumer goods generally decline last of all.

HAWTREY'S THEORY

According to Professor, R.G. Hawtrey the trade cycle is a purely momentary phenomenon. Certain non-monetary factors like wars, earthquakes, strikes, crop failures etc. may cause a partial and temporary depression in particular sectors of the economy but they can not cause a full and permanent depression involving general unemployment of the factors of production in the form of trade cycle. In contrast, changes in the flow of the money are exclusive and sufficient cause of the changes in the economic activity, of the alteration of prosperity and depression and of good and bad trade. The upward phase of the trade cycle is caused by an expansion of money and bank credit and also by an increase in the velocity of circulation of money supply. Similarly, the downward phase of the trade cycle results from a contraction in the supply of money and bank credit, and a decline in the velocity of circulation of money. Cyclical fluctuations are caused by factors which produce expansions and contractions in money's circular flow. The fluctuation in the income-expenditure flow are caused by changes in the supply of bank credit.

According to Hawtrey, business cycle is a small scale replica of an outright money inflation and deflation. The upswing of the trade cycle is caused by an expansion of credit and continues so long as the credit expansion goes on or, at least, is not followed by credit contraction. Expansion of bank credit causes a decline in the rate of interest and induces the banks to grant loans on more liberal terms, which induces merchants to increase their inventory holdings. The result is that they begin to place large orders with the manufacturers who, in order to execute the orders, expand production by employing more resources into production. This increases the demand for factors of production and hence higher income and employment which causes a further increase in the demand for goods. In course of time, cumulative trend is set into motion. As the volume of business expands and factors of production are fully employed, the prices further increase and induce further upward expansion, which leads to inflationary conditions or boom conditions.

The prosperity phase, however, is not without limits. According to Hawtrey, prosperity comes to an end when credit expansion ends. As the banks go on increasing credit, their cash reserves decline and they are compelled to reduce credit and raise interest rates in order to discourage the demand for new loans. The contraction of credit exerts a deflationary pressure on prices and profits, on consumers' income and outlay. The rise in interest rates charged by banks discourages traders to hold large stocks and their demand for credit decreases. Prices and profit start declining. This leads the traders to further reduce stocks and stop ordering goods. Consequently, producers curtail their output and employment. The incomes of the factors of production decline. When consumers' income and outlay decreases, effective demand decreases, stocks and output decreases, prices decline and profits decline and so on. Thus there develops a cumulative downswing. In short, it is the shrinkage of effective demand reflected in reduced outlay by consumers and increased holding of cash balances in view of growing credit contraction which causes a vicious circle of deflation leading to severe depression.

During depression, as traders experience slackness in the demand for their goods, they try to dispose of goods at whatever price they fetch and repay bank's loans. When loans are repaid, money gradually flows from circulation into reserves of banks. As depression continues, banks will have more and more idle funds. The credit creating capacity of banks increases and, in order to stimulate borrowing, they lower their interest rates. This would encourage traders to increase their inventories and the whole process of expansion will be once again set into motion.

Hawtrey does not deny that non-monetary factors (like inventions, bumper crops etc.) may influence productive activity but believes that their effects will be synchronised only with the monetary effects. Non-monetary causes have no periodicity; the periodicity which appears in business cycles is owing to monetary effects and can be overcome with the help of a suitable monetary policy. Hawtrey is of the view that it is only the flexibility and inherent instability of bank credit which seizes on fluctuations in business and turns them to rhythmic changes. If instability of bank credit is eliminated by a suitable banking policy, the cycles would disappear.

CRITICAL APPRAISAL

That an expansion of business activity is sometimes caused by an expansion of credit cannot be denied. Expansion of credit is very necessary for the development of the boom. Trade cycles are mainly caused by non-monetary factors. Monetary influences may make a boom possible and change the amplitude of fluctuations of the business cycle.

No doubt, the banking system plays an important role in financing trade activities, but it would be wrong to say that banks cause business cycles. Borrowing and investment are not determined by the interest rate alone as believed by Hawtrey. A high rate of interest will not deter borrowing for investment if the profit prospects are very good. Similarly, a low rate of interest may not induce people to borrow if profit prospects are dark. To cite Haberler, "His (Hawtrey's) contention that reasons for the breakdown of the boom is always monetary one and that the prosperity could be prolonged and depression stayed off indefinitely, if the money supply were inexhaustible, would certainly be challenged by most economists."

Hawtrey exaggerates the importance of wholesalers, leaving capital goods industries and other parts of the economy in an insignificant position.

It is not necessary that the wholesalers hold stocks only with funds borrowed from banks. They may finance their inventories largely with their own capital rather than by borrowing. In cases where they finance their inventories with their own capital and reinvested earnings, they may not respond to changes in the interest rates as much as they would when they mainly depend on borrowed funds.

The wholesalers' decisions about their inventories are generally governed by the factors like the expectations about price changes, cost of storage etc. rather than by changes in interest. Thus Hawtrey's assumption of decisions being sensitive to changes in interest rate is open to question.

In Hawtrey's theory, changes in inventories are the sole initiator of the cumulative movement in the economic activity. But, in actual practice, changes in inventory investments are not capable of producing major cycles; they can produce at the most minor cycle. And minor cycles cannot be considered as business cycles.

Some economists have pointed out that monetary inflation and deflation are not the causes as believed by Hawtrey, but the result of business cycles. In fact, credit expansion follows business expansion, and once it takes place, it accentuates the rate of business activity. Similarly, monetary deflation is preceded by business contraction.

According to Hawtrey, a rise in the rate of interest acts as the turning point from boom to depression. The general experience, however, shows that a rise in the rate of interest occurs after the crisis and not before it. This happens because the crisis produces a collapse of credit. Thus, change in the rate of interest is not generally a cause of the crisis but a consequence of it.

The initiating role assigned by Hawtrey to the monetary system is obviously questionable. Actual experience shows that expansionary movements are not likely to arise simply as a result of easy money policy (*i.e.,* increase in the supply of money). In fact, many a times the money supply adjusts itself to the changing conditions resulting from non-monetary causes.

It would be taking a too narrow view of business cycles to assume that business cycle are a purely monetary phenomenon. Hawtrey, however, realises this in his recent writings when he states, "The monetary theory offers an explanation of one important class of economic disorders, and indicates the remedy for them. It does not mean that a community perfectly free from monetary fluctuations would have no economic disorders at all." It may be concluded that expansion and contraction of bank credit can be a supplementary cause but not the main and sole cause of business cycle.

MONETARY OVER-INVESTMENT THEORY

Hawtrey's purely monetary theory of trade cycle, as we have seen, views cycles as a product of the breakdown in the monetary system owing to inherent instability of bank credit. In the same manner, the monetary over-investment theory also traces the ultimate cause of cycles in the instability of credit system but holds that the real problem is a breakdown in the production system than in the monetary system. Unlike Hawtrey's theory it traces the consequences of changes in money supply not through changes in the volume of real investment, *i.e.,* the sale and production of capital goods. The best known exponent of the monetary over-investment theory is the Austrian-economist, F.A. Hayek.

Broadly speaking, Hayek's theory centres on the analysis of equilibrium between production of capital goods and consumption goods. When the structure of production is in equilibrium, the production of capital goods and consumption goods takes place in precisely the same proportion as the distribution of monetary demand by consumers between consumption and saving. In Hayek's view, cyclical fluctuations are the results of the shortening and the lengthening of the process of production which are caused by an expansion of money supply leading the market rate of interest to decline below the natural or equilibrium rate of interest. A decline in interest rate brings about changes in the structure of production.

During depression, which is caused by the shortening of the structure of production, the market rate of interest declines below the natural rate of interest owing to banks' increasing the supply of money in excess of the supply of voluntary or real savings.[18] This leads to a sudden spurt in the investment activity. There takes place

18. The equilibrium or natural rate of interest is the rate of interest at which the demand for loanable funds just equals the supply of voluntary savings. And the market rate of interest is that which prevails in the market and is determined by the supply of and demand for money.

investment which could not have occurred had not the market rate of interest declined below the equilibrium rate of interest. Thus, monetary investment tends to exceed real savings, the difference being financed by the new bank credit. The increase in investment lengthens the process of production. Hayek believes that this lengthening of the process of production not financed by voluntary savings cannot be sustained and must necessarily be followed by shrinkage in the structure of production which must cause depression. In other words, boom brought about by an increase in the money supply by the banks must cause in turn depression because the boom can continue only so long as the market rate of interest continues to remain below the natural rate of interest and this cannot continue permanently because banks cannot increase the supply of money indefinitely. The question arises: How does an increase in the supply of money which initially brings about a boom by inducing the entrepreneurs to lengthen the process of production ultimately ends in depression by compelling them to shorten the process of production?

The banks may cause an increase in the supply of money in two ways—it may be made available either to the entrepreneurs through whom it ultimately reaches the consumers in the form of incomes of factor owners or it may be made available directly to the consumers. Whatever way is adopted, the ultimate outcome would be the same. When the increased money supply is made available to the entrepreneurs by lowering the market rate of interest, they increase their investment. Increase in investment lengthens the process of production. As a result, the demand for capital goods rises relatively to prices and profits of consumer goods. This leads to a diversion of resources from consumer goods industries to capital goods industries. The result is that consumer goods industries starve for want of resources and hence the supply of these goods declines. On the other hand, when incomes of workers employed in capital goods industries increases, their demand for consumption goods is increased. When the supply of consumer goods fall short of the demand for these, the prices of consumer goods rise. Thus the profits in consumer goods industries rise and attract producers' attention. The consumer goods industries start competing with the capital goods industries for obtaining resources. This competition bids up factor prices. The costs in capital goods industries rise and consequently profit margins decline. In the meantime, the banking system decides to reduce the rate of credit expansion. Consequently, the market rate of interest rises above the equilibrium rate. This leads to a decline in investments. In view of shortage of capital, producers try to substitute labour for capital. In other words, they try to produce more consumer goods by shortening the process of production. Ultimately, the recession begins leading to depression.

If the increased money supply is made available to the consumers directly, there would occur an increase in the demand for consumer goods in relation to the demand for producer goods. The result would be a rise in the prices of goods of the lower order in relation to the prices of goods of the higher order. This would encourage producers of consumer goods to produce more consumer goods by making increasing use of those methods of production which yield quick results in terms of output, though these methods might not be the most efficient ones. Thus the process of production would be shortened leading to depression.

It may be pointed out that in Hayek's theory it is the shortage of savings (or capital funds) that brings the boom to an end. When the expansion of credit stops, a decline in investments financed through credit becomes inevitable unless there is a sufficiently large volume of savings which constitutes capital funds. Since the savings do not take place in a sufficiently large volume, there occurs a shortage of capital funds. Interest rates rise, investment falls and the downswing begins. Thus, the monetary over-investment theory is also known as the shortage of capital theory of business cycles.

In Hayek's analysis, the business cycles are caused by failure of the banking system to keep the supply of money neutral. The appropriate remedy to eliminate business cycles is, therefore, to follow 'natural money policy'. To keep the money neutral, Hayek suggested that the supply of money should be kept constant except for such increases or decreases as may be necessary to offset changes in the velocity of money and to offset these changes in the coefficient of money transactions which may be owing to such reasons as the amalgamation of firms.

CRITICAL APPRAISAL

Hayek's theory makes some important contributions to the understanding of the nature of business cycles. It shows how the business cycles can be explained by integrating monetary and real factors through cost-price relationship. The theory provides some new insights to the structural distortions which may develop in relation to cyclical fluctuations. The theory brings out the fact that sectoral balance in the economic system is necessary for smooth and steady growth.

The theory, however, has certain weaknesses, important of which are mentioned below:

(i) The theory assumes that the utilisation of investment would encroach upon the resources employed for the production of consumer goods. But in a situation where resources are not fully employed, investment and consumption are complementary rather than competitive. Since the resources are never fully employed, the fundamental assumption of the theory does not hold good.

(ii) The theory assumes that the saving and investment are in equilibrium and that the equilibrium is disturbed by the banking policy, which is not correct.

(iii) It is not easy and always possible, as assumed by Hayek, to shift, as and when desired, factors of production from consumption goods industries to capital goods industries and conversely.

(iv) Hayek wrongly assumes that the increase in demand for consumer goods causes a shortening of the process of production and fall in the investment in capital goods industries. He fails to recognise that increase in consumption demand would raise the marginal efficiency of capital which would in turn encourage investment rather retarding it.

(v) The theory does not explain almost entirely major phases of the cyclical process, particularly the contraction phase.

(vi) It overemphasizes the role of the rate of interest in determining the volume of investment. It ignores other factors which influence the volume of investment, *e.g.*, technological changes, innovations etc. According to Hayek, the sole cause of changes in the volume of investment lies in the variations in the market rate of interest in relation to the equilibrium rate of interest. The theory does not mention the way in which investment is related to consumer demand. In fact, investment is influenced not only by changes in the market rate of interest but also by non-monetary factors.

In order to overcome the problem of cyclical fluctuations, Hayek suggests that money supply should be kept neutral because if it is not done investment will be either stimulated (when the supply of money expands) or discouraged (when the supply of money contracts) and this would cause economic fluctuations. In this connection, it may be pointed out that it is not the changes in the volume of investment as such but only those particular changes which are not financed by voluntary savings which have destabilising influence on the economy. And it is these changes in the volume of investment which are induced by an increase in the supply of money.

NON-MONETARY OVER-INVESTMENT THEORY

This theory, like Hayek's monetary over-investment theory, states that the boom is accompanied by an excessive amount of investment and that this over-investment is the basic cause of depression. But it differes from Hayek's theory in that it does not attach much importance to the monetary factors as causing expansion and contraction in the economy. The theory regards the money system as a part of the response mechanism in the process of business cycle, but not as a causative factor. The chief formulators of this theory are Spiethoff, Cassel and Robertson.

SPIETHOFF'S ANALYSIS

Spiethoff gives a real over-investment theory of business cycles. He refers to several real factors as the cause of the business cycles. The core of Spiethoff's analysis rests upon the disproportionate development of the different sectors of the economy. He divides the economy into the following four sectors:

1. Non-durable consumer goods industries.
2. Durable and semi-durable consumer goods industries.
3. Durable capital goods industries.
4. Industries producing materials supplied to capital goods industries.

These four sectors are so inter-linked that expansion and contraction take place through movements within and among these four sectors of the economy.

Spiethoff holds the view that the upswing starts because of the opening of new investment opportunities in sector 3. This causes a disproportion in the development of different goods in the capital goods industry during the expansion phase. It is the shortage of consumption goods during the early expansionary period which stimulates entrepreneurs to invest more in capital goods. When the upswing begins, sector 3 (*i.e.* capital goods industries) start expanding leading to expansion of supplementary industries (sector 4) also. This raises the level of income and employment in these sectors. Consequently, the consumption expenditure increases and expansion begins in sectors 1 and 2 also. But, when more and more plants begin production, the prices of consumer goods start declining and over-investment in capital goods industries is experienced. The prospecting comes to an end.

Thus, during depression, there exists an excess capacity in sector 3 (*i.e.* durable capital goods industries). No investments are made, therefore, in sector 3 or even in sector 4 (*i.e.* industries producing material supplied to capital goods industries). As a result, production in these sectors reaches a low ebb, causing decline in employment and income in the economy, thereby leading to contraction in sectors 1 and 2.

CASSEL'S APPROACH

The approach of Gustav Cassel is similar to that of Spiethoff excepting that he differs with Spiethoff on the question of expansion turning into contraction. While according to Spiethoff, as we have seen above, the basic cause of upswing turning into a downswing is overinvestment in the consumer goods industries, Cassel believes that the cause of the turning point is not over-investment in consumer goods sector but general over-investment which is unwarranted by the volume of total real savings available in the economy.

ROBERTSON'S APPROACH

Robertson's approach represents a synthesis of the real (or non-monetary) and monetary factors. According to Robertson, non-monetary factors are responsible for causing trade cycles but monetary system also contributes to them. In his *Banking Policy and the Price Level*, published in 1926, he disagrees with the stress laid on the monetary policy in the 1920s and advocates for laying more emphasis on real as against monetary or psychological causes of fluctuations.

According to Robertson, the course of economic progress rarely runs smooth and some fluctuations are, in fact, desirable for growth. The problem, however, arises when these desirable fluctuations invoke excessive responses which cause destabilising fluctuations in the economy. The invoking of these excessive responses leading to inappropriate fluctuations is partly owing to the existence of "indivisibility" in certain investments. Certain projects require lumpy investment. Once such an investment is undertaken, a large lump sum is involved which may be excessive in relation to the current position of demand for the output of such investment. But, owing to the indivisible nature of investment, a smaller amount of investment would not be able to deliver the goods.

This is not the end of the problem. Not only many investments are lumpy but they are also time-consuming. These investments have abnormally long 'gestation period', *i.e.,* a long period of time must elapse between the date on which the work on the project is initiated and the date on which the project starts yielding output. The gestation period obscures the amount of realised investment, the results of which are not yet visible. Meanwhile, other investors in a competitive system go ahead with their own capital-forming actions which consequently leads to over-investment creating the problem of glut of new goods in the market.

Robertson holds the view that monetary factors may give a further fillip to fluctuations caused by the non-monetary factors. Thus the banking system might, by putting more money in circulation, further the already existing state of imbalance. The increase in the supply of money will raise the prices which may mislead the entrepreneurs with optimism of profits leading to further over-investment and hence accentuation of the crisis. Thus Robertson integrates the real and monetary factors causing trade cycles. Since he makes a clear distinction between monetary and real forces as the causal factors, his analysis is superior to that of Spiethoff.

According to the advocates of non-monetary over-investment theory, it is the excess of real investment which causes the upper turning point. While Spiethoff believes investment to be excessive in relation to consumption, Gustav Cassel feels that the problem arises because the amount of investment is excessive relatively to the total real saving. The theory does not provide a complete explanation of the cause of lower turning point.

OVER-PRODUCTION OR COMPETITION THEORY

This theory states that the business cycles are caused by over-production resulting from competition in a capitalist economy. In a capitalistic economy, it is the individual entrepreneur who decides what to produce and what not to produce and each one of them attempts to capture as much of the market as he possibly can. In this attempt, each producer tries to excel others and this leads to overflooding of the market. This tendency is more forceful during periods of prosperity when prices show an upward trend and the profit prospects improve. The volume of goods produced exceeds the actual demand. Increase in production leads to an increase in demand for the factors of production, which raises their prices and hence the costs of production. On the consumption side, the excessive production leads to a fall in prices. Thus there appears a glut in the market owing to miscalculation of demand by each individual producer.

Even when the producers realise that their products are being produced in excessive quantities, they continue the same scale of production for some time, probably at a loss, because it is not possible for them to shift immediately large quantities of fixed capital to other uses. Marginal producers are driven out of the market. Then follow the others; the process once started, feeds itself and competition and over-production come to play the role of the villain.

CRITICAL APPRAISAL

The theory can be supported on many grounds. Since competition is found in every country (excepting socialist countries), the theory establishes the universality of trade cycles. It explains that economic fluctuations must occur in a competitive society. It also offers explanation for upward and downward tendencies in business.

But, at the same time, the theory suffers from certain weaknesses. It does not explain how fluctuations take place in all trades simultaneously. It does not explain whether it is the general over-production or specific over-production which initiates a business cycle. The theory does not explain the periodical recurrence of trade cycles. It attributes business cycles only to unco-ordinated and unplanned production but this is not the only cause of business fluctuations. The theory ignores, for instance, the banking policy as a cause of prosperity or depression. Since the theory does not explain regularity of trade cycles, its explanation is unsatisfactory and incomplete.

KEYNES ON TRADE CYCLE

In fact, Keynes does not develop a complete and systematic theory of trade cycle. Nevertheless, in chapter 22 entitled "Some Notes on Trade Cycles" in his *General Theory*, he makes significant contribution to the theory of trade cycle. Keynes' explanation of trade cycle is a byproduct of his main theory of income and employment propounded in the *General Theory*. Since the *General Theory* provides an explanation of the determinants of the level of employment and income at any time, logically it is also capable of explaining the phenomenon of the trade cycle, because a trade cycle is nothing more than a rythmic fluctuation in the aggregate level of income, output and employment. Dudley Dillard, however, believes that Keynes' work is much more and also much less than a theory of the business cycle. "It is more than a theory of business cycle in the sense that it offers a general explanation for the level of employment, quite independently of the cyclical nature of change in employment. It is less than a complete theory of the business cycle because it makes no attempt to give a detailed account of the various phases of the cycle, and does not examine closely the empirical data of cyclical fluctuations. Something which any complete study of the business cycle would presumably do."[19]

In Keynes' analysis, the level of income and employment is determined by three independent variables: (i) the propensity to consume, (ii) the liquidity preference, and (iii) the marginal efficiency of capital. Of these three, the first two, *viz.* the prospensity to

19. Dudley Dillard, *The Economics of John Maynard Keynes* (London, 1960), p. 167.

consume and the liquidity preference, however, are relatively stable phenomenon in the short-run. It is the marginal efficiency of capital which is subject to short-term instability and long-term decline. It is, therefore, the marginal efficiency of capital which is the real strategic variable determining the investment function which in turn determines the level of employment and thereby plays a major role in trade cycle. Thus the basic cause of trade cycle is the instability of the marginal efficiency of capital. To cite Keynes, "The trade cycle is best regarded as being occasioned by a cyclical change in the marginal efficiency of capital, though complicated and often aggravated by associated changes in the other significant short-period variables of the economic system."[20]

As seen earlier, the marginal efficiency of capital asset depends upon two factors *viz.* (i) the prospective yield and (ii) the supply price of the capital asset. But the supply price of the asset does not change in the short period. It is, therefore, fluctuations in the prospective yield (expectations) which make a marginal efficiency of capital very unstable and subject to violent fluctuations. Thus the trade cycle results from fluctuations in expectations. The downswing of the business cycle results from a collapse of the MEC and the upswing is brought about by the revival of the MEC. By introducing the concept of the marginal efficiency of capital, Keynes has, in fact, provided a more refined explanation of the psychological theory of trade cycle.

Having given a brief outline of the so-called Keynes' theory of trade cycle, let us now turn to the explanation of how collapses and revivals in the MEC come about, or in other words, to the courses and phases of business cycle. Following Keynes, we may begin with the expansion phase. This phase of the cycle is occasioned by a high value of the marginal efficiency of capital in relation to the rate of interest. A high marginal efficiency of capital leads to a fast increase in the rate of investment, which increases income and employment. Each increase in investment leads to a manifold increase in income through the operation of the multiplier. Thus, a cumulative rising trend spurts during the expansion phase. In this phase, businessmen are optimistic about the future and expect higher and higher profits. The result is a progressive expansion in business activity. The

---

20. J.M. Keynes, *General Theory of Employment, Interest and Money* (London, 1951), p. 313.

process of cumulative economic expansion goes on till the peak level of the boom is reached.

This process of cumulative expansion cannot continue indefinitely. As the expansion enters the boom stage, certain economic forces come into operation which tend to lower the marginal efficiency of capital. In the first place, as more and more capital goods investment is made, the scope for new investment goods becomes less and less as all remunerative openings for investments are being progressively utilised. The prospective yield on investment goods, therefore, tends to decline. Secondly, increase in the volume of investment goods increases their cost of production; this happens because after a certain stage the process of expansion faces bottlenecks and shortages of labour and raw materials. The combined operation of these two forces depresses the marginal efficiency of capital. The businessmen are always highly sensitive to a decline in the marginal efficiency of capital and adjust their activities accordingly, which means a decline in investment. But the basic factor which sets limits to the expansion is Keynes' concept of the consumption function which lays down that the consumption increases with an increase in consumption but by a smaller proportion. As a consequence, during the expansionary phase, there is the possibility of over-production, leading to a decline in prices. This would depress the marginal efficiency of capital at the peak of boom, which would dampen the spirit of enterprise. Optimism gives place to scepticism and then to pessimism. At this point, Keynes feels that the marginal efficiency of capital collapses all a sudden. Keynes explains the sudden collapse of the marginal efficiency of capital by the fact that an atmosphere of optimism prevails in the later stages of the boom and, therefore, the decline in the expected profitability of capital goods investment is not visualised for some time. But "doubts suddenly arise concerning the reliability of the prospective yield, perhaps because the current yield shows signs of falling off, as the stock of newly produced durable goods steadily increases."[21] Kevnes, however, holds the view that all of the psychological forces which are so important in the erratic behaviour of the stock exchange play a leading role in explaining the decline in

21. Keynes, *op. cit.*, pp. 316-17.

the marginal efficiency of capital. To cite him, "It is of the nature of organised investment markets...that, when disillusion falls upon an over-optimistic and over-bought market, it (MEC) should fall with sudden and even catastrophic force." Further, the decline in the marginal efficiency of capital is followed by a substantial increase in liquidity preference, and hence a rise in the rate of interest. Thus a declining marginal efficiency of capital combined with a rising rate of interest may seriously aggravate the decline in investment.

Thus, the collapse of the marginal efficiency of capital is the predominant cause of the crisis. Since the collapse of the marginal efficiency of capital is sudden, the change from an upward to a downward tendency occurs suddenly and in this regard differs from the lower turning point (revival) which occurs gradually and imperceptibly.

During the contraction phase, which begins on account of the collapse of the marginal efficiency of capital, the investment declines, which leads to a decline in income and employment. A cumulative downward tendency gathers momentum because of the rise in the rate of interest with the declining marginal efficiency of capital, and hence a larger fall in the rate of investment as well as the backward working of the multiplier effect. Every decline in income leads to a rise in the rate of interest when the multiplier operates in the reverse direction. The rate of interest rises further because of increasing liquidity preference of the people in view of the falling prices of the assets and securities. It may be pointed out that the rise in the rate of interest, according to Keynes, becomes important only after and not before, the decline in the marginal efficiency of capital. Thus, the decline in the marginal efficiency of capital below the current rate of interest is accentuated, and the decline in investment aggravated. Keynes believes that at this stage a reduction in the rate of interest is neither easy nor adequate to restore confidence and revive investment. According to Keynes, the length of the contraction period is conditioned by the time required to absorb excess stocks of goods left over from the boom. Keynes estimates such a period to be of three to five years.

Just as the collapse of the marginal efficiency of capital is the main cause of the upper turning point, so the lower turning point (*i.e.* change from recession to recovery) is caused by the revival of the marginal efficiency of capital. In contrast to the fall in the marginal efficiency of capital, which is sudden, its recovery takes time. The time required for the recovery of the marginal efficiency of capital depends partly upon the magnitude of the normal rate of the growth of the economy and partly upon the length of life of durable assets. The shorter the length of life of durable assets, the shorter the depression. Similarly, the more rapid the rate of growth, the shorter the depression. Further, in regard to inventories, the duration of depression is influenced by the carrying costs of surplus stocks. The decline of investment, income, and sales leads to an accumulation of undesired inventories the carrying costs of which are seldom less than 10 per cent per annum. The carrying costs are quite high to hasten the process of liquidation. The sellers would, therefore, be prepared to sell of these surplus stocks at a declining price. The decline in their price will have to be adequate so that they can be absorbed within a period of say 3 to 5 years. For 3 to 5 years, therefore, the disinvestment in stocks would continue and this will have an adverse effect upon employment and income. Once the stocks have been absorbed, negative investment on this account will come to an end. Thus, the marginal efficiency of capital will revive from its depressed state on two accounts: firstly, as the time lapses in depression, the existing capital assets become worn-out and need to be replaced, creating demand for new capital goods; secondly, the surplus stock of other goods (consumption goods) will also be exhausted with the lapse of time. When the surplus stocks get exhausted, the prices tend to rise. Further, during depression, when the factor prices have fallen, the cost of production also declines and as such the supply price of capital assets is low. All these have a tendency to raise the marginal efficiency of capital, which tends to promote new business activity. In the meantime, the rate of interest also declines because the liquidity preference starts declining as a consequence of the rising marginal efficiency of capital and rising prices. As a result, the business confidence is restored, optimistic outlook is developed and economic activities gather momentum. The operation of multiplier magnifies the income generation of each initial investment outlay and a cumulative expansion follows. Once again expansion sets in reaching to boom. This is how the trade cycle operates.

Prof. Hansen brilliantly summarizes the essentials of Keynes' discussion of trade cycle as below:[22]

1. The cycle consists primarily of fluctuations in the rate of investment.
2. Fluctuations in the rate of investment are caused mainly by fluctuations in the marginal efficiency of capital.
3. Fluctuations in the rate of interest have indeed at times played a significant role, but, more typically changes in the liquidity preference schedule, induced by fluctuations in the marginal efficiency of capital, reinforce and supplement the primary factor (*i.e.* changes in the marginal efficiency of capital).
4. Fluctuations in the marginal efficiency of capital are due to (a) changes in the prospective yields of capital goods (b) changes in the replacement cost of capital goods. Fluctuations in the cost of capital goods are due to changes in the rate at which investment is produced in a given period, in other words, to the extreme pressure placed upon the capital goods industries during the boom. Fluctuations in costs are secondary and supplementary to the primary initiating factor, which is the fluctuation in the prospective yields of new capital goods.
5. Towards the end of a boom the decline in prospective yields on capital is due in the first instance to the growing abundance (and therefore lower marginal productivity) of capital goods. This is an objective fact, which in turn may induce a wave of pessimistic expectations (a psychological factor) so that the anticipated yield, once the turning point is past, is usually lower than the facts, coolly considered, justify.
6. In the absence of more thoroughgoing measures (*e.g.* fiscal policy) a variable rate of interest may be useful as a means to stabilize the cycle. Keynes, however, prefers a maintained low rate of interest in conjunction with other more radical measures designed to regularize the cycle.

---

22. A. H. Hansen, *A Guide to Keynes* (New York, 1953), pp. 213-14.

7. Even boom time levels of investment have typically failed to produce full employment. Thus in order to achieve sustained full employment it is not even enough to keep the boom going. Accordingly, Keynes did not believe it to be a sound policy to choke off the boom. He was not impressed with the analysis which alleged that the depression is the inevitable consequence of the distortions of the boom. Any distortions that might exist could progressively be overcome by a programme of sustained full employment. Merely to choke off the boom by an increase in the rate of interest "belongs to the species of remedy which cures the disease by killing the patient."

CONTRIBUTION OF KEYNES TO BUSINESS CYCLE THEORY

According to Prof. Metzler, Keynes was largely responsible for at least two fundamental changes in the theory of business cycles.[23] The first fundamental change was in the definition of the 'normal' or 'equilibrium' level of economic activity, about which the economic system tends to fluctuate. This equilibrium level of economic activity was represented by that level of income where intended savings are equal to non-intended investment. While this definition of equilibrium, according to Prof. Metzler, "presented a number of serious statistical problems such as the difficulty in distinguishing between induced and non-induced investment, it nonetheless represented an important advance in the theory of business cycle."[24]

The second important contribution of Keynes to the theory of business cycles was in the explanation of turning points of the cycle. Before the publication of the *General Theory* there were a large number of business cycle theories but none of these provided any satisfactory explanation of the turning points of business cycle. It was Keynes who with the help of his consumption function provided a convincing explanation of the upper and lower turning points of cycle. According to him, the upper and lower limits of the cycle are set by the marginal propensity to consume being less than one.

---

23. Llyod A. Metzler, "Keynes and the Theory of Business Cycle", in S.E. Hariss (ed.), *The New Economic* (London, 1960), pp. 437-38.
24. *Ibid.*, 438.

With the help of the concept of multiplier, Keynes explains the cumulative nature of expansion and contraction.

Keynes also explained another important characteristic of the business cycle—"some recognisable degree of regularity in the time-sequence and duration of the upward and downward movement." He determined the duration of boom roughly by the time necessary to produce a sufficient increase in capital assets to cause break in the marginal efficiency of capital which again leads into depression. The duration of depression is conditioned by (i) time necessary for the wearing out and obsolescence of the capital assets and (ii) the time that elapses before excess stock which accumulates towards the end of the boom can be exhausted. Thus Keynes explained the observed periodicity of the boom and depression.

Keynes also threw light on a special characteristic of business cycle while the transition from boom to slump is violent and sudden, that from slump to boom is gradual and imperceptible. This is owing to the highly conjectural nature of the marginal efficiency of capital.

Lastly, Keynes' contribution to the theory of business cycles consisted more in the stimulus which he gave to the work of other economists. Many economists, like Samuelson, Hansen and Hicks, explained trade cycles by combining the principle of acceleration with the Keynesian consumption function.

CRITICISM

The concept of the marginal efficiency of capital, which forms the core of Keynes' business cycle theory, is vague and has been used in different senses. To cite Hazlitt, "At one time it seems to mean the actual present yield of capital assets; at another time the expected future yield of specific capital assets; and at still another time it seems to mean merely the outlook for business profits, regardless of the specific return to a specific capital asset. If we give "the marginal efficiency of capital" this broad meaning, it does not make much difference whether we say changes in the marginal efficiency of capital cause the trade cycle, or the changes in the trade cycle cause changes in the marginal efficiency of capital because in this broad sense changes in the marginal efficiency of capital and changes in the business outlook turn out to mean pretty the same thing. If, however, Keynes' proposition were that trade cycle movements are caused, initiated and led by (independent) changes in specific returns to specific capital assets it would be too implausible on its face to be worth disproving."[25]

Keynes' theory does not explain periodicity which is an important characteristic of a trade cycle. His belief that "there is some recognizable degree of regularity in the time sequence and duration of the upward and downward movement" of the business cycle is also debatable. "The closer the investigations", says Hazlitt, "the less regular the duration that seems to emerge."[26]

Keynes believed that "the duration of the downward movement... which shows some regularity of habit lies between, let us say, three and five years." "Characteristically", says Hazlitt, "he presents no statistical evidence of this, nor does he refer to any source where the statistical evidence can be found." Geoffrey H. Moore finds that average duration of the downward movement of the 24 cycles during the period 1854-1954 was just 20 months.

Keynes concludes "that the duration of the slump has a definite relationship to the length of durable assets and also to the carrying costs of surplus stock. Here again, as Hazlitt points out, no statistical evidence is provided and it may be questioned whether any is possible. There is no meaningful 'average' length of life of 'durable assets' and no meaningful 'average' period for getting rid of 'surplus stock.'[27] No doubt, the length of the life of durable assets bears some relation to the duration of a slump, but it is only one of the many factors and seldom the most important.

According to Keynes the predominant reason for the crisis is the sudden collapse of the marginal efficiency of capital, which he attributes to lack of confidence or pessimistic expectation—a psychological phenomenon. Thus Keynes' theory is very similar to the Psychological Theory associated with the names of Professors Pigou and Hobson. In explaining crisis, Keynes ignores the real factors underlying these psychological shifts.

---

25. H. Hazlitt, *The Failure of "New Economics"* (New York, 1960), pp. 317-18.
26. *Ibid.*, p. 327.
27. *Ibid.*, p. 327.

Hazlitt finds contradictions in Keynes' theory of business cycle. "The interest according to him should be low in the depression, low in boom and, low in crisis. His remedy to keep the boom going by encouraging over-investment and mal-investment, and then, when the boom cracks to keep the boom going by lowering the rate of interest still more to encourage still more over-investment and mal-investment."

Keynes explains the cumulative nature of trade cycle with the help of his concept of the multiplier. But multiplier alone does not offer a complete and satisfactory explanation of the cumulative nature of the trade cycle. In fact, it is explained by the interaction between the multiplier and accelerator.

Lastly, many economists do not agree with Keynes' advocacy of cheap money policy or low interest rates as a remedy for economic crisis. They hold the view that a cheap money policy encourages excessive borrowing and undue credit expansion, unhealthy speculations and instabilities in the economy with inflationary spirals.

SELF-GENERATION THEORY OF W.C. MITCHELL

The self-generation theory of trade cycle is associated with the name of Prof. W.C. Mitchell. He is of the view that each phase of the trade cycle automatically generates the other. According to him, trade crisis are but one feature of a recurrent cycle. A crisis is expected to be followed by depression, depression by recovery or revival, revival by prosperity and prosperity by crisis, and so on. Business cycles often differ not only in length but also in their violent effect and the relative prominence of their phases. This difference in business cycles is owing to different business situations which are influenced by complex forces. The factors which slacken or quicken the pace of economic activity include internal political conditions, changes in monetary and banking systems, war or peace, new industrial methods, international relations etc. It may be pointed out that different industries are affected differently by trade cycles. Some are hit hard and are affected quickly by a decline in economic activity while others are only slightly affected.

Mitchell's explanation of the cycle is eclectic. He does not emphasize one factor alone to the exclusion of all others. He believes in drawing his generalisations from the observed behaviour of the economy. He is of the view that instability is inherent in a business economy. Economic activity in a free enterprise economy depends upon income and profit motive. Profits in turn are determined by the cost-price relationship which might not turn out to be what the entrepreneurs had expected when they undertook investment. Mitchell also stresses the interdependence between different parts of the economy in a way that maladjustments begun in one sector of the economy spread throughout the economy.

Mitchell holds the view that depression eventually creates conditions for the onset of a new upswing. During depression, costs are reduced, profit margins eventually improve, inventories are low and eventually require restocking, weak firms are weeded out, banks become more willing to lend as excess reserves accumulate and so on. A business economy thus tends to generate conditions favourable for revival, and external events may also intervene. Once the revival starts, the economy grows in a cumulative manner. Increase in production increases the incomes of the factors of production and thus expands sales which leads to replacement of worn-out equipment and depleted inventories. The business optimism generally improves. Prices start rising and the expectation of further price increases stimulates business demand still further. Rising profit margins and increased volume of business cause profits to increase rapidly; improved profits cause business investments to expand; incomes, spending, production, and prices act and react on each other and rise further in a cumulative manner.

According to Mitchell the downswing is caused by "a slow accumulation of stresses within the balanced system of business-stresses which ultimately undermine the conditions upon which prosperity rests."[28] Mitchell emphasizes that as expansion continues in a cumulative manner, there ultimately develop unfavourable cost-price relations, which impair profit margins. Overhead costs rise ultimately and more important, operating costs rise fast owing to pressure of output on capacity, rising wage rates, decreased labour efficiency, and rising raw material costs. The boom generates other stresses like limited bank reserves, growing tightness in the market for long and short-term funds, and rising costs of new construction and equipment. Though he does not mention this in his

---

28. *In Readings in Business Cycle Theory*, p. 50.

1913 volume[29], Mitchell later takes into consideration the operation of the acceleration principle, which leads to a decline in new orders for capital goods simultaneously with the development of other stresses mentioned above.

Ultimately, some industries discover that their selling prices cannot be raised adequately to allow continuation of satisfactory results. Deteriorating profits prospects, reinforced by growing monetary stringency, lead to contraction of credit in some sectors. New orders decline, output is reduced, lenders refuse new loans and seek repayment of old debts. Thus liquidation begins; and since the economy is tied together in a network of commercial and financial relationships it spreads fast to other firms. There is a scramble for liquidity; efforts are made to reduce inventories and new orders are substantially reduced; price declines feed on themselves and affect more and more commodities; production, employment, and income fall. The decline continues until the economy builds up corrective forces strong enough to start a new recovery.

According to Keynesian analysis business cycles can be analysed in terms of the relationship among a few aggregative variables. In contrast to this, Mitchell is of the view that trade cycle in an extremely complex phenomenon which cannot be analysed in terms of a few aggregative variables. According to him trade cycles results from the action on business profits of the whole complex of trading and financial relationships which make the economy a compact whole. Discussing the difficulty of explaining the cycle in the present state of knowledge Mitchell writes, "But, despite these advances theorists who sought to explain business cycles were insufficiently informed about the phenomena with which they were dealing, and had to reason for the most part from untested assumptions. The complexity of economic organisation suggested to ingenious minds an embarrasing array of plausible hypotheses. No one could determine which among these jostling competitors was least inadequate, or whether any combination of them would account for what happens."[30]

---

29. *Reprinted as Business Cycles and Their Causes*, 1941.

30. W.C. Mitchell, *What Happens During Business Cycles*, p. 3.

CRITICISM

The major weakness of the 'business economy' theory of Mitchell is that it fails to tell the whole story. While the stress laid on the cost-price relationships and expectations and also mention of the fact of interdependence of different sectors of the system are all right, the theory fails to analyse the underlying real factors which bring about turning points. Errors of optimism and pessimism and the possibility of horizontal maladjustments (partial over-production) on which the theory depends can help explain only relatively mild savings in the investment activity; these are inadequate to explain wide fluctuations in the level of investment activity which cause the turning points of the major cycles.

The theory treats the cyclical movement as the movements of a machine which is not correct. To cite Professor Knight, "This theory likens the economic mechanism to a perpetual motion machine. And no machine will run indefinitely on the power which originally sets it into motion unless, like a clock, it is periodically rewound. It will run down because of friction. The cycles of the economic machine like the revolutions of clock would become successively weaker if no fresh facts are imported to them."[31]

EXOGENOUS AND ENDOGENOUS THEORIES

Business cycle theories have sometimes been classified into (i) theories explaining fluctuations in terms of exogenous factors and (ii) theories explaining fluctuations in terms of endogenous factors. Many non-mathematical theories depend heavily upon exogenous factors for explaining both the cumulative process and the turning points. Econometric theories in contrast emphasize endogenous movements.

Econometric theories emphasize the systematic movements which originate from the internal nature of the economic structure. This structure can be described in terms of a system of relations between various economic variables. Econometric analysis shows that "constant relationship can produce a fluctuating process", once an initial shock has disrupted equilibrium. The econometric approach emphasizes the effect of the economic structure on cyclical fluctuations or, to put the things in more precise manner, it

31. P.W. Knight, *Economic Principles in Practice*, p. 412.

tries to explain how cyclical movements result from the response of the economic structure to random shocks.

A strictly exogenous theory considers economic fluctuations as "nothing but a purely arbitrary and random succession of change."[32] Fluctuations in the 'data' or exogenous variables would produce corresponding fluctuations in the economy as a whole if the system responds immediately to changes in the data. But, in actual practice, this is not so. The economic structure adapts itself more or less slowly to external disturbances. As soon as lags are introduced, we are immediately involved with endogenous factors in cyclical behaviour. It must, however, be emphasized that an endogenous theory cannot ignore external disturbance to which the economic system responds in a way which sets into motion cyclical movements.

Exogenous theories place primary emphasis upon changes in the data while endogenous theories stress the lagged reactions of the economic structure (with constant internal relationships) to such changes. Exogenous theories explain the turning points in the cycle by reference to some external factor. Endogenous theories explain the turning points by reference to the internal functioning of the system itself.

The system of internal relationships may, however, be such that the endogenous movements are of a unilateral character, consisting simply of a cumulative process upward or downward. If still a cyclical movement takes place, the turning points must then be explained by exogenous factors. In this case, we have a mixed theory. In general, there is probably a tendency in literature on business cycle to emphasize the role of exogenous factors at the lower turning points, and to emphasize the role of endogenous factors at the upper turning points. The endogenous forces that lead to recovery are at any rate often considered as weaker than those which terminate a boom.

COBWEB THEORY

The theory was developed in thirties. It was advanced independently by three economists almost at the same time. The theory is associated with the names of Henry Schultz, Jan Tinbergen and Arthur Hanau, though the term 'Cobweb Theorem' was first

32. Tinbergon and I.J. Polak. *The Dynamics of Business Cycles* (University of Chicago Press, 1950), p. 253.

suggested by Professor Nicholas Kaldor in 1934. The theory represents an important advancement in the development of the dynamic explanations of the cyclical fluctuations. The earlier explanations of cycles were static in nature. They analysed the economy as at a point of time ignoring completely the movements of the economy through time. They assumed that the adjustments between supply and demand take place instantaneously and ignored the time-lag. The cobweb theory, in contrast, provides us an illustration of the dynamic process or adjustment movements through time.

The cobweb theory is based on the foundation of the concept of 'lag'. It stresses that the supply adjusts to changing conditions of demand which are reflected through price changes not instantaneously but after a certain period of time. This time, taken by the supply to adjust itself to changes in demand, is known as lag. Thus the quantity supplied during any given time period is the function of the price ruling in the preceding time period *t-l* whereas the demand depends upon the price which prevails in the period *t* itself.

The cobweb theory has its major application in the field or agricultural products, the supply of which can be varied only after a certain time-lag. Most of the products can be sown and reaped only once a year. If the price of wheat rises in April, 1973, for instance, the supply will not increase instantaneously. No doubt, a larger acreage would be devoted to the cultivation of wheat in the next crop-season but it will take one year before the supply can be increased in response to a rise in price. Thus the supply of wheat in 1974 would depend on the price of wheat which prevailed in 1973 and induced the producers to devote a larger acreage to the cultivation of wheat. In case of some products like tea or rubber, the time-lag involved is five years or more. In general terms, if it takes *H* months to produce and bring to market a commodity, the quantity sold *now* would be a function of price *H* months ago and the cycle would necessarily be of 2*H* months' duration.

Tinbergen visualises the tremendous implications of this type of analysis and extends its application to the supply of durable goods which responds to changes in demand after a considerable time-lag because, owing to the long gestation period, their is considerable lag between the decision to produce and the actual deliveries of the durable goods. Since perishable goods are consumed in a single go, the total supply is purely the result of price prevailing H months ago. But since the durable goods continue giving service for a long time, the previous price determines no supply but rather the additions to the total stock. As such, the supply Q in the cobweb theorem is replaced by the *rate of increase* of stock K at time t, or $\frac{dk}{dt}$. As a result, the rate of increase of the stock depends on the total stock some time ago. Tinbergen shows that this could cause oscillations of a duration longer than $2H$ because of the durability of the good.

Cobwebs have been divided into (i) converging cobwebs, (ii) diverging cobwebs and (iii) continuous cobwebs. In case of continuous cobwebs, the fluctuations in price and output continue repeating about the equilibrium at the same level. In case of converging cobwebs, the economy, when disturbed from equilibrium position, has a tendency to regain it through a series of oscillations. Each fluctuation is more damped than the one preceding it. The amplitude of the fluctuations narrows down when the slope of the supply curve is steeper than the slope of the demand curve. In the case of diverging cobwebs, the amplitude of the fluctuations increases with the passage of time. Once disturbed from the equilibrium position, the economy moves away cumulatively into the doldrums of disequilibrium. This happens when the slope of the supply curve is less than the slope of the demand curve. Figures 17.7(*a*), 17.7(*b*) and 17.7(*c*) depict the continuous, converging and diverging cobwebs respectively.

In case the elasticity of supply is equal to the elasticity of demand the series of reactions work out as shown in the figure 17.7 (*a*). The quantity in initial period (Q_1) is large, resulting in a relatively low price where it intersects the demand curve at P_1. This low price, intersecting the supply curve calls forth a relatively short supply Q_3 in the next period. This short supply leads to a high price P_2 where it intersects the supply curve. This high price calls forth a corresponding increased production Q_3 in the third period, with a corresponding low price, P_3. Since this low price in the third period is identical with that in the first, the production and price in the fourth, fifth, and subsequent periods will continue rotating around the path Q_2, P_2, Q_3, P_3 etc.

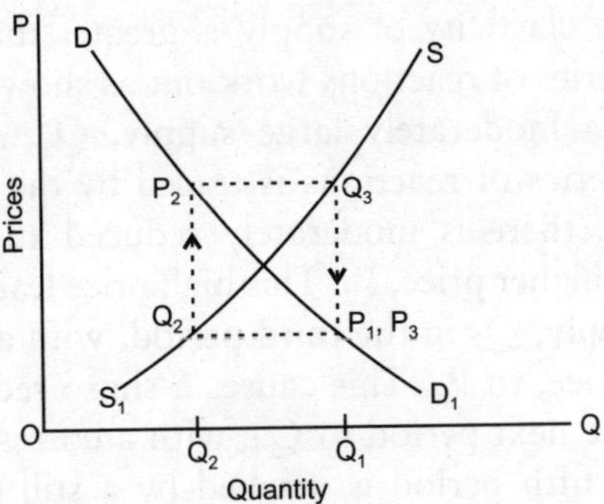

Fig. 17.7 (a)

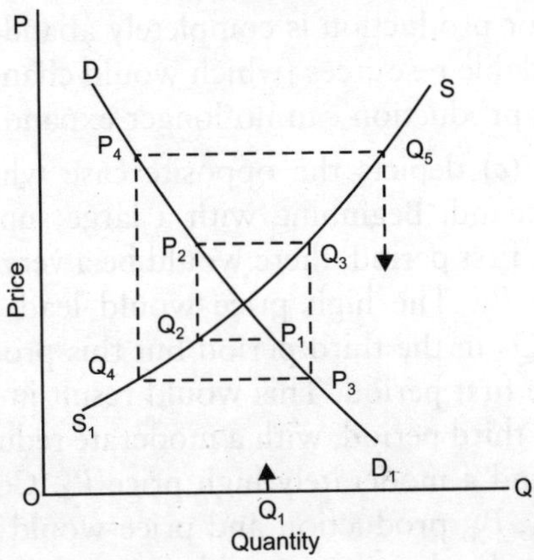

Fig. 17.7 (b)

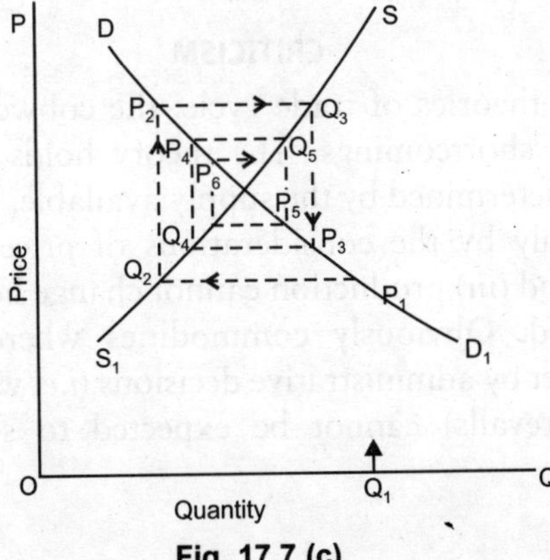

Fig. 17.7 (c)

In case the elasticity of supply is greater than the elasticity of demand, the series of reactions work out as shown in figure 17.7(*b*). Starting with a moderately large supply, Q_1, and corresponding price P_1, the series of reactions is traced by the dotted line. In the second period, there is moderately reduced supply, Q_2 with the corresponding higher price, P_2. This high price leads to a considerable increase in supply, Q_3 in the third period, with a resulting material reduction in price, to P_3. This causes a sharp reduction in quantity produced in the next period to Q_4, with a corresponding very high price, P_4. The fifth period is marked by a still greater increase in supply to Q_5 and so on. Under these conditions, the situation might continue to grow more and more unstable until the price declines to absolute zero, or production is completely abandoned, or a limit is reached to available resources (which would change the elasticity of supply) so that production can no longer expand.

Figure 17.7(*c*) depicts the opposite case where supply is less elastic than demand. Beginning with a large supply, Q_1, and low price, P_1, in the first period, there would be a very short supply, Q_2, and high price P_2. The high price would lead to an increase in production to Q_3 in the third period but this production is smaller than that in the first period. This would result in a moderately low price, P_3, in the third period, with a moderate reduction to Q_4 in the fourth period and a moderately high price P_4. Continuing through Q_4, P_4, and Q_5, P_5, production and price would tend to approach more and more closely to the equilibrium condition where further changes would occur. Of the three cases considered above, only the last one behaves in the manner assumed by the equilibrium theory.

CRITICISM

Like other theories of trade cycle, the cobweb theory also has certain serious shortcomings. The theory holds good only where (i) the price is determined by the supply available, (ii) the production is governed only by the considerations of price as under perfect competition, and (iii) production cannot change before the expiry of one full period. Obviously commodities where either price or production is set by administrative decisions (*i.e.* where monopolistic competition prevails) cannot be expected to show the cobweb reaction.

Even for the commodities which approximately fulfil the assumptions, however, the theory is of limited application. In many commodities, once the farmers have made their initial commitment in acreage sown or in animals bred, it may not be able for them to increase their future production, but they can decrease production at any time until the product is finally marketed, by ploughing up portions of the crop or letting it go unharvested, by slaughtering breeding stock, or by slaughtering pigs young instead of fattening them. Thus there does exist some elasticity of response in the downward direction, at least.

An even more serious limitation is that imposed by natural conditions affecting production. The volume of production depends not only on the acreage but also on the yield per acre; and the yield per acre is substantially influenced by the weather conditions. Unusual weather may occasionally change what would otherwise be a large crop to a normal one, and thus restore price to a point where subsequent variation will be slight until another abnormal yield occurs. Most of the time, however, natural variations may cause unduly high or unduly low production, and thus set a new cycle of response in reaction. Even in commodities which follow the convergent pattern, the actual cycles may be quite similar to those of either of the other types, if abnormally large or small crops occur frequently enough to cause a marked departure from normal and to start again a long series of convergent cycles before stability is again approached. The combination of cobweb reactions with occasional crop disasters or gluts may be enough to produce recurring cyclical changes in production and prices, rather than stability, as the normal situation over a considerable number of commodities.

The theory is based upon the assumption that the crop which farmers sow in 1973 depends entirely on the price prevailing in 1972. In fact, this is not true. No doubt, the price prevailing in 1972 influences decisions regarding the 1973 crop, producers are also influenced by their expectations. Producers' decisions in regard to production during any given period are influenced not only by prices in the past period but also by the prices expected in the next period. If this year's price is high, the producers may foresee some reaction to the high price and anticipate increased production by their competitors in the next year. Further the decisions in regard to the production may be influenced not only by the price of the commodity itself but also by the prices of the inputs required for the production of the commodity.

There is no commodity which satisfies the condition that supply alone sets the price. The prices of commodities are influenced by changes in the supply of competing products, changes in the prosperity or income of consumers, and changes in institutional factors affecting their markets, such as tariff quotas, freight rates, weather conditions, and even style changes.

If we look at diagram 17.7 (*b*) showing diverging cobwebs, we find that once the disequilibrium begins, it continues indefinitely. The curves show that once the equilibrium is disturbed, the system falls into a series of unending cycles. In actual practice, however, this is most unlikely to happen. Commonsense tells that this cannot happen. Actually the shape of the curves is such as to make continued divergence impossible.

It can also be argued that even the constant type of cobwebs would not continue indefinitely. This is obvious from the diagram 17.7 (*a*). In case of constant cobweb cycles, producers experience alternating years of profits and losses but the losses always exceed the profits. Bankruptcy would ultimately put an end to a cycle of this type. Thus it is in a way correct to assert that in so far as the cycles of the cobweb take place in actual practice, they are either converging cycles that tend towards a new equilibrium position or temporary affairs in economic world limited by the ultimate bankruptcy of people in industry and business.

To conclude, in spite of its weaknessess, the cobweb theory is important as an explanation of agricultural products markets. It concentrates attention on the important fact that the present events are determined by the past happenings. It furnishes us with a technique to demonstrate the process of change over time.

Economic Stabilisation

18

ITS MEANING

The goal of economic stability can be resolved into twin objectives of sustained full employment and avoidance of wide fluctuations in the general level of prices. The opinion is more or less unanimous on this. We want to keep the economy continuously at the full-employment level and at the same time avoid marked variations in prices in either direction. In other words, the objective is to avoid both deflation and inflation.

Before the World War II, the problem of economic stability was considered to be that of preventing depressions. The Great Depression of the thirties, as well as earlier experience with cyclical downswings, focussed our attention on preventing unemployment on a mass scale. But since the World War II, while not forgetting the danger of unemployment, we have been more concerned with the threat of continuing inflation. A policy of economic stabilisation must aim at attaining both full employment and price stability. In recent years, there has been much discussion of a third objective, namely, the attainment of a satisfactory rate of economic growth.

The meaning of full employment has already been discussed in detail in an earlier chapter. As regards price stability, it means absence of any marked trend or sharp short-term movements in the general price level. This, of course, does not mean interference with the flexibility of individual prices. The relative prices of particular commodities should be free to shift widely in response to changes in consumer tastes and cost conditions.

The goal of economic stability has a short-run as well as a long-run aspect. This is true of both the objectives *viz.* (1) full employment and (2) price stability. The goal of short-term economic stability is basically the goal of eliminating (or at least moderating) cyclical fluctuations in business activity. But this is not enough. We also want to control the long-run level around which the permissible fluctuations are to occur. We do not want stability of output or employment at a level significantly below that of full employment. Nor do we want a "creeping" sort of inflation that may double the price level every 30 years or so. While seeking cyclical stability, we also want to avoid both secular stagnation and secular inflation.

There is no particular problem in regard to the full-employment objective. The goal obviously means short-run stability and full employment. Secularly, employment would rise with the growth of the labour force. Output would rise with the increase in employment and in labour productivity. Appropriate adjustments would have to be made for any reduction in the number of hours worked; some output may be forgone for additional leisure.

Though the desirable long-run objective is cleat and unambiguous in respect of employment, the same is not true in case of the price level The short-run stability of prices may be sought on a horizontal secular trend or on a slowly rising or slowly falling one. Some economists believe that the full employment can be maintained only if the government assumes a responsibility for deliberate slow inflation so that consistently rising prices will induce adequate amounts of investment. They would presumably give the government a specific price-level responsibility, but it would be a mandate to inflate rather than to keep prices stable. Their argument is that major economic units—labour, business and farm—have now so effectively organized important sectors of the market that they are able to maintain prices and wages at levels higher than those which will be consistent with maximum sales and production. In such a situation, it will not be possible for the government to maintain full employment without expanding the supply of money and deliberately inflating prices.

Some economists hold the view that moderate inflation simply cannot be held to moderation. Creeping inflation gathers momentum particularly if the economy ever accepts the view that such inflation is a matter of deliberate intent by the government. These economists also advocate the assignment of specific price-level responsibility of the government but differ from others in that they would stipulate a responsibility for the stabilisation (rather than inflation) of prices.

Experience, however, shows that some rise in prices is unavoidable during pursuit of the goals of full employment and rapid economic development. In such a situation, there is more or less consensus of opinion that a high level of employment and a satisfactory rate of economic growth is a more important objective than long-run constancy in the price level.

Any stabilisation programme which aims at freezing the economy at full employment level of a particular period would be based upon an erroneous concept of the objective of economic stabilisation. Such a stabilisation programme would attain stability at the cost of economic growth. Stabilisation is very much different from freezing. Long-run economic growth considerably depends upon the maintenance of sufficient economic flexibility, so that same industries will be encouraged to expand and bid resources away from others which are less efficient or whose products no longer have their former appeal in the market place. A stabilisation programme must be administered in a flexible manner so as to allow reasonable movement among the self-adjusting forces of the economy.

METHODS OF ECONOMIC STABILISATION

An economic stabilisation programme requires the maintenance of an effective balance between aggregate demand and aggregate supply. Such a programme can, therefore, be administered by measures which influence the aggregate supply of goods and services in the economy and/or the aggregate supply of money which bids for such goods and services.

The aggregate purchasing power in the economy can be influenced by changes in the level and types of taxes. A decrease in taxes will leave more money with people for the purchase of goods and services. An increase in taxes will reduce disposable income and would probably also raise the cost of goods purchased. Changes in the relative importance of different kinds of taxes may alter the relative availability of funds for consumption as contrasted with investment spending.

The government may alter the flow of funds it sends into the private economy by varying government expenditures. It may alter the kind of spending it does, putting more money into some sectors of the economy and less into others. The quantitative and qualitative adjustments of taxes and public expenditures are one of the most important instruments of economic stabilisation.

The monetary authorities may vary the amount of money available to the economy by varying the terms on which credit is available, by instituting outright restrictions upon the quantity and kinds of available credit, and by direct purchase and sale operations in the open market. Monetary policy is the second important tool of economic stabilisation.

In certain situations, the aggregate tools alone may not be adequate to stabilise the economy. The disequilibrating forces may be much more marked in certain key areas of the economy and overall monetary and fiscal measures may not be appropriate to control such forces. Under such circumstance, it may become necessary to introduce direct controls, which may take the form of price ceilings, wage ceilings, allocation programmes for materials, consumer rationing, or direct credit controls.

STABILISING CONSUMERS' EXPENDITURE

The volume of consumers' expenditure in any period depends on two sets of influences: (i) those determining the level of disposable income after personal taxes and (ii) those determining the ratio of consumers' expenditure to disposable income (the propensity to consume). The most important factor responsible for cyclical changes in consumption is the fluctuations in the level of disposable income. If it is desired to stimulate or reduce consumption, it would have to be done mainly by changing the volume of income available to consumers.

MEASURES TO STABILISE DISPOSABLE INCOME

The cyclical instability in consumers' incomes can be moderated in a number of ways. Particularly important in this context are social security programmes, especially unemployment insurance, and income taxes, especially on a "pay-as-you-go" basis. Social Security contributions by employers and employees rise and fall along with the rise and fall in the level of employment. Social security payments by the government, particularly unemployment insurance payments, move inversely with the fluctuations in the volume of employment. Thus during periods of declining economic activity, the government increases payments to the unemployed at a time when its social security collections are declining because fewer people have full-time jobs. A liberal and widespread programme of unemployment insurance can be an important instrument of holding up personal incomes during periods of declining economic activity.

A similar automatic stabilising influence is attained through a "pay-as-you-go" income tax. This is particularly true when tax rates are highly progressive and personal exemptions are well above zero. In this case income tax payments decline relatively faster than aggregate personal incomes during the recession and rise relatively faster during the boom period. The result is that the disposable incomes fluctuate less than do the total incomes before taxes; as such consumption becomes more stable than it would otherwise be.

Corporate income taxes also have a similar stabilising effect. In fact their stabilising effect is much more important than that of the personal income tax for corporate profits fluctuate very widely over the cycle. An appreciable part of any decline in corporate income before taxes is offset by a decline in corporate income-tax liabilities.

The stabilising effects described above are attained without any change in tax rates. Such effects can be further enlarged by raising tax rates and reducing exemptions during booms and following the reverse policy during depressions.

INFLUENCING PROPENSITY TO CONSUME

Redistribution of income is one of the possible ways of changing the fraction of disposable incomes which consumers spend. Normally, the poor classes have a tendency to spend a larger fraction of their incomes than the rich classes. As such the measures which tend to equalise personal incomes will tend to raise the ratio of consumption to income for the economy as a whole. This, however, is not a very practicable method of moderating short-run cyclical fluctuations in consumption. The most direct way of changing the distribution of incomes is through making the tax structure more or less progressive. But it is neither practicable nor desirable to introduce radical changes in the tax structure every year or two making it more progressive when recession starts and less progressive when recovery begins. Not only would the political and social repercussions be an obstacle to doing this frequently but also frequent changes in the tax structure would create uncertainty which would ultimately decrease the volume of private investment. It is also doubtful if moderate changes in the tax structure, which did not at the same time change the total yield of taxes, would appreciably affect the level of consumption.

Though changes in the progressiveness of the tax structure are not a suitable instrument of moderating cyclical fluctuations, they may be useful in dealing with long-run trends. This mainly depends on how progressive the tax structure already is. If the economy is facing secular stagnation, the tax structure might be made more progressive. This would permanently reduce the volume of savings at a given level of income. This may, however, at the same time lead to a reduction in the volume of investment, which would offset the favourable effect of any increase in consumption brought about by it. In a country already having a high and very progressive tax structure, the opportunities are limited in this regard.

Another way of changing the distribution of income is to alter the division of national income between wages and profits. An increase in wages at the cost of profits would tend to increase consumption. But this step may also reduce investment of incentives and thereby the value of private investment. Thus we find that measures aimed directly at the redistribution of incomes are not an effective way of reducing fluctuations in consumption.

A more direct way of influencing the propensity to consume is to tax consumption and saving at different rates. One suggestion put forward during World War II, for instance, was that a special tax should be levied on consumer's expenditure in addition to the regular income tax.[1] Another proposal is that a part of person's saving should be exempted from income tax, which would provide greater incentive to save.[2]

A third suggestion is that of compulsory saving whereby, in addition to income tax, the tax payers are required to deposit with the government a certain percentage of their income to be repaid at some stipulated time in future.[3] A similar scheme was introduced in the year 1963-64 but was withdrawn the following year because of great opposition from the public.

---

1. Articles by Milton Friedman and K.E. Poole in *The American Economic Review* (March 1943), pp. 50-73.
2. S.H. Slichter, "The Problem of Inflation", *Review of Economics and Statistics* (February, 1948), p. 5.
3. James Tobin, "Taxes, Savings and Inflation", *American Economic Review* (December, 1949), pp. 1223-32.

All of these proposals were put forward to combat inflation and were not designed to fight depressions as well as booms. These proposals can, however, be reversed during deflationary periods. Any plan which requires frequent changes in the tax structure would not be acceptable on practical grounds. Besides the administrative difficulties involved, it is doubtful if some of these plans would have the desired effectiveness. The plans for special taxes on consumption or for compulsory saving should be introduced only during emergency situations when the threat of inflation is very great and when it is not possible to raise income taxes substantially on political or economic grounds.

Particularly unstable is the consumer's expenditure on durables like automobiles, radios, television sets, refrigerators, furniture etc. A substantial part of such goods is bought on credit which adds instability to this type of expenditure. Control can be exercised over type of expenditure by regulating the terms on which credit is made available. Such "selective controls" were used in the United States during the World War II (until 1947), briefly during 1948-49, and again after the Korean crisis. The Board of Governors of the Federal Reserve System specified minimum down payments and maximum repayment periods for consumers' loans used to buy various kinds of durable goods. This measure has been used in other countries also. It is an effective method of reducing a particularly volatile type of expenditure during inflationary periods. During the recession periods, consumption can be stimulated by relaxing such controls over consumer credit; but the stimulus will not be very effective if the consumers do not want to buy even on easy credit terms or if the lenders are not willing to give credit on these terms.

CONTROL OF INVESTMENT

Investment is the most volatile component of aggregate demand and attainment of economic stability through the stabilisation of private investment is the most difficult task. The very nature of technological progress causes private investment to occur in spurts, and the volatility of business expectations adds a further element of instability. But still something can certainly be done. Greater stability and steady growth in other components of aggregate demand would have a tendency to make investment somewhat more stable.

We have already examined the various measures which can be taken to stimulate investment during the depression period. In inflationary periods, the problem is to curtail private investment. For this purpose concessions mentioned earlier can be withdrawn. Some countries have curtailed investment by some form of an investment tax and some have directly controlled the floatation of new securities. If the inflationary stimulus is very strong, and particularly if private investment competes with government for strategic materials needed for military or other vital purposes, it may become necessary to use direct controls as is often done during wartime. But in a private-enterprise economy such controls should be used only during emergencies.

Monetary Policy

19

MEANING AND INSTRUMENTS OF MONETARY POLICY

Monetary policy refers to measures designed to influence the cost and availability of money with a view to influence the working of the economy. In other words, monetary policy consists of all those measures which help the central banking authority of a country to manipulate the various instruments of credit control. The instruments of monetary policy are the same as the instruments of credit control at the disposal of a central bank referred to as the quantitative credit controls. The second category of instruments consists of consumer credit control, real estate credit control, stock credit control, marginal requirements etc. referred to as qualitative controls. The quantitative instruments are so called because they regulate the total quantity of money available and the qualitative measures because they are employed to restrict the total quantity of money available for certain specific purposes even though plenty of money may be available for other purposes.

OBJECTIVES OF MONETARY POLICY

The objectives of monetary policy have been different in different countries and at different times in the same country depending on the nature of the problem confronting the country. At times, these objectives may not be compatible with each other. The major objectives of the monetary policy, however, are as mentioned below:

(i) stability of exchange rates,

(ii) price stability,

(iii) neutral money,

(iv) income stabilisation,

(v) full employment, and

(vi) economic development.

EXCHANGE RATE STABILITY

The traditional objective of the monetary policy has been the achievement of stable exchange rates. The government of every country is generally faced with the problem of a choice between a stable price level and a stable foreign exchange rate. Such a problem of course, would not arise if prices all over the world remained stable. This is, however, wishful thinking and, in fact, the prices all over the world continue changing.

Changes in the rate of exchange lead to a number of difficulties. They give rise to a lot of speculative activity in the foreign exchange market which hinders the inflow of foreign capital and stimulates outflow of capital. There develops an unprecedented drain on the limited foreign exchange reserves of the country. The repeated runs that were made on the currencies of the 'Gold Block' countries during the financial crisis of thirties provide ample evidence to show that fluctuating exchange rates produce very unpleasant long period effects. The gains which can be made from unexpected depreciation or appreciation of a currency attract the attention of the speculators all over the world and they try to keep their funds in as liquid form as possible so that the same may be converted at the first sign of danger into some other currency which is likely to offer greater security and return. This desire for liquidity on the part of the investors leads to the hoarding of gold on a very large scale and considerably strengthens the tendency towards deflation particularly in the gold standard countries.

For countries which are small in size and in whose economy foreign trade plays a large part (*e.g.* Denmark and England) stabilization of exchange rate is the only wise policy. If such countries do not follow this type of policy, fluctuations in the rate of foreign exchange will disturb their entire trade and thereby their economic prosperity. They must sacrifice stability of internal prices in favour of the stability of foreign exchange rate particularly if they considerably depend on foreign capital. Owing to the paramount importance of international trade in the economies of leading countries like England, Denmark, Japan etc., this objective was primary while that of stability of prices and output was secondary.

If the financial position of a country is weak there develops a crisis of confidence, the consequences of which can simply be disastrous for the country. Even a slight change in the rate of exchange has a very bad effect on the domestic prices because it is clearly noticed by all.

Exchange stabilisation as an objective of the monetary policy much advocated in the nineteenth century and early decades of the twentieth century has lost much of its force today. Although no longer advocated as the best goal of a country's monetary policy, for a considerable time before the great depression most leading countries of the world were on gold standard and consequently followed a policy of exchange rate stability. Though a policy of stable exchange rates promotes world trade and international lending, it is open to severe criticisms on other grounds. Such a policy creates a more difficult problem of domestic price instability. This was an important drawback of the gold standard. Under gold standard, exchange stability was attained at the heavy price of unstable prices within the country. The price instability tended to be severe when the other countries of the world did not observe the so-called "sacred rules of the gold standard game." The establishment of the International Monetary Fund has further reduced the importance of this objective of the monetary policy.

PRICE STABILITY

During and after the Great Depression of thirties price stability and control of business fluctuations became the prime objects of monetary policy. Price instability has very unpleasant economic effects. A rising price level causes great economic hardships to some sections of the society, *e.g.*, wage-earners, rentiers, consumers etc. The decline in prices creates complicated problems of production and distribution. What is worse is price instability is cumulative in nature. Once started it gathers momentum, threatening, in course of time, the entire economic, social and political stability of the country. World economic history shows that the periods of fluctuating prices have been the periods of great economic and political upheavals.

On the suggestion of late Lord Keynes, the United States' government officially recognised in 1937 the objective of price stability for the New Deal Recovery Programme. To quote from the annual address that late President F. D. Roosevelt gave to the American Congress on January 6, 1937, "It is to the interest of the nation to have government help private enterprise to gain sound general price levels, and to protect these levels from wide perilous fluctuations." But this objective of the monetary policy proved to be shortlived because of a number of reasons, *e.g.*, difficulties involved in determining a satisfactory price level at which the prices are to be stabilised, disappearance of indirect business incentives provided by a rising price level. Further, the prices in different sectors of the economy vary considerably and exhibit different trends.

The objective of price stability has been criticised on a number of grounds. The objective of monetary policy today is no longer restricted only to the stabilisation of internal prices but covers the stabilisation of economic activity consistent with full employment and growth within the system. The policy of price stabilisation does not make a distinction between price changes that are due to non-monetary causes and those which are due to monetary causes. Some economists are of the opinion that the objective of the monetary policy should be stabilisation of the prices of factors of production and not the prices of the commodities.

In fact, changes in prices in different sectors in response to changes in demand or supply conditions are helpful in correcting maladjustment in the economy.

Moreover, stability of prices does not necessarily lead to stability of business conditions. An ideal situation would be that in which full employment is achieved simultaneously with price stability. It is, however, generally agreed that if the two objectives cannot be attained simultaneously, the objective of price stability would be the one to be sacrificed. This objective has thus been replaced by the objective of full employment with stability.

Price stability as the objective of monetary policy is suitable for those countries which are agricultural and large in size, and in the economy of which foreign trade plays an unimportant role.

NEUTRALITY OF MONEY

The term neutral money which originated from Wicksteed was made popular by the Dutch economist Koopmans. Recent advocates of neutral money policy include Hayek and Robertson. The basic idea of the policy is that money should be controlled in such a way that its quantity in circulation does not affect the prices.

The idea of neutral money is clearly connected with the philosophy of *laissez faire*. The quantity of money would be so controlled as to have the result that the total output, the purchases and sales and the prices of goods and services are exactly what they would be in a non-money using economy in which, however, the shortcomings of barter are overcome. The idea is that the motivation of private gain and the automatic regulative forces of competition would lead to an equilibrium adjustment of production and consumption. In the absence of distorting stimulus of credit creation and credit destruction, the economy would be completely stable, subject to only those changes which result from such fundamental factors as alterations of consumers' preferences or improvements in the arts or acts of God.

The advocates of neutral money believe that the worst disturbances in a modern economy are those originating in monetary changes. If disturbances caused by creation or destruction of money are ruled out, there would be no business fluctuations but only comparatively smooth adjustments to changes in technology or other data.

Money divides the actions of barter into purchases and sales which are individually independent of each other but equal as a total for the whole economy. If new money is created, it leads to new demand which is not immediately and precisely matched by an equal increase in the supply of goods and services at prevailing prices. Similarly, if some money is removed out of circulation, existing supply does not find its demand counterpart on the markets without painful downward price adjustment. Creation as well as destruction of money disturbs the equality between demand and supply.

The above, however, should not be taken to mean that neutral monetary policy implies a completely stable quantity of money. In the first place, the monetary authority would have to be authorised to counterbalance changes in the velocity of circulation of money arising from factors like hoarding and dishoarding by the public. Secondly, unless fundamental changes in the economy structure—population, technology, integration of industrial organisation—are compensated by changes in the quantity of money, there will result disturbances, precisely contrary to neutral monetary theory.

Professor Hayek vehemently criticises inflationism. He rejects as basically inflationism even those theories "which have led to the belief that, by stabilising the general price level, all the disturbing monetary causes would be eliminated."[1] He further remarks:[2]

> If we have to recognise that, on the one hand, under stable price level, relative prices may be changed by monetary influences, and on the other, that relative prices may remain undisturbed only when the price level changes, we have to give up the generally received opinion that if the general price level remains the same, the tendencies towards economic equilibrium are not disturbed by monetary influences, and that disturbing influences from the side of money make themselves felt otherwise than by causing change of the general price level.

Relative inflation and deflation are considered to be manifestations of non-neutral money. An inflationary situation is that in which the supply of money exceeds the condition of neutrality whilst deflation exists when the supply of money falls short of the amount corresponding to the principle of neutrality. The zero mark of inflation and deflation is thus made identical with the 'ideal' of neutral money supply.

This type of reasoning suffers from a number of weaknesses. The neutral money is a corollary of the old quantity theory of money, which establishes a direct relation between the quantity of money in circulation and the level of prices. Without going into the discussion of the validity of the old quantity theory of money, it may be mentioned that the prices may fluctuate even when the money remains neutral on account of changes in the volume of transactions. The policy of neutral money may be applied to a static society in which population, production technology etc. remain unchanged and not to a dynamic society. If money were neutral since 1914, the manifold increase in production would have resulted into a serious decline in prices. Thus the neutral money policy though aiming at elimination of inflation or deflation, actually leads to deflationary tendencies which might discourage economic development.

---

1. F.A. Hayek, *Monetary Theory and the Trade Cycle,* p. 16.
2. *Ibid*., p. 24.

But the supporters of the neutral money policy argue that a fall in prices which is due to technological progress and increased productivity of the factors of production is not at all dangerous. If the unit costs of production decrease and if the prices are forced down by competition to a correspondingly low level, there is no reason why production should be affected adversely.

> When the decline of prices is due to improvements in industry and agriculture which have lowered production cost, the decline of prices is, on the whole beneficial, for it is in this way that the fruits of industrial and agricultural progress are made available to the society as a whole.... It is only when the attempt is made to sustain prices in the face of decreasing production costs that disequilibrium occurs, for this encourages overproduction and causes an accumulation of goods which results ultimately in a breakdown.[3]

The above argument, however, holds true only when prices adjust themselves in the downward direction to the reduced cost of production instantaneously through competition. But in the actual world, prices do not adjust themselves readily and immediately to the cost of production because of the existence of several frictions. Professor Hansen has criticised the neutral money theory on the ground that it

> presupposes...that prices are, in point of fact, reduced at once wherever technical improvements lower cost. Under the modern development of cartels, and other monopolistic and quasi-monopolistic organizations, this assumption does not correspond to reality...It is not possible for the central bank to lower the individual prices of those commodities which, as a result of technical progress, are produced at a lower unit costs. All the banking system can do is to keep money constant (or, more accurately speaking, natural). The price level will, in consequence, fall, but there is no assurance that the decline will take place in the commodities produced at lower costs. If the prices of these commodities are held above cost the effects of a neutral money policy

3. Gold Delegation of the League of Nations, *Final Report* (Geneva, 1932).

> will be to force down the prices of commodities whose costs have not fallen at all.[4]

The decline in prices, apart from being due to increased productivity of the factors, may also be because of, unit cost of production remaining unchanged, increases in production. The volume of production in India today, for instance, is much larger than what it was hundred years ago. In such cases, if the quantity of money remains neutral in the sense of fixed quantity, prices would fall even if there is no decline in the unit cost of production. This tendency of the prices to fall as a result of the increase in production would cause a vicious process of contraction. In such a situation, new money will have to be introduced in the economy so as to maintain the old ratio between prices and quantity of money. But such a step would be against the concept of neutral money. Prices may also change because of changes in the velocity of circulation of money. During recession when people prefer hoarding to spending, even though the quantity of money may remain neutral, prices may decline because of a decrease in the velocity of circulating media.

The above discussion leads to the conclusion that the neutral money policy cannot solve the problem of economic fluctuations. If prices are to be kept stable under neutral money policy, the quantity of the money will have to be continuously changed through the conscious and deliberate decision of the monetary authority so as to adjust to the continuous changes in the volume of production. In fact, the policy of neutral money and that of economic stabilisation are inconsistent. Because of its serious shortcomings, the policy of neutral money has never gone beyond the stage of academic discussions.

INCOME STABILISATION

Stability of income has been proposed as an objective of the monetary policy by those economists (*e.g.* Hawtrey) who consider trade cycle to be a purely monetary phenomena. They are of the view that to avoid or mitigate the evil effects created by cyclic fluctuations, the credit must be controlled, *i.e.*, an overissue of credit must be avoided under all circumstances. The objective of income stabilisation makes the banking system of the country

4. A.H. Hansen, *Full Recovery or Stagnation* (New York, 1938), pp. 78-79.

equally sensitive to deflationary fluctuations. If some quantity of money is hoarded, it will disturb the level of income and investment. In such a situation, the monetary authority should adopt the policy of credit expansion so that the former level is restored.

This objective of the monetary policy has been criticised on two major grounds. In the first place, to stabilise incomes, the level of employment will be taken as stabilised but the present level of employment is far from satisfactory because there exists considerable unemployment. Secondly, since the present distribution of national income is unfair, the maintenance of existing level cannot be justified.

FULL EMPLOYMENT

In recent years, price and exchange stabilities have been relegated to the background and achievement of full employment has assumed great importance as the goal of monetary policy. Prof. Crowther is of the opinion that the main object of monetary policy of a country is to bring about equilibrium between saving and investment in the country at the level of full employment. In the words of Keynes, "the object of a monetary policy should be to reduce the ebb and flow of the trade cycles, and bring about equilibrium between savings and investment at the point of full employment."[5]

Keynes was one of those economists who directed their efforts not only in diagnosing the ailments of the economy but also in prescribing right remedies for them. The 'pre-Keynesian' classical type of monetary policy tried to cure depression simply by making more central bank funds available at low rates of interest. But the inadequacy and ineffectiveness of such a policy during depression was demonstrated both by the Keynesian analysis and the actual experience of depression when the desire for liquidity made it impossible to increase funds for investment. Thus the objective of monetary policy is not only to cure booms and depressions when they have already occurred but to check the recessionary or inflationary tendencies in their initial stages.

According to Keynes, full employment of available resources, which will automatically lead to maximum output, can only be

5. J.M. Keynes, *A Tract on Monetary Reforms,* 1923.

attained by maintaining an adequate volume of expenditure in the country. In order to cure unemployment, the monetary policy should aim at expanding consumption (C) and investment (*I*) expenditure. Since the consumption function is more or less stable in the short period, the monetary policy should aim at increasing investment expenditure. To increase the volume of investment, cheap money policy should be followed so as to stimulate borrowing for investment which in its turn through multiplier-acceleration effect will lead to increased level of employment. Once the level of full employment is attained, then through equality between saving and investment, monetary policy tries to maintain it.

The concept of full employment which calls for the employment of all the available resources of a country is somewhat vague. Instead, we should have optimum employment, *i.e.*, a level of utilisation of economic resources which leads to the highest national income, but if we try to fully utilise the labour force, "we might be forced to choose combinations of the factors of production which yield a considerably smaller social product (*i.e.* national income) than the optimum combination which leaves some of the available means of production unemployed."

MONETARY POLICY DURING DEPRESSION

Depression is characterised by low marginal efficiency of capital on account of falling prices, incomes, output and employment and the resulting uncertainties. It is period of low interest rates and unusually high liquidity preference. The objectives of monetary policy during depression are to offset the decline in velocity of money, to satisfy demands for hoarding including precautionary and speculative motives, to strengthen the cash position of banks and non-bank groups, stimulating lending for investment and consumption purposes, bringing down the structure of interest rates with a view to encouraging investment etc.

Limitations of Monetary Policy in Stimulating Recovery: Today it is widely believed that the monetary policy is ineffective in lifting an economy out of the depth of depression. The interest rates are already very low during depression and cannot be depressed further. Injections of cash and other liquid securities into the economy are absorbed by firms, banks and individuals in strengthening their liquidity position, in changing from risky and liquid assets to less risky and more liquid ones because of a general wave of pessimism and uncertainty which shrouds the future. The attempts to increase the amount of money in a slump may merely increase liquidity. Even if it is accepted that the monetary authority can lower the rate of interest, the effects on investment may be negligible because the marginal efficiency of capital continues to be low. Businessmen borrow when business is expanding and not when it is declining. A decline in interest rate cannot make unwilling and nervous borrowers to borrow. One can take the horse to water but can not make it drink. Moreover, there is a minimum beyond which the rate of interest cannot be lowered by increasing the supply of money. Thus monetary policy may not be very effective in lifting the economy out of depression.

It would, however, be a gross mistake to regard monetary policy as absolutely ineffective and useless. The cheap money policy does affect private investment demand for durable consumer goods. Low interest rates stimulate sale of durable goods like automobiles, television sets, refrigerators etc. which are purchased on credit. Low interest rates also stimulate long-term investments. Investment in public utilities, for instance, is highly interest-elastic.

When a cumulative business contraction has got under way, monetary policy alone may be enough to reverse the decline and other measures may not be required to increase aggregate spending. But even in this case monetary policy can play an important role. During the downswing, there is generally a scramble for liquidity. The monetary authorities should attempt to offset this increase in liquidity preference to the maximum possible extent. The central bank should pump reserves into the banking system so as to induce banks not to liquidate their earning assets; it can supply cash to banks as well as to the non-banking public through large open-market operations. By lowering interest rates and holding up bond prices, it can help in maintaining confidence in the financial and business community and thus reduce the general desire to hold cash rather than securities and goods. By prompt and vigorous action, the central bank can reduce the strength of the cumulative deflationary forces at work—though it cannot eliminate them altogether. But if the central bank does this much, the task to be done by other measures would be very much facilitated.

MONETARY POLICY DURING INFLATION

Inflation is characterised by high marginal efficiency of capital as a result of rising prices, incomes, output and employment. There is all-round optimism and business activity expands rapidly. Banks release more and more cash making additions to consumer's income and expenditure. Traders faced with reduced stocks of goods and continuously rising demand make frantic efforts to obtain and hold additional stocks. The improved prospects of business and high values of securities on the stock exchanges make the banking authorities willing to expand their credit which is used for additions to fixed capital, plant and machinery. Both consumer spending and investment spending reach a high pitch making credit conditions extremely tight. Banks find it difficult to meet the increased demand for credit. Under such conditions, the objective of monetary policy should be to slow down the rate of expansion of money, to reduce the velocity of circulation of money, to contract the volume of liquid assets and to reduce consumption and investment spendings through higher interest rates. The objective should be to check off the inflation and to level off the boom conditions.

Effectiveness of Monetary Policy in Checking Inflation: Monetary policy is more effective in checking inflation than in curing a depression. It is easier to raise interest rates than to lower them. This is followed by open market operations to curtail the liquidity of banks and non-bank groups, thereby further reducing lending and investment. Further margin requirements and consumer credit conditions may also be tightened. If even then expenditure on consumption and investment is not reduced, there remains the power to raise reserve requirements to check further expansion of bank credit. Thus monetary policy, if applied quickly and judiciously, can be fairly successful in preventing booms from developing into inflation.

Though monetary policy is more effective in checking inflation than in curing deflation, it is not without limitations. Interest on capital constitutes only a small part of the total cost of production. In a period of rising prices and high profit expectations, a rise in interest rates may not be successful in discouraging investment. If interest rates are substantially raised to have any effect, the effect will be first felt by small business. In order to check speculative investment genuine borrowers may be hurt first. If the banks possess excess reserves, the measures adopted by the central bank may fail in reducing the volume of credit and raising the rate of interest. An increase in bank rate may be ineffective if commercial banks do not follow the rise in the bank rate by raising their own interest rates. Since monetary policy is not very effective, more and more reliance has been placed on direct controls over prices to check inflation.

EFFECTIVENESS OF MONETARY POLICY

The success of monetary policy considerably depends on the influence which the rate of interest can be expected to wield on the investment and consumption decisions of the community. While the contact between the monetary authority and consumption is indirect, roundabout and remote, since consumption is a function of income, the relationship between monetary policy and investment is direct and effective in so far as it can influence the rate of interest with the changes in the quantity of money.

Is investment in stocks interest-elastic? The total cost of holding stocks includes cost of warehousing, insurance against fire, theft etc., allowance for depreciation of quality and the risk of the price of the commodity falling while it is being held. These other charges may constitute a large percentage of total cost and as such the interest may form only a small part of total costs. If this is the case, changes in the rate of interest will not appreciably affect the holding of stocks.

A trader may by and large finance his business from his own internal resources instead of being dependent on the bank credit. In such a case he may not bother much about the rise in the rate of interest. This, however, does not mean that interest rate considerations do not matter at all in such cases. Entrepreneurs with liquid cash, obtained through the ploughing back of profits, must calculate the cost of these resources on the basis of their earnings in alternative investments. If the rate of earnings on the use of this liquid cash in the security investment exceeds the rate of profits on their employment in holding stocks, the difference between the two rates will be reckoned as a loss to the firm which possesses the funds.

Before 1920 or so when the quantity theory of money dominated the scene, there was little doubt about the effectiveness of monetary policy. It, however, failed to control the unprecedented hyper-inflation of Germany. It could not revive economic activity during the depression of thirties. Keynes openly questioned the efficacy of monetary policy and advocated fiscal policy to bring about economic stability and full employment. In the fifties, opinions changed again in favour of monetary policy, countries raised rediscount rates, sold securities and tightened the money markets in their efforts to control the post-war inflation. An important reason for the renewed emphasis on the monetary policy is that since the World War II the problem faced by the world is that of inflation and not depression. Radcliffe Committee expressed the opinion that monetary policy consisting of the bank rate and selective credit controls may be quite effective in checking an inflationary situation but it cannot be expected to act quickly enough or alone to bring about a complete recovery during depression. Keynes and his followers—Hansen, Kurihara, Lerner etc.—maintain that monetary policy alone cannot cure business cycle and generate full employment for, according to them, business cycle is not a monetary phenomena. Even they, however, believe that it can assist towards that end. Though monetary policy alone cannot eliminate business fluctuations, if applied skillfully, it can certainly reduce the amplitude of fluctuations. It suitably combined with fiscal and other measures can eliminate business fluctuations and generate full employment.

While a flexible countercyclical monetary policy is certainly desirable, a number of cautions should be borne in mind. Monetary policy cannot be considered in isolation from the fiscal policy but must be synchronized with the latter. Secondly, monetary policy alone cannot be relied upon for fighting inflation, particularly because the inflation that is being faced today is due to more than a simple excess of aggregate demand. Thirdly, monetary policy cannot be divorced from debt management; and as such the freedom of monetary authorities is restricted by the need to maintain a smoothly functioning market for government securities, including the steady flow of new securities that the Treasury must issue to replace those that mature. Finally, the aggregate spending can change because of changes in velocity as well as in the supply of money. While monetary measures can contribute something to the stabilisation policy, they cannot by themselves stabilise velocity. Cyclical instability reflects changes in velocity more than in the quantity of money and the rise in prices since the World War II has been more owing to the rise in velocity than owing to increase in the supply of money.

MONETARY POLICY AND ECONOMIC DEVELOPMENT

The nature of unemployment in a developing country, as already seen, is different from that in an advanced country and its basic solution lies in accelerating the rate of capital formation and rapid economic growth. In an underdeveloped country cheap money policy would lower the rate of interest and thereby stimulate investment. In case it leads to misdirection of investment, the central bank can apply selective credit controls so as to direct investment into desirable channels. In an underdeveloped economy, private investment may not be forthcoming in adequate amounts and as such public investment on a large scale may become necessary. Cheap money policy would promote public investment by keeping the burden of interest on public borrowing low.

Some economists have suggested that the underdeveloped countries should follow a policy of high interest rates. According to them, a high rate of interest would limit the allocation of scarce capital only to the most productive uses and avoid wasteful use of resources. It would also serve as an effective anti-inflationary measure by restricting undesirable investment and stimulating saving. A policy of high interest rates, however, does not appear to be in the interest of the underdeveloped countries. No doubt high interest rates may check inflation by curtailing investment, it is not desirable for an underdeveloped country to resort to a general restriction of investment just for controlling inflation. On the contrary, a mild doze of inflation generates forced savings which can be utilised for purposes of investment. A better and more effective method of checking investments in undesirable directions would be to resort to direct controls and control over capital issues. Further the qualitative methods of credit control can be so handled as to ensure reasonable control over investment without producing any adverse effect on investment in desirable directions. As regards the argument of stimulating saving, it may be mentioned that the volume of savings depends more on the capacity to save and the facilities for saving than on the rate of interest. Further, as already seen, an increase in the rate of interest will lead to a decline in the volume of savings in case of people who save with the objective of having a certain specified amount of income in years to come. A high rate of interest can, of course, be used a shock tactic. When speculation in goods and securities becomes ripe and gets beyond control by other means, the rate of interest may be employed for pricking the bubble. The monetary policy can influence economic growth by helping to create favourable environments for saving and investment. Past history tells us that rising prices have a tendency to discourage saving. When the money is expected to depreciate in value, people have a tendency to spend it rather than saving it. This is particularly the case when the prices are rising very fast. Inflation is a tax on cash balances. Stable prices, in contrast, promote savings which are the principal source of investible funds.

The monetary policy can perhaps be most useful in shaping the character of investment. This will, of course, depend on the range of credit institutions that exist, and the forms of credit controls that are adopted. In most of the underdeveloped countries, the commercial banks provide only short-term credit which is primarily used for carrying inventories, purchasing land and real estate, or financing the production of export crops. The banks are reluctant to provide medium-term and long-term finance on the required scale and as such there is a shortage of finance for public utilities, for purchase of raw materials, and for manufacturing in general. To induce banks to provide more medium-term and long-term loans of a productive nature, the government may make appropriate guarantees or provide rediscounting facilities. Joint loans by commercial banks and state-managed development finance institutions can be another method.

Selective credit controls can be used to influence the pattern of investment and production. By differentiating between the cost and availability of credit to different sectors, selective credit controls can influence the allocation of credit and thereby the pattern of development. This selectivity can be introduced in credit policy by directly stipulating the loans that can be made, the amounts, the rates of interest, the duration, the type that is not desirable, the amount of collateral, and other provisions. Alternatively, if the central bank has adequate powers of control over the commercial banks, such controls may be exercised selectively so as to indirectly influence the behaviour of the banks; rediscount rates, for instance, may vary according to the type of loan, or some selective exceptions may be made on reserve requirements.[6]

A developing country has a tendency to get into balance of payments difficulties. In such a situation, in addition to exercising direct controls on foreign exchange, the monetary authority should help in improving the balance of payments position by using traditional methods of control like raising the bank rate etc.

The role of monetary policy should not, however, be overestimated. As an instrument of promoting capital formation, monetary policy is not as effective as the fiscal policy. An easy money policy makes credit more readily available but this credit will not be utilised unless profit expectations are sufficiently high. Moreover, such a policy will lead to inflationary pressures which may harm the process of economic development.

To permit the use of monetary policy, the underdeveloped countries must first improve their currency and credit system. There is the need for banks and financial institutions which will increase credit facilities and channel actual and potential voluntary savings into productive uses. At present the credit system is limited to providing credit for large estates, plantations and foreign traders. Adequate credit facilities are not available for peasants, small industry and small traders. There is the need to extend commercial banks and to introduce savings banks, co-operative savings societies and mutual societies. The need is particularly urgent in rural areas.

In order to control the supply and uses of money, the central banks must work in an effective manner. Though central banks exist in all countries, their working is far from satisfactory because of the particular characteristics of their money markets. Firstly, there is a vast non-monetised sector where the changes in the quantity of money or interest rates do not exert any influence upon the nature and level of economic activity. Secondly, the proportion of credit policy presupposes the existence of a developed money market which is conspicuous by its absence in underdeveloped

---

6. I.G. Patel, "Selective Credit Controls in Underdeveloped Economics" *International Monetary Fund Staff Papers* (September, 1954), pp. 76-77.

countries. The underdeveloped countries are marked by an underdeveloped money market having the following characteristics:

(1) It lacks a highly organised banking system.

(2) It is not composed of specialised sale markets like bill market, bond market, call-loan market etc.

(3) The different sub-markets are not well integrated. There are sub-markets which often occupy significant positions, but are not linked with or influenced by the banking system, *e.g.*, Indian indigenous bankers.

(4) Because of the various rigidities and bottlenecks which hamper the mobility of capital funds, an underdeveloped money market is rather insensitive to the impact of international influences.

RECONCILIATION OF CONFLICTING OBJECTIVES

Normally, the different objectives of monetary policy discussed above (*viz.* price stability, exchange rate stability, full employment and economic growth) are not inconsistent with each other. Sometimes, however, these objectives may conflict with each other. In the post-war recessions, for instance, prices of consumer goods continued to rise for several months after production, employment and income started declining. In such situations, the objective of price stability calls for a tight money policy while declining business activity and employment require an easy money policy. At such times, the objectives of monetary policy are in conflict and the monetary authority has to make choices. In making choices, the objective should be to aim at that combination of objectives which in the prevailing conditions would be in the best interest of the country.

Fiscal Policy

20

INTRODUCTION

The fiscal policy as an instrument of economic stabilisation has assumed great importance since the depression of 1930s. This is owing to several reasons *viz.* limited effectiveness of monetary policy in initiating revival of economic activity, the new emphasis placed on the concept of aggregate demand in economic analysis, and the growing size of the government budget relative to the national income.

OBJECTIVES OF FISCAL POLICY

The fiscal policy aims at different objectives depending upon the particular circumstances of the country. Following may be mentioned among the important objectives of fiscal policy:

(1) It may aim at increasing the efficiency of productive resources like men, money, materials etc.

(2) Its objective may be an equal distribution of wealth and income. It means that differences in payments to the factors of production should be minimised and inequalities in income should be reduced by transferring wealth from the rich to the poor.

(3) The aim of the fiscal policy may be to maintain price stability. A decline in prices leads to a sharp decline in business activity and the level of employments. On the other hand, a rise in prices hits hard the fixed income classes and may benefit the speculators and traders. The fiscal policy should, therefore, aim at maintaining a reasonably stable general price level.

(4) The most important objective of fiscal policy is the attainment and maintenance of full employment. According to classical economists fiscal policy was neither to encourage nor to discourage the level of economic activity. In regard to economic activity, it was to be strictly neutral. The classicists considered the functions of the state pertaining to taxation and expenditures as a necessary evil.

They advocated strict restriction of the functions of state so as to permit the market mechanism to operate freely and smoothly. They believed that taxes result in a wrong diversion of resources and wanted that the public spending should be minimum possible. They further believed that the budget should be balanced. Keynes exposed the fallacy of the classical neutral fiscal policy and considered positive fiscal policy as a balancing factor to bring about an adjustment between the propensity to save and the inducement to invest. Under the institutional arrangements of the capitalistic economy, there is no market mechanism which acts as a balancing factor between the disproportions of the desire to save and the desire to invest. Investments may be so large as to generate inflationary pressures or so low as to result in chronic unemployment. In the former case, the state should cut down its spending and raise taxes and in the latter case, it should increase its spending and lower taxes and thus rectify the disequilibrium between saving and investment at the full employment level.

It is, however, not necessary that the different objectives of fiscal policy should be compatible with each other. There may arise conflicts between certain objectives of fiscal policy. The objective of equal distribution of income, for instance, may come in conflict with the objectives of economic efficiency and economic growth. The objective of equal distribution of income would require such a taxation policy as transfers income from the rich to the poor but this type of policy will adversely affect savings and consequently the rate of capital formation.

INSTRUMENTS OF FISCAL POLICY

The instruments of fiscal policy are taxes, expenditure and public debts which constitute the nations's budget. The expenditures include normal government expenditures, capital expenditure on public works, relief expenditures, subsidies of various types, transfer payments and social security benefits. While the government expenditures are income generating, the taxes are primarily income reducing. Management of public debt has become an important instrument of fiscal policy in most of the countries. It aims at influencing aggregate spending through changes in the liquid asset position.

CONTRA-CYCLICAL FISCAL POLICY

Contra cyclical fiscal policy means that taxes (*T*) and government spending (*G*) be varied to an anti-cyclical direction. *G* being cut and *T* increased in the expansion phase of the cycle and *G* increased and *T* cut during the contraction phase. In this way booms can be cut down and the troughs of depression filled in. In other words, the objective of the fiscal policy is to "chop off the hills to fill in the valleys." To put in simple words, when total private spending on consumption and investment is too high (*i.e.* is at inflationary level), the state should compensate by curtailing public investment and expenditure and increasing its tax collections—it should withdraw funds from income stream by taxing away more than it spends, generating a negative multiplier effect. At the extreme, it may simply hold or destroy this net surplus or it may use the surplus to pay off public debt, hoping that the bond holders will not rush out and spend the funds they receive. On the other hand, when private spending on consumption and investment is too low (*i.e.* is at deflationary level), the state should compensate by stepping up its previously postponed expenditures and by reducing its tax collections—it should inject more funds into income stream by spending more than it currently collects in taxes, generating a positive multiplier effect. At the extreme, it may finance this net addition by creating new money so as to ensure a net addition to private spending or it may borrow existing funds from the public hoping to draw on funds that would not otherwise be spent. When the government is following contra-cyclical compensatory policy of taxing and spending, the government budget would rarely be in balance. Since taxes are increased and government expenditure reduced on the upswing, there would emerge a surplus of revenue over expenditure during this period. In contrast, the downswing would be characterised by revenues falling short of expenditures, because during this period the spending is increased and taxes reduced. The budgets are to be balanced neither yearly nor cyclically. They are to be so managed as to compensate under-spending or over-spending in the private sector of the economy so as to achieve the objective of economic stability and full employment.

We briefly discuss below the various instruments of fiscal policy and see to what end they could possibly be put and with what results.

BUDGETARY POLICY

Budget is an important instrument of fiscal policy and it shall have to be readjusted to fight both deflation and inflation. From time to time, several budgetary principles have been put forward *viz.* annually balanced budget, cyclically balanced budget, fully managed compensatory budget.

Annually Balanced Budget: The classical economists advocated a policy of balanced and small budgets. Until the 1930s, hardly anybody questioned the policy advocated by the classical economists. There were at least two reasons for the acceptance of the proposition that the budgets should be balanced every year, *viz.* (i) an analogy with personal finance, where a person's income must cover his expenditures if he is to stay on good terms with his creditors; and (ii) a pervasive feeling that by and large the economic system automatically corrects any deviation from full employment without help from government fiscal policy. The state is to feed into the income stream just what it withdraws and no less. Thus a balanced budget appears appropriate when an economy is satisfied with the existing level of total expenditures, or in other words, the economy is in a state of full employment without inflation. But when the economy is suffering from inflation, the principle of balancing the budget annually runs contrary to the goal of economic stability because it well have destabilising effects which would tend to intensify the trade cycle. During the inflationary period a surplus budget is likely to arise because of increasing tax revenues. The principle of annually balanced budget requires an increase in government expenditure or a reduction in taxes to bring the budget into balance which would intensify inflation. The proper course during inflation would be to increase tax rates or to reduce government expenditure. Similarly, during a deflationary period a deficit will automatically be created because of decline in tax revenues. The principle of annually balanced budget requires that the state must raise taxes to get more money and reduce expenditures to match its reduced tax receipts. Increase in taxes and reduction in expenditure in a contraction period in order to balance the budget would have further negative multiplier effects which would intensify deflation. But the right course during depression is to reduce tax rates and to increase government spending. Thus we find that the policy of balancing the budget in each fiscal year is a wrong prescription for stabilisation purposes. It rather intensifies the cyclical fluctuations.

Cyclically Balanced Budget: According to this approach which was first adopted in Sweden during thirities, the budget need not be balanced in each fiscal year but it should be so over the length of the business cycle. During the inflationary period, the budget must show a surplus of tax receipts over expenditure so that the public debt can be reduced. During the deflationary period, in contrast, the budget must show a deficit of taxes over expenditures, with public debt returning to its previous level. The budget should, of course, be balanced over the whole business cycle. Such a policy would permit state fiscal policy to play a positive stabilising role and at the same time maintain the basic character of a balanced budget. The principal of cyclically balanced budget is based on the assumption that surpluses of booms are cancelled by later depression deficits or depression deficits are matched by boom time surpluses.

The policy of cyclically balanced budget would work smoothly only if the booms and slumps were of equal duration and intensity or if the differences in duration were precisely offset by those in intensity. There would arise a problem if the depression and boom are of different durations and the differences in their duration are not offset by differences in their intensity. For instance, if the government runs a big deficit fighting a long and severe depression and then the following boom is very moderate, should the government feel obliged to collect a large surplus to match the preceding deficit?' The principle of cyclically balanced budget would reply in the positive but commonsense would rebel at the idea of a big government surplus when the problem is to avoid slipping back into large-scale unemployment. Further cyclically balanced budget may succeed in stabilising the level of economic activity but it cannot guarantee that the level at which income is stabilised is that of full employment.

Fully Managed Compensatory Budget: The policy of managed budgets consist of a deliberate attempt to adjust revenues, expenditures and public debts in a way so as to provide full employment without inflation. This policy became popular with the appearance of *Keynes' General Theory*. It advocates that we should forget about balancing the budget as a separate goal and make use of state budget in whatever way is necessary to provide full employment without inflation. If the economy stagnates, it will not mind more deficits than surpluses; a rising government debt is not a very big price for the elimination of mass unemployment. On the other hand, if the economy inflates, continued government surpluses are welcome. Budgetary balance is considered of only secondary importance. Much more importance is attached to the attainment and maintenance of full employment.

The policy of managed compensatory budget has been criticised on a number of grounds. In the first place, it is argued that the government should not give a blanket guarantee against unemployment because it would pressurise the bargaining power of monopolistic groups which would lead to inflation. Secondly, it is argued that there is such a long lag between the time when such a policy is needed and the time when its effects will actually be felt that the policy might in practice turn out to be destabilising as it is not automatic. The third argument is that since budgetary balance is given a secondary role, the managed budget policy may lead to a long-run growth in the national debt. In spite of these criticisms the managed budget policy has been favoured as an important instrument of fiscal policy to influence the level of income, output and employment. Further, it also includes compensatory budgets under which certain automatic stabilisers are built into the revenue and expenditure systems of the state.

TAXATION

The structure of tax rates has to be adjusted in the context of conditions prevailing in an economy. Changes in tax rates affect the level of disposable income and thereby the level of consumption. During depression tax policy has to be such as to encourage private consumption and investment. During inflation, in contrast, the tax policy should discourage consumption and investment. During depression taxation burden on the community should be reduced. The commodity taxes should be reduced to the minimum so as to stimulate increased consumption. Reduction in excise duties, sales tax etc. will go a long way in increasing community's consumption demand. Economists like Hansen and Musgrave favour reduction in corporate and income taxes because it will leave higher disposable incomes with the public for more consumption and also because low corporation and business taxes will encourage 'rich enterprise' and 'venture capital' and thereby promote investment. But economists like Kalecki have expressed grave doubts in the supposed stimulating effect of tax reductions on the volume of investment. They point out that even heavy tax reductions do not go to alter the decisions of entrepreneurs. They hold that the policy of tax reductions to increase C and I is no solution for unemployment because in that case income tax will have to be continuously reduced. It cannot be denied, however, that in the short period it is wise to encourage private investment by manipulating business tax rates and to encourage consumption by lowering sales tax and excise duties. It may also be desirable to manipulate a certain amount of redistributive taxation to stimulate consumption function. The idea is to tax the rich (having a low propensity to consume) at a progressive rate in order to subsidise the poor (having a high propensity to consume) so as to stimulate consumption expenditure. Redistributive taxation, however, may lead to a counteracting decline in saving and investment spending by the rich. Further, the difference in the marginal propensities to consume of the poor and rich families is far less than that in their average propensities to consume and the net effect of income redistribution on consumption depends on the comparative marginal propensities of the families concerned.

During inflation, on the other hand, the taxes should be increased to wipe off the surplus purchasing power. Care should, however, be taken not to raise the taxes so high as to stifle new investment or generate a business recession. Expenditure tax and excise duties are anti-inflationary in character. During inflation the fiscal authority should levy such taxes as go to reduce current incomes and demand for particular commodities rather than the aggregate demand. Perhaps the most effective anti-inflationary tax is personal income tax with steep rates and high surcharges. It would reduce the disposable income in the hands of the people and thus help in curbing inflationary pressures. While taxes should be increased, customs duties on essential imports should be reduced so as to encourage increased imports to increase the supply of goods at home to match the increased demand. While raising taxes to curb inflationary pressures, care should, however, be taken that money incomes are not so much deflated as to generate a recession. Experience has shown that manipulation of tax rates is a more powerful and effective anti-cyclical instrument than interest rates.

PUBLIC SPENDING

Public expenditure is the most important instrument of fiscal policy. These days government expenditure forms a very important part of the total expenditure in the economy and an increase or a decrease in it can cause significant variations in income, output and employment. Any increase in government spending has multiplier effect like private investment. Similarly, a decline in government spending will set in operation multiplier in the backward direction.

If private demand is not adequate to maintain income and output at full employment level, the government should spend an amount equal to the deflationary gap in order to restore full employment. The positive multiplier effects of government expenditure will counteract or offset the negative multiplier effects of decline in private demand and restore the economy to a level of full employment national income. On the other hand, if private demand is excessive or inflationary, the government should reduce its own expenditure to counteract or wipe off this inflationary gap. In this way, the government spending can act as a balancing to disequilibrium between *S* and actual *I*.

The principal cause of inflation in a country is the excessive aggregate spending. During inflation, therefore, the wise policy is to reduce government expenditure by giving up those schemes which are justified during deflation and by postponing the construction of various types like school buildings, hospital, parks, etc. Simultaneously, with the reduction in expenditure, attempts should be made to increase revenue to generate a budget surplus. Though there is a minimum below which the government cannot reduce its spending, yet it can vary its expenditure to some extent to overcome inflationary pressures.

A distinction is often made between two concepts of public spending *viz.* (1) 'pump priming' and (2) 'compensatory spending': The term pump-priming implies that a certain amount of public spending, varying under different conditions, will have the effect of setting the economy going on the way toward full utilisation of resources on its own power without further aid from governmental spending.[1] The concept does not amply, as has sometimes been suggested, that only a very small amount of public spending will set

1. Alvin H. Hansen. *Fiscal Policy and Business Cycle* (New York, 1941), p. 262.

the economy operating at full capacity. A pump may require much or little priming, depending upon a variety of conditions; similarly, the concept of pump-priming carries with it no implication as to the amount of spending necessary, but only the implication that, whatever the amount required, sooner or later the economy can operate on its own motive power.

Pump-priming is intended to be a remedy for a temporary maladjustment which prevents the economy from functioning in a normal manner so as to move out of depression. The economy needs to be shoved off dead centre, so as to resume the normal movement from depression to revival and recovery. It may be that the missing spark is a maladjustment in the cost-price structure, which rigidities in the system make it difficult to overcome without the application of a special remedy. In this case, public expenditures may have the effect of temporarily increasing income and output in the depressed areas, thereby facilitating a readjustment of the price structure towards a more normal relationship. It may be that the missing spark is lack of confidence on the part of business entrepreneurs on account of depressed conditions. A certain amount of public expenditure may start activity in the upward direction and encourage people to a less pessimistic and truer view of future prospects. It may be that the accumulation of replacement needs owing to depreciation and obsolescence has reached a point favourable to larger capital expenditures, or that the accumulation of innovations with respect to new products and new techniques has reached a point favourable to new investment. But these investment opportunities may await a determined and vigorous leadership behind which a host of timid entrepreneurs are ready to follow. Such leadership, however, may for various reasons not be forthcoming from private entrepreneurs, but may require government action. Under such conditions, pump-priming may prove very effective.

The concept of 'pump-priming' differs from 'compensation' in that the later has no implication in regard to setting the system going on its own momentum. The latter concept implies simply that the public expenditure may be used to compensate the shortfall in private investment. The extent of effectiveness of the compensation is not in question. A policy of compensation may be said to accomplish its purpose even though the public expenditures do not succeed in bringing the economy to full recovery. It may be said to be successful even though it succeeds in achieving a rise in the national income no greater than the volume of expenditures made.

As the long black years of 'thirties' dragged on, faith in government pump-priming weakened. Talk of the stagnant economy and chronic deficiency in private investment spread. Emphasis shifted to continuing compensatory spending. According to advocates of compensatory spending, the private economy cannot carry itself forward to prosperity even when primed by doses of public spending. Public deficit spending should be continued as long and as heavily as necessary to attain and maintain full employment. Compensatory spending, through its multiplier and acceleration effect, will raise the levels of income, output and employment.

The compensatory spending by the state during depression may take two forms (i) expenditure on public works like roads, schools, parks, buildings, airports, post offices, hospitals, canals etc. and (ii) transfer payments such as interest on the public debt, pensions, subsidies, relief payments, unemployment insurance, social security benefits etc. It has been suggested that the government should keep ready with them a list of public works, which may be taken up, the moment the economy shows signs of recession. These public works will provide employment to the unemployed workers not only directly but also indirectly through the expansion of secondary industries whose products are utilised in the construction of these public works. Such a programme of public works will boost up the sagging morale of businessmen who will start undertaking investments which would create increased employment opportunities in private industries. The primary employment in public works programmes will, in turn, induce secondary employment and thereby raise the level of business activity. As soon as the private investment become normal and the economy is put on the track, such programmes may be slackened and may be stopped completely during inflation so that at such a time public investment may not compete with private investment and may not lead to inflationary pressures. By proper timing of public works, the booms would be levelled off and the troughs of depression filled in.

The funds for such public works are to be raised by loans or by the creation of new money so that the total volume of spending is increased. If the funds are raised by taxation, public spending will simply replace private spending. Public expenditure through created money is called "interest-free financing" because no interest is payable on such monies.

Public works projects during depression are supported on the grounds that they (1) provide jobs for otherwise unemployed workers; (2) help to maintain the morale, self-respect and skills of workers; (3) directly stimulate the durable and constructional industries where unemployment is usually centred; (4) give us something to show for our money because modern schools, highways and bridges are valuable in their own way in addition to providing help in putting people back to work; (5) do not come in competition with private investment; (6) increase purchasing power and thereby stimulate demand for consumption goods.

Though an effective anti-depression weapon, they are subject to serious limitations. Important of such limitations are mentioned below:

In the first place, there is the problem of forecasting the coming depression or inflation. It may not be possible to accurately forecast their advent. But the effectiveness of public works programme depends on its proper timing.

Secondly, even if it is possible to accurately forecast the coming of depression, it may not be possible to undertake the public works programmes immediately to check it. Public works are clumsy and slow moving. They take time to get ready and to turn off. In spite of the best preparations made by the state, some delay in starting such projects is more or less inevitable.

Thirdly, the timing of public works projects cannot be adjusted easily to the movement of cycle. Many projects like dams etc. take a long time for completion and many others like schools and hospitals cannot be postponed or held till the emergence of depression. In case they are needed, they will have to be undertaken irrespective of whether the economy is suffering from inflation or deflation. It is not practical to cut off many projects short of their completion, once they are started. A bridge half way across a river or a half-built railway line must be completed to avoid wastage of country's precious productive resources. This difficulty is inherent in the construction activity.

In spite of the difficulties mentioned above, something can certainly be done to improve the timing of public works. As a minimum, the government agencies can plan work in such a way as not to accentuate short-term stability. There is often a tendency, particularly among state and local governments, to plan public work in way that accentuates short-term instability. The revenues of the governmental bodies rise during boom periods and they have a tendency to undertake more projects during such periods with increased revenues. Similarly, their expenditure on public works declines during the slump periods with the decline in their revenues.

In addition to what can be done in the field of 'heavy' public works, 'light' public works offer some scope for cyclical variation in government expenditures, particularly if a 'shelf' of such works is kept ready for use as and when the need arises. Light public works include projects like maintenance and improvement of roads, irrigation works and buildings, soil conservation and flood control etc., which can be started quickly and completed within a short period.

Fifthly, public projects become subjects for political pressures; every state, locality and political group demands its share.

Sixthly, these projects may perpetuate cost-price maladjustments in heavy industries where public works spending is centred. Wages and many monopolised prices is construction industry rise rapidly during the boom but stay far out of line when recession forces move flexible prices downward. Large government construction projects keep these costs up.

Seventhly, some types of public works may compete with, rather than induce, private investment. This objection has particularly been advanced against construction of low-cost housing etc.

Eighthly, it is unlikely that all the resources unemployed by a decline in aggregate demand will find employment in public works projects. "An advertising executive will probably not be a very good brick-layer...."[2]

2. Bach, *Economics*, p. 261.

Ninthly, the public works projects may lead to heavy debt burden for they are partly financed by public borrowing.

Finally, they may lead to misallocation of resources because the projects may be located in one region while the unemployed resources are located in another region and their mobility may be difficult to achieve.

Social Security Measures: In view of the limitations and practical difficulties of public works mentioned above, some economists favour a comprehensive programme of social security measures, like pensions, subsidies, relief payments, unemployment insurance etc. While it is desirable to change the volume of transfer payments as a part of a compensatory fiscal policy, the scope for this is limited. Social security programmes should be planned on a long-term basis and there should be no drastic changes in the provisions of these programmes with the changes in the volume of economic activity. The major scope for deliberately changing the amount of transfer payments lies in the field of consumers' subsidies to provide for the needy who are not covered by unemployment insurance and to supplement the benefits being received by those who are covered.

Different types of expenditures have different indirect effects on private investment. Normally, the stimulation effect of public works expenditures is likely to be more powerful than that of transfer payments of equal value. Public works expenditures stimulate the construction industries, which fluctuate widely over the cycle. During slump, increased expenditure on public works means substantially large orders for building materials and constriction equipment; these may induce firms to replace worn-out equipment and to accumulate inventories. As against this, an increase in transfer payments, even if entirely spent by the initial recipients, may only lead to a small increase in consumption, which may be met by a reduction in inventories by retailers and manufacturers; in any case it is not likely to provide a strong stimulus to investment expenditures by firms in the consumer-goods industries.

We have seen above the pros and cons of both the public works programmes and social security measures as instruments of counteracting fluctuations in economic activity. The best results would, however, be realised if the two types of measures are combined in a judicious manner.

BUILT-IN-FLEXIBILITY

Built-in-flexibility is another tool of fiscal policy. One of the practical difficulties of government expenditure and taxation to compensate for deficiencies or excesses in private spending is that of making the fiscal tools flexible enough for prompt and effective use. The tempo of business activity may change suddenly exhibiting itself in booms and slumps but fiscal tools cannot be geared immediately to cope with such situations for they lack flexibility. This practical difficulty has led to the suggestion for introduction of built-in-flexibility in the fiscal system. Under the built-in-flexibility system the tax rates are so fixed that in the upward phase of the business cycle with every increase in the national income the tax yield going to the government exchequer would automatically go up at a faster rate than increase in national income without any changes in the tax rates, while the government expenditure on relief, unemployment benefits, etc., would decline automatically with the rise in national income. As a result of the two forces operating simultaneously the budget would automatically show a surplus without any action by the government and thus the upswing would be automatically controlled. Similarly, in the downswing phase of the cycle, without any change in the tax rates, the tax yield would fall at a faster rate than the decline in national income and government expenditure on relief and unemployment benefits would go up and thus the budget would automatically show a deficit which would tend to counteract the downswing. The built-in-flexibility works without changes in the tax rates and thus avoids elaborate legislative procedure which such rate changes involve.

The built-in-flexibility has a number of advantages. It eliminates the need for making forecasts, which may turn out to be wrong, before action can be taken. Secondly, automatic stabilizers operate promptly without involving administrative delays which normally accompany discretionary changes in tax rates and expenditure programmes. Thirdly, such a policy by keeping tax rates unchanged and avoiding large and frequent changes in government spending programmes, creates conditions favourable to private investment. Fourthly, it is the simplest way of integrating short-run and long-run fiscal policy.

The effectiveness of the bulilt-in-flexibility depends upon the elasticity or the tax receipts (*i.e.* the rate at which the tax receipts change with changes in the national income) and the size of the tax revenue relatively to the national income. The larger the elasticity of tax receipts and the larger the ratio of tax revenue to income, the greater will be effectiveness of the built-in-flexibility in mitigating the amplitude of the upswings and downswings.

The experience of fiscal authorities even in advanced countries with sufficiently developed tax collection machinery, not to speak of the underdeveloped countries, shows that the elasticity of tax receipt is not sufficiently high to warrant an automatic regulation or business fluctuations with the help of built-in-flexibility measures alone. Such measures, therefore, have generally to be supplemented by formula flexibility under which tax rates are also increased in the upswing phase of the business cycle and reduced during the downswing phase according to some pre-determined formula which links the variations in tax rates with the fluctuations in national income. Since the elasticity of tax rates is likely to be greater under formula flexibility than under built-in-flexibility, the former is likely to be more effective in controlling the business swings than the latter. Similarly, the government expenditure may be varied counter-cyclically according to some pre-determined rule such as if the national income rises by such and such percentage, the government expenditure would be decreased by such and such percentage. In the case of built-in-flexibility, the parameters of fiscal policy like the tax rates are kept constant and the budget is made to work anti-cyclically through changes in the endogenous variables like, for example, the tax yield following the change in tax base, while in the case of formula flexibility the parameters themselves are varied in a counter-cyclical manner. In the case of formula flexibility, however, the parameter manipulations are not left to the discretion of the executive; such manipulations are made according to some pre-determined rules linking the parameter manipulations to the fluctuations in income, employment, price level etc.

COMPENSATORY SPENDING AND TAX POLICY

If the relation between expenditures and receipts is to be deliberately changed in order to counteract fluctuations in private spending, should we rely on changes in tax rates or changes in the volume of expenditure? Economic thinking on this matter has change somewhat in recent years. During the thirties, emphasis was placed on the possibilities of moderating cyclical fluctuations by varying the amount of government spending, which would be increased during depressions and reduced during booms. Particular emphasis was placed on the stimulating effect of increased expenditure on public works during depressions. But in recent years emphasis has been shifted to the results that can be obtained by changing tax rates.

Whether cyclical fluctuations can better be moderated by changes in tax rates or by changes in the volume of government expenditure depends particularly on (i) the multiplier effects of the proposed tax and expenditure changes, (ii) questions of timing and flexibility, and (iii) possible indirect repercussions on private spending. Pure multiplier analysis suggests that a certain increase in public expenditure on goods and services would have a greater impact on the gross national product than a decline in tax revenues of the same amount. The amount of difference would depend on, among other factors, the types of taxes involved. Let us illustrate it with the help of a simple example. Suppose, in order to raise the level of employment, the Government increases its expenditures on new goods and services by Rs. 4000. The tax rates remain unchanged. Further suppose that the marginal propensity to consume is 3/4. The additional expenditure would raise the gross national product by Rs. $4000 \times \frac{1}{1-\frac{3}{4}} =$ Rs. 16000. Now let us suppose that Rs. 4000 stimulus is attained through an appropriate reduction in the rate of personal income tax. The initial effect is to increase disposable incomes. Only thereafter there would be any increase in spending and further multiplier effects on the gross national product. If we assume that marginal propensity to consume disposable income is 8/10 and the marginal propensity to consume gross national product is ¾, the rise in gross national product brought about by a Rs. 4000 reduction in taxes would be Rs. $4000 \times \frac{8}{10} \times \frac{1}{1-\frac{3}{4}}$ or Rs. $4000 \times \frac{8}{10} \times 4/1$ or Rs. 12800. While disposable income rises initially by Rs. 4000, Rs. 800 of this is saved and only Rs. 3200 spent and are thus available to generate a multiplier effect.

The above conclusion, however, is based upon a number of assumption which, if dropped, may lead to even opposite conclusion. In the above example, for instance, it was assumed that a part of the tax reduction by the government (namely Rs. 800) is not spent by the recipients of the concession but is saved by them. In fact, this need not necessarily be so. If whole of the tax relief is spent by the beneficiaries, the increase in national income would amount to Rs. 4000 and hence a government expenditure programme and an equivalent tax relief programme would yield the same result. Further, in the above example, we have assumed that all persons in the community have the same marginal propensity to consume irrespective of their income. In actual practice, this is not likely to be true. If the recipients of government expenditure have a lower marginal propensity to consume than the recipients of tax concession then again a programme of government expenditure may be less expansionary than that of tax relief, since the higher multiplicand in the former case may be more than offset by a multiplier smaller than in the latter case. In addition, we shall have to see how different sections of the community gain or lose through the successive spending of the proceeds of the government expenditure and tax relief, since different sections in the community may have different marginal propensities to consume, with the result that the size of the multiplier may itself vary according to the nature of the distribution of the income and the purchasing power following the injection of fresh units of money into the economy as a result of the government expenditure of tax concession measures. Last, but not the least, we have to take into consideration the repercussions of the government expenditure or tax concession measures on the volume and nature of the private investments for a full understanding of the relative effectiveness of the measures. The above leads to the conclusion that though, other things remaining the same, a government expenditure programme has a tendency to be more expansionary than an equal-amount tax reduction programme, other things do not generally remain the same, with the result that by *a priori* reasoning we can not say that one method of expansion is always superior to another method.

While theoretical multiplier analysis favours changes in government spending as an instrument of compensatory fiscal policy, considerations of timing and flexibility go in favour of changes in tax rates. A reduction in tax rates, for instance, becomes operative promptly while it normally takes considerable time to plan and carry out changes in expenditures. Similarly, a change in tax rates can be reversed more quickly. One of the shortcomings of fighting recession by increasing public expenditures is that the major stimulating effect of such expenditures may be felt only after the next upswing is well under way. This is particularly the case with the heavier types of public works.

ALTERNATIVE FISCAL POLICIES FOR FULL EMPLOYMENT

In an economy with unemployed resources and manpower owing to deficiency in the volume of effective demand, fiscal policy may be used in any of the following three ways so as to attain full employment.

(i) *Deficit Spending:* When the sum of private consumption, private investment, government consumption and government investment is less than full employment income and as such there is a deflationary gap in the economy causing unemployment, the government may increase its expenditure either on consumption or on investment without an increase in taxation and thereby incur a deficit in the budget, the deficit being covered either by the creation of new money or by government borrowing. Assuming that the marginal propensity to consume of the economy is 3/4 and hence the multiplier 4, an additional government expenditure of Rs. 100 would lead to an increase in national income worth Rs. 400 which would consequently increase employment. This result is very likely in view of the fact that if the budget deficit is financed by the creation of money, there would be no reduction in the consumption of any other section, and if the deficit is covered by borrowing, the bond holder's marginal propensity to consume is not likely to be reduced thereby because the bonds are in all probability held out of funds which would otherwise have been saved.

Deficit without Spending: The second method by which the government can rectify unemployment is by reducing taxation without any increase in government expenditure and thereby creating a budget deficit. If taxes are reduced, the disposable income in the hands of the public increases and since at least a part of the increased income in the hands of the public is likely to be consumed, the total consumption of the community would be boosted up which would increase income and employment.

Spending without deficit (or the Balanced Budget Multiplier): The third type of expansionist fiscal policy, namely, the balanced budget multiplier, is the most interesting. Under such a policy an increase in government expenditure is matched by an equal increase in taxes and still there is a net increase in income. This happens because, in all probability, the marginal propensity to spend of the government is greater than that of the tax-payers. The government normally spends all the money that it raises in the form of taxes. But those who pay the tax do not reduce their consumption by the whole of tax payment.

If the marginal propensity to consume of the recipients of government expenditure and that of the tax-payers are identical, the balanced budget multiplier will be equal to one. If the marginal propensity to consume of the recipients of government expenditure is higher than that of the tax-payers, the balanced budget multiplier will be greater than one. If the marginal propensity to consume of the recipients of government expenditure is less than that of the tax-payers, the balanced budget multiplier will be less than one.

Secondly, the alternative fiscal policies assume that a government expenditure programme has no secondary effects on private investment and consumption expenditures. This is not realistic. In case the government investment expenditure, for instance, competes with the private investment expenditure, the latter may be so much discouraged that the government expenditure programme may have little, no, or even negative expansionary effect on the economy. Similarly, the government entry in fields traditionally dominated by the private enterprise may result in such adverse psychological effects on private investors that the expansionary effect of public investments may be largely offset by the contractionary effect of a fall in private investments. As against the latter possibility, we should also take into consideration another alternative possibility that the public investment may be of such a nature as facilitates private investment and increases its profitability. During a depression period, the public investment programme may be viewed by private investors as a symbol of determination of the government to fight the depression with all seriousness which would bring back recovery. Such considerations would raise the marginal efficiency of capital and thereby stimulate private investment.

Thirdly, the alternative fiscal policies do not take into consideration the differences in the effect of the possible ways in which the budget deficits are financed. In actual practice, this may appreciably affect the expansion of income and employment. If, for instance, budget deficit is covered by the creation of new money, the effect is likely to be more expansionary than if it is financed by the creation of public debt through government borrowing. This would be so because in the former case the increase in the money supply is likely to lower interest rate and thereby stimulate private investment but in the latter case since the government competes with the private investors for funds, the rate of interest is likely to rise which would discourage private investment. In other words, liquidity effects of fiscal policy will have to be taken into account, *i.e.*, we will have to study not only how the government revenue-expenditure process affects national income directly but also how the budget deficit is covered and how the latter affects the private consumption and investment properties which may have very important secondary effects on the levels of national income and employment.

Effect of an Increase in Debt Supply on Consumption: Previously it was assumed that an increase in debt supply amounts to an increase in the total wealth holding by the community which leads to an increase in consumption. But in this connection, we should take into consideration two more factors. In the first place, an increase in the total volume of public debt may lead to a rise in the rate of interest which may either stimulate or discourage consumption—a factor about which nothing definite can be said. Secondly, an increase in the amount of public debt may lead to a rise in the rate of interest and hence a fall in the prices of the outstanding securities, which may actually reduce the wealth of the holders of the outstanding securities, with the result that the consumption of such security holders may be reduced—a factor which should be offset against the likely increase in the consumption propensity of the holders of the newly issued securities as a result of the wealth effect on them.

Effect of an Increase in Money Supply on Investment: Previously it was assumed that an increase in money supply leads to a decline in the rate of interest which stimulates investment. This will not hold true in the "special Keynesian case" of deep depression when the liquidity preference schedule becomes absolutely interest-elastic or the marginal efficiency of investment schedule becomes absolutely interest-inelastic in which event no amount of increase in money supply would increase private investment.

Effect of an Increase in Debt Supply on Investment: Previously we assumed that an increase in debt supply would lead to a decrease in investment through a rise in the rate of interest. This again will not hold good in the "special Keynesian case" when the liquidity preference schedule is absolutely interest-elastic so that a decrease in the supply of money for speculative purposes consequent upon an increase in debt supply will not raise interest rate and hence will not discourage investment.

Fourthly, it should be noted that the expansionary effect of the balanced budget multiplier will be different under different types of taxes. If, for instance, taxes fall more on savings, the expansionary effect of a government spending programme will be much greater than if the taxes fall more on consumption.

Fifthly, the psychological effect of a compensatory fiscal policy is also important. A vigorous fiscal policy may adversely affect the psychology of the private inventors and this may obstruct business recovery. In fact, President Roosevelt's New Deal Programme failed largely on this account.

Sixthly, a vigorous use of fiscal measures designed to attain full employment may result in balance of payment difficulties because a part of the newly created purchasing power is likely to be spent on imported goods.

Finally, it should be noted that, these days, government investment expenditures are guided by broader social considerations and made under a programme of planned economic development. As such, changes in such investments on short-term considerations for avoiding cyclical fluctuations in income and employment, as assumed by the advocates of compensatory fiscal policy, are not always practicable.

ALTERNATIVE FISCAL POLICIES FOR CURING INFLATION

Though the fiscal techniques were discovered and first made use of during the great depression of thirties, it has been shown that the techniques are capable of being applied perhaps equally effectively during inflationary periods. In fact, fiscal techniques were extensively used to control inflation during the inflationary years of the Second World War as also during the post-war period in a large number of countries including the United Kingdom and the United States. In the United States, for instance, during the Second World War period monetary policy in the form of discount rate variations, open market operations and changes in reserve requirements of commercial banks could not be used for controlling the inflationary impact of the war on the economy because it was felt that a tight money condition would result in a disorderly situation in the wide market for government securities by raising the rates of interest and interfering undesirably with the pattern of the interest rates from the shortest-dated to the longest-dated securities which the U.S. Treasury had set up and which the Treasury wanted to maintain at all costs. Similar was the situation in the United Kingdom during the Second World War and the post-war period until September 1951, when the severe inflationary impact of the Korean boom led to a revival of monetary policy after practically twenty years of disuse. Even after the revival of monetary policy, during the fifties, extensive use is still being made of the fiscal techniques in conjunction with monetary techniques.

There are alternative fiscal policies for curing inflation similar to alternative fiscal policies remedying unemployment. The alternative fiscal policies for fighting inflation are:

1. A decrease in government spending without any change in the tax rate is the first method by which the total volume of effective demand may be reduced and thus the inflation may be controlled. The reduction in government expenditure without being accompanied by a change in the tax rates leads to a surplus budget which mops up purchasing power from the economy, and as a result of the operation of multiplier in the negative direction, there is a decline in national income and employment which tends to mitigate inflation.

2. The policy would be more effective if a decrease in government spending is accompanied by an increase in tax rates; in this case the budget surplus would be larger and hence the contraction in effective demand and volume of income and employment would be greater than under case (1) above.
3. If, however, the government expenditure is inflexible as, for instance, during the war period then a reduction in the effective demand might be possible by an increase in the rates only. An increase in tax rates will reduce the private disposable income and hence private consumption and investment expenditures which would check inflation. In fact, during the Second World War period, the United States considerably relied on increasing tax rates for siphoning off purchasing power from the hands of people; more than 43 per cent of the cost of the war was financed out of tax proceeds.
4. We saw in the balanced budget multiplier case that an increase in government expenditure accompanied by an equal increase in tax revenue increases national income. Similarly, a decline in government expenditure even when followed by an equal decrease in tax receipts would lead to a net decline in money national income during an inflationary period if the recipients of tax concession and the receivers of the proceeds of the government expenditure have the same marginal propensity to consume. Thus, unlike in the previous three cases above, in this case there is a reduction in the effective demand and hence in the force of inflationary pressures even without any budget surplus or decrease in budget deficit. This is so to say, the case of a balanced budget multiplier working in the downward direction. In case a reduction in government expenditures and tax receipts by equal amounts results in a redistribution of the national income in such a way that the net consumption propensity of the community as a whole is reduced, the reduction in national income will be greater than the reduction in the government expenditure. In other words, the multiplier in this case will be greater than unity and the anti-inflationary impact of the fiscal policy will be correspondingly greater.

It is generally held that consumption tax is more effective as an anti-inflationary measure than income tax. The argument is that the consumption tax, by definition, is paid in full at the expense of the consumption of the tax-payers (*i.e.* the whole of the consumption tax reduces consumption) while income tax, which falls both on savings and consumption, is paid partly at the expense of consumption. During inflationary periods, for reducing the total volume of effective demand, it is essential to reduce consumption but the portion of tax which is paid at the expense of saving does not help in controlling inflation. It is, therefore, concluded that an expenditure tax is more effective than an equal-yield tax on income.

The above conclusions are valid only in the absence of money illusion of the consumers. In other words, it is the money illusion which makes the consumption tax more effective as an anti-inflationary instrument than an income tax. This so because the changes in income tax leave the price level unaffected and as such there arises no problem of money illusion. In contrast, an increase in consumption tax leads to a rise in price level while the money income remains unchanged. If it is assumed that the consumer operates under a money illusion, he disregards this change in the price level and continues to spend the same amount of money income. Since the consumption tax constitutes a diversion of consumer expenditure, the consumer expenditure in real terms is decreased by the amount of tax. The required reduction falls short of that needed under the income tax. Hence with money illusion consumption tax will be more effective per unit of increased yield than is the income tax.

Let us now compare the two taxes if there is no money-illusion. Since we have assumed that the income tax leaves the price level unchanged, the required increase in the income tax yield is the same with or without the money illusion. The increase in consumption tax, however, becomes less efficient per rupee if the money illusion is removed. In the absence of money illusion the consumer is aware that the real value of a given money income has declined as prices have risen. He will adjust himself to this change and the consumption function in money terms will shift upwards. He will raise his expenditure out of a given money income by dissaving, thus resisting government's move to cut his consumption in real terms. The above leads to the conclusion that the effectiveness of consumption tax in curbing inflation is more limited without money illusion than with money illusion.

FUNCTIONAL FINANCE

If total expenditure is inadequate, the government can increase it in three ways.[3] In the first place, the government can increase total expenditure directly by increasing its own purchases (or offset the insufficiency in demand in relation to supply by reducing its own sales of goods and services). Secondly, the government can increase aggregate expenditure indirectly by inducing individuals to spend more. This can be done either by giving away more money (in pensions, subsidies, social security benefits etc.) to people who will spend it (or part of it) or by taking away less money from people in taxes so that more remains with them for spending. Thirdly, the government can increase aggregate expenditure still more indirectly by entering the loan market and lending money or by paying back some of its existing debt with newly issued money. This would lower the rate of interest which would, in turn, induce more investment which was not considered worthwhile at the old rate of interest.

In the same manner, if the aggregate expenditure is excessive, the government can reduce it in three ways. In the first place, it can reduce total spending directly by spending less itself (or offset the excessive demand by selling more goods itself). Secondly, it can decrease total spending indirectly by inducing individuals to spend less. This can be done by reducing payments to them (in pensions, subsidies, social-security payments, and social dividends) or by taking more money away from them (in taxes). Thirdly, it can enter the loan market to borrow money which would raise the rate of interest and thereby discourage investment. This reduction in investment is the indirect subtraction from total spending.

Thus there are three pairs of fiscal instruments at the disposal of the government: (i) buying and selling; (ii) giving money to and taking from citizens; and (iii) lending and borrowing.

---

3. Abba P. Lerner, *Economics of Employment* (New York, 1951), pp. 126-27.

The idea of functional finance rules out the traditional concept of sound finance, *i.e.*, the government must collect in taxes all the money that it desires to spend or that it must keep its spending within the range of its tax revenues or that the budget must be balanced. If the six fiscal instruments mentioned above are employed for controlling deflation or inflation, the expenditure may exceed or fall short of the amount raised in taxes. The balancing of the budget is not the only idol that falls when the functional approach is applied to fiscal policy. There are also some other implications of functional finance.

One such implication is that taxes should be imposed only when their social effects are desirable. They should never be imposed for the sake of tax revenues. If the sole objective is to obtain money the government can print it. The important effect of taxation is the effect on the public in influencing their economic behaviour. Taxes, for instance, may be used to control inflation by leaving less money in the hands of people which they can spend. If these effects are not desired, if, for instance, the total expenditure is inadequate which an increase in tax would make worse, it would not be wise to suffer this deflation just because the government needs some money which can easily be printed.

Another implication of functional finance is that the government should borrow only when the effects of the borrowing are desired. Government borrowing, for instance, may be used to control inflation by making it difficult for people to borrow and invest or inducing people to lend money to the government instead of spending it. But if its effects on the economy are not desired, borrowing, like taxation, should never be undertaken simply because the government needs money. Similarly, if deflationary conditions call for lending money and there happens to be no money around, there should be no hesitation in printing it. The size of the stock of money as well as the size of national debt are subsidiary to functional finance.

The functional finance, of course, does not interfere with other objectives of the government. The prevention of inflation and deflation, though important, does not constitute the only objective of a good government. There are many more things which the government has to do in the general interest. Functional finance, in fact, is in one sense the last thing for the government to think about.

The government must first of all decide on all the other reasons for buying the various things or for taxing certain activities or for applying any of the other instruments of fiscal policy. When all these decisions have been made, there results a certain volume of aggregate expenditure. Then it is considered whether this total expenditure is deficient or excessive, whether it would result in deflation or in inflation, or whether perhaps it turns out just the right amount of total spending which will cause neither inflation nor deflation. If this last is the actual situation, there is nothing for the functional finance to do. But if, as is very likely, the resulting total spending is not exactly at the leavel which avoids inflation on the one hand and deflation on the other so as to give us full employment, the government has to press into service functional finance to raise or to lower total spending to the required level. Though functional finance may be the last thing for government to think about, it is certainly not least important of the government responsibilities. In fact, it is considered neither first nor last but together with all the other objectives in arriving at a general policy.

Functional Finance and Public Debt: According to "sound finance" taxation is the normal and proper way for the government to get the money it needs, borrowing is only for emergencies, and printing money is unthinkable. But there are situations in which functional finance would lead to borrowing and an increase in the national debt. Such a situation would arise if the government wanted to spend more than it collected in taxes but did not want to cover the difference by the issue of new money. Excess of expenditure over revenue collected in taxes would be necessary only if otherwise aggregate spending would have been too little. The borrowing would be necessary only if covering the deficit by issuing new money would lead to too much liquidity, too low a rate of interest and excessive investment. Investment is excessive if it involves the elimination of some other and socially more desirable expenditure while permitting both would means too much spending and inflation. Government borrowing then raises the rate of interest and cuts out some of the investment. It is then possible, without making total spending excessive, for the government either to spend more itself or lower taxes and thereby enable others to spend more on the socially more desirable alternative.

Under certain circumstances, functional finance may lead to a large and growing national debt. This, however, need not be a cause of alarm. Most people who worry about the national debt do so because of the analogy with personal debt. They know that it is imprudent for an individual to get into debt and they assume that this must also be true in the case of a nation. This analogy is so inappropriate that economists are sometimes tempted to say that there is no need to bother about the national debt, howsoever large it may be, because as a nation, "We owe the debt to ourselves."

The proper analogy would be a debt by one nation to another nation. The debtor nation, like individual debtor, is poorer because of his debt. The creditor nation, like the individual creditor, is richer for the same reason.

If no arbitrary limit is fixed to the growth of national debt, would the national debt grow indefinitely. No, there is a natural limit to the growth of national debt. The national debt makes the individual members of society feel themselves richer and as such they have a tendency to spend more. When the national debt has grown so large that people feel themselves so wealthy that they spend enough to provide full employment, there is no need for any further deficits. At this stage, functional finance prescribes the balancing of the budget and the national debt stops growing. The national debt has reached an equilibrium level which is its natural limit.

What is true of national debt also holds in case of issue of money. The government may correct a deficiency in aggregate expenditure by deficits covered not by borrowing but by printing additional money. The stock of money, however, would not increase indefinitely but tend to reach a natural or equilibrium limit. This happens because of two reasons. Firstly, an increase in money relatively to other assets increases liquidity, lowers the rate of interest, and stimulates private investment. Secondly, an increase in money makes its possessors feel wealthy and, therefore, increases their propensity to consume. Both the increase in private investment and the rise in the propensity to consume mean an increase in aggregate expenditure and as such less need for government spending to maintain full employment and so less need for the issue of new money for this purpose. When the stock of money and the induced private investment and consumption have grown larger enough to ensure adequate spending for full employment, there will be no need for government spending of newly created money. At this stage, functional finance prescribes an end to the issue of new money. An equilibrium or natural limit to the size of the money stock has been reached.

The natural limits to deficits covered by borrowing and to deficits covered by issuing new money would also make themselves felt in the more normal case where deficits are covered partly by borrowing and partly by issuing money. The deficits by governments would increase national debt as well as the stock of money, and both would stop growing when the increased wealth and the increased liquidity have between them raised private spending to the full employment level where no further government deficits are needed.

We have seen that borrowing has deflationary effects because it puts government securities into the hands of the public in place of money so that there is a loss of liquidity and a reduction of investment. But the larger the national debt, the greater is the remaining wealth effect and, therefore, the higher the propensity to consume. It can, therefore, be said that although borrowing, or increasing the national debt, is deflationary, the existence of debt is inflationary. Not only that, but the interest payments which have to be made as long as the debt stands are also inflationary. An increase in national debt leads to more spending both because of the wealth effect (people feel richer and would consume more out of the same income) and because of the income effect (the interest payments constitute additional income some of which is consumed).

With this additional spending a full-employment policy, keeping aggregate spending at the full-employment level, will have to reduce spending elsewhere by a corresponding amount. Either the government will have to spend less or others will have to be induced to spend less, *e.g.*, by taking away more of their money in the form of taxes. Thus a larger national debt necessitates a higher rate of taxation.

This looks like a return from functional finance to 'sound finance' because the latter says that more taxes will be necessary to raise additional money for making interest payments. But the resemblance is only superficial. In fact, what is needed is not the collection of more revenue but a higher tax rate which would reduce spending by the public. An increase in purchase tax, for instance, which the public evades by spending less, will do the trick even if it reduces the amount of money raised by the Government. In contrast, a tax which raises revenue but does not reduce spending (*e.g.*, a tax falls on savings) will not help.

National debt has three disadvantages which become more serious, the larger is its volume. In the first place, the government will have to reduce its spending on matters which presumably were considered desirable. Secondly, the public will have to be induced to cut their spending below what they considered desirable. Thirdly, the tax will interfere with the proper working of the price mechanism. Against the first two disadvantages, we must set the advantages enjoyed by the owners of the government debt out of their increased spending. But there remains the third disadvantage, the harm done by the additional taxation in raising some prices in relation to others and in disturbing the proper incentives for economic activities. Other things remaining equal the smaller the volume of national debt, the better it is for the economy.

But the evils of national debt can be avoided only by having depression, the consequences of which are much more disastrous. In fact, the evils are the result not of national debt but of prosperity.

LIMITATIONS OF FISCAL POLICY

A fairly correct forecasting of the future course of business cycles is very necessary for an effective use of the compensatory fiscal policy. Such forecasting is, however, seldom possible, or, in any case, an extremely difficult job which renders the application of fiscal techniques a rather difficult art.

Even when we know what lies ahead, we are not sure of the exact impact of different combinations of taxes and government spending. The higher taxes fall partly on consumption, partly on saving and partly investment. It is difficult to find taxes which will fall solely on saving without affecting consumption and investment. It is impossible to prophesy as to how much investment would be inhibited as compared with the amount of savings forgone. Similarly, it is not possible to ignore the possible effects upon investment of a sustained high level of total demand resulting from full employment fiscal policy.

There are political and administrative delays in taking measures, particularly when legislative approval is required for effecting changes in the rates and structure of taxes and expenditures on public works projects.

There is a lot of uncertainty in regard to the time-lag between the initiation of fiscal measures and their full impact on income, output and employment.

An increase in public investment may be accompanied by a decline in private investment. If the government's demand for labour and raw materials comes in competition with that of private industries, the latter would be discouraged by a rise in prices and costs.

A vigorous pursuit of the compensatory fiscal policies for fighting unemployment may adversely affect the psychology of private investors and this may frustrate the very objectives of these policies. The fiscal policy may be ineffective particularly in deep depressions and run-away inflations because of the peculiar business psychology.

Full employment fiscal policy may be impaired by rising wages. Rising wages may also reduce the amount of secondary employment, *i.e.*, the employment resulting from the spending of those who receive the government funds.

Monopoly prices which increase rapidly with the increase in total demand resulting from fiscal measures can be as great a hindrance to full employment as rising wages. If with the increase in demand, the monopolists simply increase their prices instead of expanding their output, there will be no additional secondary employment in the monopoly industries. Thus wage or price inflation can be an important hindrance to the achievement of full employment through fiscal measures.

Fiscal measures may succeed in curing unemployment which is due to deficiency of demand but may fail in curing unemployment which is owing to other reasons. Public spending or deficit spending may not succeed in curing (1) structural unemployment, (2) wage-distortion unemployment, and (3) monopoly restrictions unemployment.

A vigorous pursuit of fiscal remedies for unemployment may result in balance of payments difficulties in an open economy because a part of the new purchasing power is likely to be spent for the purchase of important goods. The increase in imports and the decline in exports may also partly counteract the effect of increase in public spending.

Adjustment of government expenditures on public projects for curbing inflation or deflation may not always be possible because such expenditures are guided more by broader social and economic considerations.

Changes in taxation and public debt policies may be such a time-consuming process particularly in a democratic country that the practical application of the compensatory fiscal techniques may be extremely difficult. In fact, the administrative lag of fiscal policy is certainly more than that of monetary policy and this often tends to offset the advantage of the former policy over the latter policy in point of the operational lag.

A vigorous pursuit of the anti-depression fiscal policy may lead to a vast increase in the public debt with the associated problems of debt management.

INTERRELATION OF FISCAL AND MONETARY POLICY

Since fiscal policy is concerned with money flows into and out of the Treasury, the government's budgetary operations have a monetary side which cannot be ignored. Fiscal policy creates two types of monetary problems. The first problem is as to how to finance deficits and what to do with the funds resulting from a budgetary surplus. Secondly, the mere existence of a large public debt, even if it is not growing gives rise to important monetary issues. It is, therefore, important to study the interrelations between monetary policy, on the one hand, and fiscal policy and debt management, on the other.

Financing a Deficit: The stimulating effect of a budgetary deficit partly depends on the way it is financed. The deficit can be financed in a number of ways. The government may simply print paper money to finance the excess of expenditure of tax receipts. This possibility can, however, be ignored for countries having well-developed banking system. All other alternatives involve the sale of securities, that is, an increase in the interest-bearing public debt. The government can borrow from three types of lenders *viz.* (i) the non-banking public, *i.e.*, individuals, corporations, institutional investors like life insurance companies etc.; (ii) the commercial banks; and (iii) the central bank. It also has the choice in regard to the kind of securities to be sold, that is, long-term vs. short-term, marketable vs. non-marketable, and so on.

The stimulating effect of the deficit is the greatest if the securities are sold to the central bank and least when these are sold to the non-banking public. When the government sells securities to the central bank, the latter creates deposit to the Treasury account. Spending of this deposit would put funds into the hands of the public which are deposited in the commercial banks. The result is that the public's demand deposits rise and member-bank reserves expand by an equal amount. With the present system of fractional reserves, this means that the banks have reserves on the basis of which they can create additional deposits either by lending to business or by buying securities. Thus this method of financing injects a double monetary stimulus into the economy. In this case, the government's borrowing operations make it easier rather than more difficult for private borrowers to obtain funds.

Let us now consider the case when Treasury sells securities to the commercial banks rather than to the central bank. Demand deposits rise by a corresponding amount and pass into the hands of the public as the government spends the money. But there is no change is the bank reserves. While total reserves remain unchanged, there is an increase in the deposit liabilities of the banks; this means that the banks' ability to advance loans is impaired. This method of financing the deficit, therefore, is less stimulating than direct borrowing from the central bank, though both the methods lead to an increase in the supply of money.

The increase in the holding of securities by the banks leads to another problem. The banks may do one of the three things with their government securities: hold them to maturity, sell them to the central bank, or sell them to the public. If they hold them, the situation remains as described above. However, as the government securities are highly liquid and can readily be converted into cash, the banks have larger secondary reserves than before. As such their willingness to lend is likely to increase; and, if they do expand their loans, they may try to turn some of their securities into additional cash reserves. Thus new problems of debt management are created for the treasury of the central bank. The banks can sell their securities, to the central bank, thereby secure new cash reserves, and then expand their loans by several times this amount. They may choose to do this not when business is slack and such action would be welcomed but later when business is booming and credit expansion strengthens the inflationary forces then at work. In case the central bank refuses to purchase the securities, the banks may sell them to the non-banking public. The public gives up demand deposits in exchange. If the public is unwilling to buy and the banks insist on selling, prices of securities will fall and interest rates will rise. In case, the decline in the prices of securities is quite substantial, it may result in some degree of financial disorganization, which may impair the solvency of some financial institutions.

The above shows that deficit financing leads to not one but two major monetary problems. One is how to obtain the immediate monetary effects that are desired. This involves the decision as to whether to bring about an expansion in demand deposits and whether bank reserves should be increased. The other monetary problem relates to the future. What will be the future monetary repercussions of the present increase in debt? Will the present buyers of the government securities be content to hold them, and how will the enlarged supply of liquid assets affect the economy's propensity to spend in the future as business conditions change?

Let us now study the case when the government finances the deficit by selling securities to non-bank investors. This leads to a transfer of deposits from the public to the Treasury. When the government spends the money, these deposits again come into the hands of the public. In this case, there is no net increase in the supply of money, nor any change in the reserves of the banks. Among the three ways of financing the deficit, this is obviously the least inflationary.

Deficit spending by the government would increase aggregate demand only if MV rises. As seen above the last way of financing the deficit does not lead to an increase in *M*. The gross national product can rise, therefore, only if there is a change in the income velocity of money. If the new government securities are exchanged for money which would have otherwise remained idle, there would be a rise in velocity. But if the public buys securities by reducing its own spending, velocity remains unchanged and the increase in government spending is counteracted by a decline in private spending. During recession periods, it is very likely that the funds used for buying the government securities would have otherwise remained idle and the desired rise in velocity does therefore occur. Further, it is safe to assume that during such periods the government can sell large amounts of securities to the public without causing any significant rise in interest rates, as such public borrowing does not make it more difficult for private borrowers to obtain funds. In addition the monetary authorities can take measures to ensure that the rate of interest does not rise.

As in the case of bond sales to the banks, the monetary situation is affected by the fact that the rise in public debt expands the supply of liquid assets in the economy, and the fact that the larger supply will continue into the future. This tends to stimulate private spending. Though the supply of money has remained unchanged, there is a rise in the total stock of liquid assets. Since highly marketable bonds, particularly short-term securities, help to satisfy the desire for liquidity, the public's business to spend its present cash holdings is likely to increase. During periods of declining economic activity, this will have favourable effects. It would strengthen the stimulating effect of the government's deficit spending. Unfortunately, this effect will be felt more strongly after business conditions improve and a boom has got under way. It is during this period that the large supply of liquid assets is most likely to increase the public's willingness to spend.

Thus, large-scale deficit financing, whether securities are sold to banks or to non-banking public, leads to the problem of debt management and monetary policy for the future. Sale of securities to the non-banking public is the least inflationary way of financing a deficit; but even this method, by increasing public's supply of liquid assets, creates problems of monetary control for the future. How inflationary are the ultimate effects of deficit financing depends on how much the supply of money and liquid assets increases relative to the national income, on the government's ability to reduce the debt during boom periods, and on the underlying non-monetary forces that determine the volume of private spending, particularly the cyclical and secular influences operating on business expectations.

Budgetary Surplus: Monetary problems are created not only by a deficit but also by a surplus in the budget. The deflationary impact of a surplus largely depends on what the Treasury does with the excess receipts. A number of alternatives are possible here. The Treasury may simply accumulate idle deposits at either the commercial banks or the central bank. Or, what is more likely, it may reduce the public debt by retiring securities held by the central bank, by the commercial banks, or by the non-banking public. The maximum deflationary effect will be caused if it accumulates the idle deposits at the commercial banks or redeems securities held by the central bank. The deflationary effect is somewhat less powerful if it accumulates the idle deposits at the commercial banks or retires securities held by the latter. The deflationary effect is minimum if the excess tax receipts are used to retire debt held by the non-banking public.

The excess of government's tax receipts over its expenditures leads to a decline in public's debts and an increase in those of the Treasury. Let us assume that these deposits are transferred to the central bank and left idle there. This would lead to a two-fold result. Public has less money in its possession and the reserves of the member-banks are reduced correspondingly. The effect is the same if the excess receipts are used to retire bonds held by the central bank. There is a decline in both the demand deposits and bank reserves. The result is that the commercial banks have smaller excess reserves. If they were fully loaned up before, they must now liquidate some earning assets. In this case the Treasury's handling of the surplus results into a tightening of the money market, the effect of which is added to that resulting from the initial decline in the public's cash holdings.

If the Treasury uses the surplus to retire bonds held by the commercial banks, the latter's deposits decline by an equal amount; but the total reserves of member-banks remain unchanged. With a decline in deposit liabilities and unchanged reserves, the banks have higher reserve ratios which they can use to expand their earning assets if they desire so. Their secondary reserves, however, decline by the amount of bonds retired. In case the Treasury simply accumulates idle deposits at the banks but does not retire any bonds, the reserve position of the banks remains unchanged. The only effect is to transform some of the public's active deposits into idle Treasury deposits; there is a decline in the velocity of the total supply of money.

Let us now consider the case when the Treasury retires debt held by the non-banking public. In this case, there is no change in either the money supply or bank reserves. What the government takes away in taxes it returns to the public in exchange for some of the latter's holdings of securities. The former owners of government bonds now acquire additional cash; which they may leave idle, spend on goods, or put into other securities. Only a small amount is likely to go into consumption. Most of the investors obtaining cash in exchange of their securities would use it to buy corporation securities or other government securities that are still outstanding. This would lead to an increase in the supply of loanable funds. Interest rates will have a tendency to decline and security prices will tend to rise. The overall result would be a stimulation of private investment. Here we have an inflationary influence which may partly offset the original deflationary pressure exerted by the budgetary surplus. The extent of the offset would depend on how eager investors are to exchange their cash for securities and on how responsive private investment is to the greater ease in the money market.

INTEGRATION OF MONETARY AND FISCAL POLICY

Monetary policy has the advantage over fiscal policy that it is more flexible and affects broader stratum of economic units. It can be altered quickly in response to changing needs. It is impersonal and non-discriminatory in nature (excepting selective credit controls) and involves minimum possible state interference. Though monetary policy cannot cure trade cycle, it is not entirely useless. Keynes admits, that a suitable monetary policy can assist the attainment of full employment by maintaining the rate of interest at a low level. The weakness of monetary policy strengthened the case for fiscal policy as a powerful weapon of fighting depression. But fiscal policy is weak in applying sufficient restraint in inflationary periods. Thus we find that both the policies have their limitations and weaknesses. But a judicious combination of the two provides a strong weapon to fight against unemployment and inflation. The two policies are complementary to some extent and, therefore, both of them will have to be taken together.

The fiscal authorities take a monetary decision when they decide how to finance a deficit or what to do with a surplus. In a full-fledged compensatory policy, deficits should be financed so as to have the maximum immediate stimulating effect but due consideration should be given to the possible latter repercussions from a large increase in the public's or the bank's holding of liquid assets. Surpluses should be handled so as to have the maximum immediate deflationary effect, without causing any disorganising effect on the financial and money markets. In the case of both deficits and surpluses the monetary authorities should pursue a policy that strengthens the effect being sought by budgetary action. During depression periods, the central bank should provide enough reserves to the commercial banks so that they can freely buy the securities being offered by the Treasury. During boom periods, the government should put pressure on bank reserves so that the commercial banks cannot readily replace the earning assets which they lose through the government's debt-retirement programme. In case the public debt is very large and both the banks and public possess liquid assets, the monetary authorities should take measures to ensure that these securities remain in stable hands and are not transferred into cash and spent. In particular, this means that the commercial banks should not be allowed to unload government securities on the central bank in exchange for additional reserves.

Fiscal Policy and Economic Development

21

INTRODUCTION

The fiscal policy can affect the rate of economic development in four important ways. It can (i) affect the allocation of resources, (ii) change the distribution of income, (iii) accelerate the rate of capital accumulation, and (iv) control inflation.

The expenditure by government in a particular sector of the economic tends to attract resources into that sector while taxation of a sector has the reverse effect. In this general sense, by affecting factor mobility among industries and occupations, the pattern of government revenues and expenditure affects the allocation of resources. More particularly from the point of view of development, land and property taxes can affect the system of land tenure, tax exemptions and tax discrimination can influence the direction of investment to particular sectors, taxes can discourage investment in industries with social costs, and subsidies can stimulate investment in industries offering social benefits.

Fiscal measures can alter the distribution of income by changing the institutional environment through which the distribution of income comes about, or by changing the resultant distribution. The government expenditure on health and education, for instance, may increase occupational mobility and allow an upgrading of workers; land taxes may affect the distribution of land ownership; and a system of taxes and subsidies can change the degree of competition in various sectors of the economy. Alternatively, the resultant distribution can be made more equal by increasing the degree of progressivity in the tax structure or by directing government expenditure towards the benefit of low-income groups.

The use of fiscal policy for promoting capital formation and controlling inflation are, however, much more important than those for affecting resource allocation and income distribution. The rate of capital formation is the most important factor governing the rate of economic development. Capital formation can take place through private investment financed either by an increase in savings or by credit creation, by an inflow of foreign investments, or by public investment financed through tax revenue, borrowing or deficit financing. The scope for investment through an increase in savings is limited because of very low level of incomes in underdeveloped countries. There are hardly any chances for an inflow of capital from advanced to the underdeveloped countries on a fairly large scale.[1] The responsibility for capital formation, therefore, largely rests, with the government.

TAXATION

If wisely conceived and skillfully used, taxation can become a very effective instrument of policy. The structure of public finance in many underdeveloped countries has grown up haphazardly, influenced by historical accidents, the example of other countries, the thinking of foreign rulers, and the exigencies of the moment. Though many productive sources of revenue have been tapped, the systems of taxation have not generally been evolved on sound principles suited to the requirements of rapid economic growth. A rational reorganization of the structure of taxation will not only accelerate the rate of economic development but also make possible to raise more revenue in the long run. To cite Buchanan and Ellis, "While neither ideal equity nor optimum yield may be expected to the tax systems in many countries, the improvement of revenue systems throughout the underdeveloped world offers one of the greatest unexploited instruments of economic progress.[2]

The role of taxation in raising the resources for economic development is widely recognised. The trend of opinion, however, appears to be in favour of collective compulsory saving through taxation. In the words of Heller: "To break out this (vicious)[3] circle, apart from foreign aid, calls for vigorous taxation and government development programmes; on this point, expert opinion is nearing a

---

1. For details see K.R. Gupta, *International Economics* (Delhi, 1968), pp. 325-41.
2. Narman S. Buchanan and Howard S. Ellis, *Approach to Economic Development* (New York, 1955), p. 333.
3. Words within parentheses added.

consensus."[4] This consensus in favour of collective saving means that emphasis is placed on stepping up public investment and financing it through higher taxation. A number of arguments have been advanced in support of public investment financed through taxation.

The basic reason for the low rate of investment in underdeveloped countries is the low level of domestic savings. Personal savings in the countries of South Asia are estimated to stand between 1 and 2 per cent of national income. Business savings also are not very large. Small businesses predominate and large-scale corporate enterprises which can be expected to generate a sizable volume of savings, cover only a small part of the economy. As such, private savings and investment are not forthcoming at the desired scale. Further whatever little investment is there is mostly directed into unproductive channels. A major portion of the business savings is not invested in agriculture, transport and industry. It is used for speculative purposes and for investment in commerce and real estate. The inference is drawn that public investment has to be stepped up even at the cost of private investment. To quote from Economic Bulletin for Asia and Far East, "Taxation, therefore, remains as the only effective financial instrument for reducing private consumption and investment and transferring resources to the government for economic development."[5]

A country's "taxation potential" depends upon a number of factors, *e.g.*, the level of per capita real income, the degree of inequality in the distribution of income, the structure of the economy, the political leadership and administrative powers of the government. In most of the underdeveloped countries the actual ratio of tax revenue to the national income is at present less than the tax potential.[6]

> Underdeveloped countries are under no illusion that they can—or should—push their tax ratios of 10 to 15 per cent of national income to the 30 to 40 per cent levels reached in

4. *Taxes and Fiscal Policy in Underdeveloped Countries*, p. 3.
5. "Taxation and Economic Development in Asian Countries", *Economic Bulletin for Asia and Far East*, Vol. No. 3, Nov. 1953.
6. Gerald M. Meir, *Leading Issues in Development Economics* (New York, 1964), p. 113.

> such advanced countries as Austria, Belgium, France, Germany, the Netherlands, Norway, the United Kingdom, and the United States.[7]

The potential can be more fully exploited particularly if the increase in taxation is gradual and spread over a number of years.

In view of a number of considerations, taxation is a highly desirable method of financing economic development. In the initial stages of development, a considerable amount of expenditure has got to be incurred for the building of economic and social overhead *viz.* transportation and communications, electricity, irrigation works, health services, vocational and general education etc., which yields very little direct returns. Because the benefit from such projects is primarily social and not private, these projects are not attractive to private entrepreneurs. These, therefore, have got to be undertaken by the state. It is not wise to undertake these projects with borrowed funds, because these do not yield direct returns necessary for the repayment of borrowed funds and the interest thereupon. Such investments can best be financed through taxation.

Inequalities in the distribution of income are larger in underdeveloped countries than in developed countries. The higher-income groups lavishly spend on luxury articles, a considerable portion of which is imported from abroad. Investment in luxury industries does not lay sound foundations for rapid economic development. Importation of luxury articles leads to a wastage of the precious foreign exchange resources which can be used for the importation of equipment, technical know-how and essential raw materials required for development programmes. Taxation of higher incomes, thus, will not only provide funds for economic development but also release badly needed foreign exchange. Rapid development requires considerable sacrifice from the poorer classes which constitute an overwhelming majority of the total population and on whose sweat and toil depends the development of the country. Poorer classes cannot agree to make sacrifices when a few rich

---

7. Walter W. Heller, "Fiscal Policies for Underdeveloped Economies" in *Conference on Agricultural Taxation and Economic Development* edited by Haskell Q. Waid (Cambridge, 1954) Reprinted in Gerald M. Meir, *Leading Issues in Development Economics* (New York, 1964), p. 115.

people are rolling in luxuries. Reduction of inequalities will thus provide a better atmosphere for enlisting the co-operation of the masses. Inequalities create political unrest which is highly inimical to development.

When reducing inequalities, care should be taken that only those inequalities are reduced which arise from inheritance and do not perform any useful function. Functional inequalities (*i.e.* inequalities arising from hard work, education, skill, intelligence etc.) have an important role to play in the development process and should be permitted to the reasonable extent. Functional inequalities highly prize the enterprising and not the idle classes. Functional inequalities, of course, should not be permitted to go beyond what is necessary. In case there occurs a temporary shortage of certain skills, for instance, reward to workers possessing such skills should not be permitted to rise according to the forces of demand and supply. Wage differentials between different occupations should not exceed those necessary to call forth sufficient supply of labour to these occupations under normal conditions.

Taxation was not very important during the development phase of the present developed countries because most of the development took place through private enterprise. Recently, it has been widely realised that development process can be considerably accelerated by an active participation by state in economic activity. As a result of this realisation, state participation has considerably increased in almost all developing economies. Further socialism and classless society have been declared to be the goals in several underdeveloped countries. Extension of public sector is very essential for the achievement of socialism and a classless society.

High taxes on the richer classes involve the risk that these may adversely affect their savings and investment. To avoid such adverse effects, types of taxes and tax exemptions should be properly selected. Taxes on property and consumption have lesser adverse effects than those on incomes and profits. Taxes which decrease private investment by an amount far larger than the amount of revenue collected by the state should be avoided. If the decrease in private savings and investment is almost equal to the revenue collected, taxes won't be harmful because the decrease in private investment would be offset by an increase in the government investment.

The principle should be to collect from taxes as much as is possible without adverse effects on the development process. Application of the principle, however, is not so easy as its formulation. Governments, particularly in democratic countries, have to face considerable opposition from the public in imposing new taxes and raising the rates of old taxes. Any considerable overall increase in taxes may lead the people to overthrow the government. Theoretically, it is possible to step up the rate of capital formation but cutting the consumption of the masses below its present level, or at least, by preventing the masses from consuming whole of the increased output, but it is very difficult to achieve this in actual practice. On the contrary, some democratic countries are faced with the problem of consumption rising faster than the production. It may not be desirable to reduce the consumption of the poorer classes because of their extremely low standard of living. Middle and higher income-groups are well-known for their conspicuous consumption and offer scope for increased taxation. It is, however, not easy to tax the middle and higher classes. These classes play an important role in formulating and executing the development programmes of the country in the capacity of administrators, educationists, scientists and private entrepreneurs. Government, therefore, has to be very cautious in encroaching upon the consumption of middle and higher classes, lest they withhold their co-operation. In many underdeveloped countries, the government is dominated by the wealthy classes and, therefore, it avoids taxing the richer classes as far as possible. Further, it is doubtful if the rate of capital formation can be stepped up by increasing taxation on the richer classes. Richer classes will pay increased taxes by reducing not consumption but savings. Unnecessary consumption of the richer classes can be checked only by direct controls on the production, import and consumption of luxury articles.

In selecting among the various types and kinds of taxes, the governments of different countries should take into account matters like their particular legal system, balance of political and social power within the country, the administrative ability to enforce the tax comprehensively and justly, the effects of different taxes on incentives, and the objectives of a proper balance between short-term revenue raising measures for financing urgent development projects and long-term tax reforms which will give steady encouragement to economic development over the longer pull.[8]

Though there are differences in the taxable capacity and types of taxes that can be used in different countries, it can generally be said that the present tax system of the underdeveloped countries does not satisfy to the desirable extent such criteria as yield, equity, simplicity and certainty of enforcement, and minimum negative effects on incentives. An important problem of fiscal policy is to find a sufficient number of taxes which will satisfy these criteria. No doubt, there are great difficulties in accomplishing this, but there are some possibilities.

The tax structure should be based on the principle of mobilisation of the economic surplus. Taxation must mop up a great part of the surplus which is not being used for productive investment. The problem is to discover the surplus and channel it into investment without, in the process, destroying or seriously damaging its generation.

Each person should be made to contribute to taxation in accordance with his unused capacity or ability to contribute to economic development. This ability can be measured in terms of that part of the economic surplus accruing to him which he is not already, on his own, utilising for productive investment. A person's income can be said to contain a surplus if it is above the level needed to maintain the minimum consumption necessary for efficiency and for incentives.

The taxation must mobilise the increases in the surplus that result from initial development efforts. In other words the taxation system should be such as prevents consumption from increasing proportionately with increases in income in the initial stages of development.

The taxation should be income-elastic, that is, with the rise in income, the share of taxation in total incomes must rise. This requires that the tax structure should possess built-in-flexibility. To impart the needed flexibility to the tax system, it is necessary to tax goods that have a high income elasticity of demand and also adopt

8. *Conference on Agricultural Taxation and Economic Development* (Cambridge, 1954), p. 17.

a progressive scale of income taxation. Since the marginal rate will be higher than the average rate, the share of the government will increase more than proportionately as income increases.

It has been suggested that taxation for economic development must fall on the economic surplus and mobilise it for investment, and that it must be so designed as continually to enlarge the surplus. This requires that taxation should be levied on a progressive scale on that part of the income (above a certain level) which is not used for desired investments, and that the manner of taxation must be such as to encourage individuals to save. In other words, savings which are invested in the socially desired directions should be exempted from income taxation.

Such total exemption would be justified only if we view taxation solely as a tool for promoting economic development. Taxation, however, also provides funds for financing governmental services and for public investment in social overheads. A compromise solution, therefore, would be to grant only a partial but adequate exemption.

It is not intended to argue against progressive taxation. It may mean that the tax system will be highly regressive in relation to incomes. But the system will be highly progressive in regard to that part of the income which is not being invested productively. This scheme serves a double purpose; if a large portion of the income is not saved, a significant part of it will go to the state; on the other hand, if the income is to escape heavy taxation, it will have to go into investment. Either way the surplus is mobilised for economic development.

Such exemptions must benefit all type of income-tax payers and not only recipients of dividends and owners of corporations. Since encouragement to investment must be given at the individual as well as at the business level, the scheme would require modifications in the taxation of both personal and business income.

If savings are granted partial exemption, there is no doubt that the income tax will be less effective in reducing inequalities of wealth. But since the rates of income tax can be stepped up under the scheme, inequalities in the standard of consumption will be reduced. This appears to be the best that can be done for the masses in the short run. For reducing inequalities in the distribution of wealth and for preventing perpetuation of inequalities, reliance would have to be placed on wealth and inheritance taxation. If a country wants to use private enterprise, there is no escape from permitting accumulation of wealth in private hands upto a certain point. If a country desires economic development without inequalities in the distribution of wealth, it would be possible only by adopting a socialist system of society.

Two important objections may be raised against exemption of savings. The first objection is that the scheme would make the state lose a considerable amount of revenue. This objection does not have much force. As stated above, the tax rates can be raised which would, at least partly, compensate the reduction in revenues. Even if this is not done, there is no reason to suppose that the long-term yield of taxation would be any less; in fact, to the extent the scheme promotes investment, the yield may be higher because of larger taxable profits.

The second objection to the scheme is that the tax system, instead of reducing economic inequalities, would actually increase them. This objection certainly has some force. Therefore, unless measures are taken to counteract the growth of inequalities, the scheme may not be acceptable to the general masses. A scheme of progressive income taxation which favours savings together with a suitable pattern of commodity taxation can considerably help in reducing disparities in the standards of consumption of different classes. Much depend also on the pattern of investment that is promoted through planning or otherwise. The standards of consumption of the poorer classes will improve if fairly high priority is given to investment in wage-goods industries, in education, and in measures designed to reduce the rate of growth of population.

Personal income taxation may play some role but it cannot be expected to be a major source of revenue in many underdeveloped countries. The scope for personal income tax is restricted because of a number of reasons. The majority of the people are just on the subsistence level and, therefore, cannot be taxed. A major portion of the income does not come through the commercial channels but is directly consumed by the producers. The people are by and large illiterate and as such unable to maintain adequate records necessary for assessment of income. There is a lack of integrity, efficiency and technical competence required for administering the tax. Although personal income tax may not yield a large amount of revenue, it does provide an element of equity in the tax system. Since there exist extreme inequalities in the distribution of income and consequently strong feelings of injustice, the underdeveloped countries might use personal income tax as a way of strengthening equity; if not as an important source of revenue.

In this connection, consideration should be given to the effects of taxation on the incentives to save. If the recipients of high incomes are indulging in luxury consumption, hoarding, capital flight or unproductive speculative investment, taxing their incomes will not adversely affect the rate of capital formation. If, however, the recipients of high incomes have a high propensity to save, and these savings are invested in a productive manner, care would have to be taken to ensure that the source of these savings is not adversely affected. In such a case, there may be a conflict between the desire for equity and the desire to raise the level of savings. With a view to avoid any adverse effects on savings, it has been suggested that taxation should be not on personal income but instead on expenditure through excise and other indirect taxes.

Even though income taxation cannot be used widely, it may be desirable to tax certain forms of income, *e.g.*, the sizable income derived from land rents and interest. Land rents may form an important part of the country's income, and if the rents accrue to inactive landlords who are not contributing anything to the productivity of land, an effective income tax would yield funds for capital formation without involving any adverse effects on economic activity. Progressive income taxes on landlords may also encourage sale, or at least discourage further accumulation, of large land-holdings. Reform of the tax system may also reduce the tax burden on small farmers and tenants who normally bear a high burden of taxation. Money lenders may also be subjected to a steeply progressive income tax on the usurious interest payments which they receive for private credit. Such tax could divert these usurious gains into productive investment.

It would also be desirable to introduce a greater degree of progressivity into the tax system through inheritance taxes. This would not only increase tax revenue but also decrease the wide inequalities in the distribution of incomes and wealth by limiting huge concentrations of wealth to be passed from one generation to another. Though easier to administer than an income tax, the inheritance tax may arouse strong social opposition and as such the government may be unwilling to adopt such a measure.

It may not be very desirable to heavily tax business profits. Taxation of profits may reduce the incentive to invest and may also reduce the ability to finance new investment from undistributed earnings. The sacrifice of equity resulting from low taxes on profits can be compensated to some extent by high inheritance taxes.

Some underdeveloped countries have taken advantage of the temporary or permanent improvement in the terms of trade for raising funds for financing development. The method has been either to impose a tax on exports varying according to the foreign price of the article or to establish a state trading agency which buys at a lower price and sells abroad at a higher price. This, however, is not a very sound method of financing economic development because of the highly fluctuating nature of terms of trade of the primary-producing countries. Development requires stable sources of financing.

In some underdeveloped countries, foreign companies earn and export fabulous profits. Often the fabulous profit aries because the local governments signed certain natural resources (like minerals) or monopolies (like public utilities) without demanding adequate royalty or rental in return. Such contracts were made through genuine ignorance, through corruption of the local government, or through foreign political pressure. Sometimes, the contracts were reasonable at the time of execution but later on became highly unprofitable because of the phenomenal rise in prices, the amount of rental or royalty remaining fixed. Taxes should be used to siphon off unreasonable profits of the foreign firms. A standard income tax may be applied to foreign investors but special taxes may be levied on excessive profits arising from royalties. It would, however, be necessary to strike a balance between the need for preventing the profits of foreign enterprises from being repatriated without benefit to the underdeveloped country and the need for maintaining sufficient fiscal incentives to attract foreign capital. As in the case of domestic enterprises, foreign companies can also be granted taxation immunity for a certain period of time if they are embarking on new and essential enterprises and they can be granted liberal tax allowances when they reinvest their business profits. These measures, however, are liable to be inequitable and tend to encourage vested interests who prevent the eventual removal of these discriminatory benefits. On this account, subsidies may be preferable because they make the benefits explicit.

There also exists a case for property taxes. Since the distribution of real property in most underdeveloped countries is more unequal than the distribution of income, a proportional property tax with a relatively high level of basic exemptions would be more progressive than an income tax. Such a tax would also be easier to administer. It would also discourage use of savings in the acquisition or construction of real property, thereby permitting savings to be directed into more productive investments. A capital gains tax can also be used as a supplementary measure to discourage excessive speculation particularly in real estate during inflationary periods. As a substitute for a capital gains tax on speculative sales of buildings, a transfer tax can be imposed on the sale of buildings, applying high rates in cases where the interval between two sales is short and lower rates in those cases where it is long.[9]

Though there is scope for increasing revenues by making improvements in income and business taxes, the major reliance will have to be placed on agricultural and indirect taxes. Land taxes can be a form of property tax levied on the value of land, or it can be levied on annual production or on the rent from land. Japanese development during the latter part of the nineteenth century is a classic case in which the government imposed heavy land taxes to divert a major part of the increase in agricultural productivity to capital formation. Another argument in favour of land tax is that since development generally results in an appreciation of real estate values, the government is justified in appropriating a part of the windfall in the form of land taxes. Large land-owners and even medium-sized farmers might be subjected to such taxes but small farmers and tenants should be excluded from taxation because of their low levels of income.

Indirect taxes like the excise and sales taxes have the merit of falling on consumption rather than on saving, but suffer from the

9. United Nations, *Taxes and Fiscal Policy in Underdeveloped Countries* (New York, 1954), p. 36.

disadvantage that they raise prices and the cost of living, and the sales tax tends to make the tax structure regressive within particular income brackets. To minimise these disadvantages, excise and sales taxes should be used selectively. They should discriminate in favour of necessary commodities and against luxuries. The government should also avoid adding new taxes and supplementary rates on top of old ones to such an extent as to complicate the tax system and reduce its efficiency.

The tax policy may be used to counteract the inflationary pressures arising from economic development by reducing overall effective demand. The tax policy can be used in two ways for controlling inflationary pressures. Greater reliance should be placed on progressive direct taxes the yield of which changes more than in proportion to changes in the tax-base as a result of monetary and price changes. Commodity taxes provide an instance of such taxes. The automatic capacity of the tax system to cope with economic fluctuations, however, is limited by considerations of administrative efficiency and other objectives of a sound tax system. A resort to the second method, therefore, becomes necessary when strong inflationary pressures appear in the economy. Changes are made in the prevailing general framework of tax system to deal with inflationary situations. Taxes which mop up additional incomes and commodity taxes on the increase in general purchasing power will have definite anti-inflationary effects. Special anti-inflationary taxes such as excess profits tax and commodity taxes on luxury articles may be imposed.

The tax system should provide positive inducement to desirable investment in the private sector. This can be accomplished by differential rates of taxation, a discriminatory tax system or the grant of tax exemption in suitable directions. Opinions, however, differ in regard to the desirability and effectiveness of special tax concessions for channelling investment in suitable directions. One school of thought holds that such concessions are relatively ineffective either because tax burdens in underdeveloped countries are not high enough to discourage investment to any significant extent or because other factors like political instability and foreign exchange restrictions overshadow tax barriers. In regard to the desirability of special tax concessions, it is held that these are more or less a disguised government expenditure and at par with subsidies. In view of extremely limited resources, the public exchequer in underdeveloped countries cannot afford a reduction in its tax revenue. Tax concessions are sometimes misused to evade taxes by meeting the formalities of the concession provisions. Tax administration in most of the underdeveloped countries is not adequately efficient for practising finer arts of taxation.

In spite of the defects mentioned above, tax concessions and exemptions are strongly pleaded in underdeveloped countries as inducements to investment in the private sector. The implementation of a development tax policy requires, of course, a careful analysis and planning, skilful structuring of taxes, and competent and clean tax administration.

The conditions prevailing in most of the underdeveloped countries are not very congenial for using tax policy as an instrument for mobilisation of resources for economic development. The existence of a large non-monetary sector in the underdeveloped countries is a great obstacle in modernising the tax system. The real income of the subsistence farmers cannot be satisfactorily assessed and, therefore, the rural population, excepting peasant proprietors paying land revenue, remains outside the scope of the income tax. In many underdeveloped countries, the privileged groups are still in political power and, to protect their positions, oppose any programme of modernising tax policy. The machinery for administering tax policy lacks honesty and efficiency. Voluntary compliance by the tax-payers is very much lacking in underdeveloped countries. Tax evasion is quite widespread. People are illiterate and, therefore, unable to maintain proper accounts which are very necessary for taxing income or production.

BORROWING

If taxation revenue is less than government expenditures, the gap can be covered by mobilising savings through voluntary loans. Financing through borrowing is not harmful so long as it is used to finance long-term projects which ultimately yield enough to repay the capital and interest thereupon. The main difficulties involved in borrowing by the government in underdeveloped countries are dearth of savings, lack of organised markets for government securities, lack of demand for government securities on the part of commercial banks and insurance companies, and inflation. Another important obstacle in the way of government in borrowing is the comparatively far higher rates of return obtainable on alternative investments. Government, generally, pays 3 to 4 per cent interest on its securities. But a person can obtain a far higher return by investing the money in a house, in business, or by lending it to a trader or a farmer. In spite of a far higher rate of return obtainable on alternative investments, government securities do find a market because of a number of reasons:

(1) Investment in government securities is the safest form of investment. It does not involve risks usually involved in alternative investments yielding a higher rate of interest.

(2) Public might be induced to invest in government bonds on patriotic grounds because the funds raised are utilised for the development of the country.

(3) Government bonds provide investment opportunities to persons possessing a small amount of money which may not be sufficient for alternative investments yielding a higher return *viz.* housing, business etc. Further, persons possessing a limited amount of funds may not like to invest their hard-earned savings in risky investments yielding a high rate of return.

(4) While small investors are likely to be long-term holders of government securities, large private investors may hold these as a transitional investment to be disposed of at an opportune moment.

(5) Public may be offered bonds at rates of interest more attractive than those at which these are offered to financial institutions.

The government bonds meant for sale to public differ from those meant for sale to financial institutions in three main respects *viz.* denomination, rate of interest and maturities. Bonds for public are generally of smaller denominations than those meant for institutional investors. Bonds issued specifically for public carry a higher rate of interest. Long-term bonds are issued for public while short-term and medium-term bonds are issued for financial institutions because of their preference for liquidity. Normally, long-term bonds carry a higher rate of interest than the short-term bonds. Government should try to sell as many bonds as possible to public and sale to banks and other deposit-creating institutions should be the last resort because it has a tendency to create inflationary pressures with all their evil consequences.

Measures for Increasing Sales of Government Bonds: There are two fundamental prerequisites for the establishment of an extensive public market for government bonds. First, the public should have a firm belief in the creditworthiness of the government and hence in the credit standing of the government bonds. Secondly, the government should offer rate of interest and other terms no less favourable than those obtainable on alternative investments.

Creditworthiness of the government and credit standing of its bonds cannot be established overnight. It is built through traditions over a long period. Establishment and maintaining creditworthiness requires a number of things. Public should have confidence in the stability of the constitutional process of the government. Public won't be willing to invest in the government bonds if it is feared that the next government will repudiate the old debts. It should avoid unnecessary expenditures and resolutely collect taxes. It should control inflation lest the purchasing power of money invested in securities declines.

To safeguard the real value of savings, sometimes, it has been suggested that the bonds should include provisions to the effect that the face value of bonds and interest thereupon shall fluctuate according to fluctuations in the general level of prices. There are, however, a number of objections to such a procedure. It may involve unpredicted liabilities on the government in case of a rise in prices which is very likely in developing economies. This difficulty would be particularly great because the government revenue is not very elastic to a rise in prices. A number of taxes (*e.g.* land revenue) in underdeveloped countries are specific and do not increase at all with a rise in prices. The inclusion of escalator provisions in the bonds would accentuate inflation. This may be taken as a signal for a fall in the value of money and thus undermine the confidence of the people in the stability of currency. It may lead to similar demands on the part of other groups of population (*e.g.* wage and salary earners) and thus restrict government's freedom in pursuing the most appropriate monetary and price policy. In case of a rise in the value of money, decrease in the face value of deposits may cause adverse psychological effects on the depositors. Such a provision would be resented by private financial institutions, competing for the same saving, whose co-operation is very essential for development programmes. It would involve very difficult statistical problems of calculating changes in the general level of prices. In view of the objections mentioned above, such a provision is not desirable.

The best course is that government should keep the price level under control by taking effective measures against inflation. Government should take measures to stabilise the domestic market for government securities. Any unreasonable fall in the value of government securities will discourage investment in these. In this connection, consideration may be paid to the establishment of a stabilisation fund for preventing an undue fall in the value of government securities owing to panic. Whenever the value of government securities falls, independently of the trends in other sectors of the market, owing to a lack of confidence in government securities, the stabilisation fund should be used to buy the securities at the normal market rate.

Attractive terms should be offered, particularly to small savers. This may be done either by exempting investment in government bonds from income and other taxes or by offering higher rates of interest. Profitability of different investments does not vary according to their essentiality for the economy. Often, less essential investments (*viz.*, investment in the production of luxury articles, in estate, in hoarding and speculation etc.) yield far higher returns than some of the most essential investments. In a competitive economy, inessential investments may outcompete essential investments in attracting savings. Government should, therefore, take direct and indirect measures for controlling the flow of savings towards private industries which offer very high rates of return but are not essential for the development of the country.

The government should provide securities of a wide variety in respect of dates of maturity, ease of cashing, use as collateral for credit, rates of interest, capital appreciation, lottery features, etc., so as to meet the requirements of different types of savings and savers. Securities catering to the special needs of the small savers should be issued. To increase the liquidity of the securities, adequate facilities should be provided for the encashment of the securities or for loans against securities.

A lottery system has been successfully used for encouraging savings in Mexico. Under the system, participants make regular contributions similar to deposits and receive a certain amount of money after five or ten years if their bonds are not drawn in the lottery. In case their bonds are drawn, they receive the money much earlier. The system is popular among the masses because of the elements of chance. A different lottery system was used in Palestine. Loans were floated at very low rates of interest. The money which would otherwise have been paid as interest was distributed as prizes to be drawn in lottery. The element of chance in lottery system should be kept within narrow limits. Normally, it should be limited to a part of the interest and in no case should it touch the safety of capital. Large element of chance may encourage a desire in public for growing rich quickly which is not consistent with the requirements of economic development. In countries in which lottery feature is contrary to social customs, it may retard the long-term growth of the market for government bonds by impairing the dignity of bonds.

Subscriptions to public loans have successfully been attracted by linking specific savings with specific investment fields or specific investment projects. Savings collected from rural areas by institutionalised bonds are mostly taken to metropolitan areas and invested in commerce and industry which does not directly benefit the rural savers. Incentive for subscribing to loans will be larger if it is known that the funds thus raised will be used for local development which would benefit local people. This method, however, has its limitations. It may not result into an optimum allocation of resources. Potentialities for local development may not coincide with the capacity to save in different localities. There may exist little scope for development projects in some localities inhabited by rich people having considerable capacity to save. On the other hand, there may be considerable scope for development projects in localities inhabited by the poor people having little capacity to save. Similarly, projects which succeed in attracting savings may not be the most essential ones from the point of view of the economy as a whole. Further, to a large extent, the investors are guided by the financial soundness of the authority floating the loan rather than by the specific project or its location. A more important aspect of the problem is that of preservation of national savings for local development. Regulations for local investment of national savings are prescribed not only in underdeveloped countries but also in some developed countries.

Measures should be taken to establish and strengthen the market for government securities. This would facilitate the sale of government securities.

In selling bonds, government should seek the co-operation of institutional investors, particularly of banks. Banks have a direct contact with the public. They can sell government bonds to their customers. In the initial stages when the government securities are not popular among the public, the government may sell its securities to the public through banks and other financial institutions.

An extensive education and publicity campaign should be organised to promote in masses the habit of thrift and investment in government bonds. Government should seek the co-operation of various organisations and influential individuals for the sale of government bonds. A small commission may be paid to postal staff and others for inducing them to sell government bonds.

Certain people have acquired huge incomes through illegal means or, to avoid taxes, have inadequately reported their incomes. They are afraid of buying registered bonds lest their incomes should get government recognition. Bonds payable to the bearer may be issued to induce such people to invest their bonds. Bearer bonds, however, may encourage efforts to obtain income through illegal means and to avoid taxes. Further these may be widely used as means of payment in black market transactions.

Issuing of gold certificates and mortgage certificates has, often, been proposed to overcome the strong preferences of savers to invest in hoarding gold and in real estate. It is, however, doubtful if the problem of hoarding gold can be tackled by issuing gold certificates. There arises the question as to whether the payment of gold certificates is to be made in gold or in currency. If the government undertakes to pay the certificates in gold it cannot use the gold so obtained because it will have to hold it against the certificates for making payments which might be demanded at any time. In case the payment is to be made in currency, there will be hardly any differences between the gold certificates and the ordinary bonds. Preferential treatment to certain savers in the forms of gold certificates may lead the masses to suspect the security of ordinary bonds. If gold is hoarded because of the past history of repudiation of government bonds, the same suspicion would prevail about the gold certificates.

Deficit Financing

22

DEFINITION

In the United States, the term 'deficit spending' or 'deficit financing' is generally used to mean any expenditure by the Government in excess of its current revenues. As such, expenditure that is financed by borrowing from the public would be included in the measures of deficit in the budget. In India, however, expenditure financed by borrowing from the public does not constitute deficit financing. Thus only expenditure in excess of current revenues and non-bank borrowings is included in deficit spending. According to this definition, the term deficit is applied to expenditure financed only by those means which have a tendency to increase the total outlay in the community.

If a deficit is defined this way, expenditure financed by borrowing from the public can be excluded from the deficit only on the assumption that such expenditure, since it is financed out of genuine savings has no tendency to increase aggregate outlay. This assumption, however, is not completely valid. In addition, it is difficult to classify government borrowing according to the type of lender. To cite the Planning Commission, "While the monetary impact of government's borrowing will differ according to the type of subscriber, it would clearly be impracticable to record government's borrowing operations on this basis. Nor does the ownership of public debt remain with the same persons or institutions that bought it to begin with."[1] As such, this definition of deficit is only "a convenient convention which under prevailing practices gives as near an approximation to the purpose in hand as possible."[2]

---

1. Government of India, *Second Five-Year Plan* (New Delhi, 1956), p. 84.
2. *Ibid.*, p. 84.

A deficit thus defined can be financed in one or more of the following ways: (1) borrowing from the central bank; (2) withdrawal of cash balances; (3) borrowing from the commercial banks; (4) issue of new currency by the government. Except for the issue of one rupee note amounting to Rs. 5 crores per annum in recent years, the last method is not employed in India. Further in governmental accounting practice borrowing from the public and from the banks are combined together as "market borrowings." The figures of annual deficits released by the government or the Reserve Bank of India include only withdrawal of cash balances and net borrowing from the Reserve Bank.

NEED FOR DEFICIT FINANCING

For economic development the under developed countries or developing countries need resource mobilisation which is done through taxation, borrowing, surpluses from public enterprises, etc. To accelerate economic development, investment in different sectors is only the way. Additional resources are necessary to create so as to step up the rate of investment in order to bring rapid economic development. But where from are the developing countries to create the additional resources? In the absence of sufficient foreign aid forthcoming from friendly countries and international organisations, the required fund should come from domestic resources. To raise domestic resources, voluntary savings should be encouraged through national small savings schemes in order to add to the resources available to the government.

But in the underdeveloped or developing countries where a majority of the people are living at the subsistence level or below poverty line, the difference between income and consumption is very low. Hence, voluntary savings, though it is encouraged, cannot provide sufficient resources for development. The government has to attempt to impose additional taxes to increase the volume of resources. But due to extreme poverty of a majority of the people, additional taxes beyond a point creates problems economically or politically. Public borrowing fails also to meet the fund required for development. Therefore, the government has to resort deficit financing to implement development schemes.

CREATION OF DEFICIT

The deficit in the budget may be created either through an increase in public expenditure or a reduction in public revenues. Each of these methods has its merits and demerits. The following are the important advantages claimed for the method of reducing revenue:

1. To some extent it works automatically. The decline in income, output and employment would necessarily lead to a decline in revenues. With the decline in employment, there is bound to be a decline in tax receipts, net surpluses earned by public enterprises and the employee and employer contributions to social insurance funds. The extent of the automatic effect can be further enlarged by reshaping the tax structure in such a way as increases its sensitivity to changes in income. Normally, the more progressive is the tax structure, the larger would be the income-elasticity of revenue receipts. A broad-based and highly progressive income tax collected on a pay-as-you-earn basis appears to be ideal for this purpose. The yield of such a tax declines more than proportionately to the fall in income. A capital gains tax also increases the income-elasticity of the revenue system. Another method of attaining the same objective would be to peg the rates of certain taxes to an index of unemployment or income. To the extent the revenue system can be made income-elastic, it works automatically and provides a sort of built-in stabilizer.

2. The scope for a fast increase in socially useful public investment and hence in aggregate public expenditure is limited in countries where the size of the public sector is limited, or the public authorities have not prepared in advance an adequate number of suitable investment projects, or the available public projects are such on which the work cannot be easily accelerated or slowed down in accordance with requirements of the economy, or a level of development has been attained where the basic problem before the economy is a higher rate not of capital accumulation but of private consumption. In such countries, reduction in revenues will be a better method of creating the required budget deficit.

3. The public investment may compete with private investment and thus discourage the latter. The method of reducing revenues does not involve such a threat.

4. It is easier to expand public expenditure but difficult to curtail it. As such, if the increased demand is created through increased public expenditure, there is the risk that this may permanently increase the share of the state in the economic activities of the country which is inconsistent with the assumptions of a private economy. The revenue method does not suffer from this drawback.

5. Under the revenue method the decision regarding the use of the resources which, in the absence of positive action, are likely to remain idle lies with the public and not with the authorities. This, it is claimed, provides greater scope for directing production in accordance with the consumers' preferences.

6. A public works programme may lead to corruption, favouritism and wastes. This risk is particularly marked in underdeveloped countries which generally lack a honest and efficient administration.

Following may be mentioned among the important advantages claimed for creating a budget deficit by the method of increased expenditure:

1. A certain amount of deficit created through increased public outlay is likely to have more stimulating effect on aggregate demand than an equal amount of deficit created through a reduction in revenue receipts. The extent to which this is true depends upon the method of financing the deficit, the direction of increased public outlays and the type of tax receipts foregone. The stimulating effect of increased public outlay would be maximum if it is financed with created money and is directed to industries with a high ratio of wages to total costs or to sectors of the economy with the highest incidence of unemployment or takes the forms which induce a relatively large private investment of consumption. An important disadvantage of the revenue method is that the expenditure cannot be directed precisely to sectors of the economy where it will have the maximum stimulating effect and where it will yield the maximum social advantage.

2. Not to talk of underdeveloped countries, even advanced countries offer considerable scope for improvement in existing facilities in regard to housing, education, medical, public utilities etc. There is thus considerable scope for increased socially useful

public expenditure in sectors which lie outside the field of private enterprise.

3. Transfer expenditures, particularly for social security and welfare, provide great scope for increased public expenditure in all countries. To the extent such expenditure is inversely related to changes in income and employment, it provides a sort of built-in stabiliser for the economy.

4. In case private consumption occupies a higher place in the scale of social priorities, this may be attained by granting substantial subsidies on a wide range of consumer goods and services. This provides another socially useful outlet for increased public expenditure.

Maximization of social welfare requires that the two methods should be combined in a judicious ratio.

FINANCING OF BUDGET DEFICIT

It is very essential that an appropriate policy is adopted for financing the deficit budget. Such a policy should keep the interest rates low and stable. If the government borrowing to finance the deficit raises interest rates, it will have unfavourable results. The interest charges on public debt will rise. The investors will suffer heavy losses through capital depreciation. Private investment will tend to be discouraged. Unstable interest rates will disrupt the security markets and have unfavourable effects on private investment.

The financial technique followed in the United Kingdom and in other countries during the Second World War appear to be quite suitable for a budget deficit aimed at creating additional demand. Under this technique, long-term and short-term papers are offered on 'tap'. The excess of the budget deficit over subscriptions to the tap issues is covered by borrowing from the Central Bank. In this way, the deficit is met partly by borrowing the genuine savings of the public and partly through monetary expansion while keeping the rate of interest low and stable. If the government could convince the public of its determination to prevent a further rise in the rate of interest, there will be a decline in the assets-demand for money, and hence in the rate of interest, unless it is already very low.

ADVERSE EFFECTS OF DEFICIT BUDGETING

The commonly mentioned limitations of deficit financing are increase in public debt, possible adverse effects on private enterprise, the fear that increased public expenditure may prevent desired cost reductions from being effected and its inflationary impact. These are briefly discussed below.

Increase in Public Debt: Since the public securities are held mostly by the richer classes either directly or indirectly (*i.e.* by holding deposits with banks, or owning stocks and shares of companies which hold public securities as one of their assets), it leads to an increase in inequalities in the distribution of income before tax. And since an increase in inequalities in the distribution of income raises the propensity to save, the offset to private saving currently provided by a deficit budget is at the expense of raising the propensity to save in future.

Since public securities are likely to be held by the older generation in the community, public debt would lead to a transfer of wealth from the younger to the older generation. And since the younger generation has greater capacity to enjoy wealth than the older generation, it would diminish aggregate economic welfare of the country. But to the extent, family and other liabilities of the older generation are larger than those of the younger generation, the transfer of wealth from the latter to the former is justified.

Adverse Effects on Private Enterprise: Deficit budgeting creates adverse effects on private enterprise in a number of ways. In the first place, the government's desire to direct increased public expenditure into socially useful investment may lead it to encroach upon fields which normally fall within the province of private enterprise. Secondly, the growing public debt, and the prospect of larger amounts required to service, it may lead to fears of higher taxation in future. Such fears, whether imagined or real, tend to discourage investment. To the extent, for one reason or other, increase in public expenditure discourages private investment, the deficit budgeting will prove self-defeating.

Obstruction of Desirable Cost Reduction: In case particular costs—say wages of a particular type of labour or prices of particular raw materials—are out of line with the general cost-price structure and costs as such exercise a depressive influence on the industry concerned, they must be lowered so as to help the revival of the industry. If the increased public spending obstructs such adjustment, it would tend to retard self-sustained recovery.

Deficit Financing and Inflation: Does deficit financing inevitably lead to inflation? No, it may be used without inflationary pressures if it is kept within the limits permitted by the following factors:

(1) *Growth of Production:* Increased supply of money is essential to match the increased production if deflation is to be avoided.

(2) *Increase in Population:* Increase in population increases the demand for money for holding cash balances. To the extent, the increased supply of money meets the increased demand for it, there will be no tendency towards inflation.

(3) *Replacement of Subsistence Economy by Exchange Economy:* Underdeveloped countries are characterised by a marked degree of self-sufficiency, workers consume a considerable part of their produce at home and sell very little in the market. With the development process, subsistence economy gives place to exchange economy. To the extent exchange requires money, demand for money is increased.

(4) *Extension of the Monetary Sector to the Barter Economy:* In underdeveloped countries, a considerable portion of the transactions is carried out without the intervention of money. With the development process, barter economy gives place to monetary economy and thus the demand for money is increased.

(5) *Excess of saving over Investment:* Habit of hoarding money is very common in underdeveloped countries. To the extent the deficit financing offsets hoarded money, there will be no tendency towards inflation. It may, however, be mentioned that with economic progress, the people may realise the loss from hoarding and actually there may occur dishoarding instead of hoarding. Savings may remain unutilised, also, because of lack of profitable investment opportunities or because of the underdevelopment of the monetary organisation through which small savings are transformed into investment.

(6) *Excess of Imports over Exports:* Excess of imports over exports may be made possible by the use of old foreign exchange balances (*e.g.* sterling balances in case of several Commonwealth

countries) or foreign loans. To the extent the additional supply of money is matched by the additional imported goods, there will be no inflationary pressure.

The extent to which deficit financing may lead to inflation depends upon a number of factors:

(1) *Elasticity of Production:* The greater the elasticity of production, the greater will be increase in production and smaller the rise in prices as a result of deficit financing. Production in underdeveloped countries, however, is comparatively inelastic because of the lack of excess capacity, shortage of complementary factors and other bottlenecks.

(2) *Nature of Investment:* If the newly created money is used to finance projects which would soon start producing consumable goods, there won't be much inflationary pressure. Generally, there is a time-lag between the employment of additional labour and the increased demand for goods resulting from additional income. Firstly, there is a time-lag between the employment of labour and the payment of wages. Secondly, there is a time-lag between the receipt of wages and the incurring of expenditure. If the projects financed with the newly created money start producing goods during this time-lag, there may occur no inflation. On the other hand, if the newly created money is used to finance the production of capital goods, there may occur strong inflationary pressures. The extent to which additional labour can be employed for the production of consumption goods, however, is strictly limited because of the dearth of capital goods which are essential for the production of consumption goods. Cottage industries employing a small amount of capital and producing goods for which there exists a ready demand offer some scope for creating additional employment through deficit financing.

(3) *Credit Creation:* Generally, a certain amount of deficit financing results into a much larger increase in the supply of money through credit creation. The larger the degree of credit creation, the larger will be the increase in the supply of money resulting from a certain amount of deficit financing.

(4) *Strength of Trade Unions:* Increase in prices leads the labour to demand higher wages. The stronger the trade unions, the larger will be the increase in wages that labour can obtain. The larger the increase in wages, the larger will be the inflationary pressure.

DEFICIT FINANCING AND ECONOMIC DEVELOPMENT

Deficit financing to a certain extent is justified for rapid economic development. The danger of financing leading to inflation is more in underdeveloped countries than in developed countries. In underdeveloped countries, the marginal propensity to consume is very high. On the other hand, supply is comparatively inelastic because of lack of excess capacity, shortage of complementary factors and other bottlenecks. Inflation has been described as a maiden who devours her own lover. It discourages voluntary savings. No doubt, it forces people to save, but over a long period of time, it becomes increasingly difficult for them to maintain their saving rate against rising prices. Inflation may even lead to a decrease in the total supply. With the rises in prices and incomes, the agriculturists may consume more at home or they may prefer leisure to additional income leading to a decrease in total production. Rising prices offer an incentive for hoarding leading to a reduction in the volume of goods brought to the market.

Inflation distorts the profitability of different investments. It induces people to invest in gold, foreign exchange, real estate, hoarding and speculation which offer prospects of fabulous profits rather than in fields which constitute a strong foundation for rapid and balanced economic development. Continuous inflation may endanger the stability of the currency with all its disastrous consequences.

No doubt, a rise in money income raises the revenue and still more revenue can be obtained by certain changes in the tax structure. But the cost of development projects may rise much more because of a rise in wages and in prices of equipment and materials and the government may not be able to carry out the planned programme.

It encourages imports and discourages exports and thus causes balance of payments difficulties. Continuous adverse balance of payments weakens the domestic currency in the world market and thus discourages the inflow of foreign capital

No doubt, for political and administrative reasons, capital formation on the required scale cannot be undertaken by orthodox financial measures, it should not be forgotten that the very simplicity and convenience of deficit financing may lead to extravagance and inefficiency and to neglect of the possibilities for tapping savings and collecting high taxes that exist even in underdeveloped countries.

It is argued that as the projects financed by deficit financing are completed, they would have the effect of increasing production and thereby of increasing savings and tax yields which ould provide finance for development, in the next period. In underdeveloped countries, increased production, however, may not necessarily lead to a significant increase in savings. It is primarily the entrepreneurial class which gains from inflation. This class in predominantly agrarian societies consists largely of poor peasants and merchants with high marginal propensity to consume. Any increase in their income, therefore, is more likely to be consumed than invested. Moreover, the merchants rarely invest in productive enterprises.

The tax system in most of the underdeveloped countries is very inelastic. Many taxes, like land revenue, are difficult to revise upwards in money terms with the rise in prices. In fact the rise in prices caused by deficit financing may decrease government's command over real resources through taxation.

In the ultimate analysis, inflationary financing requires some groups to suffer a decline in their standard of living. But there is no surety that it will elicit the sacrifices from the required groups. In primarily agricultural countries, the classes which have to bear the burnt of inflationary financing are not many. The peasants, merchants and the few rich entrepreneurs do not suffer much loss in real income through rising prices. The only classes which have to sacrifice are the small class of professional men, government employees, and the industrial proletariat. It is difficult to justify a method of enforcing savings which elicits sacrifices from only a few people.

Apart from this, the classes which are adversely affected by inflationary financing—professional men, government employees and industrial proletariat—play an important role in the process of economic development. Their co-operation and support for any programme of development is very essential. For this reason, to neutralise the effect of rise in prices, the governments often introduce measures like price control, rationing, cost of living allowances etc. The result is that almost everybody's income increases *pari passu* with rising prices, and there is very little forced saving, but a maze of administrative problems.

'Created money', if injected into the economy in moderate doses at intermittent intervals, can certainly induce resources into the productive system and generate more capital even in the underdeveloped countries. Much depends upon the timing and quantity of doses of 'created money' and the watch kept over the reactions they produce on the economic system.

Public Debt

23

BURDEN OF PUBLIC DEBT

In an earlier chapter we saw how budget deficits and surpluses might be varied and how consequently the size of the public debt might be altered to control the business fluctuations. While doing so, we did not, however, study the implications of the size of the public debt either from the point of view of equity or from that of economic efficiency. We shall do so in this chapter.

A very important and much controversial question is whether public debt imposes any burden on the community concerned, or any portion thereof, and also whether the burden, if any, of the public debt can be shifted to a subsequent generation.

An extreme form of opinion on the issue is that an internally held public debt imposes a burden just like a private debt. This, however, is not true because in the case of private debt the debtor has to pay the interest and the principal to the creditor who is a different person while in case of public debt the tax-payers pay the interest and the principal to the bond-holders, and since tax-payers and bond-holders belong to the same state this imposes no burden on the state as a whole in the sense a private debt does on the debtor.

Another extreme opinion is that since an internally held public debt requires a transfer of funds from tax-payers to bond-holders in the same state, it is very similar to the transfer of money from one pocket to another pocket of the same person, with the result that such a debt imposes no burden whatsoever. This view is also not correct. Though the tax-payers and the bond-holders belong to the same state, they are different groups of people and the satisfaction lost by one group may not be the same as gained by the other group and as such the state as a whole may suffer a net loss or make a net gain.

The relevant factors which should be taken into consideration while determining as to whether an internally held public debt imposes a burden, and if so how much, are as follows:

(1) The nature of the burden of an internally held public debt is different from that of an externally held public debt. In the case of a foreign debt the interest and the principal have to be paid by the debtor countries to the creditor countries through the creation of an export which means transfer to real resources from the debtor countries to the creditor countries. In the case of internal public debt, in contrast, the resources remain within the country and have only to be transferred from the tax-payers to the bond-holders in the form of interest payments to the latter.

(2) Who owns the government debt obligations and who pays taxes required to service the interest on debt is a matter of great importance. Though "we owe it to ourselves" and not to a foreign country, it is significant who among us holds the bonds and who pays the taxes. To quote from the Annual Report of the Secretary of the Treasury to the Congress, January 3, 1945:

> The payment of interest is a transfer operation by which the amount of interest is collected from tax-payers and paid to the holders of the debt, who are also numbered among the tax-payers. The burden of the debt, therefore, consists of the necessity of collecting a large amount of money from some persons and repaying it to others, and of the possible adverse economic effects of the resulting redistribution of income upon the amount of the national product.[1]

The size as well as the distribution of public debt has a substantial effect on the economy. It can have adverse effects upon production and employment resulting from the redistribution of income on account of the manner in which debt is held and the taxes are collected. It can have adverse effects if it grows to a size, in relation to real income, so large that the holdings of liquid assets become inflationary. It is essential that the volume of production should be adequate to give real value to the liquid assets to which the debt gives rise.

---

1. Cf. Alvin H. Hansen, *Economic Policy and Full Employment* (London, 1947), p. 267.

The burden of public debt would not be absent, if the bondholders were to pay in tax just the amount which they received in the form of interest. This is because of the frictions of levying and collecting taxes and because of the differences in the subjective effects of paying taxes and receiving interest. Moreover, the existence of a large public debt limits the government's freedom of action and may preclude effective control of the monetary and banking system.

(3) The net burden incident to the public debt is considerably less than the total interest charges in view of the fact that the holders of the bonds will pay a considerable amount of tax on the interest earning received. Further, in terms of disposal of the interest payments as between saving and expenditures, the data points to the conclusion that the net deflationary effect of the total transfer from tax-payer to interest recipient is relatively small. The conclusion dos not take into consideration on the one hand the contractionist effect of the impact of the added net tax burden upon new investment and new industry, nor on the other hand the expansionist effect of increased liquidity and financial security upon the propensity to spend out of current income. Taking into account all the factors, it is highly probable that the net effect of a large public debt is likely to prove, on balance, expansionist.

(4) Prof. Domar holds that the burden of public debt should be defined as the ratio of the total debt to the total national income, *i.e., Total Debt/Total National Income*. If the total amount of national income remains constant and the total amount of public debt increases year after year, the burden of debt would increase. But if the national income also rises, say, by a constant absolute amount together with the increase in the amount of public debt by a constant amount, then in spite of the increase in the volume of public debt, the burden of public debt, defined as to the total amount of public debt divided by the total amount of national income will actually fall. This will be more so if the national income rises by a constant relative amount along with the rise in the amount of public debt.

The criterion of a "reasonable" ratio of debt to income need not defeat the ends of fiscal policy. A full-employment programme in view of growth (i) in labour force and (ii) in productivity would lead to an ever-rising income. Thus, even if the interest rates do not fall, tax rates needed to finance debt interest might well be reduced, the more so if the tax structure is progressive. In case interest rates decline, this would be still more the case. Thus an ever-growing debt would not, within the limits of what is probable, necessarily mean higher tax rates. If higher rates prove to be necessary, the problem is not unmanageable, but is nonetheless still a problem.

(5) It is sometimes held that a large amount of public debt increases the inequalities in the distribution of income in favour of bond-holders because the bond-holders are generally the richer people while there are limits upon which the taxes may be made progressive without seriously impairing the incentives to work, to save and to take risks. Lerner, however , does not agree with this view and holds that it is because of the inequality of income distribution that public debt is held by the richer people in large quantities. In other words, inequalities in the distribution of income are the cause and not the effect of the concentration of public debt in the hands of a few rich people.

Another controversial question is as to whether the system of financing a project by means of public debt shifts the burden to the future generation. The traditional argument is that if taxes are used to finance a project, people pay for the project now; but if the project is financed by borrowing, the present generation escapes the cost and the burden is shifted to the future generation which pays the interest and the principal.

The above argument, however, is not considered to be correct. The real burden of the project must be borne in the period in which expenditure is made because it is in this period that resources are diverted from private to public use. The real burden of a war, for instance, consists of the use of productive resources for the production of war materials instead of civilian goods and this is borne during the period of the war in the form of reduced consumption, regardless of the method of financing employed. The financing through borrowing, beyond any doubt, results in some problems for the future generations in the form of adverse effects on the economy flowing from the taxes necessary to pay interest and principal to the bond-holders, inflationary effects of the existence of debt etc., but there is no shifting of the basic burden to the future. While the future generations inherit the obligation to pay interest and principal on the debt, they also inherit the bonds themselves and as such receive the interest payments and principal repayments.

This view, however, does not take into consideration that even if the real burden of financing a project consists in the sacrifice of private consumption, the same may be out of present or future consumption. The burden cannot be same in the two cases. The theory of shifting of burden has thus revived in new forms discussed below:

Ricardo-Pigou Thesis: According to it, if the government expense is financed by taxation the first generation hands on to the second nothing but tax receipts; if the expense is financed by issue of bonds, the first generation bequeaths the bonds to the second generation, but along with them a tax liability represented by the annual charge on the debt for interest and, if the bonds are not perpetuities, for redemption and amortisation. The welfare of the second generation, however, depends not on whether it inherits tax receipts or government bonds, but on what it inherits in the way of real stock of capital; the inheritance of stock of capital depends on the reaction of the first generation to the taking away of the real resources by the government. The first generation is likely to cut its consumption more and investment less if it receives only tax receipts from the government than if it receives bonds because it fails to give full-weight to the task ahead of servicing the bonds. This failure is because of the fact that no one individual can be sure of the amount of tax he will have to pay towards the servicing of the bonds each year in the future. Every individual may have a tendency to believe that he is richer with the bonds with an unidentified future tax obligation than he would be with tax receipts and no such future obligation. In case of bond financing, therefore, the individual, feeling richer, may reduce his consumption less. The result would be that a smaller amount of capital stock would be passed on to the second generation. The burden in this case consists in inheriting by the second generation a smaller amount of capital stock than otherwise.

Buchanan Thesis: Prof. Buchanan is of the opinion that financing through borrowing does shift a burden to the future generations. According to him, the concept of burden should be interpreted in terms of the individual attitudes towards their economic well-being rather than in terms of changes in private-sector outputs and real income because of the inheritance by the latter generations of a larger or smaller amount of capital instruments. Buchanan believes that during the period in which the project is financed and borrowing takes place, no burden of any type is created. People who subscribe to government loans voluntarily exchange liquid funds for less liquid government bonds instead of using the funds for obtaining consumption and/or investment goods. Since this is done voluntarily by the individuals concerned, they do not feel themselves to by any worse off. The repayment of bonds in the future generation, however leads to a transfer of funds from the tax-payers to the bond-holders. The result is that the tax-payers feel themselves to be worse off while the bond-holders do not feel better off because they have now merely changed bonds for cash. As such the society as a whole becomes worse off during the future generations. In other words the burden is shifted to the future generations.

Musgrave Thesis of Inter-generation Equity: Prof. Musgrave formulates a model in which, irrespective of the reaction of Generation I to tax finance and loan finance, loan finance always divides the cost among generations and tax finance can never do so. In this sense loan financing does shift the burden to the generations to come.

Musgrave considers a long-lived government facility, the cost of which is to be distributed equitably amongst those who make use of it. Suppose that the project has a life of three periods and each generation has a life span of three periods. As period I opens. Generation I, already in its last period, is on the scene; so also are Generation II with one more period to go, and Generation III, in its initial period. In the second period, there exist Generation II in its last period as also Generation III and IV. In the third period. there will be Generations III, IV and V respectively in their third, second and first periods.

The problem is how to take from the Generations in question their due shares of the cost of the project, namely, the following:

Generation I	1/9th
Generation II	2/9th
Generation III	3/9th
Generation IV	2/9th
Generation V	1/9th

the due share being proportional to the period or periods for which the service of the facility is enjoyed by each Generation, Musgrave's solution is to require Generation I to pay 1/9th of the cost in taxation and so on. As to financing the project in its year of construction 6/9th must be covered by loan; but no part of the loan can be demanded from Generation I, since it is already in its last period and thus could never be repaid. Generation I is vanishing at the end of the first period. So, 6/9th is financed by loans from Generation II and III who are repaid before they vanish. Thus every body gets his money back, except to the extent that he is required to pay tax, and the tax is distributed over time in accordance with the degree of service use.

BDK Thesis: A corollary of the Ricardo-Pigou thesis is that a project financed by public debt will not shift any burden to the future generation if initially it is financed entirely by a reduction in private consumption. This contention has, however, been challenged by Bowen, Davis and Kopf, who have shown that even if a project is financed entirely by a reduction in consumption by Generation I, a burden is shifted to future generations. Suppose, for instance, in a country producing only timber, in year 1900, a quantity of 100 tons of timber is consumed by the Government for meeting, say, war needs and the "project" is "financed" wholly by a reduction of 100 tons of timber consumption by Generation I. Supposing that the life span of each Generation is 44 years and assuming that the reduction in the consumption of timber made by each Generation at the time of its appearance is met by a corresponding increase in its consumption before it passes away, the pattern of timber consumption by three Generations will be as follows:

Year	*Generation*	*Timber Consumption*
1900	I	–100
1944	I	+100
	II	–100
1988	II	+100
	III	–100

In the above example, though the government consumption of timber has been financed entirely by a reduction in the consumption of timber by Generation I, the consumption of every generation is deferred by 44 years; and this will be continued until the debt floated by the government for consuming the timber initially is amortised. This deferring of consumption, according to *BDK*, is a burden, even though the entire consumption of timber by the government is matched by a corresponding decrease in the private consumption.

MANAGEMENT OF PUBLIC DEBT

The basic prerequisite for an efficient management of the public debt is that the debt should be so issued, the pattern of maturity structure of the bonds should be so fixed, the interest rates should be so managed, taxes should be so devised and the bonds should be so redeemed that the strains and frictions are kept at the minimum.

The most important requirement for an efficient management of public debt is that the interest rates on the government obligations should be kept as low as possible and the pattern of interest rates on different maturities of the securities should be so worked out as would most nearly conform to the preference pattern of the individuals. The lower the average rate of interest on the government securities, the smaller will be the required amount of the recurring transfer of resources from tax-payers to the bond-holders and as such, other things remaining unchanged, the less will be the strains and frictions associated with a given amount of public debt. In addition, individuals and institutions generally like to hold debts of different maturities from the shortest to the longest so as to strike an optimum balance in their portfolios between the conflicting interest of liquidity and solvency on the one hand and the highest possible interest income on the other. The managers of the public debt should so fix the pattern of interest rates on the different maturities of government securities that the bond-holders are able to attain the highest possible indifference surface by the holding of a mix of different types of available public debt.

With a view to make the structure of public debt conform to the preference pattern of the individuals, one of the techniques commonly used by the government is what is known as "swapping operation." The operation consists in a simultaneous purchase and sale by the central bank of government securities of different maturities, leaving the total volume of the securities unchanged and hence without releasing in or absorbing from the economy any additional bank reserves, but altering the composition of the securities and hence the pattern of interest rates on such securities.

Empirical evidence shows that the general strategy of the governments in countries, which have substantially relied on deficit financing, has been to maintain a very low rate of interest on the shortest-term securities and to increase the rate gradually, and sometimes by discontinuous spurts, as the maturity period of debt lengthens. This may lead to such wide differences between short-term and long-term rates of interest as to induce pattern-playing switching over from the shorter ends to the longer ends of the market by the holders of the public debt, with the accompanying problem of debt management and the ineffectiveness of the monetary policy.

The shorter the duration of public debt, the greater will be the ratio of matured debt to total debt at any point of time and as such the greater will be the obligation of the government at any point of time to repay the amount to the lender. This will necessitate either fresh taxes and/or fresh floatation of debts. This advantage of short-term debts should be weighed against the advantage of the comparatively smaller interest obligation on such debts. The longer-term debts, in contrast, involve a comparatively smaller repayment obligation but, again, this advantage has to be offset by the higher interest obligation on such debts.

Thus any system of public debt under which the holders of the debt are free and/or induced to monetise their debt obligations before their maturity period would create more problems for the managers of public debt than any system under which such freedom and/or inducement is limited or absent. Besides the adverse effects on an effective exercise of monetary policy which the monetisation of public debt involves, monetisation of debt on a large scale by the holders thereof would result in great strain on the central banking system of the country which these days is generally entrusted with the task of floatation and redemption of public debt on behalf of the government. The managers of public debt should therefore be careful that such freedom of and/or inducement to monetisation of public debt is kept at the minimum. In fact, various devices have been worked out to this end. One such device is to fix interest rates on intermediate and long-term government obligations in such a way that the rate of interest per annum on each type of government securities rises progressively with the increase in the period for which the security is held. Thus though the holder of the security is often given option to monetise his debt holdings before the expiry of their maturity period, he is penalised in the shape of receipt of a very low interest income if he actually monetises it "too early", and he is rewarded in the shape of a higher interest rate if the monetisation is deferred to or near the maturity period of the securities. Another device is to float non-marketable securities; but in this case the advantage of non-monetisation should be weighed against the disadvantage of the higher levels of interest rates which would be necessary on such securities. A third way is to combine a system of non-marketability of the securities for a particular period from the date of floatation of the securities with the feature of progressive interest rates, the rate of interest increasing with the increase in the period for which the security is held.

Now we come to the problem of management involved in the issue and redemption of a large amount of public debt as also in the existence of a large amount of public debt.

Other things remaining unchanged, the issue of a large amount of public debt is likely to create a shortage of funds in the private capital market. This will be so because assuming that there are not much idle funds in the capital market, the debt floated by the government will be held by the individuals, banks and non-bank financial intermediaries out of the funds which would have otherwise gone to the private capital or money market. The stringency of funds in the private capital market is likely to raise the rate of interest. Such a rise in the rate of interest is highly detrimental to a sound policy of debt management. A rise in the rate of interest in the private capital market inevitably leads to an upward pressure in the government credit market which enhances the burden of public debt. Further, it is an accepted objective of debt management policy that there should be an "orderly condition" in the government security market. The "orderly condition" would prevail only if the government can successfully assure the investors in government securities of the continuation of the level and pattern of interest rates stipulated on the government securities so that the investors need not be afraid that after they have purchased the securities there would be a rise in the level of interest rates involving a capital loss.

A major plank of a sound debt management policy is a co-operating monetary policy. With the wide powers which the governments now-a-days possess over the central banking organisations, there has been no difficulty in obtaining such co-operation. In fact, the central banking system is often made the residual purchaser of government securities at par so that whenever there is an excess supply of government securities resulting from their holders' willingness to monetise them, the central bank stands ready to purchase them. The purchases by the central bank wipe out the excess supply and thereby check the downward pressure on the security prices and upward in the interest rates. With the extensive authority of the government-dominated central banking system to engage in open-market purchase and sale of government securities, it has not been difficult to maintain stable prices of government securities and an orderly condition in the government security market. Thus the floatation of public debt is generally accompanied by required degree of purchase and, redemption by sale, of government securities in the open market by the central bank so that the people's liquidity preference is just satisfied by the injection of money into, and withdrawal thereof from, the system at the prevailing rate of interest.

The above policy, while easing the task of management of public debt, has resulted in major obstacles in the way of an effective exercise of the monetary policy. Though the floatation of public debt is deflationary, the existence of a large amount of public debt has great inflationary potential so much so as to defy its effective control by a vigorous use of monetary policy. This is so because, apart from the destabilising effect on government credit market which a rise in the rate of interest following a vigorous use of monetary policy entails, the presence of a large volume of government securities considerably eases the access of the spending units to money from government securities, because of the latter's characteristics of high liquidity and risklessness which make them close substitutes of money. We should also take into consideration the fact that under factorial reserve banking system adopted by a central banking organisation, any increase in the holding of public debt by the central bank and the consequent increase in its liability correspondingly increases the cash assets of the commercial banks on the basis of which such banks may make a multiple increase in their deposit liabilities with their consequent expansionary potential. Further, a substantial increase in the volume of public debt and the fluctuations in their demand, supply and prices over the business cycles tend to amplify the magnitude of the business fluctuations. In the earlier phases of the boom, the economic units expecting a rise in the commodity prices but no change in security prices, want to hold commodities only by disposing of both securities and money. While an excess supply of securities tends to lower their prices and thus raise the rate of interest, an excess supply of money tends to lower the rate of interest. In the initial phase of the upswing, the second effect is likely to more powerful than the first one and as a result the rate of interest is likely to be reduced. This is followed by a next stage in the upswing when the economic units expect both the commodity and the security prices to go up and as such they want to purchase both commodities and securities at the cost of money. A rise in the demand for securities causes further decline in the interest rates which adds further momentum to the upswing. In the next stage, expectation changes for a decline in security prices accompanied with a rise in commodity prices which induces the economic units to hold commodities and money by disposing of the securities. This causes a decline in the prices of the securities or a rise in the rate of interest. As the rise becomes sufficient and as it is accompanied with an expectation of a fall in the commodity prices, the downswing sets in. During the downswing phase, there is first a shift from the holding of commodities to both securities and money and consequently the interest rate rises. This is followed by a shift from both commodities and securities to money in anticipation of a decline in security prices also which causes a rise in the interest rate aggravating the downturn. The expectation of a rise in the security prices revives gradually in the depth of the depression inducing in the next stage the economic units to shift from both money and commodities to securities which lowers the interest rate and eventually facilitates the recovery.

Another important problem relates to the choice between different types of public debt. While maintaining a given level of private expenditure or securing a given change, the mix of claims might be made to include more money and less liquid debt, less money and more liquid debt, a large and less liquid debt, a smaller and more liquid debt and so forth. The determination of the most efficient mix of public debt involves two steps. In the first place, there is the appraisal of market preferences, or the cost at which various types of obligations may be placed. Secondly, there is the more difficult task of appraising the relative degrees of liquidity, or non-spending, that are secured by borrowing a given amount through the sale of various types of obligations.

In purchasing liquidity, the government may enter into a wide variety of debt contracts. These may differ with regard to maturity, marketability, and many other features.

Maturity: Most important is the choice between obligations of differing maturity. The claims may range from obligations of zero maturity over obligations of finite maturity including short-term and long-term obligations, to obligations of infinite maturity or consoles. Claims of zero maturity include savings bonds payable at a specified price on demand. In case of finite maturities, it is not necessary to fix a single date at which the debt must mature. The terms may be such as to fix the maximum maturity date while an option to terminate earlier is left either to the Treasury or to the lender. Alternatively, the terms of debt may entitle the lender to refund at a later date into specified issues to be made available at that time.

At sometimes, the Treasury may have to pay more for placing short issues and, at other times, more for placing long ones, the latter being the more normal case. The problem, then, is to determine in which case more liquidity is surrendered by the investor per rupee of coupon payment. This determination of the proper maturity mix has, perhaps, been the most important problem of debt management.

Marketability: Variations in the degree of marketability is another aspect of debt policy. In case of marketable issues, the contract of the Treasury is with the bearer and the original buyer of the claims is of no importance. In the case of non-marketable issues, the contract is with the original buyer of the claims who must hold the claims till the Treasury redeems it. The non-marketability is a great disadvantage to the investor and must be compensated for by higher returns or by granting him an option to terminate the contract at an earlier date. From the Treasury's point of view, such concessions must be weighed against the advantages expected from the issue of non-negotiable claims.

The treasury can also issue debt of restricted marketability. In this case the Treasury differentiates between groups of lenders and permits marketability only among eligible investors. Only non-bank investors, for instance, may be declared eligible for holding certain types of securities. From the eligible lenders' point of view, restriction on marketability is a disadvantage; but it is beneficial for him to the extent he is accorded a favourable treatment. It is advantageous to the Treasury to the extent it is enabled to discriminate between different markets so as to implement subsidy objectives through debt policy.

Differences between Lenders: In selling claims, the Treasury does not face a homogeneous body of lenders or a homogeneous mass of private debt which is to be replaced by public debt. Different lenders have distinct preferences for various types of debt, public and private. By issuing debt that appeals to one or the other group, the Treasury may influence the particular type of private debt for a restricted market, as well as the particular type of private expenditure that is to be reduced. The additional sale of long-term claims by the government would tighten the terms at which private debt of long maturities may be placed. If the government sells short-term claims, it will tighten by and large the private market for short-term debt. A lengthening of the structure of public debt will tend to raise long-term rates relative to short-term rates and ease the market, for short-term private debt relative to that for long-term private debt. This will affect the availability of funds to those who want to borrow short relative to those who want to borrow long. This will in turn affect the flow of expenditures between investments that depend upon short-term and long-term financing. Though long-term investments may be financed by short-term funds, and vice versa, the type of public debt does affect the flow of private investment expenditures.

More or less the same reasoning applies to exchanges between money and debt as applies to exchanges between long-term and short-term debt. Substitution of short-term public debt for money tends to curtail the market for private short-term debt, while substitution of long-term public debt tends to curtail the market for private long-term debt.

Similar considerations bear on the choice between marketable and non-marketable securities and among other technical features of debt issues that appear in varying degrees to various types of lenders. The particular preferences of lenders differ with their business or personal positions and depend upon the constraints that the liability side of their balance sheets places upon them. Commercial banks with short-term liabilities will be cautious in undertaking long-term investment. Insurance companies having long-term contracts would prefer long-term investments.

The above shows that the simple requirement of minimum cost ignores an important aspect of the problem. If all private debt were of the uniform type, the choice of public debt would not affect the type of private borrowing that is reduced. If there were only one type of private investment, there would be no qualitative effect on the curtailment in expenditure by the lender. In such a situation, the objective would simply be to determine the structure of public debt that attains the desired reduction in private expenditures at the least cost. But there arise complications if we take into consideration the fact that the private debt obligations that are replaced, and the expenditures that these obligations may generate, are not homogeneous. Keeping in view the lack of homogeneity, the pattern that emerges if a certain curtailment in private expenditure is attained at the minimum cost may not be the optimal one; a different pattern may be more desirable even if it involve a higher cost.

Anti-cyclical Debt Management: A proper management of public debt (public borrowing and repayment) is an important instrument to fight inflation and deflation and to bring about economic stability and full employment. During depression, as we have seen, taxes are reduced and public expenditures are increased; thus budget deficits are created which are financed by borrowings. While borrowing funds from the public, the state should keep two things in view. Firstly, to keep the burden of public debt low, the state should aim at a policy of low rates of interest during depression. Secondly, the state should try, as far as possible, to borrow from those sections of people with whom the funds are lying idle so as to avoid adverse effects on private spending. Borrowing from the commercial banks has also a positive multiplier effect. As soon as the money is created and spent by the state, it stays in the hands of the public as part of an enlarged money supply. The larger the public's cash balances, other things remaining unchanged, the higher will be its propensity to consume and invest. To have the desired effects, the state borrowing must avoid replacing loans to private borrowers. The state may also borrow from the central bank directly in exchange for bonds. This method is certainly good during depression because new funds are treated for the state without any reduction in the public's spending power. Further during depression public debt should be funded into short-term debt in the hope that the long-term funds released will be driven into capital formation.

During inflation public debt should be managed in such a way as to reduce money supply in the economy and restrict expansion of credit. New borrowing should be avoided and old debts should be retired by a budget surplus created by reducing expenditures and increasing tax rates and levying new taxes. Furthermore, during inflation public debt should be lengthened so that holding long-term debt becomes attractive to capital formation.

Evaluation of Keynesian Theory of Employment

24

ACHIEVEMENTS OF KEYNES

No other economist in the present era has so profoundly influenced both economic thought and policy as Keynes did. In the words of Hazlitt[1]:

> The most famous economist of the twentieth century is John Maynard Keynes;....Open any issue of almost any of the scholarly economic journals, and you will find his name and the phrases that he coined or popularised sprinkled generously through its pages. Open the newspaper, and you will find interpretations of current economic events, or proposals for economic and monetary policies, that owe at least their unequity, if not their origin, to his writings.

Alvin H. Hansen, considered to be a leading American disciple of Keynes, speaks of the *General Theory* thus[2]:

> There are few who would deny, as of now, seventeen years later, that the book has had a greater impact on economic analysis and policy even in this short time than any book since Ricardo's Political Economy. It may be a little too early to claim, that along with Darwin's *Origin of Species* and Karl Marx's *Das Capital*, the *General Theory* is one of the most significant books which have appeared in the last hundred years,......But......it continues to gain in importance.

To city Dudley Dillard[3]:

---

1. Henry Hazlitt, *The Failure of "New Economics"* (New York, 1959), p. 1.
2. Alvin Hansen, *A Guide to Keynes* (New York, 1953).
3. Dudley Dillard, *The Economics of John Maynard Keynes* (New York, 1948), pp. vii and 102.

> By any test, Keynes ranks as one of the great economists of all times and as the most influential economic thinker the twentieth century has so far produced......
>
> Within the first dozen years following its publication, John Maynard Keynes' *The General Theory of Employment, Interest and Money* (1936) has had more influence upon the thinking of professional economists and public policy-makers than any other book in the whole history of economic thought in a comparable number of years. Like Adam Smith's *Wealth of Nations* in the eighteenth century and Karl Marx's *Capital* in the nineteenth century, Keynes' *General Theory* has been the centre of controversy among both professional and non-professional writers. Smith's book is a ringing challenge to mercantilism, Marx's took is a searching criticism of capitalism, Keynes' book is a repudiation of the foundation of *laissez faire*. Many economists acknowledge a heavy debt to the stimulating thought of Lord Keynes.
>
> If the influence of Lord Keynes were limited to the field of technical economic doctrine, it would be of little interest to the world at large. However, practical economic policy bears even more deeply than economic theory the imprint of Keynes' thought.

Having had a detailed and over-all picture of the Keynesian Economics, let us now evaluate its achievements and failures. We begin with his achievements. Keynes has certainly made some advances in the economic theory, important of which are briefly stated below:

(1) *The Underemployment Equilibrium:* This is considered to be one of the important contribution of Keynes to Economics. Keynes strongly refuted the earlier classical assertion that in a *laissez faire* economy there was always a tendency towards full employment and maintained that a state of underemployment was the more likely case.

(2) The consumption function or the propensity to consume is another important contribution of Keynes to economic theory. In recent years many empirical studies have been made both in the United Kingdom and the United States, which support Keynes' psychological law of a stable consumption function.

(3) *The Multiplier:* Closely connected with the consumption function, the Multiplier (*K*) is considered Keynes' path-breaking contribution to the economic theory. It is an integral part of the modern theory of employment and business cycles.

(4) *The Liquidity Preference Theory of Interest:* This again is an important contribution of Keynes to economic analysis. In contrast to the classical view, Keynes considered interest to be a monetary phenomenon and explained it as such. His analysis of the liquidity preference of the community into three motives—the transactions motive, the precautionary motive and the speculative motive—is comprehensive and illuminating.

(5) *Dynamic Element:* An important contribution of Keynes lies in the introduction of dynamic element in economic analysis. He stressed the important role which future expectations play in the taking of investment decisions.

(6) *The 'General' Nature of Keynesian Theory:* Keynes' theory is 'general' in the sense that it is equally applicable to all sorts of situations—under-employment, full employment, and overfull employment situations. The classical theory, in contrast, was special theory applicable to a full employment situation.

(7) *Emphasis on Investment:* Keynes stressed the importance of investment as a determinant of employment. Of the two determinants of employment, consumption is more or less stable and can be varied easily. In contrast, investment is a highly variable factor. By increasing or decreasing it, the government can ensure full employment or economic stability as the need may be.

(8) *Macro Approach:* An outstanding contribution of Keynes lies in the adoption of macro analysis approach. As against this the pre-Keynesian Economics was by and large based on the micro approach.

(9) *Tools of Analysis:* Keynes, like Marshall, has contributed a number of tools to the tool-box of the modern economic analysis, *e.g.*, propensity to consume, inducement to invest, marginal efficiency of capital etc.

PRACTICAL IMPORTANCE OF KEYNESIAN THEORY

(1) Keynes gave a fatal blow to the old discredited policy of *laissez faire*. He demonstrated that in a private enterprise economy full employment will not prevail automatically and for attaining full

employment, the state may have to step up investment by active participation in economic matters.

(2) The Keynesian theory showed that a balanced budget was not always the best policy for the government. According to Keynes, the budgetary policy would have to be decided in the light of the economic situation prevailing in the country. He showed that in certain circumstances the policy of deficit budget was the most appropriate for stepping up the volume of income, output and employment in the economy. The credit for the present popularity of a policy of deficit budgeting during recessionary periods rightly goes to Keynes.

(3) Keynes assigned an important role to fiscal policy in his programme of full employment. He greatly contributed to the evolution of President Roosevelt's 'New Deal' Policy. His policies of government intervention and public works were given a fair trial in the United States which succeeded in pulling the country out of the depth of depression. These days governments in almost all countries have accepted public works as an important part of their unemployment fighting programme. The Keynesian remedies have been equally effective in tackling the problems of an inflationary economy. In his pamphlet, "How to Pay for the War" (1940), Keynes suggested ways and means to the British Government for financing the cost of the Second World War. To check inflation, he suggested the suppressing of Consumption and investment both through monetary and fiscal measures. For suppressing consumption he made a revolutionary suggestion of compulsory saving or deferred payment. The scheme was that a compulsory deduction should be made from current wages and salaries and deposited in a blocked saving account which could not be withdrawn during war. The idea was to cut down purchasing power in the hands of public with the objective of reducing national consumption. The scheme was adopted by the British Government, though only to a limited extent and was quite successful. In 1963, the Government of India adopted the scheme of compulsory saving with the objective of mobilising resources for development and defence but was discontinued after a year.

FAILURES AND WEAKNESSES OF KEYNES

So far we were examining the important achievements of Keynes in the field of theory as well as in that of policy. In order to make a fair assessment of Keynes' contribution, let us briefly examine his failures and weaknesses also.

(i) According to Prof. Hazlitt[4], Keynes' objective of 'full employment is neither definable, nor attainable, nor even desirable'. He scraps the concept of full employment' and uses instead the concept of "optimum employment" and so does Prof. Halm. According to Dr. Klein and Sweezy—both Keynesians—Keynes does not provide a comprehensive solution of the problem of unemployment. A complete theory of employment should tell us as to how to sustain full and fair employment. Keynes failed to tackle the technological and frictional unemployment. Thus Keynes' theory is not a complete theory of employment.

(ii) Like the old classical economics, the theory is based on the unrealistic assumption of perfect competition. Keynes overlooked the problems of monopolistic concerns which occupy a dominant position in the capitalist countries.

(iii) Though Keynes assumed the existence of a functional relationship between effective demand and the volume of employment, he never attempted to test it by statistical evidence. Prof. Hazlitt remarks that there is, in fact, no reason to assume that any functional relationship exists between 'effective demand' and the 'volume of employment'. The volume of employment does not vary directly with the volume of 'effective demand'. In fact, everything depends upon the inter-relationship of wage-rates, prices and the supply of money. Prof. Hazlitt is of the opinion that it is possible to have full employment even when the effective demand is low provided wage-rates are flexible enough to be adjusted quickly to the prices.[5] In short, the volume of employment is not a function of effective demand but depends on the existence of a fluid and dynamic element among prices, wages etc.

4. Hazlitt, *The Failure of "New economics"* (New York, 1958), pp. 339-408.
5. Hazlitt, *The Failure of 'New Economics'* (New York, 1959), p. 433.

(iv) The classical theory suffered from the weakness that it overemphasized the micro aspect of economic analysis. But Keynes erred on the other side by overemphasizing the macro analysis. In a private enterprise economy, which Keynes was trying to preserve the economics of an individual firm cannot be ignored. We must clearly understand functional distribution and realise that the factors of production are paid for their functioning. Higher wages can be justified only by an increase in productivity. The macro economic thesis that higher wages may be paid to maintain effective demand is only a half-truth. In a private enterprise economy, the level of wages cannot be isolated from the level of productivity. Thus the macro-economic analysis alone may lead to economic disorder.

(v) Thinking that the postulates of the classical theory are applicable only to a special case and not to the general case, Keynes claimed his theory to be a "general theory."[6] Actually, Keynes' theory is a static theory because it is mainly concerned with equilibrium positions. Arthur Smithies regards Keynesian analysis a special case of a general dynamic theory.[7] Keynes' analysis is concerned primarily with the short period. He takes "as given the existing skill and quantity of available labour, the existing quality and quantity of available equipment, the existing technique, the degree of competition, the tastes and habits of the consumer, the disutility of different intensities of labour and of the activities of supervision and organisation, as well as the social structure......which determine the distribution of the national income."[8] Growth, however, is concerned primarily with the long period and to a considerable extent depends on changes in the basic factors assumed by Keynes to be given. Keynesian analysis, thus, is not very relevant to the problems of growth.

In the long period, changes in the basic factors considerably affect the volume of employment. An increase in the degree of

---

6. J.M. Keynes, *The General Theory of Employment, Interest and Money* (London, 1957), p. 3.
7. Arthur Smithies, "Effective Demand and Employment" in Seymour E. Harris (ed.), *The New Economics* (London, 1949), p. 568.
8. J.M. Keynes, *The General Theory of Employment, Interest and Money* (London, 1936), p. 245.

monopoly, for instance, may lead to a restriction of production and thereby to a decline in the volume of employment. Similarly, an increase in the quantity of capital equipment available would make possible a larger volume of employment where the unemployed labour (as in underdeveloped countries) could not be employed because of a shortage of capital equipment. The volume of employment may decline if the labour-intensive techniques of production are replaced by the capital-intensive techniques.

(vi) Keynes' choice of units for economic measurement is highly confused. What he calls a "quantity of employment" turns out, on his own definition, to be not a quantity of employment but a quantity of money received by labourers who are employed.

(vii) Keynes' definitions of his key terms—income, saving, and investment—are circular in nature; they are all defined in terms of each other. He so defines saving and investment that they are not only necessarily equal but identical. At the same time, while he approves of investment, he treats saving with contempt.

(viii) Keynes' list of eight motives for saving is arbitrary. It can either be expanded to a much larger number or reduced to a much smaller one. Keynes ignores the motive to capitalistic saving, that is, to make possible roundabout methods of production.

(ix) In Keynes' model, the supply of labour is perfectly elastic at the ruling money wage-rate. In advanced countries, which Keynes had in mind while formulating his theory, the current money wage rate provides a standard of living higher than the subsistent level and, consequently, there is scope for a cut in the real wage rate. Supply of labour, therefore, won't decrease much with a cut in the real wage rate, money wage rate, remaining unchanged. In underdeveloped countries, in contrast, the prevailing money wage rate provides a bare subsistence level. Physical existence of labour is not possible at a lower real wage rate. Supply of labour, therefore, will be perfectly elastic not at the prevailing money wage rate but at the prevailing real wage rate. It is not possible to permit the price level to rise so long as the money wage rate remains unchanged.

(x) According to Keynesian analysis, the rate of interest is determined by the demand for and supply of money. Demand for money arises out of three motives *viz.* (i) transactive-motive, (ii) precautionary-motive and (iii) speculative-motive. Demand for money owing to transactive-motive and precautionary-motive is a relatively stable function and changes in this part of the total demand for money evoke quick response in the supply of money; this part of the total demand for money, therefore, does not exert an important influence on the rate of interest. It is the demand for money for speculative-motive which exerts the most important influence on the rate of interest. In underdeveloped countries, the speculative activity is not very important. Rate of interest in these countries is influenced more by customs, tradition and institutional factors than by the demand for money for speculative motive. Demand for money for investment also exerts an important influence on the rate of interest.

Further, it is not helpful to explain interest rates as "the reward for parting with liquidity" any more than it would be to explain the price of a car as the "reward" to the buyer for parting with cash for it. There can be no liquidity to part with without previous saving. If Keynes' theory of interest were correct, interest rates would be highest at the bottom of a depression and lowest at the peak of a boom, which is precisely the opposite of their actual tendency. Keynes is also wrong in regarding interest as a purely monetary phenomenon. His fallacy consists in assuming that because monetary factors can be shown to affect the rate of interest, "real" factors can safely be ignored or even denied. Whatever is true in Keynes' theory of interest was already recognised by Knut Wicksell and is fully taken account of in the works of the best contemporary economists.

Keynes attacks the classical theory of the rate of interest but actually there is no uniform classical theory of interest. Current theories of interest can be divided into three broad categories: (1) productivity theories, (2) time-preference or time-discount theories, and (3) theories which combine productivity and time-preference. Since a borrower of funds in effect buys or borrows time, or the use or enjoyment of goods before he could otherwise use or enjoy them, 'time preference' or 'time usance' must be recognised as the chief factor in explaining interest and the rate of interest. But 'investment opportunity', the prospective 'rate of return over cost' (or the expected net value productivity of specific new capital codes) also plays a role, because of its influence on the demand for loans and the rate the borrowers are willing to pay. Any complete theory of interest must deal not only with "real" but also with monetary factors.

(xi) According to Keynes, rate of interest, along with the marginal efficiency of capital, is an important determinant of the rate of investment. The influence of the rate of interest on the rate of investment, however, has been doubted even in advanced countries. The inquiry conducted by the Oxford Economists Research Group revealed that the investment decisions of the businessmen are not significantly affected by the rate of interest.[9] Interest-elasticity of investment is likely to be lower in underdeveloped countries because of a number of factors. Firstly, the risk factor is more important in an economy passing through a transitional stage than in an advanced economy which is comparatively stable and in which the path of growth can be predicted much more safely. The more important the risk factor, the smaller will be the influence of the interest rate. Secondly, the interest rate is more important in case of long-term investment than in case of short-term investments. In underdeveloped countries, the long-term projects like railways, roads, irrigation, electricity etc. are, generally, undertaken by the state which is guided more by the welfare considerations than by the profit and loss calculations based on interest rate. Thirdly, the rate of interest is more important in case of investments undertaken with borrowed funds than in case of those financed through internal resources. In underdeveloped countries, investment through borrowed funds is relatively less important.

(xii) To expand the volume of employment, Keynes depended almost exclusively on investment function since he considered consumption function to be stable in the short run. This has been criticised by economists like Pigou and Eric Roll. They point out that other determinants of employment (consumption function, liquidity function etc.) should also be acted upon. "It is by the inter-relations among these several elements not by the individual state of anyone of them the volume of employment is determined."[10] Many

---

9. J.E. Meade and P.W.S. Andrews, "Summary of Replies to Questions on Effects on Interest Rates", T. Wilson and P.W.S. Andrews (eds.) *Oxford Studies in Price Mechanism* (Oxford, 1952), pp. 28-30.

10. A.C. Pigou, *Keynes General Theory*, p. 27.

economists have suggested that the propensity to consume should be raised by redistributive taxation and other means.

(xiii) Prof. Hazlitt considers consumption function only a truism put forward under the guise of a great discovery—a self-evident truth known in a loose general form since times immemoral. He also criticises the concept on the ground that it is cast purely in quantitative terms "whereas every civilised human being conceives his actual consumption just as much in qualitative terms." He wants better food, better clothing and better housing. In fact, there are no assignable limits to the possible improvements in the quality of consumption. Prof. Hazlitt further points out that actual experience and statistical evidence also fail to support Keynes' consumption function and for this reason he dubs it as 'useless and illegitimate concept.'

(xiv) An important characteristic of Keynesian Economics is that it is short-run in character. Keynes once remarked, "In the long-run, we are all dead." Some economists have taken Keynes to task for the short-run character of his theory and for ignoring the long period altogether. Prof. F.A. Hayek, an important critic of Keynes, remarks: "I cannot help regarding the increasing concentration on short-run effects...not only as a serious and dangerous intellectual error, but as a betrayal of the main duty of the economist and a grave menace to our civilisation."[11] According to Hayek, it is the duty and privilege of the economist to study and stress the long-run effects which are likely to be hidden to the untrained eye rather than concentrating on short-run forces.

(xv) An important omission on the part of Keynes is that he developed his theory on the basis of a closed economy. This is a very unrealistic assumption since modern economies are open economies. In an open economy a favourable or an unfavourable balance of trade has important repercussions on the volume of employment. A favourable balance of trade amounts to a fresh injection of purchasing power in the economy which through the working of multiplier has the same effect on the level of employment as domestic investment. Similarly, an unfavourable balance of trade has the same effect as domestic disinvestment.

11. Hayek, *The Pure Theory of Capital* (1941) p. 409.

(xvi) Keynes' theory is not general in the sense that it is applicable anywhere and everywhere. Its application is at best limited to advanced capitalistic economies like the United Kingdom and the United States. As already seen the Keynesian theory of employment is not much relevant to underdeveloped countries. Nor is it applicable to the socialist countries like the Soviet Union and China. In socialist countries, the investment is undertaken by and large by the state and as such does not fluctuate much in response to market forces. Harris aptly remarks, "Those who seek universal truths, applicable in all places and at all times, had better not waste their time on the *General Theory*."[12]

(xvii) Keynes did not take into account the acceleration principle in his *General Theory*. This is considered to be a serious omission on his part. Keynes considered only the principle of multiplier which states the effect of an increase in investment on the level of income. But to consider the total effect of increase in investment on income Keynes should have taken into account the fact that the increase in income brought about by an increase in investment will also induce private investment and thus start another round of the process of income expansion. Keynesians attribute this omission to an oversight on the part of Keynes.

(xviii) According to Hazlitt, Keynes is not successful in refuting the most strongly established principle in economics that if the price of any commodity or service is kept too high some of that will remain unsold. When wages are too high, there will be unemployment. Adjusting the myriad wage rates to their respective equilibrium points may not always be a sufficient step to the promotion of full employment but it is an absolutely necessary step. Keynes tried to substitute general monetary inflation for piece-meal wage-and-price adjustment. But inflation cannot bring about full employment without wage-price co-ordination.[13]

One of the important sources of Keynes' error in his discussion of wages and employment is his failure to distinguish, most of the time, between wage rates and total wage payments.[14] This is

12. S.E. Harris (ed.), *The New Economics* (London, 1949), p. 40.
13. Henry Hazlitt (ed.), *The Critics of Keynesian Economics* (London, 1960), p. 5.
14. Henry Hazlitt, *Ibid.*

because he habitually uses the ambiguous word 'wages' to describe either or both. This in turn leads him tacitly to assume that a reduction in wage rates means a corresponding reduction in wage income, and hence 'reduces purchasing power' and 'effective demand' and leads to a descending spiral without limit. But the classical contention is simply that those wage rates which are above the equilibrium level should be reduced to that level in order to restore employment and to *increase* and *maximise* the aggregate of wages paid.

(xix) Keynes is hailed by his admirers almost as if he alone had discovered the importance of 'expectation' in economics. But, on the contrary, the fact is that he did not adequately recognise that role. He saw that expectations affected current price and employment, but appeared to forget that they are also embodied in every current price, interest rate, wage rate. It is partly because he under-rated the central importance of expectations that he denounced 'liquidity preference' and 'speculation'. He failed to see that speculative anticipations and risks are necessarily involved in all economic activity, and somebody must bear these risks.

(xx) Keynes' rejection of Say's law is considered to be one of his outstanding attainments. But he rejects this law in a sense in which no serious economist ever held it.[15] The law was designed to point out mainly that there cannot be an overproduction of all commodities. It never stated that the money was never hoarded or that depression was impossible. Prof. Hutt remarks that Keynes never understood Say's Law.[16] "Keynes' attack on the law was illustrated by a quotation not from Say himself, but from J.S. Mill and it was a quotation which, as B.M. Anderson, Emil Korner and Patinkin have pointed out, was torn from its context...J.S. Mill was a poor exponent of say in his *Principles*. But had Keynes read Mill's treatment of the topic in his *Unsettled Questions in Political Economy* he would, I think, have dropped his attack on the Say's law."[17]

(xxi) Keynes' discussion of the relation of 'saving' and 'investment' is very much confused. He constantly altered between

15. *Ibid*., p. 6.

16. *Ibid*.

17. Hutt, *Keynesianism—Retrospect and Prospect*, p. 387.

two mutually contradictory contentions: (1) that saving and investment are "necessarily equal" and "merely different aspects of the same thing," and (2) that saving and investment are "two essentially different activities" without even a "nexus", so that saving not only can exceed investment but chronically tends to be so, and hence brings on deflation.

(xxii) Keynes did not realise the importance of saving on which depends the rate of capital formation and the rate of economic growth which also influences to a large extent the volume of employment in underdeveloped countries. He regarded saving as something merely negative, a mere non-spending, forgetting that it was an inseparable first-half of the completed positive act of investment.

What Keynes failed to recognise was that, normally, to save is to spend: but to spend on capital goods rather than on consumer goods. And even if, in abnormal conditions, saving takes merely the form of monetary hoarding, it does not lead to unemployment, as Keynes supposed, *unless wages (or prices) are inflexible* in the downward direction. Otherwise, the result would be merely the continuance of the same volume of output and employment at lower prices and wages.

On the whole Keynes' *General Theory* is considered to be vague and full of inconsistencies and fallacies. In the words of Samuelson, "...the General Theory...is a badly written book, poorly organized; any layman who, beguiled by the author's previous reputation, bought the book was cheated of his five shillings... It is arrogant, bad tempered, polemical, and overly generous in its acknowledgements. It abounds in mares' nests or confusions..."[18]

WEAKNESS OF KEYNESIAN FULL EMPLOYMENT POLICY

Criticism has been levelled not only against Keynes' theory of employment but also against the policy measures suggested by him for attaining full employment. We briefly examine below some of the important criticisms levelled against the policy measures suggested by him.

---

18. Paul A. Samuelson, "The General Theory (3)" in Seymour E. Harris, *The New Economics* (London, 1966), pp. 148-49.

(1) It is feared that the departure from the "sound" rules of balanced budget may provide the government an opportunity to indulge in extravagance which may lead to serious evils.

(2) The increase in the progressivity of the tax structure as an instrument of raising the national propensity to consume may have unfavourable effects on capital formation and private investment.

(3) Keynes was so much pre-occupied with fiscal policy that he paid inadequate attention to monetary policy which is an important instrument of fighting cyclical unemployment.

(4) The *General Theory* hardly says anything on principles of planning investment.

(5) The possibility of a large scale investment by the government may discourage private investment. The businessmen may be afraid of competition from the Government.

(6) As we have already seen, the nature of unemployment in underdeveloped countries being different from that in advanced countries, the Keynesian remedies for fighting unemployment are not of much use to the underdeveloped countries.

CONCLUSION

We have examined both the merits and weaknesses of the Keynesian Economics. The extreme Keynesians find in the *General Theory* a panacea for all economic ills of the society—may it be inflation or deflation, may it be over-full employment or under-full employment. The extreme anti-Keynesians dub the *General Theory* as simply 'a huge joke', 'a mockery' and 'one of the great intellectual scandals of out age' (Hazlitt). Keynesians consider their master's doctrine both original and true but anti-Keynesians 'could not find in it (*General Theory*) a single doctrine that was both true and original' (Hazlitt). In the opinion of anti-Keynesians 'where he (Keynes) was right, he was not original and that where he was original he was wrong' (Hutt). Keynes' admirers find in his work new economic tools, new definitions, new terminology, new economic policies while the anti-Keynesians find 'an incredible number of fallacies, inconsistencies, vaguenesses, shifting definitions and usages of words and plain errors of fact' (Hazlitt).

Admittedly "Keynes, indeed, also had lost many battles and made many errors. He also, however, had won the war. Out of the straws of his predecessors, with some additions of his own, he had built a structure which no economist or economic practitioner can afford not to inspect and use" (Harris). The persistence of critics, the attention given to Keynes' writings, the mobilisation of virtually all economic criticism on the pastime of examining Keynes' writings, are ample evidence of an underlying agreement that what Keynes had to offer was of transcendent importance" (Harris). Even Pigou does not deny Keynes the credit that is due to him when he remarks, "when a man has devised a new way of tackling an unclimbed mountain, we may, indeed, regret that this way has not led him to the top. But for the effort which has advanced him towards the top, nothing is due but praise." No doubt Keynes made important contributions to economic theory and policy, but what he said should not be considered as the final word. What Keynes said requires a lot of supplementation and amplification. In the words of Smithies, "Great though it is, the *General Theory* is not the last word in Economics. But, in the present stage of capitalism, it should be the first word... The *General Theory* is a most constructive tool for those who are aware of its limitations, but a dangerous one for those who ignore them."

Growth Models

25

HARROD-DOMAR MODEL

Harrod and Domar are mainly concerned with the conditions required for smooth and uninterrupted growth in national income.[1] Both of them developed their models of steady growth independent of each other. Harrod, of course, published his theory earlier than Domar. Though the models of Harrod and Domar differ in details, the basic idea is very similar in the two.

In Harrod-Domar model, capital accumulation plays a crucial role in the process of economic growth. The distinctive feature of this model is that it considers both the sides of the investment process while the earlier writers concentrate only on the one side. The classical economists consider only the capacity side of capital accumulation and, believing that supply creates its own demand, do not consider it necessary to pay attention to the demand side. Keynesians, on the other hand, err in the opposite direction. Concerned primarily with the short period, they consider only the adequacy of demand and neglect the problem of increase in capacity through investment in the long run. Harrod-Domar model integrates the classical and Keynesian analysis of economic growth.

The essence of the Harrod-Domar model is, starting from a full employment equilibrium level of income, continuous maintenance of this equilibrium requires that the volume of spending generated by investment must be sufficient to absorb the increased output resulting from investment. Given the marginal propensity to save, the more the capital is accumulated and the larger the initial national income, the larger must be the absolute volume of net investment. Maintenance of full employment, therefore, requires an

1. R.F. Harrod, *Towards a Dynamic Economic* (London, 1948) and Evsey D. Domar, *Essay in the Theory of Economic Growth* (New York, 1957).

ever-expanding amount of absolute net investment. This, in turn, requires a continuous growth in rear national income. Capital accumulation and growth of income must go side by side. An increase in capital expands the productive capacity of the economy. If it is not accompanied by an increase in income, any of the following three things may happen: (1) the new capital may remain unutilised; (2) the new capital may replace old capital depriving the latter of its labour and/or markets; (3) the new capital may be substituted for labour (and possibly for other factors). Thus increase in capital unaccompanied by an increase in income would result into an unemployment of capital and/or labour. Harrod and Domar are afraid that excessive accumulation of capital would result into overproduction and consequently into a fall in investment leading to depression.

DOMAR MODEL

The fundamental question around which Domar builds his model is: Investment leading to an increase in productive capacity and income, what should be the rate of increase in investment which would equalise the increase in income and the increase in productive capacity, so that full employment is maintained?[2] To answer this question, Domar tries to link between aggregate supply and aggregate demand through investment. The model is based on the following main assumptions: (1) an initial full employment level of income has already been achieved; (2) absence of government and foreign trade; (3) there are no lags in adjustment; (4) the average and marginal propensities to save are equal; (5) the propensity to save and the capital co-efficient (ratio of capital stock to output) are constant. All these assumptions, however, are not necessary. Some of these are made just for simplifying the analysis and can be relaxed in a more complicated analysis. Income, investment and saving are all used in the net sense, *i.e.,* gross minus depreciation. The model is in the form of an equation. Let us set up this equation. Increase in Productivity Capacity: Let investment proceed at an annual rate of I and let annual productive capacity per dollar of newly created capital be equal on average to S. In other words, S is the ratio of increase in real income or output to an increase in capital, *i.e.,* the reciprocal of acceleration or the

2. Domar, n. 1, p. 89

marginal capital co-efficient. Thus if capital worth 3 dollars is required for producing output worth one dollar, S will be 1/3 or 33.3 per cent per year. The productive capacity resulting from an investment of I dollar will, thus, be IS dollars per year.

But the operation of new capital may, at least to some extent, be at the cost of previously existing capital. In other words, the new capital may replace some of the existing capital by depriving the latter of its market and factors of production (particularly labour). If so happens, the increase in productive capacity resulting from an increase in investment will not be IS; it would be a smaller amount say $I\sigma$ dollars per year. Thus S stands for the increase in productive capacity per dollar invested in only new plants while σ stands for the increase in productive capacity per dollar invested of the whole economy. Since a part of the increase in capacity in new plants is offset by a decrease in capacity in the existing plants, σ is less than S. σ should be distinguished from the traditional concept of the marginal productivity of capital. The concept of the marginal productivity of capital is based on the assumption that the quantity of other factors of production and the state of techniques remain unchanged while σ makes no such assumption. Thus σ stands for the productive capacity which *accompanies*, rather than which is caused by, each dollar invested. Further it may be mentioned that σ stands for productive potential of the economy (*i.e.* capability of the economy to increase output) and not an actual increase in output. Whether or not the productive potential results into an increase in output depends on the behaviour of money income. Domar defines the symbol σ as the potential social average productivity of investment.

The expression $I\sigma$ is the supply side of the system, *i.e.*, the total net increase in output that the economy can produce. Required Increase in Aggregate Demand: The demand side of the economy is the familiar Keynesian multiplier. If investment increases at an absolute annual rate of ΔI and the corresponding absolute annual increase in income is indicated by $\Delta\gamma$,

(1) $\Delta\gamma = \Delta I \dfrac{1}{\alpha}$ where α is the propensity to save and, therefore, $\dfrac{1}{\alpha}$ the multiplier.

Equilibrium

If the economy is initially in a state of full employment equilibrium, so that its income equals its productive capacity, the maintenance of the state of full employment requires that the income and the productive capacity should increase at the same rate. $I\sigma$ being the annual increase in potential capacity and $\Delta I\left(\frac{1}{\alpha}\right)$ the annual increase in actual income, the full employment equilibrium will be maintained only if

$$(2)\ \Delta I \frac{1}{\alpha} = I\sigma$$

Multiplying both sides of the equation by α and dividing by I, we obtain

$$(3)\ \frac{\Delta I}{I} = \alpha\,\sigma$$

The left side of the equation (3) is the absolute annual increase (or the absolute rate of growth) in investment—ΔI—divided by the volume of investment itself; or in other words, it is the relative increase in investment, or the annual rate of growth of investment. This shows that the maintenance of full employment requires that the investment should grow at the annual relative rate of $\alpha\sigma$. Let us now turn to the income. Suppose that the marginal and average propensities to save are equal and constant, *i.e.,* income is a constant multiple of investment. Therefore, income must also grow at the same annual relative rate of $\alpha\sigma$. In short, maintenance of a continuous state of full employment requires that investment and income grow at a constant annual relative (or compound interest) rate equal to the product of the propensity to save and the average productivity of investment. Let us illustrate the analysis with the help of a numerical example. Let σ = 25 per cent per year, α = 12 per cent, and γ = \$ 150 billion per year. The investment required for the maintenance of full employment is $\frac{150\times 12}{100}$ or \$18 billion. This would raise productive capacity by the amount invested σ times, that is, by $\frac{150\times 12\times 25}{100\times 100}$ or \$4.5 billion. If unused capacity is to be prevented, national income would have to rise by 4.5 billion. But the relative increase in income would equal the absolute increase divided by the income itself, *i.e.:*

$$150\times\frac{\frac{12}{100}\times\frac{25}{100}}{150}=\frac{12}{100}\times\frac{25}{100}=\alpha\sigma=3 \text{ per cent.}$$

Thus if full employment is to be maintained and unused capacity avoided, the income must grow at the rate of 3 per cent per annum. The above results are based on the assumption that α, the propensity to save, and σ, the average productivity of investment, remain constant. This assumption, however, is not essential for the analysis and the whole problem can be easily reworked with variable α and σ.

Let us contrast this long-period analysis with the Keynesian short period analysis which neglects growth. In the short-period analysis, to maintain a level of income, investment must offset saving, or the savings of yesterday must be invested today. To maintain full employment over a long period of time, however, offsetting yesterday's savings by today's investment is not sufficient; investment of today must exceed saving of yesterday. Further, investment must grow at an increasing absolute rate (or constant compound interest rate).

As is clear from equation 3, the larger is the α, the larger would be the amount of investment required for the maintenance of the income. Similarly, the larger is σ, the greater is the increase in productive capacity resulting from investment and therefore the larger is the rise in income required for avoiding unused capacity. But, since rising income depends on a rising rate of investment, if income is to grow, investment must also grow. The required amount by which the investment must grow is given by the product $\alpha\sigma$.

Thus the economy faces a serious dilemma: if sufficient investment is not forthcoming today, unemployment will occur today; but, if enough is invested today, still more will be needed tomorrow in order to increase demand so that the expanded capacity can be utilised and excessive capital accumulation avoided tomorrow; otherwise, the excessive capital accumulation will cause a fall in investment leading to a depression day after tomorrow. To stay at the same place, therefore, the economy must move faster and faster otherwise it will slip downward.

In contrast to the situation in which a depression occurs, when investment is below the required rate, too rapid a rate of growth strains existing capacity and stimulates investment, which in turn accelerates the growth of output and increases the strain on capacity all the more. Elimination of idle capacity, therefore, requires building of more capital (assuming a given propensity to save or that the propensity to save does not decline sufficiently rapidly). Avoidance of capital shortage requires a reduction in investment. This conclusion sounds paradoxical. For understanding this paradox, we have to consider the effect that an increase in output or investment has on demand. Too rapid an increase in output or investment will increase the quantity to be sold, but it will also raise the demand even more and, therefore, there would be underproduction and a capital shortage. For eliminating this capital shortage, investment would have to be reduced which would, in turn, reduce demand and the pressure on capacity. Similarly, for eliminating idle capacity, more investment is needed which would, in turn, lead to increase in demand.

After considering the rate of growth of income required for maintaining full employment equilibrium over time, Domar considers the question as to whether or not sufficient investment would be forthcoming for allowing the required increase in income. Unlike the classical analysis leading to the stationary state, or the Marxian analysis leading to the inevitable downfall of capitalism, Domar's model shows that there is no inherent logical impossibility in conceiving a capitalist system enjoying continuous expansion, or in other words, the downfall of capitalism is not inevitable. Nevertheless, it demonstrates that there is no automatic tendency for capitalist system to keep moving 'onwards and upwards' and that certain special conditions are necessary for continuous expansion.

Domar states that the growth of monopoly leads to increasing unemployment of capital, and by retarding innovation, may also cause unemployment of labour. If this inhibition to new investment resulting from a developing of idle capacity in monopolistic industries is not offset by exogenous forces like territorial, technological and population expansion, there may occur chronic depression and increasing unemployment.

HARROD MODEL

Like Domar, Harrod is concerned primarily with conditions for a steady rate of growth and demonstrates the possible paths along which the economy might grow. Once the steady growth (i.e., equilibrium) is disturbed, the cumulative forces will lead the economy either to secular deflation or secular inflation. He tells us three types of the rates of growth: (1) The actual rate of growth; (2) The warranted rate of growth; and (3) The full employment or the natural rate of growth.

THE ACTUAL RATE OF GROWTH

He starts his model with the fundamental equation.

(i) $GC = S$

In this equation C stands for the rate of growth of output, *i.e.*, ratio of increase in output to total output in any period or $\frac{\Delta\gamma}{\gamma}$; C stands for the increase in capital during the period divided by the increase in output in the period or $\frac{I}{\Delta\gamma}$; *s* is the average propensity to save or $\frac{S}{\gamma}$. The equation (i) can be written as $\frac{\Delta\gamma}{\gamma}.\frac{I}{\Delta\gamma} = \frac{S}{\gamma}$ or $\frac{I}{\gamma} = \frac{S}{\gamma}$ or $I = S$. Thus this equation is a mere truism, that is, *ex post* (on actual or realised) savings equal *ex post* investment.

Harrod then postulates two important behaviour relations *viz.* (1) savings depend on the level of income and (2) investment depends on the rate of growth of income. Second relation involves the acceleration principle, *i.e.*, increase in the rate of output that is taking place induces the increase in the stock of capital that makes it possible. Maintenance of full employment requires that the *ex ante* (or desired or intended or planned) savings out of full employment income must be offset by an equal amount of *ex ante* investment. For inducing the required investment, income must be growing.

THE WARRANTED RATE OF GROWTH

Harrod states a second fundamental equation

(ii) $GwCr = s$

This equation expresses the equilibrium conditions for a steady growth. *Gw*, the "warranted rate of growth" defined as the rate of growth $\left(i.e.\ \frac{\Delta\gamma}{\gamma}\right)$ which satisfies entrepreneurs and thereby leads to its own perpetuation. *Cr*, the "capital requirement" is defined as the capital coefficient $\left(i.e. \ \frac{I}{\Delta y}\right)$ required for sustaining the warranted rate of growth. The definition is based on two assumptions *viz.* (1) that innovations are neutral and (2) that the rate of interest is constant. Under these assumptions the capital/income ratio will remain constant, *i.e.*, the length of production process will remain unchanged. If capital/income ratio remains constant, the existing output can be sustained with the existing capital and the additional output can be required for sustaining only the additional output. Harrod assumes that saving intentions are always realised and, therefore, *ex ante* savings are equal to *ex post* savings, *s*, therefore, is the same in both the equations. Thus in dynamic equilibrium $\left(\text{stable value of } \frac{\Delta y}{y}\right) GwCr = GC$; the actual or *ex post* value of $\frac{I}{y}$ equals the equilibrium value, which is a subjective phenomenon. Further *G* must equal *Gw* and *C* must equal *Cr*.

If *G* (the actual rate of growth) exceeds *Gw* (the warranted rate of growth that would give steady advance), *C* (actual capital accumulation) must be less than *Cr* (required capital accumulation for steady advance). In other words, actual amount of capital goods will be less than the desired amount of capital goods, *i.e.*, there would occur a shortage of capital. This situation would lead to a chronic inflationary gap because desired investment would be greater than desired saving, and production would be less than the aggregate demand.

In contrast, if *G* falls short of *Gw*, *C* must be greater than *Cr*. This situation would lead to a chronic deflationary gap, *i.e.*, desired saving would be greater than desired investment, and businessmen would not be able to sell all that they have produced.

Deviations of *G* from *Gw* are unstable, *i.e.*, once *G* departs from *Gw*, the gap between the two would continue widening cumulatively. "Around the line of advance, which, if adhered to, would alone give satisfaction, centrifugal forces are at work, causing the system to depart farther and farther from the required line of advance."[3] If *G* is greater than *Gw*, desired investment is greater than desired saving, and this, in turn, stimulates further

3. Harrod. n. 1, p. 86.

growth. In contrast, if G is less than Gw, desired saving exceeds desired investment, inventories accumulate, entrepreneurs become pessimistic, they keep the rate of increase in output below Gw, and this results in a further retardation of growth.

Harrod realises that the equation $GC = s$ may be criticised for laying too much emphasis on the acceleration principle. To avoid this criticism, he suggests that this equation may be rewritten as $GC = s - k$ when k is the investment not required by the current increase in output. k is, in fact, the investment of a long run character and is not justified within a fairly short period. In the long run, k will be zero because in the long run all investment is put to some or the other use and, therefore, is justified.

THE NATURAL RATE OF GROWTH

The third fundamental equation in Harrod's model is

(iii) $GnCr = or \neq s$

Gn, the natural rate of growth, is the maximum possible rate of advance determined by the fundamental conditions *viz.* growth of population and technological investments. This is the ceiling above which the rate of advance cannot go, "...it excludes the possibility of 'involuntary' unemployment."[4]

Gn may or may not be equal to Gw. If Gn exceeds Gw, there is no reason why G should not exceed Gw for most of the time. We saw earlier that when G exceeds Gw, there tends to occur a cumulative boom. Therefore, when Gn exceeds Gw, a boom will tend to develop. In contrast, if Gw exceeds Gn, G must be below Gw for most of the time because the average value of G over a period cannot exceed that of Gn. We saw earlier that when G falls short of Gw, there tends to occur a cumulative recession. Therefore, when Gn falls short of Gw, a recession will tend to develop. This sounds a little paradoxical. Apparently, if desired rate of growth exceeds the rate of growth permitted by fundamental conditions, we should expect inflationary pressures. But penterating analysis demonstrates that, in fact, quite the opposite happens. This paradox is very similar to contrast between Keynesian economics and classical economics. When Gw is below Gn, we will have boom conditions and a tendency to approach full employment; but this

4. *Ibid.*, p. 87.

high employment will be of an inflationary and hence unhealthy character. Under these cirumstances, savings are desirable because these enable us to have a high level of employment without inflationary pressures. In contrast, when *Gw* is above *Gn*, savings will have a tendency to accentuate depression.

Harrod uses his analysis to explain trade cycles. While doing so, of course, he fully recognises that no theory of business cycles can be complete without taking into account lags and psychological, monetary and other factors. In the recovery phase, because of the existence of unemployment productive resources, *G* is above *Gn*. When full employment is reached, *G* becomes equal to *Gn*. If *Gw* exceeds *Gn* at the full employment, slump is inevitable. Since *G* has to fall below *Gw*, it will, for the time being, be driven progressively downwards. Further, *G* itself fluctuates during the course of the business cycle. Savings as a fraction of income, though fairly steady in the long run, fluctuate in the short run. In the short run, savings tend to be residual between the earnings and normal consumption. Companies, also, are likely to save a large portion of their short-period increases in net receipts. Thus, even if *Gw* is normally below *Gn*, it is likely to rise above *Gn* in the later stages of advance, and, if it so happens, a vicious spiral of depression is inevitable when full employment is reached. If *Gw* does not rise above *Gn*, in the course of the advance, there would be continued pressure to advance when full employment is reached; this would lead to inflation and consequently, sooner or latter, to a rise of *Gw* above *Gn* resulting, ultimately, into a vicious spiral of depression. Actually, *G* may be reduced before the full employment is reached because of immobilities, frictions and bottlenecks and, if it so happens, depression may come before full employment is reached. If *Gw* is far above *Gn*, *G* may never rise far above *Gw* during the revival and the depression may be precipitated long before full employment is reached.

Actually, business cycles are constrained and are not free to move beyond certain limits. The upper limit is provided by the *Gn*. In the short run, real income cannot rise beyond the full employment ceiling. The lower limit is set by a 'floor' of autonomous investment, the 'break-even point' of the consumption function, the impossibility of gross investment being negative (disinvestment cannot exceed the rate of depreciation), and eventually replacement investment.

For making allowance for inventions which are not neutral, Harrod introduces another symbol in the fundamental equation, *d* stands for the fraction of income needed for capital involved in lengthening the production process. *d* will be negative if the inventions are 'capital saving'. To take into consideration such inventions, the equation will have to be rewritten as

$$GwCr = s - d$$

Capital saving inventions enhance the equilibrium rate of growth (*Gw*) and thus aggravate any tendency towards chronic unemployment resulting from $Gw > Gn$. *d* may be positive because of the nature of inventions or because of falling rate of interest which tends to lengthen the period of production. For preventing depression, we should try to get such a progressive reduction in the rate of interest that

$$GwCr = s - d = GnCn$$

So far we were considering a closed economy. In an open economy, the fundamental equations will have to be rewritten as $GC = s - b$ and $GwCr = s - b$, where *b* stands for foreign balance. Thus, in a country suffering from a chronic unemployment, $Gw > Gn$, a positive value of *b* (*i.e.* favourable balance of payments) would reduce the deflationary gap. In contrast, in a country suffering from an inflationary gap, a positive value of *b* will accentuate the inflationary gap. Thus a country with $Gw > Gn$ should try to achieve a favourable balance of payments and a country with $Gw < Gn$ should aim at an unfavourable balance.

After explaining business cycles, Harrod discusses policies for filling a chronic deflationary gap. Regarding wage policy, he states that once for all wage reduction is not effective. A year by year wage reduction would not affect *Gn* directly. It would not depress *Gw*. On the contrary, it would raise *Gw* by raising the goods value of money and thereby accentuate the tendency towards depression. Harrod considers interest rates to be an effective way of preventing unemployment. But he is doubtful if the system will of its own secure a sufficient fall in the interest rates.

In a later article[5] published in 1960, Harrod stressed the need for elaborating the supply side of his growth equation in order to

5. R.F. Harrod, "Second Essay in Dynamic Theory", *Economic Journal*, June, 1960, pp. 277-93.

make it more relevant to the conditions prevailing in underdeveloped countries. He particularly studies the role of the rate of interest in determining the availability of savings and the demand for savings for implementing plans of investment. In his earlier essays, *Cr* indicates the optimum amount of capital required at the warranted growth rate of income. But the amount of savings available and as such the magnitude of investment that is possible are both influenced by the rate of interest. Similarly, the natural rate of growth of income requires a certain volume of savings. Given the other resources in the economy like labour and natural resource, actual rate of growth can reach the level of natural rate only if a corresponding amount of savings is forthcoming. Further, the natural rate of growth itself will not be determinate unless the rate of interest is specified. Harrod, therefore, conceives of natural rate of interest which he defines as the one that conforms to the natural growth of income and is determined by the natural rate of growth of per capita output (*Pc*) and the elasticity of the schedule of the diminishing utility of income (*e*). Thus a large value of *e* means that the utility of income falls rapidly when income grows. Hence the natural rate of interest is

$$r_n = \frac{P_c G_n}{e}$$

With given values of P_c and G_n the natural rate of growth will be low if *e* is large and *vice versa*. *e* is supposed to be generally less than one. The capital intensity of the methods of production employed by the entrepreneurs and as such the amount of capital required will be determined by the rate of interest. Generally C_r or the capital requirements would be a decreasing function of r_n, *i.e.*, $C_r = f(r_n)$. Corresponding to the natural rate of output there would be the required rate of savings and also the natural rate of interest. It is not necessary that the fraction of income actually saved (*S*) should tend to equality with the social requirement (S_r). *S* may be greater or smaller than S_r. In case *S* exceeds S_r, the warranted rate of growth will be above the natural rate of growth, *i.e.*, the entrepreneurs will like to increase their investment because larger savings are available. There is an important difference in the way the natural rate of growth and the warranted rate of growth are determined. The natural rate of growth is determined by labour and technological resources. Given these resources, the level of natural rate of growth would require a certain rate of savings. The warranted rate of growth is determined by the actual rate of savings (S).

What would happen if S exceeds or falls short of S_r. In case S exceeds S_r, the warranted rate of growth would be higher than the natural rate of growth. As the natural rate is the highest which can be attained in the long run, it is not possible for the excess of warranted rate to continue. The actual rate of growth would hit the full employment ceiling and thereafter it will have to decline below the warranted rate of growth and a depression will ensue. In contrast, if S falls short of S_r, investment will exceed savings and as such there will be a chronic tendency to inflation, which is an important characteristic of developing economies. If the rate of growth is low because of a shortage of savings, there would result underemployment and unemployment. It may, therefore, be expedient to raise S towards the level of S_r by surplus budgetting or compulsory levy. Harrod, however, stresses the need for social and institutional changes to bring about growth in underdeveloped countries. Growth may not be limited by savings. A low rate of growth may be the result not of a shortage of S compared with S_r but of a shortage of technical skill or of institutional and social hindrances. Owing to these reasons, the required rate of savings will be low in underdeveloped countries and actual level of savings may not fall short of it.

CRITICISM OF HARROD-DOMAR MODELS

The models assume key parameters, like the propensity to save and the capital-output ratio, to be constant. In reality, these are very likely to change over the long run. Changes in these parameters would change the requirements for steady growth.

Because the variables in the models refer only to aggregates, a model constructed on the basis of such aggregates cannot show the inter-relations between the sectors and as such is not meant for demonstrating the structural changes which constitute a basic aspect of the economic development of underdeveloped countries.[6] Harmonious growth of different sectors of the economy is very important for steady growth. Deviations from steady growth may be caused by a lack of harmony between the growth of different

6. *Economic Bulletin for Asia and Far East* (New York, 1955), pp. 34-40.

sectors even when aggregative requirements for stability are fulfilled.

The models assume the production function to be fixed and, therefore, there is no scope for substitution between different factors. Actually different factors of production, at least to a limited extent, can be substituted for each other. If labour can be substituted for capital, the requirements for steady growth would not be so rigid. Substitutability between different factors increases the flexibility of the economy and thereby decreases the possibilities of cumulative deviations from the path of steady growth. In fact, such substitution is regularly taking place and constitutes an essential feature of economic growth. Technological changes and improvements in the methods of organisation bring about a shift in the pattern of production. It is, therefore, not correct to make use of a fixed production for explaining long-term growth. The capital-output ratio and the accelerator are also not constant in the real world. In fact, the contribution of capital to production is not clearly known. Lundberg states that recent statistical studies pertaining to Norway and the United States indicates that contribution of capital accumulation to the growth rate of these economies has been small as compared with the contribution of shifts in the production function, technical research, administration and investment in education.[7] The variables in the models are expressed in real terms which rules out the influence of monetary and price factors on investment, savings and demand. In fact, the accelerator is not a non-monetary element in the business cycle. Businessmen's willingness and ability to invest is influenced by price expectations, interest rates, credit policies and condition of stock market. If these factors influence savings and investment, changes in them may bring about equilibrating adjustments in savings and investment when there is a deviation and check on the cumulative working of the factors of deviation. It is held that, in fact, instability is very much exaggerated in the growth models. Small deviations from the equilibrium path need not carry the economy headlong in either direction. Instability, in fact, is caused by the entrepreneurial behaviour and the lag

7. Erik Lundberg, "The Profitability of Investment", *Economic Journal,* December, 1959, pp. 653-77.

between investment decisions and capital outlays.[8] Yeager criticises the use of the concept of natural growth in Harrod's model.[9] He points out that the upper limit to growth is not rigidly fixed by labour and natural resources. Even if it is assumed that labour and natural resources are fixed, the output that can be obtained from these resources would vary according to the method of utilizing the resources. Improvements in technology and the methods of organisation would increase the productivity of both capital and labour and thus the maximum output possible with a given supply of productive resource can be increased. Yeager also points out that the cumulative upward and downward movements supposed to describe the real world are only a theoretical derivation from certain basic assumptions and are not supported by empirical evidence. He criticizes models also on the ground that many of the concepts like warranted rate of growth in Harrod are fuzzy and incapable of being assessed objectively.

The concept G_w "warranted rate of growth" has an important place in Harrod's model. Harrod, however, has not elaborated the meaning of this concept. He defines G_w "as the over-all rate of advance which, if executed, will leave entrepreneurs in a state of mind in which they are prepared to carry a similar advance."[10] In his earlier article in *Economic Journal*, he defines G_w as "that rate of growth which if it occurs, will leave all parties satisfied that they have produced neither more nor less than the right amount." Harrod does not tell as to what are the determinants of G_w. It is very important to know as to what determines the G_w. C_r depends on G_w; in fact, it is defined in terms of G_w. The values of G and C depend on entrepreneurial decisions which in turn depend on G_w. G_w is, in fact, the core of the model. Though Harrod says nothing regarding the determinants of G_w, he, in the course of discussion, gives a number of relationships between G_w and other variables. G varies (1) inversely with Cr (capital requirements); (2) directly with s (the average propensity to save); (3) inversely with the volume of

8. H. Rose, "The Possibility of Warranted Growth", *Economic Journal*, June, 1959, pp. 313-32.
9. Leland B., Yeager, "Some Questions about Growth Economics", *American Economic Review* (March, 1954), pp. 53-63.
10. *Ibid*., p. 82.

public works; (4) inversely with the volume of investment, that is, independent of the current rate of growth, *k*; (5) directly with the rate of interest *r* (since *k* and *Cr* vary inversely with *r*, and *s* probably varies directly with *r*). These relations, however, are not truly causal, with meaning in terms of entrepreneurial behaviour.

The models pay attention only to the requirements for steady growth and neglect the rate of growth. The models are more useful for developed countries whose main aim is stability and not the rate of growth. In contrast, underdeveloped countries are interested more in the rate of growth. They would not mind following policies which create fluctuations if these considerably raise the rate of growth.

Preclusion of autonomous investment makes Harrod's concept of 'warranted' rate analytically inadequate for the purposes of underdeveloped economies.[11] Hicks feels that there is too much instability in Harrod's model of an economy advancing at the 'warranted' rate, and, therefore, considers it essential to introduce automonous investment as a stabilising force.

The 'required' rate of growth of investment in Domar's mode fails to solve the problem of structural underemployment. What it meets is the problem of unemployment due to an insufficiency of effective demand. But if population grows faster than accumulation of capital, which is not uncommon in underdeveloped countries, there would arise structural unemployment owing to a shortage of capital equipment.

Domar's attitude towards technology leaves much to be desired Being primarily concerned with an insufficiency of effective demand Domar considers technological progress mainly as 'the creator of investment opportunities'. As regards an underdeveloped country technological progress is desired for its productivity effect, irrespective of whether or not effective demand is increased thereby.

The Harrod-Domar growth models are purely *laissez faire* ones based on the assumption of fiscal neutrality and designed to indicate the conditions of progressive equilibrium for an advanced economy. Their policy implications, therefore, are not very relevant to the underdeveloped countries.

---

11. *Development* (London, 1961), pp. 62-71, 153.

JOAN ROBINSON'S THEORY OF CAPITAL ACCUMULATION

Joan Robinson's model[12] of economic growth is based on two fundamental factors *viz.* (i) the capital formation depends on the manner of distribution of income and (ii) the rate at which labour is utilised depends upon the supply of capital and that of labour. The model is based upon the following assumptions: (i) Total income in real terms is distributed between only two classes—the workers and the entrepreneurs. The workers spend their entire income on consumption and save nothing. The entrepreneurs spend their entire income (from profits) on investment or capital formation and consume nothing. If they have no profits, the entrepreneurs cannot accumulate and if they do not accumulate, they have no profits. (ii) Capital and labour are the only productive factors. They are combined in fixed proportions and there is no technological-change. (iii) There is a *laissez faire* closed economy.

In Robinson's Model, net national income is the sum of total wage bill and total profits. Total wage bill is the real wage rate multiplied by the number of labourers. Total profits are the profit rate multiplied by the volume of capital. Algebraically, the net national income may be expressed as

$$\gamma = wN + pK$$

where γ stands for the net national income, W for the real wage rate, N for the number of workers employed, P for the rate of profit, and K for the amount of capital. The profit rate, which is a strategic factor in the theory of capital accumulation, would, therefore, be

$$P = \frac{\gamma - \omega N}{K}$$

Thus profit rate is the ratio of total income minus the total wage bill to the amount of capital utilised. As the profit per labourer employed is the difference between the output per labourer and the real wage, profit rate would depend on labour productivity, the real wage rate and the quantum of capital per worker or the capital-labour ratio. Hence the profit rate can increase if the income remains constant and the wage rate decreases or if the income increases and the wage rate remains constant. The rate of profit can

12. Joan Robinson, *The Accmuulation of Capital* (London, 1956).

also rise by a decline in the capital-labour ratio. In this way the entrepreneurs maximise their profits.

On the expenditure side, net national income (Y) is equal to the sum of consumption expenditure (C) and investment expenditure (I). Algebraically speaking

$$Y = C + I$$

Since Joan Robinson assumes that savings out of wages are zero, savings are done only by the entrepreneurs, and profits are meant only for investment, we have

$$S = I$$

This saving-investment relation may be shown as:

$$S = pK$$

and $$I = \Delta K \qquad (\Delta K \text{ is increase in real capital})$$

$$\therefore \quad pK = \Delta K \qquad (\because\ S = I)$$

or $$P = \frac{\Delta K}{K}$$

which is the growth rate of capital or the rate of capital accumulation. The growth rate of capital ($\Delta K/K$) being equal to p (rate of profit), it depends on the same factors on which depends the latter.

In addition to the rate of growth of capital ($\Delta K/K$), another factor on which depends the rate of growth of the economy is the rate of population growth. An increase in population and in labour force without being accompanied by an increase in capital would lead to a decline in labour productivity, and if the real wages are constant, would lower the margin of profit and thus widen the difference between capital and labour supply. It would also lead to unemployment. Full employment, therefore, is possible only if the growth rate of population is matched by the growth rate of capital. Algebraically speaking, if

$$\frac{\Delta N}{N} = \frac{\Delta K}{K}$$

there would be full employment of both labour and capital. Joan Robinson calls this the 'GOLDEN AGE'. To cite Joan Robinson:[13]

13. *Ibid.*, p. 99.

> When technical progress is neutral and proceeding steadily without any change in the time pattern of production, the competitive mechanism working freely, population growing (if at all) at a steady rate and accumulation going on fast enough to supply productive capacity for all available labour, the rate of profit tends to be constant and the level of real wages to rise with output per man. There are then no internal contradictions in the system. Provided that political events cause no disturbances, and provided that the entrepreneurs have faith in the future and desire to accumulate at the same proportional rate as they have been doing over the past, there is no impediment to prevent them from continuing to do so. Total annual output and the stock of capital (valued in terms of commodities) then grow together at a constant proportionate rate compounded at the rate of the labour force and the rate of increase of output per man. We may describe these conditions as a *golden age*...

If the economy goes off the path of golden age, there is possibility of its coming back to this path under certain conditions. Thus, if the rate of increase in population exceeds that of capital $\left(i.e.\ \frac{\Delta N}{N} > \frac{\Delta K}{K}\right)$, a return to the golden age equilibrium is possible only if the profit-wage relation behaves in an equilibrating manner. Thus excess of labour supply would lower the wage rate and if prices are unchanged, will reduce the real wages, and by increasing the amount of profits may increase the rate of growth of capital so that it would catch up with the increase in population. The equilibrating mechanism, however, will not work if real wages fail to decline either because of rigidity of money wage rates or because price level falls in the same proportion as the money wage rates. Normally, increase in prices assists capital formation so long as there is not a corresponding increase in wages. Increase in unemployment, while prices and wages are rising, is a common phenomenon in underdeveloped countries.

In contrast, if the capital grows faster than population, it is possible that the equilibrium may be restored through technological improvements and the shifting of the whole production function so that the economy gets itself adjusted to a higher capital-labour ratio. Joan Robinson, however, observes that the mechanism by which the rate of accumulation is adjusted to the rate of increase in the supply of labour is more reliable when what is required is a reduction in the rate of accumulation than when a rise is required; it is only too easy for a surplus of labour to grow, relatively to the stock of capital, while investment fails to increase and the economy sinks into stagnation; whereas entrepreneurs will not accumulate and maintain rebundant capital, so that when the rate of accumulation is too high (relatively to the labour force) one way or another it is certain to be cut down."[14]

Joan Robinson considers an economy in the golden age when 'potential growth ratio' is being realized. The potential growth ratio is the highest rate of capital accumulation which can be permanently maintained at a constant rate of profit. The conditions of a golden age require the growth ratio to be steady because frequent change in the growth ratio disturb the tranquility of a golden age. This tranquility, however, may not be possible even when the growth ratio is stable. An increase in the total stock of capital is likely to slacken the urge to accumulate so that a stage of stagnation starts and the economy deviates from the part of golden age. The golden age is not an ideal. It only represents a state of equilibrium growth at any conceivable rate so that each rate of growth will have its appropriate golden age.

Though broadly speaking Robinson's Model comes to the same thing as those of Harrod and Domar, there are some important differences between them.[15] Joan Robinson makes capital accumulation depend explicitly on the profit-wage relation and the labour productivity, which brings her theory nearer a real market economy. In contrast, Harrod and Domar make capital accumulation depend on the saving ratio (related to national income and not to profit income alone) and capital productivity (or its reciprocal) which transcend all economic systems, capitalistic or socialistic. While Joan Robinson approaches the question of capital accumulation from the standpoint mainly of labour, Harrod and Domar approach it from that of capital.

14. *Ibid.*, p. 18.

15. Kenneth K. Kurihara, *The Keynesian Theory of Economic Development* (London, 1961), pp. 79-80.

Joan Robinson's principal contribution lies in the fact that she has integrated classical value and distribution theory and modern Keynesian saving-investment theory into one coherent system. This, however, appears to be also the major shortcoming as far as policy application is concerned. Unlike the Harrod-Domar models, the Robinson model is not capable of being modified so as to introduce fiscal-monetary policy parameters—unless labour productivity, the wage rate, the profit rate and the capital-labour ratio could be considered as subjects of practical policy—as they might be so regarded in a completely planned economy.

MEADE'S NEO-CLASSICAL THEORY OF ECONOMIC GROWTH

Professor Meade's model[16] of economic growth is based on the following assumptions: (1) There is a closed economy without any economic or financial relationships with other economies. (2) There are no state or governmental economic activities involving taxation or state expenditure. (3) There prevails perfect competition (with its corollaries of prices equal to marginal costs and net factor rewards equal to the value of their marginal net products). (4) The production is subject to the law of constant returns. (5) Only two commodities are produced in the economy *viz.* consumption goods and production goods. The consumption goods satisfy all final human needs for food, clothing, shelter etc. and capital goods are used to help the further production of consumption goods for capital goods. (6) In addition to machines, there are only two other factors of production, *i.e.,* land and labour. (7) There is a constant money price for consumption goods and full employment of labour and land available at any moment of time is attained by the adjustment of money wage per worker and money rent per acre of land. (8) All machines are alike and the ratio of labour to machinery can be varied with equal ease in the short period as in the long period. (9) There is perfect substitutability in production between capital goods and consumption goods. (10) Each year some percentage of machines wear out which requires replacement.

In an economy of the type envisaged above, the net output produced depends upon four things *viz.* (i) the amount of the existing stock of machines; (ii) the amount of labour available for

16. J.E. Meade, *A Neo-Classical Theory of Economic Growth* (London, 1961).

productive employment; (iii) the amount of land or natural resources available for productive use in the economy; and (iv) the state of technical knowledge which is assumed to be improving through time. This simple relation may be put in the form of a production function as below:

$$Y = F(K, L, N, t)$$

where Y stands for net output or real national income, K for the existing stock of machines, L for the amount of labour, N for the amount of land and t for time, since the mere passage of time brings technical progress and allows Y to be raised even without any increase in K, L, or N.

With the passage of time, three things can happen to raise Y. In the first place, the stock of machines (K) may increase because the community is saving part of its income and is thereby accumulating real capital. Assume that in a year the stock of machines increases by ΔK. This would lead to an increase in output equal to $V\Delta K$, where V is the marginal net physical product of a machine.

Secondly, the working population (L) may grow. If in anyone year the amount of labour productively employed rises by ΔL, it would lead to an increase in output equal to $W\Delta L$, where W stands for the marginal product of labour.

Thirdly, it is assumed that the amount of land or natural resources available to the community is fixed and, therefore, there is no change in N to affect the level of Y. But with the passage of time (as t grows), Y would rise even if K, L, and N remain unchanged because of technological improvements. The term $\Delta Y'$ may be used to indicate the amount by which net output Y would rise in anyone year because of technical progress.

If the changes which occur in any one year are not very great, it can be assumed that the total change in net output (ΔY) is equal to the sum of three influences mentioned above. Algebraically speaking,

$$\Delta Y = V\Delta K + W\Delta L + \Delta Y'$$

The above equation can be written as:

$$\frac{\Delta Y}{Y} = \frac{VK}{Y} \cdot \frac{\Delta K}{K} + \frac{WL}{Y} \cdot \frac{\Delta L}{L} + \frac{\Delta Y'}{Y}$$

where $\frac{\Delta Y}{Y}$ is the annual proportionate rate of growth of output, $\frac{\Delta K}{K}$ the annual proportionate rate of growth of the stock of machinery, $\frac{\Delta L}{L}$ the annual proportionate rate of growth in the working population, and $\frac{\Delta Y'}{Y}$ the annual proportionate rate of growth of output solely due to technical progress. Let us call these four proportionate rates of growth y, k, l, and r respectively. The proportion of national income going to each factor in the form of remuneration is the ratio of the marginal product of the factor times the factor to total income. Thus the amount of income paid as profit is $V.K/Y$. Let this be called the proportional marginal product of capital (as distinct from net marginal product) and expressed as U. Similarly, Q represents the proportional marginal product of labour. The basic relationship can, therefore, be written as

$$y = Uk + Ql + r$$

which shows the growth rate of output (y) as being the weighted sum of three other growth rates, namely the sum of the growth rate in the stock of machines (k) weighted by the proportional marginal product of capital (U) plus the growth rate of population (l) weighted by the proportional marginal product to labour (Q) plus the growth rate of technical progress (r).

The basic relationship $y = Uk + Ql + r$ can be written as:

$$y - l = Uk - (l - Q)\, l + r$$

In the above equation $y - l$ is the difference between the growth rate of total output and the growth rate of the working population and, therefore, it approximately measures the growth rate of real income per head. It is the growth rate in this real income per head which is most important. According to our basic relationship, the growth rate in real income per head ($y - l$) is the result of three factors *viz.* (i) it is raised by the growth rate in real capital (k) weighted by its proportional marginal product or by proportion of the net national income which would be paid to profits in a competitive equilibrium (U); (ii) it is depressed by the growth rate in the working population (l) weighted by one minus the proportional marginal product of labour ($l - Q$); (iii) it is raised by the technical progress; and (iv) the second element—$(l - Q)\, l$—which tends to depress the growth rate of real income per head is the familiar tendency for diminishing returns to labour set in as more and more labour is applied to any given amount of land and capital equipment.

In the basic relationship $y - l = UK - (l - Q)\, l + v$ the element Uk can be expressed in other forms, U, as has been seen is $\frac{VK}{Y}.k$, the growth rate of the stock of machines, equals $\frac{SY}{K}$, where S is the proportion of the net national income which is saved; since SY would equal the amount of net real output which is added to the stock of machines in the course of a year so that $\frac{SY}{K}$ would equal the proportionate increase in the stock of machines over the year. Thus $Uk = US\frac{Y}{K} = SV$, which expresses in three forms the same thing, namely the contribution which capital accumulation is making to the growth rate of final output. The basic relationship can then be expressed between the growth rate of real income per head and its three basic determinants in three different forms:

$$y - l = UK - (l - Q)\, l + v$$

$$y - l = US\frac{Y}{K} - (l - Q)\, l + v$$

$$y - l = SV - (l - Q)\, l + v$$

After discussing the main factors which determine the rate of growth of real income per head, Meade passes on the conditions which may lead to a rise or decline in the rate of economic growth over time. If growth of population and development of technology (*i.e.* l and v) are constant, the change in the growth rate would depend on changes in the values of V, S and Q over time. If population and technology remain unchanged but savings rise, capital per head would increase and the marginal product of capital would decline. This decline in V will, however, be less if it is possible to substitute capital for land and labour. Also if technical progress takes place, the decline in the marginal product of capital will be offset. But the volume of land and labour being fixed in the economy, more capital per head will be used and at the same time technical progress will tend to raise V. Under these conditions, the rate of growth of income per head over time would rise which would in turn tend to raise S. S will tend to rise still further owing to a change in income distribution towards larger profits resulting from the factors mentioned above. In other words, if population above is assumed to be constant, real income per head would depend upon the rate of capital accumulation (VS) and the technical progress (r), which can be expressed as

$$y = VS + r.$$

Next Prof. Meade examines the conditions of a state of steady economic growth, where population is growing at a constant proportionate rate while the rate of technical progress is constant. Obviously, the income per head will be constant under these conditions only if the rate of growth of total output is constant. But under what conditions would the growth rate of total output be constant? This question is examined under the following assumptions: (i) all elasticities of substitution between the various factors are equal to unity; (ii) technical progress is neutral towards all factors; and (iii) the proportions of profits saved, of wages saved, and of rents saved are all three constant.

Let the proportion of national income saved out of profits, wages and rents be Sv, Sw and Sg respectively. Then total savings or $S = SvU + SwQ + SgZ$. As l and r are assumed to be constant, the U and Q will be constant. Since proportional marginal products U, Q and Z are constant, and Sv, Sw and Sg are also constant, S as a ratio of Y will be constant.

Now the rate of growth of output is given by our basic relationship

$$y = Uk + Ql + r$$

and y will be constant if and only if k is constant. We have assumed that l and r are constant and also conditions (i) and (ii) mentioned above mean that the proportional marginal products U and Q will be constant. It is, therefore, only if k is constant, that y will be constant.

But k, the growth rate of the capital stock, equals $\frac{SY}{K}$, since SY represents the amount annually added to the capital stock K through savings. Since conditions (i), (ii) and (iii) above mean that S is constant $\frac{SY}{K}$ or k will be constant, if and only if $\frac{Y}{K}$, the ratio of annual national income to the value of the capital stock, is constant. But $\frac{Y}{K}$ will be constant only if Y and K both grow at the same proportional rate per annum. In other words, $\frac{Y}{K}$ will be constant if $y = k$. The conclusion, therefore, is that if the growth rate of the capital stock is equal to the growth rate of the national income, the growth rate of income will be constant and hence given a constant proportionate rate of growth of population, the per capita growth of income will be constant and steady.

This equilibrium position ultimately depends upon the rate of accumulation of the capital stock. There is a *critical growth rate* of the capital stock which makes the growth rate of income equal to the growth rate of the capital stock. A higher or lower growth rate in the capital stock than this 'critical growth rate' will not bring about the equality of y and k. If the 'critical growth rate' is denoted by a, the basic relationship will be

$$a = Ua + Ql + r$$

or

$$a = \frac{Ql + r}{l - U}$$

If at any time there is any deviation from this level of steady growth, forces will set in to bring the growth rate of the capital stock at the equilibrium level of $\frac{Ql + r}{l - U}$. Suppose k or $\frac{SY}{K} > \frac{Ql + r}{l - U}$

Since $\frac{Ql + r}{l - U}$ is, as already seen, the rate of accumulation of capital which causes income (Y) and capital stock (K) to grow at the same proportionate rate, a rate of accumulation of capital greater than this critical rate will cause the capital stock (K) to grow at a greater proportionate rate than income (Y). So long, therefore, as $\frac{SY}{K} > \frac{Ql+r}{l-U}$, Y will be growing at a lower proportionate rate than K, $\frac{Y}{K}$ will be falling and with S constant $\frac{SY}{K}$ will be falling. In other words, if k starts above the critical steady-growth level of $\frac{Ql+r}{l-U}$, the capital stock will grow more rapidly than income; and since savings grow only in proportion to income, the ratio of savings to the capital stock or the growth rate of capital will be declining towards the critical level $\frac{Ql+r}{l-U}$.

Similarly, if k starts at a figure below the critical steady-growth level of $\frac{Ql+r}{l-U}$, the income would grow more quickly than capital, so that savings would grow more quickly than the capital stock and the rate of growth of the capital stock would in consequence rise towards the critical level $\frac{Ql+r}{l-U}$.

The conclusion, therefore, is that if the growth rate of population is constant, if the three elasticities of substitution between the three factors land, labour and machinery are all unity, if the technical progress is at a constant rate and neutral towards all factors, and if the proportions of profits, of wages, and of rents saved were all three constant, then the growth rates of real income and of the stock of machinery would both tend towards a constant level equal to $\frac{Ql+r}{l-U}$.

The significance of Meade's model lies in showing the influence of population growth, capital accumulation and technical progress on the growth rate of national income and real income per head. The model follows the classical tradition of a closed *laissez faire* economy where there is perfect competition and constant returns to scale. It thus ignores the important role played by social, political and religious institutions and international forces in the process of economic development.

MAHALANOBIS MODEL

Mahalanobis started with a very simple model, *i.e.,* single sectoral model.[17] In this model, β is the ratio of the increase in net national income per unit of time to the investment associated with this additional income, *i.e.,* inverse of the marginal capital co-efficient; α is the rate of net investment, *i.e.,* fraction of net national income used for investment. Thus the rate of the growth of the economy is $\alpha\beta$. If ρ is the rate of increase of population, the rate of increase in income per capita would be $\alpha\beta - \lambda$. This model is similar to the growth models of Harrod and Domar. While formulating his model, Mahalanobis, however, was not aware of the existence of the models of Harrod and Domar.

Then he introduced a two sector model. In this model, he divides the total net investment into two components. One part of this investment (say λ_k) is used to increase the production of basic capital or investment goods (which may be called the *K* sector) and the other part (say λ_c) is used to increase the production of consumption goods (C-sector). Because λ_k and λ_c are fractions of total investment $\lambda_k + \lambda_c = 1$. Appropriate fractions of investment in industries manufacturing intermediate (producer) goods should be allocated to λ_k and λ_c in proportion to the value of such intermediate goods used in the capital goods (*K*-sector) and consumer goods (C-sector) industries respectively. The division of investment between the production of consumer goods and capital goods depends upon the choice of the planners. But once the value of λ_k is decided, the supply of domestic investment goods becomes fixed; the supply of investment goods can be changed only through imports or exports.

Let λ_t = national income, C_t = consumption, and K_t = investment and time *t*; with y_o, C_o, and K_o, as the corresponding values at the initial period. As already mentioned, λ_k and λ_c (with $\lambda_k + \lambda_c = 1$) are fractions of investment allocated to industries producing capital goods (*K*-sector) and consumer goods (C-sector) respectively. Let β_k be ratio of increment of income to investment in industries

17. P.C. Mahalanobis, "The Statistical Basis of Plan Frame", *Sankhya* (December, 1955).

producing investment goods; β_c be ratio of increment of income to investment in industries producing consumer goods; β be ratio of increment of income generated to total net investment in the economy as a whole.

Thus $\beta = \lambda_k + \beta_k + \lambda_c\beta_c$

We also have $K_{t+1} - K_t = \lambda_k\beta_k K_t$

$C_{t+1} - C_t = \lambda_c\beta_c K_t$

We then get $K_t = (1+\lambda_k + \beta)\, K_o$

$$Y_t = Y_0\left[1+\alpha_0\ \frac{\lambda_k\beta_k + \lambda_c\beta_c}{\lambda_k\beta_k}\left\{\left(1+\lambda_k\beta_k\right)^t - 1\right\}\right]$$

giving national income in terms of the initial income Y_0, the initial rate of investment α_0 and the allocation parameters $\lambda_k + \lambda_c$ (which are not our choice), and the contingent co-efficients β_k and β_c (which are determined by the pattern of investment and conditions of production).

Later on, Mahalanobis introduced a four-sector model. In this model, the allocation to industries producing capital goods (λ_k) is decided with the help of the two-sector model. The industries producing consumer goods and services are divided into three sectors *viz.* factory production of consumer goods (sector C_1); the production of consumer goods (including agricultural products) in small and household industries (sector C_2); and services such as health, education etc. (sector C_3).

In this model an additional set of parameters θ's; the net investment required per engaged person, is introduced. The number of jobs created in any sector, which may be called n, is simply λ/θ per unit investment where λ is the fraction of investment allocated to the sector under consideration. Subscript k is used for industries producing investment goods (k sector); subscripts 1, 2 and 3 used for industries producing consumer goods and services in the three sectors C_1, C_2, C_3, respectively. λ_k, λ_1, λ_2 and λ_3 are fractions of investment allocated to sectors K, C_1, C_3, and C_2 respectively; with $\lambda_k + \lambda_1 + \lambda_2 + \lambda_3 = 1$. β_k, β_1, β_2 and β_3 are the ratios of increment of income to investment; and θ_k, θ_1, θ_2, and θ_3 are the net investment required per engaged person respectively in the four sectors. If n_k, n_1, n_2 and n_3 are the number of additional persons engaged respectively in the four sectors over a five-year period and A is the total investment over the same period, then

$$n_k = \lambda_k A/\theta_k,\ n_1 = \lambda_1 A/\theta_1,\ n_2 = \lambda_2 A/\theta_1,\ n_3 = \lambda_3 A/\theta_3$$

If N is the total number of additional persons engaged over the period under consideration, and E is the increase in income over the whole plan-period, then

$$N = n_k + n_1 + n_2 + n_3$$

$$A = n_k\theta_k + n_1\theta_1 + n_2\theta_2 + n_3\theta_3$$

$$= \lambda_k A + n_1\theta_1 + n_2\theta_2 + n_3\theta_3 \textit{ since } n_k\theta_k = \lambda_k A \text{ (as shown earlier)}$$

$$E = \beta_k\theta_k n_k + \beta_1\theta_1 n_1 + \beta_2\theta_2 n_2 + \beta_3\theta_3 n_3 \equiv Y_0[(1+n)^5-1], \text{ say}$$

If we assume a constant annual rate of growth of income of, say n per cent per year, then E can be derived from the initial income per year Y_0 by applying the n ratio to Y_0.

For applying the above model, we will have to substitute statistical estimates for the various algebraic symbols in the equations. The increase in national income E, the investment A, and the employment N, are the variables. The ratio of net income generated to capital investment β_k, β_1 β_2 and β_3 and the net investment required per engaged person θ_k, θ_1, θ_2, θ_3, respectively for each of the four sectors behavs as parameters, that is, they are given in the sense that their respective values are assumed to remain more or less constant and are not sought to be influenced by planning during the period under consideration. Allocation ratios λ_k, λ_1, λ_2, and λ_3 also are parametric in the sense that they do not change during the period of time under consideration. There is, however, one important distinction. The income-investment ratio β's are determined by the conditions of production (and the pattern of investments within each of the four sectors) and are not directly influenced by planning during the period under consideration. These, of course, are indirectly influenced by planning since the pattern of investment itself is determined by the programme of investments resulting from planning. The allocation ratios λ's on the other hand, are at the choice of the planner within certain limits. The proportion of total investment allocated to investment goods industries λ_k must be decided from considerations of long period changes; and the allocation ratios for the other sectors λ_1, λ_2 and λ_3 then be obtained as solutions of the set of simultaneous equations given above. For example, the rate of increase of income or the employment generated may be treated as 'variables' to which desired values may be assigned. The model would then enable us, with the help of numerical estimates of the various parameters, to study how the allocation ratio λ's that is, the proportions of total investment going into the different sectors should be chosen so that the desired aim can be realized.